Essential Letters

Augustinian Heritage Institute

Board of Directors:

+John E. Rotelle, O.S.A. (1939–2002), founding director

Joseph L. Farrell, O.S.A.
David Hunter
Joseph T. Kelley
Patricia H. Lo

Jane E. Merdinger
Boniface Ramsey
James Wetzel
Jonathan Yates

THE WORKS OF SAINT AUGUSTINE
A Translation for the 21st Century

Essential Letters

THE WORKS OF SAINT AUGUSTINE
A Translation for the 21st Century

Essential Letters

Selected and Introduced by
Przemysław Nehring

translation and notes by
+Roland Teske, S.J.

edited by
+ John E. Rotelle, O.S.A. and Boniface Ramsey

New City Press
Hyde Park, New York

Published in the United States by New City Press
202 Comforter Blvd., Hyde Park, New York 12538
©2021 Augustinian Heritage Institute

Library of Congress Control Number: 2021910807
Augustine, Saint, Bishop of Hippo.

    Essential Letters
    The Works of Saint Augustine.

    "Augustinian Heritage Institute"

ISBN 978-1-56548-508-2 (paperback)
ISBN 978-1-56548-511-2 (e-book)

Contents

Acknowledgements 1

General Introduction 2
   1. The ancient letter as a literary genre: theory and practice 2
   2. Christian letters before Augustine, and his contemporary epistolographic tradition 7
   3. The correspondence of Augustine 11
   4. Augustine as philosopher... 23
   5. Augustine as theologian.. 26
      5.1. On the Holy Trinity against the Arians 27
      5.2. On the validity of baptism and the unity of the Church against the Donatists 28
      5.3. On grace and free will against the Pelagians 31
   6. Augustine as bishop.. 35
   7. Augustine as exegete 37
   8. Augustine as monk and monastic founder.. 41

LETTERS

Augustine as Philosopher

Letter 3: Augustine to Nebridius, Augustine's close friend (387) 49
Letter 4: Augustine to Nebridius (387) 53
Letter 7: Augustine to Nebridius (388-391) 54
Letter 18: Augustine to Celestine, a deacon, possibly the future pope (390-391) 58
Letter 118: Augustine to Dioscorus, a young man, Greek by nationality (410-411).. 59
Letter 120: Augustine to Consentius, a Catholic layman from the
   Balearic Islands (410).. 81
Letter 148: Augustine to Fortunatian, the bishop of Sicca (413-414) 93
Letter 155: Augustine to Macedonius, the vicar of Africa (413-414) 103

Augustine as Theologian

On the Holy Trinity against the Arians 115
Letter 238: Augustine to Pascentius, an Arian count
   from the imperial court (400-410)... 115
Letter 239: Augustine to Pascentius (404)... 129
Letter 241: Augustine to Pascentius (404) 131
Letter 242: Augustine to Elpidius, an Arian from North Africa
   (during Augustine's episcopacy) 133
Letter 170: Alypius and Augustine to Maximus,
   a physician from Thaenae in Byzacena (after 415) 136

On the validity of baptism and the unity of the Church against the Donatists 141
Letter 23: Augustine to Maximinus, the Donatist bishop of Siniti
in Numidia (391-395) 141
Letter 33: Augustine to Proculeian, the Donatist bishop of Hippo (396-397)..........147
Letter 34: Augustine to Eusebius, a Roman official in Hippo (396-397)................150
Letter 35: Augustine to Eusebius (396-397)..153
Letter 43: Augustine to a group of Donatist leaders (396-397)................................156
Letter 44: Augustine to a group of Donatist laymen (396-397) 172
Letter 51: Augustine to Crispinus, the Donatist bishop of Calama (399-400) 181
Letter 52: Augustine to Severinus, Augustine's relative and a Donatist (399-400) .185
Letter 87: Augustine to Emeritus, the Donatist bishop of Caesarea
in Mauretania Caesariensis (405-411)..187
Letter 89: Augustine to Festus, a Roman official in Africa (405-411) 194
Letter 93: Augustine to Vincent, the Rogatist bishop of Cartenna
in Mauretania Caesariensis (407-408)...199
Letter 108: Augustine to Macrobius, the Donatist bishop of Hippo (409-410) 231
Letter 185: Augustine to Boniface, the tribune of Africa (417) 247
On grace and free will against the Pelagians 276
Letter 146: Augustine to Pelagius (410)..276
Letter 157: Augustine to Hilary, a Catholic layman from Syracuse (414-415)........278
Letter 178: Augustine to Hilary, the bishop of Narbonne in Gaul (416)..................302
Letter 179: Augustine to John, the bishop of Jerusalem (416)..................................304
Letter 186: Alypius and Augustine to Paulinus, the bishop of Nola (416) 309
Letter 188: Alypius and Augustine to Juliana, the widow of Olybrius
and daughter-in-law of Proba (417-418) 330
Letter 193: Augustine to Marius Mercator (418) 338
Letter 194: Augustine to Sixtus, the future pope (418) 345
Letter 214: Augustine to Valentine, the abbot of the monastery
of Hadrumetum (426-427)..367
Letter 215: Augustine to Valentine, the abbot of the monastery
of Hadrumetum (427)..371
Letter 215A: Augustine to Valentine, the abbot of the monastery
of Hadrumetum (soon after Letter 215) 375
Letter 217: Augustine to Vitalis, a Catholic layman in Carthage (426-427)............376
Letter 4*: Augustine to Cyril, the bishop of Alexandria (417)..................................391

Augustine as Exegete

Letter 28: Augustine to Jerome (394-395)...397
Letter 71: Augustine to Jerome (403)...401
Letter 149: Augustine to Paulinus, the bishop of Nola (416)....................................404
Letter 5*: Augustine to Valentinian, the primate of Numidia (?)..............................422

Augustine as Bishop

Letter 96: Augustine to Olympius, a Catholic layman and a high official
at the imperial court in Ravenna (408) 427
Letter 97: Augustine to Olympius (408) 429
Letter 113: Augustine to Cresconius, a Catholic layman and tribune
of the harbor at Hippo (409-423) 432
Letter 114: Augustine to Florentinus, an imperial official (soon after Letter 113) ... 433
Letter 153: Augustine to Macedonius (413-414) 434
Letter 209: Augustine to Celestine, the pope (423) 449
Letter 7*: Augustine to Faustinus, a deacon in Hippo (426-427) 454
Letter 8*: Augustine to Victor, an African bishop
(sometime during Augustine's episcopacy) 456
Letter 9*: Augustine to Alypius, Augustine's closest friend
and the bishop of Thagaste (422-429) 458
Letter 14*: Augustine to Dorotheus, a Catholic layman and landowner
in the neighborhood of Thagaste (419) 461
Letter 15*: Augustine to unnamed clerics in Thagaste (419) 462
Letter 20*: Augustine to Fabiola, a Roman laywoman (422-423) 464

Augustine as Monk and Monastic Founder

Letter 48: Augustine to Eudoxius, the abbot of the monks
on the island of Capraria (398) 481
Letter 60: Augustine to Aurelius, the bishop of Carthage
and primate of Africa (401-402) 484
Letter 83: Augustine to Alypius (404-405) 486
Letter 210: Augustine to Felicity, the superior of the women's monastery
at Hippo (423) 490
Letter 211: Augustine to the nuns of the women's monastery at Hippo (424) 492
Letter 243: Augustine to Laetus, a young man who left the monastery in Hippo
(during Augustine's episcopacy) 502

Select Bibliography 509

Index of Scripture 514

General Index 524

Acknowledgements

I would like to thank David G. Hunter, my dear friend and a distinguished Augustinian scholar, and also a member of the board of directors of the Augustinian Heritage Institute, for his inspiration and encouragement to work on this volume, all his consultation while the book was being written, and above all for the great work he put into the proofreading of my English. Without David's kind and generous help, this volume would never have been finished.

I also want to thank Rafał Toczko, once my student and today my closest friend, a colleague at Nicolaus Copernicus University and an outstanding expert on Augustine's letters. I appreciate very much his excellent collaboration in the *Scrinium Augustini. The World of Augustine's Letters* project, which several years ago marked the beginning of our shared fascination with Augustine's correspondence.

My thanks go to Claude Blanc and his colleagues at New City Press for trusting me with the work on this volume and then patiently tolerating my rescheduling of subsequent deadlines. I hope that in the end I was able to satisfy their hopes for a book that meets the high standards of this series.

Finally, I sincerely thank my wife Barbara for her love, friendship, and understanding. May this book be a gift to celebrate the thirtieth anniversary of our marriage, which gave the world Grzegorz and Antoni, our two wonderful sons.

General Introduction

Saint Augustine played a key role in the history of Western Christian civilization,[1] and his letters reflect almost all of the important areas of his intellectual and institutional activity as well as everyday practice. On the one hand this correspondence belongs to the rich tradition of ancient epistolography in general, and on the other it is the best-preserved collection of Latin early-Christian letters. Augustine was a professor of rhetoric and hence an author deeply immersed in the Latin literary tradition, but he was also a Christian bishop aware of his own authority and very much involved in theological debates and ecclesiastical activity. Both of these facts should be borne in mind when reading his letters, which are of extraordinary value to us. However, before we discuss the essential features of this particular collection and the most important problems of interpretation that are associated with it, let us briefly take a look at the ancient theory and practice of epistolography that Augustine followed.

1. The ancient letter as a literary genre: theory and practice

In Greco-Roman antiquity the letter was much more than just a medium through which one person communicated various types of information to another person with whom he had no direct contact at a given moment. Many representatives of the cultural and political elite, especially during the time of the Roman Empire and Late Antiquity, treated maintaining regular correspondence as a kind of obvious duty, allowing them to build and then strengthen the network of formal and informal personal connections within the social circles to which they belonged. Thanks to such an approach to writing letters, this form of communication gained great popularity in antiquity and attracted the theoretical interest of rhetoricians; it also created, to some extent, the specific schematic character of the genre.

The extant collections of Greek and Latin letters, as well as remarks on the art of letter writing that we can trace in textbooks of rhetoric, allow us to treat the ancient letter as a full-fledged and also very specific literary genre. Despite having a vast and rich source base, it is not easy for us to define clearly its genealogical profile. This is not an exceptional situation, because literary genealogy in the case of ancient genres, especially prose ones, often encounters such prob-

---

1. The classic and still highly-recommended monograph dedicated to Augustine remains Peter R. L. Brown, *Augustine of Hippo: A Biography. A New Edition with an Epilogue* (Berkeley and Los Angeles 2000). Of the latest books on the life and work of the Bishop of Hippo, Miles Hollingworth's work deserves special attention: *Saint Augustine of Hippo. An Intellectual Biography* (London 2013).

lems. But the letter, due to its occasional and very often personal character, particularly eludes unambiguous qualifications. The fact that ancient letters differ a great deal, not only in style and topics but also in such features as their degree of fictitiousness or simply length, makes formulating general comments on this issue rather difficult. What they certainly have in common, though, is that the structure of the individual letter very often reproduces a similar pattern. This applies to the earliest letters known to us as well as to the Late-Antique examples of this literary form.

An ancient letter almost always begins with a more or less extensive greeting, in which the names of the sender and recipient are necessarily mentioned, followed by the introductory part, which usually includes references to the health and wellbeing of the sender and the addressee, and often also their emotional and social relations. We can discern then the main part of the letter with its principal subject and the final greeting to the addressee, sometimes combined with a request to forward such a greeting to others. Although it would be hard to identify indisputably all the formal features listed above in every ancient letter, nevertheless they are so repeatable that we can talk about them as specific genre determinants.

Among the ancient writers who undertook a theoretical reflection on epistolography,[2] the most important are three theorists of rhetoric. The first is Ps.-Demetrios, a Greek author who was active probably in the second century BC and who included remarks on this subject in chapters 223-235 of his book *De elocutione*. The other two are the late-antique writer Ps.-Libanios, author of the short treatise *De forma epistulari*, in some manuscripts identified with a fourth-century Antiochene master of rhetoric named Libanios and in others with the Neoplatonic philosopher Proclos, and the late antique rhetorician Caius Iulius Victor, who published an excursus on the subject of the style and types of letters in his *Ars rhetorica* 27. Their studies, of course, differ in many respects, but they all identified several general and common features of letters, which they also found normative for this genre. The basic assumption they adopted was treating the letter as a kind of remote conversation between the sender and the addressee. This approach to the problem determined their comments on the style characteristic of this type of writing. Therefore, according to all of them, the author of the letter should on the one hand avoid a style that was too high, but on the other hand he should particularly care about the clarity of what he said. The assumption that the addressee should understand what the sender had to convey to him without any doubt was of fundamental significance. An important feature of the style employed in the letters was also its adjustment to the person of the recipient. Writing to people who occupied a higher position in

---

2. For a collection of ancient sources on the theory of epistolography in English translation see Abraham J. Malherbe, *Ancient Epistolary Theorists* (Atlanta 1988).

the social hierarchy was quite a different art than writing to equals and to those who had a lower status.

Ps.- Demetrios and C. Iulius Victor generally agreed that all letters could be divided into two groups: private letters, which were sent to persons with whom the sender enjoyed a certain intimacy, and public or official letters, which were sent to persons or institutions that the writer should address in a much more official way. Ps.-Libanios not only listed in his book as many as forty-one different types of letters, distinguished by him according to their functions, but also included examples of each of them. This meticulous typology, however, can hardly be put into practice when analyzing the Greek and Latin letters that have been preserved, because various functions very often appear side by side or intertwine in them.

This methodology, as it seems, was primarily descriptive rather than prescriptive, but the studies mentioned above show that in rhetorical schools of Late Antiquity reflection on the letter as a literary genre was vital. Moreover, this issue was not simply discussed from a theoretical perspective, because students, even at the middle level of education, were also taught how to construct letters in practice. Among the rhetorical exercises that were referred to as *progymnasmata* (in the Latin form, *praeexercitamenta*), as we know them from the late-antique school textbooks, there was, for example, an exercise called *ethopoeia* (personification), which consisted in composing a fictional speech or a letter of some historical or literary character in order to give an accurate account of his nature and personality.

The theorists mentioned above all raised the topic of letter size, which should not exceed reasonable limits. The general principle of brevity as a feature of good style, which was widely discussed by rhetoricians, took on special significance in this case. It was particularly important in private letters, which should not be overloaded with rhetorical decoration or the discussion of secondary topics, often completely inappropriate for correspondence, which were suitable rather for elaboration in separate treatises. But Ps.-Libanios warned against dealing with this principle too dogmatically. He recommended adjusting the length of the letter to its subject and not judging its size as a simple qualification of good or bad style. According to him, the clarity and completeness of the message contained in the letter were much more important than its conciseness.

Theoretical observations of a genealogical nature on epistolography can also be found in various ancient writers and rhetoricians who themselves were very successful in this literary form. One of these Latin authors must be mentioned here because of the popularity and literary authority that he enjoyed with later writers, including Augustine. This is Cicero (106-43 BC), who was undoubtedly aware of the formal and stylistic conventions of this genre. Although he himself did not compose any separate treatise on this topic or devote special attention to it in any of his writings on the theory of rhetoric, nevertheless several passages in his letters indicate that he knew the tradition of this subject as it was transmitted in Greek textbooks. For Cicero, too, the letter was a form of long-distance conversation, which in its style had to be adjusted to the special circumstances that such an exchange of thoughts accompanied, as well as to the anticipated mood in which the recipient of the letter would read it. Therefore, private and official letters had to be different. He also clearly divided them into two other groups: those that had a purely informational function and those in which the sender communicated his emotions to the addressee.[3]

The late-antique theorists of this genre mentioned above, as well as the well-educated practitioners whose letters have survived to our times, also referred to earlier epistolographic practice, formed by collections of letters known to them that were already considered exemplary in their times. In the Latin world, two such collections were perceived very early as classics of the genre and models to be imitated. The first of them was authored by Cicero himself, and the second by Pliny the Younger (61-112 A.D.). Both figures were not only outstanding authors but also public personalities and prominent politicians of their epoch. This contributed greatly to the interest they enjoyed publicly both in their lifetimes and beyond. We do not know, of course, the actual motivation of the authors of the letters, their addressees, or of other people who decided to collect these letters, store them in private archives, and finally publish them, but in the case of people occupying a prominent place in the social hierarchy such decisions are quite easy to understand. A typical decision of this sort would have been based on the desire to preserve the reputation of a famous letter writer, to commemorate his activities, to document important historical events in which he had actively participated, to pass on valuable instructions that were found in the letters, or to provide an example of his literary style.[4]

The two collections referred to above represent two different traditions of gathering letters, each of which had its followers in Late Antiquity. Cicero, although he mentioned at the end of his life that he had intended to supervise the publication of a collection of his letters,[5] probably did not manage to do so, and their transfer to posterity is due to their later publishers. Today we have 914 letters making up this collection (about ninety of them being letters to which Cicero was an addressee), divided into several subsets, according to addressees: sixteen books of letters to family and friends (*Ad familiares*), sixteen books to Atticus, his close friend (*Ad Atticum*), one-and-a-half books to Marcus Brutus (*Ad Marcum Brutum*), as well as three addressed to his brother Quintus (*Ad Quintum fratrem*); and to some extent according to the subject of the letters themselves. An important role in the process of publishing these books of letters was prob-

---

3. See *Epistulae ad familiares* 2,4,1; 4,13,1; *Epistula ad Atticum* 12,53
4. See Michael Trapp, ed., *Greek and Latin Letters: An Anthology with Translation* (Cambridge 2003) 12.
5. See *Epistula* 16,17; *Epistula ad Atticum* 16,5.

ably played by Tiro, a freedman and secretary of Cicero, who shortly after the death of his protector prepared the edition of his letters for Cicero's friends and his brother. Other books that have reached our times, but also those that we do not have today, were published later, certainly well before the end of the first century A.D.[6]

The second of these two letter-writers, Pliny the Younger, a Roman author and politician who was active in the first decades of the second century A.D., took care of publishing his letters himself. The collection we know today under his name consists of 368 letters gathered in ten books, of which the first nine contain letters addressed to various recipients, while the tenth, the only one he may not have published personally, contains correspondence with the emperor Trajan from the time when Pliny was holding the office of governor of Bithynia-Pontus. Contrary to what the author himself writes in the first letter that opens the entire collection, his placing of individual letters in specific books was not by chance but seems to have been the result of a very thoughtful selection, based on several criteria. The succession of individual books is chronological, as modern researchers have shown, but the arrangement of the letters within these subsets corresponds rather to their themes. The author's care to preserve the thematic balance and diversity of this collection can be treated as a principle he had followed when selecting letters. Pliny also played a kind of intertextual game with the reader, both within the collection itself and with other literary texts. By using his own letters Pliny was undoubtedly trying to build up his image as a Roman aristocrat who was successful in the various fields of his activity.[7]

Regardless of whether the author himself prepared for publication a collection of his own letters, as did Pliny, or whether it was done later by a publisher who cared about the author's reputation, as was the case with Cicero, the selection of letters and probably also their final form was the result of a deliberate publishing project in which the chronological order that usually characterizes modern collections of letters did not matter much. The key according to which ancient publishers arranged individual letters into larger collections was usually the recipient and/or the subject. Such a compositional principle helped them to achieve various didactic and persuasive goals they had set for these projects.[8] We should remember this whenever we try to treat this quasi-documentary literary genre as a kind of biography/autobiography of a letter's author or as a historiographic genre. This remark also applies, and perhaps even more, to early Christian epistolographic collections that have been preserved to our times.

---

6. See Peter White, *Cicero in Letters: Epistolary Relations of the Late Republic* (Oxford 2010).
7. See Roy K. Gibson and Ruth Morello, *Reading the Letters of Pliny the Younger: An Introduction* (Cambridge 2012).
8. See Roy Gibson, "On the Nature of Ancient Letter Collections," in *Journal of Roman Studies* 102 (2012) 56-78.

2. Christian letters before Augustine, and his contemporary epistolographic tradition

In the first centuries of Christianity, this literary form enjoyed immense popularity and played an important role in promoting the principles of the new religion, in integrating its followers' environments in the face of all kinds of external threats, and in administering the structures of the emerging Church.[9] The vast majority of the books that constitute the canon of the New Testament have the form of letters; additionally, apologetic texts, writings concerning martyrs, and hagiographic texts very often took this form. In the world of both Greek and Latin patristics, collections of letters were authored by eminent writers and theologians who occupy a key place in the history of the Church. Among the Greeks, for instance, there are such personages as Basil of Caesarea, Gregory of Nazianzen and John Chrysostom, and, among those writing in Latin, Cyprian, Ambrose, Jerome, Augustine, and Gregory the Great.

From a formal point of view, the early Christian letter was not a new genre but instead represented a stage in the development of the literary model that had been functioning in the Greco-Roman world for centuries. Some classic epistolographic motifs were peculiarly Christianized in it. For instance, the spiritual co-presence of both correspondents evoked unity in God's spirit, and mentioning the friendship of the correspondents was an occasion to discuss the love of Christ.

In order to understand the historical and literary context in which Augustine's correspondence arose, it is necessary to mention the collections of Christian letters that, at least to a limited extent, he had known, and that came out of the scriptoria of authors who were considered to be great figures for the Latin Christian tradition. This list is opened by Cyprian (c. 200-258), a martyred bishop of Carthage and an undisputed authority in North Africa, whose writings, including letters, Augustine knew and cited.[10] Three other authors of epistolographic collections were themselves Augustine's correspondents. His exchange of letters with Ambrose (c. 340-397) has not been preserved, but, as will be noted, we are certain that there was such an exchange. We are fortunate to have some examples of his correspondence with Paulinus of Nola (c. 354-431) and also an extremely interesting exchange of letters with Jerome (c. 347-420).

The letters of Cyprian were collected and published posthumously.[11] We do not know by whom this was done or exactly what the original collection, or collections, looked like. The letters were probably gathered by those who want-

---

9. See Trapp, *Greek and Latin Letters* 17-18.
10. See Letter 157,34, where he quotes Cyprian, Letter 11,1; Letter 108,10-11, where he quotes Cyprian, Letter 54,3; and Letter, 93,41, where he quotes Cyprian, Letter 55,21. Augustine's references to Cyprian in his anti-Donatist writings are extensive.
11. See Graeme W. Clarke, trans., *The Letters of St. Cyprian of Carthage* I (New York 1984) 4-11.

ed to commemorate the figure of the bishop-martyr and pass on to posterity his teaching on many issues that were crucial for the emerging Western theology. Today we have eighty-two letters associated with the name of Cyprian, of which sixty were authored by him, while the rest are writings addressed to him or that belong to the category of official church letters. All these letters come from the time when Cyprian was holding the office of bishop of Carthage (250-258), but these are certainly not all the letters that he wrote and that were kept in his archive or the archives of his addressees. But those that have survived have one important feature in common, namely, they are texts that can be treated as a form of Cyprian's episcopal teaching, which he had intended to be disseminated well beyond their specific recipients. He also used letters as a means of comprehensive pastoral influence in his diocese at the time when he left Carthage to take refuge from the persecution of the emperor Decius (249-251). Defending himself against the charge of abandoning the Church entrusted to him, he argued in a letter addressed to the Roman clergy that he was in constant contact with his flock in Carthage by means of correspondence.[12] The whole collection, or perhaps different sets of his letters, enjoyed extensive use in the decades and centuries after his death, and not only in North Africa. This is best demonstrated by the more than 150 extent manuscripts containing various sets of these letters and also by the testimony of other ancient writers who referred to them. At the end of the fourth century, Rufinus of Aquileia wrote that "the entire body of correspondence of the holy martyr Cyprian is usually contained in one codex,"[13] but we are not certain if all the letters of his that are known to us today were part of this collection, nor do we know if there were any others in it that have not survived. The extraordinary popularity of these writings is also evidenced by the fact that, as Augustine notes, they were translated very early into other languages (most probably Greek) and available outside Africa.[14]

Augustine himself referred to Cyprian's letters several times and, as he confirms, had in his library a selection of them, which he knew was incomplete.[15] They could have been for him a perfect example of pastoral correspondence in which a Christian bishop raises key theological issues and whose individual character yields to the universality of the teaching contained therein. Augustine, too, composed lengthy theological treatises using this literary form. An example that we could mention here is Letter 140, which functioned in the Augustinian tradition as a separate book entitled *On the Grace of the New Testament*, or Letter 187, also called *On the Presence of God*.

The other collections of Latin Christian letters that are worth mentioning in the context of presenting the historical and literary background in which Au-

---

12. See Letter 20,2.
13. See *On the Adulteration of Origen's Books* 12.
14. See Sermon 310,4.
15. See *Baptism* VI,15,24-27.

gustine's correspondence appeared came from the pens of authors who were not only his contemporaries but also belonged to the circle of his correspondents. The first of them is Ambrose (c. 340–397), the great bishop of Milan, who, according to the account of Augustine himself, played a huge role in the process of his final conversion and for the rest of his life was for him a major authority in theological matters. Although any correspondence between these two monumental figures for the history of Western Christianity has not survived, we know that at least once an exchange of letters occurred. In *Confessions* IX,5,13 Augustine mentions that during a breakthrough period of his life, after he had decided to quit his career as a professor of rhetoric and devote himself entirely to God, he asked the bishop of Milan by letter to give him advice on the most appropriate reading for him at that time, and in response Ambrose recommended the Book of Isaiah.

Ambrose's correspondence, as we have it today, comprises 91 letters, of which 71 constitute the basic collection, consisting of a selection of letters from the period in which he held the office of the bishop of Milan (374-397).[16] It is probably just a fraction of all the letters that came from his pen during his busy life. As is apparent from the words of Ambrose himself, most probably in the last years of his life he personally took care of publishing a set of his letters,[17] which recalls the earlier case of Pliny the Younger. Additionally, the collection preserved under the name of the bishop of Milan was divided—it seems by Ambrose himself—into ten books, with the last one containing the letters that refer mainly to his political activity. Such a division of the corpus of correspondence, also reminiscent of Pliny, was not something unique in this era. For example, Memmius Symmachus did the same, when after the death of his father, the Roman senator Aurelius Symmachus, he published the letters of the elder Symmachus in ten books, including his correspondence with the emperors in the last of them.

It is hard to discover the principle according to which the individual letters were grouped in the first nine books of Ambrose's collection; the chronological order of their composition was certainly not followed. Some of the books are comprised of letters addressed to specific recipients, but Ambrose was not consistent with this selection rule. If he deliberately imitated Pliny, then perhaps, following in his footsteps, he intended to keep thematic diversity as a selec-

---

16. See J. H. W. G. Liebeschuetz, "Letters of Ambrose of Milan (374-397). Books I-IX," in *Collecting Early Christian Letters from the Apostle Paul to Late Antiquity*, ed. by Bronwen Neil and Pauline Allen (Cambridge 2015) 97-112; idem, "General Introduction," in *Ambrose of Milan: Political Letters and Speeches*, trans. with introduction and notes by J.H.W.G. Liebeschuetz with the assistance of Carole Hill (Liverpool 2005) 27-46; Gérard Nauroy, "The Letter Collection of Ambrose of Milan" in *Late Antique Letter Collections. A Critical Introduction and reference Guide*, ed. by Cristiana Sogno, Bradley K. Storin and Edward J. Watts (Oakland 2017) 146-156.
17. See Letter 32 (48),7.

tion criterion. This hypothesis, however, has been subjected to serious criticism and is now being treated with increasing scepticism. Ambrose was undoubtedly trying to present in his collection the most important areas of his activity as an exegete and moralist and also as a widely respected authority and guardian of orthodoxy.[18] We can observe that here he paid less attention to presenting his episcopal duties, and he certainly did not want to create an autobiography through the letters.

The collection of letters authored by Paulinus of Nola came to exist in a completely different way than Ambrose's.[19] This well-educated and influential aristocrat, who was also an ascetic and a bishop, did not collect his letters in a private archive, and he was even surprised that others were interested in doing so.[20] His position in the hierarchical Church, his authority and his literary proficiency were so remarkable, however, that even during his lifetime his addressees were collecting and most likely disseminating these writings. About fifty letters have been preserved under Paulinus's name, and among his correspondents were such prominent personalities of that time as Sulpicius Severus, Rufinus of Aquileia and Augustine himself. Due to the fact that Paulinus did not pay much attention to gathering his own letters, this collection has survived to the present day in a very incomplete state. For example, we do not have his letters to Jerome, although the responses that he received from him are available to us.[21]

Jerome, the great exegete and polemicist, included information about his authorship of two sets of letters—*One Book of Letters to Marcella* and *One Book of Letters to Various People*—in a brief note, dedicated to himself and closing his book *On Illustrious Men*, in which he presented the history of Christian literature in the form of short biographies of Christian writers. The titles of these collections clearly indicate that the criterion he used to arrange them was who the recipients of his letters were.[22] Marcella, a Roman aristocrat and patron of Jerome, we know very well from the letters to her that have survived, while we can only guess who the addressees of the writings contained in the second set were. Although the subject matter of the fifteen letters to Marcella seems to be very diverse at first glance, together they form a group whose common feature is the idealized self-presentation of the author, who had experienced life as a monk in the Syrian desert of Chalkis. We have no doubt, therefore, that this outstanding Latin writer, well aware of his own literary talent and rhetorical skill, took care to

---

18. See Nauroy, "The Letter Collection of Ambrose of Milan" 156.
19. See Catherine Conybeare, *Paulinus Noster: Self and Symbols in the Letters of Paulinus of Nola* (Oxford 2000); Sigrid Mratschek, *Der Briefwechsel des Paulinus von Nola. Kommunikation und soziale Kontakte zwischen christlichen Intellektuellen* (Göttingen 2002); Dennis Trout, "The Letter Collection of Paulinus of Nola," in *Late Antique Letter Collections* 254-268.
20. See Letter 41,1.
21. Letters 53;58;85.
22. See Andrew Cain, *The Letters of Jerome. Asceticism, Biblical Exegesis, and the Construction of Christian Authority in Late Antiquity* (Oxford 2009).

publish and arrange his letters in such a way as to present his own activities in the most favorable way. However, it is not known how the entire collection of 123 letters, which was handed down in a rich manuscript tradition, was established. Most probably only a part of it is due to the author himself and a part to its later publishers, who added subsequent letters or sets of letters to it.

The collections of Latin letters known to us from the end of the fourth and the beginning of the fifth century enable us to evaluate and appreciate all the fields of activity of their authors, thanks to which they entered the history of Christianity. The same applies, naturally, to the largest group of Christian letters from that time, namely, Augustine's correspondence.

3. The correspondence of Augustine

The collection of correspondence published in modern times under Augustine's name contains 309 letters, of which 252 are of his own authorship, 49 are writings addressed to him, and eight have Augustine neither as sender nor as addressee.[23] Its last enlargement occurred relatively recently, in 1981, when the Austrian philologist, Johannes Divjak, published 31 original letters by Augustine that he had discovered in libraries in Spain and France.[24] We cannot reliably answer the question of what proportion of all his actual letters has been preserved until today. The data on the basis of which we could make some estimates in this matter are so ambiguous that scholars trying to resolve this problem have come to fundamentally different conclusions: from the optimistic hypothesis that we can read today half of all letters written by him to the pessimistic assumption that we know only one-eighth of them.[25] Regardless of these estimates, it is a huge selection which, even in its preserved form, has no equal among the collections of ancient Latin Christian letters known to us.

The intensity with which Augustine wrote and sent his letters to places both within and outside of Africa is so high that a question must arise about the technical and logistic side of his letter-writing. Like other ancient authors, he dictated his writings, and if he added some handwritten notes or greetings or signed the letter himself, he drew the attention of the recipient to this only on rare occasions.[26] In this way he emphasized the authenticity of his letter, if for some rea-

---

23. For general information on the collection of Augustine's letters see Johannes Divjak, "Epistulae," in *Augustinus-Lexicon* II 5/6 (2001) 893-1057; Robert B. Eno, "Epistulae," in *Augustine through the Ages*, ed. by Allan D. Fitzgerald (Grand Rapids, Mich. 1999) 298-310, esp. 299-305; Jennifer V. Ebbeler, "The Letter Collection of Augustine of Hippo," in *Late Antique Letter Collections* 239-253.
24. Augustinus, *Epistolae ex duobus codicibus nuper in lucem prolatae*, ed. by J. Divjak (Vienna 1981).
25. See Frank Morgenstern, *Die Briefpartner des Augustinus von Hippo. Prosopographische, sozial- und ideologiegeschichtliche Untersuchungen* (Bochum 1993) 5.
26. See, e.g., Letters 44,6; 61,2; 238,26; 19*,4.

son it could be questioned by his correspondent, or gave his views the status of authoritative statements that the addressee could later use as arguments for his own purposes. The risk of forgery of the letter, in whole or in part, was inscribed in the imperfect process of delivering correspondence in Antiquity. Fabricating the name of the alleged sender, especially if it was a person of undisputed authority, could be very attractive to the real author of a letter.

In the famous correspondence of Augustine with Jerome, the authenticity of the letters of the former was questioned several times by the latter, who asked Augustine to autograph his writings that were forwarded to him.[27] So, when Augustine sent him some examples of his anti-Pelagian works, he signed them all by hand to testify to the completeness, intact character and above all the truthfulness of the attached set of texts.[28] In his exchange of letters with Pascentius, an Arian who was also a high imperial official, which concerned the most important issues in the dispute between Arians and Niceans, namely, the nature of Christ and the mystery of the Holy Trinity, Augustine always autographed his writings and ensured that he had read the dictated letters before signing.[29] Writing to a certain Theodore, who was expected to influence some Donatist clergy on his behalf to embrace the Catholic side, Augustine sent him an autograph of his letter, which Theodore was to use in his mission as a reliable declaration of the openness of the bishop of Hippo to their merciful reception.[30]

When sending his letters Augustine could not use the state post, which was reserved exclusively for official imperial correspondence, so he had to rely on trusted messengers who were to deliver letters to his addressees and bring him back their answers. In one of his letters to Jerome, delivered by Paul Orosius, he defined the requirements that he expected the messengers to meet.[31] The letter-bearer should be a man in whose actions he had full confidence, who was characterized by zealous obedience and also by a facility in travel. Trust in the messenger and his obedience were of key importance here, because very often Augustine not only addressed the recipient by way of the letter itself but also transmitted orally some content that Augustine did not want to include in written form for various reasons.[32] He knew perfectly well that in practice there was no secrecy of correspondence in his day, and therefore his letters would not be read only by their addressees. Not much had changed since the time of Cicero, who wrote in one of his letters to Atticus that it was difficult to prevent any mes-

---

27. See Augustine, Letters 68.1; 72.2-3.
28. See Letter 19 *,4
29. See Letters 238, 29; 239.3; 241, 2
30. See Letter 61,2.
31. See Letter 166,2.
32. See Sigrid Mratschek, "The Unwritten Letters of Augustine of Hippo," in *Scrinium Augustini. The World of Augustine's Letters. Proceedings of the International Workshop on Augustine's Correspondence, Toruń, 25-26 June 2015*, ed. by Przemysław Nehring, Mateusz Stróżyński and Rafał Toczko (Turnhout 2017) 57-77.

senger from reading the letter he was to deliver.[33] In fact, Augustine often even encouraged his correspondents to disseminate widely the content of his letters, especially when he wrote on important doctrinal issues.[34] It also happened quite often that the bearer brought with him a copy of another of Augustine's writings or a gift intended for the addressee. Finding the right man to undertake such a mission, therefore, played an important role in the correspondence process. Sometimes Augustine mentioned the courier by name within the letter, usually emphasizing his trust in him.[35] In this way he not only credited the authenticity of the letter itself but also encouraged its recipient to show the highest kindness and trust to the man who had carried it. Of course, he himself also treated with respect and trust those couriers who delivered letters to him. Answering Paulinus of Nola and his wife Therasia, he wrote that he had seen the monks Romanus and Agilis, sent by them as couriers, as a "talking letter" and as a substitute for their personal presence.[36]

Many correspondents of Augustine, who himself stayed permanently in Africa, were in places that could only be reached after crossing the sea. Therefore, both the letters he sent to Sicily, Italy, Spain or Gaul, as well as the responses he received from there, were delivered to their addressees only during the period of open navigation on the Mediterranean, in other words, approximately between March and November. This circumstance, combined with finding the appropriate messenger at the time, had an obvious impact on the regularity of Augustine's correspondence with individual recipients. It was also a good excuse for the author of the letter, invoking the haste forced by the messenger waiting for departure, to excuse himself for his not quite polished literary style.[37] We can certainly count this type of statement as a rhetorical commonplace of the introduction, which was aimed at gaining the favor of the recipient by the exaggeratedly modest presentation of the author's own literary abilities. Its obvious effectiveness was undoubtedly based on the tacit reference to the experience of every person sending letters overseas who always had to take into account the complex logistics of such a practice.

The question of the role of Augustine himself in the formation of the collection of his letters and how it received its present shape is extremely difficult, if not impossible, to answer. We are sure that Augustine not only kept copies of his letters in his archives (though probably not all of them) but also that he treated them as an important part of his legacy, which at the end of his life he intended to examine critically, in the same way as he did his other works. He announced this task in the introduction to the *Revisions*, where he divided all his

---

33. See *Epistula ad Atticum* 13,1.
34. See Letters 55,39;58,3;61,1;89,8;93,53; 141,13; F. Morgenstern, *Die Briefpartner* 5, n. 68; 157.
35. See, e.g., Letters 110,1;145,1; 189,1
36. See Letters 30,3; 31,2.
37. See Letters 139,34; 149,2.

literary output into three formal categories—treatises (*libri*), letters (*epistulae*) and sermons (*tractatus*). In one of his letters, written about 428 to the deacon Quodvultdeus, he mentioned that he had read many of his letters again, but the dispute with Julian of Eclanum, in which he became deeply involved at the end of his life, did not allow him to take care of them in the same methodical way as he did his other writings.[38]

The *Indiculum* (or *Indiculus*), a list of Augustine's works prepared posthumously by his biographer and friend, Possidius, bishop of Calama,[39] on the basis of the books stored in the library in Hippo, adds to the letters known to us eighty-nine more that have not survived; on the other hand, almost the same number of authentic letters of Augustine have survived which were not listed there.[40] This clearly shows that only part of this collection was preserved, but also that the currently available set of letters had not been formally gathered by Possidius or by any other people who had access to his archive.

Research on the very rich manuscript tradition—numbering hundreds, and if we count those containing fragments of at least one letter of Augustine, then even thousands of manuscripts, along with testimonies appearing in other late-antique and early-medieval authors—has allowed scholars to formulate various hypotheses regarding the shaping of this collection, although, it should be emphasized immediately, there is no final solution in this matter. Donatien DeBruyne's[41] theory that Augustine himself published some selection of his own letters does not stand up to criticism; nor does the theory of Hans Lietzmann,[42] who claimed that before Carolinigian times there did not exist any collection of this kind. Johannes Divjak, analyzing both the structures of collections handed down in the earliest manuscripts and also information about letters missing today but certainly existing in Late Antiquity, convincingly proved that the hypotheses referenced above are very unlikely, if not completely excluded.[43] However, according to Divjak, a rather extensive set of Augustine's letters appeared very early, based primarily on the resources stored in the archive at Hippo, which became the nucleus of all later collections.[44] In Possidius's *Indiculum*, a good

---

38. See Letter 224,2.
39. Possidius Calamensis, *Operum S. Augustini Elenchus: a Possidio eiusdem discipulo Calamensi episcopo digestus-post maurinorum labores*, ed. by André Wilmart in *Miscelannea Agostiniana* II (Rome 1931) 149-233. For an English translation see St. Augustine, *Revisions*, trans. by Boniface Ramsey (Hyde Park, N.Y. 2010) 169-202.
40. See Ebbeler, "The Letter Collection of Augustine of Hippo" 241.
41. See Donatien De Bruyne, "Les anciennes collections et la chronologie des lettres de Saint Augustin," in *Revue Bénédictine* 43 (1931) 284-295.
42. See Hans Lietzmann, "Zur Entstehungsgeschichte der Briefsammlung Augustins," in *Sitzungsberichte der Preussischen Akademie der Wissenschaften* (Berlin 1930) 356-388.
43. See Johannes Divjak, "Zur Struktur Augustinischer Briefkorpora," in *Les lettres de Saint Augustin découvertes par Johannes Divjak : communications présentées au colloque des 20 et 21 septembre 1982* (Paris 1983) 13-27.
44. See ibid. 26-27; Ebbeler, "The Letter Collection of Augustine of Hippo" 243.

proportion of the letters was thematically grouped with other writings of Augustine regarding the various theological debates he conducted during his life, but we have no subsequent testimonies that they were distributed in such groups. In the same ancient catalog of his works there is also a section in which Possidius listed a series of over 200 letters, grouping them by the names of the recipients, marking each with information on how many letters to the specific recipient he knew. He mentions, among others, ten letters to Nebridius, six to Jerome, eight to Paulinus of Nola, and three to Evodius. We can assume, therefore, that at the early phase of the formation of this collection, which would have been consistent with the tradition widely present in ancient epistolography, there were series of letters gathered under the names of their individual recipients, both letters sent to them and answers received by Augustine. The most probable—although still quite speculative—theory about the creation of the currently available collection of Augustine's correspondence seems to be, as Jennifer Ebbeler has suggested, based on the practice of copyists, who gradually added smaller or larger sets of letters, or even individual letters, to the pre-existing collections.[45]

When the Benedictine monks from the Abbey of St. Maur began in the seventeenth century to work on the first critical edition of Augustine's letters, they adopted the chronological order as the key to their arrangement, in keeping with the standards of their time. Although this principle was actually uncommon to ancient publishers of such collections, its application to this particular set of writings could easily be justified. If Augustine had had time to complete the task that he announced in the introduction to the *Revisions* and had systematically revised his letters, he certainly would have arranged them like the rest of his own writings discussed there, that is, in chronological order. The first modern publishers of this corpus explicitly referred to this argument in the introduction to their edition. This close connection of the letters with Augustine's biography could also help readers to follow the development of his views on the most important theological issues he had dealt with during his long life. The chronological order was later adopted by Alois Goldbacher in his edition for the *Corpus Scriptorum Ecclesiasticorum Latinorum*[46] and by Klaus D. Daur, the latest publisher of the letters, who also followed the chronological order in the *Corpus Christianorum. Series Latina*,[47] which included the letters discovered by Johannes Divjak that had been previously published separately.

It should be emphasized here that dating particular letters of Augustine is not an easy task, because he himself never specifically dated them, nor did he directly indicate the place from which he sent them, which could sometimes help to solve this problem. Not recording a date was the usual practice in the case of the ancient epistolographic collections that have been preserved; only Cicero

---

45. See Ebbeler, "The Letter Collection of Augustine of Hippo" 244.
46. Augustinus, *Epistulae,* ed. by Alois Goldbacher (Vienna 1895-1923).
47. Augustinus, *Epistulae,* ed. by K. D. Daur (Turnhout 2004-2005).

included some indication of this type in approximately one-third of the letters of his that are known to us. Hence, the chronology of individual writings constituting the corpus of Augustine's correspondence has been and still is the subject of scholarly discussion. Despite all the interpretative problems in this matter, however, we can assume that the preserved collection covers the period from 386/7 to 430, in other words, to the end of his life.[48] Certainly before 386 he also wrote and received letters, but unfortunately none of them has survived. Perhaps he had not considered it necessary to archive his letters before he began to treat them as a medium for building and maintaining a network of contacts relevant to his involvement in theological issues and related to his pastoral activities.

It is worth recalling that it was in the autumn of 386 that the famous "Take and read" scene described in *Confessions* VIII,12,29 occurred, after which Augustine resigned from the post of professor of rhetoric in Milan and went with a group of friends to the estate of Verecundus in Cassiciacum. Two years later, in 388, he returned from Italy to his native Africa to begin his ascetic Christian life and shortly afterwards an ecclesiastical career. It was only the archive in Hippo that turned out to be the place where, as is apparent from both the *Revisions* and the evidence of Possidius, the legacy of its famous bishop was systematically collected.

The temporal scope of Augustine's surviving letters more or less overlaps the period of his other literary activity, confirmed in the preserved works that begin with the so-called philosophical dialogues created at Cassiciacum. It is also a period that is not chronologically covered by the autobiographical narrative in the *Confessions*, which concludes shortly before the year 400. Therefore, next to *The Life of Augustine* by Possidius, who began his hero's biography at the point where he stopped talking about himself in the *Confessions*, the letters seem to be an obvious source for learning about the historical figure of the bishop of Hippo. It is not surprising, therefore, that their modern publishers could not resist arranging this collection in chronological order, in other words, in close relation to his biography.

Augustine undoubtedly knew the correspondence of Cicero, which was already a standard for the art of letter-writing in his time.[49] But as a professor of rhetoric he was also aware of the existence of basic rules that had to be followed in a well-written letter, as well as how this literary form should be distinguished from treatises or sermons. From Augustine's point of view, a very simple but also sufficient determinant in classifying a work as a letter was whether it started with the address formula, namely, the information about who was writing to whom.[50] He knew very well that in the customary greeting one should mention

---

48. In this book I follow the dating established in Eno, "Epistulae" 299-305.
49. See Letter 242,5.
50. See *Revisions* II,20 (47).

the merits of the addressee, which we see not only from his regularly observing this practice but also from the explicitly formulated remark he made in one of his letters to Volusianus, a pagan intellectual.[51] He usually began his letters with fairly formal introductions, focused on the recipient and the relationship with him. This convention was so obvious to him and his correspondents that, when one of them, his close friend Nebridius, left out this part of the letter, he considered it appropriate to explain the omission.[52] Augustine usually closed his letters in an equally conventional way, summarizing the most important content of the letter, repeating the greeting or expressing hope for the soonest possible response or a personal meeting with the addressee.

Augustine was aware that the characteristic feature of this literary genre should be brevity. He mentioned it many times, usually in the context of excusing himself for excessively long letters that he had to write because of the seriousness of the matters at hand.[53] In another letter to the aforementioned Volusianus he invoked as a good example of such practice the letters of the apostles and of other Christian authors who had discussed theological problems in this literary form. From his point of view, following the traditional theory of this genre, the most important qualities should be clarity and unambiguity, traits that had to be subordinated to the appropriate length of a particular letter.[54] Sometimes Augustine asked his recipients for forgiveness for having sent letters longer than they might have expected.[55] This often happened when he wrote to high-ranking people in the social or ecclesiastical hierarchy, and it was rather an element of topics aimed at gaining the benevolence of the recipient rather than a statement that we should take literally. Having anticipated the use of the same convention by Jerome, he asked him in one of his letters for the broadest possible explanation of his exegetical ideas, at the same time flattering his literary vanity by stating that in the case of such an excellent author no letter could seem too long.[56]

Like all of his ancient predecessors, Augustine considered a letter a kind of long-distance conversation. Writing to Jerome, he called this form of communication a *litteraria collocutio*, which could be a substitute for a real discussion.[57] He was aware of the obvious limitations of it but also, on the other hand, of the specific advantage that an exchange of letters might have over a personal talk, especially in the case of disputes on serious doctrinal topics conducted with heretics or schismatics.[58] First of all, the presentation of the position in the discussion,

---

51. See Letter 132, 1.
52. See Letter 8,1: "Since I am in a hurry to get to the point, I want no introduction, no beginning."
53. See Letters 120,20; 155,5.
54. See Letter 137,19.
55. See, e.g., Letters 115,2,5; 162,9; 177,19; 6*,8.
56. See Letter 40,1.
57. See ibid.
58. See Rafał Toczko, "Debating through the Letters vs. Live Discussions. The Patterns of *ars disputandi* in Augustine's Correspondence," in *Scrinium Augustini* 149-178.

which was recorded in correspondence, allowed one to avoid the casual remarks characteristic of a lively conversation and, even more importantly, the misrepresentations that could appear in later accounts of such debates. The unambiguous formulation of one's own views in writing had an additional advantage, namely, that the addressee of the letter could later disseminate them or use them himself in discussions with his doctrinal opponents. Augustine willingly emphasized this value of letter-writing by referring to discussions with the Donatists, whose position before 411 was strong in North Africa and with whom he had to compete very seriously in both the theological and the institutional spheres.[59]

A significant issue is whether, as a perfectly educated rhetorician, Augustine used in his correspondence the appropriate composition schemes and argumentative themes characteristic of the various types of letters described in rhetorical textbooks.[60] The collection preserved under his name includes examples of such writings, which can be classified, either in whole or in parts, as consolatory letters,[61] exhortatory letters,[62] commendatory letters[63] or congratulatory letters.[64] In a characteristic way, Augustine combines in them classic school theory with arguments based on the Scriptures and theological reasoning. A good example of such practice is Letter 263, in which he consoles the virgin Sapida after the death of her brother Timothy, who was a Carthaginian deacon. This letter, after a conventional introduction, is clearly divided into two parts: in the first part (2-3) Augustine presents a number of specific arguments that are to be a consolation for a sister suffering after her brother's death, and in the second he tries to make the case that death as such should not be a cause for concern at all (4). This structure, present in the classic consolation letters, of which Seneca's writings are the best-known examples, evokes the rhetorical theory of the schools, while the concrete arguments presented by him belong exclusively to the Christian sphere, because he seeks consolation only in the Scriptures and in God himself.[65]

The same applies to two other categories of letters, which the ancient theorists of this genre specified, namely, private letters and official letters. This division was based on a stylistic differentiation of letters depending on the persons to whom they were addressed and what matters were covered in them. With respect to Augustine's correspondence, we are often unable to decide absolutely whether the subject of an individual letter falls in the first or second of these categories,

---

59. See Letters 19; 29,1; 33,4; 51,1; 58,2; 61,1; 61,2; 87,1; 89,8.
60. See Maria Pia Ciccarese, "La tipologia delle lettere di S. Agostino," in *Augustinianum* 11 (1971) 471-507.
61. See Letters 92; 252; 263.
62. Exhortatory elements can be found in Letters 19; 76; 100; 112; 132; 170; 210; 218; 220; 232; 247.
63. Commendatory elements can be found in Letters 96; 113; 116; 206; 212; 215.
64. Congratulatory elements can be found in Letters 41; 58; 142; 144; 191.
65. See Ciccarese, "La tipologia delle lettere di S. Agostino" 477-480.

although the classification of their addressees due to their degree of intimacy with the bishop of Hippo seems to be much easier.

Among the huge number of Augustine's 197 correspondents whom we can identify by name, representing the whole social cross-section of those times, are his friends and people with whom he had personal relations based on partnership principles, the clergy and the laity under his jurisdiction, and also prominent representatives of the church hierarchy as well as high-ranking state officials. Such a large number of addressees and their enormous social diversity clearly makes this collection different from other collections of Latin correspondence, such as the those of Ambrose or Jerome.

It is not easy to reconstruct the functioning of the social network either centered around Augustine or of which he was only a more or less active member. As regards his relationship with the African bishops who were his contemporaries, for example, Claire Sotinel notes that, of his correspondents known to us today, only twenty-nine belonged to this group, and only fifteen of them could be combined into a more complex network of interrelationships. The comparison of this number with the total number of African bishoprics (in Augustine's day estimated at about 600, including Donatist bishops) may indicate how incomplete this picture of his actual relations with other representatives of the African episcopate is.[66]

With respect to Augustine's correspondents, it is also worth emphasizing that, apart from one example of a relative named Severinus whom he tried to divert from Donatism,[67] there is no member of his own family among them. This does not necessarily mean, of course, that he did not correspond at all with his brother, sister, or other close or distant relatives; rather, it reflects the transmission tradition of this collection, whose core was probably made up of letters kept in the archives of Hippo, in which were placed letters related primarily to Augustine's official activities as a bishop and those containing his clear theological positions.

An interesting subgroup of Augustine's addressees consists of women. Among them there are representatives of rich and very influential Roman families, such as Albina and Melania the Younger,[68] who were descendants of the famous ascetic Melania the Elder, along with other Roman aristocrats like Proba, with her daughter-in-law Juliana and her grandniece Demetrias,[69] and Fabiola, a

---

66. See Claire Sotinel, "Augustine's Information Circuits," in *A Companion to Augustine*, ed. by Mark Vessey (Chichester 2012) 133; Gillian Clark, "Influential Friends? Augustine's Episcopal Networks," in *Episcopal Networks in Late Antiquity*, ed. by Carmen A. Cvetkovic and Peter Gemeinardt (Berlin 2019) 63-81.
67. See Letter 52.
68. See Letters 124; 126 (to Albina, Melania the Younger and Pinian, Melania's husband).
69. See Letters 130-131 (to Proba); 150 (to Proba and Juliana); 188 (to Juliana concerning Demetrias).

Roman laywoman of some standing.[70] Although the social status of their families was far superior to that of Augustine himself, the bishop of Hippo addresses them in a much more paternalistic way than he does his male correspondents. In this case it is difficult to talk about friendly relations based on the principles of equality.[71] In his letters to women Augustine discussed a number of theological matters, especially in the context of polemics with heretical groups like the Pelagians,[72] the Priscillianists,[73] and the Novatianists,[74] and disciplinary and moral issues as well. These writings testify to the high literary education of his female correspondents and also to their theological culture and their lively interest in the doctrinal disputes of the time. Addressing women, Augustine devotes a great deal of space to sexual ethics, the virtue of virginity, widowhood, and possible sexual abstinence in marriage.[75] Two of the letters belonging to this group—Letter 210 to Felicity, the superior of the women's monastery in Hippo, and Letter 211 to the nuns from this convent, which contains the female form of the so-called *Rule of Augustine*—constitute basic evidence of the birth of institutional female monasticism in North Africa in Augustine's day.

The degree of stylistic officiality of the bishop of Hippo's letters increased depending on whether he wanted to be perceived in them as an equal partner of his correspondents in discussing various theological and moral issues; or as an authority aware of his institutional position, who had the right to address disciplinary or administrative matters; or as a petitioner, seeking high-ranking persons to settle a problem that was beyond his episcopal jurisdiction. Belonging to a completely separate category in this respect are the letters in which the common position of Numidian bishops or clerics from Hippo with regard to various local problems was formulated and sent to the bishop of Rome or other overseas bishops. These writings, signed by a group of bishops or clerics, usually have the distinctive mark of Augustine's own style, which proves that he was not only an active participant in the meetings during which such issues were discussed but also served as one of the editors of the documents that they generated. Examples of such records are present in the collection given under his name.[76]

Among Augustine's letters we also find those which, due to their length and the richness of the discussed topics, can be classified as treatises. A good example of such a treatise-letter, which Augustine himself describes in his *Revisions*

---

70. See Letters 267; 20*.
71. See Maureen A. Tilley, "No Friendly Letters: Augustine's Correspondence with Women," in *The Cultural Turn in Late Ancient Studies*, ed. by Dale B. Martin and Patricia Cox Miller (Durham, N. C. 2005) 40-62.
72. See Letter 188.
73. See Letter 264.
74. See Letter 265.
75. See Letter 262.
76. See Letters 88; 141; 175; 176; 177; 219.

as a *libellus* (small book), is Letter 140, *On the Grace* of the New Testament,[77] sent in 411 or 412 to a catechumen from Carthage named Honoratus. In it he responds to a number of his addressee's doubts related to the understanding of various biblical passages and also discusses at length the concept of grace in the New Testament. Letter 157, written in 414 or 415, is similar; it is addressed to Hilary, a lay correspondent from Sicily, and in it Augustine extensively explains some questions related to the emergence of Pelagian teaching in Syracuse. It is probably this letter that Augustine was referring to as a book in his treatise *The Deeds of Pelagius* 11,23.

The rhetorical style and form of Augustine's letters were influenced by some other factors. He adapted them, for instance, according to whether he was writing to friends, to Catholic clergy, to heretics and schismatics, or to pagans who often held important state offices. The differences can be seen in the kind of greetings that begin individual letters, in the titles specifying recipients, and in the ending formulas. When Augustine addressed a friend who was not yet baptized, he usually referred to him as *filius* (son); if he identified his correspondent with the epithet *honorabilis* (honorable), it meant a member of the aristocracy; and if the term *frater* (brother) appeared, it was usually in connection with another bishop or a monk.[78] The introductory formulas are so characteristic in his letters that on the basis of their analysis one can form a hypothesis regarding not only the existence of monastic communities in the sees of bishops but even whether they consisted of lay monks or local clergy.[79] In his polemical and doctrinal letters he used a whole arsenal of arguments well-rooted in the biblical context, which we also know from his theological treatises, and when writing to pagans he referred to a common rhetorical and literary tradition.

The differences in the style of letters addressed by Augustine to different groups of addressees can be seen in the vocabulary he used and also in the syntax of the sentences he constructed.[80] Writing to well-educated persons, such as Paulinus of Nola or Jerome, he employed less frequently than elsewhere the grammatical forms and non-classical syntax that were characteristic of late Latin. Striving for maximum clarity in his message, he tried to adapt his language accordingly when addressing people with a lesser literary culture. However, he never went to extremes in this respect; for example, he did not use an excessive number of sophisticated archaisms and neologisms, nor did he follow classical syntax strictly, nor did he, on the other hand, use the so-called Late Latin.

---

77. See *Revisions* II,36 (63).
78. See Divjak, "Epistulae" 902-903.
79. See Paul Monceaux, "La formule *Qui mecum sunt fratres* dans la correspondance de saint Augustin," in *Mélanges Paul Thomas* (Bruges 1930) 529-537.
80. See Ludovic-Jules Wankenne, "La langue de la correspondance de Saint Augustin," in *Revue Bénédictine* 94 (1984) 102-153.

When analysing the language of Augustine's letters, one can also notice his gradual transformation from a philosophizing professor of rhetoric, to a Christian neophyte, and then to the sophisticated theologian and bishop of Hippo who was well-read in Christian literature. This change is clearly visible at the level of the philosophical and theological terminology employed in his letters. Over time it shifted from the vocabulary characteristic of classical philosophy and religion to concepts of a strictly Christian character that already existed in Latin. An illustrative comparision can be made, for example, in the way in which Augustine spoke of Christ's assumption of human form in an early letter to Nebridius, written probably in the late '80s of the fourth century, and in a letter to Volusian composed more than twenty years later. In the former he used the expression *in mysteriis et sacris nostris*, strongly resonating with Latin pagan religious literature, and described the process of Christ's adoption of human nature by the theologically neutral term *suscipere hominem/susceptio hominis*.[81] In the latter, however, he employed the term *incarnatio*, which belonged completely and exclusively to the Christian theological lexicon.[82]

In selecting the essential letters of Augustine to be found in this volume, I had, it seems, a choice of two obvious formats for dividing the collection into smaller parts. The first format, which could be called chronological/biographical, would follow the stages of Augustine's life, marked by the development of his ecclessiastical career. The first subgroup would then include examples of his letters from 386 to 391, that is, from his conversion in Milan to his ordination as a presbyter in Hippo; the second subgroup would cover the next few years of his life, when he was not yet a bishop; and the third would contain letters from 395 to 429, when he served as the bishop of Hippo, first as an auxiliary bishop and then as the ordinary. This last and longest period, represented by the largest number of letters, could be further divided into two smaller parts by accepting as a caesura the Carthaginian Conference of 411, which marked the end of Augustine's intense polemics with Donatism. Such a chronological approach would probably make it easier for the reader to use this volume as a source for learning about the biography of the bishop of Hippo during the period that he did not narrate himself in his *Confessions*.

However, the wealth of sources in this collection is much greater than its usefulness in reconstructing Augustine's biography, especially since both the relative and absolute dating of individual letters remains a highly debated issue in scholarship. Hence, I decided on the second obvious format for the division of this collection, namely, thematic, in accordance with which the letters would be divided into groups that illustrate several important areas of Augustine's in-

---

81. See Letter 11,2.
82. See Letters 137,12; 137,15; Wankenne, "La langue de la correspondance de Saint Augustin" 152.

tellectual and practical activity. This methodology reflects to some extent the plan of Possidius, the author of the *Indiculum*, and therefore perhaps also the arrangement of the letters as they were collected in the library of Hippo. Thus I have followed the format proposed by Goldbacher, Divjak and Daur in their editions of the letters, with each subgroup in chronological order. The compositional principle I have adopted will, I hope, enable the reader to perceive and appreciate the specific character and the vast scope of Augustine's letters without losing sight of the chronological aspect.

This format causes two editorial problems, namely, determining which areas of Augustine's intellectual and practical activity deserve to be included in it, and then selecting specific writings that best illustrate the predefined categories. First of all, the thematic homogeneity of individual letters is not at all obvious, and often assigning them to only one thematic group may raise justified doubts. Secondly, some of the categories proposed here are so copiously represented in this corpus that the selection of representative sets of letters is necessarily arbitrary, and any such selection carries the risk of inadequacy. Faced with the two difficulties mentioned above, I made use of a digital tool, which was created within the framework of the project that I had the opportunity to direct, the *Scrinium Augustini. The World of Augustine's Letters* database (www.scrinium.umk.pl). This database allows us to determine easily not only the dominating thematic content of individual letters but also to combine them into larger groups in which the selected topic is particularly richly represented.

In 2009 Fr. Roland J. Teske S.J., an excellent patristic scholar and a brilliant translator of Augustine's writings, including the letters contained in the present volume, published a collection of his articles dedicated to the bishop of Hippo. He divided his book into three parts, on Augustine as philosopher, as exegete and as theologian.[83] I took over these titles for the individual chapters of the volume presented here, in which I collected letters showing these areas of the Bishop of Hippo's intellectual and ecclesiastical activity. To these I added two more categories with analogous titles that touch on Augustine as bishop and as monk and monastic founder, for which I gathered examples of letters related to his administrative activity in the Church and to his role in the formation of Western monasticism.

4. Augustine as philosopher

Writing about Augustine as a philosopher, we may expose ourselves to the accusation of an anachronistic classification, which consists in separating what was inseparable in his thought, namely, a discourse inspired by philosophy, especially in its Neoplatonic spirit, from theological inquiries aimed at understanding

---

83. Roland J. Teske, *Augustine of Hippo. Philosopher, Exegete, Theologian. A Second Collection of Essays* (Milwaukee 2009).

and precisely formulating the truths of faith.[84] All of his preserved writings, even his early so-called philosophical dialogues, date to a time when he was already a declared Christian, and this circumstance had a great influence on the content and form of his intellectual inquiries. And yet it seems worthwhile to make such a distinction in order to show, also by way of his letters, how one of the most important Christian thinkers in the history of Western civilization engaged with the views of the most influential ancient philosophical schools and also how he adapted, interpreted, and passed on ideas and reasoning present in the world of Greek philosophy, as it was known to him.

The first important turning point in Augustine's intellectual and spiritual life was, according to his own words, his exposure to Cicero's now-lost philosophical dialogue *Hortensius* at the rhetorical school in Carthage.[85] This encouragement to philosophy was to be of the utmost importance in the process of his gradual conversion to God, as narrated in the *Confessions*. Inspired by *Hortensius*, he decided to abandon his ambitions for success in a secular career, and for the first time in his life he reached for the Bible. Although this earliest encounter with the Scriptures was a disappointment to him, the seed had already been sown. Reading the *Hortensius* aroused his interest in philosophy as such. Many years later he cited this work in a letter to the widow Proba, in which he discusses, among other things, what constitutes a happy life.[86] The scepticism of the New Academy, which he encountered in other writings of Cicero, strongly influenced his critical attitude towards the Manicheans, with whom he had been fascinated for about ten years.[87] He owed almost his entire knowledge of classical and Hellenistic Greek philosophy, which he had acquired in the early period of his intellectual development, mainly to Cicero and, to a lesser extent, to the Roman encyclopaedist Varro (first century B.C.).

The greatest influence on Augustine's philosophical formation, however, was his encounter with Neoplatonism (which Augustine refers to simply as Platonism) that took place in Milan, where in 384 he was appointed professor of rhetoric. This religiously flavored interpretation of Plato's thought, whose main author was Plotinus, a Hellenistic philosopher from Roman Egypt, gained extraordinary popularity in the intellectual world of Late Antiquity, both pagan and Christian. In Augustine's early writings the names of several Christian intellectuals whom he met at that time appear in a Neoplatonic context. We do not know whether this was, as is often accepted in the Augustinian scholarship, a Neoplatonic circle whose members included Simplicianus, Manlius Theodorus, Zenobius, Hermogenianus, Celsinus and even Ambrose himself, or

---

84. On Augustine's understanding of the relationship between philosophy and faith see John Rist, *Augustine. Ancient Thought Baptized* (Cambridge 1994).
85. See *Confessions* III,4,7.
86. See Letter 130,10.
87. See *Against the Academics* I,3,7; *Confessions* V,10,19; 14,25.

rather whether the references to them that can be found in Augustine's so-called philosophical dialogues made them a compact intellectual environment in the eyes of later scholars. Augustine mentions in *Confessions* VII,9,13 that in 386, during his stay in Milan, he received from an anonymous man "Platonic works translated from Greek into Latin." Perhaps he was speaking of Plotinus' *Enneads*,[88] which were probably translated into Latin not long before by Marius Victorinus, but these could also have been works by Porphyry or Iamblichus. Augustine later had no doubt that his discovery of Neoplatonic concepts had a decisive influence on his conversion process, and he saw Neoplatonism not only as convergent with Christianity in many points but also as a peculiar interpretative key to its understanding. Traces of his deep fascination with Neoplatonism can be seen in his *Confessions* and so-called philosophical dialogues and also in his correspondence—mainly, although not exclusively, in letters from the earliest period of his literary activity.[89]

In Letter 118, written in 410, in which he was asked for advice by Dioscorus, a young man who was Greek by nationality and went to Africa for studies, Augustine argued that he should focus on Christian truth rather than on the understanding of philosophical issues contained in Cicero's dialogues. He systematically criticized the teaching of several of the most important ancient philosophical schools that Cicero had mentioned, including the Presocratics, the Epicureans, and the Stoics. However, he deliberately excluded the Neoplatonists from this criticism and praised them for their perception of God as the supreme good, which is both an immaterial and unchangeable entity and the source of all existence.

Augustine critically analyzed ethical views proclaimed by various philosophers or entire philosophical schools in several other letters. It was indisputable for him that, without a Christian perspective in which God was the supreme good, true happiness could not be achieved. While writing to Macedonius, a well-educated official of the imperial administration, he warned against the absurd consequences of following moral principles based exclusively on philosophical foundations without any reference to God. Such an attitude could, in his opinion, result in a rational justification or even affirmation of suicide. According to him, Plato's four cardinal virtues—prudence, courage, temperance and justice—could only flourish fully if they were linked to Christian faith in God and the hierarchy of values resulting from it.[90]

A strong Neoplatonic inspiration can be seen especially in Augustine's early letters, in which he correspondedd with his friends from the Milanese circle and particularly with Nebridius, who had accompanied him since his student days

---

88. See *The Happy Life* 4.
89. See Mateusz Stróżyński, "Neoplatonism in Augustine's Letters," in *Scrinium Augustini* 113-148.
90. See Letter 155.

in Carthage. In them he addressed such cosmological and ontological issues as the separation of the material from the spiritual world,[91] the incorporeality of the soul and the hierarchy of beings,[92] and recorded his epistemological reflections on memory and the possibility of knowing what is material and spiritual.[93]

Augustine also invoked the Neoplatonic theory of cognition with some respect in Letter 120, probably dating from 410, without mentioning this philosophical school by name. He responded here to the doubts of a man named Consentius concerning, among other things, how to understand the unity of the Trinity. He claimed that the cognitive dilemma which a Christian may face as a result of following either reason or faith was in fact only an illusory problem. Reasonable knowledge must always, according to him, be preceded by faith. On this occasion he mentioned people who, while not possessing the Christian faith, had access through contemplation to a true knowledge of the invisible, unchangeable and incorporeal nature.[94] The reference to contemplation as a source of cognition of the supra-sensual world is undoubtedly a clear allusion to the Neoplatonism of Plotinus.

Another matter to which Augustine paid attention in his letters to well-educated persons was the omnipresence of the immaterial God in human souls and in the world, as well as the participation of souls in the perfect Divine Being. Presence and participation, which are concepts of Platonic provenance, appear in a whole series of his letters, in which he reflected on fundamental ontological problems.[95]

Augustine, as the reader of the letters chosen in this volume will easily notice, was convinced that the Neoplatonic philosophy, although closest to Christianity, could not lead people to salvation or even to temporal happiness.[96] Nevertheless, he valued it highly as one of the keys to cognition and to understanding both material and spiritual reality, including their most important elements, namely, God and the soul.

5. Augustine as theologian

The fundamental achievements of Augustine's theology, such as his teaching on the unity of the Trinity, the salvific role of grace and the status of free will, as well as his sacramentology and ecclesiology in the broad sense, are still the pillars of Christian doctrine in the West. The letters are not, of course, such a systematic interpretation of his theological views as can be found in his

---

91. See Letters 3; 4.
92. See Letter 18.
93. See Letters 4; 6; 7.
94. See Letter 120,4.
95. See, e.g., Letters 92; 120; 148; 153; 187.
96. See Letters 3; 118; 120.

monumental doctrinal works and polemical treatises. Nonetheless, they constitute special evidence of how in the course of a discussion, and often an acute polemical dispute, Augustine was formulating very clear views, which became significant for the history of later theology. The exemplary letters selected for this volume focus above all on the bishop of Hippo's teaching on baptism and the unity of the Church, which he developed in his dispute with the Donatists, and on his theory of grace, free will and predestination, which was the main subject of his long-standing battle with Pelagius and the Pelagians. But to illustrate even better his polemical competence and theological precision, I decided to add a few of his letters in which he discusses the Arian perception of the person of Christ as a being originating from God the Father and therefore not equal but subordinate to Him.

5.1. On the Holy Trinity against the Arians

In formulating in *The Trinity* a doctrinal position on this theme, Augustine did not refer directly to the Arian controversy, which at the beginning of the fourth century had not only caused a real earthquake in christology but also had a great influence on relations between the Roman Empire and the Church in the post-Constantine era. In his native North Africa it did not provoke such emotions as it did in the East and later in Gaul and Italy. Nonetheless, Augustine had to deal with it, especially when Arian Goths appeared in Africa at the end of his life.[97] Among his works we can find the *Debate with Maximinus*, an account of a dispute he had with the Arian bishop Maximinus, who had arrived with the Goths toward the beginning of 428, and also a separate polemical treatise against him in two books, the *Answer to Maximinus*. But this was not his first theological confrontation with a high-ranking Arian, because already at the beginning of the fifth century in Carthage he had been summoned to a public debate by a certain Pascentius, an imperial official, who was using his position to mock and fight Catholic bishops.[98] Since it was agreed at the request of his rival that no record of the meeting would be made, Augustine decided to present his position and the accompanying arguments in several letters signed by himself and addressed to Pascentius. This correspondence[99] is not only a perfect testimony to Augustine's Trinitarian views but also shows the strategy adopted by him, namely, of arguing that the essential equality of the individual persons of the Holy Trinity had biblical foundations, contrary to Arian teaching, and that its understanding required openness to the spiritual reality of God while also being subject to rational examination. According to Augustine, this dispute should not be restricted to a debate of a terminological nature, because the interpretation of even such key concepts

---

97. See William A. Sumruld, *Augustine and the Arians: The Bishop of Hippo's Encounters with Ulfilan Arianism* (Selinsgrove, Penn. 1994).
98. See Possidius, *The Life of Augustine* 17,1.
99. See Letters 238-239; 241.

as the Greek term ὁμοούσιον (consubstantial) contained in the Nicene Creed was not obvious, especially if the discussion were held in Latin.

Interestingly, in another piece of correspondence concerning the Arian controversy, written by Augustine together with Alypius to the newly converted physician Maximus,[100] Augustine readily referred to the terminological interpretation and exact meaning of a Greek noun. In this case it was λατρεία, meaning, in both the Septuagint and the New Testament, worship given to God. Congratulating Maximus on his conversion, he showed him both the inconsistency of the Arian understanding of the Trinity and the rationality of the Catholic position. The letter's argumentation is largely based on the literal understanding of the noun λατρεία, which was used by Arians in relation to both God the Father and Christ.

The theological discussion between the Arians and Augustine, and the seriousness with which they treated him as an opponent in the dispute, is evidenced in Letter 242, written by him to an otherwise unknown Arian named Elpidius. We learn from it that his addressee, by sending him Arian writings, hoped to convince him to accept this doctrine, and that Elpidius himself mediated the transmission of Augustine's theological writings to well-educated Arians living overseas. The bishop of Hippo presented here his firm position on the essential equality of God the Father and Christ, the Father's eternal Word, by whom all things were created.

5.2. On the validity of baptism and the unity of the Church against the Donatists

Donatism, a schism that at the beginning of the fourth century divided the North African Church into two factions that sometimes even engaged in physical violence, was a major controversy.[101] Augustine's correspondence contains more than thirty anti-Donatist letters and is one of the most important sources for the history of this schism. Its origin was the appointment of Caecilian as bishop of Carthage, somewhere between 306 and 312. His opponents accused him of betrayal during the recently concluded persecutions and, considering him unworthy of episcopal ordination, they chose another bishop, Majorinus, to replace him. When the latter died unexpectedly, they appointed Donatus, after whom the schism was named. It should be emphasized, though, that this name was used only by the opponents of the Donatists, who never spoke of themselves as Do-

---

100. See Letter 170.
101. On the history and characteristics of Donatist controversy see William H.C. Frend, *The Donatist Church: A Movement of Protest in Roman North Africa* (Oxford 1952, repr. 1970); Maureen A. Tilley, *The Bible in Christian North Africa: The Donatist World* (Minneapolis 1997); eadem, "General Introduction," in *The Donatist Controversy* I, trans. by Maureen Tilley and Boniface Ramsey (New York 2019) 13-28.

natists and always regarded themselves as authentic members of the Church and not as dissidents. As a result of the aforementioned events, two succession lines of bishops—Caecilianists, whom later orthodox Christians would identify with the Catholic side, and Donatists—began to function side by side in North Africa. In the majority of cities there existed simultaneously the structures of both Churches, each with its own bishops, clergy and even separate martyr traditions.

Until the beginning of the fifth century the Donatist side seemed to have enjoyed both a numerical superiority and greater material resources in North Africa, although it was not free of internal divisions and disputes. Augustine, with a certain degree of malice, noted that the Donatists themselves were unable to count how many schismatic groups emerged from their circle.[102] We can say something about two such groups. The first one, whose true scale we cannot define, was initiated in the '60s of the fourth century by Rogatus, a bishop of Cartenna in Caesarean Mauritania. The only thing we know about his supporters, the so-called Rogatists, is that they opposed the use of any kind of violence in religious disputes. The second group, however, which originated in Carthage in the last decade of the fourth century, had a very strong impact on the Donatist Church. It began with a dispute over the succession of the long-term Donatist bishop of Carthage, Parmenian, who was replaced by Primian in 391, elected to this post despite a very strong opposition, of which a deacon named Maximian was one of the leaders. Primian excommunicated his opponents, which was fiercely opposed by many bishops, who first condemned him in 393 at the synod in Cebarsuss of Byzacena and then consecrated Maximian himself as a bishop of Carthage. The so-called Maximianist schism was in later years resisted by the Donatists themselves, who also sought the support of the state authorities against it. Augustine mercilessly used internal disputes within this rival Church as an argument against it.[103]

Eventually the Donatists were outlawed by a decision of Emperor Honorius after a conference held in Carthage in 411, in which Augustine himself played a very important role. Information about what happened during this meeting was contained in an open letter to the Donatists, which was signed by several bishops including Augustine and very probably drafted by Augustine himself.[104]

Mutual accusations of betrayal at the time of the persecution of Decius, with which both sides equally charged each other, became a historical flashpoint of controversy. However, the most serious doctrinal consequence was the dilemma, known in Africa since Cyprian's times, of whether to re-baptize those who fell during the persecution or were baptized by unworthy ministers. Augustine, as bishop, was faced with a situation in which two competing churches existed

---

102. See Letter 93,25.
103. See Letters 93; 108; 185.
104. See Letter 141.

side by side, both in Hippo and in the capital city of Carthage, and as a theologian he had to confront the question of the validity of the sacrament of baptism when bestowed in varying situations, as well as the importance of universality as a fundamental characteristic of the Church. He dealt with these issues in a number of his polemical writings against the Donatists and also in many letters preserved to this day. His correspondence therefore not only gives an insight into the history of the controversy itself and the related ecclesiastical and state jurisdictions[105] but also reveals in detail the doctrinal positions that he took on the key theological issues of Donatism and shows his polemic strategy in this dispute. Among his correspondents were Donatist bishops,[106] prominent lay representatives of this Church,[107] and Catholic imperial officials in Hippo who could mediate in contacts with the other side or cooperate with him in dealing with the Donatists;[108] one was even a member of Augustine's family, a certain Severinus, whom he tried to persuade to abandon the Donatist sect.[109]

While still a presbyter Augustine wrote a letter to Maximinus, a Donatist bishop of Siniti in Numidia, in which he strongly opposed the practice of rebaptism and its validity; he also encouraged peaceful reconciliation and forgetfulness of the violence that both sides experienced from each other in the past.[110] Around 396, at the beginning of his term as bishop in Hippo (we do not know whether he was still an auxiliary bishop or already the administrator of the diocese after Valerius's death), he wrote a letter to Proculeian, the Donatist bishop of Hippo, in which he invited him to take part in a discussion aimed at bringing the conflicting parties closer together.[111] In his Letters 34 and 35, sent at the same time to Eusebius, a Roman official from Hippo, he mentioned two shocking affairs related to the conversion to the Donatist Church of young people with dubious moral attitudes and their rebaptism there. The first of them, which discredited the Donatist side, involved a young man who had physically tormented his mother, and the second had to do with a subdeacon who was charged with some inappropriate behavior towards nuns. Augustine hoped not only that his addressee would inform Proculeian about these scandalous cases but also that he would persuade Proculeian to discuss with him matters that were important to both sides.

---

105. See Letters 43;44;141.
106. See Letters 23 (to Maximinus, a Donatist bishop of Siniti); 33 (to Proculeian, a Donatist bishop of Hippo); 51 (to Crispinus, a Donatist bishop of Calama) 87 (to 51; Emeritus, a Donatist bishop of Caesarea in Mauretania Caesariensis); 108 (to Macrobius, a Donatist bishop of Hippo, who succeeded Proculeianus).
107. See Letters 43; 44.
108. See Letters 34; 35; 89.
109. See Letter 52.
110. See Letter 23.
111. See Letter 33.

Letters 43 and 44 were sent by Augustine at the beginning of his episcopal career to a group of well-off Donatist laypeople from Numidian Thiave, with the hope that he would be able to convince them to return to the unity of the Church. Recalling the earliest history of this schism, he drew their attention to the controversial condemnation of Caecilian, which was its original cause, and, reminding them of the dispute he had with Fortunius, a Donatist bishop of Thiave, he argued that the Donatists were mistaken regarding their relationship with overseas churches. He also questioned their belief that they were the persecuted church, because only those who suffered persecution for the sake of righteousness could think of themselves in this way.

In his anti-Donatist letters Augustine used a very efficient rhetorical argumentation,[112] but he also had no doubt that the civil law of the state could and should be applied with all its severity against his opponents. In particular, the violence that the so-called Circumcellions (pro-Donatist gangs that were alleged to have committed robberies and physical attacks on Catholics living in rural areas) required in his opinion a harsh response. The circumcellions owe their terrible reputaton to Augustine's letters, in which they are usually portrayed as insanely cruel criminals linked to the Donatists.[113] Very interesting in this context is Letter 185, written in 417 by Augustine to Boniface, a military tribune and later the count of Africa, who was to supervise the implementation of the restrictions set by the emperor against the Donatists. In this document, which because of its length Augustine described in *Revisions* II,48 (75) as a separate treatise entitled *On the Correction of the Donatists*, he presented the substance of the dispute itself and in particular justified the severe imperial repression imposed on that rival church.

5.3. On grace and free will against the Pelagians

The most important and profound theological controversy that Augustine faced for many years arose from the teaching of Pelagius and his closest followers and interpreters.[114] Pelagius himself was a monk from Britain who came to Rome at the end of the fourth century and probably in Rome formulated his theological views, which were the basis of the doctrine later called "Pelagianism." Apart from him, several other figures deserve to be mentioned here as the doctrine's influential representatives: the somewhat mysterious Rufinus

---

112. See Rafał Toczko, *Crimen obicere. Forensic Rhetoric and Augustine's anti-Donatist Correspondence* (Göttingen 2020).
113. See Letters 23; 29; 35; 43; 44; 76; 88; 93; 105; 108; 111; 133; 134; 185.
114. There is a very abundant literature on both Pelagianism and the role that this controversy played in shaping and clarifying Augustine's key theological views. For the most recent monograph on the subject published in English see Stuart Squires, *The Pelagian Controversy: An Introduction to the Enemies of Grace and the Conspiracy of Lost Souls* (Eugene, Oregon 2019).

the Syrian,[115] Caelestius, a Roman aristocrat and lawyer, and Julian, a bishop of Eclanum in Italy.

Pelagius and Caelestius left Rome after it was sacked by Alaric in 410, and together with a group of rich refugees they departed for North Africa. Pelagius stayed in Hippo for some time but did not have the opportunity to meet Augustine there. Then he went to Carthage, from where he sailed to Palestine, where he spent several years. In Palestine he had to face accusations of heresy twice, but neither a council in Jerusalem (415) nor a council in Diospolis (415) found him guilty. Despite this fact, the African bishops, undoubtedly under Augustine's leadership, tried to have Pope Innocent I condemn Pelagius. His successor in Rome, Zosimos, rehabilitated both Pelagius and Caelestius in 418, causing a sharp reaction in Africa, where another council gathered in Carthage and confirmed their condemnation as heretics. Zosimos finally changed his mind and declared the teaching of the Pelagians to be heretical.

Having read the files of the Council of Diospolis that had been sent to him, Augustine decided to deal systematically with the teaching of Pelagius, and in 417 he wrote a treatise *On the Deeds of Pelagius*, which was addressed to Aurelius, bishop of Carthage. In 418 Emperor Honorius issued a rescript condemning Pelagius and his followers as heretics. The controversy did not stop completely, however, and its next stage was the dispute between Augustine and Julian, a bishop of Eclanum in Italy, who did not accept the position of Pope Zosimos and spoke out strongly against Augustine and other opponents of Pelagius, accusing them of condemning marriage and proclaiming Manichean views. The dispute with Julian totally absorbed the bishop of Hippo in the last years of his life.

The Pelagian controversy had several phases, but it always focused on the question of the conditions necessary for human salvation. Augustine claimed that God's grace, which by its very nature is free and therefore independent of human will and efforts, could be considered the only such condition. Because of the universality of the sin that all people had inherited from Adam and the limitations to which free will was subject, it was God alone who assigned some people to salvation and sentenced others to condemnation. This teaching of Augustine, who in the first decades of the fifth century enjoyed great theological authority not only in his native Africa but also in Italy and Gaul, faced significant criticism. There were those who could not accept the consequences of it, such as the fact that God would have given commandments that human beings were not able to observe and that he would condemn people for what they did not really have influence over. It is not at all certain, however, that at the beginning of the fifth century Pelagius himself was particularly interested in doctrinal polemics with Augustine and in the undermining of his teaching about the salvific role of

---

115. In his article "Rufinus the Syrian: Myth and Reality," in *Augustiniana* 59 (2009) 79-157, Walter Dunphy convincingly proves that this character should be identified with Rufinus of Aquileia.

grace. Such interest would be indicated by the testimony of the bishop of Hippo from the treatise *The Deeds of Pelagius 22,46*. But we might as well interpret it as an attempt, formulated by him after years of polemical struggles, to present the history of this controversy in a coherent way and to justify a strong engagement in a polemic with the adversary who was supposed to attack him from the very beginning of his teaching. Pelagius himself often cited Augustine's writings with the utmost respect in his work *On Nature*, which seems to speak in favor of a positive attitude to his teaching, at least in the first period of his activity, rather than harsh criticism.

Pelagius's name first appears in a short, rather conventional letter addressed to him by Augustine in 410, in which, in response to a letter that is lost today, he called him *my beloved lord and brother for whom I long very much*.[116] It seems to suggest that he did not treat him at the time as a definite doctrinal opponent, and it is also apparent from this concise answer that Pelagius in his letter had referred to the bishop of Hippo with great respect.[117]

Pelagius's views are often known first-hand, which is a rarity in the case of ancient Christian authors who were considered heretics during their lifetimes. We can learn them from his finished works, from fragments, or from testimonies given by other sources. The most important book of his that has survived is the *Commentary on the Letter to the Romans*, which dates to the first years of the fifth century and was written in Rome. We can also learn much about his doctrinal position from a short exposition of faith, *A Pamphlet on the Faith*, addressed by him to Pope Innocent I in response to the pope's demand. This text, in which Pelagius defends the orthodoxy of his faith, has been preserved in many manuscripts, probably because its authorship was often attributed to Augustine himself or to Jerome. There is also universal agreement among the scholars that the so-called *Book Addressed to Demetrias* was written by Pelagius. In this letter he encourages a young girl from a very well-off Roman family to undertake an ascetic lifestyle, and he pays particular attention to the character of human nature and the role of free will, which God has given equally to men and women. A number of excerpts from his other writings have been given to us by authors arguing against him, particularly Jerome and Augustine. Some quite extensive paragraphs from his treatise *On Nature* are quoted by the bishop of Hippo in his work *On Nature and Grace*, dating from 415.

Due to the nature of the preserved writings of Pelagius and the fragmentary state of some of them, it is difficult for us to reconstruct a coherent theological doctrine, if such existed at all. Even if it was not on topics of prime importance to him, however, he propounded views that called into question the clarity of

---

116. Letter 146, salutation.
117. See ibid. 1: "At the same time I admonish you rather to pray for me so that the Lord might make me the sort of person you think me already to be."

Augustine's teaching about the universality of sin and the exclusive role of grace in the process of human salvation. Contrary to what the common opinion attributes to him, Pelagius appreciated both the obvious importance of grace and also the free will by which human beings, relying on reason and knowledge received from God, could make completely sovereign decisions regarding good or evil. The good deeds that resulted from such choices, therefore, had to have an impact on the salvation of individual persons. He disagreed with Augustine's teaching on the inheritance of original sin, believing that infants were born in the same innocent state that Adam possessed before his sin. Moreover, he quite often used expressions in his writings indicating his belief that it was possible to live a sinless life. The apostle Paul was for him an obvious example of such a holy and perfect man. According to him, human beings, guided by free will, could follow either Adam, the beginning and symbol of sin, or Christ, the beginning and symbol of righteousness. Spiritual death and salvation were therefore the consequences of human choice.

Augustine authored a number of theological and polemical treatises in which he sharply attacked the views of Pelagius and other Pelagians.[118] But we would not be able to fully understand the dynamics of this dispute, its historical and social conditions and consequences, if we did not have access to Augustine's correspondence. He entered for the first time into a polemic with Pelagian teaching about 415 in an extensive letter addressed to Hilary, a Catholic layman from Sicily,[119] who was concerned about the views voiced there to the effect that sinlessness was possible, that human beings could fulfill the commandments through their own efforts, and that original sin did not exist.[120] The name of Pelagius does not appear in this letter, and the only person who is referred to as an advocate of these views is Caelestius, his Roman disciple. Caelestius had sought ordination to the presbyterate in Carthage a few years earlier, but his efforts were unsuccessful because of his controversial views on grace and his questioning of the teaching on original sin. Augustine suspected that Caelestius was now causing turmoil in Sicily by his preaching.[121]

Pelagius is mentioned as a heresiarch, alongside Caelestius, in three letters addressed to Pope Innocent, in which the African bishops inform him of their position on this heresy, which they had developed during the councils held in the autumn of 416 in Carthage and Milevis. The signatories of these writings—including of course Augustine—warned Innocent about the danger posed to the Church by this heresy, which declared, among other things, that free will without the support of grace might suffice for salvation and that the baptism of infants

---

118. For the English translation of Augustine's anti-Pelagian writings see St. Augustine, *Answer to the Pelagians* I-IV, trans., intro. and annot. by Roland J. Teske (New York 1997-99).
119. See Letter 157.
120. See Letter 156 (authored by Hilary).
121. See Letter 157,22.

was irrelevant to the attainment of eternal life.[122] Letter 177, the last of this series, signed by Augustine and five other bishops, is the most extensive and is particularly interesting. Its senders requested Innocent to intervene actively in the dispute with Pelagius and his followers. They attached a copy of Pelagius's *On Nature* and Augustine's treatise *On Nature and Grace*, which was composed in response to it, and they asked him to call Pelagius to Rome and demand a clear position from him—either a meticulous explanation of his worrisome views on grace or their official denial. This letter deals with the most important controversial issues of the conflict, namely, the understanding of grace, free will and justification, and the possibility of human sinlessness.

In the years 416-418 Augustine wrote several other letters to prominent representatives of the Church, in which he explained how dangerous Pelagius's teaching was and how cunning the heresiarch himself was, who was able to deceive the judges gathered in Diospolis and avoid explicit condemnation there. Special attention should be paid to two letters sent to Italy and one to Alexandria. In 416 Augustine and his friend Alypius wrote Letter 186 to Paulinus of Nola, and in 418 Augustine addressed Letter 194 to Sixtus, a Roman presbyter who later became pope. Both included systematic criticism of Pelagius's teachings as found in his work *On Nature* and a presentation of the extremely dangerous consequences that it could lead to. In 417 Augustine wrote Letter 4* to Cyril, the bishop of Alexandria, referring to the doubts that had arisen in the East about the authenticity of his writing *The Deeds of Pelagius*, in which he had stated that not every sinner would be condemned. He presented the possibility of human sinlessness as an essential problem in the Pelagian controversy.

6. Augustine as bishop

As the administrator of his diocese, Augustine had to face problems far removed from theological considerations, doctrinal disputes, and exegetical complexities. It was the bishop's responsibility to enforce discipline in the Church.[123] In addition to vigilance over doctrinal issues, he oversaw the conduct of the clergy within his jurisdiction. He intervened both when he observed that good morals were being infringed and when he had to react to violations of ecclesiastical or civil law committed by his clergy. Both criminal and civil charges against clergymen were referred to the bishop's tribunal, and in North Africa, by force of synodal regulations, the clergy were forbidden to appeal to civil courts.[124] Although we know that the bishop's jurisdiction played an important role in the legal system

---

122. See Letters 175-177.
123. See Daniel E. Doyle, *The Bishop as Disciplinarian in the Letters of St. Augustine* (New York 2002).
124. See *Breviarium Hipponense*, ed. by Charles Munier in *Concilia Africae a.345–a.525* (Turnhout 1974) 36.

of Late Antiquity, our knowledge of its scope still remains uncertain and limited.[125] We cannot even take as certain the authenticity of the rule ascribed to the emperor Constantine according to which bishops were expected to embrace full judicial capacity in cases where only one of the contesting parties was willing to have the case heard by a bishop.[126] There must have been, however, a considerable number of such instances, as Augustine was often annoyed by the burden of deciding cases, and his biographer Possidius did not fail to note that hearing the testimonies of witnesses and other judicial work used to take several hours of his time every day.[127]

Letters contained in this volume show how Augustine had to face serious disciplinary problems, what actions he took in such situations, and what difficulties he encountered. The scandalous and extremely complicated case of Antoninus, who was brought up in Augustine's monastery and who, thanks to his assistance, became the bishop of Fussala and then terrorized the inhabitants of the diocese under his control, occupies a special place among the matters discussed in this source material.[128] In the letters we will meet some other clergymen who exceeded the moral norms accepted by the bishop of Hippo or committed acts directly forbidden under ecclesiastical or state jurisdiction. When dealing with such cases, which included instances of sexual misconduct as well as financial misdeeds and criminal acts of violence, he always took into account the good reputation of the Church as an institution that was seriously jeopardized when the clergy engaged in any sort of misconduct.[129]

Augustine's duties as a bishop also involved representing the Church and intervening in various ways before the secular authorities and other high-ranking persons in the affairs of people who, in his opinion, deserved such mediation.[130]

---

125. On this topic see Eva M. Kuhn, "Justice Applied by the Episcopal Arbitrator: Augustine and the Implementation of Divine Justice", in *Etica & Politica / Ethics & Politics* 9/2 (2007) 71-104; John C. Lamoraux, "Episcopal Courts in Late Antiquity", in *Journal of Early Christian Studies*, 3/2 (1995) 143-167; Noel Lenski, "Evidence for the Audientia episcopalis in the New Letters of Augustine," in *Law, Society, and Authority in Late Antiquity*, ed. by Ralph W. Mathisen (Oxford 2001) 83-97; Caroline Humfress, "Bishops and Law Courts in Late Antiquity: How (Not) to Make Sense of the Legal Evidence," in *Journal of Early Christian Studies*, 19/3 (2011) 375-400.
126. A. J. B Sirks, "The *episcopalis audientia* in Late Antiquity," in *Droit et cultures* 65/1 (2013).
127. See *The Life of Augustine* 19, 2-3.
128. See Letters 209; 20*. On the case of Antoninus of Fussala see Jane E. Merdinger, *Rome and the African Church in the Time of Augustine* (New Haven and London 1997) 154-182; Neil McLynn, "Augustine's Black Sheep: The Case of Antoninus of Fussala," in *Istituzioni, carismi ed esercizio del potere, IV-VI secolo*, ed. by G. Bonamente and R.L. Testa (Bari 2010) 305-321.
129. See Przemysław Nehring, "Misbehaviour of Clergy in the Light of Augustine's Letters," in *Scrinium Augustini* 79-112; David G. Hunter, "Between Discipline and Doctrine: Augustine's Response to Clerical Misconduct," in *Augustinian Studies* 51 (2020) 3-22.
130. See Stanisław Adamiak, "Asking for Human Mercy. Augustine's Intercession with the Men in Power," in *Scrinium Augustini* 19-40.

As Possidius writes, the bishop of Hippo saw this activity as particularly significant.[131] On the one hand it reflected the social client-patronal relations characteristic of the functioning of the Late Empire; on the other it was a sign of a certain instability of the Roman legal system in the early fifth century, when it was possible to obtain special treatment on the basis of informal contacts, or even exemption from the legal consequences for a person who violated the law. Letters were an excellent tool used by Augustine in such situations. We do not know what part of all his interventions finally proved to be effective. The replies to only a few of his writings of this kind have survived, and we have no other information available to settle this question definitively. If, however, we were to draw conclusions from the extant letters, we would have to assume that in most such cases the power of his authority and argumentation guaranteed the success of his interventions. This was even the case when he tried to convince a high-ranking representative of the secular authorities to spare the punishment of a man whose guilt was undisputed. Macedonius, the imperial vicar of Africa, wrote about such a case in a letter in which he favourably treated the request addressed to him by Augustine.[132] In response to Macedonius, Augustine composed a kind of short treatise to justify the reason and the need for this sort of action to be taken by a Christian bishop.[133] In his opinion, a bishop should follow the example of Christ, who forgave public sinners and taught that every human being should be forgiven for his or her own sin, even though sin itself always requires condemnation. In this letter Augustine expressed his full acceptance of the existing legal system, including the use of torture in justified cases, but also his firm conviction that mercy could be applied to mitigate the severity of state jurisdiction. The spectrum of cases in which he intervened with the men in power was very wide, ranging from financial issues such as unpaid debts and various types of tax evasion,[134] through legally questionable acquisitions,[135] to cases of physical violence[136] and even rape.[137]

7. *Augustine as exegete*

One of the breakthroughs on his path to conversion, which Augustine describes and analyzes in the *Confessions*, was his encounter with the allegorical exegesis of Scripture practiced by Ambrose. The method of interpretation employed by the bishop of Milan in his sermons had a great impact on him, first and foremost because it allowed him to understand the consistency of the biblical

---

131. See *The Life of Augustine* 20.
132. See Letter 152 (authored by Macedonius).
133. See Letter 153.
134. See Letters 96-97; 247.
135. See Letter 8*.
136. See Letter 9*.
137. See Letter 15*.

message[138] and also to grasp the spiritual, or figurative, meaning of the seemingly absurd teaching contained in the Old Testament.[139] Only now could he abandon the Manichaean belief that the Old Testament should be rejected completely. The figurative method of explaining the various biblical passages was widely used in his exegetical writings, starting with the first work of this series, *On Genesis against the Manicheans*, composed in 388/9. Not only in works dedicated to specific biblical books, however, but in his overall output he built a persuasively efficient argumentation based on the authority of Scripture and on examples from both Testaments.[140]

The most comprehensive presentation of the principles of biblical interpretation, both figurative and literal, and of Christian teaching on this subject, founded on his own ecclesiastical practice as well as on his deep knowledge of ancient rhetoric, was laid out in *Teaching Christianity*. The first three books of this treatise were written in 397, at the beginning of his episcopal ministry, and the last one in 426, toward the end of his life. It was in this work that he formulated the programmatic exegetical principle that whatever in the Scriptures was not directly related to good morals or to the truthfulness of faith should be seen in a figurative way.[141]

Many statements about Scripture as the most important authority in Christian teaching, along with countless examples of interpretations of specific biblical passages, can be found in Augustine's letters. Augustine often answered questions asked by friends and other correspondents about his understanding of difficult passages, and he himself would sometimes question the interpretation of a biblical text that led, or could lead, his correspondent to erroneous conclusions. Letter 149, addressed to Paulinus of Nola in 416, is a good example of a letter explaining some problematic passages in the interpretation of both Testaments. At the request of Paulinus, not only a friend of Augustine but also a very well-educated writer and intellectual, he interpreted a series of verses from various Psalms as well as several passages from Paul's letters and some from the Gospels. As was customary in his exegetical practice, Augustine tried to seek arguments for his interpretation, regardless of whether it was figurative or literal, in the Scriptures themselves. The exegesis of verses from the Old Testament was therefore often supported by texts from the Gospels and Paul's letters; conversely, ambiguities in the understanding of the New Testament texts were clarified by the evidence of the Old Testament. In this way Augustine demonstrated the coherence of the Bible and at the same time the persuasive power inherent in its words. In the letter to Paulinus mentioned above, he repeatedly referred to the authenticity of the Greek Scriptures, not only the New Testament, which was

---

138. See *Confessions* V,14,24.
139. See ibid. VI,4,6.
140. See Michael Cameron, "Augustine and Scripture," in *A Companion to Augustine* 200-214.
141. See *Teaching Christianity* III,10,14.

originally written in Greek, but also the Septuagint, a Greek translation of the Old Testament that in the first centuries of Christianity was commonly considered divinely inspired. It was the Greek text that he treated as the basic one for understanding the biblical message, and he verified the existing Latin translations with philological accuracy by comparing them to the Greek manuscripts. This was the case with both the originally Greek-written letters of Paul and the Greek translation of the originally Hebrew-written Psalms.

The authority of Scripture and especially of the Septuagint was one of the key themes that became the starting point of the controversy that arose between Augustine and Jerome and that is known to us from their correspondence,[142] which lasted with varying intensity for more than ten years.[143] Thanks to this source we can understand better the principles on which Augustine based his exegetical method and appreciate its practical implementation.

While working from 394 to 395 on his *Commentary on the Letter to the Galatians*, Augustine came across a commentary on the same biblical book written by Jerome.[144] The interpretation of Galatians 2:11-14 that he found there was particularly objectionable to him. According to Jerome, while Peter was living among the gentiles he only pretended to keep Jewish customs and to require them to be kept by the converted gentiles. Morever, Jerome argued that Paul in fact did not rebuke Peter for such hypocrisy, but, in agreement with him, gave a kind of performance whose aim was to gain the favor of the Jews converted to Christianity. Augustine read this chapter from the Letter to the Galatians literally and did not even consider that the Scriptures, whose credibility must be boundless, might be deceptive at a given place. Neither in his *Commentary on the Letter to the Galatians* nor in his treatise *On Lying*, written at about the same time, in which he argued for the inadmissibility of lies under any circumstances, did he mention Jerome by name as the author of a contrary position, but he took up this polemic in his correspondence. In these letters, Augustine attacked Jerome as a camouflaged defender of the so-called "useful lie,"[145] and he also challenged the need to translate the Old Testament directly from the Hebrew text, questioning the sense of the work undertaken by Jerome. He believed that the Greek Septuagint rather than the Hebrew original should remain the standard point of

---

142. See Jennifer V. Ebbeler, *Disciplining Christians. Correction and Community in Augustine's Letters* (Oxford 2012) 101-145.
143. The preserved correspondence between Augustine and Jerome can be divided into two groups of letters. The first one includes an exchange of eleven preserved letters from 394/5 to 405 concerning the dispute over the exegesis of Gal 2 and the issue of the Jerome's translation of the Old Testament from the Hebrew against the authority of the Septuagint (Letters 28; 39; 40; 67; 68; 71; 72; 73; 75; 81; 82). The second group, comprising correspondence from 415 to 420, consists of only seven letters (123; 166; 167; 172; 195; 202; 19*) and is closely linked to Augustine and Jerome's involvement in the Pelagian controversy and such topics as the origins of the soul and original sin.
144. See Letters 28,3 and 40,3, addressed to Jerome.
145. See Letters 28,3; 40,3; 82,21-22.

reference for guaranteeing the uniformity of biblical teaching in the world of Latin Christianity. Moreover, he considered that Jerome's new Latin translation, which was not based on the Greek text that had been known for centuries, could create unnecessary tensions with people accustomed to specific biblical formulations and could consequently reduce the authority of Scripture and cause a rift between the Greek-speaking churches in the East and the Latin-speaking churches in the West. To illustrate this problem, he wrote about the confusion that had occurred in the city of Oea (now Tripoli), where the bishop read in church Jerome's translation of the Book of Jonah, which was very different from the well-known earlier Latin version based on the Greek. The outraged faithful, who were familiar with another translation, demanded that the bishop consult Jews who knew Hebrew; these Jews allegedly said that the old Latin translation and also the Greek text of the Septuagint better expressed the Hebrew original than the new translation that was presented to them.[146]

Augustine, appreciating Jerome's linguistic mastery, urged him to translate into Latin Eastern exegetical works, probably the writings of Origen, and also to retranslate the entire Old Testament from the Septuagint and to prepare this work in such a way that it would be known where the Greek version differed from the Hebrew one. He invoked as a good example of such a translation the Book of Job, which Jerome had translated from the Septuagint and then critically elaborated.[147]

The dispute between Augustine and Jerome was quite turbulent, mainly, it seems, due to the impulsive character of Jerome, who felt himself to be the object of the criticism contained in Augustine's letters. The situation was complicated further by the fact that one of Augustine's letters (28) was not delivered to Jerome at all, while another (40), before it was in his possession, had already been widely read in Rome and been perceived there as an attack on Jerome. Augustine tried to soften the sharp edge of this dispute by asserting that it merely dealt with exegetical principles, but Jerome reacted angrily and unyieldingly: not only did he not withdraw from his interpretation of the conflict between Paul and Peter as described in Galatians 2:11-14, but he also strongly defended the idea of translating the Bible directly from the Hebrew, and he even accused Augustine of heresy.[148]

Augustine was convinced that any interpretation that undermined the authority of the Bible was a threat to his pastoral activity. He believed, as he explicitly wrote in *The City of God*, that the implausible legend of the origins of Septuagint was true and gave this translation the status of a work inspired by God.[149] The different versions of the Greek text that existed in manuscripts, in his

---

146. See Letter 71,5.
147. See Letter 28,2.
148. See Letter 75,16.
149. See *The City of God* XV,14.

opinion, should be critically analyzed in order to eliminate any possible mistakes of the copyists, but comparing the Septuagint with the Hebrew text should not result in adding or subtracting from it any words or content but only in marking in an appropriate way the variations noted between these versions.[150] Even if such discrepancies existed, there was a prophetic inspiration behind them, which required acceptance and reflection by Christians.

8. Augustine as monk and monastic founder

Augustine's spectacular conversion, described in his *Confessions* in the famous "take and read" scene,[151] was ascetic in charater, and his entire later life, even during the period of his highest ecclesiastical activity, was strongly marked by a monastic element. Yet he had had no direct experience of an already functioning Christian monastic institution, and we can say very little about his possibly having taken inspiration from Eastern monastic literature. According to Augustine's account in the *Confessions*, the story of the conversion of Anthony,[152] the protagonist of Athanasius's *Life of Anthony*, made a great impression on him and was supposed to have contributed to his own conversion, but we have no evidence that Augustine himself actually read this work. Other mentions of Eastern monastic practices that can be found in his writings are rather of a secondary nature or are a repetition of common opinions. He based his completely original concept of monastic life on a few biblical passages, the most important of which was Acts 4:31-35, on references to philosophical tradition, and on the experience of ascetic life in the community of friends gathered around him first in Cassiciacum and then in his family estate in Thagaste. Perhaps Augustine's lengthy exposure, during the course of his Manichean years, to Paul's dichotomy between the spiritual and the physical person man and his engagement in various ascetic practices could also have played a role in this matter.[153]

There is no evidence of any kind to indicate that in North Africa, before the communities under Augustine's patronage were established, there was an institutionalised monastic life. The monastery of lay brothers founded by him in the garden of the church in Hippo, the community of clerical monks in his bishop's house, and the female monastery originally led by his sister, are therefore the earliest monastic institutions in the region that our sources speak of. Augustine's monastic writings are thus of great value to us,[154] especially inasmuch as the

---

150. See ibid. XVIII, 42-43.
151. See *Confessions* VIII,12,29.
152. See ibid. VIII,6,15.
153. See Adolar Zumkeller, *Augustine's Ideal of the Religious Life* (New York 1986); George P. Lawless, *Augustine of Hippo and His Monastic Rule* (Oxford 1987).
154. See Przemwsław Nehring, "Literary sources for everyday life of the early monastic communities in North Africa," in *La vie quotidienne des moines en Orient et en Occident* I: *Etat des sources*, ed. by Olivier Delouis and Maria Mossakowska-Gaubert (Cairo 2015) 325-336.

so-called *Rule of Augustine*, which is the earliest document of its kind in the Western tradition, left an enormous mark on the institutional development of European monasticism.

Several of Augustine's letters are closely connected with the monastic sphere of his activity, and one of them, Letter 211, written about 424 and addressed to the nuns of the Hippo monastery, contains the feminine form of the so-called *Praeceptum*, the most important text in the dossier of the *Rule of Augustine*. Its feminine specificity is mainly due to the use of the term "sister" instead of "brother," some verb forms, and a few minor differences in content, such as the recommendations for modest clothing, which include typical female headwear like a veil or a hair net. Although the authorship of the original form of this prescriptive document, the date of its origin, and the sequence of the male and female variants, belong to the most discussed issues in Augustinian research, Letter 211 has always been handed down as a coherent whole in the manuscript tradition. Its first part comprises the so-called *obiurgatio*,[155] an admonition addressed to nuns who, after the death of their superior, Augustine's own sister, refused to obey their new superior, and the second part contains the female form of the *Rule*.[156] Even if Augustine himself or someone very close to him was the original author of the *Praeceptum*, written as early as the last decade of the fourth century for monks living in a monastery adjacent to the church in Hippo, the insertion of its female version into Letter 211 probably already occurred in antiquity, and perhaps it was Augustine himself who was responsible for it.

Letter 210, whose main theme is the appropriateness and principles of punishment in the convent, was also addressed to the nuns of Hippo. Since no one, including of course monks and nuns, could be free from sin, they should sometimes be subject for their own good to reprimands and punishments from their superiors. Only in this way could they receive a chance for improvement and in consequence avoid the punishment that awaited people after death. It is possible that the scandalous disobedience referred to by Augustine in the first chapters of Letter 211 was also the direct inspiration for sending this letter, but we cannot be certain of it.

Other letters in this volume speak of the bishop of Hippo's attitude to monastic issues, such as the need for a balance between the contemplative and the active life[157] and the humility that monks, who were just as exposed to sin as other Christians, had to observe.[158] Their author also confirmed the principle, which he followed in the church that he administered, that only those brothers who were trained in monastic life could become priests.[159] He required not only

---

155. See Letter 211,1-4.
156. See Letter 211,5-16.
157. See Letter 48.
158. See Letter 111.
159. Letter 60.

that candidates for ordination should have had monastic experience but also that they would live with him as clerics in the monastic community that he presided over in the bishop's house.

Augustine insisted on the complete renunciation of private property by those who decided to enter the monastic life.[160] Failure to meet this requirement could result not only in exposing the monk to pride, which was disastrous for his soul, but also to a whole range of practical problems, one of which had to do with the inheritance of a deceased monk's estate, the right to which would be claimed not only by his legal heirs but also by the monastic community in which he lived and sometimes even by the local church for which he was once ordained as presbyter. Such a situation is discussed in Letter 83, addressed around 405 to Augustine's closest friend Alypius. Here Augustine stated his position concerning the property left by Honoratus, a monk from the community in Thagaste run by Alypius, who had previously been ordained for the church in Thiave; his suggestion for dealing with this took into account both the civil legal system and the customs practiced in the church. Twenty years later, in Letters 355-356, Augustine dealt with a similar situation, this time concerning a monk from his own monastery, the presbyter Januarius, and here he expressed his radical view that for a monk to keep even a small amount of property was a scandal that damaged not only the good name of the deceased but also that of the entire Christian community of Hippo.

From Letter 243 we learn that someone's decision to enter a monastery might arouse a negative reaction, especially if the person in question was a young man for whom his family might have had other plans. The addressee of this letter was Laetus, a young man who left the monastery for some time to meet his mother, who tried to dissuade him from the way of life he had undertaken. Augustine clearly expressed his view here that the biblically motivated breaking of all ties with the temporal world was not only justified but also desirable.

---

160. See Przemysław Nehring, "Disposal of Private Property: Theory and Practice in the Earliest Augustinian Monastic Communities," in *La vie quotidienne des moines en Orient et en Occident* II: *Questions transversales*, ed. by Olivier Delouis and Maria Mossakowska-Gaubert (Cairo 2019) 393-411.

LETTERS

AUGUSTINE AS PHILOSOPHER

LETTER 3

Augustine to Nebridius, Augustine's close friend (387)

In early 387 Augustine replies from Cassiciacum to a letter of Nebridius that has not survived. He tells his friend that he does not deserve to be called happy (paragraph 1). He explores where one may find the happy life (paragraphs 2 and 3) and appeals to a favorite argument to show that happiness is to be found in the immortal mind (paragraph 4). Finally, Augustine wonders whether his friendship with Nebridius should not be counted as a good of fortune, the sort of good a wise man should not desire (paragraph 5)—a topic that raises a point of Latin grammar.

Augustine sends greetings to Nebridius.[161]

1. I remain uncertain whether I should think it the effect, so to speak, of your persuasive words or whether it really is the case. For it came upon me suddenly, and I did not sufficiently consider to what extent I ought to believe it. You are waiting to find out what this is. What do you think? You almost convinced me, not, of course, that I am happy—for that is the lot of the wise man alone—but that I am at least like someone happy, as we say that a man is like a man in comparison with that true man whom Plato knew, or that those things that we see are like something round or something square though they are far distant from those that the mind of the few sees.[162] For I read your letter after supper by lamplight; it was almost time for bed, but not also time to go to sleep. Once having gotten into bed, I long considered with myself and had these conversations, Augustine with Augustine: Is what Nebridius holds not true, namely, that we are happy? No, of course not. For even he does not dare to deny that we are still foolish. Well, then, do the foolish also attain the happy life? That is hard to accept. As if folly itself is a small unhappiness or as if there is any other unhappiness but folly. Why, then, did he think this? Did he, after reading those writings of mine, dare to believe that I was happy? He is not reveling in premature joy, especially since we well know the ponderousness with which his thoughts proceed. This, then, is the answer: He wrote what he thought would be most pleasing to us. Because whatever we put in those writings was also pleasing to him, he wrote filled with joy, and he was not concerned about what he should have committed to his joyous pen. What if he read the *Soliloquies*?[163] He would have rejoiced much more

---

161. Nebridius was a close friend of Augustine from his student days in Carthage.
162. Augustine alludes to the Platonic doctrine that things in this sensible world are merely copies or images that resemble their true archetypes, the Ideas, which are seen only by the minds of the few.
163. Augustine wrote the two books of the *Soliloquies* in 387; *The Immortality of the Soul* was intended as a draft for a third book.

exuberantly, and he would not have found anything better to call me but happy. He, therefore, quickly bestowed that title on me, and he did not hold back anything that he might say of me if he were even more joyous. See the effects of joy!

2. But where is this happy life? Where? Where is it? Oh, if only it consisted in rejecting the atomism of Epicurus![164] Oh, if only it consisted in knowing that there is nothing below but the world! Oh, if only it consisted in knowing that points on the top and bottom of a sphere turn more slowly than those around the middle! And other similar things that we know. But now, how am I happy or what sort of a happy person am I who do not know why a world this great exists? For the intelligible patterns of the shapes that cause it to exist do not in any way prevent its being greater to the extent anyone might wish. Or would it not be objected to me—in fact, would we not be forced to admit that bodies are divisible to infinity so that from a given base, so to speak, we would get a determinate number of bodies of a determinate quantity? Hence, since no body is permitted to be the smallest, how shall we allow one to be the largest than which there cannot be one larger? Unless perhaps what I once said to Alypius[165] in complete secrecy has great force, namely, the intelligible number increases to infinity, but is not, nonetheless, decreased infinitely, for it is not possible to break it down past the monad.[166] A sensible number, on the other hand, can decrease infinitely, but cannot increase infinitely. For what else is a sensible number but the quantity of bodily things or of bodies? And perhaps for this reason philosophers rightly assigned riches to intelligible things and neediness to sensible ones. After all, what is more wretched than always to become less and less? What is better than to increase as much as you wish, to go where you wish, to return when you wish, as far as you wish, and to love very much that which cannot be decreased? For whoever understands those numbers loves nothing so much as the monad, nor is this surprising since it is what makes the other numbers loveable. But why, nonetheless, is the world this great? For it could be larger or smaller. I do not know; for it is this way. And why is it in this place rather than in that? We should not raise a question on this point, for whatever the answer to it might be, there would still be a question. That one idea bothered me much, namely, that bodies should be infinitely divisible. And I have perhaps got an answer to it from the contrary power of intelligent numbers.

3. But wait a minute; let us see what this idea is that comes to mind. Certainly the sensible world is said to be the image of an intelligible one. What we see, however, in the images reflected by mirrors is surprising. For, though the mirrors are huge, they do not reflect images larger than the bodies set before

---

164. Epicurus (ca. 342/1-271/270 BC) was an Athenian philosopher who defined philosophy as the attempt to gain happiness, understood as freedom from fear (ἀταραξία) and the absence of pain (ἀπονία).
165. Alypius was a friend of Augustine from boyhood; he became the bishop of Thagaste
166. The monad here seems to be the intelligible One of Plotinian thought; see *True Religion* 32, 60-34, 63, where Augustine uses similar language in speaking of the One.

them, even if the bodies are very small. But in small mirrors, such as in the pupil of the eyes, a very small image is formed in accord with the size of the mirror, even if a large face is set opposite it. Hence, the images of bodies may become smaller if the mirrors are smaller, but they cannot become larger if the mirrors are larger. There is surely something hidden here, but now I must go to sleep. I do not, after all, seem happy, even to Nebridius, when I am seeking something, but I do perhaps when I find something. But what is that something? Is it perhaps that little argument which I often cherish as my sole resource and in which I take too much delight?

4. Of what are we composed? Of soul and body. Which of these is better? The soul, of course. What is praiseworthy in the body? I see nothing else but beauty. What is beauty in the body? The harmony of the parts along with a certain pleasing color. Is this form better where it is true or where it is false? Who has any doubt that it is better where it is true? Where is it true? In the soul, of course. The soul, therefore, should be loved more than the body. But in what part of the soul is the truth found? In the mind and intelligence. What is opposed to this? The senses. Must, then, one resist the senses with all the strength of the mind? Obviously. What if sensible things cause too much delight? Let them stop causing delight. How does this come about? By the habit of doing without them and of desiring better things. What if the soul dies? The truth, therefore, dies, or the intelligence is not truth, or the intelligence is not in the soul, or something can die in which there is something immortal. But none of these is possible. Our *Soliloquies* already contain this, and it has been sufficiently proven. But because of our familiarity with evils we are frightened and wavering. Finally, even if the soul dies, something that I see cannot happen in any way, it has been sufficiently shown in this period of leisure that the happy life does not consist in the enjoyment of sensible things. For these and similar reasons I perhaps seem to Nebridius to be happy or at least somewhat happy. I wish that I seemed so to myself as well. What do I lose from this, or why should I refrain from having a good opinion of myself? I said these things to myself; then, I prayed as was my habit and went to sleep.

5. I wanted to write these things to you. For I am delighted that you thank me when I conceal from you nothing that crosses my mind, and I am happy that I please you in that way. In whose eyes, then, should I more willingly write nonsense than in the eyes of him whom I cannot fail to please? But if it lies in the power of fortune that one person loves another, see how happy I am who find so much joy in goods of fortune, and I desire, I admit, that such goods of mind richly increase. But the most truly wise men, whom alone one may call happy, wanted that the goods of fortune neither be feared nor desired—you worry about whether "desired" should be *cupi* or *cupiri*.[167] This is fortunate. For I

---

167. Augustine is apparently puzzled over whether the present passive infinitive of *cupio* should be formed as a verb of third or fourth conjugation.

want you to inform me about the conjugation of this verb. For when I conjugate similar verbs, I become uncertain. After all, *cupio* is like *fugio*, like *sapio*, like *jacio*, and like *capio*, but I do not know whether the infinitive mood is *fugiri* or *fugi*, *sapiri* or *sapi*. I could have followed *jaci* and *capi*, if I were not afraid that someone would catch me and throw me where he might want,[168] as if in a game, if he proved that the supines *jactum* and *captum* are different from *fugitum*, *cupitum*, and *sapitum*. Likewise, I do not know whether these three should be pronounced with a long and accented penultimate syllable or with a short and unaccented one. I would like to provoke you to write a longer letter. I beg that I may read your writing for a little longer. For I cannot say how great a pleasure it is to read your letter.

---

168. The infinitives *capi* and *jaci* are from verbs that mean "to catch" and "to throw."

LETTER 4
Augustine to Nebridius (387)

Again writing to Nebridius from Cassiciacum, most probably in early 387, Augustine explains the slow progress he has made in distinguishing sensible and intelligible natures (paragraph 1) and appeals to a short argument from the superiority of the mind or intelligence to the eyes of the body and their gaze, an argument that convinces him that eternal things are as present to us as we are to ourselves (paragraph 2).

Augustine sends greetings to Nebridius.

1. It is at least surprising how unexpectedly it happened that, when I asked which of your letters was left for me to answer, I found only one that still holds me indebted to you. In it you ask that, with our leisure, a leisure as great as you think you have or desire that we have, we indicate to you the progress we have made in distinguishing sensible nature and intelligible nature. But I do not think that you are unaware of the fact that, if anyone is more deeply immersed in false opinions to the extent that he is involved with them longer and with greater familiarity, the same thing happens much more readily to the mind with the truth. In that way, nonetheless, we gradually make progress with age. Though there is, of course, a great difference between a boy and a young man, no one who is asked daily from boyhood on will on a certain day say that he is now a young man.

2. I do not want you to interpret this in the sense that you think that we have come by the strength of a more solid intelligence, as it were, to a certain manhood of the mind. For we are boys, but, as it is often said, good boys and not bad ones. For the troubled eyes of my mind are filled with the concerns of wounds inflicted by the senses, but they are often revived and raised up by that little argument, which you know so well, that the mind and intelligence are better than the eyes and this ordinary looking. This would not be the case, unless those things that we understand had more being than these things which we see. I ask that you consider with me whether there is any strong opposition to this argument. Meanwhile, refreshed by this argument and having implored God's help, I begin to be raised up both to him and to those things that most truly are true, and I am at times filled with so great a foretaste of imperishable things that I am surprised that I at times need that argument in order to believe that those things exist that are in us with as much presence as each of us is present to himself. Please check for yourself—for I admit that you are more cautious about this matter than I am—lest, without knowing it, I am still owe you answers. For the sudden release from so many burdens, which I had at one point counted, does not make me confident about this, though I do not doubt that you have received letters from me for which I do not have replies.

LETTER 7
Augustine to Nebridius (388-391)

Between 388 and 391 Augustine replied to Nebridius' letter (Letter 6) in which his friend asked him for his views concerning the nature of memory and imagination; Augustine explains how there can be memory without images (paragraph 1). He appeals to the Platonic doctrine that intellectual learning is only remembering to show that we remember present intelligible things, though, he insists, our original vision of them was in the past (paragraph 2). He argues against Nebridius's idea that we can form images of sensible things without having previously used our senses (paragraph 3). The images we have can be divided into three kinds: those derived from previous sensations, for example, the image of a person I have seen; those we make up, for example, my image of Aeneas or of Medea; and those arrived at by reason, such as the image we form when reasoning with numbers and mathematical figures (paragraph 4). Augustine then shows that the soul has none of these kinds of images before it makes use of the senses of the body (paragraph 5). We can imagine things that we have never sensed because the soul has a power of diminishing and increasing images of things we have seen and of combining them in new ways, but we could never imagine the taste of strawberries or cherries before tasting them, just as someone born blind has no idea of colors (paragraph 6). Augustine tells Nebridius that he should not be surprised at how we can imagine things that we have never experienced through the senses since the soul has many activities that are free from images. Finally, he warns him to avoid entering into friendship with the shadowy images of sensible things (paragraph 7).

Augustine sends greetings to Nebridius.

1, 1. I shall refrain from any introduction and immediately begin what you impatiently want me to say, especially since I am not going to come to an end soon. You think that there can be no memory without images or representations of the imagination, which you chose to call "fantasies." I disagree. First, then, we must see that we do not always remember things that pass away, but very often things that last. Hence, though memory claims for itself a hold on past time, it is clear that memory, nonetheless, is in part memory of those things that leave us and in part memory of those things that we leave. For, when I remember my father, I, of course, remember someone who has left me and is no more, but when I remember Carthage, I remember something that still is and that I have left. In both of these kinds of things, however, memory holds onto the past time. For I remember both that man and this city from what I have seen, not from what I see.

2. Here you perhaps ask, "Where is this going?" especially since you observe that each of these can enter memory only by that representation of the

imagination. It is, however enough for me for the time being to have shown that one can say that there is also memory of those things that have not yet perished. But make yourself more attentive in order to hear how this helps me. Some speak falsely against that truly remarkable discovery of Socrates by which he maintains that those things that we learn are not impressed upon us as new, but are recalled into memory by recollection. These objectors say that memory is of past things, but that these things that we learn by understanding, on the authority of Plato himself,[169] last forever and cannot perish and, for this reason, are not past. They do not notice that this vision is past, because we once saw these things by the mind. And since we have flowed down from them and have begun to see other things in another way, we see them again by remembering them, that is, through memory. Hence, if—to leave other things aside—eternity itself lasts forever and does not require any products of the imagination upon which, as if upon vehicles, it might enter the mind and cannot, nonetheless, come into the mind unless we have remembered it, there can be a memory of certain things without any imagination.

2, 3. But your idea that the soul can imagine bodily things without having used the senses of the body is shown to be false in this way: If, before the soul uses the body for sensing bodily things, it can imagine the same bodily things and if—as no one in his right mind doubts—the soul was in a better state before it was entangled in these deceptive senses, the souls of the sleeping are in a better state than the souls of those awake, the souls of madmen are in a better state than those who are free from this plague. For the sleeping and the insane are affected by these images by which they were affected before having used the senses, these most deceptive messengers. And either the sun that they see will be truer than the sun that the sane and the awake see, or false things will be better than true ones. If these ideas are absurd, as they in fact are, that imagining, my dear Nebridius, is nothing but a wound inflicted by the senses, and they do not, as you write, produce a certain reminder so that such images are formed in the soul, but they cause the very introduction or, to put it more clearly, the impression of this falsity into or upon the soul. It, of course, bothers you how it happens that we think of those faces and shapes that we have never seen, and you are right to be bothered. I shall, therefore, do what will extend this letter beyond the usual limit, but not for you, for whom no page is more pleasing than one which brings you more words from me.

4. I see that all these images, which you call "fantasies" along with many people, are most suitably and truthfully divided into three kinds. One of these is impressed by things we sense; the second by things we think of; the third by things we reason to. Examples of the first kind are found when my mind pictures in itself for me your face or our late friend, Verecundus,[170] and anything else

---

169. See Plato, *Phaedrus* 72E; 75C.
170. Verecundus was a Milanese teacher of grammar who loaned Augustine and his friends his villa

of lasting or mortal things that I have, nonetheless, seen and sensed. Those fall under another kind that we suppose to have been or to be in a certain way, for example, when for the sake of argument we imagine certain things that in no sense are an obstacle to the truth, the sort of things we picture when we read histories and when we hear or compose or invent myths. For I picture for myself the face of Aeneas,[171] as I want and as it comes to my mind, the face of Medea[172] with her winged serpents bound to the yoke, the faces of Chremes and a certain Parmenon.[173] In this kind there are also included those that were substituted for the truth either by the wise who disguise a truth in such figures or by the foolish who found various superstitions, such as Phlegethon of the underworld, the five caves of the nation of darkness, the North Pole that holds up the heaven, and a thousand other portents of the poets and heretics.[174] We say even in the midst of an argument: Suppose that there are three worlds, one on top of the other, such as this one world is; suppose that a square shape encloses the earth, and the like. We frame and think of all these as the mood of our thought would have them. For with regard to the things that pertain to the third kind of images we deal most of all with numbers and dimensions. In part we do this in the real world, for example, when we discover the shape of the whole world, and there follows upon this discovery an image in the mind of the thinker. In part we do this in the disciplines, for example, in geometrical figures, musical rhythms, and the endless variety of numbers. Though they are in my opinion grasped as true, they, nonetheless, give rise to false imaginings, which reason itself scarcely resists. And yet it is not easy even for the discipline of logic to be free of this evil, since we imagine certain tokens,[175] as it were, in distinctions and conclusions.

5. In this whole forest of images I do not believe that you think that the first kind belongs to the soul before it is joined to the senses, nor is there need to discuss this further. With regard to the other two kinds one could still correctly pose the question, if it were not evident that the soul is less subject to falsity when it has not been exposed to the deceptiveness of sensible things and of the senses. But who has any doubt that these images are less true than these sensible things? For those things that we suppose and believe or invent are in every respect absolutely false, and those things that we see and sense are certainly far more true, as you recognize. Now in that third kind whatever bodily space I picture, though thought seems to have given birth to it by the principles of scientific disciplines,

---

at Cassiciacum where Augustine composed the earliest of his dialogues. See *Confessions* IX, 3, 5-6.
171. Aeneas is the hero of Virgil's epic poem, the *Aeneid*, on the founding of Rome.
172. In Greek mythology Medea helped Jason steal the golden fleece from her father.
173. Chremes and Parmenon are characters in a comedy of Terence.
174. Phlegethon is one of the rivers of the underworld; see Virgil, *Aeneid* VI, 551. The five caves are part of the Manichean myth.
175. Pebbles were used as tokens on a counting-board as a means of calculation in somewhat the same way the beads are used on an abacus.

which involve no deception, I prove it to be false by arguments from the same principles. As a result of this, I do not by any means believe that the soul lay in such a great ignominy of falsity, when it was not yet sensing by means of the body, when it was not yet pummeled through the deceptive senses by a mortal and fleeting substance.

6. How, then, does it come about that we think of things we have not seen? What do you suppose but that there is a certain power implanted in the soul for decreasing or increasing, a power that the soul carries with it wherever it goes? This power can be especially observed in the case of numbers. It, for example, causes the image of a raven set, as it were, before our eyes, which is, of course, familiar to our sight, to be transformed by adding and subtracting certain elements and to be turned into any image whatever that has absolutely never been seen before. It brings it about that shapes of this sort spontaneously, as it were, invade the thoughts of souls that habitually indulge in such things. By subtracting from or adding to, as was said, what sensation has brought to it, the soul that uses the imagination may, therefore, bring forth those things that it attains by no sense in their totality. But it had attained parts of them in this or that thing. In that way we children who were born and raised inland could already imagine seas just from seeing water in a small cup, though the taste of strawberries or cherries would never have entered our mind before we tasted them in Italy. This is the reason why those blind from infancy do not find anything to answer when they are questioned about the light and colors. For they never experience any colored images if they have not sensed any.

7. Do not be surprised at how those things that are formed in the nature of reality can be imagined, though the soul which is present in all does not first ponder them within itself, since it never perceived them externally. For, when in anger or joy or any of the other emotions of the mind we form in our body many expressions and hues, our thought does not first conceive that we can produce such images. These follow upon our emotions in those marvelous ways that are to be left to your consideration, when numbers hidden in the soul are brought on stage without any shape of bodily falsity. From this I would like you to understand that, since you experience so many acts of the mind free from all the images about which you are now asking, the soul acquires the body by any action other than by thinking of sensible forms, for I do not think it experiences these in any way before it has use of the senses of the body. Hence, by our friendship and by our very fidelity to the divine law I earnestly warn you, my very dear and most delightful friend, not to enter into friendship with these shadows of the lower world and not to hesitate to break off that friendship you have begun. For in no way do we resist the senses of the body, which is for us a most sacred duty, if we show fondness for the blows and wounds they inflict.

LETTER 18

Augustine to Celestine, a deacon, possibly the future pope (390-391)

During 390 or 391 Augustine wrote this letter to Celestine, possibly the same deacon and future pope to whom he wrote Letter 209. He asks Celestine to return his books on the Manicheans and sums up in a nutshell his view of the hierarchy of being and the task of the Christian life in relation to it.

Augustine sends greetings to Celestine.

1. How I wish I could constantly say one thing to you! But that one thing is that we should strip ourselves of empty worries and clothe ourselves in useful ones. For, with regard to a freedom from all worries, I do not know whether we should hope for any in this world. I wrote to you, and I did not receive a reply. I sent the books against the Manicheans that I could send once they were ready and corrected,[176] but nothing of your judgment or of your impression of them has been conveyed to me. It is now time for me to ask them back and for you to return them. I beg, therefore, that you do not delay to send them back with your reply from which I want to know what you are doing with them or what weapons you think you still need to defeat that error.

2. Since I, of course, know you well, receive this small, but important idea. There is a nature mutable in terms of places and of times, such as a body. There is also a nature mutable in no way in terms of places, but only in terms of times, such as the soul. And there is a nature which cannot be changed either in terms of places or in terms of times; this is God. What I have here said is mutable in some way is called a creature; what is immutable is the creator. But since we say that everything that we say is existing exists insofar as it lasts and insofar as it is one, and since unity is the form of all beauty, you, of course, see what exists in the highest manner, what exists in the lowest, but still exists, and what exists in an intermediate manner, greater than the lowest and less than the highest. That highest being is happiness itself; the lowest is what can be neither happy nor unhappy. That in the middle lives unhappily by turning to the lowest, but lives happily by conversion to the highest. One who believes in Christ does not love the lowest, is not proud over the intermediate, and thus becomes fit to cling to the highest. And this is the whole of what we are commanded, admonished, and set afire to do.

---

176. See *On the Catholic Way of Life and the Manichean Way of Life.*

LETTER 118

Augustine to Dioscorus, a young man, Greek by nationality (410-411)

In late 410 or early 411, Augustine replied to Dioscorus, a Greek by nationality, who was in Africa for studies, and sent him a list of questions on the philosophical works of Cicero. (Letter 117). This letter lacks the usual salutation. He complains that Dioscorus has asked him to answer many difficult questions, though Augustine would prefer to rescue him from such curiosity (paragraph 1). Augustine admonishes Dioscorus about the impropriety of a bishop's neglecting the care of his church in order to answer questions on the dialogues of Cicero (paragraph 2). He further admonishes him because Dioscorus' chief concern is that he might appear ignorant and stupid if he is unable to answer questions about these dialogues (paragraph 3). He accuses Dioscorus of being motivated only by the desires for praise from others and for freedom from their criticism (paragraph 3) and of acting for a childish, useless, and vain goal (paragraph 5). He urges Dioscorus to work for a goal that is firm and unchanging (paragraph 6).

Perhaps Dioscorus wants to avoid the appearance of stupidity and ignorance in order to gain an entrance to the minds of others in order to help them to learn some beneficial and salutary knowledge (paragraphs 7 and 8). In any case Dioscorus is not likely to encounter the sort of questions about Cicero in the Eastern lands where he is headed (paragraph 9), where people are more likely to question him about the original Greek texts from which Cicero drew his philosophy (paragraph 10). Furthermore, it is more important to know the salutary truth that Dioscorus wants to teach than the means to attract listeners (paragraph 11). And if this salutary truth is the truth of the Christian faith, Dioscorus would do better to learn about the various heresies than about the ancient Greek philosophers (paragraph 12).

As Themistocles was not ashamed of not knowing how to play the flute, since he knew how to govern a state, so Dioscorus should not be ashamed of any ignorance of Cicero, since he knows how to attain the happy life, which consists in the possession of the highest good (paragraph 13). The highest good, Augustine argues, is not to be found in the body or in the soul, but only in immutable wisdom, the creator, and by clinging to him the soul attains happiness (paragraphs 14 and 15). The Platonists held that our supreme good will be the enjoyment of God, who made us and all things. Hence, they opposed the Stoics who located the highest good in the soul and the Epicureans who located it in the body (paragraph 16). But the Platonists were unable to become living examples of true reason as the others were living examples of their error, because the Platonists did not have the example of the humility of our Lord, Jesus Christ, and without that example they could not persuade the people about the truth they attained about morality (paragraph 17), about nature (paragraph 18), and about logic (paragraph 19).

Hence, the Platonists chose to conceal their views and argue against those who claimed to have discovered the truth, namely, the Stoics and the Epicureans (paragraph 20). Augustine claims to have demonstrated the errors of the pagans, especially in the Stoics and the Epicureans who have now fallen silent so that no new error arises without claiming for itself the Christian name (paragraph 21).

Augustine urges Dioscorus to take the way Christ provided for us: humility, humility, humility (paragraph 22). To the humility of Christ there is opposed an ignorant knowledge that rejoices to know about the Greek philosophers inorder to appear learned. In fact, the teachings of Christianity are quite sufficient. Augustine insists, for example, that Anaximenes' view that God was air should not be of concern to someone who knows that God is incorporeal (paragraph 23). So too, there is no need to quarrel with Anaxagoras over a word for saying that mind is truth or wisdom (paragraph 24). Augustine uses Cicero's comments on Anaxagoras to emphasize the difficulty of thinking of non-bodily realities (paragraph 25). For the Stoics and the Epicureans maintained that there are only bodily things, while Anaxagoras held that there is a pure and simple wisdom and truth, saw that it was God, and called it a mind (paragraph 26). Yet, we are not learned because of the knowledge of Anaxagoras, much less because of that of Democritus (paragraph 27).

Augustine points to the difference between Democritus and Epicurus on nature (paragraph 28) and expresses surprise that Democritus did not see the falsity of his view of mind from the images that enter it (paragraph 29). Cicero refutes the account Democritus and Epicurus give of the production of images by atoms flowing from bodies (paragraph 30). It is deplorable that such ideas cannot be immediately rejected once they are explained, but need to be refuted at length (paragraph 31). Because of the great blindness of human minds, Dioscurus should realize that our race could be helped in no better way than by the Truth becoming man to teach people who are incapable of understanding through wisdom that they should believe for their salvation (paragraph 32).

The Platonists who did not have such a divine person concealed their views then, but began to disclose what Plato held after the coming of Christ and his Church (paragraph 33). Finally, Augustine tells Dioscorus that he may have preferred other things in this letter, but that what he has written will do him more good. Some questions, however, he declines to answer since they are not suited to his calling as a bishop (paragraph 34).

1, 1. You thought that I should be suddenly besieged or rather overwhelmed by a horde of countless questions, as if you believed that I was unemployed and at leisure. After all, when could I in any amount of leisure resolve so many knotty problems for someone in such a rush and, as you write, already departing at the moment? For I would be prevented by the number of the questions, even if the problems were easy to resolve. But they are wrapped in such complexity and knotted with such tightness that, even if they were few and found me completely at leisure, they would weary my mind by the great amount of time they would take and would wear my finger to the bone. But I would like to snatch you from the midst of your delightful questioning and surround you with my worries in order that you might learn not to be uselessly curious or to impose the feeding and nuturing of your curiosity upon those who have it among their cares, or even as their greatest care, to repress and to hold in check the curious. How much better, after all, how much more fruitful it would be if the time and effort spent in writing any letter to you were spent rather on trimming back your vain and deceitful desires! These are the more to be avoided the more they readily deceive, when veiled and covered by some shadow of morality and by the name of the liberal arts. How much better this would be than that our ministry and, so to speak, complicity should arouse more vehemently those desires so as to weigh down so fine a mind as yours.

2. Look, if all the dialogues[177] that you read have helped you in no way to see and grasp the end of all your actions, tell me, what good do they do you? For you clearly enough indicate by your letter where you locate the end of this whole most burning desire of yours, which is both fruitless for you and bothersome for us. For, when you were doing everything you could with me by letter concerning the solution of the questions which you sent me, you wrote as follows, "I could have," you said, "pleaded with you more and through many of your friends, but I know your mind. You do not desire to be begged, but to give to all, provided only that there is nothing improper involved, and in this matter there is absolutely nothing improper. Nevertheless, whatever it is, I am about to set sail and I ask that you give it to me."[178] In these words of your letter you are, of course, correct in thinking that I desire to give to everyone, provided that nothing improper is involved, but it is not evident to me that there is nothing improper involved in this matter. For my mind fails to find a proper appearance of things when I think that a bishop, torn this way and that by noisy concerns of the Church, holds himself back from all these, as if he suddenly became deaf, and explains minor questions about the Ciceronian dialogues to a single intellectual. Although, caught up in the ardor of your desire, you do not want to notice how improper this is, even you, nonetheless, see it. For what else does it indicate that, when you said that "in this matter there is absolutely nothing improper," you added immediately, "Nonetheless, whatever it is, I am about to set sail and I ask that you give it to me." For this sounds as though it seems to you, of course, that there is nothing improper in this matter, but whatever impropriety there is, you ask that I give it to you, who are about to set sail. But why is it that you added, "who am about to set sail"? Ought I not to give you anything if you were not going to set sail? You, of course, suppose that the sea water will wash away the impropriety. If that were

---

177. Augustine is referring to the philosophical works of Cicero.
178. Letter 117.

the case, certainly my impropriety, for I am not about to set sail, would remain without being wiped away.

3. You also write that I know how much you dislike to be a burden to anyone, and you declare that God alone knows that you did this, driven by great necessity. When I read your letter, I, of course, applied my mind to know your necessity when, look, you present me with the following, "You are familiar with the behavior of human beings: They are inclined to be critical, and if someone is asked a question and does not reply, they will consider him unlearned and stupid." At this point I burned with the desire to reply to you, for with that malady of your mind you penetrated my heart and burst into my concerns so that I could not ignore healing you to the extent that the Lord might help. It was not that I had in mind resolving and explaining your questions; instead I wanted to tear your happiness—dependent, as it is, upon the tongues of human beings and fluctuating accordingly—away from so unfortunate a hawser and tie it to a site that was utterly unshakeable and stable. And you, O Dioscurus, do not notice your Persius,[179] not mocking you with his clever verse but pummeling and twisting your boyish head, if you have any sense, with a fitting slap. Your knowledge amounts to nothing Unless someone else knows that you know it.[180]

You have, as you said above, read so many dialogues; you have filled your heart with the arguments of so many philosophers. Tell me, which of them place the end of their actions in popular acclaim or in the tongues of human beings, even the good and the wise ones? But you—and this is something more shameful—on the verge of setting sail declare that you have made quite excellent progress in Africa, while you state that you are being a burden to bishops, men extremely busy and attending to other far different matters, in order to have them explain Cicero[181] to you for no other reason than that you are afraid of people inclined to criticize, who might think that you are unlearned and stupid if they asked you a question and you could not reply! O what a task to keep bishops awake and worried over at night!

4. To me you seem to think of nothing else day and night but that you may be praised by human beings in your studies and learning. And what I judged to be something perilous for those whose goals are certain and correct, I, nonetheless, find, especially in your case. It is only because of that destruction that you have not, after all, seen the motive that could move us to give you what you asked. For you are wrongly caught up in learning those things that you are asking for only in order that you might be praised or not criticized by human beings, and you also just as wrongly think that we are moved by such reasons as you alleged

---

179. Persius (Aulus Persius Flaccus, A.D. 34-62), a Stoic, was a Roman poet and satirist.
180. Persius, *Satires* 1, 27.
181. Cicero (Marcus Tullius Cicero, 106-43 B.C.) was a Roman statesman, rhetorician and philosopher who, among his numenrous achievements, brought the Greek philosophical tradition to Rome.

in your request. And would that we could bring it about that you also would not be moved by so empty and fallacious a good as human praise when we indicate to you that we are not moved to give you what you ask for because you write this about yourself, but to correct you! "The behavior of human beings," you say, "is inclined to criticize." So what? "If someone is asked a question and does not reply, they will consider him unlearned and stupid." Look, I am asking you a question not about the books of Cicero, the meaning of which his readers perhaps cannot discover, but about your own letter and about the meaning of your words. For I ask why you did not say, "They will prove that one who does not reply is unlearned and stupid," but said rather, "They will consider him unlearned and stupid," unless you yourself understand well enough that someone who does not give such answers is not unlearned and stupid, but thought to be. But I warn you that someone who fears to be cut by the tongues of such thinkers, as if by scythes, is dry wood and, therefore, is not merely thought to be unlearned and stupid, but is truly so and proven to be so.

5. Perhaps you will say, "But since I am not dull-witted and I study precisely so that I may not be, I do not want even to be thought such." Good, but for what purpose do you not want this? That is what I ask. For you did not hesitate to be a burden to us in our resolving and explaining those questions, and you said that this reason and this purpose was so necessary that you called it a great necessity, namely, that human beings inclined to criticize would not consider you to be unlearned and stupid, when you are questioned about these matters and do not reply. I, however, ask whether this is the whole reason why you want this from us, or do you also want to avoid being thought unlearned and stupid for some other reason? If this is the whole reason, you see, I think, that this is the goal of this intense desire of yours, because of which you are also a burden to us, as you admit. But what from Dioscorus can be a burden for us except what weighs down Dioscorus even without his knowing it? He will not feel it unless he wants to rise up. And would that these burdens were not so tied on that he tries in vain to shake them from his shoulders! I do not say this because you are learning the answers to those questions, but because you are learning them for such a goal. For you surely see that this goal is childish, useless, and vain. It has a swelling under which a cancer also grows, and the pupil of the mind is blocked in order not to see the richness of the truth. Believe me, my Dioscorus; it is true. I pray that I may enjoy your friendship in the desire for the truth and in the dignity of the truth, by whose shadow you are turned away. For I find no way save this to convince you about this matter. After all, you do not see it, nor can you in any way see it as long as you pile up crumbling joys from the tongues of human beings.

6. If, however, the goal of these actions and of this desire is not found there, but you do not want to be thought unlearned and stupid for some other reason, I ask what it is. If it is so that you might have easier access for acquiring temporal riches, for winning a wife, for procuring honors and other such things,

which rush away in a swift stream and carry those who have fallen into it to the bottom, it is not fitting for us to be of service to you for that purpose; in fact, it is fitting that we even turn you away from it. After all, we are not prohibiting you from locating the goal in the incertitude of fame so that you move from the Mincius to the Eridanus[182] in order that perhaps the Mincius might not soak you when you move from it. For, since the vanity of human praise does not satisfy the hungry spirit because it offers nothing to eat except what is hollow and full of air, the hunger itself forces it to appeal to something else as richer and more fruitful. If this, nonetheless, is carried off by the flow of time, it is as if one river leads to another so that there is no end of misery as long as the goal of our duties is located in something unstable. We, therefore, want you to fix the abode of your utterly constant purpose and the most secure repose of all your good and honest actions in some firm and unchangeable good. Or if by a breeze of favorable popularity or even by opening the sails to the winds you could arrive at this earthly happiness, which I mentioned, do you think that you can refer this to another certain, true, and complete good? But it does not seem so to me, and the truth itself absolutely denies that such great wandering leads to the truth, which is so near, or that such great expenses are needed for the truth, which is so free.

7. Or do you think that you should use human praise as a means to prepare the entrance way to the minds of human beings for persuading them of what is true and salutary, and are you afraid that, when they think that you are unlearned and stupid they will think you someone unworthy for them to offer a very attentive or very patient hearing, whether you exhort someone to good deeds or upbraid the malice and wickedness of a sinner? If you were thinking of this goal of righteousness and beneficence in asking those questions, we have not been treated well by you. For you did not set forth in your letter the motive that might move us either to give gladly what you are asking for or not to give it on the grounds that some other cause perhaps prevented us. After all, it would be shameful not only to cater to your vain desire but even not to resist it. For how much better and more conducive to salvation would it be, I ask you, to accept the rules of the truth! How much more certain and brief it would be to accept by themselves those rules by which you could refute all those errors! Otherwise, and this is something false and shameful, you will think that you are learned and intelligent if you have learned those old, worn-out errors of many people with a more proud than prudent zeal. But now I do not think that you hold this. For we have not in vain stated so many truths to Dioscorus for so long a time since we began this letter.

2, 8. Hence, let us now see that other point, since you by no means judge yourself unlearned and stupid because of ignorance of these matters but rather because of ignorance of the truth. For, whoever has written or will write on these matters, either they are what you now hold with certitude, or you are safely ignorant of them if they are false. Then you will not waste away with worry about

---

182. Eridanus is the classical name for the Po; the Mincius is a tributary of the Po.

knowing the diversity of other views for fear that you remain as if unlearned and stupid. Since this, then, is the case, let us also see that issue, if you please. I mean whether the false judgment of others who, as you write, are inclined to criticize so that, if they perceive that you do not know these things, they will think, though falsely, that you are unlearned and stupid, ought to disturb you to the point that you act appropriately in asking bishops to explain them to you. For we believe that you now desire these things with the goal of helping those people to convince them of the truth and to correct their lives. After all, if they think you unlearned and stupid regarding those books of Cicero, they will not consider you someone valuable from whom they think that they should learn for themselves any beneficial and salutary knowledge.

9. Believe me that is not the case, first, because I do not at all see that in those lands where you are afraid to be seen as unlearned and dull there are men who will ask you anything about these topics. For both here, where you came to learn these matters, and in Rome you experienced how lightly they are valued and, for this reason, are neither taught nor studied. And in Africa you suffer from no questioner on these matters to the point that you do not find anyone who will put up with you, and because of that dearth you are forced to send those questions to bishops for an explanation. You suppose that, even if these bishops, when young, took care to learn these matters as something important with the same ardor or rather error of mind by which you are carried off, they allowed them to remain in their memory until their episcopal heads were gray with age and while they sat upon their ecclesiastical seats. Or, if these men wanted them to remain, would not greater and more serious worries drive them from their hearts, even if they did not want that to happen, or if some of these things remained in their minds because of ingrained habit, would they not prefer to bury them in utter oblivion, when they come to mind, than to reply to foolish questions. For even in the superficiality of the schools and in the chairs of rhetoric they seem to have met with silence and lack of interest to the point that people think that such questions should be sent from Carthage to Hippo in order to be answered. But here they are so unusual and utterly foreign that, if I wanted to look at a text in my concern to reply, desiring to see how the author came from the previous statement to the one I am supposed to explain or how the argument continues from there, I could not in fact find the text of Cicero. If, however, those professors of rhetoric at Carthage were of no help in this study of yours, I not only do not blame them, but even give them my approval, if they perhaps recall that these debates were customarily held not in the forums of Rome but in the gymnasiums of Greece. But when you turned your thoughts to the gymnasiums and found them also bare as well and cold to such matters, the basilica of the Christians at Hippo occurred to you as the place to deposit your concerns, because there now sits in it a bishop who once sold such ideas to children.[183] I, however, do not want you to be a child,

---

183. Augustine is referring to his secular career as professor of rhetoric.

and it is not proper that I hand out childish nonsense as I once sold it. Since this is so, that is, since two great cities, masters of Latin literature, Rome and Carthage, neither worry you with questions on these points nor care about your worries so they listen to your questions about them, I am amazed more than I can say that you, a young man with a fine mind, are afraid that in Greek and Eastern cities you will encounter any troublesome questioner on these matters. You will more readily hear horns in Africa than this sort of talk in those parts.

10. Second, suppose that I am wrong and that someone there asks such questions, someone more of a pest to the extent that in those places he is more inept. Would you not be afraid that once you, who have been trained in the Greek language from early on, found yourself in Greece, there would much more likely be Greeks there who might ask you some questions about the very books of the philosophers that Cicero did not quote in his writings? But if this happens, what are you going to answer? That you preferred to know these things in the books of Latin authors rather than in those of the Greeks? By that answer you will first of all offend Greece, and you know how those men do not tolerate this. Then, once they have been offended and angered, how quickly they will judge you stupid—precisely what you want to avoid in every way—because you preferred to learn the teachings of Greek philosophers or rather certain tiny pieces of their teachings torn from them and scattered about in Latin dialogues rather than to learn the whole of them in their proper setting in the Greek books of their own authors. How quickly they will also judge you unlearned because, though you do not know so many things in your own language, you have set out to gather crumbs of those same things in a foreign language. Will you perhaps answer that you have not scorned the Greek books on these topics, but took care to learn the Latin ones first, and that you want to study the Greek ones now that you are learned in the Latin books? If you, a Greek, are not ashamed to have learned the Latin works as a boy and now want to learn the Greek works as a man, will you be ashamed not to know some things in the Latin books that very many learned Latin speakers do not know along with you? Or are you aware of this from the very fact that you say that you are under such great necessity to be a burden to us because you find yourself at Carthage among so great a multitude of learned men?

11. Finally, suppose that you could reply, when questioned, on all those points about which you ask us. See, you will now be called very learned and very clever; see, a little Greek flattery already lifts you skyward with praises. Only remember your seriousness and the end for which you wanted to earn that praise, namely, in order that you might teach something very important and salutary to those people who are easily awed by trivia and hang upon your every word with much good will and great eagerness. I would like to know whether you possess and know how to hand on that very important and salutary something, whatever it is. For, when you learn many superfluous things precisely in order to prepare the ears of others for necessary things, it is ridiculous not to possess those necessary things, for the reception of which you prepared their ears by superfluous things.

And, while you are busy learning how to make them attentive, it is ridiculous for you to refuse to learn what you should teach them once you have their attention. But if you say that you already know this and reply that it is the Christian teaching, for we know you prefer it to all others and that you are confident that it alone contains the hope of eternal salvation, it requires no knowledge of Cicero's dialogues and of a collection of contradictory maxims begged from others in order to gain hearers. Let those who are going to receive from you such a teaching become attentive because of your moral conduct. I do not want you first to teach something that must be unlearned in order that you may teach the truth.

12. For if the knowledge of other dissident and contrary views in some way helps the teacher of the Christian truth to know how to destroy opposing errors, it helps at least so that anyone arguing in opposition does not set his eye only on refuting your views while he carefully hides his own. For the knowledge of the truth is able to detect all errors and to destroy them, even those that were previously unheard of, if they are only brought forth. But in order not only that those that are known might be combatted but also that those that are hidden might be uncovered, if there is need to know the errors of others, raise up your eyes and ears, I beg you, and see and hear whether anyone brings forth any objection against us from Anaximenes and Anaxagoras,[184] when not even the ashes of the much more recent and much more loquacious Stoics or Epicureans[185] are warm enough that a spark can be stirred from them against the Christian faith. But the noise of battle is heard here from the circles and assemblies, partly in flight, partly also boldly advancing, of the Donatists, Maximianists, and Manicheans,[186] and also in the flocks and peoples to whom you are going, those of the Arians, Eunomians, Macedonians, Cataphrygians,[187] and the other plagues in countless numbers. If you are too lazy to learn the errors of all these, why does it fall to us to investigate what Anaximenes thought for the sake of the defense of the Christian religion and to rehash out of empty curiosity quarrels that have long since fallen asleep, while nothing is now said of the disagreements and questions of certain heretics, such as the Marcionites and Sabellians[188] and many others who glory in the Christian name. If, nonetheless, it is necessary, as I said, to know in advance and to have a thorough examination of some views opposed to the truth,

---

184. Two of the earliest Presocratic philosophers, Anaximenes and Anaximander, both of Miletus, flourished in the 6th century B.C.
185. The Stoics were founded by Zeno of Citium (ca. 362/357–264/259 B.C.); the Epicureans were founded by Epicurus of Athens (341-270 B.C.). Their followers were opposed to one another on many points, as Augustine indicates.
186. For the Donatists see *Heresies* 69; the Maximianists split away from the Donatists. For the Manicheans, see Heresies 46.
187. Augustine mentions a series of Eastern heresies. For the Arians see *Heresies* 49; for the Eunomians see ibid. 54; for the Macedonians see ibid. 52; for the Cataphrygians see ibid. 26.
188. For the Sabellians and the Marcionites see ibid. 41 and 22 repectively.

we ought to give thought to the heretics who call themselves Christians rather than to Anaxagoras and Democritus.[189]

3, 13. Whoever he may be who asks of you the questions you ask of us, let him hear that you are more learned and more wise in your not knowing them. For Themistocles[190] did not care that he was considered rather ignorant when he refused to play the lyre at a banquet, and, when he said that he did not know how to do that, he was asked, "What, then, do you know?" He answered: "To make a great state out of a lesser one."[191] Should you, then, hesitate to say that you do not know these things, since you could reply to someone who asks what you know that you know how a human being can be happy even without these things? And if you do not yet have this knowledge, you are as misguided in seeking these other things as you would be misguided, when you are afflicted with some dangerous illness of the body, in seeking delicacies and finery rather than doctors and medicine. For you must by no means postpone this knowledge or prefer those other things to it, even in the order of learning, especially at this age. But see how easily you could know this if you wanted. For one who asks how to come to the happy life asks, of course, for nothing else but where the ultimate good is, that is, where the highest good of a human being resides, not according to a wrong or rash opinion but according to certain and unshakable truth. And no one finds any place where it resides except either in the body or in the soul or in God or in any two of them or surely in all of them. But if you have learned that neither the highest good nor some part of it is in the body, two possibilities remain: the soul and God, in one or two of which it might reside. If, however, you go on and learn that the same thing holds true of the soul as of the body, what else besides God comes to mind as that in which the highest good of a human being resides? It is not that other things are not good, but that is said to be the highest good to which the rest are ordered. Each is happy when enjoying that for the sake of which he wants to have all the other things, while that is now loved, not for the sake of something else, but for its own sake. And the end is said to be there, because one finds nowhere further to go or to be directed. There is rest from seeking; there is security in enjoying; there is the utterly tranquil joy of a complete good will.

14. Give me, then, someone who is quick to see that the body is not the good of the soul but that the soul, rather, is the good of the body. He will immediately cease from asking whether that highest good or some part of it is in the body. For it is most foolish to deny that the soul is better than the body. It is likewise most foolish to deny that what gives the happy life or some part of the happy life is better than what receives it. The soul, therefore, does not receive from the body either the highest good or some part of the highest good. Those who do not

---

189. Democritus of Abdera (494-404 B.C.) was the leading atomist among the Greek philosophers.
190. Themistocles (524-460 B.C.) was an Athenian politician who saved Greece from subjection to the Persian empire at the Battle of Salamis
191. See Plutarch, *Themistocles* 2; Cicero, *Tusculan Disputations* I, 2, 4.

see this are blinded by the sweetness of carnal pleasures, which they do not see comes from the lack of good health. But the perfect health of the body is that powerful a nature that from its full happiness, which is promised to the saints in the end of time, there will also overflow into the inferior nature, that is, into the body, not the happiness that is proper to one who enjoys and understands, but the fullness of health, that is, the strength of incorruptibility. Those who do not see this, as I said, fight with restless quarrels, each one locating, according to his grasp, the highest good of human beings in the body, and they stir up the masses of carnal and rebellious people. Among these the Epicureans[192] enjoyed a more excellent authority in the eyes of the unlearned multitude.

15. Likewise give me someone who is quick to see that, when it is happy, the soul itself is not happy because of its own good; otherwise, it would never be unhappy, and it would cease from asking whether that highest and, so to speak, beatifying good or some part of it is in the soul. For, when the soul rejoices in itself, because of itself, as if then because of its own good, it is proud. But when it sees that it is changeable, at least because of this one fact, namely, that it becomes wise from foolish, and when it sees that wisdom is immutable, it ought at the same time to see that wisdom is above its own nature and that the soul more richly and more certainly rejoices because of partaking of it and because of being illumined by it than because of itself. Ceasing in that way and subsiding from its own boasting and inflatedness, it strives to cling to God and to be re-created and re-formed by that immutable being, from whom it already grasps that there comes not only every form of all the things that are attained either by the senses of the body or by the intelligence of the mind, but also that very capacity for formation before it is formed, when it is said to be something unformed that can be formed. In that way the soul perceives that it is less stable to the extent that it clings less to God, who exists in the highest way, and that he exists in the highest way because he neither makes progress nor fails because of any mutability. The soul perceives, however, that it profits from that change by which it makes progress so that it clings to God perfectly and that the change that consists in its failing is full of defects. But every defect tends toward destruction, and even if it is not clear that a particular thing comes to destruction it is, nonetheless, clear to everyone that destruction brings it to the point that it is no longer what it was. Hence, the soul concludes that things fail or can fail for no other reason than that they were made out of nothing and that the fact that they are and last and are ordered toward the harmony of the universe in accord with their defects pertains to the goodness and omnipotence of him who exists in the highest way, the creator, who is able to produce not only something out of nothing but even something great out of nothing. But the first sin, that is, the first voluntary defect, is to rejoice over one's own power, for in this case one rejoices over something smaller

---

192. The followers of Epicurus were thought to have located the highest good in pleasures, especially those of the body.

than if one rejoiced over God's power, which is, of course, greater. Those who do not see this and who look upon the powers of the human soul and the great beauty of its words and deeds and who locate the highest good in the human soul, though they were ashamed to locate it in the body, have certainly located it lower than where it ought to be located by reason at its clearest. Among the Greek philosophers who think this way, the Stoics have predominated in number and in the subtlety of argument, but because they think that everything in the natural world is bodily, they were better able to turn the soul away from the flesh than from the body.

16. Among those who say that our one and supreme good will be to enjoy the God by whom both we and all things have been made, the Platonists[193] were preeminent among them. With good reason they thought that it was their duty to resist the Stoics and Epicureans chiefly and almost exclusively. The Academics are, of course, the same as the Platonists, as the very sequence of disciples teaches us. For Arcesilas[194] was the first who, having concealed his own opinion, decided to do nothing but refute those people. Ask whose place he took, and you will find Polemon; ask whose place he took, and you will find Xenocrates.[195] But Plato left his school, the Academy, to his disciple, Xenocrates. Insofar, then, as it pertains to the highest good of human beings, remove the individual human beings and consider the argument itself. You will find, of course, that the two errors collide with each other head-on, one that locates the highest good in the body, the other that locates it in the soul. But the nature of the truth, by which God is understood to be our highest good, resists both of these, not teaching the truth, however, before it refutes their errors. Consider the argument again with the individual persons included, and you will find that the Epicureans and the Stoics are fighting bitterly with each other, but that the Platonists, while trying to settle the argument between those two, still conceal their own views while accusing and refuting the vain confidence in error on the part of the others.

17. But the Platonists were not able to become the living example of true reason as those other philosophers were able to become living examples of their errors. For they were all lacking the example of divine humility, which was revealed at the most opportune moment by our Lord Jesus Christ. Before that one example all pride yields, is broken, and dies in the mind of anyone, no matter how terribly arrogant. And so the Platonists were unable by their authority to bring the masses blinded by a love of earthly things to a faith in invisible things. For they saw that the masses were moved, especially by the Epicurean arguments, not only to experience bodily pleasure, which they willingly pursued, but

---

193. The term "Platonists" refers to all the followers of Plato, though for Augustine the principal Platonists were Plotinus (204/205-270 A.D.) and Porphyry, his student, who organized Plotinus' teachings in the *Enneads*.
194. Arcesilas of Pitane (c. 315-241 B.C.) is regarded as having founded the New Academy.
195. Polemon of Athens was converted to philosophy by Xenocrates, whom he followed as head of the Academy from 314 to 270 B.C.

even to defend it to the point that they located in it the highest good of a human being. But they saw that those who were roused against this pleasure by the praise of virtue contemplated it with less difficulty in the soul of human beings, from which there proceed good deeds, about which they were somehow able to judge. At the same time they saw that, if they tried to teach them about some reality that was divine and immutable above all things and that was attained by no bodily sense, but understood by the mind alone, a reality that, nonetheless, surpasses the nature of the mind, the people would not understand. If they tried to teach them that this reality is God, who is promised for the enjoyment of the human mind that has been purified from every stain of human desires, in whom alone all our longing for happiness would come to rest, and in whom alone we would have the attainment of all goods, the people would not understand and would ascribe victory to the Epicureans or to the Stoics, their opponents, much more readily than to the Platonists. Therefore, the true and salutary teaching would become scorned by the mockery of peoples, something that is most harmful for the human race. And this holds for morality.

18. But on questions about nature the Platonists said that incorporeal wisdom is the creator of all natures, while those others never moved away from bodies, since some assigned the principles of things to atoms and others to the four elements, among which fire was the most important for making all things. Hence, who would not see which side the multitude of the foolish, who are completely given over to bodies, would be most drawn to support, since they cannot see the incorporeal power that is the creator of things?

19. There remained the part with questions on logic. For you know that whatever is sought in order to acquire wisdom poses a question either about morals, or about the natural world, or about reason. Since, then, the Epicureans said that the bodily senses are never deceived, while the Stoics admitted that they are deceived at times, though they both, nonetheless, placed the criterion of grasping the truth in the senses, who would listen to the Platonists, given the opposition of these philosophers? Who would think that they should be included not only in the number of the wise but in that of human beings at all, if they said right off that there is not only something that can be perceived neither by the touch of the body nor by smell or taste, nor by these ears or eyes, and is not thought of at all by some imagining of the sort of things that are sensed in that way, but that it alone truly exists and it alone can be perceived? For it is immutable and everlasting but perceived by the intelligence alone, by which the one truth is attained, however it is attained.

20. Since the Platonists, then, held such views which they would not teach to human beings completely given over to the flesh, and since they did not enjoy such great authority among the people that they persuaded them to believe such who boasted that they had discovered the truth, though they located the discovery of the truth in the bodily senses. And how is it relevant to examine what their plan was? It certainly was not divine or endowed with divine authority.

Consider only the fact that Cicero most clearly shows in many ways that Plato located the highest good and the causes of things and the trustworthiness of reason in wisdom, not human wisdom but clearly the divine wisdom by which human wisdom is kindled, that is, in wisdom that is absolutely immutable and in the truth that is always the same.[196] Consider, too, that the Platonists attacked in the name of the Epicureans and Stoics those who located the highest good, the causes of things, and the trustworthiness of reason in the nature of the body or of the mind. Consider that in the course of time the situation came to the point that, at the beginning of the Christian era, faith in invisible and eternal realities was proclaimed through visible miracles for their salvation to human beings, although they could neither see nor think of anything besides bodies. And consider that these very same Epicureans and Stoics are found to have in the Acts of the Apostles opposed the blessed apostle Paul who was spreading that same faith among the nations.[197]

21. In this argument it seems to me that I have demonstrated sufficiently the errors of the pagans, whether on morals or on the nature of reality or on the method of investigating the truth. Though these errors were many and varied, they stood forth, nonetheless, principally in these two sects and, despite the attacks of the learned who were overthrowing them with such a great subtlety and abundant argument, they lasted, nonetheless, even into the Christian era. We see that now at least in our age they have fallen silent so that in the schools of rhetoric it is now hardly so much as mentioned what their views were. The debates, nonetheless, have been eradicated and removed even from the most garrulous gymnasiums of the Greeks so that, if any erroneous sect now emerged in opposition to the truth, that is, in opposition to the Church of Christ, it would not dare to step forth for battle if it were not clothed with the Christian name. From this it is understood that those philosophers of the Platonic school, having changed a few things of which Christian discipline disapproves, ought to bow their pious necks to the one king, Christ, and to understand that when he, the Word of God clothed with a man, commanded faith, the people believed what the Platonists were afraid even to state.

22. I wish, my Dioscorus, that you would be subject to him in complete piety and would not construct another way to reach and to gain the truth than that way which he constructed who, as God, saw the weakness of our steps. That first way, however, is humility; the second way is humility, and the third way is humility, and as often as you ask, I would say this. It is not that there are no other commandments that should be mentioned, but unless humility precedes and accompanies and follows upon all our good actions and is set before us to gaze upon, set alongside for us to cling to, and set over us to crush us down, pride tears the whole benefit from our hand when we rejoice over some good deed. We must

---

196. See Cicero, *The Ends of the Good and the Evil* V, 15, 43.
197. See Acts 17:18.

fear the other vices in sinful actions, but pride even in good deeds. Otherwise we will lose, because of the desire for praise, those things that were done in a praiseworthy manner. And so, when that most distinguished orator was asked what he thought one ought first of all to observe in the rules of eloquence, he is said to have answered, "Delivery." And when he was asked what came second, he said again, "Delivery." And asked what came third, he said only, "Delivery."[198] So too, if you ask and as often as you ask about the rules of the Christian religion, I would answer only, "Humility," even if necessity would perhaps force me to say something else.

4, 23. Our Lord Jesus Christ humbled himself in order to teach us this most salutary humility. To this humility, I say, there is strongly opposed a certain most ignorant knowledge, so to speak, when we rejoice that we know what Anaximenes, what Anaxagoras, what Pythagoras,[199] and what Democritus held and other things like this in order that we may appear learned and educated, though this is far distant from true learning and education. After all, one who has learned that God is not extended or spread out in places, whether finite or infinite, as if he were larger in one part and smaller in another, but is present as whole everywhere, like the truth, of which no one sensibly says that a part is in this place and a part is in that place, for the truth is, of course, God, will in no way be disturbed about what he thought about the infinite air, whoever thought that it was God. What difference does it make to him if he does not know what these men say is the form of the body—they, of course, say that it is that which is limited on all sides—and whether for the sake of refutation Cicero, like an Academic, objected to Anaximenes that God must have form and beauty like bodily beauty, thinking that Anaximenes had said that God was bodily?[200] For air is a body. Or did he hold that the truth has an incorporeal beauty by which the mind is informed and by which we judge that all the actions of a wise person are beautiful so that Cicero said not merely for the sake of refutation, but also with complete truth, that it is right that God have a most beautiful appearance, because nothing is more beautiful than intelligible and immutable truth? But the fact that Anaximenes said that air, which he, nonetheless, thought was God, is generated does not in any way bother a man who understands that the Word of God, God with God, was not generated in the way in which air is generated, that is, caused to be by some cause, but in a far different way, which no one will understand except one whom God himself inspires. But who would not see that Anaximenes is unwise even regarding bodies themselves, since he says that air is generated and wants it to be God, but says that the source from which air is generated—for it cannot be generated from nothing—is not God? But when he says that air is always

---

198. See Cicero, *The Orator* III, 56, 213, where he reports that Demosthenes said that acting was of such importance for the orator.
199. Pythagoras of Samos flourished in the middle of the 6th century B.C.; he is best known for his doctrine of the transmigration of souls.
200. See Cicero, *The Nature of the Gods* I, 26.

in motion, he will in no way confuse someone so that he thinks it is God, if he knows that the motion of every body is inferior to the motion of the soul, but that the motion of the soul is far more sluggish than the motion of the highest and immutable truth.

24. Likewise, if Anaxagoras or anyone says that mind is the truth and wisdom,[201] why should I quarrel with the man over a word? It is, after all, evident that it produces the arrangement and measure of all things and that it is not incongruously said to be endless, not in space, but in its power, which human thought cannot comprehend. Nor does it follow that this wisdom is something formless, for this characteristic pertains to bodies, namely, that whichever bodies are without limit are also formless. But in his desire, it seems, to refute his adversaries who thought only of bodily things, Cicero denies that anything can be joined to something unlimited, because in bodies on that side on which anything is joined to something there must be some limit. Hence, he says that he also did not see that "there cannot be any motion united with sensation or connected," that is, clinging with a continuous union, "to the infinite,"[202] that is, to some unlimited thing, as if he were dealing with bodies, to which nothing can be united except through spatial limits. But he added as follows, "Nor can there be any sensation at all without the whole of nature sensing the repercussion,"[203] as if Anaxagoras had said that the mind, which orders and governs all things, had sensation like that which the soul has through the body. For it is evident that the whole soul senses when it senses something through the body. After all, the whole soul is aware of whatever it is that is sensed. But Cicero said that the whole of nature senses precisely to deprive Anaxagoras, as it were, of his claim that mind is without limit. For how does the whole mind sense if it is without limit? After all, bodily sensation begins from some place, and it does not run through the whole except of that thing to whose end it comes, and that thing cannot be called endless. But Anaxagoras had not spoken about bodily sensation, and an incorporeal whole is spoken of in another way, because it is understood to be without limits in space so that it can be said to be both whole and endless: whole because of its entirety and endless because it is not circumscribed by spatial limits.

25. "Then," he says, "if he intended this mind to be like some living being, there will be something interior because of which it will be called a living being,"[204] so that this mind is like a body and has within it a soul, because of which it is called a living being. See how he speaks out of the habit of dealing with bodies, in the way in which living beings are often viewed, on account of the

---

201. Anaxagoras held that that there is an infinite mind (νοῦς) that has power over all things. Augustine draws his information on Anaxagoras from the previously mentioned passage of Cicero's work.
202. Cicero, *The Nature of the Gods* I, 26.
203. Ibid.
204. Ibid.

obtuseness, I think, of those against whom he is speaking, and he, nonetheless, mentioned something that, if they were alert, would have sufficiently warned them, namely, that everything like a living body that comes to mind must be thought to have a soul and is a living being rather than a soul. For this is what he says, "There will be something interior because of which it is called a living being." But he adds, "What is more interior than the mind?"[205] A mind, therefore, cannot have an interior soul so that it is a living being because it is itself interior. Hence, it has a body outside in relation to which it is interior in order that there may be a living being. For this is what he says, "It is, therefore, clothed with a body externally,"[206] as if Anaxagoras said that a mind could not exist unless it belonged to some living being. It could be that Cicero held that the mind was itself the highest wisdom, which does not properly belong, so to speak, to any living being, because the truth offers herself in common to all souls who are able to enjoy her. And for this reason, see how acutely he concludes: "And since this is not acceptable," that is, it is not acceptable to Anaxagoras that the mind, which he calls God, is clothed with a body externally by reason of which it can be a living being, "a pure and simple mind without anything united to it by which it could have sensation," that is, without any body united to it by which it could have sensation, "seems to escape the power and grasp of our intelligence."[207]

1. There is nothing more true than that this escapes the power and grasp of the intelligence of the Stoics and Epicureans who can only think of bodily things. But when he said, "our," he wanted us to understand, "human," and he rightly did not say, "escapes," but, "seems to escape." For it seems to them that no one can understand this, and for this reason they think that there is nothing of the sort, but it does not escape the intelligence of certain persons, to the extent that this is granted to human beings, that there is a pure and simple wisdom and truth, which is not proper to any living being but by which every soul that is capable of this is in common made wise and true. And if Anaxagoras held that it exists and saw that it is God and called it mind, we are not made learned and wise by the name of Anaxagoras, which all the little masters happily trumpet about, if I may use military language. We are not made learned and wise even by that knowledge of his by which he knew that it is true. After all, truth ought not to be dear to me because Anaxagoras knew it but because it is the truth, even if none of those philosophers knew it.

27. If, then, neither the knowledge of that man, who perhaps saw the truth, nor the full reality of the truth, which can make us truly learned, ought to fill us with pride so that we think that we are learned because of it, how much less can the names and teachings of those men who were in error help our learning and make hidden matters known! For, if we are human beings, it is proper that we

---

205. Ibid.
206. Ibid.
207. Ibid. 50.

be saddened by the errors of so many and such illustrious men, if we happen to hear them, rather than that we eagerly seek them out precisely in order to spout them with most hollow boasting among those who are ignorant of them. After all, how much better it would have been had I never heard the name of Democritus instead of thinking that he was someone considered great in his times. He thought that the gods were images that flowed from solid bodies, though the images were not them- selves solid, and that, by going about this way and that by their own motion and by slipping into the minds of human beings, they make them think of the divine power, even though that body, of course, from which the image flows is thought to be more excellent to the extent that it is more solid! Hence his opinion was wavering, as they say, and in doubt so that at times he said that God was a certain nature from which the images flowed. And yet God could not be thought of save by means of those images which he pours out and emits, that is, which emerge from that nature, which Democritus considers to be somehow bodily and everlasting and, for that reason, also divine. They are carried in a continuous semblance and emanation as if of vapor, and they come and enter our minds so that we can think of God or of the gods. For these people conceive no other cause of any thought of ours except that images come and enter our minds from these bodies we think of, as if those who know how to think of such things do not think of many and almost countless things, such as wisdom itself and truth, in a non-bodily and intelligible way. If they do not think of this, I wonder how they argue about it at all, but if they do think of it, I wish they would tell me either from which body the image of truth comes into their minds or what sort of image it is.

28. And yet Democritus is also said to differ from Epicurus on questions about nature by the fact that he thought that there is present in the coming together of the atoms a certain animal and vital force, and I believe that he says that "the images are endowed with divinity" by that force—not the images of all things, but those of the gods—and that in the universe there are "the elements of mind," to which he attributes divinity, and "living images, which often either benefit us or harm us."[208] But Epicurus does not maintain anything in the elements of things besides atoms, that is, certain bodies so small that they cannot be divided or perceived by sight or by touch. And he says that the fortuitous coming together of these tiny bodies produces countless worlds, living beings, souls themselves, and the gods, which he locates not in some world, but outside the worlds and between the worlds in human form. And he absolutely refuses to think of anything besides bodies. He says, nonetheless, that in order to think of them, images flow from the things, which he thinks are formed from atoms, and they enter the mind as more subtle than those images that come to the eyes. For he says that the cause of our seeing is "certain images so large that they embrace

---

208. Ibid., 120.

the whole external world."²⁰⁹ But you already understand, I think, the images that these people have in mind.

29. I am surprised that Democritus did not notice that what he says is false by the very fact that such great images coming into our mind, which is so small, cannot wholly touch it, if the bodily mind, as they claim, is enclosed in so small a body. For, when a small body is touched by a large body, it can by no means be touched by the whole large body at the same time. How, then, are those images thought of as whole at the same time, if they are thought of to the extent that they touch the soul by coming and entering it? For they can neither as whole enter through so small a body nor as whole touch so small a soul. Remember that I am saying this in accord with their way of thinking, for I do not think that the mind is that sort of thing. Or, if Democritus thinks that the mind is incorporeal, only Epicurus can be refuted by this argument. But why did Democritus not also see that there is no need, nor is there any possibility, that an incorporeal mind think as the result of the arrival of bodily images and contact with them? Both of them are certainly refuted from the vision of the eyes. For such enormous bodies of these images can in no way as whole touch such small eyes.

30. But when they are asked why we see one image of some body from which images flow in countless number, they reply that, because of the fact that images flow forth frequently and intersect, their accumulation and density brings it about that one image is seen from the many. Cicero refutes this nonsense in such a way that he denies that their God can be thought to be eternal by the very fact that he is thought of as the result of countless images that flow forth and slip away. And they say that the everlasting forms of the gods are produced by the help of countless atoms, since certain tiny bodies leave the divine body so that others take their place and do not allow that nature to be destroyed by their succession. He says, "All things would be eternal,"²¹⁰ because nothing lacks this countless number of atoms that would make up for the constant loss of them. Later, he asks how this god would not fear that he would perish "since he is struck incessantly and disturbed by the endless influx of atoms."²¹¹ He says that this body is struck because it is beaten by the incoming rush of atoms and is disturbed because it is penetrated by them. Then he adds, "Since the images," about which we have already said enough, "are always flowing into him,"²¹² how can he be confident of his immortality?

31. Among all these crazy ideas of those who think this way, it is especially deplorable that it is not enough to explain them in order for them to be rejected without any argument to the contrary from anyone. But the minds of very intelligent men have also taken up this task of extensively refuting these

---

209. Ibid.
210. Ibid. 109; 105.
211. Ibid. 114.
212. Ibid.

ideas that even the slowest minds ought to have mocked and rejected as soon as they were stated. For, if you grant that there are atoms, if you also grant that they push and shove one another by their fortuitous coming together, is it also allowed to grant that, in colliding fortuitously, atoms produce something so that they limit it with form, determine it with shape, adorn it with equality, brighten it with color, and enliven it with soul? For all these things are produced only by the art of divine providence. Anyone who loves to see with the mind rather than with the eyes and asks for this from the God who made him sees this truth. For one should not grant in any way that those atoms exist; see how easily this can be shown in accord with the opinion of these philosophers, even if one leaves aside the subtle arguments that the learned pass on concerning the division of bodies. The learned, of course, say that all the things that belong to nature are nothing other than bodies, the void, and accidents of them, and I believe this means motion, thrust, and the resulting forms. Let them say, then, in which kind they put the less solid images themselves, which they think emanate from more solid bodies so that they can only be perceived by contact with the eyes when we see and with the mind when we think, if these images themselves are also bodies. For they think in that way that they can leave a body and come to the eyes or to the mind, which they nonetheless say is bodily. I ask whether the images flow forth from the atoms themselves. If they do, how can they be atoms, if some bodies split off from them? If they do not, either something can be thought of without images—an idea which they strongly reject—or how do they know about atoms, which they cannot even think of? I, however, am now embarrassed to refute these ideas, though they were not embarrassed to hold them. But since they have dared to defend them, I am embarrassed not over them but over the human race, whose ears were able to tolerate them.

5, 32. Since, then, there exists such a great blindness of minds because of the filth of sin and the love of the flesh that even these monstrous views could consume the leisure of the learned in arguments, will you, Dioscurus, or anyone endowed with a mind that is alert, doubt that for following the truth the human race could not have been helped better in any way than if the Truth himself assumed in an ineffable and wondrous way a man who bore his person on earth? By commanding what was right and by doing the works of God, he persuaded people to believe for their salvation what they could not yet understand through wisdom. We ourselves serve his glory; we urge you to believe without wavering and with constancy this man through whom it has come about that not a few but even whole peoples who are unable to settle these questions by reason believe[213] with faith until, aided by his saving precepts, they emerge from these perplexities into the brightness of the most pure and most sincere truth. And we ought to obey this authority with greater devotion to the extent that we see that

---

213. R. Teske has translated *credant,* which is found in the older editions, rather than *inrideant,* which is found in the CSEL text.

no error dares to raise its head to gather to itself crowds of uneducated people without seeking to cloak itself with the Christian name. From the old peoples, however, only those people continue apart from the name of Christ and gather somewhat more frequently in their synagogues who possess those scriptures by which the Lord Jesus Christ was foretold, though they pretend that they do not understand and see this. But those people who are not in the unity of the Catholic community, though they boast of the Christian name, are forced to be opposed to those who believe, and they dare to attract the uneducated by the semblance of reason, especially when the Lord came with this medicine that was precisely to demand faith. But these heretics are forced to do this, as I said, because they see that they have no standing whatsoever, if their authority is compared with the Catholic authority. They try, therefore, to overcome the most stable authority of the most well-founded Church as if by the mention and promise of reason. This rashness is like a general rule for all heretics. But that most merciful sovereign of our faith has both fortified the Church with a fortress of authority through crowded communities of peoples and nations and the very sees of the apostles and armed the Church with abundant means of defense by invincible reason through a smaller number of learned and truly spiritual men. This, then, is the most correct practice: to receive the weak as much as possible into the fortress of faith in order to fight the battle on their behalf by the strength of reason, once they have been placed in safety.

33. But the Platonists, who were at that time surrounded by the yapping errors of the false philosophers, did not have a divine person by whom they might demand faith. Hence, they preferred to conceal their view as something to be sought out rather than to expose it to profanation. But when the name of Christ had become more frequently heard to the wonder and confusion of earthly kingdoms, they began to come forth to disclose and explain what Plato had held. Then the school of Plotinus flourished in Rome and had as disciples many very keen and clever men. But some of them were corrupted by curiosity concerning the arts of magic, while others, knowing that the Lord Jesus Christ bore the person of the immutable truth and wisdom, which they were trying to attain, entered into his army. And so the whole summit of authority and the light of reason for the re-creating and re-forming of the human race was located in that one saving name and in his own Church.

34. Though you perhaps would have preferred other things, I do not regret having stated these ideas for you at such great length in this letter. For you will appreciate these ideas more to the extent that you make progress in the truth, and then you will appreciate my advice, which you now think has contributed less to the good of your studies. And yet I also tried to reply, as well as I could, to those very questions of yours, not only to certain ones in this letter, but also to almost all the rest, by making brief notes on the very pages on which you sent them. If you think that with these questions I have done too little or something other than you wanted, you are not thinking correctly, my Dioscorus, about the one whom

you are now asking these questions. But I have passed over all the questions about *The Orator* or from the books of *The Orator*. For I would have seemed a trifler in my own eyes if I had gone on to explain them. Concerning the others I could, after all, be appropriately questioned if anyone presented me with the issues to be examined and resolved not from the books of Cicero but by themselves. But in those books the issues are less suited to our calling as a bishop. I would not, however, have done all this if I had not withdrawn for a while from Hippo after the illness that I had when your man had come to me. During these days I was again stricken with problems of health and fevers. Hence, the result is that this letter is being sent to you later than it could have been. I ask that you let me know how you find it.

LETTER 120

Augustine to Consentius, a Catholic layman from the Balearic Islands (410)

In 410 Augustine replied to the questions of Consentius, a Catholic layman from the Balearic Islands, raised in his letter (Letter 119). Augustine urges Consentius to come to him so that they may converse about these questions (paragraph 1). He advises Consentius that he should not scorn either faith or reason (paragraph 2) and points out that believing should precede understanding in questions pertaining to salvation (paragraph 3), though the apostle Peter warned that we should be ready to give an account of our faith and hope (paragraph 4). There are, nonetheless, some mysteries of which a rational account cannot be given (paragraph 5). True reason leads to a love for understanding, and faith prepares the mind for true reasoning (paragraph 6).

Augustine warns Consentius that because of our familiarity with bodily things we find it difficult to think of God as non-bodily (paragraph 7). He discusses the relations between reason and faith and insists that a believer ought to desire to see what he can now only believe (paragraph 8). We can only believe past visible events, but we believe in visible events to come, such as the resurrection, so that we hope to see them. Invisible realities are seen when they are understood (paragraph 9). We now believe in some lasting visible realities, such as Christ's risen body, which we hope to see with the eyes of our risen bodies (paragraph 10).

Augustine distinguishes three kinds of things we see: bodies, images or likenesses of bodies, and things that are neither bodies nor likenesses of bodies (paragraph 11). The Trinity might seem not to belong among the third kind of reality because it is so different from goods of our mind like justice and charity (paragraph 12). Augustine urges Consentius to hold to the faith in God as one and three and to drive from his mind any images in thinking about the Trinity (paragraph 13). He discusses the sense in which God is in heaven, though he is whole everywhere (paragraph 14), and warns that we should not think of Christ's risen body as seated at the Father's right hand in a bodily sense (paragraph 15).

Augustine warns Consentius that he must reject the view that the Father as one person in the Trinity is in heaven, while his divinity is everywhere, as if divinity were a quality common to the Father and the Son (paragraph 16). He explains that the divinity of the Trinity cannot be a quality but must be the substance of the Trinity (paragraph 17). Augustine then deals with Consentius' problem in thinking of God as being like righteousness, which he regards as lifeless (paragraph 18). He insists, rather, that God is righteousness that is living through itself and immutably (paragraph 19). Even though God's righteousness is vastly superior to our righteousness, the righteousness in us is the beauty of our soul, and our soul is made to the image of God (paragraph 20).

To Consentius, his most beloved brother who is to be honored in the heart of Christ, Augustine sends greetings in the Lord.

1, 1. I asked you to come to visit us precisely because I was greatly pleased with your talent revealed in your books. Hence I wanted you to read certain small works of ours, which I thought to be very useful for you, not while you were situated far from us, but rather in our presence. In that way you could, while present, ask without any difficulty about those ideas that you might perhaps understand less well, and from our discussion and conversation with each other you yourself would recognize and you yourself would correct, to the extent that the Lord granted me to explain and you to grasp, what needed correction in your books. You certainly have the ability to explain what you held; you also have the goodness and humility to merit to hold the truth. And I am now of the same opinion, which ought not to displease you either. For this reason I recently advised you that in these works of ours, which you are reading at home, you should make marks at those passages that trouble you and that you should come to me with them and ask about each of them. I urge you to do what you have not yet done. You would be right, of course, to be shy and to hesitate to do this if you had chosen to do so even once and had found me difficult. I had also said, when I heard from you that you were tired of very defective manuscripts, that you should read ours, which you would discover have fewer errors than the others.

2. But you ask that I carefully and prudently discuss the question of the Trinity, that is, of the unity of the divinity and the distinction of the persons, in order that the clarity of my teaching and mind may, as you put it, wipe away the fog of your mind so that you may be able to see somehow with your eyes what you cannot now imagine, after I have clarified it by the light of intelligence. See first whether this request is in harmony with your earlier conviction. Earlier in the same letter in which you make this request, you say that you had determined for yourself that "the truth about things divine must be attained more by faith than by reason. For," you say, "if the faith of the holy Church were grasped by reasoned argumentation and not by pious belief, no one except philosophers and professors would possess happiness. But because it pleased God, who chose the weak things of this world in order to confound the strong,[214] to save through the foolishness of preaching those who believe,[215] we should not so much require reasoning concerning God as we should follow the authority of the saints."[216] See, then, whether in accord with your words you ought not rather, especially on this topic in which above all our faith consists, to follow only the authority of the saints and not ask of me a rational account in order to understand it. For, when I begin to introduce you to some extent to an understanding of this mystery—and if God does not help interiorly, I shall be utterly unable to do so—I

---

214. See 1 Cor 1:27.
215. See 1 Cor 1:21.
216. See Letter 119, 1.

shall do nothing else in my explanation than give a rational account to the extent I am able. And if you not unreasonably demand of me or of any teacher that you may understand what you believe, correct your conviction, not so that you reject faith, but so that what you already hold with the firmness of faith you may also see with the light of reason.

3. Heaven forbid, after all, that God should hate in us that by which he made us more excellent than the other animals. Heaven forbid, I say, that we should believe in such a way that we do not accept or seek a rational account, since we could not even believe if we did not have rational souls. In certain matters, therefore, pertaining to the teaching of salvation, which we cannot yet grasp by reason, but which we will be able to at some point, faith precedes reason so that the heart may be purified in order that it may receive and sustain the light of the great reason, which is, of course, a demand of reason! And so, the prophet stated quite reasonably, *Unless you believe, you will not understand* (Is 7:9 LXX). There he undoubtedly distinguished these two and gave the counsel that we should believe first in order that we may be able to understand what we believe. Hence it was reasonably commanded that faith should precede reason. For, if this command is not reasonable it is, therefore, unreasonable. Heaven forbid! If, then, it is reasonable that faith precede reason with respect to certain great truths that cannot yet be grasped, however slight the reason is that persuades us to this, it undoubtedly also comes before faith.

4. Hence the apostle Peter warns that we should be ready to respond to everyone who asks us for an account of our faith and hope[217] because, if an unbeliever asks me for an account of my faith and hope and I see that, before he believes, he cannot grasp it, I give him this very argument by which he may, if possible, see how preposterous it is to demand before faith an account of those things that he cannot grasp. But if a believer asks for an account in order that he may understand what he believes, we must look at his ability in order that, when an account has been given in accord with it, he may derive as great an understanding of his faith as is possible: a greater understanding if he grasps more, a smaller understanding if he grasps less. Yet until he comes to the fullness and perfection of knowledge, let him not depart from the journey of faith. This is the reason why the Apostle says, *And even if you have some other ideas, God will also reveal it to you; let us, nonetheless, continue to walk in the path to which we have come* (Phil 3:15-16). If, then, we are already believers, we have come to the way of faith, and, if we do not give it up, we shall undoubtedly come not only to as great an understanding of incorporeal and immutable things as can be grasped in this life, though not by all, but also to the peak of contemplation, which the Apostle calls *face to face* (1 Cor 13:12). For certain people, even the simplest who, nonetheless, walk with great perseverance in the path of faith, come to that most blessed contemplation. But there are those who somehow already know what the invisible, immutable, incor-

---

217. See 1 Pt 3:15.

poreal nature is and refuse to hold onto the way that leads to so great an abode of happiness, because it seems foolish to them. That way is Christ crucified. And hence they cannot arrive at the temple of that rest by the light of which their mind is now touched as it sheds its ray from afar.[218]

5. There are, however, certain things to which, when we hear them, we do not give credence, and after a rational account has been given, we know that those things that we cannot believe are true. None of God's miracles are believed by those without faith precisely because they do not see their rational explanation. And there really are some for which a rational explanation cannot be given, though there is one. After all, what is there in the world that God has created without a reason? But it is even beneficial that the reason for some of his marvelous works is to some extent hidden so that the knowledge of that same reason does not make them seem worthless in the minds of the bored and jaded. For there are not only a few, but many, who are drawn more by a wonder over things than by a knowledge of their causes, which makes miracles cease to be sources of amazement. And it is necessary to arouse them to a faith in invisible things by visible miracles in order that, having been purified by love, they may come to where they cease to be filled with wonder because of familiarity with the truth. For human beings are filled with wonder at the tightrope walker in a theater, and they are delighted by musicians. In the first case they are awed by the difficulty; in the latter the sweetness of the sounds holds and nourishes them.

6. I wanted to say these things in order to encourage your faith toward a love for the understanding to which true reasoning leads and for which faith prepares the minds. For there is a reasoning that leads to the belief that, in that Trinity which is God, the Son is not coeternal with the Father or is of another substance and the Holy Spirit is unlike in some respect and in that way inferior. So, too, there is a reasoning that leads to the belief that the Father and the Son are of the same substance but the Holy Spirit is of another substance. Such reasoning, it must be said, is to be shunned and detested not because it is reasoning but because it is false reasoning. For, if the reasoning were true, it would not, of course, have fallen into error. Hence, just as you ought not to avoid all speech because there is also speech that is false, so you ought not to avoid all reasoning because there is also reasoning that is false. I would say this of wisdom as well. After all, wisdom is not to be avoided because there is also wisdom that is false, a wisdom for which Christ crucified is foolishness,[219] though he is the power of God and the wisdom of God.[220] And so through this foolishness of preaching it pleased God to save those who believe, because the foolishness of God is wiser

---

218. Augustine is alluding here to the Neoplatonic theory of contemplation as a means to recognize the transcendent reality.
219. See 1 Cor 1:18.
220. See 1 Cor 1:24.

than human beings.²²¹ Certain philosophers and professors who were following not the true way but one like the truth, and who were misleading themselves and others by it, could not be convinced of this, but some of them could be. And, for those who could be, Christ crucified is neither a scandal nor foolishness; they are, after all, among the Jews and Greeks who have been called and for whom he is the power of God and the wisdom of God.²²² On that way, that is, in the faith of Christ crucified, those who were able to grasp its correctness by the grace of God, even if they were called philosophers or professors, certainly confessed with humble piety that fishermen had preceded them, who were more excellent than they were not only by the most firm strength of believing but also by the most certain truth of understanding. For when they learned that the foolish and weak of the world were chosen in order to confound the strong and the wise,²²³ and when they realized that they were wise with false wisdom and strong with a feeble strength, they were confounded with a saving confusion, and they became foolish and weak in order that through the foolishness and weakness of God, which is wiser and stronger than human beings, they might become truly wise and really strong among the foolish and weak whom God has chosen.

2, 7. Faithful piety, however, respects only the truest reason so that we do not hesitate to overthrow a certain idolatry that the weakness of human thought tries to build up in our heart because of our familiarity with visible things and so that we do not dare to believe that the invisible, incorporeal, immutable Trinity, which we worship, is like three living masses, though very large and beautiful, each bounded by the limits of its own space and clinging to one another by close proximity in their places. It makes no difference whether one of them is located in the middle so that it separates the two joined to it on each side or whether, arranged like a triangle, each touches the others so that none is separated from another. We do not dare to believe that those three great and good persons, though in very great masses, still bounded on top, on the bottom, and on every side, have the one divinity as a fourth something, not like one of them, but common to all of them as the deity of all, whole in all and in each one, and that because of this one divinity the same Trinity is said to be one God. We do not dare to believe that its three persons are nowhere but in the heavens, while that divinity is absent nowhere but is present everywhere. We do not dare to believe that for this reason it is correct to say that God is both in heaven and on earth on account of that divinity that is everywhere and common to the three, but that it is not correct to say that the Father or the Son or the Holy Spirit is on earth, since this Trinity has its abode only in heaven. When true reason begins to undermine this construction and vain figment of carnal thinking, let us immediately hasten, with the interior help and enlightenment of him who does not want to dwell in our hearts along

---

221. See 1 Cor 1:21.25.
222. See 1 Cor 1:24.
223. See 1 Cor 1:27.

with such idols, to smash them and to shake them from our faith so that we allow not even any dust of such phantasms to remain there.

8. Hence, in order to clothe us with piety, faith had to precede in our heart the reasoned argumentation by which, once we have been admonished externally, we see that these ideas are false because the truth shines interiorly. If faith had not come first, would we not have heard the truth to no purpose? And for this reason, because faith did what pertained to it, reason followed along and found some of those things that it was seeking. We ought undoubtedly, therefore, to prefer to false reasoning not only the reasoning by which we understand what we believe but also the very faith in those things we have not yet understood. For it is better to believe what is true, though it is not yet seen, than to think you see something true, which is in fact false. For faith has eyes of its own by which it somehow sees that what it does not yet see is true and by which it most certainly sees that it does not yet see what it believes. But one who now understands by true reason what he before only believed should certainly be preferred to one who still desires to understand what he believes. But if he does not even desire to understand and thinks that those things which should be understood ought only to be believed, he does not know the benefit faith brings. For pious faith does not want to be without hope and love. A believer, therefore, ought to believe what he does not yet see in such a way that he both hopes for and loves that vision.

9. And for past visible events, which have passed away in time, there is only faith, because we no longer hope to see them but believe that they happened and passed away. Such is the fact that Christ once died for our sins and rose, that he now no longer dies, and that death will no longer have dominion over him.[224] But we believe in those events that are not yet, but are future, such as the resurrection of our spiritual bodies, in such a way that we also hope that we will see them. Yet we can now in no way point to them. Those things that exist so that they neither pass away nor are in the future, but last eternally, however, are in part invisible, like justice and like wisdom, and they are in part visible, like the body of Christ, which is now immortal. But invisible things are perceived when they are understood, and for this reason they are seen in a manner appropriate to them. And when they are seen, they are much more certain than those things that the senses of the body attain, but they are called "invisible" because they cannot be seen at all by these mortal eyes. But those lasting things that are visible can, if they are shown to us, be perceived even by these mortal eyes. In that way the Lord showed himself to the disciples after the resurrection,[225] and in that way he showed himself to the apostle Paul[226] and the deacon Stephen after the ascension.[227]

---

224. See Rom 6:9-10; 1 Pt 3:18.
225. See Mt 28; Mk 16; Lk 24.
226. See Acts 9:3-4.27.
227. See Acts 7:55.

10. Hence, we believe in these lasting visible things so that, even if they are not shown to us, we hope that we will at some time see them, and we do not try to grasp them by reason or intellect except in order that we might think of them as more distinct from invisible things, since they are visible. And when in thought we imagine what they are, we know quite well that we do not know them. For I think of Antioch, which I do not know, but not in the way in which I think of Carthage, which I do know. For my thinking fashions for itself that former vision, but recalls the latter; I in no way, nonetheless, doubt what I have believed about the former on the basis of many witnesses or what I have believed about the latter on the basis of my own eyes. But we do not imagine justice and wisdom and other things of that sort in one way and gaze upon them in another, but we perceive these invisible things, which are understood by the simple attention of the mind and reason, without any bodily forms or masses, without any lines or shapes of members, without an spatial areas, whether finite or infinite. The very light by which we distinguish all these, in which it is quite clear to us what we believe though it is unknown, what we hold as known, what form of a body we recall and what we make up in thought, what the sense of the body attains and what the mind imagines like a body, what the intelligence contemplates as certain and utterly unlike all bodies—this light, then, in which all these things are distinguished is not, of course, poured out like the brightness of this sun or of any bodily light through stretches of space and in every direction. And it does not illumine our mind as if by a visible splendor but invisibly and ineffably, and it shines, nonetheless, in an intelligible manner. It is as certain for us as it makes certain for us what we see in accord with it.

11. There are three kinds of things that are seen. The first kind includes corporeal things like this sky and this earth and whatever the senses of the body see or touch in them. The second kind includes those things like bodies, such as we think up and imagine in the spirit or that we contemplate as if they were bodies, whether they are recalled or are presented to us. From these there also come the visions that in dreams or in some transport of the mind are presented with these seemingly spatial quantities. A third kind distinct from both is neither a body nor has likeness to a body, such as wisdom, which is perceived as understood by the mind and in whose light we truthfully judge concerning all these things. In which of these kinds are we to believe that this Trinity that we want to know is found? Surely it is either in one of them or in none. If it is in one, it is in that which is more excellent than the other two, as is wisdom. If it is his gift in us, it is also less than that highest and immutable wisdom, which is called the wisdom of God. I do not think that we ought to suppose the giver to be less than his gift. But if it is a ray of that wisdom in us, which is called our wisdom, to the extent that we can grasp it through a glass and in an enigma[228] we must distinguish it both from all bodies and from all likenesses of bodies.

---

228. See 1 Cor 13:12.

12. But if this Trinity should not be thought to be in any of these kinds, and if it is invisible in such a way that it is not seen even by the mind, much less should we have concerning it such an opinion that we believe it is like corporeal things or like the images of corporeal things. For it does not surpass bodies in the beauty or greatness of its mass but in the dissimilarity and unlikeness of its nature. And we, of course, do not value by the mass of their body the goods of our mind, like wisdom, justice, love, chastity, and the others of this sort, nor do we represent them in thought by corporeal forms of them. Rather, when we correctly understand them, we see them in the light of the mind without any bodily nature and without any likeness of a bodily nature. If the Trinity differs in comparison with such goods of our mind, how much does it differ in comparison with all bodily qualities and quantities! And yet the Apostle bears witness that it is not utterly alien to our intellect when he says, *For his invisible reality is seen as understood from the creation of the world through those things which have been made, even his everlasting power and divinity* (Rom 1:20). And for this reason the same Trinity, which made both the body and the soul, is undoubtedly more excellent than both of them. If, then, we consider the soul, especially the human, rational, and intellectual soul, which was made to his image, and if it does not surpass our thoughts and intelligence, but we can apprehend by the mind and intelligence the soul's principal part, namely, the mind and intelligence, it will perhaps not be absurd that we should consider raising it up to understand its creator with his help. But if it fails in itself and succumbs to itself, let it be content with pious faith as long as it is on its journey away from the Lord until there comes about in the human being what God promised, when he brings it about *who is able to do more than we ask for or understand* (Eph 3:20).

3, 13. Since that is so, I want in the meanwhile for you to read those many things that we have already written pertinent to this question as well as those that we are still working on and cannot yet resolve on account of the magnitude of so great a question. But now hold with unshakeable faith that the Father and the Son and the Holy Spirit are a trinity and that there is, nonetheless, one God, not that the divinity is common to these as if it were a fourth, but that it is itself the ineffably inseparable Trinity. Hold that the Father begot the Son, that only the Son was begotten of the Father, and that the Holy Spirit is the Spirit of both of them. And when you think of it, drive away, remove, deny, spurn, cast aside, and flee whatever comes to mind with the likeness of a body. For it is no small beginning in the knowledge of God if, before we can know what he is, we already now begin to know what he is not. But love understanding very much, because even the Holy Scriptures themselves, which exhort us to have faith before the understanding of important realities, cannot be useful to you unless you correctly understand them. All the heretics who accept them as authoritative think that they follow them, though they follow their own errors instead, and for this reason they are heretics, not because they scorn the Scriptures but because they do not understand them.

14. But you, my dearest friend, pray vigorously and faithfully that the Lord may give you understanding and that what the care of an instructor or teacher applies externally can thus bear fruit, for *neither the one who plants nor the one who waters is of any importance, but God who gives the increase* (1 Cor 3:7). To him we say, *Our Father who art in heaven* (Mt 6:9), not because he, who by his incorporeal presence is whole everywhere, is there and is not here, but because he is said to dwell in those pious souls in whom he is present. And these are most of all in the heavens, where our citizenship is also,[229] if our lips truthfully reply that we have our heart lifted up.[230] For even if we interpret carnally the words of Scripture, *The heavens is my chair, but the earth is the stool for my feet* (Is 66:1), we ought to believe that he is both there and here, though he is not whole there because his feet are here, and he is not whole here because the upper parts of his body are there. Again, the words of Scripture about him, *He who has measured the heavens with the palm of his hand and the earth with his fist* (Is 40:12), can drive from us that carnal way of thinking. After all, who would sit in the space of a palm of the hand or put his feet in a place as small as his fist can grasp, unless perhaps the vain flesh has gone so far that it is too little for it to ascribe human members to the substance of God, if it does not also make them monstrous so that the palm is wider than the hips and the fist is wider than two feet joined together? But these things are said so that when what we hear is inconsistent, if it is taken in a carnal sense, we are admonished by it to think of ineffably spiritual things.

15. Hence, even if we think of the body of the Lord, which he raised from the tomb and carried up to heaven, only in terms of human form and members, we should not think that he sits at the right hand of the Father[231] so that the Father seems to sit at his left. In that blessedness, of course, which surpasses all human understanding, there is only the right hand, and that same right hand is the term for that blessedness. Hence we should not interpret those words that he spoke to Mary after his resurrection, *Do not touch me, for I have not yet ascended to my Father* (Jn 20:17), in such an absurd manner that we think that he wanted to be touched by women after he had ascended, though he allowed himself to be touched by men before he had ascended. But when he said that to Mary, who, of course, symbolized the Church, he wanted her to understand that he had then ascended to the Father when she recognized him as equal to the Father and touched him with such faith conducive to salvation. Otherwise she would not touch him in the right way if she believed that he was only what she saw in the flesh. In that way the heretic Photinus[232] touched him who believed that he was only a man.

---

229. See Phil 3:20.
230. An allusion to the beginning of the preface at Mass.
231. See Mk 16:19.
232. Photinus was a fourth-century heretic; he was bishop of Sirmium in Pannonia and condemned for holding that Christ was only an extraordinary man who was adopted as God's son.

16. Even if something more suitable and better can perhaps be understood from these words of the Lord, we must, nonetheless, undoubtedly reject the opinion that holds that the substance of the Father were in heaven insofar as the Father is one person in the Trinity, but that the divinity is not only in heaven but everywhere, as if the Father were one thing and his divinity, which is common to him along with the Son and with the Holy Spirit, were another. For it implies that the Trinity itself is equivalently in bodily places and bodily, while the one divinity of the three persons is present everywhere and that it alone, as incorporeal, is whole everywhere. After all, if it were a quality of them—and heaven forbid that in the Father or the Son or the Holy Spirit quality should be one thing and substance another—if, nonetheless, it could be a quality of them, it could, of course, not be anywhere more fully than in its own substance. But if it is a substance and is other than they are, it is another substance, and that is a completely false belief.

17. But if you perhaps understand less well the difference between a substance and a quality, you certainly more readily notice the fact that the divinity of the Trinity—which is thought to be other than the Trinity itself and, on this account, is said to be not three gods, but one God, because it is one and common to the three—is either a substance or is not a substance. If it is a substance and is other than the Father or the Son or the Holy Spirit or than the Trinity itself taken together, it is undoubtedly another substance. The truth, however, refutes and rejects this. But if this divinity is not a substance and is God because it is whole everywhere, but that Trinity is not, then God is not a substance. What Catholic would say this? So too, if this divinity is not a substance and if the Trinity is one God because of it, because this divinity is one in the three, the Father and the Son and the Holy Spirit ought not to be said to be of one substance, but of one divinity, which is not a substance. But you acknowledge in the Catholic faith that it is true, that it is reaffirmed as true, that the Father and the Son and the Holy Spirit are one God, because they are the Trinity, for they are inseparably of one and the same substance or—if this is a better term—essence. After all, some of ours, especially the Greeks, said that the Trinity that is God is one essence rather than one substance, supposing and understanding that there is some difference between those two terms. On this issue there is no need to argue at present, and even if we said that this divinity, which is thought to be something other than the Trinity itself, is not a substance, but an essence, the same error would result. For, if it is other than the Trinity itself, it will be another essence. Heaven forbid that a Catholic should think that! It remains, then, that we should believe that the Trinity is of one substance in the sense that the essence itself is not other than the Trinity. However much we may advance toward seeing this in the present life, it will be in a glass and in an enigma that we shall see it.[233] But when we begin to have a spiritual body, which is promised in the resurrection, whether we see it by the mind or in a wondrous way also by the body, since the grace of a spiritual

---

233. See 1 Cor 13:12.

body is ineffable, we shall in accord with our capacity, nonetheless, see it, but not in various places nor as smaller in one part and larger in another, because it is not a body and is everywhere whole.

4, 18. But you put in your letter that you think or rather that you thought "that nothing living is present according to substance in righteousness" and that you "still cannot think of God, that is, a living nature, as being like righteousness, because righteousness," as you say, "is not living in itself, but in us. In fact, we rather live in accord with it, but righteousness does not live at all by itself."[234] In order that you may reply to yourself, look at whether one can correctly say that life itself, which causes to live whatever we do not falsely say is alive, does not live. For I think that it seems absurd to you that life causes things to live and does not itself live. But if life itself by which everything living lives is especially living, recall, please, the souls that the divine scriptures call dead; you will, of course, find that they are unjust, impious, and unbelieving. And by reason of them the bodies of the impious live of which it was said, *Let the dead bury their dead* (Mt 8:22), and there even wicked souls are understood not to be without some life. For bodies could not live because of them in any other way than because of some sort of life, which souls cannot completely be without. For this reason they are rightly called immortal. They are, nonetheless, said to be dead after having lost righteousness for no other reason than that righteousness, as the life of their lives, is a truer and greater life, even for souls that are living immortally by some sort of life. Since souls are in bodies, the bodies themselves are also alive, though they cannot live by themselves. Hence, if souls cannot but somehow live in themselves, because by reason of them even bodies live, and bodies die when they are abandoned by souls, how much more must true righteousness be understood also to live in itself, since by reason of it even souls live so that, if this righteousness is lost, they are called dead, although they do not cease to live with some sort of life.

19. But that righteousness that lives in itself is undoubtedly God, and it lives immutably. However, just as, though it is life in itself, it also becomes life in us, when we become partakers of it in some way, so though righteousness exists in itself, it also comes to be in us when we live righteously by clinging to it, and we are more or less righteous the more or the less we cling to it. Hence Scripture says of the only-begotten Son of God that, though he is the wisdom and righteousness of the Father and always exists in himself, he became *for us wisdom and righteousness from God and sanctification and redemption, in order that, as Scripture says, He who boasts may boast in the Lord* (1 Cor 1:30-31). You yourself saw this, of course, when you added and said, "Unless righteousness is said to be not the righteousness of this human equity but only that righteousness that is God."[235] That God most high is clearly true righteousness, and that true

---

234. See Letter 119, 5.
235. See ibid.

God is the highest righteousness. To hunger and thirst for it[236] is, of course, our righteousness during this sojourn, and to have our fill of it afterwards is our full righteousness in eternity. Let us, then, not think of God as like our righteousness, but let us rather think of ourselves as more like God, the more we can be more righteous by participation.

20. If, then, we must avoid thinking that God is like our righteousness because the light that enlightens[237] is incomparably more excellent than that which is enlightened, how much more ought we to avoid believing that he is something inferior and somehow more degenerate than our righteousness is! But what else is righteousness when it is in us, or any other virtue by which one lives correctly and wisely, than the beauty of the inner person? And we were surely made to the image of God in accord with this beauty rather than in accord with the body. For this reason we are told, *Do not be conformed to this world, but be reformed in the newness of your mind that you may test what is the will of God, what is good and pleasing and perfect* (Rom 12:2). If, then, we say or know or want the mind to be beautiful, not in its mass nor in parts spatially separated, as we distinguish or think of bodies, but in its intelligible virtue, such as righteousness, and if we are reformed in terms of this beauty to the image of God, surely the beauty of God himself, who has formed us and is reforming us to his image, is not to be looked for in some bodily mass, and he must be believed to be incomparably more beautiful than the minds of the righteous, insofar as he is incomparably more righteous. With respect to the usual length of letters this letter is perhaps longer than you expected, but with respect to the inquiry about so important a topic let it suffice to have briefly reminded Your Charity, not in the sense that it should suffice for your education, but in the sense that, after having been carefully instructed by reading or hearing other works, you yourself may more extensively correct your own statements made in another vein. That is, of course, better to the degree that it is done with more humility and more faith.

---

236. See Mt 5:6.
237. See Jn 1:9.

LETTER 148

Augustine to Fortunatian, the bishop of Sicca (413-414)

In 413 or 414 Augustine wrote to Fortunatian, bishop of Sicca. In *Revisions* II, 41 (68) Augustine mentions that he found this memorandum in a manuscript with the Letter 147 (*A Book on Seeing God*) and says that it was listed neither among his works nor among his letters. The memorandum is clearly related to that letter.

Augustine begins by asking Fortunatian to apologize to "our brother," presumably a fellow bishop, whom he has offended by his harsh language in maintaining that God is not and will not be seen by these bodily eyes (paragraph 1). As long as one does not hold that God is a body, it is somewhat tolerable, though incorrect, to suppose that our body will be so transformed that we will be able to see the incorporeal God with such new, but bodily, eyes (paragraph 2). Augustine, nonetheless, points to the absurdities that follow from supposing that the risen body will be so transformed that we can see the invisible God with our new bodily eyes (paragraph 3). Augustine begs for forgiveness for having given offense by his letter and hopes that his brother bishop will pardon him (paragraphs 4 and 5). He nonetheless goes on to cite passages from Ambrose and Jerome in support of his own position (paragraphs 6 and 7). He warns that we should not take the Scripture's words about a face-to-face vision of God to imply that God has a bodily face (paragraph 8). Augustine cites other passages from Jerome, Athanasius, Phoebatius of Agen, whom he takes to be an Eastern bishop named Gregory, probably Gregory Nazianzen, and Ambrose, all of whom maintain that God is seen by the eyes of the mind, not of the body (paragraphs 9 and 10).

The Apostle linked together God's invisibility and immutability; hence, God will remain invisible but will be seen by the eyes of the heart (paragraph 11). Ambrose too taught that God will be seen, but only by the clean of heart (paragraph 12). Augustine explains how we are to understand the anthropomorphism of the Scriptures (paragraph 13). He cites a passage from Jerome in which the latter speaks against those who think of God as having a human form (paragraph 14). Augustine explains why he has cited so many ecclesiastical writers and insists that their authority must never be set on a par with the canonical Scriptures (paragraph 15). Finally, Augustine admits that he still does not know all of what will be involved in the transformation of our body into a spiritual body (paragraph 16). Even if God will somehow be seen exteriorly by the eyes of the spiritual body, he will surely continue to be seen interiorly by the eyes of the mind (paragraph 17). Whether we can discover the nature of the spiritual body or not, we should still believe the clear statements of Scripture that the interior self will see God (paragraph 18).

A Memorandum for his holy brother, Fortunatian

1, 1. As I asked when present, I also now exhort you to be so good as to see our brother about whom we were talking in order to ask him to pardon me if in that letter, which I do not now regret having written, he found anything said to him rather sternly and harshly. For I said that the eyes of this body do not see and will not see God. Of course I added the reason why I said this, namely, so that God himself would not be thought to be bodily and visible in a stretch or area of space. After all, the eye of this body cannot see anything in any other way. And I said it so that the words, *face to face* (1 Cor 13:12), would not be interpreted in the sense that God is limited by the members of a body. Hence, I do not regret having said that; otherwise, we would have so wicked an idea of God himself that we would think that he is not whole everywhere, but divisible in areas of space. Such things we, of course, know with these eyes.

2. On the other hand, inasmuch as I think nothing of the sort about God but believe him to be an immutable and incorporeal spirit who is whole everywhere, if anyone considers that there will be so great a change of this body when it is made a spiritual body from a natural one that we will also be able to see by such a body an incorporeal substance not divisible in areas and stretches of space or limited by the lines and bounds of members, but whole everywhere, I want him to teach me whether he holds the truth. But if he holds a false opinion on this, it is far more tolerable to add something to a body than to take something away from God. And if this opinion is true, it will not be opposed to the words of mine that I put in that letter. For I said that the eyes of this body will not see God, having in mind that the eyes of this body cannot see anything at all but bodies that are apart from our eyes at some spatial distance. For if there were no distance between them, we would not even see bodies by them.

3. But if our bodies will be changed into something so unlike what they are now that they will have eyes by which they will see that substance which is not either spread out or bound by stretches of space, which does not have one part here and another there, a smaller one in a smaller space and a larger one in a larger space, but is everywhere whole in a non-bodily way, these bodies will be something far different and will not be themselves. They will be something else not merely because of the removal of their mortality, corruption, and heavy weight, but they will somehow be transformed into the power of the mind, if they will be able somehow to see in a way in which the mind will then be able to see, but now not even the mind can see. For, if we say that a man is not the man he was after he has changed in his morals, if we even say that a body is not what it was when its age has changed, how much more will the body not be itself if it has been transformed by so great a change that it not only lives immortally but also sees the invisible? Hence, if they see God, the eyes of this body will not see him, because in this respect it will not be the same body if it has been transformed into that power and potency, and this opinion will not be opposed to those words of my letter. If, however, the body will not be the same because it is now mortal and

will then be immortal, because it now weighs down the soul and then without any weight will be most agile for any movement, but is the same for seeing those things that are viewed in stretches and areas of space, it will by no means see an incorporeal substance that is whole everywhere if it is not something other than what it is. Whether this opinion or that one is true, according to both of them it is true that the eyes of this body will not see God. For they will either be the eyes of this body, and they will not see him, or they will not be the eyes of this body if they do see him, because by such a great transformation they will be the eyes of a far different body.

4. If this brother knows something better on this issue, I am ready to learn it either from him or from the one from whom he learned it. But if I were speaking ironically, I would even say that I am prepared to learn that position about a bodily God who is divisible by his members in space. But I do not say that, because I am not speaking ironically, and I have no doubt that God is not like that at all. And I wrote that letter in order that no one would believe that he was like that. Since I was concerned with giving a warning in the letter that I wrote without mentioning any names, I was excessive and imprudent in rebuking, and I did not, like a brother and a bishop, bear in mind the person of a brother and bishop, as was fitting. I do not defend this but blame it. I do not excuse this but accuse it. I ask him to forgive, to recall our earlier love and to forget the recent offense. Let him at least do what he is angry that I did not do; let him have a gentleness in granting pardon that I did not have in writing that letter. I ask by means of Your Charity what I wanted to ask when I was present before him if I had the opportunity. I tried this by having a venerable man, one preferable to all of us in honor, write to him, but he refused to come, perhaps having suspected, I suppose, some trick against him, as often happens in human affairs. Make him believe, to the extent you can, that I am far from behaving like that, for as someone present you can do so more easily. Tell him of the great and true sorrow of which I spoke with you about the offense to his feelings. Make him realize that I do not hold him in contempt and how much I revere God in him and bear in mind our head in whose body we are brothers. I thought that I should not go to his place of residence for fear that we might produce a spectacle to be laughed at by others, to be deplored by our friends, and to be ashamed of by us. By means of Your Holiness and Charity the whole situation can be handled correctly; God, of course, handles it, who dwells by his faith in your heart, and I believe that our brother does not hold the Lord in contempt in you since he recognizes him in himself.

5. I at least have not found anything better to do in this case than to ask pardon from a brother who has complained that he was injured by the harshness of my letter. And he himself will do, I hope, what he knows is commanded by him who speaks through the Apostle. He says, *Pardon one another if one of you has a complaint against another, just as God has pardoned you in Christ* (Col 3:13). *Be imitators, then, of God, like most beloved children, and walk in love, as*

Christ has also loved us (Eph 5:1). Walking in this love with greater care, if we can, let us with oneness of heart investigate the spiritual body that we will have in the resurrection. For, even if we should have some other ideas, God will also reveal this to us, if we remain in him.[238] But one who remains in love remains in God, and God remains in him, because God is love[239] either because he exists like its ineffable fountain or because he bestows it on us through his Spirit. If, then, one can show that love will at some time be seen by bodily eyes, God will perhaps also be seen. But if love will never be seen, much less will its fountain be seen or anything else more excellent and more fitting that can be said about it.

2, 6. Certain great men who are also most learned in the Holy Scriptures, who have by their writings greatly helped the Church and the sound studies of the faithful, when they were given the opportunity, have said that the invisible God is seen in an invisible way, that is, by that nature that is also invisible in us, namely, by a clean mind or heart. When blessed Ambrose was dealing with Christ insofar as he is the Word, he said, "Jesus is seen, after all, not with bodily but with spiritual eyes." And a little later he said, "The Jews did not see him, for their foolish heart was blinded,"[240] here showing how he might be seen. Likewise, when he was speaking of the Holy Spirit, he inserted the words of the Lord where he said, *I shall ask the Father, and he will give you another comforter who will be with you for eternity, the Spirit of truth, whom this world cannot receive, because it does not see him or know him* (Jn 14:16-17). Ambrose said, "It was right that he showed himself in the body, because in the substance of the divinity he is not seen. We saw the Spirit but in bodily form; let us also see the Father. But because we cannot see him, let us listen."[241] And shortly afterwards he said, "Let us, then, listen to the Father. For the Father is invisible, but the Son too is invisible in terms of the divinity. *For no one has ever seen God* (1 Jn 4:12); since, then, the Son is God, the Son is not seen inasmuch as he is God."[242]

7. The saintly Jerome, however, says, "The eye of a human being is not able to see God as he is in his nature—not only a human being, but neither the angels, nor the thrones, nor the powers, nor the dominations, nor anything, whatever it is called. For no creature can look upon its creator."[243] With these words the most learned man showed well enough what he held concerning the world to come insofar as it pertains to our question. For, however much the eyes of our body may be improved, they will be equal to the angels. But Jerome said that the nature of the creator is invisible for them and for absolutely all the heavenly creation. Or if a question is raised on this point as well and any doubt is introduced about

---

238. See Phil 3:15.
239. See 1 Jn 4:16.
240. Ambrose, *Commentary on the Gospel of Luke* I, 5-6.
241. Ibid. II, 93-94.
242. Ibid. II, 94.
243. See Jerome, *Commentary on Isaiah* III, 1.

whether we will not be better than the angels, there is the clear statement of the Lord on this where he said about those who will rise for the kingdom: *They will be equal to the angels of God* (Lk 20:36; Mt 22:30; Mk 12:35). On this the same saintly Jerome speaks elsewhere in this way: "A human being, therefore, cannot see the face of God. The angels, however, even of the least persons in the Church always see the face of God.[244] And we see now in a glass, obscurely, but then we shall see *face to face* (1 Cor 13:12), when we shall progress from human beings into angels and shall be able to say with the Apostle, *But as we gaze upon the glory of the Lord with face unveiled, we shal all be transformed into the same image of him from one glory to another glory as if by the Spirit of the Lord* (2 Cor 3:18), though no creature sees the face of God in accord with the character of his nature, and he is then seen by the mind, since he is believed to be invisible."[245]

8. In these words of the man of God there are many points to consider: first, that in accord with the plainest statement of the Lord he too holds that we will then see the face of God when we shall progress into angels, that is, when we will become equal to the angels, something that will, of course, come about at the resurrection of the dead. Next, from the testimony of the Apostle it is quite clear that we should understand the face not of the outer self but of the inner self when we shall see face to face; the Apostle was, of course, speaking of the face of the heart when he said what I quoted on this: *But as we gaze upon the glory of the Lord with face unveiled, we shall all be transformed into the same image of him*. If anyone doubts this, let him reconsider the same passage and notice what the Apostle was speaking about, namely, the veil that remains in the reading of the Old Testament[246] until each person passes over to Christ in order that the veil may be removed. He, of course, says there: *But as we gaze upon the glory of the Lord with face unveiled,* and this face was not unveiled in the Jews of whom he says, *A veil was placed over their heart* (2 Cor 3:15), in order to show that the face of the heart has been revealed for us since the veil has been removed. Finally, so that no one less attentive to these points and with less discernment should believe that God either now is or will be visible either to the angels or to human beings when we shall have been made equal to the angels, he most clearly expressed what he held when he said, "No creature sees the face of God in accord with the character of his nature, and he is then seen by the mind, since he is believed to be invisible."[247] Hence, he sufficiently indicated that, when he was seen by human beings through the eyes of the body, as if he himself were bodily, he was not seen according to the proper character of his nature, in which he is seen by the mind since he is believed to be invisible. Invisible to what but

---

244. See Mt 18:10.
245. Jerome, *Commentary on Isaiah* I, 10.
246. See Ex 34:33-35.
247. Jerome, *Commentary on Isaiah* I, 10.

to the bodily gazes, even heavenly ones, as he said above concerning the angels and powers and dominations? How much more is he invisible to earthly gazes!

9. Hence, in another passage he says more clearly, "The eyes of the flesh are unable to see not only the divinity of the Father but also that of the Son and of the Holy Spirit, because there is one nature in the Trinity, but the eyes of the mind can. Of these eyes the Savior himself says, *Blessed are the clean of heart because they shall see God*" (Mt 5:8).[248] What could be clearer than this explanation? If he had only said: "The eyes of the flesh are unable to see not only the divinity of the Father but also that of the Son and the Holy Spirit," and did not then add, "but the eyes of the mind can," it would perhaps be said that the body should no longer be called flesh once it is spiritual. By going on, then, to say, "but the eyes of the mind can," he removed this sort of vision from every kind of body. But lest anyone should suppose that he was speaking only of the present time, he also added the testimony of the Lord, since he wanted to show which eyes of the mind he meant. That testimony states the promise not of a present but of a future vision: *Blessed are the clean of heart because they shall see God.*

10. When the most blessed Athanasius, the bishop of Alexandria, was opposing the Arians who say that only God the Father is invisible but think that the Son and the Holy Spirit are visible, he also defended the equal invisibility of the Trinity by the testimonies of the Holy Scriptures and the carefulness of his arguments. He most persistently argued that God is seen only because of his assuming a creature, but according to the proper character of his godhead God is absolutely invisible, that is, the Father and the Son and the Holy Spirit, except insofar as it can be known by the mind and spirit.[249] Saint Gregory, an Eastern bishop, says most clearly that God, that is, the Father and the Son and the Holy Spirit, is invisible by nature when he appeared to the patriarchs, just as he could have been seen by Moses with whom he spoke face to face, by assuming the disposition of some visible matter, while his invisibility remains unimpaired.[250] This is what our Ambrose also says, namely, that the Father and the Son and the Holy Spirit were seen in the form that their will chose, not in that which was proper to their nature,[251] so that it is true that *no one ever saw God* (Jn 1:18; 1 Jn 4:12), which are the words of Christ the Lord himself, and that *no human being has seen him or can see him* (1 Tm 6:16), which are the words of the Apostle; in fact, they are the words of Christ through the Apostle. And those testimonies of the Scriptures that tell of God's being seen are not rejected, because he is both

---

248. Ibid. III, 6.
249. Athanasius, *Sermons against the Arians* 1, 63; 3, 14; 4, 36.
250. Phoebatius, *The Divinity and Consubstantiality of the Son* 8. Though Augustine attributes the work to Gregory, an Eastern bishop, the work was included among the writings of Gregory of Elvira; it is now attributed to Phoebatius of Agen.
251. Ambrose, *Commentary on the Gospel of Luke* I, 11.

invisible by the proper nature of his godhead and can be seen when he wills by the assumption of a creature, as he chooses.

3, 11. But if invisibility belongs to his nature, just as incorruptibility does, that nature will not be changed in the world to come so that from being invisible it becomes visible. For it could not become corruptible from being incorruptible either. For he is at the same time immutable. And it was, of course, his nature that the Apostle emphasized when he put these two together in saying, *To the king of the ages, invisible and incorruptible, the only God, honor and glory forever and ever* (1 Tm 1:17). Hence, I do not dare to distinguish them in such a way as to say that he is incorruptible forever and ever, but not invisible forever and ever, but only in this age. Because these testimonies cannot be false, *Blessed are the clean of heart because they shall see God, We know that, when he appears, we shall be like him, because we shall see him as he is* (1 Jn 3:2), we cannot deny that the children of God will see God. But they will see him in the way that invisible things are seen, in the way he promised that he would reveal himself who was seen by human beings as visible in the flesh when he said, *And I shall love him and reveal myself to him* (Jn 14:21), who was speaking in plain sight before the eyes of human beings. How are invisible things seen but by the eyes of the heart? Of these I said a little before what Jerome understood by seeing God.

12. This is also the reason why the previously mentioned bishop of Milan said that in the resurrection it will not be easy to see God except for those who are clean of heart and that for this reason Scripture says, *Blessed are the clean of heart because they shall see God.* "How many he declared blessed, and yet he did not promise these the ability to see God!" And then he added the words, "If, then, those who are clean of heart will see God, the others, of course, will not see him." And so that we would not understand those others to be those of whom he said, *Blessed are the poor; blessed are the meek,* he immediately added, "After all, the unworthy will not see God." He, of course, wanted us to understand that the unworthy are those who, though they will rise, will not be able to see God because they will rise for condemnation, since they refused to make their heart clean by the true faith that works through love.[252] And so he goes on and says, "Nor can someone see God who has not wanted to see God." Then, because it came to mind that even the wicked all want to see God, he immediately added in order to show why he said, "Someone who has not wanted to see God," that a wicked person, of course, does not want to see God in that way, because he does not want to make his heart clean in order that he might be able to see God with it. He said, "Nor is God seen in a location, but by a clean heart. God is not sought by bodily eyes, nor enveloped by sight, nor held by touch, nor heard by words, nor perceived by his walk."[253] By these words, blessed Ambrose wanted to warn people about what they ought to prepare if they want to see God, that is,

---

252. See Gal 5:6.
253. Ambrose, *Commentary on the Gospel of Luke* I, 27.

they ought to make their heart clean by the faith that works through love by the gift of the Holy Spirit, from whom we have a pledge by which we might come to know how to desire that vision.[254]

4, 13. For Scripture often mentions the members of God, but in order that no one would believe that we are like God in terms of the form and shape of this flesh, that same Scripture said that God had wings,[255] which we, of course, do not have. Just as when we hear "wings," we think of his protection, so when we hear "hands," we ought also to understand his working. And when we hear "feet," we ought to understand his coming, and when we hear "eyes," we ought to understand the vision by which he knows. And when we hear "face," we ought to understand the knowledge by which he makes himself known. And whatever else of the sort that the same scripture mentions should, I think, be understood spiritually. Nor do I alone think this, nor am I the first, but all those do who resist by spiritual understanding those who are called anthropomorphites. I do not want to cause greater delays by mentioning many passages from their writings; I introduce only this one from the saintly Jerome in order that this brother may know that he should not argue about this issue with me rather than with earlier men, if anything inclines him against this.

14. When that man most learned in the Scriptures explained the Psalm where it says, *Understand, therefore, you who are foolish among the people, and be wise at last, you fools. Will he who made the ear not hear, or will he who fashioned the eye not see?* (Ps 94:9), he said among other things, "This passage is especially opposed to the anthropomorphites,[256] who say that God has the same members we have. For example, God is said to have eyes because the eyes of God see all things. The hands of the Lord do all things. Scripture says, *And Adam heard the sound of the Lord's feet as he walked in paradise* (Gn 3:8). These people understand these passages in a literal sense and refer these human frailties to the magnificence of God. I, however, say that God is wholly an eye; he is wholly a hand; he is wholly a foot. He is wholly an eye because he sees all. He is wholly a hand because he does all things. He is wholly a foot because he is everywhere. See, therefore, what the Psalmist says: *Will he who made the ear not hear, or will he who fashioned the eyes not see?* He did not say, 'He who made the ear, therefore, does not himself have an ear.' He did not say, 'He, therefore, does not have eyes.' But what did he say? *Will he who made the ear not hear? Will he who fashioned the eyes not see?* He excluded the members, but gave him their activities."[257]

---

254. See 2 Cor 5:4-8.
255. See Ps 16:8.
256. See *Heresies* 50 for the Audians, a sect founded by Audius of Edessa; there were also anthropomorphite monks in Egypt, but they were not Audians.
257. Jerome, *Short Commentary on the Psalms*, Psalm 93:8-9. The author of this work is most probably not Jerome.

15. I thought that I should mention all these passages from the writings of both the Latins and the Greeks who, living in the Catholic Church before us, commented on the words of God in order that this brother may know that, if he holds some view differing from these, he should investigate, learn, or teach it with a careful and tranquil consideration, with all bitterness of dissension set aside and with the sweetness of brotherly love preserved and completely restored. After all, we ought not to regard the writings of any people, though Catholic and highly praised, as being on a par with the canonical Scriptures, so that we are not permitted—always preserving the respect owed to those men—to criticize and reject something in their writings if we should perhaps find something that they held other than is found in the truth, when understood with the help of God by ourselves or by others. That is the way I am with the writings of others; that is the way I want my readers to be. Finally, in all those passages I mentioned from the works of the saints and teachers, Ambrose, Jerome, Athanasius, Gregory, and any others I was able to read but thought it would take too long to mention, by the help of the Lord I most firmly believe and, to the extent he grants, I understand that God is not a body and does not have the members of the human form, that he is not divisible by parts of space, and that he was seen by those to whom he appeared not through that same nature and substance but by a visible form he assumed as he willed, when the holy scriptures report that he was seen by the eyes of the body.

5, 16. But I confess that I have not yet read anywhere anything that I thought was enough for me for the purpose of learning or teaching concerning the spiritual body that we shall have in the resurrection. How much improvement will the body receive? Will it attain to the simplicity of the spirit so that the whole human being will then be spirit? Or, as I tend to think but do not yet affirm with full confidence, will it be a spiritual body so that it will be said to be spiritual on account of a certain ineffable agility, while it preserves its bodily substance that cannot live and sense by itself but does so by that spirit that uses it? After all, even now the nature of the soul is not the same as the body's because the body is said to be natural.[258] And if the nature of the body, though immortal and incorruptible, will be preserved, will it help the spirit for the purpose of seeing visible, that is, bodily things, just as now we cannot see anything of the sort except through the body? Or will our spirit then be able to know bodily things without the organ of the body? After all, God too does not know such things by a sense of the body. And many other issues can puzzle one on this question.

17. And for this reason if my caution of whatever kind it is does not displease this brother, let us in the meanwhile, on account of the words of Scripture, *Because we shall see him as he is* (1 Jn 3:2), prepare a clean heart for that vision

---

258. Augustine uses the Pauline expression "animal body" that in both Latin and Greek is literally "soul body." Just as "soul body" does not mean that the body is changed into the soul, neither does "spiritual body" mean that the body is changed into the spirit.

to the extent we can with his help. Let us, however, peacefully and carefully investigate with regard to the spiritual body in case God should perhaps deign to reveal in accord with his Scriptures something certain and clear, if he knows that it is useful for us. For, if a more careful inquiry discovers that the transformation of the body will be so great that it will be able to see invisible things, such a power of the body will not, I think, take from the mind its vision so that the outer self could then see God but the inner self could not, as if God would be only outside in relation to a human being and not inside within him, since Scripture says with perfect clarity, *That God may be all things in all things* (1 Cor 15:28). Or will he who is whole everywhere without any stretches of space be inside so that he can only be seen outside by the outer self but cannot be seen inside by the inner self? These ideas are most absurd. Since the saints will be more filled with God, they will not be empty on the inside and surrounded by him on the outside. Nor will they be blind inside and not see him with whom they are filled. Nor will they have eyes only on the outside and see him by whom they are surrounded. It remains that for the present we are most certain about the vision of God in terms of the inner self. But if the body will be able to do this by a wondrous transformation, some new power will be added; the former will not be taken away.

18. We do better, then, to affirm that about which we have no doubt, namely, that the inner self will see God, for now the inner self alone can see love, which Scripture praises in saying, *God is love* (1 Jn 4:8). The inner self alone sees peace and holiness, without which no one can see God. After all, no eye of the flesh now sees love, peace, holiness, and any other things like them; still, the eye of the mind now sees all these things more purely, the purer it is. Let us believe without any doubt that we shall see God, whether we discover or do not discover what we are seeking about the quality of the future body. For we do not doubt that the body will rise and will be immortal and incorruptible, because on this we possess perfectly clear and solid statements of the Holy Scriptures. But if this brother claims that what I am still seeking concerning the spiritual body is already absolutely certain for him, he will have grounds for rightly being angry if I do not calmly listen to him teach, just as he also calmly listens to me ask questions. Now, nonetheless, I beg through Christ that you obtain pardon for me from him for that harshness of my letter by which I have learned that he is not unjustly offended, and that with the help of the Lord you may bring me joy by your reply.

LETTER 155

Augustine to Macedonius, the vicar of Africa (413-414)

In 413 or 414 Augustine replied to letter from Macedonius, who was a Christian holding in the imperial administration the high position of the vicar of Africa (Letter 154). He expresses his delight over Macedonius's love for the happy life, which can be found only in Christ (paragraph 1). He points to the errors of the philosophers who thought that they could achieve happiness by their own efforts and claimed that the wise man is happy, even amid such grave pains that he is forced to commit suicide (paragraph 2). Cicero, for example, spoke of a wise man who was blind and deaf and suffering terrible pains such that he had to take himself from the life he called happy (paragraph 3). For Christians, the happy life is the reward in the next life, if they live this life and endure its evils in the hope of the next (paragraph 4).

True wisdom is the true worship of the true God, which is a gift of God, not due to our talent or merit (paragraph 5). If Macedonius loves true virtue, he should cast off the errors of the philosophers and ask for true virtue from God (paragraph 6). Augustine reminds Macedonius that the happiness of a city is to be found in God, just as is the happiness of an individual (paragraph 7). Augustine uses a Psalm to show that the happiness of a people does not come from temporal blessings (paragraph 8). We need to ask the Lord for the virtue to overcome the difficulties of this life (paragraph 9). Macedonius' virtues should not be used merely for the temporal prosperity of those he serves but should be referred to the worship of God (paragraph 10). Augustine worries that he may seem to speak with insufficient respect, but insists that his first fear is to displease God (paragraph 11). If the virtues Macedonius has are true virtues, they will increase by God's help and bring him to virtue's reward of clinging to the highest good (paragraph 12). Even in this life there is no virtue other than to love what we ought to love (paragraph 13). We ought to love God above all else and our neighbor as ourselves, and our neighbor includes everyone human (paragraph 14). We do not need a commandment to love ourselves, since we love ourselves in loving God (paragraph 15). If we lead this life with the virtues that God has given us, we have their eternal reward in the next life (paragraph 16). Piety, then, is the true worship of the true God that brings us through the difficulties of this life to the enjoyment of the highest and everlasting good in the next (paragraph 17).

Augustine, bishop and servant of Christ and his family, sends greetings in the Lord to Macedonius, his beloved son.

1, 1. Though I do not recognize in myself the wisdom that you ascribe to me, I am grateful for your great and sincere goodwill toward me, and I ought to be even more grateful. And I am delighted that the labor of my studies pleased so good and so great a man. But I am delighted much more because I recognize that your mind is filled with the love of eternity and of the truth and that the intensity of this love longs for that divine and heavenly city whose king is Christ and in which alone we will live happily forever if we live here correctly and piously. I am delighted because I see that your mind is drawing near to it and is ablaze with the desire to attain it. From it, of course, there also flows true friendship that is not to be judged by temporal advantages but is to be valued as gratuitous love. For no one can truly be a friend of another person unless he is first a friend of the truth, and if that is not done gratuitously it cannot be done at all.

2. The philosophers have also said much on this topic, but they do not have true piety, that is, the true worship of the true God, from which all the duties of leading a good life must be drawn. The reason for this, to the extent I understand it, is that they themselves wanted to construct a happy life for themselves and thought that they should procure it rather than pray for it, though only God gives it. For only he who made human beings makes them happy. After all, he bestows such great goods upon his creatures, both the good and the bad ones, that they exist, are human beings, are vigorous in their senses, able in their strength, and abounding in riches. He will give himself to the good in order that they may be happy, because it is also his gift that they are happy. But those who in this painful life, in these dying members, under this burden of the corruptible flesh, wanted to be the sources and the creators, as it were, of their own happiness, seeking after it and retaining it as if by their own powers, not asking and hoping for it from that fountain of the virtues, were unable to grasp God, who resists their pride. For this reason they fell into the most absurd error. When they claim that the wise man is happy even in the bull of Phalaris,[259] they are forced to admit that at times we should flee from the happy life. For they yield to the evils of the body that have become excessive, and they decide that they should depart from this life amid their most grievous torments. At this point I do not want to say how great a crime it is for a man to kill himself when he is innocent, since he ought not to, even when he is guilty. In that first of those three books that you read with great kindness and eagerness, we said much on this topic.[260] But at least consider and judge, not with pride but with modesty, how life can be happy if the wise man does not enjoy it when he has it but is forced to leave it by doing violence to himself.

3. There is in Cicero, as you know, in the last part of the fifth book of *Tusculan Disputations*, a passage that should be noted because of what I am saying.[261] For, when he was dealing with bodily blindness and claimed that even

---

259. Phalaris, a tyrant of Agrigento, Sicily, in the 6th century B.C., is said to have roasted his victims in a bronze bull. Epicurus taught that a wise man who has conquered the fear of death can be happy even inside the bull of Phalaris.
260. See *The City of God* I, 17-27.
261. See Cicero, *Tusculan Disputations* V, 38, 110-40, 118.

a wise man who is blind can be happy, he mentioned many things that he would enjoy perceiving through hearing. So too, if he were deaf, he transferred to the eyes the things in which he would take delight. But if he were deprived of both senses and became both blind and deaf, Cicero did not dare to state his opinion on this and call that man happy. But he also added the worst pains of the body and said that, if they did not kill him, he should kill himself and enter that harbor where no one feels anything once he has been set free by his courage.[262] The wise man, then, yields and succumbs to the worst disasters to the point that he is forced by them to commit murder against himself. Whom would he spare in order to escape those evils if he does not spare himself? Surely he is always happy; surely he cannot by the force of any disaster lose the happy life that lies in his own control. Look, in blindness and deafness and the most atrocious torments of the body he either lost the happy life, or if he is still happy amid these afflictions, the upshot of the disputations of such learned men is that at times the happy life is a life that the wise man cannot endure or—what is even more absurd—that he ought not to endure. Rather, he should flee from that life, break it off, cast it away, and take himself from it by the sword, by poison, or by another voluntary death. In that way he would be utterly non-existent in the harbor where no one feels anything, as the Epicureans and any others of the same stupidity thought, or he is happy because he was set free from that happy life as if from some plague. O the proud presumption! If the life amid bodily torture is happy, why does the wise man not remain in it to enjoy it? But if it is miserable, what, I ask you, but pride keeps him from saying so, from praying to God, from beseeching the just and merciful God? For he is able to turn aside or to lessen the evils of this life or to arm us with courage to face them or to set us entirely free from them and, after this life, to give us the truly happy life. There no evil will be allowed, and there the highest good will never be lost.

4. This is the reward of the pious; in the hope of attaining it we lead this temporal and mortal life not so much with pleasure as with endurance. And we bear its evils bravely with a good heart and by the gift of God when we rejoice over God's faithful promise of eternal goods and over our faithful expectation of them. The apostle Paul exhorted us to this; he said, *Rejoice in hope; be patient in tribulation* (Rom 12:12). For he shows why we should be *patient in tribulation* by prefacing it with the words, *Rejoice in hope*. I exhort you to this hope through Jesus Christ our Lord. For, when the majesty of his godhead was hidden and the weakness of the flesh was seen, God himself, the teacher, not only taught this by the words he spoke but also confirmed it by the example of his passion and resurrection. For in his Passion he showed us the sort of things we would have to endure; in his resurrection he showed us the sort of things we ought to hope for. Those philosophers would also merit his grace if they were not exalted and puffed up with pride and did not try in vain to produce the happy life for them- selves,

---

262. See ibid. V, 40, 117.

something that God alone truthfully promised that he would give to his worshipers after this life. That statement of the same Cicero is certainly sounder where he says, "For this life is indeed a death that I could lament if I wanted."[263] How, then, if this life is rightly lamented, is it shown to be happy? And is it not rather proven to be miserable because it is rightly lamented? Hence, I beg you, my good friend, get used to being happy for now in hope in order that you may also be happy in fact when your most constant piety receives the reward of eternal happiness.

2, 5. If I am a burden to you with a lengthy letter, you surely brought this on yourself when you called me wise. For this reason, after all, I have dared to say these things to you in order to show you not the wisdom that I have but the sort of wisdom that I ought to have. In the present age, however, this wisdom consists in the true worship of the true God in order that in the age to come its enjoyment may be certain and complete. Here there is a most solid piety, there everlasting happiness. If I have anything of this wisdom, which is the one true wisdom, I have received it from God and not presumed to have it from myself. And I hope confidently that he will bring it to completion in me, for I humbly rejoice that he has begun it in me. With regard to what he has not yet given I am not unbelieving, and with regard to what he has already given I am not ungrateful. For it is not by my talent or merit but by his gift that I am what I am, if I am in any way worthy of praise. For certain people with the keenest and most excellent minds have fallen into greater errors to the extent that they ran, as if by their own strength, with more confidence and did not humbly and sincerely ask God to show them the way. But what merits can any human beings have since he who came, not as a reward owed us but as a gratuitous grace, who was alone free from sin and our deliverer, found all of us sinners?

6. If, then, true virtue delights us, let us say to him what we read in his Sacred Books, *I shall love you, O Lord, my virtue* (Ps 18:2). And if we want to be truly happy, something we cannot fail to want, let us hold on to with a believing heart what we learned in the same Books, *Happy is the man for whom the name of the Lord is his hope and who has not searched after vanities and insane lies* (Ps 40:5). But what vanity, what insanity, and what a lie it is that a mortal human being living a painful life with both spirit and flesh subject to change, burdened with so many sins, exposed to so many temptations, subject to so much corruption, and destined for perfectly just punishments, puts his trust in himself in order to be happy, when he cannot preserve from errors even that which he has as most excellent in the dignity of his nature, that is, his mind and reason, unless God, the light of minds, gives his help! Let us, therefore, cast aside the vanities of false philosophers and their insane lies, for we will not have even virtue unless he is there to help us. Nor will we have happiness unless he is there for us to enjoy and by the gift of immortality and incorruptibility he swallows up the whole mutable and corruptible being of ours, which by itself is feeble and a veritable mine of misery.

---

263. Ibid. I, 31, 75.

7. But because we know that you love the republic, see how it is clear in those Sacred Books that a human being is happy from the same source as the city. For in them a certain man filled with the Holy Spirit says in prayer, *Rescue me from the hands of strangers whose lips spoke vanity and whose right hand is the right hand of iniquity. Their sons are like saplings strong in their youth. Their daughters are dressed and adorned like the temple. Their cellars are full and overflowing from here to there. Their sheep are fertile and are becoming many in their births; their cows are fat. Their walls are not crumbling, nor is there a hole, and there is no outcry in their streets. They called the people who have these things happy. Happy are the people who have the Lord as their God.* (Ps 144:11-15)

8. You see that a people is not called happy because of the accumulation of earthly happiness except by strangers, that is, by those who have no share in the rebirth by which we become children of God. The Psalmist prays that he may be rescued from their hands for fear that he might be drawn by them into this opinion and impious sins. While speaking vanity, they called happy the people who have these things that he mentioned above, in which is found the only happiness that the lovers of this world seek. And for this reason *their right hand is the right hand of iniquity*, because they ranked first these things that they should have ranked lower, just as the right hand is ranked above the left. For, if we possess them, we should not locate the happy life in them; they ought to be ranked below, not above; they should come later, not first. As if we said to the Psalmist, who prayed in that way and desired to be rescued and separated from the strangers who *called the people who have these things happy,* "What do you yourself think? Which people do you call happy?" he does not say, "Happy are the people who have virtue of the mind." If he had said this, he would of course also have separated these people from those other people who located the happy life in this visible and bodily happiness, but he would not yet have gone beyond all vanity and insane lies. For, as the same Books elsewhere teach, *Cursed is everyone who put his hope in a human being* (Jer 17:5). No one, therefore, ought to put his hope in himself since he too is a human being. Hence, in order to pass beyond the limits of all vanity and insane lies and to locate the happy life where it truly is, he says, *Happy are the people who have the Lord as their God.*

3, 9. You see, then, from whom we should ask for that which all, both the learned and the unlearned, desire, and because of their errors and pride many do not know from whom they should ask for it or where they can receive it. Both kinds of people, however, are reprimanded at the same time in a Psalm to God: both those who put their trust in their own virtue and those who boast over the abundance of their riches.[264] That is, both the philosophers of this world and those who hold back from such philosophy call the people happy who have earthly riches. And for this reason let us ask the Lord our God, who made us, for

---

264. See Ps 49:7

the virtue to conquer the evils of this life and for the happy life that we may enjoy after this life in his eternity. In that way both in virtue and in the reward of virtue, as the Apostle says, *let one who boasts boast in the Lord* (2 Cor 10:17). Let us desire this for ourselves; let us desire this for the city of which we are citizens. For a city's happiness comes from the same source as a human being's, since a city is nothing but a multitude of human beings with a common goal.

10. And so, if all your prudence, by which you try to provide for human affairs, if all your courage, because of which you are not frightened by the iniquity of any opponent, if all your temperance, by which you hold back from corruption amid the great disgrace of the bad habits of human beings, if all your justice, by which in judging correctly you give each his due, if all these labor for and strive after this goal—I mean that these people whose well-being you desire may be sound in body and safe and secure from the wrongdoing of anyone, that they may have sons like strong saplings and daughters adorned like the temple, that their cellars may be full and overflowing from here and to there, that their sheep may be fertile and their cows fat, that a collapse of a wall may not disfigure their property, and that the outcry of litigation may not be heard in their streets—then your virtues will not be genuine, just as their happiness will not be. Here, after all, that modesty of mine, which you praised with kind words in your letter, ought not to keep me from speaking the truth.[265] If any act of administration on your part, guided by those virtues I mentioned, is determined by the intention of this goal that human beings suffer no unjust troubles in terms of the flesh, and if you do not think it is your concern how they use this peace that you strive to give them, that is, to speak plainly, how they should worship the true God where there is found the whole benefit of a peaceful life, that great labor does you no good for the truly happy life.

11. I seem to say this with not enough respect and to have forgotten somehow the manner of my intercessions. But if respect is nothing but the fear of causing displeasure, I am not afraid when I fear in this case. After all, I rightly fear to be displeasing first of all to God and then to the friendship you have deigned to enter into with me, if I am less frank in admonishing you about what I judge because I admonish you to a most salutary purpose. Surely I may be more respectful when I intercede with you on behalf of others, but when I intercede on your own behalf I am franker to the extent I am more your friend because I am more your friend the more loyal I am. And yet I would not say these things if I were not acting with more respect. If this were not, as you wrote in your letter, "most effective for resolving difficulties among good men," may God help me with you on your behalf in order that I may enjoy you in him who has offered me this confident access to you, especially since I think that what I suggest is already easy to do for your mind, which is aided and instructed by so many gifts of God.

---

265. See Letter 154, 10.

12. For, if you realize from whom you received the virtues you have received and thank him, you would use them for his worship, even in these worldly honors you have, and you would raise up and draw human beings subject to your authority to worship him by the example of your religious life and by your zeal in providing for them, whether by showing them favor or by causing them fear. And in the life that they live in great security because of you, you would want nothing else than that, because of it, they may merit him with whom they may live in happiness. And those virtues will be true virtues and, by the help of him by whose bounty they were given, they will grow and become perfect so that they will without any doubt bring you to the truly happy life, which is none other than eternal life. In it prudence will not distinguish evil, which will not exist, from what is good, nor will courage endure adversity, because we will find there only what we love, not what we endure, nor will temperance bridle desire where we will not feel its enticements. Nor will justice aid the needy with help where we will have no one poor and needy. In that life there will be only one virtue, and it will be both virtue and the reward of virtue, something that one who loves this says in the Holy Writings, *But for me it is good to cling to God* (Ps 73:28). There this will be complete and everlasting wisdom, and this same wisdom will also be the truly happy life. It is, of course, the attainment of the eternal and highest good, and to cling to it for eternity is the goal that holds all our good. This might be called prudence because it will with perfect foresight cling to the good that will not be lost. It might be called courage because it will most firmly cling to the good that will not be torn away. It might be called temperance because it will most chastely cling to the good by which it will not be corrupted. And it might be called justice because it will with full righteousness cling to the good to which it is rightly subject.

4, 13. And yet even in this life there is no virtue but to love what one should love. To choose it is prudence; to be turned away from it by no difficulties is courage; to be turned away from it by no enticement is temperance; to be turned away from it by no pride is justice. But what should we choose that we should especially love except that than which we find nothing better? This is God, and if in loving him we prefer something else or make it equal to God, we do not know how to love ourselves. For we are better off to the extent that we advance more toward him than whom nothing is better. But we advance not by walking but by loving. We shall have him more present to the extent that we can maintain more purely the same love by which we tend toward him. For he is neither stretched out nor enclosed in bodily places. We may advance toward him who is present everywhere and whole everywhere, therefore, not by our feet but by our actions. Our actions, however, are usually judged not on the basis of what each of us knows but on the basis of what each of us loves, and only good or bad loves make good or bad actions. Because of our wrongdoing, then, we are far from the rectitude of God; hence, by loving what is right we are corrected in order that, as upright, we may cling to what is right.

14. Let us, then, work with as much effort as we can so that those whom we love as we love ourselves may attain him, if we know how to love ourselves in loving him. For Christ, that is, the Truth, says that the whole law and the prophets depend on these two commandments, namely, that we love God with our whole heart, our whole soul, and our whole mind and that we love our neighbors as ourselves.[266] We should, of course, judge who our neighbor is in this passage not on the basis of blood relationship but on the basis of our sharing in the society of reason, in which all human beings are united. For if the bond of money unites people, how much more does the bond of nature unite them, which they share not by the law of exchange but by that of birth! For this reason that famous comic playwright—for the splendor of the truth is not lacking to brilliant minds—has one old man say to another: "Do you have so much leisure from your own affairs that you busy yourself about the affairs of others that are none of your concern?" And he added the response from the other: "I am a human being; I do not regard anything human as of no concern to me."[267] They say that whole theaters, full of stupid and ignorant people, applauded that idea. The union of human minds naturally stirs the love of all human beings so that each human being in it feels that he is a neighbor of any other.

15. And though with that love, which God's law commands, a man ought to love God, himself, and his neighbor, still we were not given three commandments on this account. Nor was it said, "On these three," but, *On these two commandments the whole law and the prophets depend*, that is, on the love of God from one's whole heart, from one's whole soul, and from one's whole mind, and of one's neighbor as oneself. In that way we were, of course, meant to understand that there is no other love by which one loves himself but that by which he loves God. For one who loves himself in another way should rather be said to hate himself. He, of course, becomes unjust and is deprived of the light of justice when he turns away from the better and higher good, for, even if he turns from it toward himself, he certainly turns toward lower and lesser goods. The words of Scripture are realized in him: *But he who loves injustice hates his own soul* (Ps 11:6). Because, then, no one loves himself except by loving God, there was no need that a human being also receive a command to love himself after he had been given the commandment about the love of God, since in loving God he loves himself. He ought, then, to love his neighbor as himself in order that by consoling him through beneficence, by teaching him through doctrine, or by restraining him through discipline he may bring everyone he can to worship God, since he knows that on these two commandments the whole law and the prophets depend.

16. One who chooses this with careful discernment is prudent; one who is not turned aside from this by any affliction is courageous; one who is not turned

---

266. See Mt 22:37-38.
267. Terence, *Heauton timorumenos* I, 1, 75-77.

aside from this by any delight is temperate; and one who is not turned aside by any pride is just. By these virtues given by God through the grace of Jesus Christ, the mediator, who is God with the Father and man with us,[268] through whom we are reconciled to God in the Spirit of love after the enmities of sin—I repeat, with these virtues given by God we now live a good life, and afterwards we will be given its reward, the happy life, which can only be eternal life. For the same virtues are practiced here and will have their result there. Here they involve work; there they will be our reward. Here they are our duty; there they will be the end we attain. And so all good and holy people, even amid torments of every sort, supported by God's help, are called happy because of the hope for that end, the end in which they will be happy. For, if they were always in the same torments and the fiercest pains, no sound mind would doubt that they were miserable no matter what virtues they had.

17. Piety, then, that is, the true worship of the true God, is useful for everything.[269] It both turns aside and eases the troubles of this life and leads to that life where we will no longer suffer anything evil but will enjoy the highest and everlasting good. I exhort you, as I exhort myself, to attain that piety more perfectly and to hold on to it with great perseverance. If you did not already have a share in it and did not judge that these temporal honors of yours ought to be used in his service, you would not say to the Donatist heretics in order to restore them to the unity and peace of Christ, "On your behalf we do this; on your behalf the priests of inviolate faith labor; on your behalf the august emperor labors; on your behalf we too, his judges, labor," and many other things that you put in the same edict in order that it might be seen that in the garb of an earthly judge you have in mind to no small degree the heavenly fatherland. Hence, if I chose to converse with you longer concerning true virtues and the truly happy life, I ask that you not consider me a burden for your work. In fact, I am confident that I am not, since you have so great a mind and one so wonderfully praiseworthy that you do not abandon those concerns and you occupy yourself with these more willingly and frequently.

---

268. See 1 Tm 2:5.
269. See 1 Tm 4:8

AUGUSTINE AS THEOLOGIAN

ON THE HOLY TRINITY AGAINST THE ARIANS

LETTER 238

Augustine to Pascentius, an Arian count
from the imperial court (400-410)

In probably the first decade of the fifth century Augustine wrote to Pascentius, an Arian count from the imperial court, who had challenged Augustine to a debate in Carthage, as Possidius reports in his *Life of Augustine* 17. Since Pascentius had gone back on his earlier agreement that their words be taken down by stenographers, Augustine decided to state his faith in writing and send it to Pascentius (paragraph 1). Augustine explains the need to have what they said taken down verbatim so that neither of them could later deny what they had said (paragraph 2). Augustine gives a concrete example of how Pascentius wrote down something other than what he had said (paragraph 3). Augustine recalls Pascentius' tirade over the word ὁμοούσιον and his own attempt to explain its meaning (paragraph 4). He points out that even the Arians use expressions in speaking of God that are not found in the Scriptures (paragraph 5), though Pascentius claimed to avoid ὁμοούσιον because it does injury to God (paragraph 6). Despite the variances in Pascentius' articulation of his faith, he refused to have his words taken down by stenographers (paragraph 7). In another statement of his faith Pascentius omitted the words "God the Son," and he began to insult Augustine when this was pointed out (paragraph 8). Given the present letter, Augustine claims that Pascentius cannot truthfully claim that Augustine was afraid to state his own faith, and he expresses his wonder at Pascentius' alleged fear of attack from a bishop (paragraph 9).

Augustine states his faith in the one God, the Father, the Son, and the Holy Spirit, and explains in what sense the Son is equal to the Father and in what sense he is less than the Father (paragraph 10). He explains that what is said of God is said of each of the three persons, who are the one God (paragraph 11). As body and soul are together one human being, so the Father, the Son, and the Holy Spirit are together one God (paragraph 12). Augustine appeals to the unity of the many faithful in Christ to explain how the Father, the Son, and the Holy Spirit are one God (paragraph 13). He distinguishes the relative from the non-relative predications about the persons (paragraph 14) and shows how "spirit" is used in both ways in Scripture (paragraph 15). Augustine argues that, if the peace of Christ can make many believers to be one heart and one soul, we ought to believe that the Father, the Son, and the Holy Spirit are not three gods but one God (paragraph 16). He explains that Catholics maintain that the Son of God is also the Son of Man on account of the form of the servant that the Son of God assumed (paragraph 17).

Augustine asks Pascentius to turn his attention to the words of Scripture that demand that we confess that the Father, the Son, and the Holy Spirit are the one Lord God and resolves difficulties arising from several texts (paragraphs 18 to 20). He cites scripture texts that show that the Holy Spirit is God and equal to the Father and to the Son (paragraph 21). He deals with a passage from which one might infer that the Son is greater than the Father (paragraph 22), and he argues against the Arian claim that the Son was visible and subject to corruption even prior to the incarnation (paragraph 23). He argues that there never was a time when the Father did not have the Son, using the image of light and its brightness (paragraph 24). He challenges Pascentius to find in Scripture any passage where two things not of the same substance are said to be one without qualification (paragraph 25).

In conclusion Augustine challenges Pascentius to write out a statement of his faith and to sign it (paragraph 26). He mocks Pascentius' claim to have defeated him (paragraph 27), and he challenges him to try to defeat the words of Scripture that proclaim that the Father and the Son are one (paragraph 28). For the words *are one* are never used in Scripture of things of a different substance (paragraph 29).

Augustine to Pascentius.[270]

1, 1. As you may deign to remember, I had certainly wanted, when you begged and pleaded—indeed, considering the merit of your age and dignity, when you commanded us—to have a conversation, even face to face, about the Christian faith, insofar as the Lord might grant me the opportunity. But, since after dinner you did not want to do what we had in the morning agreed to do, namely, to have our words taken down by stenographers so that you might not say anymore what I hear that you are in fact saying, namely, that I did not dare to state for you my faith, accept in this letter what you can both read and hand on to whom you will. And you yourself may reply with what you want by writing in return. After all, it is unfair that anyone should want to pronounce judgment on another person and not want anyone to pronounce judgment on him.

2. And from our past agreement, which you were unwilling to implement at our afternoon meeting, it can be easily decided which of us lacked confidence in his faith—whether it was the one who was willing to state it but was afraid to have it preserved, or the one who was so unwilling to remove it from the judgment of the disputants that he wanted what was committed to writing to be entrusted as well to the memory of readers. In that way neither of us might be either confused by forgetfulness or annoyed by the disagreement and might

---

270. In the critical edition the letter lacks a salutation, perhaps because, as Augustine says in paragraph 26, he thought that Pascentius might not want his name on the letter. PL adds the salutation produced here.

say that something that was said was not said or that something that was not said was said. For those who desire an argument more than the truth often seek concealment for their weak defense in such places. But this could be said neither by you nor by me, neither about you nor about me, if you remained faithful to our agreement that our words be taken down and recorded, especially since you yourself changed those words in which you stated your faith as often as you repeated them, something that was not done out of deceit, I believe, but out of forgetfulness.

3. For you first said that you believed in "God the Father, almighty, invisible, unbegotten, incomprehensible, and in Jesus Christ, his Son, God born before the ages, through whom all things were made, and in the Holy Spirit." After hearing this, when I replied that you had not yet said anything that was in conflict with my faith and hence that, if you signed it, I could also add my signature, somehow or other the matter was brought to the point that you took a piece of papyrus and wanted to express by your own hand in writing what you had said. And when you gave it to me to read, I noticed that you had left out "Father" when you wrote "God almighty, invisible, unbegotten, unborn." When I mentioned this, after a brief dispute you added "Father" and "incomprehensible," which you had spoken in words but omitted in writing. But I made no mention of this.

4. Then, after I had said that I was ready to add my signature to indicate that those words could be mine as well, I first asked, lest what had entered my mind slip away, whether "unbegotten Father" was found anywhere in the Divine Scriptures. But I did this because at the beginning of our discussion, when the names Arius and Eunomius[271] were mentioned, not by me but by my brother Alypius,[272] who was asking which of them Auxentius[273] followed, a man who was extolled by you with no small praise, you immediately demanded that we condemn ὁμοούσιον,[274] as if there were any person who was called by this name, like Arius and Eunomius. Next you vigorously demanded that we show you this word in the Scriptures, and you would immediately be in communion with us. We answered that, since we spoke Latin and that term was Greek, it was first necessary to investigate what ὁμοούσιον meant and then one should demand

---

271. Arius was the fourth-century Alexandrian priest after whom the Arian heresy was named. Eunomius, also of the fourth century, taught an extreme form of Arianism, maintaining that the Son was unlike the Father. For that reason his doctrine was called Anomoeanism.
272. Alypius, Augustine's friend since his youth, was at that time bishop of Thagaste.
273. There were two Arian bishops named Auxentius. One was the bishop of Milan immediately prior to Saint Ambrose; he died in 374. The other was a Homoian Arian, the bishop of Durostorum and a disciple of Ulfilas, the apostle of the Goths, who came to Milan in 383 and attempted to obtain the basilica of Saint Ambrose through the intervention of the Arian empress, Justina. See *Confessions* IX, 7, 15. It is most likely the latter whom Pascentius had praised. Homoian Arianism held that the Son was like the Father, but not that he was of the same substance as the Father.
274. The word ὁμοούσιον, taken from the Creed of Nicaea, expressed the sameness of substance of the Father and the Son.

that it be shown to be in the Holy Books. You, on the other hand, repeated the word frequently and uttered it with hate, recalling that it was recorded in the councils of our predecessors, and you strongly urged that we show that that very word, namely, ὁμοούσιον, is in the Holy Books. We recalled again and again that, since our language was not Greek, we first had to translate and explain what ὁμοούσιον meant and then look for it in the Divine Writings. For, even if the term were not itself found there, we might nonetheless find the idea. After all, what is more a mark of quarrelsomeness than to fight over the word when we are agreed on the idea?

5. Because, then, we had already discussed this between ourselves, after we had come to the point at which you were expressing your faith in writing, as I mentioned, although I saw nothing in those words opposed to our faith and for this reason said that I was prepared to add my signature, I asked, as I said, whether God's Scripture contained the statement that "the Father is unbegotten," and, when you replied that Scripture did contain this, I asked more insistently that you demonstrate this. Then one of those who were present, someone who shares your faith, as far as I can understand, said to me, "So what? Do you say that the Father is begotten?" I replied, "I am not saying so." And he said, "If, then, he is not begotten, he is certainly unbegotten." I said to him, "You see that it is possible, however, to give an account of a word that is not in God's scripture in order to show that it is right to use it. In that way, then, even if we did not find in the Scriptures the word ὁμοούσιον itself, which we were being obliged to show was found in the authority of the Divine Books, it is possible to find that to which this word is judged to have been correctly applied."

6. After this was said, I paid attention in order to hear what you thought about this, and you said that "it was correct that 'unbegotten Father' was not used in the Holy Scriptures for fear that an injury might be done to him by such an expression." I said, "Injury is now done to God, therefore, and this by your own hand." When you heard this, you had already begun to say that you ought not to have said this yourself. But when I warned you that, if you thought this word was such that it might injure God, you should delete it there where you had written it, you considered, I think, that it could be correctly used and could be defended. And again you stated, "I certainly say this." Then I repeated the point that I had already made, namely, that it is possible that ὁμοούσιον is not found written in the Sacred Books and yet it may be defensible when uttered in the statement of the faith, just as we never read "the unbegotten Father" in those Books and yet its use is defensible. Then you took from me the sheet of papyrus that you had given and tore it up. And we agreed that in the afternoon stenographers would be present to take down our words and that we would deal more carefully with these questions between us, to the extent we could.

7. We came at the hour agreed upon, as you know; we brought along our stenographers; when yours were also present, we were seated. You again stated your faith, and in your words I did not hear "unbegotten Father." I believe that

you were thinking of what was said about this in the morning and wanted to be careful. Then you asked that I too state my faith. At this point, when I asked, recalling our agreement from the morning, that you instead be so gracious as to dictate what you had said, you shouted out that we were preparing a trap for you and, for that reason, that you wanted to have your words in writing. I do not want to recall what I said at that point, and I wish that you would not remember it either. Yet I maintained the respect due to your office, and I did not regard as an injury what I merited to hear not from the truth but from your authority. Since, nonetheless, I repeated at least those very words while saying quietly, "Are we preparing a trap for you in this way?" I ask your pardon.

8. But, when you heard this, you again repeated your faith in a louder voice and in your words I did not hear "God the Son," something that you had never omitted as often as you had stated your faith. When I asked as calmly as I could that what we had agreed upon concerning the taking down of our words be implemented, I also pointed out its usefulness from our present experience. I said that you yourself could not remember words of yours that you used very often, since you were never able to repeat them without omitting something that was very important. How much less can those who listen to us remember our words so that, if I wanted to reconsider and discuss something in your words or you in mine, they would be able to recall clearly what was said and what was not said. In such a difficulty a reading on the part of the stenographers would be of assistance to us. Then you said angrily that it would have been better if you knew me only by reputation, because you found me to be far less than it had been boasted that I was. Then I recalled that, when we greeted you in the morning and you had praised that reputation of ours, I said that the reports about me were not true. At this point you of course agreed that I was speaking the truth. Hence, since two sources have spoken different things about me, my reputation saying one thing and I another, I certainly ought to be happy that you found me rather than my reputation truthful. But because Scripture says, *God alone is truthful, but every human being is a liar* (Rom 3:4), I am afraid that you were rash also in saying this about me. After all, we are not truthful in ourselves or by ourselves when we are truthful but when he who alone is truthful speaks through his servants.

9. If you recall these actions, as I have narrated them, you see how you ought not to boast before human beings that I did not dare to state my faith for you, since you refused to keep faith with our agreement. And you, a man of such importance, who in defense of the faithfulness you owe to the state do not fear the insults of provincials, fear the attacks of bishops in defense of the faithfulness you owe Christ. Then, since you wanted men of honor to be present at our discussion, I am amazed at how, in the matter of avoiding attack, you are afraid to have your words taken down by our stenographers but are not afraid to have illustrious men hear you speaking from your own lips. Do you not realize that it is difficult for people to believe that you are so afraid of any attack from us that you refused to have your words taken down, but that, though you thought that

you were bound by your own words written down in the morning, at the same time you thought that you could not destroy the stenographers' tablets as easily as you tore up that sheet of papyrus? If, however, you say that those actions did not take place as I have narrated them, you are either misled by forgetfulness (for I do not want to say, "You are lying"), or I am likewise misled or am lying. You see, then, how correct I am in saying that the actions taken, especially on these matters, ought to be written down and recorded and how right it also was for you to have made this decision, except that your afternoon fear shattered your morning agreement.

2, 10. Listen, then, to my faith: Powerful is the mercy of God, which allows me to state what I believe so that I do not offend his truth or your graciousness. I declare that I believe in God the Father almighty and state that he is eternal with that eternity, that is, immortality, I mean, which God alone has, and I believe this of his only-begotten Son in the form of God and also of the Holy Spirit, who is the Spirit of God the Father and of his only-begotten Son. But because, *after the fullness of time came* (Gal 4:4), the only-begotten Son of God the Father, our Lord and God Jesus Christ, opportunely assumed the form of a servant,[275] for the day of our salvation, many things are said of him in the Scriptures in accord with the form of God and many in accord with the form of the servant. As an example I mention two of these in order that one may be referred to each. In accord with the form of God he said of himself, *The Father and I are one* (Jn 10:30). In accord with the form of the servant he said, *The Father is greater than I* (Jn 14:28).

11. But the words of scripture about God, *Who alone has immortality* (1 Tm 6:16), and, *To the invisible God alone be honor and glory* (1 Tm 1:17), and other expressions of this sort, we do not understand as applying to the Father alone but to the Son as well, insofar as this refers to the form of God, and to the Holy Spirit. For the Father and the Son and the Holy Spirit are one God, and the only true God, and alone immortal in accord with their absolutely immutable substance. After all, if Scripture said of the flesh, with its different sexes, *He who clings to a prostitute forms one body with her* (1 Cor 6:16), and of the spirit of a human being, which is not the same as the Lord, *But one who clings to the Lord forms one spirit with him* (1 Cor 6:17), how much more is God the Father in the Son and God the Son in the Father and God the Spirit of the Father and the Son one God, where there is no diversity of nature, since it is said of two different things that somehow cling to one another that they form either one spirit or one body.

12. And since we speak of one human being instead of a soul and a body clinging to each other, why should we not for much better reasons speak of one God when referring to the Father and the Son who cling to each other, since they cling to each other inseparably, not like the body and the soul? And since the

---

275. See Phil 2:7.

body and the soul are one human being, although the body and the soul are not one, why should the Father and the Son for much better reasons not be one God, since the Father and the Son are one according to that statement of the Truth, *The Father and I are one* (Jn 10:30)? Similarly, the interior human being and the exterior human being are not one, for the nature of the exterior is not the same as that of the interior, since the exterior along with the body that was mentioned is called a human being, but the interior is understood to be found only in the rational soul. Yet the two together are not called two human beings but one. For how much better reasons are the Father and the Son one God, since the Father and the Son are one, because they are of the same nature or substance or any other term that expresses more suitably that which God is, which is why it was said, *The Father and I are one* (Jn 10:30)? And so the one Spirit of the Lord and the one spirit of a human being are not one, and yet, when someone clings to the Lord, there are not two spirits but one spirit; and one exterior human being and one interior human being are not one, and yet on account of their connection in a natural union both together are not two but one human being. For much better reasons, then, since the Son of God says, *The Father and I are one*, God the Father is one and God the Son is one, and yet both together are not two gods but one God.

13. One faith, one hope, and one love[276] has brought it about in many holy persons, who have been called *into adoption as children* (Rom 8:17; 1 Cor 13:13) to be coheirs with Christ, that they may have *one soul and one heart* (Acts 4:32) for God. This above all forces us to understand that the nature of the divinity—if we may speak that way—of the Father and of the Son is one and the same, so that the Father and the Son, who are one and inseparably one and everlastingly one, are not two gods but one God. For, through the sharing and union in one and the same nature by which they were all human beings, those human beings were one, and if at times they were not one because of their diverse wills and views and the dissimilarity of their opinions and conduct, they will, however, be fully and perfectly one when they come to that end, *in order that God may be all in all* (1 Cor 15:28). God the Father, however, and his Son, his Word, God with God,[277] are always and ineffably one; hence, for even better reason they are not two gods but one God.

14. But human beings who understand less well what is said for that reason prefer to have hastily-formed views, and, without having carefully examined the Scriptures, they take up the defense of any opinion whatsoever and are turned aside from it either never or only with difficulty, since they want to be considered learned and wise rather than to be such. They actually want to transfer those things that were said on account of the form of the servant to the form of God, and on the other hand they want those things that were said in order to indicate

---

276. See Eph 1:5.
277. See Jn 1:1.

the mutual relations of the persons to be names of a nature or substance. But our faith consists in believing and confessing that the Father and the Son and the Holy Spirit are one God, nor do we say that he who is the Son is the Father, nor that he who is the Father is the Son, nor that he who is the Spirit of the Father and the Son is either the Father or the Son. For these names signify their mutual relations, not the very substance by which they are one. For, when he is called Father, he is called father only of a son, and the Son is understood as a son only of a father, and the Spirit, insofar as he is related to something, is a spirit of someone that breathes him forth, and the one that breathes forth, of course, breathes forth the Spirit.

15. But of God these things are not thought in a bodily fashion, nor are they understood in the usual way. As the Apostle says, *He is able to do more than we ask for and understand* (Eph 3:20). But if he can *do* more, for how much better reason can he *be* more! For in the Scriptures this term "spirit," not insofar as it is relative but insofar as it signifies a nature, refers to every incorporeal nature of spirit; for this reason this term applies not only to the Father, the Son, and the Holy Spirit but to every rational creature and soul. Hence the Lord says, *God is spirit, and for this reason those who worship God should worship him in spirit and in truth* (Jn 4:24). It is also written, *He made the spirits his messengers* (Ps 104:4). It was also said of certain human beings, *For they are flesh and a spirit that goes and does not return* (Ps 78:39). And the Apostle says, *No one knows what is going on in a human being but the spirit of the human being who is present there* (1 Cor 2:11). Likewise Scripture says, *Who knows whether the spirit of the sons of man rises upward and the spirit of an animal goes downward?* (Eccl 3:21) "Spirit" is also used in the Scriptures in accord with a certain distinction in the one soul of a human being; for this reason the Apostle says, *That your whole spirit and soul and body may be preserved for the day of our Lord Jesus Christ* (1 Thes 5:23). So too in another place he says, *If I pray with the tongue, my spirit prays, but my mind remains without fruit. What, then, shall I do? I will pray with the spirit, and I will pray with the mind.* (1 Cor 14:14-15) But in a certain proper way we speak of the Holy Spirit who is related to the Father and the Son, because he is their Holy Spirit. For, because it was once said in terms of substance that *God is spirit* (Jn 4:24), the Father is spirit, and the Son, and the Holy Spirit himself, and yet they are not three spirits but one spirit, just as there are not three gods but one God.

16. Why are you surprised? Peace has such power—not just any peace as it is usually understood, nor such peace as is praised in this life in the oneness of heart and love of the faithful, but *that peace of God that*, as the Apostle says, *surpasses all understanding* (Phil 4:7). What understanding but ours, that is, of every rational creature? Hence, as we consider our weakness and listen to the apostle saying, *Brothers, I do not think that I have attained the goal* (Phil 3:13), and, *Anyone who thinks that he knows something does not yet know how he ought to know something* (1 Cor 8:2), let us converse as well as we can with the

Divine Scriptures, at peace and without strife, not striving to outdo each other in vain and childish rivalry. In that way the peace of Christ may instead triumph in our hearts,[278] to the extent that he grants us the ability to attain it in this life. Considering what that same peace produced among the brethren from whose many souls and hearts he made one soul and one heart for God,[279] let us above all believe with due piety that in that *peace of God, which surpasses all understanding,* the Father, the Son, and the Holy Spirit are not three gods but one God in a more excellent way than those believers had *one soul and one heart,* just as *that peace, which surpasses all understanding,* is more excellent than this peace that is possessed by their one heart and one soul for God.[280]

17. We say, however, that the Son of Man is the same as the Son of God, but not on account of the form of God in which he is equal to the Father, but on account of the form of the servant by which he is less than the Father.[281] And because we say that the Son of God is the Son of Man, for this reason we also say that the Son of God was crucified, not because of the power of the divinity but because of the weakness of the humanity, not because of his remaining in his own nature but because of his taking up of our nature.

3, 18. Now consider for a while the words of Scripture that compel us to confess one Lord God, whether we are asked only about the Father or only about the Son or only about the Holy Spirit, or about the Father, Son, and Holy Spirit together. Scripture certainly says, *Hear, O Israel, the Lord your God is one Lord* (Dt 6:4). Of whom do you think it was said? If only of the Father, Jesus Christ is not our Lord God, and what happens to those words of Thomas as he touched him and cried out, *My Lord and my God*? Christ did not criticize those words but approved of them when he said, *Because you saw me, you believed* (Jn 20:28-29). But if the Son is the Lord God and the Father is also the Lord God and the two of them are two lords and two gods, how will this be true: *The Lord your God is one Lord* (Dt 6:4)? Or is perhaps the Father the one Lord, but the Son is not *the* one Lord but only *a* lord, just as there are many gods and many lords, not as there is that one Lord of whom Scripture says, *The Lord your God is one Lord*? What, then, shall we answer the Apostle when he says, *For, even if there are many who are called gods, whether in heaven or on earth, we nonetheless have one God, the Father, from whom are all things and we are in him, and our one Lord, Jesus Christ, through whom are all things and we through him* (1 Cor 8:5-6)? Now, if what is said of the one God the Father forces us to separate the Son from this, let those who dare say that the Father cannot now be understood as Lord, because Paul said, *Our one Lord, Jesus Christ.* For, if he is the one Lord, he is of the only one; and if he is the only one, how is the Father also the

---

278. See Col 3:15.
279. See Acts 4:32.
280. See Acts 4:32.
281. See Phil 2:6-7.

one Lord, unless because he and the Father are the one God and the only God, without the exclusion of the Holy Spirit? The Father, then, is the one God, and with him the Son is the one God, though the Son is not one Father with him. Likewise, Jesus Christ is the one Lord, and the Father is the one Lord with him, although the Father is not the one Jesus Christ with him, as if the Father were Jesus Christ. For Jesus Christ took this name because of the dispensation of mercy and because of the humanity he assumed.

19. Or do you perhaps, in the words of the Apostle, *Our one Lord, Jesus Christ, through whom all things come,* want to join the term *one* not to *Lord* but to *through whom all things come* in order that you can understand not *the one Lord* but *the one through whom all things come*? In that way it would not be the Father through whom all things come, but the Father alone from whom all things come and the Son alone through whom all things come. If that is the case, at long last admit that our one Lord and God is the Father and the Son. *For who has known the mind of the Lord? Or who has been his counselor? Or who first gave to him and will be repaid? For from him and through him and in him are all things. To him be glory.* (Rom 11:34-36) For he did not say, "From the Father are all things, and through the Son are all things," but, *From him and through him and in him.* Who is this but the Lord of whom he said, *Who has known the mind of the Lord?* From the Lord, then, and through the Lord, and in the Lord are all things, not in that one distinct from this one, but in the one Lord, since he did not say, "To them be glory," but, *To him be glory.*

20. But if anyone says that what the Apostle states, *The one Lord Jesus Christ through whom are all things* (1 Cor 8:6), is not understood as "the one Lord," nor as "the one through whom all things are" but as "the one Jesus Christ," and that the one Jesus Christ is also said to be the Lord, what is that person going to say when he hears the same Apostle crying out, *One Lord, one faith, one baptism, one God and Father of all* (Eph 4:5-6)? After all, since he mentions God the Father here, when he says, *One God and Father of all,* whom did he beyond any doubt want us to understand by the previous words, *one Lord,* except Jesus Christ? If he agrees, then, let the Father cease to be Lord, because Jesus Christ is the one Lord. But if that is absurd and impious to think, let us learn to understand the unity of the Father, Son, and Holy Spirit, in order that we may not be immediately kept from understanding of the Son or of the Holy Spirit what was said of the one and only God. For the Father is certainly not the Son, and the Son is not the Father, and the Spirit of both is not the Father or the Son, and yet the Father, Son, and Holy Spirit are the one Lord God, who is the only one and the true one.

4, 21. After all, if the Holy Spirit were not God and the true God, our bodies would not be his temples. The Apostle says, *Do you not know that your bodies are the temple in your midst of the Holy Spirit, whom you have from God?* (1 Cor 6:19-20) And so that no one would deny that the Holy Spirit was God, he immediately went on to say, *And you are not your own, for you were purchased at a great price. Therefore glorify and carry God in your body,* the God, that is, whose temple he had just said was our bodies. Now it is astonishing if what I hear you are saying is true—that the Holy Spirit is less than the Son, just as the Son is less than the Father. For, since our bodies are members of Christ, as the Apostle says, and since our bodies are also the temple of the Holy Spirit, as the same Apostle says,[282] I am deeply puzzled at how the members of the greater are the temple of the lesser. Or do you perhaps now want to say that the Holy Spirit is greater than the Lord Jesus Christ? After all, the following statement also seems to favor this idea: *For one who speaks a word against the Son of Man will be forgiven, but one who speaks against the Holy Spirit will not be forgiven, not in this world, nor in the world to come* (Mt 12:32; Lk 12:10). For one sins with greater peril against the greater than against the lesser, nor may one separate the Son of Man from the Son of God, because the Son of God himself became the Son of Man not by changing what he was but by assuming what he was not. But away with such impiety of believing that the Holy Spirit is greater than the Son! Let those expressions that seem to show that one is greater than another, then, not readily drive people into error.

22. For certain expressions are used in such a way that those who are less intelligent might think that the Son is greater than the Father. For, when asked which is greater, someone true or the truth, who would not rather reply that the truth is greater? After all, whatever things are true are true by reason of the truth. But it is not that way in God. For we certainly do not say that the Son is greater than the Father, and yet the Son is said to be the truth. He says, *I am the way, the truth, and the life* (Jn 14:6). But you want us to understand of the Father alone his words, *That they may know you, the one true God, and him whom you have sent, Jesus Christ* (Jn 17:3), where we understand that Jesus Christ is also the true God, so that this is the meaning: "That they may know you and him whom you sent, Jesus Christ, to be the one true God." Otherwise, the absurdity results that, if Jesus Christ is not the true God because he said to the Father, *You, the one true God*, the Father is not Lord because *one Lord* (1 Cor 8:6) is said of Christ. And yet, in accord with an incorrect interpretation or rather an error, God the truth is greater than the true God, because the true comes from the truth. The Son, therefore, is greater than the Father, because the former is the truth, while the latter is true. One who has learned that the Father is true God by begetting the truth, not by participating in it, drives this perversity from his mind. For the true Father does not have another substance than the truth he begets.

23. But, although the eye of the human heart is weak for the contemplation of these realities, it is in addition also disturbed by controversy. And when will it see them? Scripture says that the Son of God, our Lord and Savior, Jesus Christ, the Word of God, is both truth and wisdom, and some people say that through his own nature and substance, by which he is the Word of God and the wisdom of God, he was visible and subject to corruption before receiving the flesh that

---

282. See 1 Cor 6:15; 12:27.

he took from the Virgin Mary, without any assumption at all of a bodily creature. For they want what they hold to be consistent, namely, that it is said of the Father alone, *To the invisible, incorruptible, only God* (1 Tm 1:17). I ask you to see that the word of a human being is not visible, nor is the Word of God. But if that wisdom is corruptible of which it is said, *It reaches everywhere on account of its purity*, and, *Nothing impure enters into it*, and, *Remaining in itself, it renews all things* (Wis 7:24-25.27), and any other things like these, which are countless, I do not know what to say except that I grieve over the pride of human beings and am astonished at the patience of God.

24. But since it is said of that wisdom, *It is the splendor of eternal light* (Wis 7:26), not even your people, I think, now say that the light of the Father—after all, what is it but his substance?—was ever without the splendor that it begot, as these things can be believed and somehow or other understood in what is divine, spiritual, incorporeal, and immutable. For I hear that you have corrected those people. Or is it perhaps false that they once said that at some time the Father was without the Son, as if the eternal light were without the splendor it begot? What, then, do we say? If the Son of God was born of the Father, the Father ceased to beget him, and if he ceased, he began. But if he began to beget him, he was at some time without the Son. But he was never without the Son because his Son is his wisdom, which is *the splendor of eternal light*. Therefore, the Father always begets the Son, and the Son is always being born. Here we should again fear that the generation be thought incomplete if we do not say that he was born but is being born. Be patient with me, I beg, in these difficulties of human thought and expression, and let us together have recourse to the Spirit of God who speaks through the prophet, *Who will explain his generation?* (Is 53:8)

25. Meanwhile I ask that you search diligently for this one thing: whether somewhere the Divine Scripture has said of different substances that they are one. For, if we find that it is only said of those things that are clearly of one and the same substance, what need is there for us to rebel against the true and Catholic faith? But if you find that Scripture somewhere says this of different substances, then I shall be forced to search for something else by which to show that the Father and the Son were correctly said to be ὁμοούσιον. For there are some who either do not know our Scriptures or do not examine them with great care and who nonetheless say that the Son is of the same substance as and equal to the Father. Suppose that they say to those who refuse to believe this, though they believe that God the Father has an only-begotten Son: "Was God unwilling to have the Son as his equal, or was he unable? If he was unwilling, he is envious. If he was unable, he is weak. But to think either of these of God is sacrilegious." I do not know whether they can find anything to say if they do not want to say things that are most absurd and most stupid.

5, 26. There, you see, I have explained my faith to you as well as I could. And many more things, indeed, could be said and discussed with greater care. But I fear that the things that I have said may be a burden for you with all your work. Yet I not only wanted to dictate them and to have them written down, but I also took care to add my signature in my own hand, something that I had wanted to do before, if what we had agreed upon were being followed. But now I am sure that you ought not to say that I was afraid to state my faith for you, since I have not only stated it but signed the written statement of it, so that no one may say that I either said what I did not say or did not say what I said. Do this yourself as well if you are looking for judges, not ones who will reverence your person to your face but who will assert their freedom with regard to your writings. For, if you fear an attack—which I would by no means dare to say if you had not mentioned it—it is permissible for you not to sign. For I too did not want to write your name in my letter for fear that you perhaps would not have wanted this.

27. It is easy for someone to defeat Augustine; you must see whether it is by the truth or by shouting. It is not up to me to say anything but that it is easy for someone to defeat Augustine. How much more easy is it that someone should seem to have defeated me or to say that he has defeated me, even if he does not seem to have! This is easy. I do not want you to think it a great achievement; I do not want you to desire it as a great achievement. For, when on this issue people notice how much your heart is burning, many will rejoice at having found the opportunity to make a powerful man their friend with a few cries of "Good going, good going." I do not want to say that, if they do not side with you or if they express the opposite view, they could also have feared you as an enemy. They surely would do so foolishly and stupidly, but most human beings are, nonetheless, like that.

28. Do not, then, pay attention to how Augustine may be defeated, just one man of whatever sort he is. But rather pay attention to whether ὁμοούσιον can be conquered, not this Greek word, which is easy for those who do not understand it to mock, but those words of Scripture, *The Father and I are one* (Jn 10:30), and, *Holy Father, preserve those whom you gave me in your name that they may be one, just as we are* (Jn 17:11). So too, a little later it says, *But I do not ask for these alone, but also for those who will believe in me through their word, that all may be one, as you, Father, are in me, and I am in you, that they too may be one in us in order that the world may believe that you have sent me. And I have given them the glory that you gave me in order that they may be one, just as we too are one, I in them, and you in me, in order that they may be made perfectly one.* (Jn 17:20-23) See how many times he said, *That they may be one, just as we too are one.* Yet he never said, "We and they are one," but, *That they too may be one in us, just as we too are one,* because, just as they were of one and the same substance whom he wanted to make partakers of eternal life, so it was said of the Father and the Son, *We are one,* because they are of one and the same substance and are not partakers of eternal life but the very source of eternal life. And he could say in accord with the form of the servant, "They and I are one, or we are one." But he did not say this because he wanted to make known the one substance, the Father's and his own and the one substance of those human beings.

But if he had said, "That you and they might be one, just as you and I are one," or, "That you and I and they might be one, just as you and I are one," none of us would deny that different substances could also be said to be one. But now you see that this is not the case, because he did not speak in that way, and by saying it often he strongly emphasized what he said.

29. You find in the Scriptures, therefore, that "something one" is said of different natures, as we have shown above, but there is added or understood what that one thing is, just as we say that soul and body are or is one living being or one person or one human being. But if in the Scriptures you find *They are one* said without any addition of those things that are not of one substance, you will be perfectly justified in demanding that we produce another argument to illustrate the meaning of ὁμοούσιον. For there are many other things, but for the present think of this one, when you have put aside the desire to be argumentative so that you may have God's favor. The good of a human being does not consist in defeating another human being, but it is good for a human being willingly to have the truth defeat him, because it is bad for a human being to have the truth defeat him against his will. For it is necessary that the truth win out, whether one denies it or admits it. Pardon me if I have spoken too freely, not to disparage you but to defend myself. For I have presumed upon your seriousness and wisdom, since you can imagine the great obligation you imposed upon me to respond. Or if I have not done even this correctly, please also pardon it. [I, Augustine, have signed this document, which I dictated and reread.]

LETTER 239

Augustine to Pascentius (404)

About 404 Augustine wrote once more to Count Pascentius. Augustine claims that Pascentius did not state his faith, namely, the Arian aspects of his faith by which he differs from the Catholic faith, but only stated aspects that Arians and Catholics believed in common (paragraph 1). He blames Pascentius for refusing to allow stenographers to take down what each of them said (paragraph 2). Finally, Augustine delineates his Catholic faith regarding the Trinity and urges Pascentius to read the longer letter that he had sent him (paragraph 3).

Augustine to Pascentius.

1. If you say that you stated your faith for me and that I refused to state my faith for you, as I hear that you are in fact saying, recall, I beg you, how both of these assertions are false. For you refused to state your faith for me, and I did not refuse to state my faith for you. But I wanted to state it so that no one could say either that I said what I did not say or that I did not say what I said. But you would state your faith for me if you stated the reasons why you disagree with us, if you said, "I believe in God the Father who made the Son as the first creature before all other creatures, and in the Son who is neither equal to, nor like the Father, nor the true God, and in the Holy Spirit, made through the Son after the Son." For these are the things that I hear you are saying. Or, if it is false that you are saying these things, I want rather to know this from you. But if it is true that you are saying these things, I want to know how you defend them from the Holy Scriptures. But now you have said that you believe "in God the Father who is almighty, invisible, immortal, and not born from another, and from whom all things come, and in his Son, Jesus Christ, born as God before the ages, through whom all things were made, and in the Holy Spirit." This is not your faith but the faith of both of us, just as if you added that the Virgin Mary bore that same Son of God, Jesus Christ, something that we likewise believe, and any other points that we confess in common. If, therefore, you had wanted to state your faith, you would not state what is common to both of us but rather that in which we disagree with you.

2. I would say this in your presence if, as we had agreed, our words were being taken down. But because you were unwilling to do this, saying that you feared an attack from us, and withdrew in the afternoon from the agreement you made in the morning, why should I say what you might report that I said, as you want, while I would not have the means to show what I did say or how I said it? Do not, therefore, continue to boast that you stated your faith and that I did not state mine, because there are people who consider that it is really I, who wanted it to be written down, who have confidence in my faith, but that you do

not, since you feared some sort of attack. You were, therefore, ready to deny it if an objection were raised against you that you had said something contrary to my faith. See, then, what you cause people to think of you. But if you were not going to deny the objection, why did you not want what you said to be written down, especially since you greatly wanted distinguished people to be present at our discussion? Why, then, in wanting to avoid an attack, were you afraid of the pen of the stenographers, though you did not fear the testimony of such illustrious persons?

3. But if you want me to state my faith as you say that you stated yours, I can also very briefly say that I believe in the Father and the Son and the Holy Spirit. If you want, however, to hear some particular point on which you disagree with me, I believe in the Father and the Son and the Holy Spirit, and I do not say that the Son is the Father or that the Father is the Son. Nor do I say that the Holy Spirit of both of them is either the Father or the Son. And yet I say that the Father is God, the Son is God, and the Holy Spirit is God, the only God, eternal and immortal by his own substance, just as God alone is eternal and immortal by that divinity which is before the ages. If you disagree with this and you want to hear from me how it is defended from the Holy Scriptures, read as well what I wrote at greater length and sent to Your Goodness. If, however, you do not have time to read it, neither do I have time to toss about useless words. But I myself can reply to what you want by either dictating or writing to the extent that the Lord gives me the ability to either dictate or write to you. [I, Augustine, have signed this letter that I dictated and reread.]

LETTER 241
Augustine to Pascentius (404)

Around the year 404 the Arian Count Pascentius wrote Augustine an insulting letter (Letter 240) in which he challenged Augustine to tell him which of the three persons of the Trinity was the one God. He tells Augustine that, if he were confident of his faith, he and the other Catholic bishops would sit down and confer with him on matters of theology. Sometime after this letter Augustine responds to some of Pascentius' insults and denies that he believes that the person of God has three forms, as Pascentius had suggested (paragraph 1). He challenges Pascentius to explain how, though the Apostle said that someone who clings to the Lord is one spirit with the Lord, he, Pascentius, can deny that the Son, who certainly clings to the Father, is one God with the Father. Finally, Augustine invites Pascentius to reply in writing (paragraph 2).

Augustine to Pascentius.

1. Your letter could neither provoke me to return insults nor deter me from replying to your letter. The things that you wrote would certainly trouble me if they were said by the truth of God, not by the authority of a human being. You said that my "conviction is like a twisted and knotty tree that has nothing straight about it and misleads the gaze of eyes."[283] What would you say of me if I had withdrawn from the agreement that we had made between ourselves in the morning and had set twists of opposition and knots of difficulty in that very easy matter that we had rightly agreed upon? For you would not think that I had drunk heavily of polluted water but that I had drowned in the intoxication of perfidy, which is much worse, if I had not come back after dinner as the same sort of person who had left before dinner. But look: did you not write back what you wanted without fear of any attack? In the same way, then, you can write the other things as well so that there might be something for ourselves and others to consider and judge. For, as to your statement that I believe in the person of God with three forms, if you had deigned to read the other somewhat longer letter I sent and had wanted to reply to what I had written in it,[284] you would perhaps not say this. But look, you dictated, had it written down, and sent the claim that I say that the person of God has three forms, and you were not afraid of an attack. See, you have shown that what I say is true, namely, that you did not refuse to have your words taken down, as was agreed upon when we were together, because you feared an attack, but because you were not confident about the truth. Now, since you have decided to put in writing the question of whether I believe that

---

283. See Letter 240.
284. See Letter 238.

the person of God has three forms, I reply that I do not believe that. There is one form because there is, if I may say so, one deity and, therefore, one God, Father, Son, and Holy Spirit.

2. But I ask that you be so gracious as to answer briefly how you understand the words of the Apostle, *A man who clings to a prostitute forms one body with her, but one who clings to the Lord forms one spirit with him* (1 Cor 6:16-17). After all, he said that bodies of different sex clinging to each other are one body. And although the human spirit can by no means say, "The Lord and I are one," yet, when one is clinging to the Lord, one forms one spirit with him. For how much better reason are he and the Father one God, because he most truly said, *The Father and I are one* (Jn 10:30)? For he clings inseparably to the Father—at least if this term is allowed in that divinity, so that we may say that something "clings" that never was nor will be separated by any distance. Reply to this: Do you want to say that the spirit has two forms because one who clings to the Lord is one spirit? And if you do not want to say this, neither did I say that God, Father, Son, and Holy Spirit, has three forms, but that he is one God. But if you want to converse face to face, I am of course grateful to Your Grace and Benevolence. But, as you have already been so good as to write for me something else that you wanted, then be so good as to write back that we will dictate what we are going to say, and I will be ready to do what you want, to the extent that the Lord helps me. For, if our writing back and forth does not edify us, how will our spoken words to each other be edifying, when, once our words have sounded, we will not find anything we can reexamine by reading? [I, Augustine, have dictated this and have signed it after rereading it.] Let us abstain from insults so that we do not spend the time uselessly, and let us rather pay attention to the issue between us.

LETTER 242

Augustine to Elpidius, an Arian from North Africa
(during Augustine's episcopacy)

Sometime during his episcopacy Augustine wrote to Elpidius, an Arian from North Africa, who had sent him a book by an Arian bishop along with a letter in which the unnamed bishop expressed the desire to win Augustine over to the Arian faith. Augustine thanks Elpidius for the good will he has shown him, especially by even sending some of his writings overseas to two learned Arians, and hopes that Elpidius will accept in a good spirit his prayers for his conversion (paragraph 1). Then Augustine turns to a proof that the Son of God, the Word, by whom all things were made, was himself not made (paragraph 2). Hence, since nothing was made without him, he is either nothing or was not made. Since it is wrong to think that he is nothing, then one must conclude that he was not made but was born from the Father (paragraph 3). Though his generation is ineffable, he is equal to the Father. Though we now hold this in faith, we must purify our hearts so that, once they have been cleansed, we may come to see what we now believe (paragraph 4). Finally, Augustine promises to reply to the book Elpidius sent him if he finds time, and he criticizes its author for claiming to teach the bare truth, though the Apostle said that we now see through a glass in an enigma (paragraph 5).

To his excellent and rightly honorable and lovable lord Elpidius Augustine sends greetings.

1. Which of us is in error over the faith or knowledge of the Trinity is another question. Though I am unknown to you by sight, I am certainly grateful that you have tried to recall me from error, because you believed that I was in error. May God reward you for your good will and bring you to know what you think you know. For, in my opinion, the matter is difficult. And I ask you not to take it as any sort of insult that I have desired the gift of such knowledge for you. For I fear that the presumption of a knowledge that you suppose you have may drive from your hearing not true teachings, which I would never claim to teach you, but at least our good wishes, which I, though unlearned, am permitted to have regarding you. For these are not to be offered in the manner of a teacher but in that of a friend. And I fear that you may become angry at me because I have prayed that you may receive the gift of wisdom rather than congratulated you for already being someone wise. But I, who carry the burden of the title of bishop, most gladly embrace Your Benevolence because you have been so good as even to send my writings overseas to Bonosus and Jason, most learned men, as you write, in order that they may reap rich fruits from discussing them. And you also took care to have a book of a certain bishop of yours that was composed with

talent and vigor brought to me in order to clear away the clouds of all my error. How much fairer is it for you to accept with a good heart my prayer that the Lord God might grant you those gifts that can be given by no human talent and power. For the Apostle says, *We have not received the spirit of this world, but the Spirit who comes from God, in order that we may know what God has given us, and we speak of these things not in the learned words of human wisdom, but having been taught by the Spirit we prepare spiritual things for spiritual persons. But the natural human being does not perceive the things that pertain to the Spirit of God. For such a person, after all, they are foolishness.* (1 Cor 2:12-14)

2. I would prefer, if possible, to investigate with you to what extent a human being ought to be called "natural," in order that, if we are now beyond being such a person, we might perhaps rejoice to have attained to some extent those realities that remain immutably above the human mind and intelligence. For we should beware that it not seem foolish when we hear that the Son is equal to the Father,[285] precisely because we are still a natural human being, of whom it has been said that those things that pertain to the Spirit of God are foolishness to such a person.[286] Although that majesty which is high above all things can be thought of by a spiritual person but can be expressed in words by no one, it is still easy, I think, to see that he through whom all things were made and without whom nothing was made was himself not made. For, if he was made by himself, he existed before he was made so that he could make himself, something that is more absurdly said the more foolishly it is thought. But, if he was not made by himself, he was not made at all, because whatever was made was made by him. *For all things were made by him, and without him nothing was made* (Jn 1:3).

3. I am surprised that you have paid such little attention to what the evangelist wanted to teach so explicitly so as to allow no one to pretend ignorance. For it was not enough to say, *All things were made by him*, if he did not add, *And without him nothing was made*. But though I am slow and, since the fog has not yet been wiped away, my mind's eye is too weak to look upon the incomparable and ineffable presence of the Father and the Son, I nonetheless embrace with all my might what has been sown for us in the Gospel, not so that we might comprehend from it that divinity but so that we might be admonished by it not to boast rashly of our comprehension. For, if all things were made by him, whatever was not made by him was not made. But he himself was not made by himself; hence he was not made. And we are compelled by the evangelist to believe that all things were made by him; by the same evangelist, therefore, we are compelled to believe that he was not made. Likewise, if nothing was made without him, he himself is nothing, then, since he was made without himself. If it is sacrilegious to think this, it remains for us to say that he was not made without himself or

---

285. See Jn 5:18; Phil 2:6.
286. See 1 Cor 2:14.

was not made. But we cannot say that he was not made without himself. For, if he made himself, he already existed before he was made. But if, in order to make himself, he gave help to someone else by whom he was made, he already existed, nonetheless, before he was made in order that he might be made with his own help. It remains, therefore, that he was made without himself. But whatever was made without him is nothing. Either he is nothing, therefore, or he was not made. But he is not nothing; therefore, he was not made. But, if he was not made and is still the Son, he was undoubtedly born.

4. "How," you ask, "could the Son be born equal to the Father from whom he was born?" Now I cannot explain this, and I yield to the prophet who says, *Who will explain his generation?* (Is 53:8) But if you suppose that this should be understood in terms of the human generation by which the Son was born of the Virgin, examine carefully for yourself and question your soul whether, if it has failed to explain that human generation, it should dare to explain this divine generation. You say, "Do not call him equal." Why should I not say what the Apostle said? He said, *He did not consider it robbery to be equal to God* (Phil 2:6). For, though he did not explain that equality to a human mind that has not yet been purified, he stated in words what the human mind might discover in reality once it has been purified. Let us, then, work at purifying our heart in order that there may emerge from it a keenness of vision by which we may be able to see these things. He says, *Blessed are the clean of heart because they shall see God* (Mt 5:8). Thus, emerging from the cloudy images of the natural human being, we shall come to that clarity and purity by which we may be able to see what we see cannot be said.

5. For, if I have the leisure and if the opportunity is given me to reply to the individual points of the book that you were so good as to send me, I think that you will recognize that each person is less clothed in the light of the truth the more he thinks that he speaks the bare truth. For, to omit other statements and to mention for now only this one, over which I have been very greatly saddened, since the apostle Paul says, *We see now through a glass in an enigma, but then we shall see face to face* (1 Cor 13:12), who would put up with this man's saying that "he brings forth the bare truth with every veil removed"? If he said, "We see the bare truth," nothing would be more blind than this arrogant claim to see. But he did not say, "We see," but, "We bring forth," so that the truth seems not only to lie open to the gaze of the mind but also to be subject to the power of the tongue. There are many things that may be said about the ineffability of the Trinity, not in order that it may be expressed in words—otherwise it would not be ineffable—but in order that it may be understood from the words that are said that it cannot be expressed in words. But now, I think, my letter has exceeded its limit, since you advised me by yours to write briefly. Because you deigned to excuse yourself for your lack of instruction in the ancients, I shall not appear strange to you if you are willing to recall the limit of certain letters of Cicero, since you also made mention of him in your letter.

LETTER 170

Alypius and Augustine to Maximus, a physician from Thaenae in Byzacena (after 415)

Sometime after 415 Alypius and Augustine wrote to Maximus, a physician from Thaenae in Byzacena, to congratulate him on his recent conversion from the Arian heresy to the Catholic faith, though they are unhappy about those in Maximus' household who still remain Arians (paragraph 1). Augustine uses the text, *You shall adore the Lord your God and serve him alone* (Dt 6:13), to show how the Arians must either admit that the Father and the Son and the Holy Spirit are one God or not worship the Son and the Holy Spirit (paragraph 2). If, however, worship is owed to all three, then the Trinity is one God (paragraph 3). The Father did not create the Son out of nothing but generates him from his own substance; so too, the Holy Spirit proceeds from the Father and the Son and is not created by them (paragraph 4). The Trinity is not less in the individual persons than in all together and is not greater in all of them than in each person (paragraph 5). As a human being generates another human being of the same nature, so the Father generates the Son of the same nature. The two bishops distinguish names of natures from names of relations and reciprocal from non-reciprocal relations (paragraph 6). Terms that speak of the Son's generation from the Father indicate his origin, not his substance (paragraph 7). An Arian objection concerning the generation of the Son is shown to work against their position since, if God gives corruptible beings the ability to generate what they are, he himself certainly ought to be able to generate a Son of the same nature as he is (paragraph 8). Christ is said to be less than the Father on account of the form of the servant that he assumed, though he remains God along with the Father on account of the form of God that he did not lose (paragraph 9). Finally, Augustine urges Maximus to use his influence to bring his household into communion with the Catholic Church (paragraph 10).

To Maximus, our excellent and rightly honorable and pious brother, Augustine and Alypius send greetings in the Lord.

1. Since we asked from our holy brother and fellow bishop Peregrinus[287] not only about the bodily but especially about the spiritual well-being of you and your household, his replies, of course, made us happy about yours but sad about that of your household, because they have not yet been united to the Catholic Church by a conversion leading to salvation. And since we had hoped that this would soon take place, we are saddened that it has not yet occurred, my excellent and rightly honorable and pious brother.

---

287. Peregrinus was a deacon in the church of Hippo until the end of 415; he became bishop of Thaenae between then and 418. In 420 he and Alypius received Letter 22* from Augustine while they were on a mission to Italy.

2. Hence, greeting Your Charity in the peace of the Lord, we command and ask that you not put off teaching them what you have learned, namely, that there is only one God, to whom is owed the service that is called by the Greek term λατρεία. This very word is found in the law, where it says, *You shall adore the Lord your God, and you shall serve him alone* (Dt 6:13). If we say that he is God the Father alone, we shall receive the answer, "Therefore, we do not owe λατρεία to God the Son"—and that is wicked to say. But if we owe him λατρεία, how do we owe it to only one God, if we owe it to the Father and to the Son, unless the one God whom alone we are commanded to serve with λατρεία is said to be the only God in such a way that the Father and the Son and in fact the Holy Spirit as well are understood? Of him the Apostle says, *Do you not know that your bodies are the temple of the Holy Spirit in you, whom you have from God, and you are not your own? For you have been purchased at a great price. Therefore, glorify*[288] *God in your body.* (1 Cor 6:19-20) Which God is this but the Holy Spirit, of whom he had said that our bodies are the temple? We owe λατρεία, then, to the Holy Spirit. For, if we were commanded to build a temple for him out of wood and stone, as Solomon did, we would certainly be shown to offer him λατρεία by building him a temple. How much more do we owe λατρεία to him for whom we do not build a temple but are a temple!

3. And for this reason, if we owe and offer λατρεία to the Father and to the Son and to the Holy Spirit—the λατρεία of which it is said, *You shall adore the Lord your God, and you shall serve him alone*—then the Lord our God whom alone we ought to serve with λατρεία is undoubtedly not the Father alone nor the Son alone nor the Holy Spirit alone but the Trinity, one God alone, the Father and the Son and the Holy Spirit. The Father is not the Son, nor is the Holy Spirit either the Father or the Son, since in that Trinity the Father is the Father only of the Son and the Son is the Son only of the Father, but the Holy Spirit is the Spirit of the Father and of the Son. But on account of their nature and inseparable life, which is one and the same, the Trinity is understood, as far as humanly possible, through faith which must come before understanding, to be the one Lord our God of whom Scripture says, *You shall adore the Lord your God, and you shall serve him alone*, and of whom the apostle says in his preaching, *From him and through him and in him are all things; to him be glory forever and ever* (Rom 11:36).

4. For the only-begotten Son does not come from God the Father in the same way in which all creation, which he created from nothing, comes from him. For he begot the Son from his own substance; he did not make him out of nothing. Nor did he beget in time him through whom he created all times. For, just as a flame does not precede in time the brightness that it generates, so the Father never existed without the Son. For the Son is the wisdom of God the Father, of which Scripture says, *For it is the brilliance of eternal light* (Wis 7:26). It is undoubtedly

---

288. From 401 on Augustine omits as an interpolation "and carry" *(et portate)* which is found in most Latin Fathers and the Vulgate.

coeternal with the light whose brilliance it is, that is, with God the Father, and for this reason God did not make the Word in the beginning, as he made heaven and earth in the beginning. Rather, *in the beginning was the Word* (Jn 1:1). The Holy Spirit also was not made out of nothing, like a creature, but proceeds from the Father and the Son[289] without being created either by the Father or by the Son.

5. This Trinity of one and the same nature and substance is not less in each person than in all, nor greater in all than in each person, but is as great in the Father alone or in the Son alone as in the Father and the Son together and as great in the Holy Spirit alone as in the Father and the Son and the Holy Spirit together. For, in order to have the Son begotten from himself, the Father did not make himself less, but he begot from himself an other than himself in such a way that he remained whole in himself and was as great in the Son as he was alone. Likewise, the whole Holy Spirit proceeding from another whole does not precede the principle from which he proceeds but is as great together with that other as he is when he comes from it, nor does the Holy Spirit diminish whence he comes when he proceeds from it or increase it when he is united to it. And these are all one without confusion; they are not three by division. Rather, though they are one, they are three, and though they are three, they are one. Hence, how much more does he who has granted to so many hearts of the faithful that they may be one heart[290] preserve in himself that these three are individually God and all together are not three gods but the one God whom we serve with all piety and to whom alone we owe that λατρεία.

6. Since in his goodness he arranges for beings born in time to give birth to offspring of their own substance, see how impious it is to say that he himself did not beget what he himself is, since by his gift a human being begets what he is, that is, a human being, not of another nature but of the same nature as he is, although he does not beget the father of his son, which is what he himself is. For these are names of a relationship, not of a nature, and for this reason names that are at times the same and at times different are used with respect to something else or to something related. The relations are, for example, the same when a brother is related to a brother, a friend to a friend, a neighbor to a neighbor, a relative to a relative, and so forth. It would be endless if we were to run through all of them. For in these this person is to that person the same thing that that person is to this person. But other relations are different, such as father to son, son to father, father-in-law to son-in-law, son-in-law to father-in-law, master to servant, and servant to master. The first person is not the same thing to the second as the second person is to the first, and yet they are both human beings. The relation is different, not the nature. For, if you pay attention to what the one is to the other, the first is not to the second what the second is to the first, because the first is the father, the second

---

289. The expression *filioque* ("and the Son") is omitted in many manuscripts and in the CSEL edition.
290. See Acts 4:32.

the son; or the first is the father-in-law, the second the son-in-law; or the first is the master, the second the servant. But if you pay attention to what each is in relation to himself or in himself, the first is the same as the second, because the second is a human being just like the first. Hence Your Wisdom understands from this that those from whose error the Lord has set you free do not have a good reason to say that the nature of God the Father and that of God the Son are different, because the first is the Father and the second the Son and that the Father did not beget what he himself is, because he did not beget the father of his son, which is what he is in relation to himself. For who would not see that these terms do not point to natures in themselves but signify one person in relation to another?

7. Such is also what they utter with a similar error, namely, that the Son is of another nature and of a different substance precisely because the Father is not God from another God, whereas the Son is God, to be sure, but from God the Father. Here too the expression indicates not the substance but the origin, that is, not what anyone is but from where he is or is not. For it is not true that Abel and Adam were not of one nature and substance because the first was a man from the other man while the second was from no man. If, then, there is a question about the nature of each of them, Abel is a man, and Adam is a man. But if there is a question about their origin, Abel came from the first man, but Adam came from no man. And so, if there is a question about the nature of each in the case of God the Father and God the Son, each is God, and the one is not more God than the other. But if there is a question about their origin, the Father is God from whom God the Son comes, but there is no God from whom God the Father comes.

8. And so, when they try to reply to this, they say in vain, "But a man generates with passion, while God has begotten his Son without passion." For this not only does not help them but in fact helps us very much. For, if God granted to temporal and corruptible things that they generate what they are, how much more has the one, eternal, and incorruptible Father generated what he himself is, namely, his only Son. And we are filled with great amazement because he has begotten him without any passion on his part and with such equality to him that he preceded him neither by power nor by age! But for this reason the Son attributes everything he has and can do not to himself but to the Father, because he does not come from himself but from the Father. For he is equal to the Father, but he received this too from the Father. Nor did he receive equality as if he were originally unequal; rather, he has been born equal. Just as he has always been born, so he has always been equal. The Father, therefore, did not beget someone unequal and give him equality once he was born, but by begetting him he gave him equality, because he begot an equal, not someone unequal. For this reason it was not robbery but natural to him to be equal to God in the form of God,[291] for he received equality by being born and he did not falsely claim it out of pride.

---

291. See Phil 2:6.

9. Hence he says that the Father is greater[292] because he *emptied himself, taking the form of a servant* (Phil 2:7) without losing the form of God. On account of this servant's form he became less not only than the Father but also than himself and the Holy Spirit, nor did he only become less than this most excellent Trinity but he also *became a little less than the angels* (Heb 2:9). He was less than human beings when he was subject to his parents.[293] On account of this servant's form, which he received when the fullness of time came, after emptying himself, he said, *The Father is greater than I* (Jn 14:28). But on account of the form of God that he did not lose, even when he emptied himself, he said, *The Father and I are one* (Jn 10:30). That is, he both became man and remained God. For the man was assumed by God, but God was not consumed in the man. Hence it is quite reasonable that as man Christ is less than the Father and that the same Christ, himself God, is equal to the Father.

10. Since, then, we rejoice with the great exultation of the people of God that you were united to this correct and Catholic faith in our presence, why are we still saddened over the sluggishness of your household? We beg you by the mercy of Christ that with his help you remove this sorrow from our hearts. For we ought not to believe that your authority could have had such power for leading your people astray and has no power for their correction. Or do they perhaps hold you in contempt because you came into union with the Catholic Church at this ripe age, though they ought to admire and respect you more because you have conquered your very old error by a certain youthfulness? Heaven forbid that they should oppose you when you speak the truth though they agreed with you when you wandered from the truth! Heaven forbid that they should refuse to hold the correct view with you with whom they were delighted to be in error! Only pray for them and insist with them; in fact, bring them with you into the house of God since they are with you in your house. Or feel shame or embarrassment at coming into the house of God without those who were accustomed to gather in your house, especially since our Catholic mother seeks some of them from you and seeks back others of them from you. It seeks those whom it finds in your company; it seeks back those whom it lost through you. Let her not be tormented by losses but, rather, happy with gains. Let her acquire children whom she did not have; let her not mourn those whom she did have. We pray to God that you do what we exhort you to do, and we hope in his mercy that, by the letter of our holy brother and fellow bishop, Peregrinus, and by the reply of Your Charity, our heart may be soon filled with joy and our tongue with exultation over this matter.[294]

---

292. See Jn 14:28.
293. See Lk 2:51. 8. See Ps 126:2.
294. See Ps 126:2.

ON THE VALIDITY OF BAPTISM AND THE UNITY OF THE CHURCH AGAINST THE DONATISTS

LETTER 23

Augustine to Maximinus, the Donatist bishop of Siniti in Numidia
(391-395)

Between 391 and 395, while still a priest, Augustine wrote from Hippo to Maximinus, the Donatist bishop on Siniti in Numidia. He first explains the reverential mode of address that he used in writing to Maximinus (paragraph 1). Then he explains the sinfulness of rebaptizing and his reluctance to believe that Maximinus has rebaptized a Catholic (paragraph 2). He asks Maximinus to reply to him and to state whether he rebaptizes or not (paragraph 3). Augustine argues against the repetition of Christian baptism (paragraph 4) and points out that Maximinus has it in his power to set an example for the rest of Donatist Africa (paragraph 5). Augustine suggests that both parties set aside past wrongs and deal with the present case (paragraph 6). He even proposes that his letter and Maximinus' reply be read to the people when the military is not present (paragraph 7). Finally, Augustine explains that the urgency of the case demanded that he take action in the absence of his bishop (paragraph 8).

To my most beloved lord and honorable brother, Maximinus, Augustine, a priest of the Catholic Church, sends greetings in the Lord.

1. Before I come to the point about which I wanted to write to Your Benevolence, I shall give an account of the salutation of this letter lest it disturb you or anyone else. I wrote "lord" because Scripture says, *You have been called to freedom, brothers; only do not use your freedom as an opportunity for the flesh, but rather serve one another through love* (Gal 5:13). Since, then, I am serving you through love by this very duty of writing a letter, I call you "lord" without any absurdity on account of our one and true Lord who gave us these commands. But as for the fact that I wrote "most beloved," God knows that I not only love you, but love you as myself, since I am quite conscious to myself that I desire the same goods for you as for myself. But as for "honorable," which I also added, I did not add this to honor your episcopacy. After all, you are not my bishop, nor should you take this as spoken with contempt, but in that spirit by which we ought to have on our lips, *Yes, yes; no, no* (Mt 5:37; Jas 5:12). For you are not unaware, nor is any human being who knows us unaware, that you are not my bishop and that I am not your priest. I, therefore, willingly call you "honorable" on the basis of that rule by which I know that you are a human being and know

that a human being has been made to the image and likeness of God[295] and placed in a position of honor by the very order and law of nature, if by understanding what he should understand he preserves his honor. For Scripture says, *Though placed in a position of honor, man did not understand; he has been made equal to mindless animals and has become like them* (Ps 49:21). Why, then, should I not call you "honorable" insofar as you are a human being, especially since I dare not to give up hope concerning your salvation and correction as long as you are in this life? But you are not unaware that we are commanded by God to call you, "brother,"[296] so that we say even to those who deny that they are our brothers, "You are our brothers," and this holds especially true for the case on account of which I have wanted to write to Your Fraternity. For, now that I have given an account of why I made such an introduction for this letter, listen in complete calmness to what follows.

2. Though I express in the strongest words I can my hatred for the lamentable and deplorable custom of people in this region who, though they boast of the Christian name, do not hesitate to rebaptize Christians, there were some people who praised you and who said to me that you do not do that. I admit, at first I did not believe them. Then, considering that it is possible that fear of God entered the human soul reflecting on the future life so that it held itself back from a most evident crime, I gratefully believed that with such an intention you refused to be so far removed from the Catholic Church. I was, of course, seeking an occasion to speak with you in order that, if it were possible, that small disagreement that had remained between us might be removed, when, you see, a few days ago it was reported that you rebaptized our deacon in Mutugenna.[297] I was deeply saddened both over his wretched fall and over your unexpected crime, my brother. After all, I know which is the Catholic Church. The nations are the heritage of Christ, and the possession of Christ is the ends of the earth.[298] You also know this, or if you do not know, pay attention. It can be easily learned by those who are willing. To rebaptize, then, a heretical person who has already received these signs of holiness that the Christian discipline has handed down is a sin without a doubt. To rebaptize a Catholic is, however, a most grievous sin. And yet, not believing this report since I held a good opinion of you, I myself went to Mutugenna, and I could not see the poor man, but I heard from his parents that he has now also become your deacon. And I still think so well of your disposition of heart that I do not believe that he was baptized again.

3. Hence, I beg you, most dear brother, by the divinity and the humanity of our Lord Jesus Christ, to be so good as to write back to me what has happened and to write back in such a way that you bear in mind that I want to read your

---

295. See Gn 1:27.
296. See Is 66:5.
297. A town in Numidia.
298. See Ps 2:8.

letter to our brothers in the Church. I have written this so that I would not offend Your Charity, when I later do something that you hoped I would not do, and so that you would not raise a just complaint about me before our common friends. I do not see, then, what keeps you from writing back. For, if you do rebaptize, there is nothing that you should fear from the men of your company, since you will write back that you do what they command that you do, even if you do not want to. But when you maintain that this should be done with as many proofs as you can, they will not only not be angry, but will even praise you. If, however, you do not rebaptize, seize the freedom of Christ, brother Maximinus; seize it, I beg you. In the sight of Christ do not fear the reproach or do not be terrified at the power of any human being. The honor of this world is passing; its pride is passing. In Christ's future judgment neither pulpits with flights of steps nor thrones with canopies nor flocks of processing and chanting nuns will be called to our defense when our consciences begin to accuse us and the judge of our conscience begins to pass judgment. Those things which are here honors will there be burdens; those things which here buoy us up will then pull us down. These honors which are shown to us for a time on account of the good of the Church will perhaps be defended by a good conscience, but they will not be able to defend a bad conscience.

4. With regard, then, to what you do with so pious and so religious a mind, if you do in fact act in this way—I mean, if you do not repeat the baptism of the Catholic Church, but rather approve it as the baptism of the one truest mother, who offers her breast to all the nations for their rebirth and who, as the one possession of Christ that stretches out to the ends of the earth,[299] pours out in them her milk after their rebirth—if you really act in this way, why do you not burst forth in a cry that is exultant and free? Why do you cover the very useful brightness of your lamp under a bushel?[300] Why have you not torn and cast aside the old skins of timid servitude and instead put on the confidence of Christ? Why do you not go out and say, "I know of only one baptism consecrated and sealed by the name of the Father and of the Son and of the Holy Spirit? Where I find this form, I must approve. I do not destroy what I recognize as the Lord's; I do not spit[301] at the standard of my king." Those who divided the clothing of the Lord did not destroy it.[302] And they still did not believe that Christ would rise, but they saw him dying. If his clothing was not torn by his persecutors when he was hanging on the cross, why is his sacrament destroyed by Christians when he is seated in heaven? If I were a Jew in the time of the old people when I could not be anything better, I would certainly have received circumcision. That sign of

---

299. See Ps 2:8.
300. See Mt 5:15, Lk 11:33, 8:16, and Mk 4:21.
301. Literally: "I do not subject to exsufflation the standard of my king," i.e., to the baptismal rite by which the priest "blows out" the devil from the candidate for baptism.
302. See Jn 19:24.

the righteousness of faith[303] was at that time so powerful, before it was rendered void by the coming of Christ, that an angel would have suffocated the infant son of Moses if his mother had not taken a piece of stone and circumcised the boy and by this sacrament warded off imminent death.[304] This sacrament also held back the River Jordan and turned it back toward its source.[305] The Lord himself received this sacrament when he was born, although he emptied it of meaning when he was crucified. For those signs were not condemned; rather, they departed when more timely ones took their place. For, just as the first coming of the Lord took away circumcision, so his second coming will take away baptism. After all, just as now after the freedom of faith has come and the yoke of servitude has been removed, no Christian is circumcised in the flesh, so then when the righteous are reigning with the Lord and the wicked have been condemned, no one will be baptized, but what they signified, that is, the circumcision of the heart and purity of consciousness, will remain for eternity. If, then, I were a Jew at that time and if a Samaritan came to me and wanted to become a Jew after abandoning that error, which the Lord condemned when he said, *You worship what you do not know; we worship what we know for salvation comes from the Jews* (Jn 4:22)—if this Samaritan, then, whom the Samaritans had circumcised, wanted to become a Jew, he would certainly be exempt from the audacity of a repetition, and we would be forced not to repeat, but to approve that action commanded by God, though performed in a heresy. But if in the flesh of a circumcised man I would not find a place to repeat the circumcision because that member is only one, much less is a place found in one heart where the baptism of Christ might be repeated. And so, you who want to have a twofold baptism necessarily require a duplicitous heart.

5. Cry out, then, that you act correctly, if you do not rebaptize, and write back to me about this, not only without trepidation, but even with joy. Let none of your councils frighten you, my brother. For, if they are displeased with this, they do not deserve to have you, but if they are pleased, we trust in the mercy of the Lord, who never abandons those who fear to displease him and try to please him, that there will soon be peace between you and us. In that way, our dignities, a dangerous burden for which we shall give an account, will not cause the poor people who believe in Christ to take food together in their homes, but not to share together the table of Christ. Do we not deplore the fact that a husband and wife swear to one another, in most cases by Christ, that they are uniting their bodies in fidelity, and yet they tear apart the body of Christ by their different communion? If by your moderation and prudence and by the love that we owe to him who shed his blood for us, this great scandal, this great triumph of the devil, this great destruction of souls were eliminated in these regions, who would de-

---

303. See Rom 9:11.
304. See Ex 4:24-26.
305. See Ps 114:3.5.

scribe in words the palm of victory that the Lord would prepare for you because, in order to heal the other members that lie miserably wasting away through the whole of Africa, you set an example of a remedy so easily imitated? Since you cannot see my heart, how I fear that I may seem to speak to you with insults rather than with love! But I at least find nothing more that I might do but to offer for examination my words to you and my mind to God.

6. Let us remove from the center stage those empty objections that are often hurled at one another by ignorant parties. You should not raise as an objection the era of Macarius,[306] nor should I do the same with the violence of the Circumcellions,[307] if this latter problem does not apply to you, nor those earlier events to me. The threshing floor of the Lord has not yet been winnowed; it cannot be free from straw. Let us pray and do as much as we can that we may be the wheat. I cannot be silent about our deacon who was rebaptized, for I know how dangerous for me such silence is. After all, I do not plan to pass my time in the vanity of ecclesiastical honors; rather, I bear in mind that I will give an account to the prince of all pastors about the sheep entrusted to me. If you perhaps do not want me to write these things to you, you must, my brother, pardon my fear. For I fear very much that, if I am silent and pretend nothing is wrong, others will also be rebaptized by you. I have, therefore, determined to pursue this cause to the extent that the Lord offers me the strength and ability, in order that all who are in communion with us may know from our peaceful discussions how much the Catholic Church differs from heresies and schisms and how much one should avoid the destruction to come for either the weeds or the branches that have been cut off from the vine of the Lord.[308] If you enter upon this discussion with me willingly so that by our agreement the letters of both of us are read out to our peoples, I shall rejoice with unexpressible joy. But if you do not accept this calmly, what shall I do, brother, even though you are unwilling, but read our letters to the Catholic people in order that they may be better instructed? But if you refuse to reply by letter, I have decided to read at least my letter in order that, when people recognize your lack of confidence, they may at least be ashamed to be rebaptized.

7. And I will not do this when the army is present for fear that someone of yours might think that I wanted to do this with more violence than the cause of peace requires. I will do it after the departure of the army in order that all who hear us may understand that it is not part of my purpose that people be forced

---

306. Macarius and Paul were commissioners sent by the emperor, Constantius, to Africa in 347 to settle the Donatist controversy; in the following years Macarius so mistreated and persecuted the Donatists that his name became legendary among them. "In Numidia the 'Time of Macarius' was remembered by the Donatists, in the same way as the 'Time of Cromwell' was remembered in Ireland" (Peter Brown, *Augustine of Hippo: A Biography* (Berkeley 1967) 215.

307. The Circumcellions were an extremist group of the Donatists, roaming bands of men and women who often practiced savage violence against their Catholic opponents.

308. See Mt 13:24-30; Jn 15:1-8.

against their will into communion with anyone, but that the truth may become known to those who seek it most peacefully. Terror from temporal authorities will cease on our side; let there also cease on your side terror from bands of Circumcellions. Let us deal with the facts; let us deal with reason; let us deal with the authorities of the Divine Scriptures; as quiet and peaceful as we can be, let us ask; let us seek; let us knock that we may receive and find and have the door opened for us.[309] For it may perhaps be possible that, with the Lord helping our single-hearted efforts and prayers, this great deformity and impiety may begin to be wiped out from our lands. If you do not believe that I want to do this after the departure of the soldiers, write back to me after the departure of the soldiers. For, if I choose to read my letter to the people when the army is present, you can produce my letter to prove that I violated my word. May the mercy of the Lord keep this from my conduct and from the aim with which he has deigned to inspire me through his yoke.

8. If he had been here, my bishop would perhaps have rather sent a letter to Your Benevolence, or I would have written at his command or with his permission. But in his absence I did not allow this issue to cool off because of delay when the rebaptism of the deacon is or is said to be a recent occurrence, since I was aroused by the tortures of the bitterest sorrow over the true death of a brother. By the help of the Lord's mercy and providence, some compensation will perhaps soothe this pain of mine. May our God and Lord deign to inspire you with a peaceful mind, my lord and most beloved brother.

---

309. See Mt 7:7-8; Lk 11:9-10.

LETTER 33

Augustine to Proculeian, the Donatist bishop of Hippo (396-397)

In 396 or earlier Augustine wrote to his counterpart, Proculeian, the Donatist bishop of Hippo from 395 to 410. Augustine explains why he addresses Proculeian with such titles of respect (paragraph 1) and expresses his joy at hearing that he is willing to enter into a discussion of their differences (paragraph 2). He apologizes for Evodius' language, which may have unintentionally given offense (paragraph 3). Augustine spells out the conditions of a fruitful conference between them (paragraph 4) and pleads for an end to the destructive schism (paragraph 5). Finally, he pleads that they may come to an agreement for the sake of the people (paragraph 6).

To his honorable and most beloved lord, Proculeian, Augustine sends greetings.

1. I ought not to argue longer with you over the salutation on my letter on account of the vanities of ignorant human beings. For we are trying to recall each other from error, and before a complete discussion of the case some people could think that it is uncertain which one of us is in error. We, nonetheless, do each other a service if we deal sincerely with each other in order that we may be set free from the evil of discord. Even if it is not evident to many people that I do this with a sincere heart and with a fear inspired by Christian humility, he, nonetheless, sees for whom no hearts are closed. You, however, readily understand what it is in you that I do not hesitate to honor. For I do not consider the error of schism worthy of any honor; rather, I desire that all human beings be healed of it as far as this lies in my power. But without any uneasiness caused by doubt I think that I should treat you with honor, especially because you are bound to us by the bond of human society itself and because some indications of a more agreeable attitude are evident in you, because of which we should by no means give up hope that you could readily embrace the truth, once it has been shown to you. I, however, owe you as much love as he commanded who loved us up to the ignominy of the cross.

2. But do not be surprised that I have long kept my silence before Your Benevolence. I did not think that you held the view that Brother Evodius,[310] whose reliability I cannot fail to trust, joyfully reported to me. For, when it happened by chance that you gathered in one house and a discussion emerged between you about our hope, that is, about the heritage of Christ, he said that Your Grace said that you wanted to confer with us in the presence of good men. I am very happy that you have deigned to offer this to my lowly self, nor can I in any way ignore

---

310. Evodius was a friend of Augustine's since childhood, who followed him to Milan and returned with him to Africa where he would soon become bishop of Uzalis in Africa Proconsularis.

such a great opportunity afforded by your good will, namely that, to the extent that the Lord will deign to provide strength, I may seek with you and discuss the cause, the origin, and the reason for such a sad and deplorable division in the Church of Christ, to which he said, *I give my peace to you; I leave my peace with you* (Jn 14:27).

3. I heard, of course, that you complained about the brother I mentioned because he said something offensive to you in reply. I beg you not to hold that offensiveness against him, for I am certain that it did not arise from a proud heart. After all, I know my brother, but if with too much zeal in arguing for his faith and the love of the Church he perhaps said something that Your Reverence did not want to hear, it should not be called arrogance, but confidence. For he wanted to engage in a discussion with arguments, not simply to offer flattering agreement. This, after all, is the oil of the sinner with which the prophet does not want his head to be anointed. For he speaks as follows, *The righteous man will correct me with mercy and rebuke me, but the oil of the sinner will not anoint my head* (Ps 141:5). For he prefers to be corrected by the severe mercy of the righteous man rather than to be praised by the smooth unction of flattery. Hence, there is also the statement of the prophet, *Those who declare you happy lead you into error* (Is 3:12). For this reason it is also a correct and common saying, "He has a swollen head." For it was fattened by the oil of the sinner, that is, not by the harsh truth of correction, but by the smooth falsity of praise. Nor do I ask that you interpret this in the sense that I want you to understand that you were corrected by my brother, Evodius, as if by a righteous man. For I fear that you may think that I am also saying something offensive to you, something that I am trying to avoid very much. But he is righteous who said, *I am the truth* (Jn 14:16). And so, when any human being utters the truth from his lips with some harshness, we are corrected, not by that human being, who is perhaps a sinner, but by the very Truth, that is, by Christ, who is righteous, in order that our head may not be anointed by the unction of sweet, but harmful flattery, that is, by the oil of the sinner. And yet, even if Brother Evodius, a little excited in defense of his ecclesial communion, said something rather haughty because of his more agitated state, you should excuse his age and the importance of the issue.

4. I beg you to remember what you graciously promised, namely, that in the presence of those whom you choose we would investigate in harmony an issue so important and pertaining to the salvation of all. Only let our words not be futilely carried off by the breeze, but rather set down in writing in order that we may hold our conference with more tranquility and orderliness, and if something we said should slip from our memory, it may be recalled by being read back to us. Or, if you prefer, let us first confer with each other without any intermediary either by letters or by conversation and reading, wherever you wish. Otherwise, some unrestrained listeners might prefer to see a battle, as it were, between us rather than to ponder their own salvation during our discussion. The people could be informed afterward by us of the conclusion we have come to. Or, if you prefer

to use letters, let them be read out to our peoples in order that we may at you want, what you command, what you prefer. And I promise with full confidence concerning the mind of my most blessed and venerable father, Valerius,[311] who is absent at the moment, that he will learn of this with great joy. For I know how much he desires peace, and he is not tossed about by the inanity of vain pride.

5. I ask you: Of what concern to us are the old quarrels? Granted, those wounds have lasted up to the present that the hot tempers of proud men inflicted upon our members. Because these wounds have become gangrenous, we have lost the pain on account of which one usually calls in a physician. You see the great and miserable foulness that defiles Christian homes and families. Husbands and wives agree with each other about the bed, but disagree about the altar of Christ. They swear to each other by him in order to have peace with each other, and they cannot have peace in him. Children and their parents have one house of their own, but do not have one house of God. They desire to be heirs of their parents with whom they quarrel about being heirs of Christ. Servants and masters divide their common Lord *who took up the form of a servant* (Phil 2:7) in order that he might set all free by his servitude. Your people honor us; our people honor you. Your people appeal to us because of our priestly attire; our people appeal to you because of your priestly attire. We welcome the words of all; we want to offend no one. Why has only Christ, whose members we tear apart, offended us? When men need us because they want to settle their lawsuits over worldly matters before us, they call us holy men and servants of God so that they may accomplish their earthly business. Let us at last ourselves carry out the busi- ness of our salvation and theirs, not about gold, not about silver, not about estates and cattle. On account of these things we are greeted every day with heads bowed in order that we may bring the disputes of human beings to an end. But there exists between us so shameful and destructive a dispute about our head. Let those who greet us lower their heads as much as they want in order that we may bring them into agreement on earth; our head, in whom we are not in agreement, has lowered himself from heaven even to the cross.

6. I ask and beg you, if you have some of that humanity that many praise, let your goodness be seen in this case, if it is not a pretense for the sake of passing honors. May the deepest feelings of mercy be stirred in you, and may you choose that the issue be discussed, persisting along with us in prayers and discussing everything together peacefully, so that the poor people who are obedient to our positions may not cause us trouble at the judgment of God because of their obedience. May they, rather, be called back from errors and disagreements by our genuine love, and may they be guided onto the paths of truth and peace. I pray that you may be blessed in the eyes of God, my honorable and most beloved lord.

---

311. Valerius was the bishop of Hippo; Augustine was his coadjutor until Valerius' death in 396.

LETTER 34

Augustine to Eusebius, a Roman official in Hippo (396-397)

In 396 or 397 Augustine wrote to Eusebius, a Roman official in Hippo and a Catholic layman. Though he desires and prays for the unity of Christians (paragraph 1), something terrible has happened, namely, a young man who was rebuked by his Catholic bishop for beating and threatening to kill his mother has gone over to the Donatists and has been rebaptized (paragraph 2). As the young man injured his mother in the flesh, so he has tried to injure his spiritual mother, the Church (paragraph 3). The crime of the young man is too great to pass over in silence (paragraph 4). Augustine urges Proculeian, the Donatist bishop of Hippo, to hold with him the sort of discussion he promised (paragraph 5). Finally, Augustine proposes that another less learned bishop take his own place in the discussion with Proculeian (paragraph 6).

To his excellent and rightly esteemed and honorable brother, Eusebius, Augustine sends greetings.

1. God, who sees the secrets of the human heart, knows that, as much as I desire peace among Christians, I am troubled by the sacrilegious actions of those who persevere in its disruption in an unworthy and impious fashion. God knows that this attitude of my mind is directed toward peace and that I am not trying to force anyone involuntarily into the Catholic communion, but to reveal the plain truth to all who are in error. Then, once our ministry has made it evident with God's help, the very truth may be enough to persuade them to embrace and follow her.

2. After all, what is more terrible, I ask you, than what has now happened—not to mention other things? A young man is rebuked by his bishop because in his madness he constantly beats his mother and does not, even on those days when the severity of the laws pardons even the most wicked,[312] hold back his impious hands from the body from which he was born. He threatens the same mother that he will go over to the sect of Donatus and that he will kill her whom he is accustomed to beat with an incredible furor. He threatens her, goes over to the sect of Donatus, is rebaptized in his madness, and is clothed in white garments,[313] while clamoring for his mother's blood. He is placed within the altar rail where he stands conspicuously, and the eyes of all the groaning faithful have set before them, as if he were reborn in Christ, a man plotting to kill his mother.

---

312. All criminal suits ceased during Holy Week.
313. The newly baptized were clothed in white at the Easter Vigil.

3. Do you, then, a man of sound judgment, approve of these goings-on? I would never believe this of you; I know how carefully you consider things. A mother according to the flesh is struck in the members by which she bore and nourished her ungrateful child; our spiritual mother, the Church, forbids this, and she is struck in the sacraments by which she bore and nourished her ungrateful child. Does he not seem to have said, grinding his teeth for the blood of his mother, "What shall I do to the Church that forbids me to strike my mother? I have found what I shall do. I shall also strike her with whatever injuries I can. I shall do something to myself from which her members will suffer. I shall go to those who know how to drive out[314] the grace in which I was born in her and to destroy the form that I received in her womb. I shall torture both of my mothers with savage torments. Let the mother who bore me later be the first to bury me. For her sorrow I shall die spiritually; for the other's death I shall continue to live carnally." What else should we expect, my honorable Eusebius, but that, now secure as a Donatist, he is armed against the poor woman, worn down by old age and all alone as a widow, whom he was forbidden to beat by the Catholic Church? For what else did he conceive in his crazed heart when he said to his mother, "I shall go over to the Donatist sect, and I shall drink your blood"? See, now bloody in his conscience, but white in his garment, he fulfills a part of his promise; there remains the other part, namely, that he will drink his mother's blood. If, then, you approve these actions, let his clerics and sanctifiers[315] urge him to fulfill within his eight days all that he vowed.[316]

4. The right hand of the Lord is, of course, powerful to hold back the fury of that man from the poor and desolate widow and to frighten him from so wicked a plan in ways he knows. What was I, nonetheless, when stricken by so great a grief of mind, to do if I did not at least speak out? Or do those men do these actions, while I am told, "Be silent"? May the Lord turn aside from me such madness! When he himself commands me through his Apostle and says that a bishop ought to refute *those who are teaching what should not be taught* (Tit 1:11), should I be silent, because I am frightened by their indignation? I wanted that a crime as sacrilegious as that should be recorded in the public records. I wanted this precisely so that no one, especially in other cities, would think that, because I deplored these actions, I made up something when it was advantageous, since even at Hippo it is now said that Proculeian did not give the order that the public record reported.

---

314. Augustine alludes to the rite of exsufflation in which the devil was "blown out" of the candidate for baptism; when the Donatists rebaptized someone, they used this rite against the grace of the previous baptism.
315. Augustine uses "sanctifier" rather than "minister," since the Donatists held that the effect of the sacrament depends on the holiness of the minister.
316. I.e., the eight days from the Easter Vigil when the newly baptized received a white garment which they wore until White Sunday (*Dominica in albis*).

5. But how can we act with more moderation than by dealing with so serious an issue through you, a man endowed with a most illustrious office and at peace because of a most thoughtful disposition of will? I ask, therefore, as I have already asked through our brothers, good and honest men, whom I have sent to Your Excellency, that you deign to investigate whether Victor, the priest of Proculeian, did not receive this order from his bishop that he reported to the public authorities or whether, though Victor himself said something different, they charged him with falsehood in the proceedings, though they belong to the same communion. Or if he agrees that we peacefully deal with this whole question of our division, in order that the error, which is already evident, may become more evidently known, I gladly agree. For I heard what he proposed, namely, that without turmoil among the people ten serious and honest men from each side be present with us and that we investigate in accord with the Scriptures where the truth is to be found. For that suggestion that some men have again reported to me that he made as to why I should not go to Constantina since there were more of them there or that I ought to go to Milevis because they were, as they say, about to hold a council there, is ridiculous to mention, as if I personally have the care of any church but that of Hippo. For me the whole point at issue in the present question has to do especially with Proculeian. But if he perhaps thinks that he is not up to it, let him implore the help of any colleague he chooses. For in other cities we only deal with what pertains to the Church to the extent that the bishops of the same cities, our brothers and fellow priests, either permit us or ask us.

6. And yet I fail to understand what this man, who says that he has been a bishop for so many years, is afraid of in me, a mere beginner, that he does not want to hold a discussion with me. If he is afraid of my learning in fine literature, which he has not studied or has studied less, how does this pertain to this question, which must be examined either from the Holy Scriptures or from the ecclesiastical or public documents in which he has been well versed for so many years that he ought to be the more learned in them? Finally, there is my brother and colleague, Samsucius, the bishop of the church of Turris, who has acquired no literary learning of the sort this man fears. Let him be present and deal with him. I shall ask him, and he will, I trust in the name of Christ, readily grant me my request to take my place in this matter, and the Lord will, we trust, help him as he fights for the truth, a man, though not refined in his speech, learned in the true faith. There is, then, no reason why Proculeian should refer the question to any others so that we do not continue between ourselves what pertains to us. Nor, as I said, will I avoid those others if he asks their help.

LETTER 35

Augustine to Eusebius (396-397)

Shortly after the previous letter, that is, in 396 or 397, Augustine again wrote to Eusebius, asking him to pose several questions to Proculeian for him (paragraph 1). He also asks Eusebius to inform the Donatist bishop of the case of the subdeacon, Primus, who was rebaptized after abandoning the Catholic side because of penalties imposed for his improper conduct with certain nuns (paragraph 2). Augustine states his rule of not accepting into the Catholic Church someone who is under penalties from his own communion except in the status of a penitent. He also points to his own practice of not accepting back into the Catholic communion someone who is unwilling to return (paragraph 4). He again urges Eusebius to bring these incidents to the attention of Proculeian (paragraph 5).

To his excellent lord and rightly honorable and most beloved brother, Eusebius, Augustine sends greetings.

1. I have not by my bothersome exhortations and pleas imposed upon your reluctant will, as you claim, that you undertake the function of judge between bishops. Even if I had, in fact, wanted to persuade you to do this, I could perhaps have easily shown how you could judge between us in such an open and shut case, and I could have shown you what it is that you are doing, namely, that, without having heard both sides, you, who are fearful of the role of judge, do not hesitate to declare your decision for one side. But, as I said, I let this go for the time being. I had, however, asked nothing else of Your Honor and Grace but this one request, and I ask in this letter that you at least deign to give it your attention. Ask Proculeian whether he said to his priest, Victor, what the public records reported that he said to him. Or did those who were sent to do this not write down in the records what they heard from Victor, but what was false? And, finally, what would he think about discussing the whole question at issue between us? I, however, think that I do not make a man a judge if I ask him to question someone and to deign to write back the response he received. I, therefore, again ask this now, namely, that you do not hesitate to question him, because he refuses to receive my letter, as I have also learned. If he were willing to do this, I would, of course, not act through Your Excellency. But when he is unwilling, how can I proceed in a more peaceful fashion than by posing through you, a good man and a friend of his, the question that the burden of my office does not allow me to pass over in silence? A man of your character was displeased that a mother was beaten by her son, but you said, "If he[317] had known, he would have banished so

---

317. That is, Proculeian, the Donatist bishop of Hippo. See the previous letter for the Catholic lad who beat his mother and fled to the Donatist church where he was rebaptized.

wicked a young man from his communion." I reply briefly: He knows now; let him now banish him.

2. I also add another point: After a subdeacon once belonging to the church of Spanianum, by the name of Primus, was forbidden an access to the nuns that was contrary to good discipline and after he showed contempt for the sound rules and commandments, he was removed from the rank of clerics. And angered at the discipline of God, he went over to those others and was rebaptized. Either he also brought with him two nuns, fellow tenants with him on an estate of Catholic Christians, or they followed him. They too were, nonetheless, rebaptized. And now along with gangs of Circumcellions[318] amid roving bands of women who have shamelessly refused to have husbands for fear of having any discipline, he proudly exults in orgies of detestable drunkenness, happy that the freedom for an evil way of life has been opened up most widely for him, the very reason why he was excluded from the Catholic Church. Perhaps Proculeian is also unaware of this. Let it, therefore, be brought to his attention by earnestness and moderation; let him command that Primus be removed from his communion since he chose that communion only because he had lost clerical status in the Catholic Church on account of his disobedience and depraved conduct.

3. For, if the Lord is willing, I myself am going to observe this norm, namely, that whoever wants to come over to the Catholic Church after having been lowered in rank for disciplinary reasons will be received in the humble status of a penitent, to which they too would perhaps have forced him if he had chosen to remain among them. But consider, I beg you, how detestably they act when they persuade those whom we rebuke with ecclesiastical discipline for living bad lives to come to a second bath and to answer that they are pagans in order that they may deserve to receive it. So much blood of the martyrs has been shed so that those words would not come from the lips of Christians! And then, as if they were renewed and as if they were made holy, they mock the discipline that they could not bear, having, in fact, become worse under the appearance of new grace by the sacrilege of a new madness. Or, if I am wrong in my concern that these matters be corrected by Your Benevolence, let no one complain about me if I have these matters brought to the attention of Proculeian by the public records, which, I think, cannot be denied to me in a Roman city. For, since God commands that we speak and preach the word, that we refute *those who teach what they ought not* (Tit 1:11), and that we persist *in time and out of time* (2 Tm 4:3), as I prove from the words of the Lord and of the apostles, let no human being think that I should be persuaded to be silent about these matters. But if they think that they should try something in the line of violence and robbery, the Lord will not fail to protect his Church, for he has subjected all earthly kingdoms to his yoke in his embrace that extends over the whole earth.

---

318. See p. 145, n. 307.

4. For the daughter of a tenant farmer of the Church who had been one of our catechumens was won over to those people against the will of her parents, and she also donned the habit of a nun where she had been baptized. Though her father wanted to recall her by fatherly severity to the Catholic communion, I had refused that the woman, whose mind had been corrupted, should be taken back unless she were willing and desired by free choice what is better. That farmer began to insist even with blows that his daughter agree with him. I immediately and absolutely forbade that he should do this. Meanwhile, when we were passing through Spanianum, a priest of Proculeian, standing in the midst of the estate of a Catholic and praiseworthy woman, shouted out after us with a most impudent cry that we were traditors[319] and persecutors. He even hurled this abuse at that woman who belongs to our communion and in the midst of whose estate he was standing. When I heard these shouts, I not only held myself back from a fight, but also quieted the crowd that was traveling with me. And yet, if I should say, "Let us examine who are or were traditors or persecutors," they answer me, "We do not want to argue, but we want to rebaptize. We would, like wolves, prey upon your sheep, biting from ambush; if you are good shepherds, be silent." For what else did Proculeian command if it was really he who gave this command: "If you are a Christian, save it for God's judgment, but if we do this, be silent"? The same priest also dared to threaten a farmer, a man who manages the estate of the Church.

5. Let Proculeian, I beg you, also be informed by you of all these happenings. Let him restrain the insanity of his clerics, about which, honorable Eusebius, I have not kept silent before you. Please be so good, therefore, as to write back to me, not what you hold on all these matters, for I do not want you to think that I have placed upon you the burden of being a judge, but about what they reply to me. May the mercy of God keep you safe, my excellent lord and rightly honorable and most beloved brother.

---

319. The traditors were those who handed over the Scriptures or sacred vessels during the time of persecution.

LETTER 43

Augustine to a group of Donatist leaders (396-397)

At the end of 396 or early in 397 Augustine wrote to a group of Donatist leaders with an appeal for unity. He writes to them, not as to heretics, but as to men ready to be corrected (paragraph 1). He desires to be a peacemaker (paragraph 2). He recalls the beginning of the schism at which a council of seventy bishops condemned Caecilian, the bishop of Carthage (paragraph 3), which was followed by the ordination of Majorinus and the councils at Rome and at Arles, which condemned the Donatists (paragraph 4). The perfidy of Secundus of Tigisi completes the picture (paragraph 5). Augustine reminds his addressees that eternal life is at stake (paragraph 6), points out the injustices involved in the Donatist councils (paragraph 7), and explains why the Donatists rejected councils held overseas to hear their case against Caecilian (paragraphs 8 and 9). The Donatist council that condemned Caecilian was in fact composed of bishops who had themselves handed over the Scriptures (paragraph 10). In any case the council should not have condemned bishops who were not present (paragraph 11).

The case of Felix of Aptungi, who was condemned by the Donatists, but later proved innocent, shows how the Donatists could have condemned the innocent Caecilian (paragraph 12). Donatist complaints about the emperor's hearing the case against them are inconsistent (paragraph 13). They should at least listen to the decision handed down by the bishops whom the emperor appointed (paragraph 14). Augustine compares the calm judiciousness of the judges with the perversity of the Donatist accusers (paragraph 15) and points to the impartial and peaceful judgment of Pope Melchiades (paragraph 16). Augustine reminds his readers of the influence exerted by the wealthy woman, Lucilla, whom Caecilian had offended by rebuking her when he was still a deacon and who bribed the Donatist bishops (paragraph 17). Since Caecilian knew what the situation was, he wisely refused to submit to the judgment of the Donatists (paragraph 18). Furthermore, since the overseas churches remained in communion with Caecilian, the Donatists chose to take their case against him overseas where they lost at Rome (paragraph 19). Then the Donatists again appealed to the emperor who granted them another episcopal hearing at Arles where they again lost. Unwilling to give up, they forced the emperor to hear their case in Milan, where he acquitted Caecilian (paragraph 20).

Despite their crimes, the Donatists complain about the use of civil powers to correct them (paragraph 21). Augustine produces scripture texts to show how the early Church and the people of Israel tolerated sinners in their midst (paragraphs 22 and 23). The Donatists, in fact, tolerate in their midst the criminal Circumcellions (paragraph 24). Even if the Donatists cannot agree with the Catholics about the facts at the time of Caecilian, they have the present fact of the Catholic

Church's being spread throughout the world, as scripture had promised (paragraph 25). Augustine points to the similarities between the Donatists' breaking away from the rest of the Church and the Maximianists' breaking away from the Donatists (paragraph 26). Finally, Augustine urges the Donatists to return to the unity of the Catholic Church and insists that "no one wipes out from the earth the Church of God" (paragraph 27).

To his most beloved lords and his brothers who are rightly to be praised, Glorius, Eleusius, the two Felixes, Grammaticus,[320] *and all the others to whom this is pleasing, Augustine sends greetings.*

1, 1. The apostle Paul, of course, said, *Avoid a heretical man after one rebuke, knowing that such a man is perverse and a sinner and has been condemned by himself* (Tit 3:10). But people like yourselves should by no means be considered to be heretics. For you defend your view, though false and erroneous, without any stubborn animosity, especially since you did not give rise to it by the brazenness of presumption, but have received it from your parents, who were seduced and fell into error, and you seek the truth with a cautious concern, ready to be corrected when you find it. If I did not believe that you were such people, I would perhaps not be sending you a letter. And yet, just as we are warned that we should avoid the heretic swollen with odious pride and insane with the stubbornness of evil strife for fear that he may deceive the weak and the little ones, so we do not deny that we should correct him in whatever ways we can. This is the reason why we have written even to some leaders of the Donatists, not letters of communion that they now no longer accept on account of their having turned away from the Catholic unity, which is spread through the whole world, but such private letters as we are permitted to send even to pagans. And though they have at some point read these, they, nonetheless, either refused to reply to them or, as is more believable, they could not. In this way we thought that we had sufficiently fulfilled the duty of love, which the Holy Spirit teaches that we owe, not only to our people, but also to all peoples. He speaks to us through the Apostle, *But may the Lord give you increase and make you abound in love for one another and for all* (1 Thes 3:12). He also warns in another place that those who hold different views should be rebuked with moderation, *in case,* he says, *God may perhaps give them repentance to know the truth and they may escape from the snares of the devil, after have been held captive by him to do his will* (2 Tm 2:26).

2. I said this in the beginning so that no one would think that I sent this letter to you with more impudence than prudence in that I wanted to deal with you in this way about the business of your soul, since you do not belong to our communion. And yet, if I wrote something to you about the business of a farm or of settling some other financial dispute, perhaps no one would find fault. This

---

320. These are all Donatist laymen from Thiave in Numidia.

world is so dear to human beings, and they themselves have grown worthless in their own eyes! This letter, then, will be a witness for my defense in the judgment of God, who knows with what intention I acted and who said, *Blessed are the peacemakers because they will be called the children of God* (Mt 5:9).

2, 3. Be so good as to recall, then, that, when we were in your city and dealt with you about some matters concerning the communion of Christian unity, certain records were brought forth by your side from which it was read out that almost seventy bishops condemned Caecilian, then bishop of the Carthaginian church, who belonged to our communion, along with his colleagues and those who ordained him. In those records the case of Felix of Aptungi was reported as much more hateful and criminal than the others.[321] When they were all read, we replied that one should not be surprised if the persons who at that time produced that schism thought that those against whom they were stirred up by jealous and wicked persons should be hastily condemned in their absence without a hearing of their case, but not without compiling the proceedings. We, however, said that we had other ecclesiastical records in which Secundus of Tigisi, who then held the primacy in Numidia, left the traditors,[322] who were present and had confessed, to the judgment of God and allowed them to remain in their episcopal sees as they were. Their names are counted among those who condemned Caecilian, since Secundus himself presided over the same council, in which he condemned those who were absent as traditors by the votes of those whom he pardoned when they were present and confessed.

4. Then we said that, at some point after the ordination of Majorinus, whom by their wicked crime they elevated to the episcopacy in opposition to Caecilian, when they erected altar over against altar and destroyed the unity of Christ by frenzied discord, they asked Constantine, who was then emperor, for episcopal judges to act as arbitrators and to pronounce judgment on their questions that had arisen in Africa and destroyed the bond of peace. After this was granted, when Caecilian and those who had sailed from Africa in opposition to him were present, Melchiades,[323] who was then bishop of Rome, acted as judge along with his colleagues, whom the emperor had sent at the request of the Donatists. But nothing could be proved against Caecilian, and for this reason, after he had been confirmed in his episcopacy, Donatus,[324] who was at that time his opposite number, was found guilty. After this happened, since they all remained in the stubbornness of their most wicked schism, the same emperor later had the same case examined more carefully and brought to an end at Arles.[325] But they appealed the

---

321. Felix, the bishop of Aptungi in Porconsular Africa, was one of three bishops who consecrated Caecilian as the bishop of Carthage, which led to the Donatist controversy.
322. Seee p. 155, n. 319.
323. Melchiades was pope from 311 to 314; he condemned Donatism and upheld Caecilian at the Lateran Council of 313.
324. Donatus was the bishop of Casae Nigrae in Numidia, from whom the schism took its name.
325. The Council of Arles met on August 1, 314.

ecclesiastical judgment in order that Constantius would hear their case. After this came about, with both sides present, Caecilian was judged innocent,[326] and they left defeated and, nonetheless, remained in the same error. Nor was the case of Felix of Aptungi overlooked, but at the order of the same emperor he was acquitted in the proconsular proceedings.

5. But since we were only saying all this, not also reading it, you surely thought that we were doing less than you expected, given our insistence. When we perceived this, we did not delay to send for those records, which we promised to read. All these records arrived after an interval of less than two full days while we hastened off to the Church of Gelizi in order to return to your town from there. And, as you know, they were read out to you on one day to the extent that time allowed. First there was read the part where Secundus of Tigisi did not dare to remove from the college of bishops the traditors who confessed, though afterward with them he dared to condemn Caecilian and his other colleagues, who had not confessed and who were absent. Then we read the proconsular proceedings where Felix was proved innocent by a most careful examination. You remember that these were read to you in the morning. But in the afternoon we read their petitions to Constantine and, after he appointed judges, the ecclesiastical proceedings held in the city of Rome in which they were condemned, while Caecilian was retained in his episcopal dignity. Finally, we read the letter of the emperor, Constantine which showed that everything was fully attested to the highest degree.

3, 6. What more do you want, you people? What more do you want? We are not dealing with your gold and silver. It is not your land and estates, not even the health of your body that is at stake. We are challenging your souls about acquiring eternal life and escaping eternal death. Wake up at long last! We are not dealing with some obscure question; we are not searching out some hidden secrets for the penetration of which either no human hearts or very few are capable. The issue lies in the open. What stands out more clearly? What is seen more quickly? We say that innocent and absent people were condemned by a council that acted in haste, though it was one with large numbers. We prove this by the proconsular proceedings by which he was pronounced free from every crime of handing over the Sacred Books, though the proceedings of the council that your people brought forth declared him a criminal. We say that sentences were passed by confessed traditors upon those who were said to be traditors. We prove this by the ecclesiastical proceedings in which they are mentioned by name. Among them Secundus of Tigisi pardoned, as if with a view to peace, their crimes that he knew, and later, when the peace was destroyed, he condemned with them those he did not know. From this it is clear that he even at first was not concerned about peace, but was afraid for himself. For Purpurius, the bishop of Limate, had objected to him that, when Secundus himself was also arrested by an officer and his

---

326. The judgment was pronounced by the emperor at Milan in 316.

troops in order that he would hand over the Scriptures, he was released, not, of course, without reason, but because he handed them over or ordered that something be handed over. Fearing that this suspicion could easily enough be proven, having received advice from a younger Secundus, a relative of his, and having consulted others bishops who were with him, he left the most obvious crimes to be judged by God. In that way he was thought to have had an eye out for peace, but that was false since he had an eye out for himself.

7. For, if the thought of peace dwelled in his heart, he would not have later at Carthage, along with those who surrendered the Books, men whom he had dismissed when they were present and had confessed, condemned for the crime of surrendering the Sacred Books those men who were absent and whom no one had proven guilty before. He ought to have feared more that the peace of our unity would be violated to the degree that Carthage was a large and famous city, from which the evil that arose there might pour down, as if from its head, over the whole body of Africa. It was also close to the overseas regions and renowned for its very distinguished reputation. For this reason it had a bishop of more than average authority who could disregard a number of enemies conspiring against him since he saw that he was united by letters of communion to the Roman church, in which the primacy of the Apostolic See always thrived, and to the other lands from which the Gospel came to Africa. He was ready to state his case there if his opponents tried to separate those churches from him. Because he refused to come to the gathering of his colleagues, for he saw or suspected or, as they claim, pretended that they had been turned against the truth of his case by his enemies, Secundus ought all the more, if he wanted to be a protector of the peace, to have avoided condemning in their absence those who absolutely refused to appear for the judgment. For he was not dealing with priests or deacons or clerics of lower rank, but with his colleagues who could keep their case intact for the judgment of other colleagues, especially of the apostolic churches, where judgments pronounced against them, when they were absent, would be absolutely without effect. After all, they did not later leave a court that they first approached, but they never wanted to approach the court that they always held suspect.

8. This fact especially ought to have drawn the attention of Secundus, then the primate, if he was presiding over the council in order to preserve peace. For he would perhaps have keep quiet and bridled the mouths rabid against the absent, if he said, "You see, brothers, that after so great a slaughter of persecution peace has been granted through the mercy of God by the rulers of the world; we Christians and bishops ought not to destroy the Christian unity that the pagan enemy no longer attacks. And so, either let us leave to the judgment of God all these cases that the scourge of the time of unrest inflicted upon the Church, or if there are some among you who know the crimes of these men for certain so that they can easily prove them and convict those who deny them and if they are afraid to be in communion with such people, let them go to our brothers and

colleagues of the churches across the sea, and let them there first complain about the actions and contempt of these bishops, because, conscious of their guilt, they refused to come to a court of their African colleagues. In that way they might be ordered from overseas to come and reply there to the objections raised against them. But if they do not do this, their wickedness and perversity will be seen there also, and after a letter to all the churches with their name has been sent through the whole world, wherever the Church of Christ has spread, they will be cut off from communion with all the churches to prevent some error from arising in the chair of the Carthaginian church. Then we shall at last safely ordain another bishop for the people of Carthage when these people have been separated from the whole Church. Otherwise, when another has already been ordained, the new bishop might not be accepted into communion by the church across the sea, because they will not see that the present bishop has been deposed from his office, for rumor has declared him already ordained, and the church across the sea has sent letters of communion to him. And thus there might arise the great scandal of schism in the unity of Christ in a time of peace, when we wish too hastily to cast our judgments and dare to erect another altar, not over against Caecilian, but over against the world, which is in communion with him out of ignorance."

9. If any wild man refused to obey this sound and correct counsel, what was he going to do? Or how was he going to condemn some of his absent colleagues when he did not have control of the proceedings of the council since the primate was opposed? But if such a great rebellion had arisen and against the primatial see that some now wanted to condemn those whom the primate wanted to refer elsewhere, how much better would it be to disagree with such bishops who were plotting unrest and upheaval than with the communion of the whole world! But since the charges were not such that they could be proven in an overseas court against Caecilian and those who ordained him, they did not, for this reason, want the case to be brought there before they had passed sentence against him. And after they had passed sentence, they did not work with perseverance to bring to the notice of the church across the sea the traditors condemned in Africa, with whom that church ought to avoid communion. For, if they had tried that, Caecilian and the others would have defended themselves and would have won their case with a most careful examination of the issue against their false accusers before the overseas judges.

10. That perverse and wicked council, then, was, as is believed, composed mostly of traditors, whom Secundus of Tigisi pardoned when they confessed. For, since the rumor of the surrender of the Books had spread about, they tried to turn suspicion away from themselves by denouncing others, and since people who believed the bishops were saying false things about the innocent throughout Africa, namely, that they were condemned at Carthage as traditors, those bishops who really handed over the Scriptures were hiding as if in a cloud of the falsest rumor. From this you see, my friends, that what some of your people said was improbable to have happened, namely, that those very same ones who had con-

fessed their surrender of the Books, and had ensured that their case should be left to God, afterward sat to judge and condemn as traditors bishops who were absent. For they rather grasped the chance to be able to pour out false charges upon the others and in this way to turn aside from an investigation of their own crimes the tongues of human beings, once they were turned against those others. Otherwise, if it were not possible that anyone condemn in another the sins which he himself committed, Paul the apostle would not say to certain people, *For this reason you are without excuse, every one of you who judges. For in that act by which you judge another you condemn yourself. For you do the same things that you condemn* (Rom 2:1). Those bishops did precisely this so that these words of the Apostle apply to them fully and properly.

11. When Secundus left their crimes to God's judgment, he was, therefore, not aiming at peace and unity. Otherwise, he would have taken more care at Carthage that a schism not arise where no one was present whose admitted crime he was forced to pardon. Rather, as would have been most easy, the whole preservation of peace would have involved only the refusal to condemn those who were absent. And so, they would have done injustice to the innocent, even if they had chosen to pardon those who were not convicted, who had not confessed, and who were not even present. A person, of course, accepts a pardon if his wrongdoing is absolutely certain. How much more inhuman and blinder were those who thought that they could condemn those crimes that they could not even have pardoned since they were unknown! But in the former case the crimes that were known were left to God in order that no others might be looked for; in this case unknown crimes were condemned in order that those former crimes might be concealed. But someone will say, "They knew those crimes." Even if I should grant this, they ought, of course, to have spared those who were absent. For they had not fled from the court where they had never been present, nor did the Church consist of those African bishops alone so that they would seem to have avoided all ecclesiastical judgment if they refused to present themselves to their court. There were thousands of colleagues across the sea where it was evident that those bishops could be tried who seemed to hold their African or Numidian colleagues suspect. What has happened to the cry of scripture, *Before you question him, do not blame anyone, and after you have questioned him, rebuke him justly* (Sir 11:7). If, then, the Holy Spirit wanted no one blamed or rebuked if he had not been questioned, how much more of a crime is it that bishops were not only blamed and rebuked but completely condemned who, as absent, could not have been questioned about their crimes at all?

12. But these, nonetheless, say that they condemned the known crimes of those who were absent, who had not fled from the court since they were never present, and who stated that they held suspect that group of judges. How, I ask you, my brothers, did they know those crimes? You answer, "We do not know, since this knowledge was not explained in those proceedings." But I shall show you how they knew. Pay attention to the case of Felix of Aptungi, and first read

how they were more severe toward him. They, therefore, knew the case of the others in the same way they knew the case of this man, who was later proven utterly innocent by a careful and frightening inquest. When that man has been found innocent against whom they raged much more inhumanly, how much more justly and safely and quickly ought we to judge those bishops innocent since these men accused their crimes less severely and condemned them with a milder reproach!

4, 13. Or, as someone said—and you were perhaps displeased at it when it was said to you, but it still should not be passed over. For he said, "A bishop ought not to be tried by a proconsular court," as if he himself arranged this for himself and the emperor did not order that the inquest be conducted in this way. For that issue especially pertains to his care, and he will give an account to God about it. Those men made him the arbiter and judge of a case involving the surrender of the Sacred Books and schism when they sent petitions to him to whom they later appealed, and they, nonetheless, refused to abide by his judgment. And so, if he is to be blamed whom an earthly judge has acquitted, though he did not himself ask for this, how much more are they to be blamed who wanted an earthly king to be the judge of their case! But if it is not criminal to appeal to the emperor, it is not criminal to have one's case heard by the emperor. And it is not, therefore, criminal to have it heard by one to whom the emperor delegates the case. That friend wanted charges to be brought because in the case of Bishop Felix one witness was suspended on the rack and because another was also tortured with tongs. Was Felix able to oppose this so that the inquest was not carried out with such great diligence or severity, when the judge was acting to discover the facts of that case? For what else is it to refuse such an inquest but to confess to the crime? And yet amid the terrible cries of the bailiffs and the bloody hands of the executioners that proconsul himself would never condemn an absent colleague who refused to present himself to his court since he had another court where he could be heard. Or, if he did condemn him, he would certainly pay the just and due punishments even in accord with the laws of the world.

5, 14. But if you are not happy with the proconsular proceedings, yield to the ecclesiastical ones. They have all been read out to you in order. Or ought perhaps Melchiades, the bishop of the Roman church, along with his colleagues, the bishops from across the sea, not to have taken over for themselves a case that was ended by seventy Africans where the primate of Tigisi presided? What about the fact that Melchiades did not himself take it over? When asked, the emperor sent bishops as judges to preside with him and to determine what seemed just concerning that whole case. We prove this by the petitions of the Donatists and by the words of the emperor himself. For you remember that both were read to you, and you now have the freedom to inspect and copy them. Read and examine them all. See the great concern for preserving or restoring peace and unity with which everything was examined, the treatment of the legal standing of the accusers, the defects by which certain of them were disqualified, and the clear proof from the words of those present that they had nothing to say against Caecilian. Rather, they wanted to transfer the whole case to the people on the side of Majorinus, that is, to the rebellious multitude alienated from the peace of the Church. And in that way Caecilian would be accused by that crowd that they thought could turn the minds of the judges to their will by disorderly outbursts alone, without the production of any proof and without an investigation of the truth. As if an angry mob drunk from the cup of error and corruption would bring true charges against Caecilian, when seventy bishops, as it is clear concerning Felix of Aptungi, condemned their absent and innocent colleagues with such great madness! After all, they wanted Caecilian once again to be accused by the sort of mob with which they agreed in order to pronounce their sentences against innocent men who had not been questioned. But they had clearly not found the sort of judges whom they might persuade to such madness.

15. In accord with your wisdom, after all, you can note their perversity on this point and the sober sincerity of the judges who were unable up to the very end to be persuaded that Caecilian should be accused by the people on the side of Majorinus, who had no certain legal standing, and how the judges demanded of them either accusers or witnesses or people in some way necessary to the case who had come with them from Africa, and how it was said that they were present, but were withdrawn by Donatus. The same Donatus promised that he would produce them, and after he had promised that not once, but often, he refused further to approach that court where he had already confessed so much that by not approaching thereafter he seemed to want to avoid nothing else but being condemned when present. And yet, the crimes that ought to have been condemned were revealed when he was present and questioned. In addition, certain people presented a list of charges denouncing Caecilian. After this was done, you know how the inquest was reopened against Caecilian, who the people were who brought the charges, and how nothing could be proved against Caecilian. What shall I say, since you have heard all this and you can read it as often as you wish?

16. Concerning the number of seventy bishops, however, you remember what was said, since it was brought up against us as the weightiest authority, and yet very sober and sincere persons preferred to refrain from judgment about endless questions tied together as if by an inextricable chain. They did not care about how many those bishops were or from where they were assembled, since they saw that they were blinded by such great rashness that they dared to pass such precipitous sentences upon absent colleagues who had not been questioned. And yet how different was the final sentence pronounced by blessed Melchiades, how innocent, how impartial and peaceful. By that judgment he did not dare to remove from his company colleagues against whom nothing had been established, and after Donatus alone, whom he had found to be the source of the whole evil, was found especially guilty, he left to the others the free option of recovering their good health. He was ready to send letters of communion even to those who had been clearly ordained by Majorinus so that in whatever places there were two bishops as a result of the dissension, he wanted to confirm the

one who had been first ordained, but to provide for the other another people to rule. O what a fine man! O what a son of Christian peace and what a father of the Christian people! Compare this handful with that mob of bishops, and compare, not the one number with the other, but the one authority with the other—in the one case moderation, in the other rashness, in the one vigilance, in the other blindness. And in this case gentleness did not destroy integrity, nor was integrity opposed to gentleness. But in the other case fear is cloaked with fury, and fury is aroused by fear. For these bishops had come together to reject false crimes by the investigation of true ones, while those had come together to conceal true crimes by the condemnation of false ones.

6, 17. Should Caecilian have handed himself over to those men to have them hear his case and to pronounce judgment when he had such judges that, if his case were brought before them, he would most easily prove his innocence? He should absolutely not have surrendered himself to them, not even if, as coming from elsewhere, he were recently ordained bishop of the Carthaginian church and did not know what a certain very wealthy woman at that time, Lucilla,[327] could do to corrupt the minds of the evil and ignorant. For he had offended her by a rebuke in defense of church discipline when he was a deacon. This evil too contributed to carrying out that wickedness. For in that council in which the absent and innocent bishops were condemned by confessed traditors, there were a certain few who desired to cover over their own crimes by blackening the reputation of others in order that people would be distracted by false rumors and turned away from the investigation of the truth. They were, then, few in number who made this their special goal, though they had greater authority because of their fellowship with Secundus, who had spared them out of fear. But the rest, it is reported, were bought and stirred up against Caecilian especially by Lucilla's money. The proceedings exist in the possession of the governor, Zenophilus;[328] in them a certain Nundinarius, a deacon deposed by Sylvanus, the bishop of Cirta, as the proceedings show, when he tried in vain to satisfy them by letters from other bishops, disclosed many things in anger and made them public in court. Among these we read that they mention that, after the bishops were bribed in the church of Carthage, the capital of Africa, by Lucilla's money, altar was erected over against altar. I know that we did not read these proceedings to you, but you remember that there was not enough time. There was also present some mental anguish from the swelling of pride because they themselves had not ordained him bishop of Carthage.

18. Since by all these means Caecilian learned that they had come together, not as true judges, but as enemies and bribed men, how could it have happened

---

327. Lucilla was a Christian woman of senatorial rank, originally from Spain, who had settled in Carthage. Her use of wealth to promote the Donatists was mentioned also by Jerome (Letter 133, 4).

328. Domitius Zenophilus was consular governor of Numidia.

that either he himself would choose or the people over whom he presided would permit that, having left his church, he should go to a private home, not to be examined by a hearing of his colleagues, but to be slaughtered by the forces of the faction and by a woman's hatred? How could this have happened, especially since he saw that before the church across the sea, which was free from private hostilities and from both sides of the disagreement, the hearing of his case remained undamaged and unimpaired? And if the opponents refused to present a case there, they would cut themselves off from the perfectly innocent communion of the rest of the world. But if they had tried to accuse him there, then he would have been present and would have defended his innocence against all their plots, just as you learned that he did later, after they had far too late asked for an overseas trial, when they were already guilty of schism and defiled by the horrendous outrage of erecting another altar. For they would have done so in the first place if they were relying on the truth, but they wanted to come to court when false rumors had become strong with the length of time, as if the age of the rumor were the decisive factor. Or, what is more believable, after Caecilian was condemned as they wanted, they thought that they were secure, trusting in their number and not daring to present so bad a case elsewhere where, without any bribery at work, the truth could be found out.

7, 19. But after they learned by the facts that the rest of the world remained in communion with Caecilian and that the churches across the sea sent letters of communion to him and not to the bishop they had wickedly ordained, they were ashamed to continue to remain silent. For it could be asked of them as an objection why they allowed the Church among so many nations to maintain through ignorance communion with those who were condemned and why they cut themselves off from communion with innocent bishops of the world, when by remaining silent they permitted the whole world to be out of communion with the bishop whom they ordained for the people of Carthage. They chose to lodge a case, as is said, with two possible outcomes,[329] against Caecilian before the churches across the sea prepared for either of them. Thus, if they could by any trickery whatsoever of false accusation have defeated him, they would have most completely satisfied their desire; if, however, they could not, they would have persisted in the same perversity, but now as if they had gotten what they were saying, namely, that they had suffered from bad judges. That is the cry of all those who have a weak case when they have been defeated by even the most obvious truth, as if we could not also most justly say this to them, "Look, let us consider those bishops who judged the case in Rome not to be good judges; there still remained the plenary council of the universal Church where the case could be brought even against these judges so that, if they were proven guilty of having judged wrongly, their judgments would be set aside." Let them prove that they did this, for we easily prove that they did not from the fact that the whole world

---

329. The Latin has simply *ad duas*, where one manuscript adds *fraudes*.

is not in communion with them. Or if they did do this, they were defeated even there, as their separation itself reveals.

20. But what they did afterward is, nonetheless, sufficiently shown by the letter of the emperor. For they dared to accuse of judging wrongly ecclesiastical judges of such great authority, the bishops whose judgment declared Caecilian's innocence and their wickedness, not before other colleagues, but before the emperor. He granted them another trial at Arles, that is, by other bishops, not because it was now necessary, but because he yielded to their perversity and desired to restrain such impudence by all means. For a Christian emperor did not dare to take up their troublesome and false complaints in order that he himself might pronounce judgment on the judgment of the bishops who heard the case at Rome. Rather, as I said, he gave them other bishops, and they again preferred to appeal from them to the emperor, for you have heard how he warded them off on this matter. And I wish that at least by his judgment they had put an end to their most unhealthy animosity, and I wish that, as he himself yielded to them, he would have pronounced judgment concerning this case after the bishops, with an aim of seeking pardon afterward from the holy prelates. In that way, they would have nothing further to say, if they did not obey the judgment of him to whom they appealed, and in that way they would at some point yield to the truth. For he ordered that the parties meet him at Rome for handling the case. When for some reason or other Caecilian did not come there, the emperor commanded, after having been requested by them, that they follow him to Milan. Then some of them began to withdraw, perhaps angered because Constantine did not imitate them so that he right away and quickly condemned Caecilian in his absence. When the farsighted emperor learned of this, he made the rest come to Milan, escorted by guards. And after Caecilian also came, he also presented himself, as the emperor wrote, and having heard the case with the diligence, care, and foresight that his letter indicates, he judged Caecilian innocent and the Donatists most wicked.

8, 21. And they still baptize outside of the Church and, if they could, they would rebaptize the Church; they offer sacrifice in dissension and schism, and they greet with the term "peace" people whom they remove from the peace of salvation. The unity of Christ is torn in two; the heritage of Christ is blasphemed; the baptism of Christ is subjected to the rite of exsufflation.[330] And they do not want these crimes to be corrected in them by temporal scourges through ordinary human powers in order that they might not be destined for eternal punishments for such great sacrileges. We raise as objections to them the madness of schism, the insanity of rebaptizing, and the wicked separation from the heritage of Christ, which is spread through all nations. We read out, not merely from our Books, but also from theirs, the names of the churches that they read today and with which they are today not in communion. When those names are read out in their gather-

---

330. I.e., that part of the baptismal rite in which the devil is blown out of the candidate for baptism by the breathing upon him of the minister.

ings, they say to their readers, "Peace be with you," and they do not have peace with those peoples to whom that letter was written. And they raise as objections to us the false crimes of those now dead and, even if they are true, they are still the crimes of others. For they do not understand that they are all caught in those objections we make against them, whereas, in the objections they make against us, they reprehend the straw or the weeds in the Lord's harvest, but the charge does not pertain to the wheat. Nor do they consider that those who are pleased with the bad people in the unity are themselves in communion with bad people. But those who find them displeasing and cannot correct them and do not dare to uproot the weeds before the time of the harvest, *for fear that they might also uproot the wheat* (Mt 13:24-3), are in communion, not with their actions, but with the altar of Christ. In that way they are not only not defiled by them, but even deserve to be praised and lauded by the words of God. After all, they endure for the good of the unity what they hate for the good of justice in order that the name of Christ might not suffer the blasphemy of horrible schisms.

22. *If they have ears, let them hear what the Spirit says to the churches* (Rv 2:7). For in the Revelation of John we read as follows; he says, *Write to the angel of the church of Ephesus: He who holds the seven stars in his right hand, he who walks in the midst of the seven candlesticks of gold, says this: I know your works and your labor and patience and that you cannot tolerate evil persons, and you have tested those who say that they are apostles and are not, and you have found them to be liars. And you have patience, and you have put up with them on account of my name, and you have not failed.* (Rv 2:1-3) If he wanted us to understand this of an angel of the higher heavens and not of heads of the Church, he would not go on to say, *But I hold against you that you have abandoned your first love. Recall, then, from where you have fallen, and do penance, and do the works you did at first. If not, I shall come to you, and I shall move your candlestick from its place unless you do penance.* (Rv 4:5) This cannot be said to the higher angels who always retain their love; those who have fallen from there are the devil and his angels.[331] He, therefore, says *first love* because the Church endured the false apostles on account of the name of Christ, and he commands that she seek again that love and do her earlier works. And there are raised against us as objections the crimes of sinful men, not our own, but those of others, and these in part unknown. If we saw them even as true and present and tolerated them for the sake of unity, sparing the weeds on account of the wheat, whoever hears the Holy Scriptures without being deaf at heart would say that we are worthy, not only with no rebuke, but even with no small praise.

23. Aaron tolerates the many people who demand, build, and worship an idol.[332] Moses tolerates so many thousands who murmur against God and sin

---

331. See Mt 25:41; Rv 12:9.
332. See Ex 32:6.

against his name so many times.[333] David tolerates Saul who persecutes him, who abandons the things of heaven with his wicked conduct and seeks the things below by the arts of magic; he avenges him when he is slain, and even calls him the anointed of the Lord on account of the mystery of his holy anointing.[334] Samuel tolerates the wicked sons of Eli and his own evil sons; because the people would not tolerate them, the people were accused by divine truth and rebuked by divine severity. Samuel, finally, tolerates the people who are proud and contemptuous of God.[335] Isaiah tolerates those whom he accuses of many true crimes. Jeremiah tolerates those from whom he suffers so much. Zechariah tolerates the Pharisees and scribes who Scripture testifies existed at that time. I know that I have passed over many; let those who want read; let those who are able read the heavenly words; they will find that all the holy servants and friends of God always had those whom they needed to tolerate in their people. Sharing with them, nonetheless, in the sacraments of that time, they were not only not defiled, but they also endured them in a praiseworthy manner, *eager*, as the Apostle says, *to preserve the unity of the Spirit in the bond of peace* (Eph 4:3). Let them also take note of the time after the coming of the Lord when we would find many more examples of this toleration throughout the world if they could have all been written down and verified. But take note of those we have. The Lord himself tolerates Judas, a devil, a thief, and a man who betrays him for money; he allows him to receive along with the innocent disciples what the faithful know is our ransom. The apostles tolerate the false apostles,[336] and among those who seek *what is their own, not what pertains to Jesus Christ* (Phil 2:21), Paul, not seeking what is his own, but what pertains to Jesus Christ, lives a life of most glorious tolerance. Finally, as I mentioned a little before, the ruler of the church is praised by the word of God under the name of an angel because, though he hated evil persons, he tolerated them on account of the name of the Lord, after having tested and found them out.

24. In short, let them ask themselves: Do they not tolerate the slaughters and fires of the Circumcellions, those people who venerate the bodies of others who willingly throw themselves over a cliff, and the groaning of the whole of Africa under the incredible evils of the one Optatus?[337] I will not now mention the tyrannical powers of single regions, cities, and estates throughout Africa and the robberies in public view. For it is better that you yourselves mention these things either privately or openly, as you please. For wherever you turn your eyes, you will see what I am saying or rather what I pass over in silence. Nor, after all, do we accuse on this account those individuals whom you love. For they are not displeasing to us because they tolerate evil persons, but because they are intoler-

---

333. See Ex 14:11; 15:24; 16:2.8; 17:2-3; Nm 14:2; 16:41.
334. See 1 Sm 28:7-20.
335. See 1 Sm 2:27-29; 3:21; 8:1-5.
336. See 2 Cor 11:13.
337. This was the Donatist bishop of Thamugadi, the successor of Gaudentius. See *Answer to Gaudentius* 1, 18; *Answer to the Letter of Parmenian* 2, 2; Letter 53, 6.

ably evil on account of the schism, on account of their altar over against our altar, on account of their separation from the heritage of Christ spread throughout the world, as it was promised so long ago.[338] We deplore and grieve over the violated peace, the sundered unity, the repeated baptisms, and the abused[339] sacraments, which are holy even in wicked persons. If they consider these of little importance, let them look at the examples that show how important God considers them. Those who fashioned an idol were slain by the customary death of the sword,[340] but the leaders of those who chose to cause a schism were swallowed by the earth, and the crowd who agreed with them were consumed by fire.[341] The difference in their punishments reveals the difference of their merits.

9, 25. The Holy Books are handed over in the persecution; those who handed them over confess, and they are left to God's judgment. The innocent are not questioned and are condemned by rash human beings. The one who among those who were innocent and absent was accused much more intensely than the rest is proven free of guilt by reliable judges. The judgment of the bishops is appealed to the emperor. The emperor is chosen as judge; when he judges, the emperor is scorned. You have read what was done then; you see what is being done now. If you are in the least bit of doubt about those past events, look at these present ones. Let us, of course, not deal with old papers, nor with public archives, nor with judicial or ecclesiastical proceedings. Our book is greater—the world; in it I read the fulfillment of the promise I read in God's Book. It says, *The Lord said to me, You are my son; this day I have begotten you. Ask of me, and I shall give you the nations as your heritage and the ends of the earth as your possession.* (Ps 2:7-8) Let whoever does not share in this heritage, whatever Books he may possess, know that he has been disinherited. Whoever fights against this heritage proves quite well that he is a stranger to the family of God. The question, of course, centers around the handing over of the God's Books in which this heritage is promised. Let that person, then, be believed to have handed over the Testament to the flames who brings suit against the will of the testator. What has the church of the Corinthians done to you, O sect of the Donatists, what has it done to you? But what I say of this church I want you to understand regarding all such churches that are located so far off. What have they done to you? They were utterly unable to know either what you did or whom you slandered. Or has the world lost the light of Christ because Caecilian offended Lucilla in Africa? [342]

26. Let them finally realize what they have done. It is only right that after a certain period of years their action has come back to their eyes. Investigate the

---

338. See Ps 2:8.
339. Literally, "sacraments subjected to the rite of exsufflation," that is, sacraments from which the devil was expelled.
340. See Ex 32:1-28.
341. See Nm 16:1-35; 41:49.
342. See 6, 17 above for more on Lucilla.

woman through whom Maximian,[343] who is said to be a relative of Donatus, cut himself off from communion with Primian[344] and how, after gathering a group of bishops, he condemned Primian in his absence and was ordained bishop in opposition to him, just as, having gathered a group of bishops with the help of Lucilla, Majorinus condemned Caecilian in his absence and was ordained bishop in opposition to him. Or do you perhaps want it to count that Primian was acquitted by the other African bishops of his communion in opposition to the sect of Maximian, but you do not want it to count that Caecilian was acquitted by the bishops in unity across the sea against the sect of Majorinus? I ask you, my brothers, what do I ask that is so great? What do I want you to understand that is so difficult? There is, of course, a big difference, and the African church is incomparably less in authority and in number if it is compared to the others of the world. And it is far smaller, even if there were unity here, far smaller compared to all the other Christian peoples than the sect of Maximian compared to the sect of Primian. I ask, nonetheless, and I think it is just that the council of Secundus of Tigisi, which Lucilla aroused against the absent Caecilian and against the apostolic sees and the whole world in communion with Caecilian, should have as much validity as the council of the Maximianists has, which some woman or other likewise aroused against the absent Primian and the remaining multitude in Africa who were in communion with Primian. What is clearer to see? What is more just to ask?

27. You see all this, and you know it, and you groan, and yet God sees that nothing forces you to remain in so deadly and sacrilegious a schism, if in order to attain a spiritual kingdom you would overcome your carnal affection and if in order to avoid everlasting punishments you would not be afraid to offend the friendships of human beings, which are of no help in God's courtroom. There you are, go and consult; learn what can be said against these views of ours. If they produce papers, we produce papers; if they say that ours are false, let them not be angry that we say this of theirs. No one wipes out from heaven the decree of God; no one wipes out from the earth the Church of God. He promised the whole world; she has filled the whole world. And she contains both evil and good, but on earth she loses only the evil, while in heaven she admits only the good. But this discourse which we have drawn from the grace of God with a great love of peace and of you—as he knows—will be for you a source of correction, if you are not.

---

343. Maximian was a Donatist deacon of Carthage who, angered at his bishop, Primian, in 393 broke away from the Donatists and formed the Maximianists.
344. Primian was the Donatist bishop of Carhage, who succeded Parmenian as bishop in about 391.

LETTER 44

Augustine to a group of Donatist laymen (396-397)

In 396 or 397 Augustine wrote to a group of Donatist laymen about his encounter with Fortunius, the Donatist bishop of Thiave (Thubursicum Numidarum), of whom they had spoken highly. Augustine recounts his friendly meeting with Fortunius amid a turbulent crowd who were hoping to see a fight (paragraph 1). Despite Donatist opposition, some notes were taken, and Augustine has written them up in this letter (paragraph 2). The issue of the true Church is raised (paragraph 3). The Donatists claim that their being persecuted proves that they are the true Christians (paragraph 4). Augustine points out that the Donatists are not in communion with the churches overseas (paragraph 5). The Donatist appeal to the Council of Sardica to show that they were in communion with the churches overseas fails, once it is shown to be an Arian council (paragraph 6). Furthermore, persecution alone is not proof of righteousness (paragraph 7). Fortunius mentions the killing by Catholics of the administrator who was set in place by the Donatists before the ordination of Majorinus and asks how such killers can fail to be evil (paragraph 8).

Augustine argues that killings in the name of Christianity, whether by Catholics or by Donatists, are wrong, though in the Old Testament era Elijah rightly killed the false prophets (paragraph 9). In the new testament period, however, we should follow, rather, the example of Jesus with respect to Judas, his "traditor" (paragraph 10). To the Donatist complaint that they are still suffering persecution, Augustine replies that they themselves created a schism because of their intolerance (paragraph 11). As time ran out, Fortunius mentioned with apparent regret that the practice of rebaptizing Catholics who come to the Donatists has been established. Augustine urges both sides to forget past wrongs and to end the schism (paragraph 12). He insists on the importance of the pursuit of Christian unity (paragraph 13) and proposes means to continue the discussion with Fortunius or other Donatists (paragraph 14).

To his most beloved lords and esteemed brothers, Eleusius, Glorius, and the two Felixes,[345] *Augustine sends greetings.*

1, 1. When I was traveling to the church of Cirta, I made the acquaintance of Fortunius, whom you have as bishop of Tubursicum, though most hurriedly, while passing through his city. And I found him to be exactly as you usually and most kindly promise him to be. When we reported to him your conversation regarding him, he did not refuse us who wanted to see him. We, therefore, went

---

345. These are some of the same Donatist laymen to whom the previous letter was addressed.

to him, for it seemed that we ought to offer that to his age rather than to demand that he first come to us. We set out, therefore, with no small number of companions whom the circumstances had by chance found gathered around us. But after we had settled down in his home, no small crowd also assembled because of the rumor spread about. We, however, saw that there were very few in that whole crowd who desired that the issue be treated in a useful and salutary manner and that so important a question on so important an issue be discussed with wisdom and piety. But the rest had assembled for the spectacle of our quarrel, as it were, almost in manner of the theater rather than for instruction toward salvation with Christian devotion. Hence, they could neither offer us silence nor hold a discussion with us attentively or at least in modest and orderly fashion, except, as I said, for those few whose intention was seen to be religious and undivided. Therefore, everything was thrown into confusion by the noise of those speaking freely and without control in accord with the impulse of the mind of each person, and neither he nor we were able to obtain, either by asking or even at times by threatening, that they offer us a polite silence.

2. The discussion somehow got under way, and we continued for several hours in dialogue to the extent we were permitted by the voices of the uproarious when they fell silent. But we saw at the beginning of the discussion that what was said immediately slipped from memory, whether ours or that of those whose salvation we were most concerned with. Hence, in order that our discussion might be more careful and moderate and also in order that you and the other brothers who were absent might come to know by reading what we accomplished, we asked that our words be taken down by stenographers. For a long time he or those who agreed with him were opposed to this; afterward, he, nonetheless, agreed. But the stenographers who had been present and could have quickly done this refused for some reason or other to take it down. We at least got the brothers who were with us to take it down, though they could do this only rather slowly, and we promised that we would leave there the same records. They agreed. Our words began to be taken down, and some words were spoken by each side for the records. Afterward, the stenographers gave up, unable to put up with the disorderly interruptions of the uproarious and with our discussion, which was also more disorderly on this account, though we, of course, did not stop and said many things, as each of us was given the opportunity. I did not want to deprive Your Charity of all these words of ours to the extent that I could recall the discussion of the whole issue. For you can read my letter to Fortunius in order that he may agree that I have written the truth or may convey without delay anything he remembers better.

2, 3. After all, he was the first who was so good as to praise our life, which he said that he discovered from you, who perhaps recounted it with more benevolence than truth, and he added that he said to you that we could have done well all those things that you mentioned regarding us if we had done them in the Church. Then we began to seek which was that Church in which one ought to live, whether that one which, as the Holy Scriptures foretold so long ago, would spread over the whole earth[346] or that one which a small part of Africa or of the Africans would contain. Here he first tried to claim that his communion was everywhere on earth. I asked whether he could give me letters of communion, which we call "patent," for wherever I wanted, and I stated that it was evident to all that the question could most easily be brought to an end in this way. I was, however, ready, if he agreed, that such letters be sent by us to those churches which we both read in the authoritative writings of the apostles were already founded at that time.

4. But because the claim was clearly false, he quickly left the point in a confusion of words. Among these words he mentioned that gospel warning of the Lord in which he said, *Beware of false prophets; many will come to you in sheep's clothing, but within they are ravenous wolves. From their fruits you will know them* (Mt 7:15.16). When we said that the same words of the Lord can be recited by us with reference to them, he turned from there to exaggerating the persecution that he said his side often endured, wanting to show from this that their followers are Christians because they suffer persecution. When during these words I was preparing to reply from the Gospel, he was the first to mention the passage from it where the Lord said, *Blessed are those who suffer persecution on account of justice because theirs is the kingdom of heaven* (Mt 5:10). Grateful for that passage, I immediately added that we must, therefore, inquire whether they have suffered persecution on account of justice. I wanted a discussion on this question because it was, of course, clear to everyone whether the time of Macarius[347] found them situated in the unity of the Church or already divided from it by schism. Thus those who want to see whether they suffered persecution on account of justice should consider whether they rightly cut themselves off from the unity of the whole world. If they were found to have done so unjustly, it would be evident that they suffered persecution on account of injustice rather than on account of justice and, for that reason, cannot be added to the number of the blessed, of whom it was said, *Blessed are those who suffer persecution on account of justice*. Then there was mention of that surrender of the Books, which is more talked about than it is certain. But our side replied that their leaders were rather all traditors, and that, if they did not want to believe our documents on this point, we ought not to be forced to believe their documents.

3, 5. But having set aside this doubtful question, I asked how these people had justly separated themselves from the innocence of other Christians who preserve throughout the world the order of succession from the apostles and are established in the most ancient churches, though they were utterly ignorant

---

346. See Ps 2:7-8.
347. Macarius, an imperial commissioner sent in 347 to Africa along with Paul to settle the Donatist dispute, sided with the Catholics. The harshness of his methods made the time of Macarius legendary among the Donatists.

about who were traditors in Africa. For they certainly could only be in communion with those who they heard held the chairs of bishops. He answered that the churches of the regions across the sea long remained innocent until they consented to the shedding of the blood of those who, he said, suffered the persecution of Macarius. There I could have said that the innocence of the churches across the sea could not have been destroyed by the hatred of the time of Macarius, since it could in no way be proved that he did what he did under their instigation. But as a shortcut I preferred to ask whether, if the overseas churches lost their innocence by the savagery of Macarius from the time when they were said to have consented to it, it is proven that the Donatists remained in unity with the Eastern churches and the other parts of the world at least up to those times.

6. Then he brought forth a certain volume in which he wanted to show that the Council of Sardica[348] had issued a letter to the African bishops who were in the communion of Donatus. When it was read, we heard the name of Donatus among the other bishops to whom they had written. And so we began to ask that we be informed whether this was the Donatus from whose sect these people take their name, for it is possible that they had written to a Donatus who was a bishop of another sect, especially since in those names there was not even a mention made of Africa. How, therefore, could he prove that we should understand by that name Donatus the bishop of the sect of Donatus, since he could not even prove whether that letter was sent to bishops of the African churches in particular. For, though the name Donatus is usually African, it would not be impossible that either someone from those regions have an African name or that some African be made bishop in those regions. After all, we did not find in it either a date or the consul so that something clear might emerge from a consideration of its date. We had certainly heard that, after they had split from the Catholic communion, the Arians[349] at some time or other tried to make the Donatists their allies in Africa: my brother, Alypius, whispered this idea into my ear. Then, having accepted that volume, I considered the statutes of that council and read that the Council of Sardica condemned Athanasius, the Catholic bishop of Alexandria, whose conflict against the Arians in highly passionate debates is well known, and Julius, the bishop of the Roman church,[350] who was just as Catholic. Hence, it was clear to us that it was a council of Arians, whom these Catholic bishops most strongly opposed. And so, we wanted to receive and to take with us the volume for a more careful examination of the times. But Fortunius refused to hand it over, saying that we have it there when we might want to consider something in it. I also asked that he would permit me to mark it by my handwriting, for I

---

348. The Council of Sardica was convoked by Pope Julius (342-343). The Arian bishops withdrew from the council and sent the letter mentioned as if from the council.
349. The Arians originated in Alexandria with the priest Arius in the early fourth century; though condemned at the Council of Nicaea in 325, they continued to be influential well into the next century. See *Heresies* XLIX.
350. Julius I, who was the bishop of Rome from 337 to 352.

was afraid, I admit, that another volume might perhaps be produced in its place when I had to ask for it because the situation demanded, but he refused that too.

4, 7. Then he began to insist that I reply briefly to his questions, asking me whom I would consider just—the one who persecutes or the one who suffers persecution. To which I replied that he did not correctly pose the question in that way, for it is possible that both are unjust and it is also possible that the more just persecutes the more unjust. It does not, therefore, follow that anyone is more just because he suffers persecution, though that is generally the case. Then, when I saw that he was delaying much on this point because he wanted the justice of his side to be seen as certain because it suffered persecution, I asked him whether he thought Ambrose, the bishop of the Milanese church,[351] a just man and a Christian. He was, of course, forced to deny that the illustrious man was Christian and just. For, if he admitted that he was, we would immediately object that Fortunius judged that he had to be rebaptized. Since he was, therefore, forced to state those reasons why he was not to be considered Christian and just, I mentioned the great persecution he endured, when his church was surrounded even by armed troops.[352] I asked him also whether he considered Maximian,[353] who produced a schism from them at Carthage, both just and Christian. He could only say that he did not. I also mentioned that he suffered such persecution that his church was destroyed to its foundations. I was, therefore, trying by these examples to persuade him, if I could, that he should now stop saying that to suffer persecution is the most certain proof of Christian justice.

8. He also explained that in the very beginning of the schism, when his predecessors thought that they wanted in some way to hush up the guilt of Caecilian in order to avoid a schism, they gave a certain administrator[354] to the people of his community located in Carthage before Majorinus[355] was ordained in opposition to Caecilian. Hence, he said that this administrator was killed by our people in his church. I admit that I had never heard of this before, though our side rejects and refutes so many charges raised by them and hurls more and greater charges at them. But, all the same, after he told us of this, he again began to ask whom I thought to be just—the one who killed or the one who was killed, as if he had already proven to me that the crime was committed, as he had reported it. I said, therefore, that we must first ask whether it was true; for one ought not rashly to believe whatever is said, and it could, nonetheless, have been the case either that both were equally bad or even that someone bad killed someone worse. For it

---

351. Ambrose was bishop of Milan from 374 to 397; he baptized Augustine in 387.
352. See *Confessions* IX, 7, 15.
353. Maximian, a deacon in Carthage, split away from the Donatists in 397 in anger at his bishop, Primian.
354. An *interventor* administered or governed a diocese during a period when there was no bishop of it.
355. Majorinus, the first Donatist bishop of Carthage, was consecrated in 313.

is really possible that the rebaptizer of the whole person is more criminal than a slayer of the body alone.

9. For this reason he also ought not to have asked me what he later asked me. For he said that a bad person ought not to be killed by Christians and just people, as if we would call those in the Catholic Church who do this just person. They usually state these charges against us with more ease than they can prove them. For many of them, even bishops and priests and other clerics, gather crowds of highly enraged people and do not stop inflicting so much violent killing and destruction, not upon Catholics alone, but even at times upon their own people when they can. Since this is so, he feigned ignorance, nonetheless, of the most criminal deeds of his own people that he knows better than I, and he urged me to say whether a just person would kill even a bad man. Even though this had nothing to do with the present issue, for we admitted that, wherever these actions were done in the name of Christ, they were not done by good persons, we, nonetheless, replied in order to make him realize the question that should be asked. We asked whether he thought that Elijah was just, something he could not deny. Then we added how many false prophets he slew by his own hand. Here he really saw what he needed to see, namely, that such actions were then permitted to the just.[356] For they did such acts with their prophetic spirit and by the authority of God who undoubtedly knows for whom it is good even to be killed. He demanded, therefore, that I show that now in the time of the New Testament any of the just killed someone, even a criminal and wicked person.

5, 10. Then we returned to the previous discussion by which we wanted to show that we ought not to raise as objections against them their crimes, nor ought they to raise as objections against us such actions of ours, if they find any. For it cannot, of course, be shown from the New Testament that any just person killed someone, but it can be proved by the example of the Lord that innocent people tolerated criminals. After all, he allowed his betrayer,[357] who had already accepted payment for him, to be with him among the innocent up to the last kiss of peace. He did not conceal from them that there was a great criminal among them, and he, nonetheless, for the first time gave the sacrament of his body and blood to all in common, when the betrayer had not yet been excluded.[358] Since almost all were moved by this example, Fortunius tried to say that before the Passion of the Lord such communion with the criminal was not a hindrance to the apostles because they had not yet received the baptism of Christ, but the baptism of John. After he said this, I began to ask him how Scripture had, then, said that Jesus baptized more than John, though he himself did not baptize, but

---

356. R. Teske followed the CSEL reading of *alia licuisse tunc* instead of *talia eum licuisse*.
357. The Latin for "betrayer" is *traditor*. Augustine is really pointing out that Jesus tolerated his traditor, though the Donatists did not tolerate the traditors of the Sacred Books.
358. See Mt 26:14-16.20-28.

his disciples did, that is, he baptized through his disciples.³⁵⁹ How, then, did they give what they had not received, as the Donatists themselves so often say? Did Christ perhaps baptize with the baptism of John? Next I was going to ask him many questions along these lines, for example, how John was then asked about the baptism of the Lord and how he replied that the Lord had the bride and was the bridegroom.³⁶⁰ Was it then permitted that the bridegroom should baptize with the baptism of John, that is, with the baptism of a friend and servant? Finally, how were they able to receive the Eucharist when they were not yet baptized? Or how did he reply to Peter who wanted him to wash all of him, *One who has once bathed does not need to be washed again, but is entirely clean* (Jn 13:10)? For the perfect cleansing is not the baptism in the name of John, but that in the name of the Lord, if the one who receives it presents himself as worthy of it. But if he is unworthy, the sacraments still remain in him, not for his salvation, but for his destruction. Though I was going to ask these questions, he himself saw that he should not ask about the baptism of the disciples of the Lord.

11. Then we came to another topic on which many on each side spoke as they were able. Among the things said was that our people still were going to persecute them, and he said to us that he wanted to see what sort of people we would show ourselves to be in that persecution, whether we were going to assent to such savagery or were not going to give it our consent. We said that God sees our hearts, which they could not see, and that they are too ready to fear these events which, if they do come about, come from evil persons, though they themselves have worse ones than these. Nor ought we, nonetheless, to separate ourselves from the Catholic communion if anything should perhaps happen when we were unwilling or even opposed to it, if we were able, since we learned peaceful toleration from the lips of the Apostle, *Bear with one another in love; strive to preserve the unity of the Spirit in the bond of peace* (Eph 4:2-3). We said that those who produced the schism did not have this toleration and peace, while now those who are more meek among their own people tolerate more serious evils for fear that what has already been split may be further split, if they are unwilling to tolerate less serious evils for the sake of unity. We also said that in the times of the Old Testament the peace of unity and toleration was not preached with such a strong commendation as by the example of the Lord and the love of the New Testament, and yet those prophets and holy men often charged the people with crimes when they tried to remove themselves from the unity of that people and from the communion in receiving those sacraments that then existed.

12. From there we somehow or other came to mention Genethlius of blessed memory, the bishop of Carthage before Aurelius,³⁶¹ because he suppressed

---

359. See Jn 4:1-2.
360. See Jn 3:22-29.
361. Genethlius died in 391 or 392; he was followed by Aurelius, a close ally of Augustine, who remained in office until his death in 430 or 431.

a decree directed against them and did not allow its implementation. They all praised him and spoke of him with great affection. Among those praises we added that, if Genethlius himself had fallen into their hands, they would have judged that he also needed to be rebaptized. And we said these things when we were already standing because the time for departure was near. Then that old man clearly said that the rule had already been made that whoever of the faithful comes to them from us is baptized, and it was evident that he said this with as much reluctance and sorrow as possible. He, of course, very clearly deplored the many wrongs of his people and showed how removed he was from such actions, as was proven by the testimony of his whole city, and he brought forth those points that he was accustomed to say in a mild complaint to his people. Hence, we mentioned that passage of the prophet Ezekiel, where Scripture clearly says that the sin of the child will not be held against the parent, nor the sin of the parent against the child. It says there, *For, just as the soul of the parent is mine, so the soul of the child is also mine. Only the soul which sins will die* (Ez 18:4.20). Everyone agreed that in such discussions we ought not to hurl at one another as objections the violent actions of bad persons. There remained, therefore, the question of the schism. And so, we exhorted him to strive with us again and again with a calm and peaceful mind that so important an investigation might by a careful examination come to an end. At this point he was so kind as to say that it is only we who seek these goals, but that our people refuse to seek them. We departed after having promised that we would present to him many colleagues, certainly at least ten, who want to investigate the issue with such great good will and mildness and with such pious zeal as we felt that he already noticed in us and approved. He also promised this concerning the number of their bishops.

6, 13. Hence, I exhort and implore you by the blood of the Lord that you remind him of his promise and diligently insist that the task begun should be carried to completion, for you already see that it has nearly come to an end. For, in my opinion, it will be very difficult for you to find among your bishops so helpful a mind and will as we saw in this old man. On the following day, after all, he came to us, and we began to investigate these matters again. But because the necessity of ordaining a bishop was already tearing us away from there, we could not stay with him a longer time. For we had already sent to the head of "the worshipers of heaven,"[362] whom we had heard had instituted a new baptism among them, and led many astray by that sacrilege, in order that we might speak with him to the extent that the restrictions of the time permitted. After Fortunius learned that that man was coming and saw that we had taken up some other business, he left us with good will and in peace, since some necessity to depart constrained him.

14. It seems me that, in order that we may completely avoid the disturbing crowds that are a hindrance rather than a help and that we may with God's help

---

362. The *caelicolae* were a heretical group mentioned in a decree of Honorius against heretics.

continue in a truly friendly and peaceful spirit the important a task that we have undertaken, we ought to meet in a village where neither of us has a church, a village which people of our communion and of his share in common, such as the village of Titiana. Whether, then, such a place is in the territory of Tubursicum or in that of Thagaste, whether with the man I mentioned or someone else is found, let us have the canonical Books present and any documents that can be produced by the two sides. Having set aside all other concerns, let us, with no disturbances interfering, if it pleases God, devote as many days as we can to this. Let each of us pray to the Lord in the home of his host, and with the help of God, to whom Christian peace is most pleasing, let us bring so important a matter, which was begun with such good spirit, to a successful end of this inquiry. Write back, of course, what you and Fortunius think about this proposal.

LETTER 51

Augustine to Crispinus, the Donatist bishop of Calama (399-400)

In either 399 or 400 Augustine wrote to Crispinus, the Donatist bishop of Calama, a town in Numidia to the south and east of Hippo. Augustine invites Crispinus to discuss by an exchange of letters the schism that divides them, reminding his counterpart that schism was punished in Scripture more severely than idolatry and the burning of a Sacred Book (paragraph 1). Turning Donatist objections back against them, Augustine asks why they accepted back into their communion the bishops who broke away from them in the schism of Maximian (paragraph 2) and why they persecuted the members of that sect (paragraph 3). Why too did the Donatists accept the baptism of the Maximianists, though they do not accept the baptism of the Catholics (paragraph 4)? Augustine insists that baptism belongs to Christ, not to the Donatists or to the Catholics, and asks why the Donatists separate themselves from the rest of the world by a greater schism than that of Maximian (paragraph 5).

1. Because your people criticize our humility, I added this form of salutation to this letter,[363] and I might seem to have done this in contempt for you, if I do not await your reply to me. Why should I remind you at length about your promise in Carthage or our insistence? Regardless of how we acted, let those things be in the past so that they do not impede what remains. Now, unless I am mistaken, there is no excuse if God grants his help; we are both in Numidia and are near to each other in terms of locality. Rumor has reached me that you still want to examine while debating with me the question that divides our communion. See how quickly all the evasions are removed; reply to this letter if you will, and perhaps it will suffice, not only for us, but also for those who desire to hear us. Or if it will not suffice, let us continue with letters and replies until it does suffice. What greater advantage, after all, could such great nearness of the cities we inhabit offer us? For I have decided to do nothing with you on this issue except by letters so that what is said may not slip from the memory of either of us or so that interested persons, who perhaps cannot be present, may not be deprived of such information. You are accustomed to toss about false statements about past events, perhaps not because you want to lie, but because you are mistaken. Hence, if you agree, let us measure those events by present ones. You are surely aware that in the times of the people of the Old Testament the sacrilege of idolatry

---

363. Though this letter to Crispinus, the Donatist bishop of Calama in Numidia, lacks the usual salutation, Augustine often addressed the Donatists as brothers and as most dear, terms which he explained and justified in Letter 33.

was committed[364] and a contemptuous king burned the book of a prophet.[365] The sin of schism would not be punished more harshly than each of these crimes unless it were considered more serious. For you, of course, recall how the earth opened up and swallowed alive the authors of schism and how fire poured down from heaven and consumed those who had sided with it.[366] Neither the construction and worship of an idol nor the burning of a Sacred Book deserved to be punished in such a way.

2. You are often raise as objections to us charges that are not only not proven against our people, but that are rather proven against your people who were driven by fear of persecution and handed over the Sacred Books to be burned in the fire. Why, then, have you received back those whom you condemned for the crime of schism "by the true words of" your "plenary council," as it is recorded there, into the very same episcopacy in which you condemned them? I refer to Felician of Musti and Praetextatus of Assuri[367]. After all, these men were not, as you often say to the ignorant, from that number for whom your council had given a postponement and fixed a date beyond which they would be bound by the same sentence if they had not returned to your communion. They were rather from that number whom you condemned without delay on that day on which you granted a delay to those others. I shall prove this if you deny it; your council is explicit. We have the proconsular acts in our hands in which you affirmed this more than once. Prepare another defense if you can so that we do not cause delays while you deny what I prove. If Felician and Praetextatus were innocent, why were they condemned in that way? If they were criminals, why were they taken back in that way? If you prove them innocent, why should we not believe that innocent men could have been condemned on the false charge of surrendering the Books by a much smaller number of your predecessors if three hundred and ten of their successors were able to condemn innocent men on the false charge of schism "by the true word of a plenary council," as it was so pompously stated? But if you prove that they were rightly condemned, what defense remains for why they were received back into the same episcopacy except that, by emphasizing the benefit and salutariness of peace, you show that even these crimes should be tolerated to maintain the bond of unity? I wish you would do this, not with the strength of the word, but with that of the heart! You would, of course, see how the peace of Christ should not be violated by any slanders throughout the world, if it is permissible in Africa that men condemned even for sacrilegious schism are received back in the very same episcopacy to maintain the peace of Donatus.

---

364. See Ex 32:1.6.
365. See Jer 36:23.
366. See Nm 16:31-35.
367. Felician of Musti and Praetextatus of Assuri were Donatist bishops whom the Donatists tried to remove as the leaders of the Maximianist sect from their sees but later proved innocent.

3. You likewise often raise as an objection to us that we persecute you by earthly powers. On this point I do not want to discuss either what you deserve for the terribleness of so great a sacrilege or how much Christian kindness restrains us. This is what I say: If this is a crime, why did you fiercely attack the same Maximianists[368] through judges sent by those emperors, whom our communion begot through the Gospel, and why did you by the roar of controversies, by the power of ordinances, and by the assault of troops drive them from the basilicas which they had and in which they were at the time of the division? What they suffered in individual places during that conflict is attested to by recent traces of events. The records show what orders were given; the lands in which the holy memory of that notorious Optatus, your tribune,[369] is venerated cry out what was done.

4. You are also accustomed to say that we do not have the baptism of Christ and that it exists nowhere outside of your communion. I could on this issue speak somewhat more at length. But in opposition to you there is no need, for you have accepted the baptism of the Maximianists along with Felician and Praetextatus. For they baptized many when they were in communion with Maximian, though, as the records testify, you tried by a long judicial conflict to expel by name from their basilicas those very men, that is, Felician and Praetextatus. As many, then, as they baptized at that time, they now have with them and with you, not only during times of critical illness, but during the solemnities of Easter, in so many churches that belong to their cities, and even in large cities. They have those people who were baptized outside their sect in the crime of schism, and for none of these was baptism repeated. And I wish that you could prove that those whom Felician and Praetextatus baptized, as if with no benefit, outside your sect in the crime of schism were baptized again, as if to their benefit, by them when they were received back within your sect. For, if these people had to be baptized again, those bishops had to be ordained again. After all, they lost their episcopacy in withdrawing from you if they were not able to baptize outside of your communion. For, if in departing they did not lose their episcopacy, they were, of course, able to baptize. But if they lost it, they, then, ought to have been ordained upon their return in order that what they had lost might be restored to them. But have no fear. Just as it is certain that they returned with the same episcopacy with which they left, so it is certain that they reconciled to your communion without any repetition of baptism along with themselves all whom they baptized in the schism of Maximian.

5. With what tears, then, will we be able sufficiently to deplore the fact that the baptism of the Maximianists is accepted and that the baptism of the

---

368. The Maximianists were a schismatic group that broke away from the Donatists.
369. Optatus was the Donatist bishop of Thamugadi; he was also called "the Gildonian" after Count Gildo, whose rule from 395 to 397 brought persecution against the Maximianists.

whole world is subjected to exsufflation?[370] Whether after a hearing or without a hearing, whether justly or unjustly, you condemned Felician, you condemned Praetextatus. Tell me, which bishop of the Corinthians has been heard or condemned by one of yours? Which bishop of the Galatians, of the Ephesians, of the Colossians, of the Philippians, of the Thessalonians, and of all the other cities of which scripture says, *All the families of the nations shall worship in his sight* (Ps 22:28)? The baptism, then, of the Maximianists is accepted, and the baptism of those apostolic churches is subjected to exsufflation, though baptism belongs neither to these nor to those, but to him of whom it was said, *This is he who baptizes* (Jn 1:33). But I am not talking about this; turn to those matters that are at hand; look at those that strike even blind eyes. Those who were condemned have baptism, and those who have not had a hearing do not! Those explicitly named in the crime of schism and cast out have baptism, and those who are unknown, far away, never accused, never brought to trial do not! Those who were cut off from part of Africa that was already cut off from the Church have baptism, and those from whom the Gospel itself came to Africa do not have it! Why should I burden you with more? Reply to these questions. Consider the sacrilege of schism with which your council charged the Maximianists; consider the persecutions through judicial powers that you brought upon them. Consider their baptism that you accepted along with those whom you condemned, and answer, if you can, if you have some means to throw the ignorant into confusion, why you are separated from the world by a far greater crime of schism than that which you boast to have condemned in the Maximianists. May the peace of Christ win out in your heart.

---

370. Exsufflation was part of the rite of baptism; it symbolized the expulsion of the devil from the candidate.

LETTER 52

Augustine to Severinus, Augustine's relative and a Donatist (399-400)

In 399 or 400 Augustine wrote to Severinus, a relative and a Donatist, about abandoning his criminal schism. Augustine reminds Severinus that their true relationship must be in the body of Christ (paragraph 1). The sect of Donatus, Augustine explains, is a branch that does not bear fruit (paragraph 2). On the other hand, all the other churches apart from the Donatist churches are in communion with one another (paragraph 3). Finally, Augustine reminds his relative that their blood relationship is of no account toward everlasting salvation in Christ (paragraph 4).

To his much loved lord and very dear brother, Severinus, Augustine sends greetings.

1. Though the letter from you, my brother, was very late, and though it was apart from what I expected, I, nonetheless, was happy to receive it, and I was especially flooded with greater joy when I learned that your servant came to Hippo for this reason alone, that is, to bring to me your letter, my brother. I thought, after all, not without reason that the idea entered your mind to recall our blood relationship, only because you perhaps see—just as I know the considerable weight of your wisdom—how we should feel sorrow that we, who are brothers according to the flesh, do not live in the body of Christ in one society. This is especially true since it is easy for you to observe and see the city built upon a mountain, of which the Lord says in the Gospel that it cannot be hidden.[371] For it is the Catholic Church; the reason it is called καθολική in Greek is that it is spread throughout the whole world. No one is permitted to be unaware of this; for this reason, it cannot be hidden, according to the word of our Lord Jesus Christ.

2. The sect of Donatus, however, found only in Africans, slanders the world and does not consider that by that sterility, because of which it refuses to bear the fruits of peace and love, it is cut off from that root of the Eastern churches, from which the Gospel came to Africa. If a bit of soil is brought to them from those lands, they reverence it, but if a believer comes to them from there, they subject him even to exsufflation[372] and rebaptize him. The Son of God who is the truth, after all, foretold this[373] when he said that he was the vine, his children the branches, and his Father the farmer.[374] He said, *My Father will destroy the branch that does not bear fruit in me, but he will trim the branch that does bear*

---

371. See Mt 5:14.
372. See p. 167, n. 330.
373. See Jn 14:6.
374. See Jn 15:1.

fruit in me in order that it may bear more fruit (Jn 15:2). It is, therefore, not surprising if they who refused to bear the fruit of love were cut off from that vine which grew and filled all the lands.[375]

3. If the Donatists had raised as objections to their colleagues true crimes, when their predecessors created a schism, they themselves would have won their case before the church overseas, from which the authority of the Christian faith came to these parts. The result would have been that those men were excluded against whom they raised as objections those same crimes. But now when the accused are found to be on the inside in communion with the apostolic churches, whose names they have and read in the Holy Books, while their accusers are located outside and separated from that communion, who would fail to understand that they had a good case who were able to win it before impartial judges? Or if the Donatists had a good case and could not prove it to the churches overseas, how did the world do them harm since the bishops could not have rashly condemned their colleagues who had not been proved guilty before them of the crimes with which they were charged? Therefore, innocent people are rebaptized, and Christ is subjected to exsufflation in innocent people. If, however, the same Donatists knew true crimes of their African colleagues and neglected to point them out and to prove them to the churches overseas, they cut themselves off from the unity of Christ by a most wicked schism. They have no excuse, and you know it well, especially since so many criminals emerged among them and they tolerated them for so many years for fear of sundering the sect of Donatus. And they did not hesitate at that time to break up the peace and unity of Christ by hurling their false suspicions, as you yourselves see.

4. But some sort of carnal habit, brother Severinus, holds you there, and long have I grieved, long have I groaned, and long have I desired to see you in order to speak to you about this topic. After all, what good does temporal health and relationship do if we scorn in our thinking the eternal heritage of Christ and everlasting salvation? For the time being let it suffice for me to have written these ideas, which for hard hearts are very few and almost none at all, but for your mind, which I know well, they are quite many and very important. After all, they do not come from me, for I am nothing apart from what I await, namely, the mercy of God; rather, they come from almighty God, and anyone who in this age will contemn him as Father will find him as judge in the age to come.

---

375. See Ps 80:10.

LETTER 87

Augustine to Emeritus, the Donatist bishop of Caesarea
in Mauretania Caesariensis (405-411)

Between 405 and 411 Augustine wrote to Emeritus, the Donatist bishop of Caesarea in Mauretania Caesariensis.[376] Augustine explains that he has heard that Emeritus is a good man with a good mind and urges against him the argument that the presence of unknown sinners cannot defile the members of the Church (paragraph 1). Nor can known sinners be a hindrance to the good people in the Church (paragraph 2). It is not the presence of a sinner in a community, but joining in the commission of the sin or the approval of the sin that makes a person sinful (paragraph 3). The earlier Donatists did not act consistently when in order to preserve their unity they did not expel Optatus[377] (paragraph 4). The Donatists cannot plead that they did not know the crimes of Optatus and at the same time hold as excommunicated the whole world, most of which has never heard of what happened in Africa (paragraph 5). The principal question is why the schism came about (paragraph 6). Augustine appeals to Paul's words to justify the action of the earthly powers to suppress the Donatists (paragraph 7). The Catholics appeal to the Roman authorities, not in order to persecute the Donatists, but in order to defend themselves from them (paragraph 8). The Catholics want the Donatists to be united with them in order that they may have life in the Church of Christ (paragraph 9). The principal question, once again, is why the Donatists began the schism (paragraph 10).

To his lovable and beloved brother, Emeritus, Augustine sends greetings.

1. When I hear that someone endowed with a good mind and educated in the liberal arts—though the salvation of the soul is not found in them—holds another view than the truth demands on a very easy question, the more I am surprised, the more I am eager to know the man and to converse with him or, if I am unable to do this, I desire to touch his mind and be touched in turn by him, at least by letters, which speed over long distances. As I hear that you are such a man, I also grieve that you have been torn away and separated from the Catholic Church, which is spread throughout the whole world, as was foretold by the Holy Spirit.[378] But I do not know why you are separated from the Church. For it is certain that the sect of Donatus is unknown to a great part of the Roman world, not to mention the barbarian nations as well, to which the Apostle said

---

376. Emeritus was a participant at the Council of Carthage in 411; Augustine debated with him in Caesarea on 20 September 418.
377. Optatus was the infamous Donatist bishop of Thamugadi in Numidia.
378. See Ps 2:8.

that he was under obligation[379] and with whose Christian faith our communion is united. And it is certain that they absolutely do not know when or for what reasons this schism has arisen. And unless you admit that all those Christians are innocent of the charges that you hurl at Africa, you are forced to say that you are all guilty of the evil actions of all your people and are all defiled, since there are hidden among you, to put it mildly, some misguided souls. For you do not expel someone from your communion, or you only expel him after he has done that action because of which he had to be expelled. You do condemn someone who remains unknown for some time and is afterwards exposed and proven guilty, do you not? I ask, then, whether he did not contaminate you during that time when he remained unknown? You will answer, "In no way." He would, then, contaminate no one at any time, even if the sin was always unknown. For we often find out about the commission of some sins by people who are now dead, and it does not harm those Christians who were in communion with them when they were living. Why, then, have you cut yourselves off by your sacrilegious schism from communion with countless Eastern churches, which have never known and still do not know what you either teach or pretend was done in Africa?

2. It is another question, after all, whether those charges you make are true, charges that we in fact prove to be false by much more plausible proofs, and we claim that those charges that you hurl at us were better proven then against your people. But, as I said, this is another question to be undertaken and examined when there is need. Let your vigilant mind now consider this: No one can be contaminated by the unknown crimes of unknown people. Hence, it is evident that you have separated yourselves by a sacrilegious schism from communion with the world that does not know and never has known the charges, whether true or false, that you direct at Africa. And yet, it should not go unmentioned that even evil persons we know cause no harm to the good people in the Church, if there is lacking the authority to keep them from communion or if some reason for preserving the peace prevents this. For who are the ones who in the prophet Ezekiel merited to be sealed before the destruction of the wicked and to escape unharmed, when the wicked were destroyed,[380] if not, as is most clearly shown there, those who grieve and groan over the sins and injustices of the people of God that are committed in their midst? But who groans and grieves over what he does not know? For the same reason Paul the apostle tolerates false brethren. After all, he does not say of persons he does not know, *For all seek their own interests, not those of Jesus Christ* (Phil 2:21), and he, nonetheless, shows that they were with him. What sort of people are they who preferred to offer incense to idols or to hand over God's Books rather than to die but those who *seek their own interests, not those of Jesus Christ*?

---

379. See Rom 1:14.
380. See Ez 9:4-6.

3. I pass over many testimonies of the Scriptures in order not to make this letter longer than necessary, and I leave many points for you to consider with your learning. But see, I beg you, what is sufficient: If so many unjust persons in the one people of God do not make *those who testified against them* (Neh 9:26) to be as bad as they were, if a multitude of false brethren[381] do not make the apostle Paul, who was living in the one Church with them, one of those who *seek their own interests, not those of Jesus Christ*, it is evident that a person does not become the same as a bad person with whom he approaches the altar of Christ, even if the bad person is not unknown, provided one does not approve of that person and separates himself from him by a good conscience by disapproving of him. It is evident, then, that to be an accomplice of a thief is nothing other than to steal with him or to accept his theft with a consenting heart. We say this in order to remove countless superfluous questions about the actions of human beings that do not undermine our argument.

4. But unless you also hold this position, you all will be just as Optatus was in your communion, since you were not unaware of him. May God keep this from the conduct of Emeritus and such others among you who I have no doubt are far removed from the deeds of that man. After all, our objection against you is only the crime of schism, which you have also made into heresy by wrongly continuing in it. But regarding how great this sin is considered in the judgment of God, read the passage I have no doubt that you have read. You will find that Dathan and Abiram were swallowed by the earth's opening up and that all the rest who sided with them were consumed by a fire coming from the midst of them.[382] The Lord God branded that crime with an immediate punishment as an example of what we should avoid in order that, when he spares such sinners with great patience, he might show what sort of punishment he is reserving for the last judgment. Nor do we, after all, blame your arguments if at that time when Optatus is reported to have raged with his pestilential power, when he was accused by the groaning of the whole of Africa with your groans included, at least if you are the sort of person that your reputation declares you to be, something that God knows that I both believe and desire. We do not blame you, if you did not want to excommunicate him at that time for fear that he would drag with him many other excommunicated people and would split your communion with the madness of schism. But this is precisely what condemns you, Brother Emeritus: Though you saw that it is so great an evil that the sect of Donatus be divided that you thought that Optatus should be tolerated in your communion rather than that such a split be accepted, you remain in that evil that was committed by your predecessors in dividing the Church of Christ.

5. Here perhaps because of the lack of an answer, you will attempt to defend Optatus. Do not, brother, do not, I beg you. It is not fitting for your char-

---

381. See Gal 2:4; 2 Cor 11:26.
382. See Nm 16:31-35.

acter, and even if it is perhaps fitting for someone else's, if anything can be fitting for evil persons, it is certainly not fitting for Emeritus to defend Optatus. But it is perhaps fitting for you not to accuse him. Granted that it is so. Take the middle path, and say: *Each person carries his own burden* (Gal 6:5). *Who are you to judge another's servant?* (Rom 14:4). Even if by the testimony of the whole of Africa, in fact even by that of all lands, wherever the reputation of Gildo[383] spread, Optatus was also known at the same time,[384] you have never dared to pronounce judgment on Optatus for fear that you would rashly pronounce judgment on persons whom you did not know. Can we and ought we—merely on the basis of your testimony—rashly pass judgment concerning persons whom we do not know? Is it not enough that you condemn actions you do not know unless we also pronounce judgment on actions we do not know? After all, you do not defend Optatus, even if he is in danger because of misguided hatred, but you defend yourself when you say, "I do not know what sort of man he was." How much more is the Eastern world ignorant of the sort of people those lesser-known Africans were whom you accuse! And yet, from those churches whose names you have in your books and read aloud, you are separated by a wicked schism. If your bishop of Thamugadi, who was most infamous and notorious, was unknown to his colleague at that time—I do not mean in Caesarea, but in Sitifis— how was the church of the Corinthians, of the Ephesians, of the Colossians, of the Philippians, of the Thessalonians, and of the Antiochenes, the church of Pontus, of Galatia, of Cappadocia, and of the other parts of the world, which were built up in Christ by the apostles, able either to know the African traditors, whoever they were, or to deserve condemnation by you because they were not able to know them? And yet, you are not in communion with them, say that they are not Christians, and try to rebaptize them. What am I to say? What complaint am I to put forth? Or what outcry am I to make? If I am speaking with a man of intelligence, I share with you the sharpness of this indignation. For you see, of course, what I might say if I wanted to say it.

6. Or did your predecessors perhaps hold a council among themselves and condemn the whole Christian world apart from themselves? Has your assessment of the situation been reduced to the point that the council of the Maximianists, who split off from your splinter group, has no validity against you, because they were very few compared to you, while your council has validity against the nations, which are the heritage of Christ, and against the ends of the earth, which are his possession?[385] I wonder whether a person has any blood in his body who does not blush at this. Reply to these points, please; I heard, after all, from some people whom I could not fail to believe that you would reply if I wrote you. I had already sent one letter, though I do not know whether you received it or replied

---

383. Gildo was Count of Africa from 395 to 397 and sided with Optatus of Thamugadi.
384. Optatus was known as "the Gildonian" because of his association with Count Gildo.
385. See Ps 2:8.

to it and I perhaps did not receive your reply. Now I again ask that you not delay to reply to these questions what you think. But do not wander off into other questions; for the beginning of a well-ordered investigation starts with this question: Why was the schism produced?

7. For, when earthly authorities persecute the schismatics, they defend themselves by that rule which the Apostle states, *One who resists authority resists the governance of God. But those who resist bring condemnation upon themselves. For rulers cause no fear for a good work, but for an evil work. Do you want to be without fear of the authority? Do good, and you will have praise from him. For he is God's minister for your good. But if you do evil, fear. For he does not carry the sword for no reason. He is, after all, God's servant to carry out his wrath in punishing the wrongdoer.* (Rom 13:2-4) The whole question, then, amounts to whether schism is not something evil or whether you did not produce a schism, that is, whether you resist the authorities for a good work, not for an evil work, because of which you will receive condemnation. Hence, in his great providence God did not say merely, *Blessed are those who suffer persecution*, but added, *On account of justice* (Mt 5:10). I desire, then, to know from you if it is justice that you did in that act of schism, in which you also remain, in accord with what I said above. Is it wrong to condemn the whole world without a hearing, either because it had not heard what you heard or because your beliefs or accusations without certain proofs have not been made known to it? And is it wrong for this reason to want to rebaptize so many churches of the Lord that were founded by the preaching and labor of the apostles, when he was still here in the flesh? If so, why are you permitted either not to know your evil African colleagues who are living at the same time and administering the sacraments at the same time or even to know them, but to tolerate them so that the sect of Donatus is not divided, whereas those situated in the farthest corner of the world are not permitted to be ignorant of what you either know or believe or have heard or make up concerning Africans? What a great perversity it is to cling to one's own wickedness and bring accusations against the severity of the state!

8. "But," you claim, "it is not permitted that Christians persecute even bad people." Granted; it should not be permitted. But is it right to raise this as an objection to the authorities that were established precisely for this purpose? Or shall we do away with the Apostle? Or do your books lack those lines that I quoted? "But," you will say, "you ought not to be in communion with such people." What follows then? Were you not in communion with Flavian, once the vicar for Africa,[386] a man of your sect, because, in obedience to the laws, he put to death the guilty persons he had found. "But," you will say, "you stir up the Roman emperors against us." On the contrary, you stir them up against yourselves, for you have dared to tear apart with your schism the Church of which they are

---

386. Flavian (Virius Nicomachus Flavianus) was an influential Roman politician and grammarian, a pagan vicar of Africa who, according to Augustine, was partial to the Donatists.

members, as was foretold so long before. For it was said of Christ, *And the kings of the earth will adore him* (Ps 72:11). And you still stubbornly dare to rebaptize. But our people seek protection from the established authority against the illicit and private acts of violence, acts over which you yourselves, who do not do such actions, sorrow and groan. Our people do this, not in order to persecute you, but to defend themselves. The apostle Paul acted in the same way against the Jews who were conspiring to kill him, before the Roman empire was Christian, so that he was also given the protection of armed guards.[387] But at whatever occasion those emperors know the evil of your schism, they set up against you whatever they choose in accord with their concern and authority. For it is not without reason that they carry the sword; they are, after all, God's servants to carry out his wrath in punishing wrongdoers.[388] Finally, even if some of ours do these actions without Christian moderation, we are displeased, but we still do not leave the Catholic Church on account of them if we cannot cleanse it before the last day when the straw will be separated from the wheat,[389] since even you did not leave the sect of Donatus on account of Optatus when you did not dare to expel him.

9. But you say after all, "Why do you want us to be united with you if we are criminals?" Because you are still alive and can be corrected if you would want to. For, when you are united to us, that is, to the Church of Christ, the heritage of Christ, whose possession is the ends of the earth,[390] you are corrected so that you have life from the root. For the Apostle speaks in this way of the branches that were broken off, *God, after all, is able to reinsert them* (Rom 11:23). Change, then, in that respect in which you were in dissent, though the sacraments that you have are holy, since they are the same in all. Hence, we want you to change from your misguided ways, that is, so that your cut-off branches may be again attached to the root. For the sacraments, which you have not changed, are approved by us as you have them. Otherwise, when we want to correct your wickedness, we would do a sacrilegious injury to those mysteries of Christ, which were not spoiled in your wickedness. For even Saul had not spoiled the anointing he had received, the anointing to which King David, the devout servant of God, showed such great respect.[391] For this reason we, who want to restore you to the root, do not rebaptize you; we, nonetheless, accept as valid the form of the branch that has been cut off, if it has not been changed. Though the branch is whole, it still can in no way bear fruit without the root. One question concerns the persecutions that you say you suffer from such great gentleness and mildness on the part of ours, though your people actually do as private citizens forbidden acts that are worse; another question concerns baptism since we do not ask where it exists, but where it is beneficial. For wherever it is, it is the same, but the one

---

387. See Acts 23:12-24.
388. See Rom 13:4.
389. See Mt 3:12.
390. See Ps 2:8.
391. See 2 Sam 1:1-16.

who receives it is not always the same wherever he is. And so, we detest the private sinfulness of human beings in the schism, but we reverence the baptism of Christ everywhere. For, if deserters carry off with them the standards of the emperor, once they have either been punished by condemnation or corrected by pardon, the standards are received back intact, if they remained intact. And if anything needs to be more carefully investigated concerning this matter, it is another question, as I said. For in these areas we ought to do what the Church of God does.

10. The question is whether yours or ours is the Church of God. Hence, we must ask from the beginning why you began the schism. If you do not write back, I have, I believe, an easy case before God. For I sent to a man who I heard is, apart from the schism, a good and liberally educated person a letter that attempts to restore peace. It is up to you to see what you should reply to God, whose patience should now be praised, but whose judgment is to be feared in the end. But if you write back with the same care with which you see I have written to you, the mercy of God will be with you in order that at some point the error that divides us may perish out of the love of peace and by reason of the truth. Remember what I said about the Rogatists who are said to call you Firmians, just as you call us Macarians.[392] Nor have I said anything about your bishop of Rusicca; he is reported to have had an agreement with Firmus about the safety of his people so that the gates were opened for him and the Catholics were handed to him for slaughter and countless other things. Stop, then, exaggerating by these familiar arguments the actions of human beings, whether rumored or known for facts. For you see what I pass over in silence regarding your people in order that the discussion may focus on the origin of the schism where the whole case rests. May the Lord God inspire you with thoughts of peace, my lovable and beloved brother. Amen.

---

392. Rogatus was the Donatist bishop of Cartenna in Mauritania Caesariensis; disgusted with the conduct of the Circumcellions, he broke away from the Donatists with several other bishops to form the sect of the Rogatists. See Letter 93, 3, 11. Firmus was an African chief who revolted in 372; he was supported by the Donatists and persecuted the Rogatists. Macarius was the imperial commissioner who persecuted the Donatists.

LETTER 89

Augustine to Festus, a Roman official in Africa (405-411)

Between 405 and 411 Augustine wrote to Festus, a Roman official and Catholic layman in Africa. He explains to Festus the great reasonableness with which the Catholic Church works not only for her own defense against heretics, but also for the correction of them (paragraph 1). He points out the falsity of the Donatists' claim to be suffering persecution and martyrdom, since it is not suffering alone that makes a martyr (paragraph 2). The Donatists complain about the imperial laws that are brought to bear upon them, though they first appealed to Emperor Constantine against Caecilian and persisted in their position after having lost their case (paragraph 3). Furthermore, the Donatists regard the whole Christian world as guilty for not having known about the traditors in Africa, though no one is guilty because of an unknown sin (paragraph 4). Augustine argues that the validity of baptism does not depend upon righteousness of the minister of the sacrament, but upon Christ (paragraph 5). The Donatists resist the medicine of the Church either by wild savagery or by quiet lethargy, while the Church shows them her maternal love (paragraph 6). Nor does the Catholic Church receive into herself Donatist converts just as they were, but as transformed (paragraph 7). Finally, Augustine urges Festus to cooperate with him in dealing with the Donatists around Hippo (paragraph 8).

To his most beloved, honorable, and venerable lord, Festus, Augustine sends greetings in the Lord.

1. In defense of their error and damnable schism and doctrine, which has been proven false in every way, human beings are so presumptuous that they do not cease to plot against and threaten so boldly the Catholic Church, which seeks their salvation. How much more just and necessary it is, then, that those who defend the truth of Christian peace and unity, which is evident to all, even to those who pretend not to see it and who attack it, work constantly and vigorously, not only for the defense of those who are already Catholic, but also for the correction of those who are not as yet! For if stubbornness tries to maintain an insuperable strength, what great strength ought that constancy have that both knows it pleases God and certainly cannot be displeasing to prudent human beings in that good that it does perseveringly and without flagging?

2. But what is more unhappy and more perverse in the conduct of the Donatists, who boast that they suffer persecution, than not merely their failing to be ashamed over the coercion of their wickedness, but also their wanting to be praised for it? They either do not know out of an amazing blindness or pretend that they do not know out of a damnable fanaticism that it is not the punishment, but the reason for suffering it that makes true martyrs. And I would say this

against those who were only wrapped in the fog of heretical error—for which sacrilege they would pay the penalties they fully deserve–and have not dared to injure anyone out of any violent madness. But what should I say against these whose pernicious perversity is either repressed by a fear of fines or is taught by exile how the Church is spread everywhere, as it was predicted that she would be,[393] the Church that they prefer to attack rather than recognize? And if those things that they suffer through a most merciful discipline are compared to those deeds that they commit out of a mindless fury, who would not see which of us should rather be called the persecutors? After all, by the very fact that bad children live wicked lives, even if they do not lay their hands on their parents in violence, they persecute more grievously their loving parents than when a father or a mother compels them all the more to lead a good life without any pretense to the extent that they love them more.

3. There exist the most solid proofs in public records, which you can read if you wish; in fact, I beg and exhort you to read them. They prove that their predecessors who first split away from the peace of the Church dared on their own initiative to accuse Caecilian[394] by means of Anulinus, the proconsul,[395] before the emperor Constantine. And, of course, if they had won in that case, what was Caecilian going to suffer from the emperor except the sentence he pronounced against those men after they had lost? But if, for example, after they brought their accusations and won their case, Caecilian and his colleagues were expelled from the sees they held or were punished more severely, because they also continued in their rebellion—for the imperial authority could not have ignored the convicted who continued in opposition—then these people would have spread about word of their foresight and solicitous concern for the Church as something worthy of praise. But now, since they lost because they could not prove the charges they brought, if they suffer anything in return for their wickedness, they call it persecution. Nor do they hold in check such great fury of the wicked, but even seek the honor of martyrs, as if the Catholic Christian emperors carry out anything else against their most stubborn wickedness than the judgment of Constantine, before whom they were on their own initiative the accusers of Caecilian and whose authority they preferred to all the overseas bishops. For they brought a case belonging to the Church, not to them, but to Constantine. And after he granted them an episcopal court in the city of Rome in which they first lost, they again brought the accusation before him. And they appealed to him from a second episcopal court granted them in Arles, and having lastly been condemned by him, they remained in their perversity. I think that, if the devil himself were so often defeated by the authority of a judge whom he had chosen on his own, he would not be so impudent as to persist in that case!

---

393. See Ps 2:8.
394. Caecilian was the Catholic bishop of Carthage at the time when the Donatist schism began.
395. Anulinus (Caius Annius Anullinus) was the governor of Africa Proconsularis from 302 to 305.

4. But these judgments are regarded as human, and they say that the judges can be circumvented, deceived, and even corrupted. Why, then, do they still accuse the Christian world and why do they blacken its reputation by some charges against the traditors? For the Christian world, of course, could and ought to have believed only the judges who had been chosen rather than the litigants who lost their case. Those judges have to present their own case, whether good or bad, before God. But what did the Church spread throughout the whole world do? She is judged to be in need of rebaptism by these Donatists for no other reason than that in that case in which she could not judge what was true, she thought that she should believe those who were able to judge rather than those who, though they lost, did not yield. O the great crime of all the nations, which God promised would be blessed in the offspring of Abraham[396] and which he has shown us as he promised! With one voice they ask, "Why do you want to rebaptize us?" And they are told, "Because you do not know who surrendered the sacred books in Africa, and on that point on which you were ignorant you chose to believe the judges rather than the accusers." If no one is made guilty by the crime of another, how does a crime committed by anyone in Africa become that of the whole world? If no one is made guilty by a crime he does not know, how could the whole world come to know the crime of the judges or of the guilty? You who have a heart, be the judges. This is the justice of heresy: Because the whole world does not condemn a crime that it does not know, does the sect of Donatus condemn the whole world without a hearing? But surely it is enough for the world to hold onto the promises of God and to see that there is fulfilled in itself what the prophets predicted so long before. It is enough to recognize the Church in the same Scriptures in which Christ is recognized as her king. For, where we find such predictions about Christ as we read were fulfilled in the Gospel, there we read predictions about the Church that we now see are fulfilled throughout the whole world.

5. But perhaps someone among the wise will be upset because the Donatists often say of baptism that it is then the true baptism of Christ when it is conferred by a righteous person. And yet, on this point the whole world has the most evident truth of the Gospel, where John says, *He who sent me to baptize with water said to me, He upon whom you see the Spirit descending like a dove and remaining over him is the one who baptizes with the Holy Spirit* (Jn 1:33). For this reason the Church is secure and does not place her hope in a human being for fear that she may fall under that condemnation where it says, *Cursed is everyone who places his hope in a human being* (Jer 17:5). Rather she places her hope in Christ who took up the form of the servant in such a way that he did not lose the form of God.[397] Of him scripture said, *He is the one who baptizes*. Hence, it is not any human minister of Christ's baptism, whatever burden of guilt

---

396. See Gn 22:16.
397. See Phil 2:6-7.

he may bear, but it is the one upon whom the dove descended who baptizes. But such great absurdity follows upon those people who think these foolish thoughts that they find no place where they may escape from it. For they admit that baptism is valid and true when some criminal whose crimes are hidden baptizes in their sect, and for this reason we say to them, "Who baptizes in that case?" and they have no answer but, "God." For they cannot say that an adulterer sanctifies anyone. We reply to them, "If, then, when a human being who is obviously righteous baptizes, it is he who sanctifies; but when a human being who is a hidden sinner baptizes, then it is not he, but God who sanctifies; those who are baptized ought to hope to be baptized by hidden sinners rather than by obviously good persons. For God sanctifies much better than any righteous human being. But if it is absurd that anyone about to be baptized should want to be baptized by a hidden sinner rather than by an obviously chaste person, it, of course, remains that, no matter who comes along from among human ministers, baptism is valid because he upon whom the dove descended is the one who baptizes."

6. And yet, though such clear truth strikes the ears and hearts of human beings, such a great whirlpool of bad habit pulls down certain people that they prefer to resist all authorities and reasons rather than to agree. But they resist in two ways: either by wild raging or by being lazy. What, then, does the medicine of the Church do here, as she seeks the salvation of all out of her motherly love, caught up as it were among those who are manic and those who are lethargic? Ought she or can she scorn them or leave them? She is necessarily bothersome to both, because she is an enemy to neither. For the manic cases do not want to be restrained, and the lethargic do not want to be stirred up. But loving concern continues to chastise the manic and to stimulate the lethargic, but to love them both. Both are offended, but both are loved; both are bothered. As long as they are ill, they are angry, but once healed, both are grateful.

7. Finally, we do not, as they think and as they boast, receive them such as they were, but entirely changed, because they do not begin to be Catholics unless they have ceased to be heretics. For their sacraments are not opposed to us, since they are common to them along with us, because they are not human, but divine. Their peculiar error, which they have swallowed wrongly, must be removed, not the sacraments, which they similarly received. They carry and have these sacraments for their own punishment to the extent that they have them more unworthily, but they do, nonetheless, have them. After having abandoned their error and having corrected the wrong of schism, they cross over from heresy to the peace of the Church, which they did not have and without which what they had spelled their destruction. But if when they cross over they are pretending, this is not now a matter for our judgment, but for God's. And yet, though some are thought to be pretending because they crossed over to us out of fear of authority, they are later in some temptations shown to be the sort of persons who are better than certain others who were Catholics at an earlier date. It is not true that nothing is accomplished when it is accomplished with violence. Nor is the wall of hardened

habit stormed by merely human threats, but faith and mental intelligence are also instructed by divine authorities and arguments.

8. Since this is so, Your Graciousness should know that your people, who are in the territory of Hippo, are still Donatists and that your letter achieved nothing with them. There is, however, no need to write why it had no effect. But send one of your domestics or friends to whose reliability you can entrust this. Let him first come, not to those areas, but to us, without their knowing this, and after having first discussed with us a plan, let him do, with the Lord's help, what seems necessary to do. For, in doing this, we do not act only on their behalf, but also on behalf of our people who have already become Catholics, for whom their proximity is so dangerous that we absolutely cannot ignore it. I could, of course, have written this briefly, but I wanted you to have a piece of our writing by which you yourself not only might know the reason for my concern, but also might have something to reply to anyone who dissuades you from working vigorously for the correction of your people and who slanders us because we want such things. If I did that needlessly, because you had already learned such things or have yourself thought of them, or if I was a burden because I thrust upon you, who are so busy with public concerns, a long letter, I ask your pardon, provided that you do not, nonetheless, reject what I have suggested or asked for. May the mercy of God protect you in that way.

LETTER 93

Augustine to Vincent, the Rogatist bishop of Cartenna in Mauretania Caesariensis (407-408)

In 407 or 408 Augustine wrote to Vincent, the Rogatist[398] bishop of Cartenna in Mauretania Caesariensis. Augustine had, he believes, received a letter from Vincent, whom he had known from his early days in Carthage and who is now the successor of Rogatus, who had split away from the Donatists. He points out the benefit for many derived from the use of secular power to check and correct the Donatists (paragraph 1). In fact, even some of the Circumcellions have become sincere Catholics (paragraph 2). Though the use of fear does not benefit everyone, the Church should not give up all use of it (paragraph 3). God himself teaches us with both severity and gentleness (paragraph 4). Augustine turns to scriptural passages that support the use of force against the schismatics (paragraph 5) and shows how the same actions are good or bad depending on their motives (paragraphs 6 and 7). It is not always praiseworthy to suffer persecution, but only when one suffers on account of justice (paragraph 8).

Though the New Testament reveals no instance of an appeal to secular power for the Church, the Old Testament books foreshadow such action (paragraph 9). Both Catholics and Donatists favor the laws passed against the pagans, and the Donatists may very well outdo the pagans in wickedness (paragraph 10). The Rogatists are, Augustine admits, less violent that the Donatists, though that may be due to their smaller numbers (paragraph 11). The Donatists went so far as to appeal to Julian the apostate[399] for help against the Maximianists (paragraph 12). The Donatists repeatedly appealed to the emperor and still refused to abide by his decision (paragraph 13). The judgment that the Donatists demanded from Constantine, which turned out to be against them, holds against the present Donatists and Rogatists (paragraph 14). Augustine insists that, even if Caecilian were guilty as charged, his sin could not defile the rest of the Church and justify schism (paragraph 15).

The implementation of the imperial laws has brought about the conversion of many schismatics (paragraph 16). These results led Augustine to change his mind about the use of force against the schismatics (paragraph 17). Those brought into the Catholic unity through fear are now often grateful for such coercion (paragraph 18). Augustine argues that he was right not to oppose his fellow bishops on the use of force (paragraph 19). Augustine invokes Paul's admonition that we should do good if we want to be free from fear of civil authorities (paragraph 20). Though Scripture promised the spread of the Church throughout the whole world, the nine or ten remaining Rogatists are confined to Cartenna (paragraph 21).

---

398. See p. 193, n. 392.
399. Julian was Roman emperor from 361 to 363. He rejected Christianity, and because of this he became remembered as Julian the Apostate.

Given that the Christian faith has been proclaimed almost to the ends of the earth, it is ridiculous to claim that a person can be cleansed from his sins only in Cartenna (paragraph 22). Augustine rejects the Rogatist claim to being Catholic on the basis of their observance of all the commandments and sacraments (paragraph 23). The Rogatists have less claim than the Donatists to be the Church of Christ (paragraph 24). The Rogatists' argument to be the true Church can be turned against them (paragraph 25). Though the Rogatists might claim to be holier because of the fewer numbers, Augustine insists that they cannot claim to be the Church that Scripture foretold would be very numerous (paragraph 26). So too, they cannot appeal to the few who were saved with Lot (paragraph 27).

If one looks for the Church in the Scriptures, no one can justifiably separate himself from communion with the Church spread through all the nations (paragraphs 28 to 30). Augustine argues against the use Vincent made of a text from Hilary of Poitiers[400] (paragraph 31 and 32). He argues that sinners present in the Church do not harm the elect, using the parables of the weeds amid the grain, the chaff amid the wheat, and the bad fishes in the net with the good ones (paragraphs 33 and 34). Augustine warns Vincent against taking anything from writers of the Church and using it against the canonical Books (paragraphs 35 and 36). Augustine explains various texts from Cyprian that seem to favor the Donatist position (paragraphs 37 to 42). He also points to the writings of Tychonius, a Donatist, who actually defended the Catholic Church (paragraphs 43 and 44). Augustine argues that, if the sins of others defile anyone in the Church, then the Church perished long before Cyprian (paragraph 45).

Though the Donatists have the sacraments, they lack the Spirit who is the source of unity (paragraph 46). Augustine distinguishes between the baptism of John and the baptism of Christ (paragraph 47) and explains why Paul baptized people whom John had baptized, though one should not baptize again those baptized by a heretic or a drunkard (paragraph 48). After all, even among the few Rogatists there are probably some drunkards (paragraph 49). Augustine concedes that the imperial laws against the Donatists can be misused (paragraph 50) and invites Vincent to come over to the Catholic Church which he holds to be the true Church (paragraph 51). It involves no shame to be corrected (paragraph 52), and the Church welcomes those who repent (paragraph 53).

To his most dear brother, Vincent, Augustine sends greetings.

1, 1. I received a letter that seems probably to be yours, for someone who is clearly a Catholic Christian brought it, and he would, I think, not dare to lie to me. But even if it is perhaps not your letter, I thought that I ought to reply to the one who wrote it. I am now more eager for and in search of quiet than back then

---

400. Hilary was the bishop of Poitiers from about 350 to 367 and a champion against Arianism. His two great works are *On the Synods* and *On the Trinity*, which he wrote while in exile.

when you knew me as a young man at Carthage, when Rogatus, whose successor you are, was still alive. But the Donatists are excessively restless, and I think that it is not useless that they be held in check and corrected by the authorities established by God. After all, we rejoice over the correction of many who so sincerely hold and defend the Catholic unity and are happy that they have been set free from their former error so that we look upon them with great satisfaction. Given the force of habit they would, nonetheless, by no means have been changed for the better, if they were not struck with this fear and turned their worried mind to a consideration of the truth. Otherwise, they would perhaps suffer these temporal troubles with a fruitless and vain endurance, not for righteousness, but for the misguidedness and presumption of human beings, and they would afterwards find before God only the well-deserved punishments of the wicked, who scorned his gentle warning and fatherly scourges. And so, after having become docile because of this thought, they found among all the nations the Church, which was promised, not in human lies and fables, but in God's Books, and they saw it presented before their own eyes, and they did not doubt that Christ, who was foretold in those Books, is now above the heavens, even though he is not seen. Ought I to have begrudged salvation to these people and called my colleagues back from such fatherly care, as a result of which we see many blame their former blindness? They believed that Christ had been exalted above the heavens, even though they did not see this, but they denied his glory spread over all the earth, even though they saw it, though the prophet combined both of them in one sentence with such great clarity. He said, *Be exalted, O God, above the heavens, and may your glory be over all the earth* (Ps 108:6).

2. If, then, we scorned and endured these people who were once our fierce enemies and who were attacking our peace and quiet with various sorts of violence and ambushes, so that we devised and did nothing at all that might be able to frighten and correct them, we would really have repaid evil with evil. For, if anyone sees his enemy out of his mind due to dangerous fevers run toward a cliff, would he not repay evil with evil if he allowed him to run in that way rather than if he took care to catch him and tie him up? And yet, he would seem most troublesome and hostile to him at the very time when he was most beneficial and merciful. But once he had recovered his health, he would obviously thank him more profusely to the extent that he had felt that the man had spared him the less. Oh, if I could show you how many sincere Catholics we now have from the Circumcellions![401] They condemn their former life and wretched error, because of which they thought that they did for the Church of God whatever they did in their restless rashness! They would, nonetheless, not have been brought to this healthy position if they were not bound, like men out of their minds, by the chains of these laws that you find displeasing. What about that other form of the most grave disease of those who do not, of course, have this turbulent audacity,

---

401. See p.145, n. 307.

but are weighed down by long-standing apathy and say to us, "What you say is, of course, true; we have no answer to make, but it is hard for us to abandon the tradition of our parents"? Were they not to be disturbed for their salvation by the penalty of temporal chastisement in order that they might emerge, as it were, from their sluggish sleepiness and wake up in the salvation of the Church's unity? How many of them are now rejoicing with us and blame the former burden of their destructive activity! How many of them admit that we ought to have been troublesome to them for fear that they would perish in that way from the disease of longstanding habit as if from a deadly sleep.

3. But these measures, after all, do not benefit certain ones. Should we, then, neglect the art of medicine because some have an incurable plague? You pay attention only to those who are so hard that they do not accept even this discipline. For of them Scripture said, *In vain have I scourged your children; they have not accepted discipline* (Jer 2:30). I think, nonetheless, that they were scourged out of love, not out of hatred. But you ought also to pay attention to the many over whose salvation we rejoice. For, if they were frightened and did not learn anything, it would seem like a wicked tyranny. Again, if they learned something and were not frightened, they would be lazy about moving to take the path to salvation, since they were hardened by their long-standing habit. For, as we well know, when they were given reasons and the truth was shown to them by the testimonies of God, many replied to us that they desired to pass over into the communion of the Catholic Church, but feared the violent hostilities of the wicked. They, of course, ought to have scorned these hostilities for the sake of righteousness and eternal life, but we must support and not despair over the weakness of such persons until they become strong. Nor should we forget that the Lord himself said to the weak Peter, *You cannot now follow me, but you will follow me afterwards* (Jn 13:36). But when the doctrine of salvation is combined with a beneficial fear, not only so that the light of the truth drives out the darkness of error, but also so that the force of fear breaks the chains of bad habit, we rejoice, as I said, over the salvation of many who bless us and thank God. For, having fulfilled his promise that the kings of the earth would serve Christ,[402] he has in this way cured the sick, in this way healed the weak.

2, 4. Not everyone who is merciful is a friend, nor is everyone who scourges an enemy. *Better are the wounds from a friend than the spontaneous kisses of an enemy* (Prv 27:6). It is better to love with severity than to deceive with leniency. It is more beneficial to take bread away from a hungry man if, when sure of his food, he would neglect his salvation, than to break bread with a hungry man in order that he might be led astray and consent to injustice. And someone who ties down a crazy person and who rouses a lazy person loves them both, though he is a bother to both. Who can love us more than God? And he, nonetheless, does not cease not only to teach us with gentleness, but also to frighten us for our salva-

---

402. See Dn 7:27.

tion. He often adds to the gentle salves by which he comforts us the most biting medicine of tribulation; he trains even the pious and devout patriarchs with famine. He afflicts the rebellious people with more severe punishments.[403] Though he was asked three times, he does not remove from the Apostle the thorn in his flesh, in order that he may make virtue perfect in weakness.[404] Let us also love our enemies because this is just, and God commanded it in order that we might be *children of our Father who is in heaven, who makes his sun rise over the good and the evil and sends rain upon the just and the unjust* (Mt 5:45). But just as we praise his gifts, so let us bear in mind his scourges upon those whom he loves.

5. You think that no one ought to be forced into righteousness, though you read that the head of the household said to his servants, *Whomever you find, force them to come in* (Lk 14:23), though you read that he who was first Saul and afterwards Paul was forced to come to know and to hold onto the truth by the great violence of Christ who compelled him,[405] unless you perhaps think that money or any possession is dearer to human beings than this light that we perceive by these eyes. Laid low by the voice from heaven, he did not recover this light that he lost suddenly, except when he was incorporated into the holy Church. And you think that one should employ no force upon a man in order that he might be set free from the harmfulness of error, though you see that God himself, than whom no one loves us more to our benefit, does this in the most obvious examples and though you hear Christ saying, *No one comes to me unless the Father has drawn him* (Jn 6:44). This takes place in the hearts of all who turn to him out of fear of God's wrath. And you know that at times a thief scatters grain to lead cattle away and that a shepherd at times calls wandering cattle back to the herd with a whip.

6. Did not Sarah rather punish the rebellious serving girl when she was given the power? And she, of course, did not cruelly hate her since she had previously made her a mother by her own generosity; rather, she was subduing pride in her in a way conducive to her salvation. But you are not unaware that these two women, Sarah and Hagar, and their two sons, Isaac and Ishmael, symbolize spiritual and carnal persons.[406] And though we read that the serving girl and her son suffered ill treatment from Sarah, the apostle Paul, nonetheless, says that Isaac suffered persecution from Ishmael, *But as at that time the one who was born according to the flesh persecuted the one who was born according to the Spirit, so it is now* (Gal 4:29). Thus those who can may understand that the Catholic Church suffers persecution from the pride and wickedness of carnal persons, whom it tries to correct by temporal troubles and fears. Whatever, then, the true and lawful mother does, even if it is felt to be harsh and bitter, she does not repay evil with evil, but applies the good of discipline to expel the evil of iniquity, not

---

403. See Gn 12:10, 26:1, 41:54, 42:1; 43:1.
404. See 2 Cor 12:7-9.
405. See Acts 9:3-7.
406. See Gal 4:24-26.

out of harmful hatred, but out of healing love. Since the good and the evil do the same things and suffer the same things, they must be distinguished, not by their actions and punishments, but by their motives. Pharaoh wore down the people of God with hard labor;[407] Moses punished with hard chastisements the same people when they acted sinfully.[408] What they did was similar, but they did not similarly will to do good. Pharaoh was inflated with tyranny; Moses was inflamed with love. Jezebel killed the prophets; Elijah killed the false prophets.[409] I think that the merits of the agents were different and that the merits of the slain were different.

7. Also look at the time of the New Testament when the very gentleness of love was not only to be preserved in the heart, but was also to be manifested in the light of day, when Christ ordered the sword of Peter back into its scabbard and showed that it ought not to be drawn from its scabbard, not even for Christ.[410] We read, nonetheless, not only that the Jews beat the apostle Paul,[411] but also that the Greeks also beat the Jew Sosthenes in defense of Paul.[412] Does not the similarity of their action in some sense link both of them together, though the dissimilarity of their motive separates them? In fact, *God did not spare his own Son, but handed him over for all of us* (Rom 8:32). And it is said of the Son himself, *He loved me and handed himself over for me* (Gal 2:20). And it is said of Judas that Satan entered into him in order that he would hand over Christ.[413] Since, therefore, the Father also handed over his own Son and Christ handed over his own body and Judas handed over his Lord, why in this act of handing over is God loving and the man guilty, if not because in the one action that they did there is not one motive on account of which they did it? There were three crosses in the one place: on one a thief who would be saved, on another a thief who would be condemned, on the middle one Christ who would save the one and condemn the other.[414] What is more alike than those three crosses? What is more unlike than these three who hung on them? Paul was handed over to be imprisoned and chained,[415] but Satan is certainly worse than a prison guard. Paul himself, nonetheless, handed over to him a man *for the destruction of the flesh in order that his spirit may be saved on the day of the Lord Jesus* (1 Cor 5:5). And what do we say here? Look, a cruel man handed Paul over to someone comparatively gentle, while the merciful Paul handed a man over to someone crueler. Let us learn, my brothers, to distinguish the minds of the agents in their similar actions so that we do not, with our eyes closed, criticize unfairly and accuse the good-hearted

---

407. See Ex 5:6-18.
408. See Ex 32:25-38.
409. See 1 Kgs 18:4-40.
410. See Mt 26:52.
411. See Acts 16:22-23.
412. See Acts 18:17.
413. See Jn 13:2.
414. See Lk 23:33; Jn 19:18.
415. See Acts 16:23-24.

in place of the guilty. So too, when the same Apostle said that he handed over certain people *to Satan in order that they might learn not to blaspheme* (1 Tm 1:20), did he repay evil with evil, or did he rather judge that it was a good deed to correct the evil, even by means of an evil?

8. If it were always praiseworthy to suffer persecution, it would have been enough for the Lord to say, *Blessed are they who suffer persecution,* without adding, *on account of justice* (Mt 5:10). So too, if it were always blameworthy to persecute, it would not be written in the Holy Books, *I will persecute him who slanders his neighbor in secret* (Ps 101:5). At times, then, the one who suffers persecution is unjust, and the one who persecutes is just. But it is clear that the evil have always persecuted the good and the good have always persecuted the evil: the former by harming them unjustly, the latter by showing concern for them through discipline; the former savagely, the latter in moderation; the former in the service of desire, the latter in that of love. For a torturer does not worry about how he slashes, but a surgeon considers how he cuts. After all, the surgeon aims at health, the torturer at infection. Wicked men killed the prophets, and prophets killed wicked men. The Jews flogged Christ,[416] and Christ flogged the Jews.[417] The apostles were handed over by men to a human power, and the apostles handed over men to the power of Satan. In all these actions what do we consider but who acted for the truth and who for iniquity, who acted for the sake of harm and who for the sake of correction?

3, 9. Neither in the Gospels nor in the letters of the apostles is there found a case in which something was asked for from the kings of the earth in defense of the Church against the enemies of the Church. Who would deny this? But this prophecy was not yet fulfilled: *And now, kings, have understanding; you who judge the earth, be warned; serve the Lord in fear* (Ps 2:10-11). For what is said a little before in the same Psalm was still being fulfilled, *Why have the nations raged and the people plotted in vain? The kings of earth have arisen, and the princes have gathered together against the Lord and against his anointed one* (Ps 2:1-2).[418] If, nonetheless, past actions in the books of the prophets were symbols of those to come, that king who was called Nebuchadnezzar symbolized both times: both that of the Church under the apostles and that of the Church at present. During the times of the apostles and the martyrs there was fulfilled what was symbolized when the previously mentioned king forced good and righteous people to worship the idol and cast them into the flames when they refused. But now there is being fulfilled what is symbolized a little later by the same king when, after having been converted to honor the true God, he decreed in his kingdom that whoever blasphemed against the God of Shadrach, Meshach,

---

416. See Mt 27:26; Mk 15:15; Jn 19:1.
417. See Jn 2:15.
418. The Latin for "anointed one" is *Christus,* so that the Latin seems more clearly to speak of Christ.

and Abednego would face appropriate punishments.[419] The earlier time of that king, therefore, signified the earlier times of non-believing kings, under whom the Christians suffered instead of the unbelievers, but the later time of that king signified the times of the later kings, who were now believers under whom the non-believers suffered instead of the Christians.

10. But clearly with those who are misled by the wicked and go astray under the name of Christ, we use a tempered severity, or rather gentleness, in order that Christ's sheep may not perhaps wander astray and need to be recalled to the flock in such a way. Thus by the threats of exile and fines they may be warned to consider what they suffer and why and may learn to prefer the Scriptures they read to the rumors and slanders of human beings. After all, who of us and who of you do not praise the laws passed by the emperors against the sacrifices of the pagans? And in that case a more severe penalty was surely established, for that impiety was, of course, a capital offense. But with regard to rebuking and stopping you the idea was that you should rather be admonished to withdraw from error than be punished for a crime. For one can perhaps say of you what the Apostle said of the Jews: *I bear witness to them that they have zeal for God, but not in accord with knowledge. For, not knowing the righteousness of God and wanting to establish their own, they were not subject to the righteousness of God* (Rom 10:2-3). What else do you also want but to establish your own righteousness when you say that only those whom you were able to baptize are made righteous? In this statement, then, of the Apostle that he spoke about the Jews, you differ from the Jews because you have the Christian sacraments that they still lack. But with regard to his words, *Not knowing the righteousness of God and wanting to establish their own*, and, *They have zeal for God, but not in accord with knowledge*, you are absolutely on a par with them, with the exception of those among you, whoever they are, who know the truth and out of passion for their error fight against the truth, which they too know perfectly well. The wickedness of these people may, of course, surpass idolatry. But since it is not easy to prove them guilty, for this evil lies hidden in their heart, you are all restrained with a milder severity, like people who are not extremely distant from us. And I would, in fact, say this either about all heretics who receive the Christian sacraments and dissent from the truth or unity of Christ or about all the Donatists.

11. But with regard to yourselves, who are not only generically called Donatists after Donatus, but also are specifically called Rogatists after Rogatus, you certainly seem to us less fierce, since you do not run wild with the savage bands of Circumcellions, but no wild animal is called tame if it injures no one because it lacks teeth or claws. You say that you do not want to act savagely; I suspect that you cannot. For you are so few in number that you would not dare to attack the multitudes opposed to you, even if you wanted to. But let us suppose that you do not want to do what you cannot. Let us suppose that you understand the

---

419. See Dn 3:1-21.91-96.

sentence of the Gospel where it is written, *If someone wants to take your tunic and to take you to court, give him your coat as well* (Mt 5:40), and let us suppose that you hold this idea in the sense that you think that you should resist those who persecute you, not only with no injury, but not even by means of the law. Rogatus, your founder, certainly either did not have this understanding or did not live according to it. For he fought with the fiercest persistence, even in legal arguments, for some possessions that were, as you claim, yours. Suppose that he were asked, "Who among the apostles ever defended his property in a public court when it was a question of the faith?" just as you asked in your letter, "Who among the apostles ever claimed the property of another when it was a question of the faith?" He would, of course, find no example of this action in the Divine Writings. But he would perhaps find some valid defense, if he held onto the true Church and did not impudently try to keep possession of something in the name of the true Church.

4, 12. But with regard to either obtaining or carrying out the commands of earthly authorities against heretics or schismatics, those from whom you separated yourselves were certainly the most fierce, both against you, to the extent we were able to hear, and against the Maximinanists, as we prove also by certain documents from various proceedings. But you were not yet separated from them when they said in their petition to Julian, the emperor, that in his eyes only justice has a place. And yet, they surely knew that he was an apostate and saw that he was so committed to the practice of idolatry that they either identified justice with idolatry or they could not deny that they had lied in a disgraceful fashion, when they said that in his eyes only justice has a place, for they saw that in his eyes idolatry occupied a large place. Granted that it was an error in speech, what do you say about the action itself? If one should ask for nothing just from the emperor, why did they ask from Julian what they thought was just?

13. Or ought one to petition the emperor only in order that each person might recover his own goods and not to accuse someone in order that he might be coerced by the emperor? Meanwhile, in seeking the restoration of one's own goods one departs from the example of the apostles, because none of them is found to have done this. But when your predecessors accused Caecilian, who was then bishop of the Church of Carthage, with whom they refused to be in communion as if he were a criminal, before the emperor Constantine through Anulinus, the proconsul, they were not seeking the recovery of their lost property, but were slanderously attacking an innocent man, as we view the matter and as the very outcome of the judicial proceedings reveals. What could they have done more outrageous than that? But if, as you incorrectly suppose, they handed over a man who was really a criminal to be tried by earthly authorities, why do you raise as an objection against us what your leaders first presumed to do? For we would not blame them because they did this, if they had not done it with a heart filled with hatred and bent on harm, but with the desire for improvement and correction. We, nonetheless, blame you without any hesitation because you

think it a crime that we make some complaint to a Christian emperor about the enemies of our communion, though the list of charges presented by your predecessors to Anulinus the proconsul, which were to be sent on to Constantine the emperor, was entitled as follows: "The Charges of the Catholic Church against the Crimes of Caecilian Submitted by the Sect of Majorinus."[420] But we blame them more for this because, on their own initiative, they accused Caecilian before the emperor, whereas they ought, of course, first to have convicted him before their colleagues across the sea. The emperor himself, after all, acted in a far more orderly fashion in referring to bishops a case against bishops that was brought to him. Nor did they want to be at peace with their brothers after they were defeated. But they again came to the same emperor and again brought charges before an earthly king, not only against Caecilian, but also against the bishops assigned to them as judges. And again they appealed to the same emperor against another decision of the bishops. Nor did they think that they should yield either to the truth or to peace when the emperor himself heard the case between both sides and pronounced judgment.

14. But what else would Constantine have decided against Caecilian and his companions, if they lost the case to your predecessors who accused them, but what he decided against those very men who, after they had on their own initiative brought accusations against them and could not prove the accusations that they wanted to, refused to submit to the truth, even when they lost their case? That emperor was the first to determine in this case that the possessions of those who lost their case and who were stubbornly opposed to unity should be confiscated. But if the emperor, for example, decreed something of the sort against the communion of Caecilian, had your predecessors brought accusations and won their case, you would want to be called guardians of the Church, defenders of peace and of unity. But when those who on their own initiative brought accusations could prove nothing against them and refused to submit to the embrace of peace offered them by which they might be corrected and welcomed back, the emperors issued such decrees, and your people decry the infamous crime and claim that no one should be forced into unity and that no one should repay evil with evil. What else is this than what someone wrote of you, "All we want is holiness."[421] And now it would not be hard or difficult to consider and see that the judgment and sentence of Constantine has force against you, for, when your predecessors accused Caecilian so many times before the emperor and did not prove their case, it was promulgated against you, and the other emperors, especially the Catholic Christian ones, necessarily follow it as often as your obstinacy necessarily forces them to take some measures.

---

420. Majorinus was the first Donatist bishop of Carthage; when he died in 313, he was succeeded by Donatus, from whom the Donatists took their name.
421. See below, 10, 43, where this line is attributed to Tychonius.

15. It would be easy to consider these ideas so that at some point you would say to yourselves: "If Caecilian was either innocent or could not be proven guilty, how did the Christian people, who are spread so far and wide, sin in this affair? Why was the Christian world not permitted to remain ignorant of what his accusers could not prove? Why are those people whom Christ sowed in his field, that is, in this world, and whom he ordered to grow amid the weeds until the harvest,[422] said not to be Christians? Why should so many thousands of believers in all the nations, whose multitude the Lord compared to the stars of the sky and the sand of the sea, those whom he promised would be blessed in the offspring of Abraham[423] and whom he has blessed as he promised, not be said to be Christians, because in this case in which they were not present for the hearing, they preferred to believe the judges who judged at their own risk rather than the litigants who lost? Surely no charge taints one who knows nothing of it. How could the faithful spread throughout the world have known of the crime of the traditors, when, even if their accusers knew of it, they were, nonetheless, unable to prove it to them? Their very ignorance quite easily proves them innocent of this crime. Why then are innocent people accused of false charges on the grounds that they did not know the crimes of others, whether they were true or false? What place remains for innocence if it is a crime of one's own not to know the crime of another? But if ignorance itself proves that the peoples of so many nations are innocent, how great a crime is it to be separated from communion with so many innocent persons? For the actions of guilty persons that cannot be shown to the innocent or believed by the innocent do not defile anyone, if, even when known, those actions are endured on account of fellowship with the innocent. For the good should not be abandoned on account of the evil; rather, the evil should be tolerated on account of the good. In this way the prophets tolerated those against whom they said so much, nor did they abandon participation in the sacraments of that people. In this way the Lord himself tolerated the guilty Judas up to his fitting end and permitted him to share the sacred supper with the innocent. In the same way the apostles tolerated those who preached Christ out of hatred, which is a vice of the devil himself.[424] In the same way Cyprian tolerated the greed of his colleagues,[425] which he called idolatry in accord with the apostle.[426] Finally, whatever was done at that time among the bishops, even if some of them perhaps knew of it, it is now not known by all of them, provided one side is not listened to rather than the other.[427] Why then do not all love peace?" You could very easily think of these matters, or perhaps you do also think of them. But it would be better that you love earthly possessions and consent to the truth out of fear of losing

---

422. See Mt 13:24-30.
423. See Gn 22:17-18.
424. See Phil 1:15-18.
425. Cyprian, Letter 55, 27.
426. See Col 3:5; Eph 5:5.
427. See Eph 6:9; Rom 2:11; Col 3:25.

them than that you love the most empty glory of human beings, which you think you lose if you consent to the truth.

5, 16. Now you see, therefore, if I am not mistaken, that one ought not to consider the fact that anyone is constrained, but whether that to which one is constrained is good or bad. I do not say that a person can be good against his will. I say, however, that by fearing what he does not want to suffer, he abandons the stubbornness that holds him back or is compelled to recognize the truth he had not known. Thus out of fear he either rejects the error for which he was fighting or seeks the truth that he did not know, and he now willingly holds what he did not want to hold. It would perhaps be superfluous to say this with any words if it were not shown to us by so many examples. We see that, not these or those human beings, but many cities were Donatist and are now Catholic, and they intensely hate the diabolical division and ardently desire unity.[428] They nonetheless became Catholic on the occasion of this fear, at which you are displeased, through the laws of the emperor, from Constantine, before whom your people first accused Caecilian on their own initiative, up to the present emperors, who decreed that the judgment of that man whom your predecessors chose, whom they preferred to the bishops as judges, should be most justly observed against you.

17. I yielded, therefore, to these examples, which my colleagues proposed to me. For my opinion originally was that no one should be forced to the unity of Christ, but that we should act with words, fight with arguments, and conquer by reason. Otherwise, we might have as false Catholics those whom we had known to be obvious heretics. But this opinion of mine was defeated, not by the words of its opponents, but by examples of those who offered proof. For the first argument against me was my own city.[429] Though it was entirely in the Donatist sect, it was converted to the Catholic unity out of fear of the imperial laws, and we now see that it detests the destructiveness of this stubbornness of yours so that no one would believe that it was ever a part of it. And it was the same with many other cities, which were reported to me by name, so that I might recognize by the very facts that one could correctly understand the words of Scripture as also applying to this case, *Give a wise man a chance, and he will become wiser* (Prv 9:9). For how many, as we know for certain, already wanted to be Catholics, because they were convinced by the clearest truth, but because they feared offending their own people, they daily postponed doing so! How many were bound, not by the truth, in which you never had much confidence, but by the heavy chain of inveterate habit, so that those words of God were fulfilled in them, *A difficult servant will not be corrected by words, for, even if he understands, he will not obey* (Prv 29:19)! How many thought that the true Church was the sect of Donatus because

---

428. The mass conversions of Donatists took place after the laws issued against the Donatists in February 405.

429. I.e., Thagaste.

security made them uninterested, reluctant, and lazy to gain knowledge of the Catholic truth! For how many did the rumors of slanderers close the entrance way when they spread it about that we offer something else on the altar of God! How many believed that it made no difference on which side one is a Christian and, therefore, remained on the side of Donatus, because they were born there, and no one forced them to leave it and cross over to the Catholic side!

18. The fright over these laws, in the promulgation of which kings serve the Lord in fear,[430] benefited all these people so that some now say, "We already wanted this, but thanks be to God who gave us the opportunity of finally doing it and cut away time for delaying." And others say, "We already knew that this was true, but we were held back by some sort of habit. Thanks be to the Lord who has broken our chains and has brought us to the bond of peace." Still others say, "We did not know that the truth was here, nor did we want to learn of it, but fear made us concentrate on coming to know it. For we were afraid that we would suffer the loss of temporal goods without any gain of eternal ones. Thanks be to the Lord who shook us free of our negligence by the goad of fear in order that we at least might be worried and seek what we never cared to know in our security." Others say, "We were deterred from entering by false rumors, and we would not have known they were false if we did not enter, nor would we have entered if we were not forced. Thanks be to the Lord who removed our fearfulness by his scourge and has taught us by experience how vain and empty were the reports that deceitful rumors spread about his Church. For this reason we now believe that those charges were also false that the authors of this heresy raised, since their successors have made up false charges and worse ones." Others say, "We, of course, thought that it made no difference where we professed faith in Christ, but thanks be to the Lord who has gathered us back from our schism and has shown us that it is fitting that the one God be worshiped in unity."

19. Should I, then, have set myself against my colleagues to speak against them in order to impede these gains for the Lord so that the sheep of Christ, who were wandering astray in your mountains and hills, that is, in the swellings of your pride, would not be gathered into the flock of peace where there is *one flock and one shepherd* (Jn 10:16)? Should I really have spoken against this providential care so that you would not lose the possessions you call yours and so that you might securely outlaw Christ? Should I have done this so that you might create your testaments by Roman law and so that you might break by your slanderous charges the testament established by divine law with the patriarchs, where it is written, *In your offspring all nations will be blessed* (Gn 26:4)? Should I have done this so that in buying and selling you might freely make contracts and so that you might dare to divide for yourselves what Christ bought when he was sold? Should I have done this so that what any of you has given to anyone is valid and so that what the God of gods has given to his children, whom he called

---

430. See Ps 2:11.

from the rising of the sun to its setting,[431] is not valid? Should I have done this so that you are not sent into exile from the land of your body, while you try to make Christ an exile from the kingdom purchased by his blood, *from sea to sea and from the river to the ends of the world* (Ps 72:8)? On the contrary, let the kings of the earth serve Christ, even by issuing laws in Christ's favor! Your predecessors denounced Caecilian and his companions to the kings of the earth to be punished for crimes that were not true. Let the lions turn around to crush the bones of the slanderers, and let not Daniel himself, who was proven innocent and set free from the lions' pit where they are perishing, intercede for them.[432] After all, one who prepares a pit for his neighbor will himself fall into it with greater justice.[433]

6, 20. While you are still living in this flesh, rescue yourself, my brother, from the wrath to come for the stubborn and proud. When the terror of temporal authorities attacks the truth, it is a glorious trial for the brave and the righteous, but a dangerous temptation for the weak. But when the authorities proclaim the truth, it is a useful admonition for misguided, but intelligent people, and a useless affliction for the mindless. *There is, nonetheless, no authority except from God. But one who is opposed to an authority is opposed to God's governance. For princes are not a terror for good conduct, but for bad. Do you want to have no fear of authority? Do good, and you will have praise from it.* (Rom 13:1-3) For, if an authority favoring the truth corrects someone, that person who was corrected receives praise from it. Or if an authority hostile to the truth rages against someone, the person who is crowned as victor receives praise from this. But you are not doing good in order that you need have no fear of authority, unless it is perhaps good to sit and not to speak ill against one brother, but against all your brothers located in all the nations, to whom the prophets, Christ, and the apostles bore witness. For we read, *In your offspring all the nations will be blessed* (Gn 26:4), and we read, *From the rising of the sun to its setting a clean offering will be made to my name, because my name has been glorified among the nations, says the Lord* (Mal 1:11). Notice the words *says the Lord*; it does not say "says Donatus" or "Rogatus" or "Vincent" or "Hilary" or "Ambrose," or "Augustine" but *says the Lord*. And we read, *And in him will be blessed all the tribes of the earth; all the nations will proclaim his greatness. Blessed be the Lord, the God of Israel, who alone works wonders, and blessed be the name of his glory forever and for age upon age. And all the earth will be filled with his glory; so be it; so be it.* (Ps 72:17-19) And you reside in Cartenna, and with the ten Rogatists who remain you say, "Let it not be so; let it not be so."

21. You hear the Gospel say, *It was necessary that all that was written about me in the law and the prophets and the psalms be fulfilled. Then he opened up their mind so that they understood the Scriptures, and he said to them, Because*

---

431. See Ps 50:1.
432. See Dn 6:13-24;14:39-42.
433. See Prv 26:27.

it was written in that way, it was also necessary that Christ suffer in that way and rise from the dead on the third day and that repentance and the forgiveness of sins in his name be preached through all the nations, beginning from Jerusalem. (Lk 24:44-47) You also read in the Acts of the Apostles of how this Gospel began from Jerusalem, where the Holy Spirit first filled those one hundred and twenty,[434] and went from there to Judea and Samaria and to all the nations, as he told them when he was about to ascend into heaven, *You will be my witnesses in Jerusalem and in the whole of Judea and Samaria and up to the ends of the earth* (Acts 1:8), *for their voice went out into the whole world and their words to the ends of the earth* (Ps 19:5; Rom 10:8). And you contradict the testimonies of God supported with such great strength and revealed with such great light, and you try to bring Christ's heritage to reject them. For, when repentance is preached, as he said, in his name in all the nations, unless anyone roused by this preaching in any part of the world whatsoever seeks out and finds Vincent of Cartenna hiding out in Mauritania Caesariensis or one of his nine or ten companions, he cannot have his sins forgiven. What would this poor dead skin, swollen with pride as it is, not dare? To what point would the presumption of flesh and blood not hurl itself? Is this your good deed on account of which you have no fear of the authorities? Do you set such a stumbling block for the son of your mother,[435] that is, a weak and little one, on account of whom Christ has died,[436] one not yet ready for the food of his father, but still needing to be fed by the milk of his mother?[437] And you set Hilary's[438] books against me, in order that you may deny the Church, which is growing in all the nations to the end of the earth, the Church which God promised with an oath contrary to your unbelief! And though you would have been most wretched if you opposed it when it was promised, you speak against it even now when the promise is being fulfilled.

7, 22. But as a learned historian you have found something important that you think you should bring forward against the testimonies of God. For you say, "If one considers all the parts of the world, in comparison to the whole world the part in which the Christian faith is known is small." You either do not want to consider or you pretend that you do not know to how many barbarian nations the Gospel came in so short a time that even the enemies of Christ cannot doubt that in a short while there will occur what he replied to his disciples who were asking about the end of the world: *And this Gospel will be preached in the whole world as a testimony to all the nations, and then the end will come* (Mt 24:14). Go now, cry out, and argue as much as you can: "Even if the Gospel is preached among the Persians and Indians, where it has been, of course, long preached, unless whoever hears it comes to Cartenna or in the neighborhood of Cartenna,

---

434. See Acts 1:15.
435. See Ps 50:20.
436. See 1 Cor 8:11.
437. See 1 Cor 3:2.
438. See below, 9, 31, where Augustine discusses the passage from the *Synods* by Hilary of Poitiers.

he absolutely cannot be cleansed from his sins." Are you afraid to be laughed at, if you do not use this cry? And do you not ask to be wept over, if you use it?

23. But you think that you say something clever when you explain that the name "Catholic" comes not from the communion of the whole world, but from the observance of all God's commandments and all the sacraments. You suppose that we rely on the testimony of this term for proving that the Church is found in all the nations and not on the promises of God and so many and such clear prophecies of the truth, even if the Church might perhaps be called "Catholic" for the reason that it really holds the whole truth, of which some particles are also found in the different heresies. But this is the whole of which you try to convince us: that only the Rogatists have remained who should correctly be called Catholics on the basis of the observation of all God's commandments and of all the sacraments and that you are the only ones in whom the Son of Man will find faith when he comes.[439] Pardon us, but we do not believe this. For it may be that you dare to say that you should be considered to be, not on earth, but in heaven, in order in you may be found the faith that the Lord said that he would not find on earth. The Apostle, nonetheless, warned us, for he commanded that even an angel from heaven who brings us another gospel than we have received should be anathema.[440] But how can we be confident that we have received Christ so clearly from the words of God, if we have not received the Church from them with equal clarity? Whoever adds any needless complications contrary to the simplicity of the truth, whoever pours out any clouds of clever falsehood, let him be anathema, just as he will be anathema who proclaims that Christ neither suffered nor rose on the third day. For we have received in the truth of the Gospel: *It was necessary that Christ suffer and rise from the dead on the third day* (Lk 24:46). So too he will be anathema who proclaims the Church apart from the communion of all the nations, because we have received from that same truth immediately afterwards: *And that repentance and the forgiveness of sins be preached in his name through all the nations, beginning from Jerusalem* (Lk 24:47). And we ought to maintain with unshaken faith: *Let anyone who proclaims to you another gospel than what you have received be anathema* (Gal 1:9).

8, 24. But if we do not listen to any Donatists, when they substitute themselves for the Church of Christ, because they bring forth no testimony in their favor from God's Books in order to teach this, how much the less, I ask you, ought we to listen to the Rogatists who will not try to interpret in their own favor even that passage where it is written, *Where do you pasture your flocks, where do you make them lie down in the south?* (Sg 1:6) If in that passage *south* should be interpreted as Africa where the sect of Donatus is found, because it is under a hotter region of the sky, the Maximianists will surpass all of you, since their

---

439. See Lk 18:8.
440. See Gal 1:8.

schism arose in Byzacena and Tripoli.[441] But the Arzuges[442] quarrel with them and claim that it rather refers to them. Mauritania Caesariensis, nonetheless, is closer to the eastern than to the southern part; since it does not want to be called Africa, how will it boast of being called *the south*? I do not mean in relation to the rest of the world, but in relation to the sect of Donatus, from which the sect of Rogatus is a tiny fragment broken off from a larger fragment. But apart from great impudence who tries to interpret something expressed in an allegory in his own favor, unless he also has perfectly clear testimonies that cast light on the obscure passages?

25. But how much more emphatically we say to you what we usually say to all the Donatists: Suppose that some people can have a just reason, something that is not possible, for separating their communion from communion with the whole world and for calling their communion the Church of Christ, because they have for just reasons separated themselves from communion with the whole world. How do you know that in the Christian people spread so far and wide, before you separated yourselves, some others have not separated themselves for a just reason in most remote lands, from where a report of their righteousness could not come to you? How can the Church exist in you rather than in those who perhaps separated themselves earlier? Thus it turns out that, since you do not know this, you are uncertain in your own eyes, and it is necessary that this be the result for all who use, not God's testimony, but their own, in defense of their communion. Nor can you say, after all, "If this had happened, we could not fail to know it," when in Africa herself, you could not say, if you were asked, how many sects have split off from the sect of Donatus, especially since those who do this think that they are more righteous to the extent that they are fewer, and they are, of course, to that extent less known. And for this reason you are not certain that, before the sect of Donatus separated its righteousness from the sinfulness of the other human beings, some few righteous persons and, for this reason, scarcely known, somewhere far from the southern region of Africa, did not perhaps separate themselves earlier in the region of the north with a fully just reason. And you are not certain that this sect is not rather the Church of God, like the spiritual Zion, which anticipated all of you with its righteous separation and much more presumptuously interprets in its favor the words of Scripture, *Mount Zion, in the northern part, the city of the great king* (Ps 48:3), than the sect of Donatus interprets in its favor, *Where do you pasture your flocks, where do you make them lie down in the south?* (Sg 1:6).

26. And you, nonetheless, are afraid that, when you are forced into unity by the imperial laws, the name of God may for a longer time be blasphemed by the Jews and pagans, as if the Jews do not know how the first people of Israel wanted to destroy even by war those two and a half tribes that received lands beyond

---

441. I.e., the provinces of Byzacena and Tripoli, to the south and east of Carthage.
442. The Arzuges were Donatist dissents in Byzacena and Tripoli.

the Jordan, when they thought that they had separated themselves from the unity of their people.⁴⁴³ But the pagans can speak ill of you even more because of the imperial laws that the Christian emperors issued against the worshipers of idols. And yet, many of them have been corrected and have been converted to the living and true God and are being converted every day. But clearly if both the Jews and the pagans thought that the Christians were as few in number as you are, who claim that you alone are Christians, they would not stoop to speak ill of us, but would never stop laughing at us. If your small number is the Church of Christ, are you not afraid that the Jews might say to you, "Where do you find what your Paul interpreted as referring to your church where Scripture says, *Rejoice, you who are sterile, you who bear no children; burst forth and cry out, you who have no labor pains, for the children of the abandoned woman are more numerous than those of the woman with a husband* (Is 54:1; Gal 4:47), where he showed the numerical superiority of the Christians over the Jews?" Is this what you are going to say to them, "We are more righteous precisely because we are few," and do you not notice that they will reply, "However many you say that you are, you are not, nonetheless, those of whom Scripture said, *The children of the abandoned woman are more numerous*, if you have remained so few in number"?

27. At this point you are going to appeal to the example of that righteous man in the flood who was alone found worthy of being saved along with his family.⁴⁴⁴ Do you, therefore, see how far you still are from righteousness? We, of course, are not going to call you righteous until you are down to seven with yourself as the eighth, unless, as I was saying, someone else seized this righteousness before the sect of Donatus and along with his seven companions, after having been provoked by some just cause, separated himself somewhere far away and rescued himself from the flood of this world. Since you do not know whether this happened and you have not heard of it, just as many Christian peoples living in distant lands have not heard of the name of Donatus, you are uncertain about where the Church is to be found. For it will be in that place where there first occurred what you afterwards did, if there could be any just reason for which you could have separated yourselves from communion with all the nations.

9, 28. We, however, are certain that no one could have justly separated himself from communion with all the nations, precisely because each of us seeks the Church, not in our own righteousness, but in the Divine Scriptures, and each of us sees that it exists as it was promised. For she is the Church of which Scripture says, *Like a lily in the midst of thorns, so is my beloved in the midst of daughters* (Sg 2:2). They could be called *thorns* only because of their evil conduct, and they could be called *daughters* only because of their sharing in the sacraments. She, after all, is the one who says, *From the ends of the earth I have cried out to you when my heart was troubled* (Ps 61:3). In another Psalm she says, *Wea-*

---

443. See Jos 22:9-12.
444. See Gn 7:1-23.

riness grips me because of sinners who abandon your law (Ps 119:53), and, *I saw the faithless, and I wasted away* (Ps 119: 158). She it is who says to her spouse, *Where do you pasture your flocks, where do you make them lie down in the south lest I should perhaps become like a veiled woman behind the flocks of your companions* (Sg 1:6). This is what Scripture says elsewhere, *Make known to me your right hand and those learned of heart in wisdom* (Ps 90:12). In these who are brilliant with light and fervent with love you find rest as if in the south lest perhaps as a veiled woman, that is, one who is hidden and unknown, I should rush, not into your flock, but into the flocks of your companions, that is, of the heretics. And he calls these heretics companions, as he called those daughters thorns because of their sharing the same sacraments. Of these Scripture says elsewhere, *But you who are one of heart with me, my guide, my friend, you who ate with me sweet foods, in the house of the Lord we walked in harmony. May death come upon them, and may they descend alive into hell* (Ps 55:14-16), just like Dathan and Abiram, the authors of the wicked schism.[445]

29. She it is who receives the immediate reply, *If you do not know yourself, O most beautiful among women, go out in the paths of the flocks, and pasture your kids in the tents of the shepherds* (Sg 1:7). O! Reply of the most lovable spouse! *If you do not know yourself*, he says, because, of course, *A city placed upon a mountaintop cannot be hidden* (Mt 5:14), and for that reason you are not veiled so that you should rush into the flocks of my companions. For I am *a mountain prepared on the height of the mountains to which all the nations will come* (Is 2:2). *If you*, then, *do not know yourself*, not in the words of slanderers, but in the testimonies of my Books. *If you do not know yourself*, because Scripture has said of you, *Stretch out further your ropes, and strengthen your mighty fences; again and again reach out to the right and to the left. For your offspring will inherit the nations, and you will dwell in cities that were abandoned. There is nothing for you to fear, for you will prevail. Do not be ashamed that you were disgraced. For you will forget your shame forever; you will not remember the ignominy of your widowhood. I, after all, am the Lord who created you; Lord is his name. And he who rescues you will be called the God of Israel and of all the earth.* (Is 54:2-5) *If you do not know yourself, O most beautiful among women* (Sg 1:7), for Scripture said of you, *The king desired your beauty* (Ps 45:12), because it said of you, *In place of your fathers sons have been born to you; you will establish them as princes over the whole earth* (Ps 45:17). *If you do not know yourself, go out* (Sg 1:7). I do not cast you out, but, *Go out*, in order that it may be said of you, *They went out from us, but they did not belong to us* (1 Jn 2:19). *Go out in the paths of the flocks*, not in my paths, but *in the paths of the flocks*, and not of one flock, but of flocks that are divided and straying. *And pasture your kids*, not like Peter to whom it is said, *Pasture my sheep* (Jn 21:17), but, *Pasture your kids in the tents of the shepherds*, not in the tent of the shepherd, where there is one

---

445. See Nm 1:7.

flock and one shepherd.[446] For she knows herself so that this does not happen to her, because this has happened to those who have not known themselves in her.

30. She it is of whose few numbers Scripture says in comparison with the many evil persons, *Straight and narrow is the way that leads to salvation, and few are they who walk on it* (Mt 7:14). And again she it is of whose great number Scripture says, *Your offspring will be like the stars of the sky and like the sand of the sea* (Gn 22:17; Dn 3:36). The same holy and good believers are, of course, few in comparison with the evil and are many by themselves, *Because the children of the abandoned woman are more than those of the woman with a husband* (Gal 4:27), and *Many will come from the east and from the west and will recline with Abraham, Isaac, and Jacob in the kingdom of heaven* (Mt 8:11), and because *God presents to himself an abundant people who are zealous for good works* (Tit 2:14), and many thousands *whom no one can count* are seen in the Apocalypse *in every tribe and tongue, in white robes and with palms of victory* (Rev 7:9). She it is who is at times obscured and as if clouded over because of a multitude of scandals, *when sinners bend their bows to shoot in the dark moon those who are upright of heart* (Ps 11:3). But even then she stands out in her strongest members. And if some distinction is to be made in these words of God, perhaps there was a point in saying of the offspring of Abraham that they will be *like the stars of the sky and like the sand at the shore of the sea* (Gn 22:17), namely, that we understand by the stars of the sky the fewer, stronger, and more brilliant, but in the sand on the seashore the great multitude of the weak and carnal, who at times seem at rest and free because of the tranquility of the weather, but at other times are overwhelmed and churned up by the waves of tribulations and temptations.

31. Such was that time of which Hilary wrote, because of which you thought that you should attack so many divine testimonies, as if the Church perished from the whole world.[447] You can in this way say that so many churches in Galatia had ceased to exist at the time when the Apostle said, *O you foolish Galatians, who has bewitched you?* and, *Though you began with the spirit, you end up in the flesh* (Gal 3:1.3). For you in that way slander a learned man who severely reprimanded the fainthearted and timid whom he was bringing to birth once again until Christ would be formed in them.[448] After all, who does not know that at that period many people of poor judgment were deceived by obscure language so that they thought that the Arians believed what they themselves believed? But others yielded out of fear and pretended to agree with them, *not acting correctly in relation to the Gospel* (Gal 2:14), and you would have refused to pardon them

---

446. See Jn 10:16.
447. Hilary of Poitiers said in his work, *On the Synods* 65, "With the exception of Eleusius and the few with him, the ten provinces of Asia, where I find myself, do not really for the most part know God."
448. See Gal 4:19.

when they were later corrected, as they were in fact pardoned. You, of course, do not know God's Books. Read, after all, what Paul wrote about Peter[449] and what Cyprian also thought about that,[450] and do not be displeased at the gentleness of the Church, which gathers together the scattered members of Christ and does not scatter those gathered together. And yet those who were the strongest at that time and were able to understand the insidious words of the heretics were in fact few in comparison with the others, but some even bravely suffered exile for the faith, while others remained unknown in the whole world. And in that way the Church, which is growing in all the nations, is preserved in the grain sown by the Lord and will be preserved up to the end until it contains absolutely all the nations, even the barbarian ones. For the Church is found in the good seed, which the Son of Man sowed and which he foretold would grow among the weeds up to the harvest. But the field is the world, and the harvest is the end of the world.[451]

32. Hilary, then, either reprimanded the weeds, not the grain, of the ten provinces of Asia or thought that the grain itself, which was in danger due to some failing, would be reprimanded with greater benefit the more severely he rebuked them. After all, the canonical Scriptures also contain this practice of reprimanding in order that a word seemingly said to all might reach certain individuals. For, when the Apostle says to the Corinthians, *How do certain ones among you say that there is no resurrection of the dead?* (1 Cor 15:12), he, of course, shows that they were not all such people, but he, nonetheless, bears witness that such people were not outsiders, but were among them, and he warned shortly afterwards that those who did not share such ideas should not be misled by them. He says, *Do not be misled. Bad conversations ruin good morals. Be sober, you who are righteous; do not sin. For some are lacking knowledge of God; I speak to put you to shame.* (1 Cor 15:33-34) But when he says, *Since, after all, there is jealousy and strife among you, are you not carnal and do you not live in a merely human fashion?* (1 Cor 3:3), he seemingly speaks to all, and you see how serious what he says is. Hence, if we did not read in the same Letter, *I always thank my God for you because of the grace of God that has been given to you in Christ Jesus, because in every way you have become enriched in all speech and in all knowledge, just as the testimony of Christ has been confirmed in you, so that nothing is lacking to you in any grace* (1 Cor 1:4-7), we would think that all the Corinthians were carnal and merely natural, not perceiving those things that pertain to the Spirit of God, full of strife, jealous, living in a merely human fashion. And so, *the whole world has been placed in the power of the evil one* (Jn 5:19), on account of the weeds, which are spread throughout the whole world, and Christ *is propitiation for our*

---

449. See Gal 2:11.
450. See Cyprian, Letter 71, 3.
451. See Mt 13:24-30.38-39.

sins, not only for our sins, but also for those of the whole world (1 Jn 2:2), on account of the wheat, which is spread throughout the whole world.

33. *But the love of many grows cold* (Mt 24:12), on account of the abundance of scandals to the extent that the name of Christ has attained more and more glory and there are gathered into the communion of his sacraments even the evil and the persistently and utterly perverse, but like the chaff they will not be removed from the threshing floor of the Lord until the last winnowing.[452] These do not choke off the Lord's wheat, which is meager in comparison with them, but great in itself. They do not choke off the wheat plants of the Lord, which in comparison with them are few, but are many by themselves. They do not choke off the elect of God who will be gathered together at the end of the world, as the Gospel says, *from the four winds, from one end of the heavens to the other* (Mt 24:31). For this is their cry: *Save me, O Lord, because even a saint falters, for truthful- ness has decreased among the children of men* (Ps 12:2), and of these the Lord also says that amid the abundance of sinfulness *he who perseveres up to the end will be saved* (Mt 24:12). Finally, the following words inform us that not one person, but many are speaking in the same Psalm where it says, *You, O Lord, will keep us and guard us from this generation forever* (Ps 12:8). On account of this abundance of sinfulness, which the Lord foretold would exist, this passage was also written, *When the Son of Man comes, do you suppose he will find faith on earth?* (Lk 18:8). For the doubt on the part of him who knows all things prefigured our doubt in him when, because of many from whom she hoped for much, the Church was often disappointed because they were found to be other than they were believed to be and was so troubled over her members that she was unwilling readily to believe anything good of anyone. We must, nonetheless, not doubt that those people whose faith he is going to find on earth will grow along with the weeds through the whole field.

34. She, therefore, is the Church which swims along with the bad fishes within the Lord's net,[453] from whom she is always separated in heart and morals and from whom she departs *in order that she may be presented to her husband as glorious, having neither spot nor wrinkle* (Eph 5:27). But she awaits bodily separation on the seashore, that is, at the end of the world,[454] correcting those whom she can, tolerating those whom she cannot correct; she does not, nonetheless, abandon unity on account of the sinfulness of those whom she does not correct.

10, 35. Do not, therefore, my brother, desire to gather slanderous statements from the writings of bishops, whether our bishops, like Hilary, or those belonging to the unity itself before the sect of Donatus was separated, like Cyprian and Agrippinus,[455] against so many, such clear, and such indubitable testimonies of

---

452. See Mt 3:12; 13:30.
453. Mt 13:47.
454. See Mt 13:47-49.
455. Cyprian was bishop of Carthage from 248/249 to 258. Agrippinus was a bishop of Carthage

God. After all, writings of this sort are, first of all, to be distinguished from the authority of the canonical Books. For we do not read them as if a testimony is drawn from them so that we are not permitted to hold a contrary view, if those writers perhaps somewhere held some view other than the truth demands. We ourselves are, of course, included in that number so that we do not disdain to accept the Apostle's words as also spoken to us: *And if on some point you think differently, God will also reveal that to you. Let us, nonetheless, continue in that to which we have come* (Phil 3:15-16), that is, in that way, which is Christ.[456] The Psalm speaks of that way as follows: *May God be merciful to us and bless us; may he make his face shine upon us in order that we may know your way on earth, your salvation in all the nations* (Ps 67:2-3).

36. Then, if you are pleased with the authority of Saint Cyprian, the bishop and glorious martyr, which, as I said, we distinguish from the authority of the canon, why are you not pleased that he preserved by love and defended by argument the unity of the whole world and of all the nations? Why are you not pleased that he judged most arrogant and proud those who wanted to separate themselves from her as if they were righteous? He mocked them for claiming for themselves what the Lord did not grant even to the apostles, namely, that they should pull out the weeds beforetime or that they should try to separate the chaff from the wheat, as if it were granted to them to remove the chaff and clean up the threshing floor.[457] Why are you not pleased that he showed that no one can be defiled by the sins of others, the reason which all the authors of an impious rebellion take as their sole reason for separation? Why are you not pleased that on that very issue on which they held another view he decreed that his colleagues who thought differently were not to be judged or removed from the right to communion? Why are you not pleased at what he says in that very letter to Jubaianus, which was first read out in that council whose authority you say that you follow for rebaptizing?[458] For, though he admits that in the past those who were baptized elsewhere were admitted to the Church without being rebaptized and thinks that they were for this reason without baptism, he, nonetheless, sees such a great benefit and blessing in the peace of the Church that on its account he believes that they should not be excluded from offices in the Church.

37. On this point you see with the greatest ease, for I know your fine mind, that your case is completely overthrown and wiped out. For, if by admitting sinners to the sacraments, the Church, which had existed in the whole world, has, as you claim, perished—for you broke away on those grounds; it had as a whole perished earlier when, as Cyprian says, they were admitted into her without baptism. And in that way even Cyprian did not have the Church in which he might

---

before Cyprian and held views similar to his.
456. See Jn 14:6.
457. See Mt 13:28-30.
458. See Cyprian, Letter 73. The council was held in Carthage in 256.

be born. For how much greater reason did your author and father, Donatus, at a later time not have the Church! But if at that time when people were admitted to her without baptism, there was still the Church that gave birth to Cyprian and also gave birth to Donatus, it is evident that the righteous are not infected by the sins of others when they share with them in the sacraments. And for this reason you do not have any excuse by which you might excuse the separation by which you departed from the unity, and there is fulfilled in you that prophecy of the Holy Scripture: *A bad son says that he is righteous, but he does not excuse his going out* (Prv 30:12, LXX).

38. But one who does not dare to rebaptize even heretics on account of their sacraments equal to ours does not equal the merits of Cyprian, just as whoever does not force pagans to live as Jews does not equal the merits of Peter. But the canonical scriptures contain not merely that failure on Peter's part, but also his correction.[459] Cyprian, however, is found to have held other ideas concerning baptism than is contained in the norm and practice of the Church, not in canonical writings, but in his own and in those of a council. He is not, however, found to have corrected this view; it is, nonetheless, not inappropriate that we should think with regard to such a man that he corrected his view, and it was perhaps suppressed by those who were all too pleased by this error and did not want to be without so great a patron. And yet there are some who claim that Cyprian certainly did not hold this view, but that it was made up and attributed to him by bold liars. For the integrity and knowledge of the writings of one bishop, however illustrious, could not be preserved in the same way as the canonical Scripture is preserved by translations in so many languages and by the order and sequence of the Church's liturgical celebration. And yet, there were not lacking in opposition to the Scripture those who composed many documents in the name of the apostles, in vain, of course, because that scripture is so highly commended, so frequently used in celebrations, and so very familiar. But the attempt of impious audacity has shown even from this case what it could do against writings that are not founded upon canonical authority, since it did not fail to challenge those writings that were supported by so solid a basis of familiarity.

39. We, nonetheless, do not deny that Cyprian held this view. We have two reasons: because his writing has a certain character all its own by which it can be recognized and because his writing rather shows that our case against you is more invincible and undermines with great ease the grounds for your breaking away, namely, so that you would not be defiled by the sins of others. For in the writings of Cyprian we see that sinners participated in the sacraments when people were admitted to the Church who according to your opinion and, as you claim, according to Cyprian's did not have baptism, and yet the Church did not perish. Rather, the Lord's grain remained scattered through the whole world in its special dignity. And for this reason if, when upset, you take flight to the au-

---

459. See Gal 2:14.

thority of Cyprian as if to some harbor, you see there the rocks upon which your error is dashed. But if you now do not dare to take flight to him, you are shipwrecked without putting up any fight.

40. On the other hand, Cyprian either did not at all hold the view that you report that he held, or he corrected it afterwards by the rule of truth, or he covered over this view like a birthmark on his most pure heart with the richness of his love, while he both most amply defended the unity of the Church that was growing through the whole world and most perseveringly maintained the bond of peace. For it is written, *Love covers over a multitude of sins* (1 Pt 4:8). There is also added to this the fact that, if there was anything in him that needed to be corrected, the Father pruned him like a most fruitful branch with the knife of martyrdom. The Lord says, *For the Father will prune the branch that gives fruit in me in order that it may bear greater fruit* (Jn 15:2). Why, if not, because in clinging to the vine as it spread out, he did not abandon the root of unity? For, even if he handed over his body to be burned, but did not have love, it would have done him no good.[460]

41. Consider a little longer the letter of Cyprian in order that you may see how inexcusable he showed a person to be who chose to break away, as if for the sake of his own righteousness, from the unity of the Church, which God promised and has brought to fulfillment in all the nations. You will better understand how true is that statement I mentioned shortly before: *A bad son says that he is righteous, but he does not excuse his going out* (Prv 30:12, LXX). He puts in a certain letter of his to Antonian a specific point quite pertinent to the issue we are dealing with, but it is better that we include his words. He says, "Certain bishops, our predecessors, here in our province thought that they should not grant reconciliation to fornicators and that they should completely exclude a place of repentance for adulterers. They did not, nonetheless, withdraw from the college of their fellow bishops or shatter the unity of the Catholic Church either by the hardness or the stubbornness of their censure so that one who did not grant reconciliation to adulterers broke away from the Church because others granted such reconciliation. While the bond of harmony remained and the sacrament of the Catholic Church continued undivided, each bishop arranges and orders his own actions, for he will give an account of his conduct to the Lord."[461] What do you say to this, Brother Vincent? You, of course, see that this great man, a bishop of peace, and the bravest of martyrs, worked for nothing with greater intensity than to avoid breaking the bond of unity. You see him in labor, not only that little ones conceived in Christ might be born, but also so that those already born might not die, torn from the bosom of their mother.

---

460. See 1 Cor 13:3.
461. See Cyprian, Letter 55, 21.

42. But consider also the very point that he mentioned against the impious authors of schism. If those who granted reconciliation to penitent adulterers were in communion with adulterers, were those who did not do this defiled by companionship with them? But if, as the truth maintains and as the Church rightly holds, reconciliation was rightly granted to penitent adulterers, those who completely excluded a place of repentance for adulterers certainly acted impiously in denying health to members of Christ and in withholding the keys of the Church from those who knocked and in contradicting with harsh cruelty the most merciful patience of God. For his mercy allowed them to live precisely in order that they might be healed by doing penance when they offered the sacrifice of a contrite spirit and a troubled heart.[462] Nor did so great an error and impiety on their part defile these merciful and peaceful men who participated with them in the Christian sacraments and tolerated them within the nets of unity until they might be separated after being brought to the shore.[463] Or if it did defile them, the Church was already at that time destroyed by being in communion with evil persons, nor did she exist to give birth to Cyprian himself. But if the Church has remained, as is certain, it is certain that no one can be defiled by the actions of evil persons in the unity of Christ, if he does not consent to them lest he be polluted by partaking in their sins and if on account of the society of the good he tolerates the evil, like chaff on the Lord's threshing floor up to the last winnowing.[464] Since that is so, where are the grounds for your breaking away? Are you not bad sons? You yourselves say that you are righteous, but you do not excuse your going out.

43. Now I could also mention those ideas that Tychonius,[465] a man of your communion, put in his writings, a man who wrote in fact against you in defense of the Catholic Church. He uselessly removed himself from communion with the Africans on the grounds that they were traditors, and by this one fact Parmenian[466] held him trapped. What could you answer except what the same Tychonius said and what I recalled a little before: "All we want is holiness."[467] For that Tychonius, a man, as I said, of your communion, writes that a council of two hundred and seventy bishops was celebrated at Carthage and that in that council for seventy-five days, after having put aside all past norms, the position was worked out and decreed that they should be in communion with the traditors guilty of a grave sin, as if they were innocent, if they refused to be baptized

---

462. See Ps 51:19.
463. See Mt 13:47-49.
464. See Mt 3:12; 13:29-30.
465. Tychonius was a learned Donatist whose rules for the interpretation of Scripture Augustine incorporated into his own work, *Teaching Christianity*.
466. Parmenian was the Donatist bishop of Carthage at the time of Julian the Apostate. Augustine wrote three books against him in his work, *Answer to the Letter of Parmenian*.
467. See above 4, 14.

again.[468] He says that Deuterius, a bishop of Macrina, also of your communion, mixed together the assembled people of the traditors with the church and that, according to the statutes of that council celebrated by two hundred and seventy of your bishops, he established unity with the traditors and that Donatus was continually in communion with that Deuterius after this action, and not only with this Deuterius, but also with all the bishops of Mauretania for forty years, and he said that they were in communion with the traditors without rebaptism up to the persecution brought by Macarius.[469]

44. But you say, "Who is this Tychonius to me?" He is that Tychonius whom Parmenian silences when he writes back and threatens him not to write such things. But he does not refute what he writes; rather, he presses him with one point, as I mentioned above, namely, that, though he says such things about the Church spread throughout the whole world and claims that the sins of others stain no one in its unity, he removed himself from the contagion of the Africans, as if they were traditors, and become a member of the sect of Donatus. Parmenian, however, could have said that Tychonius had made up all these lies, but as the same Tychonius reminds us, there were still many alive who could prove that all these facts were most certain and well known.

45. But I will say nothing of these. Argue that Tychonius lied; I take you back to Cyprian, whom you mentioned. According to the writings of Cyprian, if anyone in the unity of the Church is stained by the sins of others, the Church already perished before Cyprian, nor was there a Church from which Cyprian himself could have come to be. But if it is sacrilegious to think that and if it is certain that the Church still remains, no one in its unity is stained by the sins of others. In vain do you, evil sons, say that you are righteous; you do not excuse, you do not acquit your going out.[470]

11, 46. "Why then," you ask, "do you seek us? Why do you so welcome those whom you call heretics?" See how easily and briefly I answer. We seek you because you were lost in order that we may rejoice over you once you have been found, you over whom we grieved because you were lost. We call you heretics, but only before you return to the Catholic peace, before you strip off the error in which you were entangled. When, however, you cross over to us, you, of course, first leave what you were so that you do not cross over to us as heretics. "Then baptize me," you say. I would do so if you had not been baptized or if you had been baptized with the baptism of Donatus or of Rogatus and not of Christ. It is not the Christian sacraments, but your wicked schism that makes you a heretic. On account of the evil that comes from you one must not deny the good that has

---

468. This Donatist council was held in 335 and presided over by Donatus.
469. Macarius was an imperial commissioner sent to deal with the Donatist schism; in 347 he fought with Donatus, the Donatist bishop of Bagai, and defeated his forces with great loss of life to the Donatist side.
470. See Prv 24:35 (LXX) and above 10, 37.

remained in you. You have that good to your own harm if you do not have it in that source from which there comes the good you have. For from the Catholic Church come all the Lord's sacraments that you possess and confer in the same way as they were possessed and conferred even before you left her. You do not, nonetheless, lack them because you are not in her from whom there comes what you have. We do not change in you those things in which you are with us, for you are with us in many things. And of such things Scripture says, *For they were with me in many things* (Ps 55:19). But we correct those things in which you are not with us, and we want you to receive here those things that you do not have there where you are. You are, however, with us in baptism, in the creed, in the other sacraments of the Lord. But in the spirit of unity and in the bond of peace, finally, in the Catholic Church herself, you are not with us. If you accept these, what you have will not only then be present, but they will then benefit you. It is, therefore, not the case, as you suppose, that we welcome your people, but by welcoming them we make our people those who leave you in order that they may be welcomed by us, and in order that they may begin to be ours, they first cease to be yours. We do not force to join us the agents of the error we detest, but we want those people to join us in order that they may not be what we detest.

47. "But the apostle Paul," you say, "baptized after John."[471] Did he baptize after a heretic? Or if you perhaps dare to call that friend of the bridegroom[472] a heretic and say that he was not in the unity of the Church, I wish that you would also put this in writing. But if it is absolutely insane either to think or to say this, Your Wisdom must consider why the apostle Paul baptized after John. For, if he baptized after an equal, you ought all to baptize after one another. If he baptized after someone greater, you also ought to baptize after Rogatus. If he baptized after someone less great, Rogatus ought to have baptized after you since you baptized as a priest. But if, though those by whom it is conferred are unequal in merit, the baptism that is now conferred has equal validity in those upon whom it is conferred, because it is the baptism of Christ, not of those who are its ministers, I think that you already understand that Paul gave to certain people the baptism of Christ, because they were baptized with the baptism of John, not with that of Christ. That baptism was called the baptism of John, as the Divine Scripture bears witness in many passages, because even the Lord said, *From where does the baptism of John come? From heaven or from human beings?* (Mt 21:25 and Lk 20:4). But the baptism that Peter conferred was not Peter's, but Christ's, and that which Paul conferred was not Paul's, but Christ's. And the baptism that they conferred who at the time of the apostles proclaimed Christ, not with the right intention, but out of envy,[473] was not theirs, but Christ's. And the baptism that they conferred who at the time of Cyprian seized estates by insidious frauds

---

471. See Acts 19:1-5.
472. See Jn 3:29.
473. See Phil 1:15-17.

and increased their capital by compound interest was not theirs, but Christ's. And because it was Christ's, though it was not conferred on them by ministers of equal merit, it, nonetheless, equally benefited those upon whom it was conferred. For, if anyone is baptized better to the extent that he is baptized by someone better, the Apostle is not correct in giving thanks that he baptized none of the Corinthians except Cripsus, Gaius, and the house of Stephanas.[474] For they would have been better baptized to the extent that Paul was better, if they were baptized by him. Finally, when he said, *I planted; Apollo watered* (1 Cor 3:6), he seems to convey that he preached the good news, but that Apollo baptized. Was Apollo better than John? Why, then, did Paul not baptize after Apollo, though he baptized after John, except that this baptism by whomever it is conferred is Christ's, but that baptism by whomever it was conferred was, nonetheless, John's, though he prepared the way for Christ?

48. It seems invidious to say, "Baptism is conferred after John's baptism, and it is not conferred after that of heretics." But it can also seem invidious to say, "Baptism is conferred after John's baptism, and it is not conferred after that of drunkards." For I do better to mention this vice, which they in whom it rules cannot hide, and who, even if blind, does not know how many drunkards there are everywhere? And still the Apostle put this too among the works of the flesh, saying that those who do them will not inherit the kingdom of God, and in the same passage he also listed heresy. He said, *The works of the flesh are evident; they are fornication, impurity, licentiousness, idolatry, sorcery, enmity, strife, jealousy, anger, dissension, heresy, envy, drunkenness, carousing, and the like. I warn you, as I warned you before, that those who do such things shall not inherit the kingdom of God.* (Gal 5:19-21) Though baptism was again conferred after the baptism of John, baptism is not again conferred after the baptism of a heretic for the same reason that baptism is not again conferred after that of a drunkard, though it is conferred after that of John. For both heresy and drunkenness are among those works that keep those who do them from inheriting the kingdom of God. Does it not strike you as intolerably improper that, though baptism is again conferred after the baptism of that man who, not drinking wine with sobriety, but not drinking wine at all, prepared the way for the kingdom of God, baptism is not again conferred after the baptism of a drunkard, who will not inherit the kingdom of God? What answer will you give here except that the former baptism, after which the Apostle baptized with the baptism of Christ, was the baptism of John, but this baptism, by which the drunkard baptized, is the baptism of Christ? Between John and a drunkard there is as great a difference as possible; between the baptism of Christ and the baptism of John there is not as great a difference as possible, but there is, nonetheless, a great difference. Between the Apostle and a drunkard there is a great difference; between the baptism of Christ that the Apostle conferred and the baptism of Christ that the drunkard conferred there is

---

474. See 1 Cor 1:14.

no difference. In the same way between John and a heretic there is as great a difference as possible, and between the baptism of John and the baptism of Christ that a heretic confers there is not as great a difference as is possible, but there is a great difference. For the essence of the sacraments is recognized as the same, even when there is a great difference in the merits of human beings.

49. But pardon me; I was mistaken when I wanted to convince you about the drunkard who baptizes; it had slipped my mind that I was dealing with a Rogatist, not with just any sort of Donatist. For you can perhaps in your few colleagues and in all your clerics find not a single drunkard. For you are the people who hold the Catholic faith, not because you are in communion with the whole world, but because you observe all the commandments and all the sacraments. In you alone he will find faith when the Son of Man will come when he will not find faith on earth. For you are not earth, nor are you on the earth, but like heavenly people you dwell in heaven! You neither fear nor pay attention to the words: *God resists the proud, but gives grace to the humble* (Jas 4:6). Nor does the passage of the Gospel touch your heart where the Lord says, *When the Son of Man comes, do you think he will find faith on earth?* (Lk 18:8). Immediately, as if he foreknew that some people would proudly claim this faith for themselves, *he told this parable to certain persons who considered themselves righteous and scorned the rest: Two men went up to the temple to pray, the one a Pharisee and the other a publican* (Lk 18:9-10), and so on. Now you yourself answer for yourself the questions that follow. Look, nonetheless, more carefully at the few of you to see whether no drunkard confers baptism among you. For this plague so widely lays waste to souls and rules over them with such great freedom that I would be greatly surprised if it has not also penetrated your little flock, even though you boast to have already separated the sheep from the goats before the coming of the Son of Man,[475] the one good shepherd.[476]

12, 50. But hear from my lips the voice of the Lord's grain that labors among the chaff up to the last winnowing on the threshing floor of the Lord, that is, throughout the whole world, for God has called the earth from the rising of the sun to its setting,[477] where even the children praise the Lord.[478] Whoever persecutes you as the result of the opportunity provided by this imperial law, not out of a desire to correct you, but out of a hatred for you like enemies, does not have our approval. And, nonetheless, no earthly possession can be rightfully owned by anyone save by God's law, by which all goods belong to the righteous, or by human law, which lies in the power of the kings of the earth, and for that reason you would wrongly call possessions yours that you do not own as righteous persons and that you are commanded to surrender in accord with the laws of the kings of

---

475. See Mt 25:32-33.
476. See Jn 10:11.16.
477. See Ps 50:1.
478. See Ps 113:3.

the earth. And you would say to no point, "We have labored to acquire them," since you read in Scripture, *The righteous will eat the labors of the wicked* (Prv 13:22). But anyone, nonetheless, who as a result of the opportunity provided by this law that the kings of the earth who serve Christ have promulgated for your correction, covets out of greed your own personal property has our disapproval. Whoever, then, holds the goods of the poor or the basilicas of congregations that you held in the name of the Church, which is the true Church of Christ, not through justice, but through greed, meets with our disapproval. Whoever welcomes someone whom you cast out for some scandal or grave sin in the same way as they are welcomed who have lived among you without serious sin, except for the error that separates you from us, meets with our disapproval. But you cannot easily prove these points, and if you should prove them, we tolerate some whom we cannot correct or punish. We do not abandon the Lord's threshing floor on account of the chaff,[479] nor do we destroy the Lord's nets on account of the bad fishes,[480] nor do we desert the Lord's flock on account of the goats that will be separated in the end,[481] nor do we move from the Lord's house on account of the vessels that were made for dishonor.[482]

13, 51. But it seems to me that if you, my brother, do not consider the vainglory of human beings and scorn the reproaches of the mindless, who are going to say, "Why do you now destroy what you were first building up?" you will undoubtedly cross over to the Church that I understand you hold to be the true Church. Nor do I have to look far for testimonies to this view of yours. In the beginning of the same letter of yours, to which I am now replying, you indeed set forth these words. You said, "Since I know very well that you were for a long time separated from the Christian faith and were once dedicated to literary studies and a lover of quiet and goodness and since you were later converted to the Christian faith, as I know from the reports of many persons, and devoted your energy to questions of God's law," and so on. Surely, if you sent that letter to me, these are your words. Since, then, you admit that I was converted to the Christian faith, and since I was not converted either to the Donatists or to the Rogatists, you undoubtedly affirm that the Christian faith exists apart from the Rogatists and apart from the Donatists. This faith, then, as we say, is spread though all the nations which are blessed according to the testimony of God in the offspring of Abraham.[483] Why, then, do you hesitate to maintain what you think, if not because you are ashamed either not to have formerly held another view than you now hold or to have defended another view, and while you are embarrassed to correct your error, you are not embarrassed to remain in your error, something over which you ought, of course, to be more embarrassed.

---

479. See Mt 3:12.
480. See Mt 13:47-48.
481. See Mt 25:32-33.
482. See 2 Tm 2:20.
483. See Gn 22:18.

52. This is a point about which Scripture is not silent, *There is a shame that leads to sin and there is a shame that brings grace and glory* (Sir 4:25). Shame leads to sin when someone is embarrassed to change a wrong opinion for fear that one will be thought to be unstable or will be thought to have long been in error because of one's own judgment. In that way they go down alive into hell,[484] that is, aware of their own perdition; Dathan, Abiram, and Korah, who were swallowed when the earth opened up, prefigured these people far in advance.[485] But shame brings grace and glory when one is embarrassed over his own sinfulness and changes for the better through repentance. You are reluctant to do this, because you are overwhelmed by that destructive shame. You are afraid that human beings who do not know what they are saying might raise as an objection to you that statement of the Apostle: *For, if I again build up those same things that I tore down, I make myself a transgressor* (Gal 2:18). If this could also have been said to those who, once corrected, preach the truth that they attacked when they were in error, it would have been said to Paul himself first of all, for in him the churches of Christ glorified God when they heard that he was preaching the good news of the faith that he once ravaged.[486]

53. Do not suppose that anyone can pass without repentance from error to the truth or from any sin, whether big or small, to correction. But it is an extraordinarily brazen error to want to speak ill of the Church, which, as is clear from so many testimonies of God, is the Church of Christ, for the reason that she treats those who abandon her in one way, if they correct this by repentance, and in another way those who were not previously in her and at that time first receive her peace. She humbles the former more to a greater degree, while she welcomes the latter more gently, loving both, working to heal both with her maternal love. You perhaps have a longer letter than you wanted. It would, however, have been much shorter, if I had only you in mind in replying. But now, even if it does you no good, I do not think that it will fail to benefit those who take care to read it with fear of God and without human respect. Amen.

---

484. See Ps 55:16.
485. See Nm 16:31-33.
486. See Gal 1:23.

LETTER 108

Augustine to Macrobius, the Donatist bishop of Hippo (409-410)

Between the end of 409 and August of 410, Augustine wrote this letter to Macrobius, the Donatist bishop of Hippo, who succeeded Proculeian. Augustine complains to Macrobius about his policy of rebaptizing someone who comes to his sect and asks for it (paragraph 1). To Macrobius' reply that he, as newly ordained, dares not to judge his predecessors, Augustine asks why the Donatists judge the Catholics concerning actions done by their predecessors of long ago (paragraph 2). Augustine argues that baptism has made them brothers, for it is Christ who baptizes. Baptism belongs to Christ, though the Donatists subject him to exsufflation when they repeat baptism (paragraph 3). The Donatist bishop, Primian, received back Felician of Musti along with all those he baptized in the sect of Maximian without rebaptizing them. Though Macrobius does not judge Primian for his actions, he judges the whole Catholic world (paragraph 4). Despite the immediate and severe condemnation of Felician, many Donatist bishops received him back in his full priestly dignity (paragraph 5).

Augustine declares to Macrobius that the Donatist case is ended and goes on to demolish the scriptural texts to which the Donatists had appealed, first regarding baptism (paragraph 6) and then regarding participation in the sins of others (paragraph 7). Augustine musters biblical examples of holy men, prophets, and apostles who complained about the mingling of good and evil persons in the world, but did not withdraw from Israel or from the Church on their account (paragraph 8). Augustine acknowledges that the Donatists appeal to the writings of Cyprian in defense of repeating baptism, but points out how much value Cyprian had placed on unity (paragraph 9). Though Cyprian deplored the sins committed by people in the Church, he insisted that one should not withdraw from unity on account of the weeds (paragraph 10). If the Donatists had borne in mind Christ's parable about not separating the grain from the weeds, they would not have split off from the Church (paragraph 11). Augustine uses the parables on the separation of the weeds from the grain, of the chaff from the wheat, of the goats from the sheep, and of the bad fishes from the good to show that schism is unjustifiable (paragraph 12). Augustine uses the case of Felician and Praetextatus to show the inconsistency in the Donatists' position (paragraph 13).

The Donatists boast of the persecutions they have suffered, though the Maximianists have surpassed them in suffering, and it is not mere persecution but persecution for the sake of righteousness that makes one blessed (paragraph 14). After the Donatists condemned Felician and Praetextatus in most severe terms, they readmitted them in their positions of honor without rebaptizing those whom they baptized in their schism (paragraph 15). Either Macrobius must not use the scripture texts the Donatists usually use against the Catholics, or he will be trapped over the case of Maximian (paragraph 16). Hence, Augustine invites Macrobius to the unity of the Church where they might together feed, not their own sheep, but Christ's (paragraph 17) and points to the harm that the loss of unity is causing (paragraphs 18 and 19). Lastly, Augustine offers a final plea for unity and for the tolerance of sinners in the Church (paragraph 20).

To his beloved brother and lord, Macrobius, Augustine sends greetings.

1, 1. Since my dearest sons and honorable men[487] brought to Your Benevolence my letter in which I admonished you and asked that you not rebaptize our subdeacon, they wrote back to me that you replied, "I cannot but receive those who come to me and give them the faith they have asked for."[488] And yet, if someone baptized in your communion, who was long separated from you, comes to you and through ignorance thinks that he has to be baptized again and asks for it, after you investigate and learn where he was baptized, you receive the person who comes to you, but you do not, nonetheless, give him the faith he asks for. Rather, you teach him that he has what he asks for, nor do you pay attention to the words of a man in error, but you apply your zeal to correct him. The one, therefore, who gives wrongly what should not now be given and who violates the sacrament that was already given is blamed for his own error; he is not excused by the error of the one making the request. Tell me, therefore, I beg you, how he who asks for it from you does not have what he had already received from me. If it is on account of the water of another and the font of another, as those who do not understand often say because Scripture says, *Keep away from the water of another, and do not drink from the font of another* (Prv 9:18 LXX), when Felician[489] was separated from you in the sect of Maximian, he was accused of being "a violator of the truth and a chain of sacrilege," according to the words of your council.[490] If he took with him your font, what was the font in which you baptized your people when he was separated? But if he baptized in the font of another, why did you not rebaptize him? For now your bishop sits together with Primian who was condemned by him and who condemned him.

2. But as our sons who saw you on this matter conveyed to me by their letter, when they asked what you would say about it, you replied that you, as recently ordained, could not be a judge of the actions of your father,[491] but that you abide by what you received from your predecessors. As a result I certainly felt sorrow over your difficult position since I consider you a young man with a good mind,

---

487. Maximus and Theodore, who wrote Letter 107 to Augustine.
488. Letter 107.
489. Felician of Musti was a Maximianist, i.e., a member of a schismatic group that split off from the Donatists in 392, when Maximian was ordained a bishop over against Primian, who succeeded Parmenian as Donatist bishop of Carthage.
490. I.e., the Council of Bagai (394)..
491. Macrobius succeeded Proculian as the Donatist bishop of Hippo.

from what I hear. For what forces you to this response but the difficulty of a bad cause? But if you pay attention, my brother, if you think correctly, if you fear God, no necessity forces you to persist in a bad cause. For this answer of yours does not resolve the question I set before you, but frees our cause from all slander from your accusations. After all, you say that, as recently ordained, you cannot be the judge of your father, but abide by what you received from your predecessors. Why, then, do we not rather remain in the Church that we have received from Christ the Lord through the apostles as beginning from Jerusalem and bearing fruit and growing throughout all the nations?[492] And why are we now judged concerning the actions of some fathers of ours that are said to have been committed almost one hundred years ago? If you do not dare to judge concerning your father who is still present in this life and whom you could question, why do you say to me that I should judge concerning someone who died long before I was born? And why do you say to the Christian peoples that they should judge concerning the African traditors[493] who died so many years before and whom so many Christians who were alive then and dwelled in very distant lands could neither hear of nor come to know, even when they were alive? You do not dare judge Primian who remains with us and is known. Why do you impose on me the task of judging Caecilian[494] who died long ago and is unknown? If you do not judge your fathers concerning their actions, why do you judge your brothers concerning the actions of others?

3. Or do you perhaps deny that we are brothers? But we do better to listen to the Holy Spirit who commands us through the prophet, *Listen, you who fear the word of the Lord. Say, You are our brothers to those who hate you and despise you in order that the name of the Lord may receive honor and may be seen by them in joy, while they are put to shame* (Is 66:5 LXX). For, if the name of the Lord truly brought more joy to human beings than the name of human beings, would Christ, who cries out, *I give you my peace* (Jn 14:27), be divided in his members by those who say, *I belong to Paul*, or *I belong to Apollos*, or *I belong to Cephas* (1 Cor 1:12) and who are torn asunder by the names of human beings? Would Christ of whom it was said, *This is the one who baptizes* (Jn 1:33), be subjected to exsufflation[495] in his own baptism, Christ of whom it was said, *Christ loved the Church and handed himself over for her in order to make her holy, cleansing her by the bath of water by means of the word* (Eph 5:25-26)? Would he, then, be subjected to exsufflation in his own bath if the name of the Lord, to whom baptism belongs, brought more joy to human beings than the names of human beings of whom you say, "What this one gives is holy, but not what that one gives"?

---

492. See Acts 1:8.
493. See p. 155, n. 319.
494. Caecilian was the bishop of Carthage at the time when the Donatist schism began; he was accused of having been ordained by a traditor.
495. The rite of exsufflation symbolized the expulsion of the devil from the person to be baptized.

2, 4. And your colleagues, nonetheless, paid attention to the truth where they wanted, and they thought that not only the baptism that Primian administered in your communion but also that which Felician administered in the sacrilegious schism of Maximian was holy on account of the holy joy over the honor shown to the Lord. And they not only did not dare to violate the character that he had received among you, but after he was corrected they also did not dare to violate that character which, as a deserter, he imprinted upon others outside your sect, because they recognized the mark of the king. You do not want to judge concerning this good action of theirs where you should laudably imitate them, and you follow their judgment in which they deserve to be despised by all. You are afraid to judge concerning Primian for fear that you might be forced to hear what you blame; judge in fact, and you will rather be able to find there what you praise. We do not, after all, want you to bear in mind what Primian did wrongly, but what he did perfectly correctly. In receiving those whom Felician, who condemned him, had baptized in his most wicked schism, he corrected the error of human beings; he did not destroy the sacraments of God. He recognized the good of Christ even in bad human beings, but he corrected the sin of human beings without violating the good of Christ. Or if this action is displeasing to you, at least pay attention to this other point; in accord with your fine mind wisely consider this: You do not judge one man, Primian, concerning the actions of Primian himself, and you judge the Christian world concerning the actions of Caecilian. You are afraid that you will be defiled if you know what you do not dare to punish; acquit the nations, then, which could not know what you accuse them of.

5. Still that was not the action of Primian alone; even you know, I believe, that almost a hundred of your bishops who conspired in that damnable schism with Maximian dared to condemn Primian, and in a council of three hundred and ten of your bishops at Bagai, as the words of its decree proclaim, "The lightning bolt of condemnation expelled Maximian, the adversary of the faith, the violator of the truth, the enemy of mother Church, the minister of Dathan, Korah, and Abiram,[496] from the bosom of peace."[497] Hence, the other twelve who were present at his ordination, when he was elevated to the bishopric in opposition to Primian, were condemned along with him without any delay. But for fear that the schism might become too great, the rest were granted an extra period of time to return by a predetermined day in possession of their full dignity, provided they returned within the time limit. Nor were the three hundred and ten afraid to call back to their company those accused of the great sacrilege of Maximian, having their eyes perhaps on the words of Scripture, *Love covers a multitude of sins* (1 Pt 4:8). But those who were granted the extra time baptized outside your communion all those whom they were able to baptize. For they could only have been invited to return within the extra time if they had been outside your com-

---

496. See Nm 16:1-17:5.
497. See *Answer to Cresconius* III,22,24.59; IV,2,5.38.

munion. Finally, before the extra time ran out and after it had, those twelve who were condemned with Maximian were accused before three or more proconsuls in order that they might be driven from their sees by the power of the courts. Among these were Felician of Musti, with whom I am presently concerned, and Praetextatus of Assuri,[498] who is recently deceased, and after his condemnation another bishop had already been ordained to replace him. Not Primian alone, but many other bishops of yours, when they were celebrating with a large crowd the birthday of Optatus of Thamugadi,[499] received back these two in their full dignities after their immediate condemnation, after the time limit that was granted to the others had run out, and after the accusation was spread about, even through the turmoil of the courts before so many consuls. And they baptized no one who had been baptized by them. If you reject this claim or deny some part of it, I will be called upon to prove what I said at the risk of losing my office of bishop.

6. The case is ended, Brother Macrobius; God has done this; God willed it. It was due to his hidden providence that in the case of Maximian a mirror for your correction was held up to your eyes in order to bring to an end all the criminal slander against us, in fact against the Church of Christ, which is growing throughout the whole world. I do not mean your own slander, for I do not want to appear insulting to you, but certainly that of your people. For nothing at all has survived of those arguments that people, who do not understand them, are accustomed to bring forth against us, as if they were drawn from the Scriptures. After all, they often have on their lips, *Refrain from the water of another* (Prv 9:18, LXX). But we answer: It is not the water of another, though it is in the hands of another. In the same way that was not Maximian's water from which you did not refrain.

Similarly, it is objected to us, *They have become for me like deceitful water that has no faith* (Jer 15:18). We reply: This was said of false human beings who had nothing to do with the sacraments of God, which cannot be deceitful even in persons who are deceitful. For they were certainly deceitful who, as you yourselves admit, condemned Primian on false charges, but the water was not deceitful in which, when separated from you, they baptized those whom they could. For, when you accepted that water in those people whom Felician and Praetextatus baptized outside your communion, you believed that the water was true in those deceitful men.

You object to us: *If one is baptized by someone dead, what good does his bath do?* (Sir 34:30). We answer: If this was written concerning the baptism by which they baptize those whom the Church has expelled as if dead, it did not say

---

498. Felician of Musti and Praetextatus of Assuri were Maximianist bishops who were accepted back by the Donatists along with all whom they had baptized without any repetition of baptism for those whom they had baptized.

499. Optatus of Thamugadi was a Donatist bishop who was notorious for his persecution of the Catholics during the time of Gildo.

that it was not a bath, but that it does no good. And we say that too. Nonetheless, when one comes to the Church with that which he received outside, it does him good within the Church, not when baptism is repeated, but when the baptized person is corrected. In that way the Council of Bagai spoke of Maximian and his companions as dead men expelled from the congregation of your communion; it says, "A true wave has cast some members onto sharp rocks as if shipwrecked. The shores are full of the corpses of those who are perishing after the example of the Egyptians; in death itself they receive a greater punishment because they do not receive burial after the loss of life in the vengeful waters."[500] From this crowd of the dead you welcomed Felician and Praetextatus back with their dignities, as if they had come back to life, and you did not rebaptize those baptized by them in that period of death, because you recognized that the baptism of Christ given outside the Church by dead ministers does not benefit those who are dead, but that the same baptism does benefit those who return to life inside the Church.

You object to us: *Let not the oil of a sinner anoint my head* (Ps 141:5). We answer: These words are understood of the smooth and deceptive agreement of the flatterer by which the head of sinners is anointed and swells when they are praised for the desires of their soul and when those who have committed iniquity are spoken well of. This is seen clearly enough from the previous verse, for the whole sentence reads as follows: *The righteous person will correct me and rebuke me with mercy, but the oil of the sinner will not anoint my head* (Ps 141:5). The psalmist said that he prefers to be worn down by the truthful severity of someone merciful rather than to be exalted by the deceptive praise of someone deceitful. But however you understand it, certainly in the case of those whom Felician and Praetextatus baptized in their sacrilege, you either welcomed the oil of sinners, or you recognized that it is the oil of Christ that was conferred even by sinful ministers. After all, they were sinners when it was said of them in the Council of Bagai, "Know that those guilty of an infamous crime have been condemned; by their deadly work of destruction they have glued together a pot filthy from collected trash."[501]

3, 7. It will suffice to have said this concerning baptism. But the reason for your schism is often made to appear good when these testimonies are not understood. Scripture says, *Do not share in the sins of others* (1 Tm 5:22). But we reply: One shares in the sins of others who consents to their evil actions, not one who, though being wheat, still shares, along with the straw, in the divine sacraments as long as the threshing-floor is being winnowed.[502] For Scripture says, *Depart from there, and touch nothing unclean* (Is 52:11), and, *One who touches something impure is impure* (Lv 22:4.6), but one who touches by consent of the

---

500. See *Answer to Cresconius* IV, 31.
501. See ibid. III, 22.59; IV,15.39; *Answer to Gaudentius, a Donatist Bishop* II, 7.
502. See Mt 3:12.

will, by which the first man was deceived,⁵⁰³ not by bodily contact, by which Judas kissed Christ.⁵⁰⁴ Those fishes, of course, of which the Lord speaks in the Gospel, good ones and bad ones within the same net, to which he compares the unity of the Church, all swim, mingled together in terms of their bodies, but separate in their morals, until the end of the world, which is prefigured by the term "shore."⁵⁰⁵ After all, Scripture says, *A little yeast corrupts the whole lump* (1 Cor 5:6), but of those who consent to evildoers, not of those who, according to the prophet Ezekiel, groan and grieve over the iniquities of the people of God, which are committed in the midst of them.⁵⁰⁶

8. Daniel too bemoans this mixture of good and evil persons; the three men also groaned over it; he did this in prayer, they did it in the furnace.⁵⁰⁷ Still they did not separate themselves by a bodily separation from the unity of the people whose sins they were confessing. What great complaints all the prophets spoke against the same people among whom they lived! Still they did not by bodily departure or separation seek another people in which they might live. The apostles themselves tolerated without any contamination of themselves that the devil, Judas, mingled with them up to the end, when he hanged himself with a noose.⁵⁰⁸ And so, the Lord said to them on account of the presence of that man in their midst, *And you are clean, but not all* (Jn 13:10). Nor was the whole lump of dough corrupted in them on account of his uncleanness, as if by the leaven of different morals. Nor can one correctly say that his wickedness escaped their notice, except perhaps that by which he was going to betray the Lord. For they wrote of him that he was a thief and had taken from the purse of the Lord everything that was put into it.⁵⁰⁹ No one slanderously applied to them the testimony: *You saw a thief and went along with him* (Ps 50:18). For one goes along with the actions of the evil not by sharing with them in the sacraments but by consenting to their evil actions. How much the apostle Paul complained about false brethren,⁵¹⁰ though he was not defiled by bodily contact with them, since he was separated from them by the difference of a pure heart! He in fact rejoiced that Christ was also preached by some of those who he knew were filled with hate,⁵¹¹ and hatred is, of course, a diabolical sin.

9. Finally, after the Church had spread more widely, there came Bishop Cyprian,⁵¹² a man closer to our times. By his authority you occasionally try to

---

503. See Gn 3:1-6.
504. See Mt 26:49; Mk 14:45.
505. See Mt 13:47-49.
506. See Ez 9:4.
507. See Dn 9:5-16; 3:28-31.
508. See Mt 27:4.
509. See Jn 12:6.
510. See 2 Cor 11:26.
511. See Phil 1:18.
512. Cyprian was bishop of Carthage; he suffered martyrdom in 258.

support the repetition of baptism, although that council or those writings, if they are really his and were not, as some think, written under his name and attributed to him, contain his great love for unity and show how he took care by his perfectly frank exhortation that even those with whom he disagreed were to be tolerated in it, for fear that the bond of peace would be broken. He was especially attentive to the fact that, if some human error crept in on certain points on which someone held another view than the truth contains, charity would cover a multitude of sins,[513] as long as fraternal oneness of heart was preserved. He so held onto charity, he so loved it that, if he held another view of baptism than is the truth, God would also reveal this to him, just as the Apostle said to the brethren living in charity, *Let as many of us as are perfect hold this view, and if any of you thinks otherwise, God will also reveal this to you. Let us, nonetheless, continue on the path on which we have come.* (Phil 3:15-16) There is also the fact that, if the fruitful branch still had something that needed pruning, it was pruned by the glorious sword of martyrdom, not because he was killed for the name of Christ, but because he was killed for the name of Christ in the bosom of unity. For he wrote and most faithfully asserted that those who are outside that unity, even if they die for his name, can be killed, but cannot receive the crown of martyrdom.[514] The love of unity has such great power either for wiping out sins if it is preserved or for reinforcing them if it is violated.

10. The glorious Cyprian deplored that many fell away when the Church was ravaged because of the persecution of the wicked pagans and attributed it to the bad morals of those who were living in the Church a life that deserved to be condemned.[515] He groaned over the conduct of his colleagues and did not cover over his groans in silence. Rather, he says that they had advanced to such great covetousness that, though people were starving, even brethren in the Church, they wanted to have money in abundance, robbed estates by insidious fraud, and increased their capital by compounding interest.[516] I do not think that Cyprian was defiled by the greed, robberies, and usury of these people, nor was he set apart from them by bodily separation but by the difference of his life. He touched the altar with them but he did not touch their unclean life, since he blamed and rebuked it in such terms. Those things are touched when they are approved; they are rejected when they meet with disapproval. Hence, that great bishop lacked neither the severity by which he reprehended sins nor the caution by which he preserved the bond of unity. We read in one of his letters that he wrote to the priest, Maximus, his clear and open view on this question; by it he absolutely commanded, while holding onto the prophetic rule, that one ought never to abandon the unity of the Church on account of the presence in it of evil persons. He

---

513. See 1 Pt 4:8.
514. See Cyprian, *The Unity of the Catholic Church* 14.
515. See Cyprian, *The Lapsed* 4-6.
516. See ibid.

says, "For, though we see that there are weeds in the Church, our faith and love ought not to be hampered so that we withdraw from the Church, because we see that there are weeds in the Church. We must only strive to be wheat."[517]

11. This law of love was promulgated by the lips of Christ the Lord, for to that love there belong the parables concerning the toleration of the weeds up to the time of harvest in the unity of the field throughout the world and concerning the toleration of the bad fishes within the net up to the time of reaching the shore.[518] If your predecessors, then, held this law in mind, if they thought with the fear of God, they would not split themselves off in a wicked schism from the Church on account of Caecilian and some other Africans, whether they were, as you suppose, truly criminals, or were accused falsely, as is more believable. Cyprian himself described that Church as shedding its rays through all the nations and extending its branches through all the earth with the abundance of its vitality. They would not, I repeat, have split themselves off in a wicked schism from so many Christian nations that were utterly ignorant of who were the accusers, what were the accusations, and who were the accused. A schism comes about only because of a private feud, not for the public benefit, or because of that vice that Cyprian himself mentioned in the following and that he warned must be avoided. For, after he commanded that we must not abandon the Church on account of the weeds that are seen in the Church, he went on and said, "We must only strive to be wheat so that, when the wheat begins to be stored in the barns of the Lord, we may receive the reward of our work and toil. The Apostle says in his letter, *In a large house there are not only vessels of gold and silver, but also ones of wood and clay, and some destined for an honorable purpose, others for a dishonorable purpose* (2 Tm 2:20). Let us work hard and labor as much as we can in order that we may be a vessel of gold and silver. But the Lord, to whom has been given a staff of iron,[519] alone is permitted to smash vessels of clay. A servant cannot be greater than his master,[520] nor can anyone claim for himself what the Father has given to the Son alone so that he believes that he can bring the winnowing fan to winnow and cleanse the threshing-floor or can separate the weeds from the wheat by human judgment.[521] This presumption is proud, and this stubbornness that a base madness takes up is sacrilegious, and since they always claim for themselves something more severe than meek justice demands, they perish from the Church. And while they insolently exalt themselves, they lose the light of the truth because they are blinded by their swollen condition."[522]

---

517. Cyprian, Letter 54, 3.
518. See Mt 13:24-43.47-50.
519. See Ps 2:9; Rv 2:27; 19:15. 34; Jn 13:16; 15:20.
520. See Jn 13:16; 15:20.
521. See Mt 3:12.
522. Cyprian, Letter 54, 3.

12. What is clearer than this testimony of Cyprian? What is truer? You see the light from the gospel and the apostles with which it glows; you see that those who, as if offended, abandon the unity of the Church for their own righteousness are themselves rather most unrighteous. You see that those who would not tolerate weeds in the unity of the Lord's field are themselves outside like weeds. You see that those who would not tolerate such chaff in the unity of a great house are themselves outside like chaff. You see how truthfully Scripture says, *A bad son says that he is righteous, but does not excuse his going out* (Prv 30:12 LXX); he does not justify, excuse, defend, or show to be pure and free from sin his going out, that is, his going out from the Church. After all, that is what *he does not excuse* means. For, if he did not say that he was righteous but was truly and genuinely righteous, he would not in a most impious fashion abandon the good on account of sinners, but would endure sinners with great patience on account of the good until at the end of the world the Lord, whether by himself or through his angels, separates the weeds from the grain,[523] the chaff from the wheat,[524] the vessels of anger from the vessels of mercy,[525] the goats from the sheep,[526] the bad fishes from the good ones.[527]

4, 13. But if you are trying to interpret in some other sense than that which the meaning of the words of God demands those testimonies of the Scriptures that your predecessors believed that they should either understand or cite in order to divide the people of God, stop this now! Pay attention to that mirror which God raised up to admonish you with a most merciful foresight, if only you will be wise. I speak of the case of Felician, "the opponent of the faith, the violator of the truth, the enemy of mother Church, the minister of Dathan, Korah, and Abiram," as was proclaimed in the Council of Bagai. They went on to add further about him that the earth did not open up and swallow him, but that he was left among the living for greater punishment. They said, "If he were carried off, he would have had his punishment in the swiftness of death, but now he will suffer more grievous penalties than death when he is dead among the living."[528] I ask you whether those who conspired with him and condemned the innocent Primian touched this man, who was then an unclean corpse. For, if they touched him, they were certainly defiled by touching someone defiled. Why, then, are those who are in communion with the same man and are separated from communion with you granted extra time for returning as if they are innocent persons, "in order that upon their return they may be assured of having their unimpaired dignity and faith"? And why did those who were not present at the ordination of Maximian deserve to hear that "the cuttings of the sacrilegious vine did not pollute them"?

---

523. See Mt 13:24-30.
524. See Mt 3:12.
525. See Rom 9:22-23.
526. See Mt 25:31.
527. See Mt 13:47-50.
528. See Augustine, *Answer to Cresconius* III, 19, 22; IV, 4, 5.

They were, after all, gathered in the same sect, in the same schism, divided from you, allied with them, together here in Africa, most well known, closest friends, and most tightly linked together. Though not present, they ordained Maximian and condemned the absent Primian on his account.

Are you going to say that the vine of Caecilian defiled countless, far distant, and completely unknown Christian peoples of the world, though many of them could not know, I do not mean his case, but not even his name? And do those who not only knew the sin of Maximian, but elevated him, raising him to the bishopric in opposition to Primian, not share in the sins of the others, while those people do share in the sins of others, who either in distant nations did not know that Caecilian was made a bishop, or who in less distant peoples only heard of it, or who in Africa simply and quietly came to know it, or who in the church of Carthage did not raise him to the episcopacy in opposition to anyone?[529] And did those not go along with a thief[530] who were in communion with the person of whom Nummasius, the lawyer, said, while speaking in defense of your present bishop, Restitutus, that "he took possession of the episcopal office by a sacrilegious and almost hidden theft"? And did not they, who were in communion with an adulterer of the truth, throw in their lot with an adulterer?[531] And was not their whole lump of dough corrupted by a little yeast[532] when they favored him, when they remained in his sect cut off from you? And it was not as if they were ignorant; rather, they took care that his sect be cut off from you and raised up against you. Finally, you yourselves invited them to return in such a way that you said that those who were in such close union with Maximian were not polluted by the vine of sacrilege. After all, you received back Praetextatus and Felician with all their dignities; you are peacefully reconciled with them; even today you see Felician seated with you. And yet you have not been stained by sharing in the sins of others; you have not been defiled by any contact with uncleanness; you have not been corrupted by the yeast of wickedness. But the Christian world is accused of the crime of others by means of these testimonies; the division of the unity is defended in your deadly schism, and the branch that remains attached to the root of its true mother is accused of being an unclean branch by the branch that is cut off!

5, 14. Why is it that you so often boast of the persecutions you have endured? If it is not the reason but the penalty that makes one a martyr, when Scripture said, *Blessed are those who suffer persecution*, it uselessly added, *on account of righteousness* (Mt 5:10). Do not the Maximianists easily surpass you in this claim to glory? After all, they underwent persecution not only afterwards with you, but earlier and at your hands. Those words that I quoted a little before are those of

---

529. The CSEL edition indicates that there is a lacuna here.
530. See Ps 50:18.
531. See Ps 50:18.
532. See 1 Cor 5:6.

the lawyer who accused Maximian in the presence of your colleague, Restitutus, who had already been ordained to succeed Salvius of Membressa, who was condemned along with those other eleven without any delay, before the date of the extension passed. Once the date of the extension was passed, Titian also accused Felician and Praetextatus in most severe terms of the whole plot against Primian. The Council of Bagai was quoted in the proconsular record, and not just once, as well as later in the municipal records. Judicial processes were set in motion; the most menacing orders were asked for and obtained; those resisting were led to punishment; the assistance of the state was granted so that the judicial decision might be carried out. Why, then, do you quarrel with us over persecution that you endured, since we shared in it with you, but not with equal justice? For, since one who undergoes persecution does not always suffer death, your clerics and the Circumcellions arranged things between us so that you would undergo persecution but that we would undergo death. But, as I said, do battle with the Maximianists over this claim to praise. For they recite against you the legal records in which you went after them by persecutions through judges, but you were clearly reconciled afterwards with certain of them, after they had been corrected by such coercive measures. Hence, we should not despair of our reconciliation if God deigns to help and to inspire you with a mind for peace. For what your sect is accustomed to say against us with slanderous rather than truthful lips, *Their feet are quick for the shedding of blood* (Ps 14:3), is something that we have rather experienced in the great pillaging of the Circumcellions and of your clerics. For they have torn apart human bodies in the fiercest slaughter and have bloodied so many places with the blood of our people. When you entered this city, their leaders accompanied you with their gangs, shouting, "Praise be to God," amid their songs, and they used these cries like trumpets of battle in all their brigandage. On another day, they were struck and stirred up by the goads of your words, which you hurled at them through a Punic interpreter with an honest and genuine indignation filled with frankness, and you were angered by their actions rather than delighted by their services. They tore themselves from the midst of the congregation, as we were able to hear from those who were present and recounted it, with the gesture of madmen. And after their feet that were quick for the shedding of blood, you did not purify the pavement of the church with any salt water—something that your clerics thought that they should do after our feet.

15. But, as I began to say, this testimony from the Scriptures that you are accustomed to toss about more by way of insult than as proof, *Their feet are quick for the shedding of blood* (Ps 14:3), was also vomited forth in that pompous statement of the Council of Bagai in its fierce attack on Felician and Praetextatus. For, after they had said what they thought should be said about Maximian, they said, "The well-deserved death for his crime not only condemns this man, but the chain of sacrilege also drags very many into complicity in the crime. Of these it is written, *The venom of vipers is under their lips, and their mouth is filled with cursing and bitterness. Their feet are quick for the shedding of blood*"

(Ps 139:3; 14:3), and so on. Then, having said that, in order to show who they were whom the chain of sacrilege drags into complicity in the crime and to condemn those united with Maximian with a similar severity, they said, "Victorian of Carcaviana, then, was guilty of the notorious crime," to whom they add the other eleven, among whom were Felician of Musti and Praetextatus of Assuri. After these things were said against them, a great reconciliation was produced with them with the result that none of them lost their dignities. No one baptized by them was judged to need baptism after the baptism of those who washed those feet that were quick for the shedding of blood. Why, then, should we despair of our reconciliation? May God turn aside the hatred of the devil, and may the peace of Christ conquer in our hearts,[533] and, as the Apostle says, *Let us forgive one another if anyone has a complaint against someone, as God has also forgiven us in Christ* (Col 3:13), in order that, as I have already said and as it must often be said, love may cover over a multitude of sins.[534]

6, 16. But, my brother, you with whom I am now dealing and over whom I desire to rejoice in Christ, as Christ himself knows, the case of Maximian is still fresh in the memory of people still living, against whom these actions were taken, and all these actions are also attested to in so many municipal and proconsular records. Hence, if you want to use the ability of your mind and eloquence to take up the defense of the sect of Donatus in the case of Maximian and if you do not want to act deceitfully, will you not take refuge in the bastion of the truth that has always warned the Catholic Church against you? Then you will admit that the passages about the water of another and about the water of deceit and about the bath of a corpse and any other passage of this sort that there may be should not be understood as you usually do. Rather it should be understood in such a way that the baptism of Christ, which was given to the Church in order that we might partake of eternal salvation, should not be judged foreign to the Church when it is conferred outside the Church and should not be regarded as belonging to others when others have it. Rather, in those outside the Church and separated from the Church it contributes to their destruction, but in those who belong to her and are her own it produces salvation. In the former, when they are converted to the peace of the Church, their error is corrected, but the sacrament is not destroyed when the error is punished. Rather, what was an obstacle for those misguided people externally begins to benefit them internally once they have been corrected. And you will not interpret those passages about not sharing in the sins of others, about separation from sinners, about not touching someone unclean and polluted, about avoiding the corruption of a measure of grain, and other such passages, as you usually interpret them. Otherwise, you will be trapped in the case of Maximian with no way of getting out. Rather, you will wisely state and will hold onto what sound doctrine teaches, what the true rule of faith proves by

---

533. See Col 3:15.
534. See 1 Pt 4:8.

examples from the prophets and apostles, namely, that we should tolerate sinners so that the good are not destroyed rather than that we should abandon the good in order that sinners be kept separate. Only let the good be separate from the reprobate in the imitation of them, in the agreement with them, and in the likeness of their life and conduct, while they both grow together, mingled together in tribulation, gathered together within the nets, up to the time of harvest, of winnowing, and of the shore. But with regard to persecutions, how are you going to defend whatever your people did by means of judges to expel and drive the Maximianists from their sees, unless you claim that your wiser leaders did this by producing a moderate fear in them with the intention of correcting them, not of harming them? But if they went beyond the human limit, as in these sufferings that the city itself testifies Salvius of Mambressa endured, what are you going to say but that this cannot be turned against the other Donatists who were living in one communion of the sacraments, as straw is mixed with the grain, but separate by the difference of their life?

17. Since this is so, I welcome this defense of yours. It will, of course, be this sort of defense if it is truthful, and it will be conquered by the truth if it is not. I welcome, I repeat, this defense of yours, but you see that it is also mine. Why, then, should we not labor together to be grain in the unity of the Lord's threshing floor? Why should we not tolerate together the chaff? Why not, I ask you? What is the reason? For whose benefit? For what advantage? Tell me! Unity is put to flight so that people purchased by the blood of the one Lamb are fired up against one another by their opposing desires, and the sheep belonging to the head of the house are divided among us, as if they were our own. He said, *Feed my sheep* (Jn 21:17); he did not say, "Feed your own sheep." And of those sheep he said, *That there may be one flock and one shepherd* (Jn 10:16). He cries out in the Gospel, *By this all will know that you are my disciples if you have true love for one another* (Jn 13:35), and *Allow both to grow until the harvest for fear that, when you want to gather the weeds, you will at the same time uproot the grain* (Jn 13:30). Unity is put to flight so that a husband goes to one church and a wife to another. He says, "Hold onto unity with me because I am your husband," and she replies, "I am staying where my father is." In that way they divide Christ in one bed, while we would detest them if they divided the marriage bed. Unity is banished so that relatives, fellow citizens, friends, guests and all united to one another in human relationships, all of them Christians, are in harmony in attending banquets, in entering into marriages, in buying and selling, in pacts and agreements, and in all their interests and affairs, but are out of harmony with regard to the altar of God. For, however great the disagreement stemming from elsewhere, people ought to put an end to the discord there and first be reconciled with their brethren and then offer their gift on the altar. But though elsewhere they are in agreement, they are in disagreement at the altar.

18. Unity is banished so that we seek civil laws against the evil actions of your people—I do not want to say your evil actions—and the Circumcellions

arm themselves against the laws, which they scorn because of that very madness by which they are aroused against you when they are in a rage. Unity is banished so that the audacity of farmhands rises up against their bosses, and in opposition to the teaching of the Apostle[535] fugitive servants not only abandon their masters but even threaten their masters. They not only threaten them but plunder them with most violent attacks, with members of your heresy as their instigators and leaders and principal agents in the crime itself. With the cry, "Praise be to God," they offer you honor; with the cry, "Praise be to God," they shed others' blood! As a result, to avoid the hatred of human beings, after having gathered your people and questioned them, you promise that you will return the estates to those from whom they were taken. And you do not, nonetheless, will this in such a way that you may be able to fulfill your promise, for fear that you would be unduly forced to offend the audacity that your priests considered necessary for themselves. They boast of their previous merits in your regard, pointing out and enumerating, prior to this law because of which you rejoice over the freedom restored to you,[536] how many places and basilicas your priests held by means of them, while ours were assaulted and put to flight. And so, if you wanted to be severe with them, you would be seen as ungrateful for their benefits.

19. Unity is banished so that whoever among us refuses to put up with discipline flees to the Circumcellions for defense and is presented to you to be rebaptized. For example, this subdeacon from the country, Rustician, on whose account I was compelled to write these things to you with great sorrow and fear,[537] was excommunicated by his priest because of his wicked and perverse behavior. He also became indebted to many in the territory, and he did not seek any other protection against the disciplinary measures of the Church and against his creditors but that he should receive a new wound to his soul from you[538] and be loved by the Circumcellions as someone utterly pure. Your predecessor already rebaptized such a deacon of ours, one who was also excommunicated by his priest, and he made him your deacon. Not many days later, having joined in the audacity of those same wicked men, as he desired, he was killed in a night attack in the midst of his robbery and arson, at the onrush of a crowd that came to help. These are the fruits of this division that you do not want to heal, since you flee from unity as you ought to flee from this division, which is ugly in itself and damnable in the eyes of God, even if other actions that are so horrible and wicked were not caused by it.

7, 20. Let us recognize, then, my brother, the peace of Christ, and let us together hold onto it, and, to the extent that God grants, let us together strive to

---

535. See Ti 2:9.
536. Toward the end of 409 the emperor, Honorius, granted some freedom to the Donatists, but it was revoked in August of 410 because of the violence of the Circumcellions.
537. See Letter 106.
538. I.e., that he should be baptized again.

be good and together strive, while preserving unity, to correct sinners with as much discipline as we can, and on account of this unity let us tolerate sinners with as much patience as we can. Otherwise, as Christ warned,[539] when we want to gather the weeds up beforetime, weeds that blessed Cyprian testified are seen and clearly seen, not outside, but within the Church,[540] we might at the same time uproot the grain as well. For you really do not have particular privileges of holiness all your own so that our sinners defile us but your sinners do not defile you, and so that the fear of the traditors from long ago, of which we are ignorant, contaminates us but the present audacity of the wicked, which you see, does not contaminate you. Let us recognize that ark that prefigured the Church; let us together be the clean animals in it, and let us not refuse also to carry in it along with us the unclean animals until the end of the flood. For they were together in the ark, but they did not together please the Lord in the odor of sacrifice. For after the flood Noah did not offer to the Lord a sacrifice from the unclean animals.[541] The clean animals did not, nonetheless, abandon the ark ahead of time on account of the unclean animals. Only the raven abandoned it and separated itself from the communion of that ark before time, but it was from among the two pairs of unclean, not from the seven pairs of clean ones.[542] Let us detest the uncleanness of this separation. For this separation by itself makes worthy of damnation those who are worthy of praise because of their conduct. For *a bad son says that he is righteous, but does not excuse his going out* (Prv 30:12 LXX), though, insolently raised up and blinded by his pride, he dares to say what the prophet foresaw and detested, *Do not touch me for I am clean* (Is 65:5). Whoever, therefore, abandons beforetime, as if on account of the uncleanness of certain people, the assembly of this unity, like the ark in the flood carrying clean and unclean animals, shows that he himself is rather what he is fleeing. The Lord willed that in this city also your people by the lips of a certain person.[543]

---

539. See Mt 13:29.
540. See Cyprian, Letter 54, 3.
541. See Gn 8:20.
542. See Gn 8:6.
543. At this point there is a lacuna of approximately twenty lines in the manuscripts.

LETTER 185

Augustine to Boniface, the tribune of Africa (417)

In approximately 417 Augustine wrote to Boniface, the tribune of Africa, who later became the count of Africa, the same man for whom he also wrote Letters 185A, 189, and 17*. As the one in charge of implementing the punishments imposed upon the Donatists, Boniface had consulted Augustine about the character of Donatism. In *Revisions* 2, 48 Augustine treated the present letter as a book and gave it the title, *The Correction of the Donatists*. He says of it: "At the same time I also wrote a book, *The Correction of the Donatists*, on account of those who refused to be corrected by the imperial laws. This book begins: 'I praise and congratulate you and admire.'"

Augustine begins by explaining the difference between the Donatists and the Arians, with whom Boniface was more familiar (paragraph 1). Scripture foretold that heresies and schisms would come to test our faith and love (paragraph 2). Along with the Catholics the Donatists recognize Christ in the Scriptures, where they should also recognize the Catholic Church, which the Scriptures foretold would spread throughout the whole world (paragraph 3). Even if Caecilian, the Catholic bishop of Carthage at the time the schism began, was guilty, as the Donatists claimed, they are still not justified in abandoning the unity of Christ (paragraph 4). It is not clear that Caecilian was guilty, but it is clear from the words of God that the Church would spread to all the nations (paragraph 5).

The Donatists were the first to appeal to the emperor when they took their case against Caecilian to Constantine (paragraph 6). The laws promulgated against the Donatists are actually for their benefit (paragraph 7). The Donatists must obey laws of the Christian emperors in defense of religious truth or submit to the penalties (paragraph 8). When the Donatists suffer under these laws, they are not martyrs because they do not suffer for the sake of justice (paragraph 9). It is not always wrong to persecute, just as it is not always right to be persecuted (paragraph 10). The wicked unjustly persecute the Church, while the Church justly persecutes the enemies of the Church (paragraph 11).

Augustine recounts the violent behavior of some of the Donatists, who have even resorted to killing themselves (paragraph 12). The laws of the emperors that force them into the unity of the Church are highly salutary (paragraph 13). The Church rightly tries to save them, even against their will and even at the risk that some will kill themselves rather than enter the Church (paragraph 14). Augustine continues his account of the Donatist violence and points out that their crimes kept many from entering into the Catholic Church (paragraphs 15 and 16). The Maximianist separation from the Donatists and their reconciliation with them provides a strong argument against the Donatists themselves (paragraph 17). Augustine explains that the terrible violence on the part of some Donatists brought the Catholics to appeal to the civil authorities (paragraph 18). The Christian emperors now use their power in the service of God (paragraph 19), as it was foretold that the kings of the earth would serve God (paragraph 20).

Though it is better to bring people to worship God by instruction than by fear of punishment and pain, the latter means are valuable too (paragraph 21). Christ himself used coercion in the conversion of Paul the apostle (paragraph 22). So, too, the Church has the right to use coercion to bring the Lord's lost sheep back to the fold (paragraph 23). Augustine explains the parable in which the Lord's servants are ordered to compel people to come in to the banquet from the roads and pathways (paragraph 24).

Augustine explains why he earlier did not want to use coercion against the Donatists and later changed his mind (paragraph 25). His earlier view failed to prevail because of the terrible way in which the Donatists treated the Catholic bishop of Bagai (paragraph 26). Augustine recounts the savage treatment that this bishop received from the Donatists (paragraph 27). Even Paul the apostle himself appealed to the protection of the emperor (paragraph 28). And great benefits have come to the church of Africa from the laws issued by the emperors (paragraph 29). For many Donatists have entered into union with the Catholic Church, though others have refused and turned to further violence (paragraph 30). The Catholic Church, nonetheless, meets their hatred and slander with love (paragraph 31).

As David in grief over the loss of Absalom was consoled by the preservation of his kingdom, so the Church is consoled by the salvation of many in her grief over the few who perish by their own hand (paragraph 32). Augustine develops a comparison between the Donatists and people who are in a building that we know is going to collapse and who threaten to kill themselves if we try to rescue them (paragraph 33). He argues that, if we could rescue even one person, we would have the obligation to do so, even if the rest kill themselves (paragraph 34).

Augustine replies to the Donatist objection that the Catholics are seeking their property (paragraph 35). If the Donatists enter the Church, they will have their own property as well as the property of the Church along with the Catholics (paragraph 36). He challenges the Donatist claim to righteousness and warns them against seeking to establish a righteousness of their own (paragraph 37). The Church in this world needs to pray daily for forgiveness of sins and will be without spot or wrinkle only in the next world (paragraph 38). All past sins are forgiven in baptism, but only if baptism is conferred within the Church (paragraph 39). For baptism makes righteous only those present in the body of Christ, which is the Church (paragraph 40). Scripture foretells the triumph of the righteous over the unrighteous, that is, of the Catholics over the Donatists (paragraph 41). For apart from the unity of Christ no one can be righteous (paragraph 42).

Augustine explains that the Donatists are not rebaptized when they enter the Catholic Church because they already have the mark of the king (paragraph 43).

Letter 185   249

He also explains why the Donatists are allowed to retain positions of honor in the Church, though the previous practice of the Church had been more strict (paragraph 44). The rigorous discipline has been relaxed in order to heal the wound of schism (paragraph 45). The Donatists are received into the Church with their full honors, but they should also do penance for their error (paragraph 46). Just as the Donatists received back the Maximianists for the peace of their sect, so the Church welcomes back the Donatists for the peace of Christ (paragraph 47).

Augustine turns to the Donatist objection that they should not be forgiven if they have sinned against the Holy Spirit (paragraph 48). He explains that the sin against the Holy Spirit that will not be forgiven is not just any sin but the refusal, up to the end of one's life, to be in the unity of Christ's body (paragraph 49). Augustine warns the Donatists that they cannot have the Holy Spirit outside the body of Christ (paragraph 50). In closing, Augustine apologizes to Boniface for the length of his letter but promises him that he will find in it the answers to the questions that the Donatists raise (paragraph 51).

A BOOK ON THE CORRECTION OF THE DONATISTS

1, 1. I praise and congratulate you and admire the fact, my most beloved son Boniface, that amid the concerns of armed warfare you intensely desire to know the things that pertain to God. From this it is truly evident that you serve the faith that you have in Christ even in a military setting. In order, therefore, to inform Your Charity briefly of the difference between the error of the Arians and that of the Donatists, the Arians say that the Father and the Son and the Holy Spirit have different substances. The Donatists, however, do not say this but confess that the Trinity has one substance. And if some of the Donatists say that the Son is less than the Father, they do not deny that he is of the same substance. But very many among them say that they believe about the Father and the Son and the Holy Spirit the same thing that the Catholic Church believes. Nor is this the question at issue with them, but to their misfortune they quarrel only about Church unity and, by the perversity of their error, carry on rebellious hostilities against the unity of Christ. But at times some of them, as we have heard, wanting to win the Goths to their side, when they see that they have some power, say that they believe the same thing as the Goths. But they are refuted by the authority of their predecessors, because not even Donatus himself is said to have held that belief, and it is his sect to which they boast of belonging.

2. But, my dearest son, do not let these things upset you. It was predicted, after all, that there would be heresies and scandals so that we might develop our minds in the midst of our enemies and that in that way our faith and love might be more tested—our faith, of course, in order that they may not deceive us, but our love in order that we may also work for their correction as much as we can, not merely striving so that they may not harm the weak and so that they may be set free from their wicked error, but also praying for them so that the Lord may open their minds and they may understand the Scriptures.[544] For in the Holy Books where Christ the Lord is revealed, his Church is also made known. But, though the Donatists come to know Christ only in the Scriptures, with an amazing blindness they do not recognize his Church through the authority of the Divine Writings but design their own church through the vanity of human lies.

3. They recognize Christ along with us when we read, *They have pierced my hands and my feet; they have numbered all my bones. But they saw me and looked upon me. They have divided for themselves my clothes, and they cast lots for my tunic.* (Ps 22:17-19) But they refuse to recognize the Church in what follows a little later, *All the ends of the earth will remember and turn to the Lord, and all the families of the nations will adore in his sight, for kingship belongs to the Lord, and he will have dominion over the nations* (Ps 22:28-29). They recognize Christ along with us when we read, *The Lord said to me: You are my Son; today I have begotten you* (Ps 2:7). But they refuse to recognize the Church in

---

544. See Lk 24:45; 1 Cor 11:19.

what follows, *Ask me, and I shall give you the nations as your heritage and the ends of the earth as your possession* (Ps 2:8). They recognize Christ along with us in what the Lord says in the Gospel, *It was necessary that Christ suffer and rise from the dead on the third day* (Lk 24:46). But they refuse to recognize the Church in what follows: *And that repentance be preached in his name through all the nations, beginning from Jerusalem* (Lk 24:47). And countless are the testimonies of the Holy Books, which I should not squeeze into this book. Just as Christ the Lord is seen in them either in his divinity equal to the Father, by which he was *the Word in the beginning, and the Word was with God, and the Word was God* (Jn 1:1), or in the lowliness of the flesh, which he assumed because *the Word became flesh and dwelled among us* (Jn 1:14), so his Church is seen to be not in Africa alone, as they rave in their most impudent vanity, but spread throughout the whole world.

4. For they prefer their contentions to the divine testimonies because, on account of the case of Caecilian, formerly bishop of the church of Carthage, against whom they brought charges that they could not and cannot prove, they split off from the Catholic Church, that is, from the unity of all the nations. And yet, even if the charges they brought against Caecilian were true and could at some point be proved to us, and we anathematized Caecilian, who is now dead, we should still not for the sake of any human being abandon the Church of Christ, which is not fashioned by quarrelsome opinions but is proved by divine testimonies, *because it is better to place one's trust in the Lord than in a human being* (Ps 118:8). For even if Caecilian sinned (and I say this without prejudice to the man's innocence) Christ did not for this reason lose his heritage. It is easy for one human being to believe true or false things about another, but it is criminal impudence to want to condemn the Church's communion, which stretches throughout the world, because of the crimes of a human being that you cannot prove to the whole world.

5. I do not know whether Caecilian was ordained by those who surrendered God's Books; I did not see it; I heard it from his enemies. It is not told me in the law of God, in the preaching of the prophets, in the holiness of the Psalms, in the Apostle of Christ, or in the words of Christ. But testimonies from the whole of the Scriptures proclaim with one voice the Church spread through the whole world, with which the sect of Donatus is not in communion. The law of God said, *In your offspring all the nations will be blessed* (Gn 22:18, 26:4). God said through the prophet, *From the rising of the sun to its setting a pure sacrifice is offered to my name, because my name has been glorified among the nations* (Mal 1:11). God said through the Psalm, *He will have dominion from sea to sea and from the river to the ends of the earth* (Ps 72:8). God said through the Apostle, *Bearing fruit and growing in the whole world* (Col 1:6). The Son of God said with his own lips, *You will be my witnesses in Jerusalem, in all of Judea, and in Samaria, and to the ends of the earth* (Acts 1:8). Caecilian, the bishop of the church of Carthage, is accused by the quarrels of human beings; the Church

of Christ, established in all nations, is praised by words of God. Piety, truth, and love do not permit us to accept against Caecilian the testimony of human beings whom we do not see in the Church to which God gave testimony. For those who do not follow the testimonies of God have lost the weight of human testimony.

2, 6. I add the fact that by their accusations they themselves referred the case of Caecilian to the judgment of Emperor Constantine. In fact, after the episcopal tribunals, in which they were not able to defeat Caecilian, they brought Caecilian himself, by their most persistent prosecution, to be examined by the aforementioned emperor. And now, in order to deceive the ignorant, they blame in us what they did first, when they say that Christians ought not to ask for anything from Christian emperors against the enemies of Christ. They did not dare to deny this in the conference that we held together at Carthage;[545] in fact, they dared to boast that their predecessors brought criminal charges against Caecilian before the emperor, adding, moreover, the lie that they won their case there and caused him to be condemned. How, then, are they not persecutors who, when they persecuted Caecilian by their accusations and lost to him, chose to claim for themselves false glory by a most impudent lie? For they not only thought it no sin if they were able to prove that Caecilian was condemned by means of their predecessors' accusations, but they even boasted of it in praise of themselves. Since the proceedings are very lengthy, especially for you who are occupied with other matters requisite for the Roman peace, it would take a great deal of time to read how the Donatists were defeated in every way at the conference itself, but you could perhaps read a synopsis of them, which I believe my brother and fellow bishop Optatus[546] has, or, if he does not have it, it could easily be obtained from the church of Sitifis,[547] since this book too is perhaps burdensome for a man with your concerns because of its length.

7. For the same thing happened to the Donatists as happened to the accusers of holy Daniel. For, just as the lions were turned against those men,[548] so the laws by which the Donatists wanted to destroy the innocent Caecilian have been turned against them. But by the mercy of Christ these laws, which seem to be against them, are rather in their favor since many Donatists have been corrected by them and are being corrected each day, and they give thanks that they have been corrected and set free from that mad destruction. And those who hated the laws now love them, and the more they hated the laws in their insanity, the more they are thankful, once they have recovered their health, that the laws so very conducive to their salvation were harsh toward them. And they are aroused by a similar love along with us for the others with whom they had been perishing.

---

545. Augustine refers to the Conference of Carthage held 1-8 June 411, at which the Donatist schism was in principle ended.
546. Optatus was the Catholic bishop of Milevis in Numidia.
547. Sitifis was the capital of Mauritania Sitifensis.
548. See Dn 6:21.

Hence, they strive equally with us in order that the others may not perish. For a doctor is troublesome to a raging madman and a father to an undisciplined son, the former by tying him down, the latter by beating him, but both because they act out of love. If, however, they neglect them and permit them to perish, this false gentleness is in fact cruel. After all, *the horse and the mule, which lack intellect* (Ps 32:9), resist with bites and kicks human beings who treat their wounds in order to heal them, and human beings are often put in danger from their teeth and hoofs and at times injured. But they still do not abandon them until they have brought them back to health by painful and tormenting medical interventions. How much more should one human being not abandon another, how much more should one brother not abandon another, lest he perish for eternity! For, once he has been corrected, he can understand what a great benefit he received when he was complaining of suffering persecution.

8. And so, as the Apostle says, *While we have the time, let us do good for all without growing weary* (Gal 6:9-10). According to what is possible in each case, whether by the words of Catholic preachers or by the laws of the Catholic emperors, in part by those who obey the teachings of God, in part by those who obey the orders of the emperor, let all be called to salvation; let all be called back from destruction. For, when the emperors establish bad laws in favor of error and against the truth, those who hold the correct faith are put to the test and those who persevere win the crowns of martyrs. But when they establish good laws in favor of the truth and against error, those who act with violence are struck with terror and those who act with intelligence are corrected. Whoever, then, refuses to obey the laws of the emperors that are issued against the truth of God earns a great reward, but whoever refuses to obey the laws of the emperors that are issued in favor of the truth of God earns a great punishment. After all, even in the times of the prophets all the kings are blamed who did not forbid or stop in the people of God practices that were instituted contrary to the commandments of God, and those who forbade and stopped them are praised beyond the merits of the others. And since King Nebuchadnezzar was a worshiper of idols, he established a sacrilegious law that the people were to worship a statue, but those who refused to obey his impious decree acted piously and faithfully. Yet the same king, once he was corrected by a miracle of God, established a pious and praiseworthy law in favor of the truth that whoever spoke blasphemously against the true God of Shadrach, Meshach and Abednego would be put to death along with his whole house.[549] If any individuals held this law in contempt and rightly suffered the penalty that had been established, they ought to have said what these Donatists say, namely, that they are righteous because they suffer persecution on account of the emperor's law. They would certainly say this if they were as insane as these Donatists are insane who divide the members of Christ, subject

---

549. See Dn 3:5.96.

the sacraments of Christ to exsufflation,[550] and boast of being persecuted because they are forbidden to do these actions by the laws of the emperors, which they established for the sake of the unity of Christ, while the Donatists deceitfully boast of their own innocence and seek from human beings the glory of martyrs, a glory they cannot receive from the Lord.

9. But they are true martyrs of whom the Lord says, *Blessed are those who suffer persecution on account of justice* (Mt 5:10). Those, then, who suffer persecution on account of injustice and on account of the impious division of Christian unity are not true martyrs, but those *who suffer persecution on account of justice*. For Hagar suffered persecution from Sarah,[551] and Sarah who did this was holy, while Hagar who suffered persecution was sinful. Is holy David, whom wicked Saul persecuted, to be compared with this persecution that Hagar suffered?[552] There is a big difference, not because he suffered persecution, but because he suffered persecution on account of justice. And the Lord himself was crucified along with thieves,[553] but the reasons for their suffering separated those whom their suffering united. For this reason we should understand in the psalm the cry of true martyrs who desire to distinguish themselves from false martyrs, *Judge me, O God, and distinguish my cause from that of an unholy people* (Ps 43:1). The Psalmist did not say, "Distinguish my punishment," but, *Distinguish my cause*. For the punishment of martyrs can be like that of the wicked, but their cause is different. And to martyrs there belongs that cry, *They have persecuted me unjustly; help me* (Ps 119:86). David thought that he was justly worthy of being helped because he was being persecuted unjustly. For, if he were being justly persecuted, he ought not to have been helped but corrected.

10. But if they think that no one can justly persecute anyone, as when they said in the conference that the true Church is the one that suffers persecution, not the one that inflicts it,[554] I omit saying what I mentioned above. For, if what they say is true, Caecilian pertained to the true Church when their predecessors persecuted him right up to the tribunal of the emperor with their accusations. For we say that he belonged to the true Church not because he suffered persecution but because he suffered on account of justice, but that the Donatists were separated from the Church not because they persecuted him but because they did so unjustly. This, then, is what we say. But if they do not look for the reasons why each person inflicts persecution or suffers it but think that it is a mark of a true Christian if one does not inflict but suffers persecution, they undoubtedly include

---

550. Exsufflation was part of the rite of baptism in which the devil was "blown out" of the candidate for baptism. In repeating baptism the Donatists subjected the baptism of Christ to such disrespect.
551. See Gn 16:6.
552. See 1 Sm 18:8-11.
553. See Mt 23:38; Mk 15:27; Lk 22:33.
554. See *Acts of the Conference* 3, 22, where the Donatist Petilian says, "For with us is found the true Catholic Church that suffers persecution, not the one that inflicts it."

in their definition Caecilian, who did not inflict but suffered persecution, but they exclude from that definition their own predecessors, who inflicted but did not suffer persecution.

11. But, as I said, I omit this. Here is what I say: If the true Church is the one that suffers and does not inflict persecution, let them ask the Apostle which church Sarah symbolized when she persecuted her serving girl. He says that our free mother, the heavenly Jerusalem, that is, the true Church of God, was in fact symbolized by the woman who mistreated her serving girl.[555] But if we examine the question more carefully, that girl persecuted Sarah more by her pride than Sarah persecuted her by restraining her. For the serving girl was doing an injustice to her mistress, while Sarah was disciplining her pride. Next I ask: If good and holy people never persecute anyone but only suffer persecution, whose words do they think are found in the psalm where we read, *I shall persecute my enemies and seize them, and I shall not turn back until they collapse* (Ps 18:37). If, then, we want to speak or recognize the truth, that persecution is unjust which the wicked inflict upon the Church of Christ, and that persecution is just which the churches of Christ inflict upon the wicked. The Church, therefore, is blessed that suffers persecution on account of justice,[556] but those people are wretched who suffer persecution on account of injustice. The Church persecutes by loving; they persecute by raging. The Church persecutes in order to correct; they persecute in order to destroy. The Church persecutes in order to call back from error; they persecute in order to cast down into error. The Church, finally, persecutes and lays hold of enemies until they collapse in their vanity so that they may grow in the truth. They return evil for good[557] because we have at heart their eternal well-being, while they try to take from us even our temporal well-being. They love murder to the point that they commit murder upon themselves when they cannot murder others. For, just as the love of the Church labors to set them free from that perdition so that none of them dies, their madness labors either to kill us in order to feed their desire for cruelty or to kill themselves lest they seem to have lost the power to kill human beings.

3, 12. But those who do not know their habits think that they are now killing themselves when, at the occasion of the laws that were established on behalf of unity, so many peoples are being set free from their utterly insane dominion. But those who know what they were accustomed to do even before these laws are not surprised at their deaths but recall their conduct. Especially when the worship of idols still existed, long columns of their crowds came to the well-attended feasts of the pagans not to smash their idols but to be killed by the worshipers of idols. For, if they chose to smash their idols when they had lawful authority, they could have some vague claim to the title of martyrs if something happened to them. But

---

555. See Gal 4:21-31.
556. See Mt 5:10.
557. See Ps 35:12.

they came only for the purpose of being killed, while the idols remained intact, for each of those very powerful young idolaters had the custom of offering to the idols as many Donatists as he killed. Certain Donatists also thrust themselves upon armed travelers in order to be killed, threatening in a terrifying manner that they would strike them if they were not killed by them. At times they obtained by force from transient judges that they be slain by executioners or the police. As a result it is reported that a certain man mocked them in ordering them to be bound as if to be killed and then left, and in that way he escaped their attack without shedding blood and without being harmed. It was a daily game for them to kill themselves by steep plunges or by water and flames. For the devil taught them these three kinds of death so that, when they wanted to die and did not find anyone to terrify into striking them with the sword, they might hurl themselves over cliffs or throw themselves into water or flames. Who are we to believe took possession of their heart[558] and taught them these things but him who suggested even to our savior, as if on the basis of the law, that he should throw himself down from the pinnacle of the temple?[559] They would drive the devil's suggestion from themselves if they carried Christ, the teacher, in their heart. But because they have given the devil a place in themselves, they either perish like the herd of pigs that a multitude of demons cast down from the mountain into the sea[560] or, having been rescued from these deaths and gathered to the loving bosom of the Catholic mother, they are set free, just as that man was set free by the Lord when his father presented him to be healed of the demon and said that he was accustomed at times to fall into the water and at times into the fire.[561]

13. Hence they were shown a great mercy when they were first rescued against their will, even by those laws of the emperors, from that sect in which they learned these evil practices through the teaching of lying demons so that later they would be healed in the Catholic Church, once they had become accustomed to her good commandments and morals. For many of them, whose pious and fervent faith and love we now admire in the unity of Christ, give thanks to God with great joy that they are free from the error in which they thought those evil practices were good. And they would not now offer thanks willingly if they had not earlier also left that wicked community unwillingly. What shall we say about those who daily admit to us that they had long wanted to be Catholics but lived among those people with whom they could not be what they wanted because of the weakness of fear? For, if they said one word in favor of the Catholics among those people, they themselves and their homes would be completely destroyed. Who is so insane that he would say that these people should not be helped by the imperial orders so that they might be rescued from such a great

---

558. See Sir 51:28.
559. See Mt 4:5-7; Lk 4:9-13.
560. See Mt 8:32; Mk 5:13.
561. See Mt 17:14-18; Mk 9:16-26.

evil, while those whom they feared are now forced to be afraid and are either themselves corrected by the same fear or at least, when they pretend that they have been corrected, spare those who have now been corrected and previously feared them.

14. Suppose that they want to kill themselves to prevent the deliverance of those who should be set free and that they want to inject fear into the piety of those setting them free in that way. And as a result, while we fear that certain wicked persons may perish, those who either had already wanted not to perish or could have been saved from perishing, if force were used, are not rescued from perdition. What does Christian love do in this case, especially since those who threaten us with their own self-inflicted and insane deaths are quite few in comparison with the people to be set free? What, then, does brotherly love do? While it fears the transitory fires of furnaces for a few, does it hand over all to the eternal fires of hell? Does it abandon to everlasting destruction all those who are now willing and were previously unable to come to perpetual life by means of the Catholic peace? Does it avoid the self-inflicted deaths of some who live as an impediment to the salvation of others whom they do not allow to live according to the teaching of Christ? For, in accord with the practice of their diabolical teaching they aim to teach them to rush at any occasion to the self-inflicted deaths that we now fear in those people. Or does it, instead, save those whom it can, even if those whom it cannot save perish by their own choice? For it ardently desires that all may live, but it labors harder that all may not perish. Thanks be to the Lord that both among us—not, of course, everywhere, but in very many places—and in other parts of Africa the Catholic peace has thrived and is thriving without any deaths of these insane people. But these crimes occur where there is the kind of crazy and hurtful persons that used to do the same things even at other times.

4, 15. And before these laws were issued by the Catholic emperors, the teaching of Catholic unity and peace was gradually growing and individuals came over to it from that sect as each of them received instruction, chose to, and was able to do so, though among the Donatists frenzied crowds of wicked men disturbed the peace of the innocent in various cases. What master was not forced to fear his slave if his slave sought refuge under the protection of the Donatists? Who dared even to threaten a rioter or the instigator of a riot? Who was able to demand a reckoning from a slave who consumed his provisions or from a debtor who asked the Donatists for help and defense? Out of a fear of clubs and fires and imminent death the records of the worst slaves were destroyed so that they might go free. Lists of what they had extorted from creditors were handed over to debtors. Whoever ignored their harsh language was forced by harsher blows to do what they ordered. The homes of the innocent who had offended them were either razed to the ground or destroyed by fires. Some heads of families, men nobly born and well educated, were carried off barely alive after their attacks and chained to a mill stone; they were forced by beatings to make it turn, as if they were mere animals. For what help from the civil authorities was able to do anything against them by means of the laws? What official breathed easily in their presence? What banker was able to demand what they were unwilling to pay? Who tried to avenge those who were slain by their attacks? And yet their own madness exacted punishment from them. Some provoked the swords of men against themselves so those whom they threatened with death would kill them, while others killed themselves, some by jumping over cliffs, others by water, and still others by fires, and they threw away their bestial lives by punishments that they inflicted upon themselves.

16. Very many people found these actions horrifying when they were actually in that heretical superstition. And since they thought that it was sufficient for their innocence that they were displeased at such actions, the Catholics said to them, "If these sins do not defile your innocence, how can you say that the Christian world was defiled by either the false or at least the unknown sins of Caecilian? How do you separate yourselves by a wicked crime from Catholic unity as if from the threshing floor of the Lord, which must until the time of the winnowing have both the grain that will be stored in the barn and the chaff that will be consumed by fire?"[562] And in that way some of them were given a reason to cross over to Catholic unity, ready to endure even the hatred of the wicked, but more of them, though they wanted to cross over, did not dare to make enemies of those men who had such license in expressing their rage. There were some, to be sure, who suffered from those most cruel men after they had crossed over to us.

17. It also happened that at Carthage some bishops of the sect of Donatus ordained a certain deacon by the name of Maximian, who arrogantly opposed his bishop, and made him a bishop in opposition to their bishop.[563] Thus they created a schism and divided the sect of Donatus among the people of Carthage. Since this displeased more of them, they condemned the same Maximian along with twelve bishops who were present and assisted at his ordination. But they gave the others who belonged to the same schismatic group the opportunity of returning by a set day. But afterward, for the sake of the peace of their sect, they received back with their full honors certain bishops from those twelve and from those given an extension who returned after the day that had been set. And they did not dare to rebaptize any whom the condemned bishops had baptized outside of their communion. This action of theirs began to serve as a strong argument against them in favor of the Catholic Church, so that their mouths were absolutely silenced. Word of this affair was spread about by every means—as it ought to have been—in order to heal the souls of human beings from schism, and it was shown, wherever it could be, by Catholic sermons and discussions that for the

---

562. See Mt 3:12; Lk 3:17.
563. In 393 Maximian was ordained bishop of Carthage in opposition to the Donatist bishop, Primian, whom Maximian and his followers deposed, thus creating the Maximianist schism in the sect of Donatus.

peace of Donatus they accepted back with their full honors even those bishops of theirs whom they condemned and that they did not dare to declare invalid the baptism that the condemned bishops or even those who were granted a delay conferred outside their church. And yet they raise as an objection against the peace of Christ the contamination of the whole world by some sins or other, and they declare invalid the baptism conferred even in those churches from which the gospel came to Africa. For these reasons many were ashamed, and in their embarrassment at the obvious truth they were corrected in greater numbers than usual and to a greater extent wherever they were able to breathe with a degree of freedom from the savagery of those people.

18. But then the Donatists became so inflamed with anger and were aroused by such goads of hatred that hardly any churches of our communion were able to be secure against their plots, acts of violence, and brazen robberies, and hardly any road was safe for those to travel who preached the Catholic peace against their madness and refuted their insanity with the plain truth. Things came to such a point that not only the laity or certain clerics but even Catholic bishops were faced with a dire situation. For either they had to be silent about the truth or they had to endure their cruelty. But, if they were silent about the truth, not only would this silence set no one free but many would also be lost through being led astray by them. If, however, the preaching of the truth provoked their fury to the point of rage, though some would be set free and our people would find strength, fear would again prevent the weak from following the truth. Since the Church was afflicted with these difficult conditions, whoever thinks that we should have endured everything rather than asking that the help of God be brought by means of the Christian emperors pays too little attention to the fact that no good reason could be given for this negligence.

5, 19. Those who do not want just laws to be established against their wickedness say that the apostles did not seek anything of the sort from the rulers of the earth. They do not take into account that it was a different time and that all things are done at their proper times. For what emperor then believed in Christ and would serve him by issuing laws in favor of piety and against impiety when those words of the prophet were still being fulfilled, *Why have the nations raged and the peoples planned folly? The kings of the earth rose up, and the princes came together against the Lord and against his anointed.* (Ps 2:1-2) There was as yet no realization of what it says a little later in the same Psalm, *And now, O kings, understand; receive instruction, you who judge the world. Serve the Lord with fear, and exult before him with trembling.* (Ps 2:10-11) How, then, do kings serve the Lord with fear except by forbidding and punishing with religious severity actions done against the Lord's commandments? For he serves in one way because he is a man, and he serves in another way because he is king. For, because he is a man, he serves him by living a life of faith, but, because he is also a king, he serves him by upholding with appropriate force laws that command what is just and forbid what is unjust. In that way Hezekiah served God by destroying the groves, the temples of idols, and the high places erected contrary to the commandments of the Lord.[564] In that way Josiah served God by also doing the same sort of actions.[565] In that way the king of the Ninevites served God by compelling the whole city to placate the Lord.[566] In that way Darius served God by entrusting the smashing of the idol to the power of Daniel and by throwing Daniel's enemies to the lions.[567] In that way Nebuchadnezzar, about whom we have already spoken, served God by forbidding with a terrifying law all those living in his kingdom to blaspheme against God.[568] Kings, then, insofar as they are kings, serve the Lord when they do those things to serve him that only kings can do.

20. Since, then, the emperors did not yet serve the Lord at the time of the apostles and were still planning folly against the Lord and against his anointed so that all the predictions of the prophets might be fulfilled, they certainly could not at that time forbid acts of impiety by the laws; rather, they committed such acts. For the order of the ages changed so that even the Jews killed those who preached Christ, believing that they were offering a service to God, as Christ had foretold.[569] And the nations raged against the Christians, but the suffering of the martyrs conquered all. After the words of Scripture began to be fulfilled, *And all the kings of the earth will adore him; all the nations will serve him* (Ps 72:11), who would say to the kings with a sober mind, "Do not be concerned about who in your kingdom defends or attacks the Lord's Church. It is no concern of yours who wants to be either religious or sacrilegious"? In the same way we cannot say to them, "It is no concern of yours who in your kingdom behaves morally or has no sense of shame." For, since God gave free will to human beings, why should adultery be punished by the laws and sacrilege be permitted? Or is it less serious for a soul to be unfaithful to God than for a woman to be unfaithful to her husband? Or, if sins that are committed not out of contempt for religion but out of ignorance should be punished more leniently, should they, then, be completely neglected?

6, 21. Would anyone doubt that it is better to bring human beings to worship God by instruction than by the fear or the pain of punishment? But because the former are better, it does not mean that the latter, who are not such, should be neglected. For it has benefited many, as we have found and continue to find by experience, to be first forced by fear or pain so that later they may be instructed or may put into practice what they have already learned verbally. Some of them quote for us the lines of a certain worldly author who said, "It is better, I believe, to hold children in check by self-respect and kindliness than by fear."[570] This is

---

564. See 2 Kgs 18:4.
565. See 2 Kgs 23:4-20
566. See Jon 3:6-9.
567. See Dn 14:21.41.
568. See Dn 3:96.
569. See Jn 16:2.
570. Terence, *The Brothers* 1, 57-58.

in fact true. But, just as they are better who are guided by love, so there are many whom fear corrects. For, to reply to them from the same author, they also read in him: "Unless you are forced by pain, you do not know how to act correctly."[571] But God's Scripture also says on account of those better persons, *Fear does not exist along with love, but perfect love drives out fear* (1 Jn 4:18). And because of those who are less good but more in number, it says, *A stubborn servant will not be corrected by words; for, even if he understands, he will not obey* (Prv 29:19). When Scripture said that he was not corrected by words, it did not command that he be abandoned; rather, it implicitly taught how he should be corrected. Otherwise, it would not say, *He will not be corrected by words*, but would simply say: *He will not be corrected*. In another passage, indeed, it says that not only a servant but even an undisciplined son should be restrained by beatings and with great benefit. For it says, *You beat him with a rod, but you free his soul from death* (Prv 23:14). And elsewhere it says, *He who spares the rod hates his own son* (Prv 13:24). Give me a man who says with right faith, true understanding, and all the strength of his soul, *My soul thirsts for the living God; when shall I come and stand before the face of God?* (Ps 42:3) and for such a person as this there is no need for fear not merely of temporal punishments or of imperial laws but even of hell. For he finds it so desirable a good to cling to God[572] that he not only holds in horror the loss of that happiness like a great punishment but also endures its postponement with difficulty. But before they say like good children, "We desire *to be dissolved and to be with Christ*" (Phil 1:23), many are first, like bad servants and in a sense like fleeing criminals, called back to their Lord by a beating with temporal scourges.

22. For who can love us more than Christ, who laid down his life for his sheep?[573] And yet, though he called Peter and the other apostles by words alone, in dealing with Paul, who was first Saul and later a great builder of his Church, but before that its fierce persecutor, he did not restrain him by words alone but laid him low by his power. And to press the man who was raging in the darkness of unbelief to desire the light of his heart, he first afflicted him with blindness of the body. If that were not a punishment, he would not have been healed of it later, and if his eyes were healthy when he saw nothing, though his eyes were open, scripture would not report that at the imposition of Ananias's hands some sort of scales that prevented his seeing fell from his eyes so that his sight might be restored.[574] What happens to their usual cry, "One is free to believe or not to believe. With whom did Christ use force? Whom does he compel?" See, they have Paul the apostle; let them acknowledge in him Christ first using force and afterward teaching, first striking and afterward consoling. It is amazing, howev-

---

571. Terence, *The Brothers* 1, 69-75; Augustine cites the words as they are abbreviated in Cicero's *Second Oration against Verres* 3, 62.
572. See Ps 72:28.
573. See Jn 10:15.
574. See Acts 9:1-18; 13:9.

er, how that man who came to the Gospel, forced by bodily punishment, labored more for the Gospel than all those who were called only by words.[575] And though greater fear drove him to love, his *perfect love cast out fear* (1 Jn 4:18).

23. Why, then, should the Church not force her lost children to return if those lost children were forcing others to perish. And yet their loving mother quite warmly embraces even those whom they did not force but only misled, if they are called back to her bosom through fearsome but salutary laws.[576] And she is much over these than over those whom she had never lost. Does it not pertain to a shepherd's care to call back to the Lord's fold, once they have been found, even those sheep that were not snatched away with violence but were led astray by seduction and gentleness, that wandered off from the flock and began to belong to others? Does he not have to call them back, even by the fear and pain of beatings, if they want to resist? He ought especially to do so if the sheep have multiplied through fertility among runaway slaves and thieves, because it is more just that the Lord's brand should be recognized on them which is not violated in those whom we receive back but still do not rebaptize. For in that way the error of the sheep is to be corrected without destroying on it the mark of the redeemer. For suppose someone receives the mark of the king from a deserter who bears that mark, and suppose they both receive pardon and the deserter returns to the army, and the other begins to be in the army, where he had not been before. The mark on neither of them is canceled. Is it not rather recognized in both of them and treated with due honor, since it is the mark of the king? Because the Donatists cannot prove that it is something evil to which they are being forced, they contend that they ought not to be forced to what is good. But we show that Paul was forced by Christ; the Church, then, imitates its Lord in forcing the Donatists. The Church earlier waited without forcing anyone until the message of the prophets was fulfilled concerning the faith of kings and of the nations.[577]

24. From this we can without any absurdity understand the statement of the Apostle where blessed Paul says, *We are prepared to punish every disobedience once your earlier obedience is carried out* (2 Cor 10:6). For this reason the Lord himself orders that guests first be invited to his great banquet and afterward forced. For, when his servants answered him, *Lord, we have done what you ordered, and there is still room*, he said, *Go out into the roads and pathways and force whomever you find to come in* (Lk 14:16.21.23). In those who were first gently invited the earlier obedience is carried out, but in those who are afterward forced their disobedience meets with coercion. For what does *force them to come in* mean after he had first said, *Invite them*, and received the reply, *We have done what you ordered, and there is still room*? If he had wanted us to understand that they were to be forced by awesome miracles, many more divine miracles

---

575. See 1 Cor 15:10.
576. See Mt 18:12-13; Lk 15:4-7.
577. See Ps 72:11.

were produced for those who were first called, especially for the Jews, of whom Scripture says, *The Jews seek signs* (1 Cor 1:22). At the time of the apostles such miracles also commended the gospel among the Gentiles so that, if the Lord ordered that guests be forced to come in by such miracles, we would rightly believe that it was rather the first guests who were forced. Hence, if the power that the Church received as God's gift through the religion and faith of rulers is at the proper time forcing to come in those found on the roads and pathways, that is, those in heresies and schisms, they should not complain because they are being forced, but they should pay attention to where they are forced to go. The Lord's banquet is the unity of the body of Christ not only in the sacrament of the altar but also *in the bond of peace* (Eph 4:3). We can indeed say of these Donatists with complete truth that they force no one to what is good, for they force whomever they force only to what is evil.

7, 25. But before these laws by which they are being forced to come into the holy banquet were promulgated in Africa, some brothers, among whom I was included, thought that, though the madness of the Donatists was raging everywhere, we should not ask the emperors to give orders that this heresy be completely eliminated by establishing a punishment for those who chose to remain in it. Rather, we thought that we should ask that they establish laws so that those who preach the Catholic truth by speaking it or who read the scriptures to determine it should not suffer the Donatists' insane acts of violence. We thought that this could be achieved in some measure if they reaffirmed more explicitly against the Donatists, who denied that they were heretics, the law of Theodosius of most pious memory, which he promulgated against all the heretics in general, namely, "that any bishop or cleric of theirs, wherever he is found, should be fined ten pounds of gold."[578] We did not want all of them to be fined in that way but only those in whose territories the Catholic Church suffered some acts of violence from their clerics, from the Circumcellions, or from their people, so that, following a complaint from the Catholics who had suffered such violence, their bishops or other ministers would be held to the payment of the fine by the care of those in charge. For we thought that, if they were thoroughly frightened and did not dare to do anything of the sort, we could freely teach and hold the Catholic truth so that no one would be forced to it, but that those who wanted would follow it without the risk of having false and hypocritical Catholics. Other brother bishops of mine thought otherwise, who were older than I and who observed the examples of many cities and locales where we saw the solid and true Catholic Church, which was nonetheless established and strengthened there by such benefits from God, when human beings were forced into the Catholic communion by the laws of earlier emperors. But we obtained what I said that we should ask for instead from the emperors; it was decided by our council, and deputies were sent to the imperial court.

---

578. *The Theodosian Code* 16, 5, 21.

26. But God knew how necessary the fear engendered by these laws and a certain remedial suffering is for wicked or tepid souls and for that hardheartedness which cannot be corrected by words but which can yet be corrected by some moderately severe discipline. His great mercy brought it about that our delegates were not able to obtain what they had wanted to obtain. For there preceded us some very serious complaints of bishops from other places, who had suffered many evils from the Donatists and been removed from their sees. In particular the horrible and unbelievable attack upon Maximian, the Catholic bishop of Bagai, caused our legation not to get what it was after. For the law had already been promulgated that the heresy of the Donatists with all its great savagery—for it seemed more cruel to spare them than they themselves were cruel—not merely be prevented from using violence but not be permitted to go completely unpunished. And yet capital punishment was not to be imposed in order to maintain Christian gentleness even toward those unworthy of it, but fines were to be levied and exile established for their bishops and ministers.

27. The aforesaid bishop of Bagai had obtained before the ordinary judge, when the sentence was pronounced between the two parties, the basilica that the Donatists had taken over when it was Catholic. While he was standing at the altar, they attacked him with terrible violence and cruel madness and beat him horribly with clubs and weapons of that sort and, finally, with pieces of wood broken off from the same altar. They also struck him in the groin with a dagger, and the blood flowing from that wound would have left him dead if their greater savagery had not saved his life. For, when they dragged the seriously wounded man over the earth, soil blocked the hemorrhaging vein and stopped the flow of blood from which he was dying. Finally, after they abandoned him, our people tried to carry him off while chanting the Psalms, but the Donatists became enraged with fiercer anger and snatched him from the hands of those who were carrying him, badly mistreating and putting to flight the Catholics, whom they surpassed by their great numbers and easily terrified by their savagery. Then, after having carried him to a tower, thinking that he had already died (although he was still alive), the Donatists pushed him off. But the bishop fell onto a pile of soft earth and was seen, recognized, and picked up by some people passing that way at night with a lamp. He was brought to a house of believers and, with much care, he recovered after many days from that desperate condition. But rumor had reported even overseas that he had been killed by the crime of the Donatists. After he arrived there, his being still alive was regarded as something completely unexpected, but by his many, large, and recent scars he proved that rumor had not without reason pronounced him dead.

28. He sought help from the Christian emperor, therefore, not for the sake of avenging himself but for protecting the church entrusted to him. If he had not done this, his suffering would not have been praiseworthy, but his negligence would have been blameworthy. For even the apostle Paul was not looking out for his own passing life but for the Church of God when he made known to the

tribune the plan of those who had plotted to kill him; as a result armed soldiers brought him to the place where he was to be brought in order to avoid their ambush.[579] He did not hesitate to appeal to Roman laws, declaring himself to be a Roman citizen, since it was not permitted to flog Roman citizens.[580] Likewise, in order that he might not be handed over to the Jews who desired to kill him, he demanded the help of Caesar, a Roman emperor but not a Christian one.[581] There he showed clearly enough what the ministers of Christ ought to do afterwards when they would find Christian emperors at a time of danger for the Church. As a result, then, when such cases were brought to his attention, the devout and pious emperor preferred to correct the error of that impiety completely by most pious laws and to bring back to the Catholic unity by terror and coercion those who bore the standards of Christ in opposition to Christ rather than merely to take away their freedom to act savagely while leaving them their freedom to be in error and to perish.

29. When the laws reached Africa, those especially who were looking for the opportunity or who feared the savagery of the Donatist fury or who were afraid of offending their own people immediately came over to the Church. Likewise many who were held in that heresy only by a habit that they inherited from their parents, people who never before knew the sort of cause this heresy had and never chose to investigate and evaluate it, became Catholics without any difficulty as soon as they began to pay attention and to find in it nothing that merited their suffering such great losses. Worry, in other words, taught those whom security had made negligent. But many who were less able by themselves to understand the difference between the error of the Donatists and Catholic truth followed the persuasive authority of all those whom we mentioned above.

30. Thus, though our true mother joyfully received great columns of people into her bosom, there remained obdurate multitudes which persisted in that plague with sorry stubbornness. From them many entered our communion as a pretense, while others remained hidden by reason of their small number. But a great many of those who entered only as a pretense were gradually corrected through becoming familiar with and hearing the preaching of the truth, especially after the conference and debate held between us and their bishops at Carthage. In certain places, however, where a more stubborn and less peaceful crowd prevailed and those fewer in number with a more positive attitude toward unity could not stand up to them, or where the crowds subject to the authority of a few persons of great power took the wrong side, the struggle lasted somewhat longer. Of these there are some with whom the struggle still goes on, and in that struggle Catholics, especially bishops and clerics, have endured many horrible and harsh sufferings, which it would take too long to discuss, when the eyes of some were put out and the hands and tongue

---

579. See Acts 23:12-32.
580. See Acts 22:24-29.
581. See Acts 25:11.

of a certain bishop were cut off. Some were even killed. I pass over the murders committed with great cruelty, the plundering of homes by attacks at night, and the burning not only of private dwellings but also of churches. And there were even some who threw the Lord's Scriptures into those flames.

31. But the ensuing results consoled us who were afflicted with such evils. For, wherever these acts were committed by the wicked, there Christian unity made progress with more fervor and perfection, and the Lord is praised more abundantly who graciously granted that his servants gain their brothers by their sufferings and by their blood gather together into the peace of eternal salvation his sheep who had been scattered by their deadly error.[582] The Lord is powerful and merciful, and we daily ask that *he grant repentance* to the rest *and that they may come to their senses from the snares of the devil by whom they are held captive according to his will* (2 Tm 2:25-26). For these people only seek ways to slander us, and they repay good with evil[583] because they do not understand the attitude of love we maintain toward them and how, in accord with the Lord's command that he gave to shepherds through the prophet Ezekiel, we want to call back the straying sheep and find the lost ones.[584]

8, 32. But, as we once said elsewhere,[585] they do not blame themselves for what they do to us, and they blame us for what they do to themselves. For who among us would want not only that one of them should perish but even that he should lose anything? The house of David only merited to have peace when Absalom, David's son, was killed in the war that he waged against his father, though David ordered his men with great concern to keep him safe and alive so that he might survive to receive pardon from David's fatherly love. What, then, remained for him but to mourn his lost son and for his majesty to be consoled by the peace that had been gained for his kingdom?[586] In the same way, none other than her children are warring against their Catholic mother, for this small branch was broken off in Africa[587] from that great tree, which in fact is spread throughout the world by the development of its branches.[588] She is now in labor to give birth to them with love so that they may return to the root without which they cannot have true life.[589] If with the loss of some she gathers together the others, who are so many, especially since they are perishing, not like Absalom by the misfortune of war but rather by a death of their own choice, she soothes and heals the sorrow of her motherly heart by the deliverance of so many peoples. If you could only see their joy, eagerness, and enthusiasm in the peace of Christ

---

582. See Mt 18:15; Ez 34:5-6.
583. See Ps 35:12.
584. See Ez 34:4-6.
585. See Letter 88, 8.
586. See 2 Sam 18:5-15.33; 22:1-51.
587. See Is 18:5; Rom 11:17.19.
588. See Lk 13:19, Mt 13:32; 24:14; Mk 4:32.
589. See Gal 4:19.

and their frequent and joyous gatherings to hear and sing hymns and listen to the word of God, and on the part of many of them the very painful recollection of their past error and the joyful consideration of the truth that they have come to know! If you could only see their anger and hatred at the lies of their teachers, of which they are now aware, and at how they spread falsehoods concerning our sacraments! If you could also hear the admissions on the part of many of them that they earlier wanted to become Catholics but did not dare to among men of such great madness! If, then, you saw at a glance the congregations of these peoples throughout many regions of Africa who had been set free from that plague, you would then say that it would have been a mark of excessive cruelty if, out of fear that some desperate persons—by no one's reckoning comparable to the countless numbers of these people—would be consumed by their own fires and by their own choice, these people were to be abandoned to perish forever and be tormented in everlasting fires.

33. Suppose that two persons were living in one house that we most certainly knew was going to collapse and that they refused to believe us when we told them of this and insisted on remaining in it. If we were able to snatch them from there, even against their will, and afterwards showed them that the collapse was imminent in order that they would not venture to return again to that danger, I think that, if we did not do so, we would be rightly judged heartless. But if one of them said to us, "When you come in to snatch us, I will immediately kill myself," but the other wanted neither to leave nor to be snatched from there, though he would not dare to kill himself, what would we choose? To leave both of them to be crushed in the collapse or to rescue at least one by our merciful effort and to allow the other to perish not by our fault but rather by his own? No one is so impaired that he would not immediately judge what ought to be done in such cases. I have set before you this example of two persons, one who is rescued and the other lost. What, then, are we to think of a certain few who have been lost and a countless multitude of those who have been rescued? For those persons who perish by their own choice are not as many as the farms, fields, villages, towns, municipalities, and cities that are rescued by means of these laws from that deadly and eternal destruction.

34. But if we weigh more carefully the matter we are discussing, I think that, if there were many persons in the house that was going to collapse and if at least one person could be rescued from it and if, when we tried to do that, the others tried to kill themselves by hurling themselves down, we would console our sorrow over the others with the safety of at least the one. But we would still not permit them all to perish without rescuing anyone out of fear that others would destroy themselves. What, then, should we judge about the work of mercy that we ought to perform for human beings in order that they may gain eternal life and avoid eternal punishment, if an argument that is true and merciful compels us to go to the aid of human beings in order to preserve their present state of well-being, which is not only temporal but also brief?

9, 35. They object to us that we desire their property and take it away. Would that they would become Catholics and possess not only their property but ours as well in peace and love along with us! But they are so blinded by their love of speaking slanderously that they do not notice how what they say is self-contradictory. They certainly say and seem to bewail that we are forcing them in a most hateful fashion into communion with us by the violent command of the laws. We would by no means do this if we wanted to own their property. Does any covetous person want a joint owner? Does anyone inflamed with the desire to have dominion or lifted up with the pride of ownership want to have a partner? Let them at least notice how those who were once their members, but who are now ours and are united with us in brotherly love, not only retain their property, which they had, but also have ours, which they did not have. Yet all those goods are now both ours and theirs if we are poor along with the poor. But if we personally possess things that are sufficient for us, those goods do not belong to us but to the poor. We somehow or other have charge of those goods, but we do not claim for ourselves ownership by an unjust appropriation of them.

36. Whatever, then, was owned in the name of the churches of the sect of Donatus the Christian emperors have by religious laws ordered to be transferred to the Catholic Church along with their churches. Since, therefore, the people of the same churches, who were being sustained by the same small properties, are now poor together with us, let the Donatists located outside the Church cease to desire the property of others but enter into the unity of our communion in order that we might together govern not just those goods that they say are theirs but also those that are said to be ours as well. For Scripture says, *All things belong to you, but you belong to Christ. Christ, however, belongs to God.* (1 Cor 3:22-23) Under that head in his one body let us be one,[590] and let us do with all such goods what is written in the Acts of the Apostles, *They had one soul and one heart, and no one called anything his own, but they held all things in common* (Acts 4:32). Let us love what we sing, *See, how good and how pleasant it is for brothers to dwell in unity* (Ps 133:1), so that they may experience and know how truthfully their Catholic mother cries out to them what the blessed Apostle writes to the Corinthians, *I do not seek your possessions, but you yourselves* (2 Cor 12:14).

37. But if we consider what is written in the Book of Wisdom, *And for this reason the righteous carried off the spoils of the wicked* (Wis 10:19), as well as what we read in Proverbs, *But the riches of the wicked are stored away for the righteous* (Prv 13:22 LXX), we will then see that we should not ask who has the possessions of the heretics but who are in the company of the righteous. We know, of course, that the Donatists claim for themselves such great righteousness that they not only boast that they have it but that they also bestow it on other human beings. They go so far as to say that someone whom they baptize is made righteous by them; here there only remains for them to say that someone who is baptized by

---

590. See Col 1:18.

them should believe in the one who baptizes him. For why should one not do so when the Apostle says, *For one who believes in him who makes the sinner righteous his faith is counted as righteousness* (Rom 4:5)? Let him, therefore, believe in him if he makes him righteous so that his faith may be counted as righteousness. But I think that even they would be horrified at themselves if they venture even to think such thoughts. For only God is righteous and makes us righteous.[591] One can, however, say of these people what the Apostle said of the Jews, namely, that *not knowing the righteousness of God and wanting to establish their own righteousness, they are not subject to the righteousness of God* (Rom 10:3).

38. God forbid that anyone of ours should say that he was righteous in such a way as to want to establish his own righteousness, that is, as if he gave it to himself, since God says to him, *What do you have that you have not received?* (1 Cor 4:7) God forbid that he should dare to say that he was without sin in this life in the same way as the Donatists said in our conference that they were now in that church that *has no spot nor wrinkle nor anything of the sort* (Eph 5:27). They do not know that this is only realized in those persons who leave this body either immediately after baptism or after the forgiveness of those debts that they ask in prayer to be forgiven. But in the whole Church it will be true that it has absolutely *no spot nor wrinkle nor anything of the sort*, when we will be able to say, *Where, O death, is your victory? Where, O death, is your sting? For the sting of death is sin.* (1 Cor 15:55-56)

39. But in this life, in which *the corruptible body weighs down the soul* (Wis 9:15), if their church is already so sinless, they should not say to God what the Lord taught us to pray, *Forgive us our debts* (Mt 6:12). For, after they have all been forgiven in baptism, why does the Church demand this? If even now in this life she has *no spot nor wrinkle nor anything of the sort*, they should disdain even the apostle John when he cries out in his letter, *If we say that we have no sin, we deceive ourselves, and the truth is not in us. But if we confess our sins, he is faithful and righteous who forgives us our sins and cleanses us from every iniquity.* (1 Jn 1:8-9) On account of this hope the whole Church says, *Forgive us our debts*, so that he may cleanse from every iniquity not those who are proud but those who confess their sins and so that Christ the Lord may present to himself on that day *a glorious Church that has no spot nor wrinkle nor anything of the sort* (Eph 5:27), the Church that he now cleanses *by the bath of water with the word* (Eph 5:26). For in baptism there is not a single past sin that is not forgiven—at least if the baptism is not conferred outside the Church in vain but is either conferred within the Church or, if it was conferred outside, the baptized person does not remain outside with it. And whatever sins those who live here after receiving baptism contract through human weakness are forgiven because of that bath. For it does not do someone who has not been baptized any good to say, *Forgive us our debts* (Mt 6:12).

---

591. See 2 Mc 1:25; Rom 8:33.

40. Thus he now cleanses his Church *by the bath of water with the word* so that he may then present her to himself *having no spot nor wrinkle nor anything of the sort*, that is, entirely beautiful and perfect, when death will be swallowed up in victory.[592] Now, therefore, insofar as our having been born of God and our living from faith is having its effect upon us, we are righteous, but, insofar as we carry with us the remnants of the mortality derived from Adam, we are not without sin. For these words are true, *One who is born of God does not sin* (1 Jn 3:9), and these words are true, *If we say that we have no sin, we deceive ourselves, and the truth is not in us* (1 Jn 1:8). And so Christ the Lord is both righteous and makes us righteous, but we have been *made righteous gratuitously by his grace* (Rom 3:24). He, however, makes righteous only his own body, *which is the Church* (Col 1:24), and for this reason, if the body of Christ carries off *the spoils of the wicked* (Wis 10:19) and *the riches of the wicked are stored up* (Prv 13:22 LXX) for the body of Christ, the wicked ought not to remain outside so that they may speak slanderously but ought rather to enter so that they may be made righteous.

41. Hence those words that were written concerning the day of judgment, *Then the righteous will stand with great constancy over against those who oppressed them and carried off the fruits of their labors* (Wis 5:1), should not be understood in the sense that Canaan will stand against Israel because Israel carried off the fruits of the labors of Canaan.[593] Rather Naboth will stand against Ahab because Ahab carried off the fruits of the labors of Naboth.[594] Canaan was indeed wicked; Naboth was righteous. In the same way the pagan will not stand in opposition to the Christian who carried off the fruits of his labors when the temples of the idols were plundered or surrendered. But the Christian will stand in opposition to the pagan who carried off the fruits of his labors when the bodies of martyrs were struck down. In the same way the heretic will not stand in opposition to the Catholic who carried off the fruits of his labors when the laws of the Catholic emperors have prevailed. But the Catholic will stand in opposition to the heretic who carried off the fruits of his labors when the madness of the Circumcellions prevailed. Indeed, Scripture itself resolves the question, for it does not say, "Then human beings will stand," but, *Then the righteous will stand* and *with great constancy*, because they will stand on a good conscience.

42. But no one is righteous here with his own righteousness, that is, as if he himself produced it. Rather, as the Apostle says, *As God has given to each one a measure of faith*. But he goes on and says, *For, just as we have many members in one body, though all the members do not have the same functions, so we, though many, are one body in Christ.* (Rom 12:3-5) And for this reason no one can be righteous as long as he is separated from the unity of this body. For, just as if a

---

592. See 1 Cor 15:54.
593. See Jos 17:12-13.
594. See 1 Kgs 21:1-16.

member is cut off from the body of a living man it cannot retain the spirit of life, so a man who is cut off from the body of the righteous Christ can by no means retain the Spirit of righteousness, even if he retains the shape of the member that he received in the body. Let the Donatists, then, enter into the frame of this body, and let them possess the fruits of their labors not out of a desire to have dominion over them but out of the piety that makes good use of them. We, however, purify our will, as has already been said, of the filth of this desire, as even an enemy would judge, when we seek, as much as we can, that those very people to whom the fruits of those labors are said to belong may along with us in the Catholic communion make use of theirs and of ours.

10, 43. "But," they say, "this is what troubles us: If we are lacking righteousness, why are you seeking us?" We reply to them, "We are seeking you who are lacking righteousness so that you may not remain without righteousness. We are seeking those who are lost so that we may be able to rejoice over them when they have been found, saying, *A brother was dead and has come to life; he was lost and has been found* (Lk 15:32)." "Why, then," he asks, "do you not baptize me in order to wash away my sins?" I reply, "Because I do not do harm to the mark of the emperor when I correct the error of a deserter." "Why," he asks, "do I not at least do penance with you?" "If, in fact, you do not, you cannot be saved. For how will you rejoice over having been corrected unless you grieve over having gone astray?" "What, then," he asks, "do we receive with you when we cross over to you?" I reply, "You certainly do not receive baptism, which you were able to have outside the framework of the body of Christ but which could not do you any good. But you receive *the unity of the Spirit in the bond of peace* (Eph 4:3), *without which no one is able to see God* (Heb 12:14), and you receive the charity which, as Scripture says, *covers a multitude of sins* (1 Pt 4:8)." Without that great good the Apostle bears witness that nothing is of any value—neither the tongues of men and angels, nor the knowledge of all the mysteries, nor prophecy, nor faith so great that it can move mountains, nor the distribution of all one's possessions to the poor, nor one's body being tormented in fire.[595] If, then, you place little or no value on so great a good, you deserve to be in error to your own misfortune; you deserve to perish if you do not cross over to Catholic unity.

44. "If, then," they ask, "it is necessary that we repent of having been outside the Church and in opposition to the Church in order that we may be saved, how may we remain among you as clerics or even as bishops after this penance?" This would not be done—because it really ought not to be done, as we must admit—if the healing brought about by the restoration of peace did not compensate for it. But let them say this to themselves, and let those who have fallen into so great a death of schism grieve deeply and humbly so that they may come to life by this wound, as it were, of our Catholic mother. For, when the branch that was broken off is grafted on, another cut is made in the tree where it can be inserted in

---

595. See 1 Cor 13:1-4.

order that the branch that will perish without the life from the root may live. But when the branch grafted on begins to live off the tree that receives it, its strength and fruit follow. If, however, the branch does not begin to live off the tree, it dries up, but the life of the tree remains. For the method of grafting is such that the branch from elsewhere is grafted on without cutting off any branch that belongs to the tree, but not without a cut in the tree, though only a very small one. In that way, then, when the Donatists come to the Catholic root and are not deprived of the dignity of the clerical state or of the episcopacy, though this follows after their penance for their error, there is produced a wound of sorts in the bark that injures the integrity of the mother tree. But because *neither the one who plants nor the one who waters is important* (1 Cor 3:7), when our prayers have been poured out to God's mercy and the branches that were grafted on have peacefully taken hold, pour *love covers a multitude of sins* (1 Pt 4:8).

45. It was not a despair of receiving pardon but the rigor of discipline that brought it about that the Church established the rule that after penance for some crime no one should enter the clerical state or return to the clerical state or remain in the clerical state. Otherwise, one will be arguing against the keys given to the Church, of which it was said, *Whatever you loose on earth will be loosed in heaven* (Mt 18:18). But for fear that, even after his crimes have been discovered, a soul swollen with pride might proudly do penance in the hope of some ecclesiastical honor, it was decreed with the greatest severity that after having done penance for some crime worthy of condemnation no one should be a cleric so that, without any hope of a temporal dignity, the remedy of humility might be greater and more genuine. For even the saintly David did penance for his mortal sins and yet remained in his position of honor and, when blessed Peter shed most bitter tears, he certainly repented for having denied the Lord, and yet he remained an apostle. But the caution of those who came later should not for these reasons be considered useless, since, while they took away nothing belonging to salvation, they added something pertaining to humility by which salvation might be more securely protected. For they learned by experience, I believe, that some men merely pretended to repent for the sake of retaining or gaining positions of honor in the Church. For experience with many illnesses creates the need to find many medicines. But in cases of this kind where, because of the grave divisions of schism, it is not a matter of danger for this or that person but of the ruin of whole peoples, we need to reduce the severity in order that sincere love may help to heal greater ills.

46. Let these Donatists, therefore, have bitter sorrow for their detestable error, just as Peter had for his denials committed out of fear,[596] and let them come to the true Church of Christ, that is, to our Catholic mother. Let them be clerics in her; let them be bishops to her benefit, though they were opposed to her as enemies. We do not hate them; in fact, we embrace them, desire them, exhort them,

---

596. See Mt 26:69-75; Mk 14:66-72; Lk 22:55-62.

and compel those whom we find on the roads and pathways to come in.[597] And in that way we still do not convince some of them that it is not their possessions but themselves that we seek. When the apostle Peter denied the Savior, wept, and remained an apostle, he had not yet received the Holy Spirit, who had been promised.[598] But to a much greater degree did these Donatists not receive him when, in separation from the frame of the body, to which alone the Holy Spirit gives life,[599] they had the sacraments of the Church outside the Church and in opposition to the Church and fought in a kind of civil war with our own standards and weapons raised against us. Let them come; let there be peace in the strength of Jerusalem, the strength that is love. To that holy city it was said, *Let peace be established in your strength, and let there be an abundance in your towers* (Ps 122:6-7). Let them not raise themselves up in pride against the motherly concern that she had and still has to gather together them and the many peoples whom they have led and are leading astray. Let them not be proud because she receives them in that way; let them not ascribe to the evil of their pride what the Church does for the good of peace.

47. It is thus that she is accustomed to help the multitudes that are perishing through schisms and heresies. Lucifer was not pleased that this practice was implemented in receiving and healing those who had perished from the Arian poison.[600] And he who was not pleased by it fell into the darkness of schism after losing the light of love. The Catholic Church in Africa observed this practice with regard to the Donatists from the beginning in accord with the decision of the bishops who heard the case between Caecilian and the sect of Donatus in the church of Rome. After a certain Donatus, who was revealed to have been the author of the schism, was alone condemned, the bishops decided that the others, once they had been corrected, should be taken back with their positions of honor, even if they were ordained outside the Church. It was not because they were able to have the Holy Spirit, even outside the Church apart from the unity of the body of Christ, but it was especially on account of those whom they, while located outside the Church, could have led astray and prevented from receiving this benefit. It was, secondly, in order that their weakness might be able to be healed within the Church, after they had been received back with much kindness, when no stubbornness any longer closed the eyes of their heart against the evidence of the truth. But what else did they themselves have in mind when they received back with their full dignities the Maximianists when they saw that their people did not abandon them? For they were afraid that all those people might perish. The Donatists had condemned the Maximianists for their sacrilegious schism, as their council indicates, and they had ordained others in place of them. And

---

597. See Lk 14:23.
598. See Jn 14:26; 16:13.
599. See Jn 6:64; 2 Cor 3:6.
600. Lucifer was the bishop of Cagliari in Sardinia from 354 to 270/371; see *Heresies* 81.

they raised no opposition to or question about the baptism that the Maximianists had conferred when they were condemned and separated from them. Why, then, are the Donatists surprised or why do they complain or slander us because we received them back for the sake of the peace of Christ? And why do they not recall what they themselves did for the sake of the vain peace of Donatus, which is opposed to Christ? If this action of theirs is held against them and intelligently defended, they will not have anything at all to say in reply.

9, 48. But they say, "If we sinned against the Holy Spirit because we used the rite of exsufflation against your baptism, why do you seek us, since this sin absolutely cannot be forgiven us, for the Lord says, *If he sins against the Holy Spirit, it will not be forgiven him either in this world or in the world to come*" (Mt 12:32)? They do not notice that in accord with this interpretation no one should be set free. For who does not speak against the Holy Spirit and sin against him, whether he is not yet a Christian or is a heretical Arian, a Eunomian, a Macedonian, who says that the Holy Spirit is a creature, a Photinian, who says that he has no reality but that the Father alone is the one God, or one of the other heretics whom it would take long to mention?[601] Should none of these be set free? Or were the Jews to whom the Lord says this not to be baptized if they believed in him? For the savior did not say, "It will be forgiven in baptism," but, *It will not be forgiven either in this world or in the world to come.*

49. Let them, therefore, understand that it is not every sin but a particular one that is meant by the sin against the Holy Spirit that absolutely will not be forgiven. For when he said, *If I had not come, they would have no sin* (Jn 15:22), he certainly did not want us to understand every sin, since they were filled with many great sins, but a particular sin which, if they did not have, all those that they had could be forgiven them, that is, the sin of not believing in him. For they would not have this sin if he had not come. In the same way, when he said, *He who sins against the Holy Spirit*, or, *He who says a word against the Holy Spirit*, he did not want us to understand every sin that is committed against the Holy Spirit by word or deed but a specific and particular sin. This sin is a hardness of heart up to the end of this life by which a person refuses to receive the forgiveness of sins in the unity of the body of Christ, to which the Holy Spirit gives life. For, after he said to his disciples, *Receive the Holy Spirit*, he immediately added, *If you forgive the sins of anyone, they will be forgiven him; if you retain the sins of anyone, they will be retained* (Jn 20:22-23). Whoever, then, resists and refuses this gift of the grace of God or is somehow apart from it up to the end of this temporal life, *it will not be forgiven him either in this world or in the world to come*, that is, this sin that is so great that all sins are retained by it and that is not proved to have been committed by anyone until he leaves the body. Yet as long as he lives here, as the Apostle says, *the patience of God leads to repentance*

---

601. Augustine mentions a series of Eastern heresies. For the Arians see *Heresies* 49; for the Eunomians see ibid. 54; for the Macedonians see ibid. 52; for the Photinians see ibid. 45.

(Rom 2:4). But if with most obdurate iniquity, as the Apostle goes on, he stores up for himself *in accord with his hard and unrepentant heart anger for the day of anger and of the revelation of the just judgment of God* (Rom 2:5), *it will not be forgiven him either in this world or in the world to come* (Mt 12:32).

50. But we should not abandon hope for these people with whom we are dealing or about whom we are dealing, for they are still living in the body. But let them seek the Holy Spirit only in the body of Christ; outside they have his sacrament, but internally they do not have the reality of him whose sacrament it is. And so they eat and drink it to their own condemnation.[602] For the one bread is the sacrament of unity, because, as the Apostle says, *We, though many, are one bread, one body* (1 Cor 10:17). Hence the Catholic Church alone is the body of Christ, and its head is the Savior of his body.[603] The Holy Spirit gives life to no one outside this body, because, as the Apostle himself says, *The love of God has been poured out in our hearts by the Holy Spirit who has been given to us* (Rom 5:5). But one who is an enemy of unity has no share in the love of God. Those, therefore, who are outside the Church do not have the Holy Spirit. Of them Scripture itself says, *Those who keep themselves separate are merely natural and do not have the Spirit* (Jude 19). But one who is in the Church only as a pretense does not receive the Spirit, because scripture says of such a person, For the *Holy Spirit of discipline will flee from a hypocrite* (Wis 1:5). One who wants to have the Holy Spirit, therefore, should avoid remaining outside the Church and should avoid entering her as a pretense, or, if he has entered her in that way, he should avoid remaining in that pretense so that he may truly grow in union with the tree of life.

51. I have sent you a long book and one that is perhaps a burden for you amid the tasks that keep you busy. If, therefore, you can read it at least in parts, the Lord will grant you understanding so that you may have answers for those who need to be corrected and healed, for our mother, the Church, commends them to you as to a faithful son in order that you may correct and heal them where you can and however you can, whether by speaking to them and replying to them or by bringing them to the teachers of the Church.

---

602. See 1 Cor 11:29.
603. See Eph 5:23.

ON GRACE AND FREE WILL AGAINST THE PELAGIANS

LETTER 146

Augustine to Pelagius (410)

In 410 Augustine wrote to Pelagius, a lay ascetic who had come to Africa after the fall of Rome. Later, when on trial for heresy at the Council of Diospolis in 415, Pelagius used this letter as testimony to his orthodoxy. Augustine commented on this letter in *The Deeds of Pelagius* 26, 51, obviously struggling to give it a meaning that is less favorable to Pelagius than a superficial reading of it might yield. His comments can serve as an Augustinian introduction to his own letter.

"I not only held myself back from praising him; I even admonished him to hold sound doctrines, as much as I could, without raising any question about the grace of God. I, of course, addressed him as 'lord' in the salutation of the letter, for in accord with the practice in letter-writing we generally write that way even to certain people who are not Christians. Nor did I do this insincerely, for in some sense we have an obligation freely to be of service to all that they may attain salvation in Christ. I addressed him as 'beloved,' and I repeat it now. And if he is angry at me, I will still say it, since, if I do not maintain my love for him despite his anger, I will do harm to myself instead. I spoke of him as someone I longed for very much, because I strongly desired to converse with him face to face. After all, I had already heard that, as soon as there was some mention made of it, he tried in open argument to oppose the grace by which we are justified. Moreover, the shortness of my letter indicates that. I thanked him for having brought me joy with his letter by assuring me of his health and that of his friends. After all, we should want those people also to enjoy good bodily health whom we want to have the correct faith. Then I expressed my hope that the Lord would reward him not with goods pertaining to bodily health but rather with those which he thought or perhaps still thinks are found only in the choice of the will and in our own power. At the same time and for the same reason I wished him eternal life. Then, because in his letter which I was answering he had extensively and kindly praised certain goods of that sort in me, I also asked him to pray for me so that the Lord might make me the sort of person that he already believed me to be. In that way I meant to admonish him—quite contrary to his views—that the very righteousness which he thought praiseworthy in me *does not depend on the one who wills or runs, but on God who shows mercy* (Rom 9:16). This is everything that my short letter contains, and that was the intention with which I dictated it."

To Pelagius, my beloved lord and brother for whom I long very much, Augustine sends greetings in the Lord.

I am very grateful that you were so kind as to bring me joy by your letter and assure me of your good health. May the Lord reward you, my beloved lord and brother for whom I long very much, with the good things by which you may be good forever and live eternally with the eternal God. Though I do not find in myself the grounds for that praise for me that your kind letter contains, I cannot fail to be grateful for your goodwill toward the slight goodness I have. At the same time I admonish you rather to pray for me so that the Lord might make me the sort of person you think me already to be.

LETTER 157
Augustine to Hilary, a Catholic layman from Syracuse (414-415)

In 414 or 415 Augustine replied to the letter from Hilary (Letter 156), a Catholic layman from Syracuse in Sicily, who had asked Augustine a series of questions about various Pelagian teachings. Augustine begins by praising Hilary's zeal for the word of God (paragraph 1). If, Augustine points out, some people claim that they can be without sin in this life, they should be confronted with the words of John, who said that they are deceiving themselves, as well as with the fact that even Daniel prayed for the forgiveness of his sins (paragraph 2). With God's help one can refrain from serious sins, but not from daily lesser sins, for which we must daily ask forgiveness (paragraph 3).

Those who claim that some persons live without sin are perhaps tolerable, but those who say that free choice is sufficient for observing the commandments, even without God's help, must be condemned (paragraph 4). With the help of God's grace free choice can perform good works, but without his help it will not attain righteousness, as the petitions of the Lord's Prayer show (paragraph 5). The benefit of the law lies in its leading us to ask for the grace to fulfill what the law commands (paragraph 6). Those who reject the medicine of Christ's grace are like sick people who are so deranged that they reject the help of a doctor (paragraph 7). Our free will is freer to the extent that it is healthier, and it is healthier to the extent that it is subject to grace (paragraph 8). Without grace the law makes sin abound, but God gives his grace that we may fulfill his commandments (paragraph 9). Grace does not take away our will but helps it (paragraph 10).

The Pelagian claim that infants who die without baptism cannot be lost because they are born without sin runs counter to the words of the Apostle (paragraph 11). Paul teaches that all human beings contract sin from Adam by birth, not by imitation of his sin (paragraph 12). As no one is born except under condemnation because of Adam, so no one is reborn for righteousness except through Christ (paragraph 13). The righteous men and women of the Old Testament were set free through faith in Christ who was to come, just as we are set free through faith in Christ who has come (paragraph 14). Through the law human beings became not merely sinners but transgressors, but the grace of Christ sets them free from all kinds of sin (paragraph 15). Human beings must not neglect what God commands and must not proudly presume upon their own ability to fulfill his commands (paragraph 16). The grace of the Savior is able to set us free from original sin and any personal sins we have added to it (paragraph 17). The Pelagians must not impede the salvation of infants by arguing that they do not need baptism (paragraph 18). From the time of Adam sin has reigned over all, even over those who did not sin like Adam (paragraph 19). The grace of Christ brings us greater benefits than the sin of Adam brought us losses (paragraph 20). Augustine again argues that the sin we derive from Adam is not contracted by imitation of his sin (paragraph 21). Caelestius had not wanted to say anything about original sin, but in saying that infants needed to be baptized in order to be redeemed he undermined his own position (paragraph 22).

Augustine turns to Hilary's question about the Pelagian claim that the wealthy must renounce all their riches if they are to enter the kingdom of heaven. He first points out that the patriarchs were wealthy men to order to show that wealth itself does not merit condemnation (paragraph 23). Though the patriarchs did not sell all they had and give it to the poor, God called himself the God of Abraham, Isaac, and Jacob (paragraph 24). In speaking to the rich young man Jesus distinguished between the commandments and the counsels of perfection (paragraph 25). In writing to Timothy Paul instructed the rich how they ought to live, but he did not command them to give up their riches (paragraph 26). And Paul certainly did not contradict Jesus' teaching (paragraph 27). Augustine presents the Pelagian interpretation of Jesus' words about selling all one has and giving it to the poor and points out that the act of abandoning one's wealth is a gift of God (paragraphs 28 and 29). According to the Pelagian teaching Paul was deceiving those who had possessions by what he said when he wrote to Timothy (paragraph 30). Augustine examines Jesus' words about abandoning all things on account of Jesus and explains the conditions under which one must do this (paragraph 31). For a person must abandon his wife, children, parents, and everyone rather than abandon Christ (paragraph 32). So too, a Christian must prefer Christ to any external possessions (paragraph 33). Augustine explains Jesus' words about the necessity of renouncing all things in order to be his disciple (paragraph 34). He also teaches how Christians may possess what they have without preferring their possessions to Christ (paragraph 35). Christians should, nonetheless, hold their wealth in contempt rather than hold Christ in contempt (paragraph 36).

Hence, the Pelagians should cease to speak against the teaching of Scripture when they exhort others to greater virtue by condemning lesser virtue (paragraph 37). Those Christians who live a life of religious poverty should not condemn other Christians who have not sold all they have and given it to the poor (paragraph 38). In the same way those who have committed themselves to lives of celibacy ought not to condemn those Christians who live in marital chastity (paragraph 39).

Finally, Augustine takes up Hilary's question about swearing and states that it is better not to swear at all than to fall into perjury, but he points out that even the Apostle swore in his letters (paragraph 40). In conclusion he asks Hilary to let him know what is being said in Gaul about the Pelagian errors (paragraph 41).

Bishop Augustine, the servant of Christ and of his Church, sends greetings in the Lord to his son, Hilary.

1, 1. From your letter I learned not only of your good health, but also of your religious zeal concerning the word of God and the pious concern for your own salvation, which is in Christ Jesus our Lord. Thanking God for this, I have not postponed giving my reply.

2. If, then, you ask whether in this life anyone advances in the perfection of righteousness to the point where he lives without any sin at all, pay attention to what the apostle John said, whom the Lord especially loved among his disciples. He said, *If we say that we have no sin, we deceive ourselves, and the truth is not in us* (1 Jn 1:8). If those, then, about whom you wrote to me, say that they are without sin, you see that they deceive themselves, and the truth is not in them. If, however, they admit that they are sinners in order that they may be able to deserve the mercy of God, let them restrain themselves from deceiving others whom they try win over to this pride. For the Lord's Prayer is necessary for all; the Lord gave it even to the rams of the flock, that is, to his own apostles in order that each would say to God, *Forgive us our debts, as we also forgive our debtors* (Mt 6:12). After all, one for whom these words in the prayer will not be necessary would have to claim to live here without sin. If the Lord foresaw that some other people of that sort were going to exist, better persons, of course, than his apostles, he would have taught them another prayer by which they would not ask that their sins be forgiven, since all their sins were already forgiven in baptism. For, if holy Daniel confessed (not before human beings as if in false humility, but before God, that is, in a prayer which he prayed to God) not only the sins of his people but also his own sins, as his truthful lips expressed this,[604] nothing else, it seems, ought to be said to these people but what the Lord commands to be said by the prophet Ezekiel to a certain proud man, *Are you wiser than Daniel?* (Ez 28:3)

3. But clearly one who is helped by the mercy and grace of God and holds himself back from the sins that are also called grievous and does not neglect to purify himself by works of mercy and by pious prayers from those sins without which no one lives here will merit to leave here without sin, though, while he lives here, he will have some sins. For, just as these sins were not lacking, so were the remedies also present by which they might be washed away. But if anyone, hearing that no one lives here without sin by means of his own choice, takes, as it were, the occasion, abandons himself to his passions and unspeakable sins, and persists in these criminal and outrageous actions until his last day, he leads an unhappy life and ends it even more unhappily, regardless of any alms that he may give.

2, 4. But these people are to be tolerated to some extent when they say that in this life there is or has been some righteous person besides the Holy of Ho-

---

604. See Dn 9:20.

lies,[605] who had no sin at all.[606] But their claim that free choice is sufficient for a human being to fulfill the commandments of the Lord, even if one is not helped for good works by the grace of God and the gift of the Holy Spirit, is absolutely to be declared anathema and to be excoriated with every form of curse. For those who assert this are completely estranged from the grace of God, for *not knowing the righteousness of God*, as the Apostle says of the Jews, *and wanting to establish their own, they are not subject to the righteousness of God* (Rom 10:3). *The fullness of the law is*, of course, *love* (Rom 13:10), and *the love of God has been poured out in our hearts* not through ourselves, nor by the powers of our own will, but *through the Holy Spirit who has been given to us* (Rom 5:5).

5. Free choice, then, is capable of good works if it is helped by God, which happens when we ask and speak humbly. But if free choice is abandoned by God's help, no matter how great is the knowledge of the law with which it excels, it will by no means have the solidity of righteousness but the bloated condition and deadly swelling of impious pride. The same Lord's Prayer teaches this. For we ask God in vain when we say, *Bring us not into temptation* (Mt 6:13), if this has been placed in our own power so that we are able to achieve this without God's help. For it says, *Bring us not into temptation*, and this is interpreted as: Do not permit us to be brought there by abandoning us. *For God is faithful*, the Apostle says, *who will not permit you to be tempted beyond that which you are capable of, but will bring about a way out along with the temptation so that you are able to withstand it* (1 Cor 10:13). Why did he say that God does this if this lies in our power alone without his help?

6. For the law itself was given as a help to those who make lawful use of it[607] in order that they might know through it either what righteousness they have already received, for which they should give thanks, or what righteousness is still lacking to them, for which they should insistently ask. But for those who hear the words of the law, *You shall not desire* (Ex 20:17; Dt 5:21; 7:25; Rom 7:7; 13:9), think that it is sufficient for them to have learned this, do not believe that they are given by the help of God's grace the strength to do what was commanded, and do not ask for it, *the law has entered in so that sin might abound* (Rom 5:20), as was said of the Jews. For it is not enough that they do not fulfill the commandment of the law, *You shall not desire*, but beyond that they also are proud, and *not knowing*

---

605. See Dn 9:24, where this Hebraism seems to apply to the Messiah.
606. Before 418 Augustine granted that some people actually did live sinless lives after baptism. See *The Perfection of Human Righteousness* 21, 44, where he says of the idea that, besides Christ, some human beings are or have been without sin after baptism, "I do not believe that one should resist this idea too much, for I know that such is the view of some whose position on this matter I dare not reprehend." Canons 6-8 of the Council of Carthage in 418, however, clearly condemned this position. Augustine was most probably influenced by Ambrose's statements in his *Commentary on the Gospel of Luke*, which Pelagius had appealed to as evidence for human sinlessness. See *The Grace of Christ and Original Sin* 1, 42, 46-46, 51.
607. See Is 8:20 LXX; 1 Tim 1:8.

the righteousness of God, that is, the righteousness that God who makes the sinner righteous gives, and *wanting to establish their own*, as if it were produced by the power of their own will, *they are not subject to the righteousness of God. For the end of the law is Christ for the righteousness of everyone who believes.* (Rom 10:3-4) He, of course, came in order that, *where sin abounded* (Rom 5:20), grace might abound even more. If the Jews, *not knowing the righteousness of God* and *wanting to establish their own*, were enemies of this grace, why are these people now also its enemies if they have believed in him whom those others killed? Is it so that those Jews may receive the reward who, after putting Christ to death, confessed their wickedness and made themselves subject to his grace once they knew it, while these present people meet with condemnation who want to believe in Christ in such a way that they try to put to death his very grace?

7. Those who believe correctly believe in him, of course, in order that they may hunger and thirst for righteousness and be satisfied by his grace. For *everyone*, as Scripture says, *who calls upon the name of the Lord shall be saved* (Jl 2:32; Acts 2:21; Rom 10:13), not, of course, with the health of the body that many have, though they do not call upon the name of the Lord, but with that health of which he says, *It is not the healthy but the sick who need a physician* (Mt 9:12). And what he said afterwards explains this; he says, *I did not come to call the righteous but sinners* (Mt 9:13). He called the righteous healthy, then, and sinners sick. Let the sick person, then, not presume upon his strength, because *he will not be saved by the greatness of his power* (Ps 33:16). For, if he presumes upon it, let him watch out lest this strength not be the sort that usually belongs to the healthy but the sort that usually belongs to the insane who, when they are sick, think they are healthy to the point that they do not even seek a doctor and go on to strike him as if he were cruel and troublesome. In the same way, with their unhealthy pride these people in a certain sense strike Christ, when they maintain that the help of his grace, which is so kind, is not necessary for acting with righteousness once they are given the commandment of the law. Let them, therefore, cease to be so insane, and let them understand, to the extent that they can, that they have free choice not in order to reject help with their proud will but to call upon the Lord with a pious will.

8. For this free will will be more free to the extent that it is more healthy and more healthy to the extent that it is more subject to divine grace and mercy. For it faithfully prays and says, *Direct my journeys according to your word, and let not every iniquity have dominion over me* (Ps 119:133). For how is it free if iniquity has dominion over it? But in order that it may not have dominion over it, see whom it calls upon. For it does not say, "Direct my journeys according to free choice because no iniquity has dominion over me," but, *Direct my journeys according to your word, and let not every iniquity have dominion over me.* It prays; it does not promise. It confesses; it does not claim. It longs for full freedom; it does not boast of its own power. For not everyone who places his trust in his own strength will be saved, but everyone who calls upon the name of the

Lord. *But how shall they call upon him,* the Apostle asks, *in whom they have not believed?* (Rom 10:14) They who believe correctly believe, therefore, so that they may call upon him in whom they have believed and may be able to do what they have received in the commandments of the law, because faith obtains what the law commands.

9. For, in order to omit for the time being the many commandments of the law and to call to mind what the Apostle chose to call to mind when the law says, *You shall not desire* (Ex 20:17), what else does it seem to command but continence with respect to illicit desires? The mind is, of course, carried by its love as if by a weight wherever it is carried; we are commanded, therefore, to take away from the weight of desire what is added to the weight of love until the former is done away with and the latter is made perfect. For *the fulfillment of the law is love* (Rom 13:10). And yet, see what Scripture says about continence: *And since I knew*, it says, *that no one can be continent unless God grants this, and it is itself a mark of wisdom to know whose gift this is, I approached the Lord and entreated him* (Wis 8:21). Did it say, "And since I knew that no one can be continent except by his own free choice, and it is itself a mark of wisdom to know that this good comes from myself"? It clearly did not say this, which some people say in their folly, but what ought to be said in the truth of the Holy Scripture. It said, *Since I know that no one can be continent unless God grants this*. God, therefore, commands continence, and he gives continence. He commands through the law; he gives through grace; he commands through the letter; he gives through the Spirit. For without grace the law makes sin abound,[608] and without the Spirit the letter kills.[609] He commands, therefore, in order that, having tried to do what was commanded, and worn out in our weakness under the law, we would know how to ask for the help of grace and, if we are able to do any good work, we would not be ungrateful to him who helps us. The one who wrote those words also did this; for wisdom taught him whose gift this was.

10. After all, the choice of the will is not destroyed because it is helped; rather, it is helped because it is not destroyed. For one who says to God, *Be my helper* (Ps 27:9), confesses that he wants to carry out what is commanded but asks for help from him who gave the command in order that he may be able to do so. So too, since that person knew that no one could be continent unless God granted it, he approached the Lord and entreated him. He willingly approached him, of course, and he willingly entreated him, nor would he have asked unless he had a will. But if he had not asked, how much would the will be able to do? For even if the will could do something before it asked, what good does it do it unless, because of what it can do, it gives thanks to him from whom it must ask for what it cannot yet do? Hence, even one who is already continent certainly does not have continence unless the will is present. But unless the will had received it, what

---

608. See Rom 5:20.
609. See 2 Cor 3:6.

would the will have? *For what do you have*, he asks, *that you have not received? But if you have received, why do you boast as if you have not received?* (1 Cor 4:7) That is, why do you boast as if you have from yourself what, if you had not received, you could not have from yourself? But the Apostle said this so that *one who boasts may boast* not in himself but *in the Lord* (1 Cor 1:31 2 Cor 10:17), and so that one who does not yet have that about which he might boast might not hope for it from himself but might ask the Lord. It is, after all, better that someone have less and ask for more from God than that he have more and attribute it to himself, because it is better to rise from below than to fall from on high. For Scripture says, *God resists the proud, but gives grace to the humble* (Jas 4:6). The law, therefore, teaches us what we ought to will in order that sins may abound if grace does not help us to be able to do what we will and to carry out what we are able to do. But grace will help us if we do not presume upon our own strength and do not have proud thoughts[610] but agree with the humble and give thanks for what we already can do, while petitioning God as suppliants with a longing will, supporting our prayer with fruitful works of mercy by giving in order that it may be given to us and forgiving in order that we may be forgiven.[611]

3, 11. They say that an infant who was not baptized because it was prevented by death cannot perish because it is born without sin. This is not, however, what the Apostle says, and I think it better that we believe the Apostle than these people. For the teacher of the nations in whom Christ spoke said, *Through one man sin entered the world, and through sin death, and in that way it was passed on to all human beings, in whom all have sinned* (Rom 5:12), and a little later he says, *For judgment comes from the one sin for condemnation, but grace comes from many sins for justification* (Rom 5:16). If these people, then, have perhaps found an infant who was not procreated as a result of the concupiscence stemming from that one man, let them say that this infant is not subject to that condemnation and does not need to be set free from that condemnation by the grace of Christ. After all, what does *from the one sin for condemnation* mean but in that sin by which Adam fell? And what does *from many sins for justification* mean but that the grace of Christ removed not only that sin by which infants are bound because they are procreated from that one man, but also the many sins that, when they are grown up, human beings add by their evil actions? And yet he says that that one sin by which the carnal offspring that take their origin from that first man are bound is sufficient for condemnation. Hence, the baptism of infants is not superfluous; for those who are held bound to that condemnation by birth are released from the same condemnation by rebirth. For, just as no human being is found who was born in the flesh except from Adam, so there is found no human being who is reborn spiritually except from Christ. Birth in the flesh, however, is subject to that one sin and its condemnation, while spiritual rebirth causes the de-

---

610. See Rom 12:16.
611. See Lk 6:37-38, 11:4.

struction not only of that one sin on account of which infants are baptized but of the many sins that by living badly human beings have added to that sin in which they were born. For this reason he goes on to say, *For if on account of the sin of one person death reigned through one person, much more will they who receive an abundance of grace and righteousness reign in life through the one Jesus Christ. Therefore, just as through the sin of one person all entered into condemnation, so through the righteousness of one all will enter the righteousness of life. For, just as through the disobedience of one man many were made sinners, so through the obedience of one man many are made righteous.* (Rom 5:17-19)

12. What will they say to these words? Or what remains for them but to claim that the Apostle was mistaken? The vessel of election, the teacher of the nations, the trumpet of Christ shouts, *Judgment comes from the one for condemnation* (Rom 5:16), and these people shout back, claiming that infants, who they admit take their origin from that one man of whom the Apostle speaks, do not enter into condemnation even if they have not been baptized in Christ. He says, *Judgment comes from the one for condemnation.* What does *from the one* mean but from one sin? For he continues, *But grace comes from many sins for justification.* Therefore, judgment leads to condemnation from the one sin, but from condemnation grace leads from many sins to justification. Hence, if they do not dare to resist the Apostle, let them explain to us why judgment leads to condemnation from the one sin, though many human beings come to judgment who will be condemned because of many sins. Or if they think that it was said because Adam produced the beginning of sin which the rest imitated, so that in that way they are dragged from that one sin to judgment and condemnation who have committed many sins by imitating him, why is the same thing not said of grace and justification? Why is it not likewise said, "And from one sin grace leads to justification"? For many sins of human beings are found between the one that they imitated and the judgment by which the many are punished. From the one they came to many so that they are brought to judgment and condemnation from many. In the same way the same many sins stand between this one sin, in imitation of which they were committed, and grace, by which they are forgiven. For from that one sin they came to many sins in order that they might come to grace to be justified from many sins. Since, therefore, in each case, that is, in the case of judgment and in the case of grace, there is one and the same proportion with regard to what pertains to the one and to the many sins, let them tell us why he said that from one sin judgment leads to condemnation but from many sins grace leads to justification. Or let them grant that it was said in this way because in this matter there are set before us two men—Adam, from whom there comes birth in the flesh, and Christ, from whom there comes spiritual rebirth. But because the former was only a man, but the latter both God and man, this rebirth does not remove the one sin which comes from Adam in the same way that that birth bound us by that sin which comes from Adam. But for that birth the connection to the one sin is sufficient for condemnation. For whatever human beings add afterward

by their evil actions does not pertain to that birth but to human living. But for this rebirth it is not sufficient to remove this one sin alone that is contracted from Adam, but whatever else is added to it afterward from the wicked actions of human life. For this reason *judgment comes from the one for condemnation, but grace from many sins for justification.*

13. *For if on account of the sin of one person death reigned through one person,* from which sin infants are cleansed in baptism, *much more will those who receive an abundance of grace and righteousness reign in life through the one Jesus Christ.* They will, of course, reign much more in life because it will be the kingdom of eternal life, but death passes in them in time and will not reign for eternity. *Therefore, just as through the sin of one person all enter into condemnation,* from which condemnation infants must be set free by the sacrament of baptism, *so through the righteousness of one all will enter the righteousness of life.* Both here and there he said *all,* not because all human beings come to the grace of the righteousness of Christ, since so many die separated from it for eternity, but because all who are reborn for righteousness are reborn only through Christ, just as all who are born for condemnation are born only through Adam. No one, of course, is born in that way apart from Adam; no one is reborn in this way apart from Christ. Therefore he says, *all* in both cases, but he afterward says that the same *all* are also *many,* when he adds, *Just as through the disobedience of one man many were made sinners, so through the obedience of one man many are also made righteous.* Who are the *many,* but those whom he had a little before called *all*?

14. See how he stresses *one* in both cases, that is, Adam and Christ, the former for condemnation, the latter for justification, though Christ came in the flesh so long after Adam. He stresses these two in order that we might know that whoever were able to be righteous among the people of the Old Testament were also set free only through the same faith by which we too are set free, that is, faith in the incarnation of Christ, which was foretold to them as it was announced to us now that it has taken place. For this reason he mentions Christ the man, though he was also God, so that no one would think that the righteous of old could have been set free through Christ as God alone, that is, as the Word, which *was in the beginning* (Jn 1:1), not through faith in his incarnation, because of which Christ is also said to be man. This statement cannot, of course, be destroyed by which he says elsewhere, *Through one man came death, and through one man the resurrection of the dead. For, just as in Adam all die, so in Christ all will also be brought to life.* (1 Cor 15:21-22) He is, of course, speaking of the resurrection of the righteous where there is eternal life, not of the resurrection of the wicked where there will be eternal death. And for this reason he says, *They will be brought to life,* because those others will be condemned. Hence, in the old sacraments it was commanded that the circumcision of infants take place on the eighth day,[612] because Christ, in whom the removal of carnal sin occurs, which

---

612. See Gn 17:12 Lv 12:3.

circumcision signifies, rose on the Lord's day, which after the seventh day of the Sabbath is the eighth day. This, therefore, was also the faith of the righteous of old. For this reason the Apostle also says, *Having the same spirit of faith on account of which it was written, I believed, and on this account I have spoken, we too believe, and on this account we also speak* (2 Cor 4:13; Ps 116:10). He would not say *the same spirit of faith* unless he were warning us that the righteous of old had the same spirit of faith, that is, in the incarnation of Christ. But because this was announced to them as future, while it is announced to us as already having occurred and because in the time of the Old Testament there was veiled what in the time of the New Testament is revealed, the sacraments of that faith were, for this reason, changed so that they were different in the Old Testament from the New, though the faith itself is not changed and is one.[613] For, *just as in Adam all die, so in Christ all will also be brought to life.*

15. To these words on which we are commenting he adds and says, *But the law entered in so that sin might abound* (Rom 5:20); this no longer pertains to that sin which is contracted from Adam, about which he previously said, *Death reigned through one person* (Rom 5:17). We should, of course, understand either the natural law, which is known by persons at those ages that are capable of using reason, or the written law that was given through Moses. For the law was not able to give life and set us free *from the law of sin and death* (Rom 8:2), which was contracted from Adam; rather it added increases in sin through transgression. *For, where there is no law*, the same apostle says, *there is also no transgression* (Rom 4:15). Hence, since there is also a law in the reason of a human being who already uses free choice, a law naturally written in his heart, by which he is warned that he should not do anything to anyone else that he himself does not want to suffer, all are transgressors according to this law, even those who have not received the law given through Moses. Of these the Psalm said, *All the sinners of the earth have been judged to be transgressors* (Ps 119:119). For not all the sinners of the earth transgressed the law given through Moses, but still, unless they had transgressed some law, they would not be called transgressors. For *where there is no law, there is also no transgression*. Because of the transgression of the law that was given in paradise, a human being is born of Adam with *the law of sin and death*, of which it is said, *I see another law in my members that resists the law of my mind and holds me captive under the law of sin that is in my members* (Rom 7:23). Yet, unless this law afterward grows strong by a bad habit, it is conquered rather easily, but only by the grace of God. Because of the transgression of the other law, however, which is found in the use of the reason of the rational soul at the age when a human being already has the use of reason, *all the sinners of the earth* become *transgressors*. But because of the transgression of the law that was given through Moses, sin abounds much more. *For if a law were given that could bring to life, righteousness would cer-*

---

613. The CSEL edition has *vera* ("true"), but R. Teske has followed here the reading *una* ("one") in PL.

tainly come from the law, but Scripture enclosed all things under sin in order that the promise might be given to those who believe on the basis of faith in Jesus Christ (Gal 3:21-22). These words (if you recognize them) are from the Apostle. Again he says of this law, *The law was established for the sake of transgression until the offspring would come to whom the promise was made, the law given by angels through the hands of a mediator* (Gal 3:19). He mentions Christ by whose grace all are saved, whether infants *from the law of sin and death* (Rom 8:2) with which they are born, or adults who, by making bad use of the choice of their will, have transgressed the natural law of reason itself, or those who have received the law that was given through Moses and, in transgressing it, were killed by the letter.[614] But when a man transgresses the commandments of the Gospel, he stinks like one who has been dead four days.[615] But on account of the grace of him who did not softly say, but shouted with a loud voice, *Lazarus, come forth* (Jn 11:43), we should not stop hoping for him.

16. *The law, therefore, entered in so that sin might abound* (Rom 5:20), either when human beings neglect what God commands or when, presuming upon their own strength, they do not implore the help of grace and add pride to their weakness. When, however, by God's calling they understand why[616] they must groan and call upon him in whom they rightly believe, saying, *Have mercy on me, God, according to your great mercy* (Ps 51:3), and, *I said, Lord, have mercy on me; heal my soul because I have sinned against you* (Ps 41:5), and, *In your righteousness bring me to life* (Ps 119:40), and, *Remove from me the way of iniquity, and by your law have mercy on me* (Ps 119:29), and, *Let not the foot of pride come to me, and let the hand of sinners not move me* (Ps 36:12), and, *Direct my journey according to your word, and let not every iniquity have dominion over me* (Ps 119:133), for *the steps of a man are directed by the Lord, and he will choose his ways* (Ps 36:23), and the many other passages that were written precisely so as to warn us that in order to fulfill what we are commanded we must ask for help from him who gave the commandments—when someone stretches out to him, therefore, and groans in that way, there will happen what follows, *Where sin abounded, grace was even more abundant* (Rom 5:20), and, *Many sins are forgiven her, because she loved much* (Lk 7:47), and the love of God is poured out in our heart,[617] as a result of which there comes about *the fulfillment of the law* (Rom 13:10), this happens not through the strength of choice that is found in us but *through the Holy Spirit who has been given to us* (Rom 5:5). He, of course, knew the law who said, *For I find delight in the law of God in accord with the inner self,* and yet he added, *I see, however, another law in my members that resists the law of my mind and holds me captive under the law of sin that*

---

614. See 2 Cor 3:6.
615. See Jn 11:39.
616. R. Teske has followed here the PL reading of *cur* ("why") rather than that in CSEL of *cui* ("to whom").
617. See Rom 5:5.

is in my members. Wretched man that I am! Who will set me free from the body of this death? The grace of God through Jesus Christ our Lord. (Rom 7:22-25) Why did he not say instead, "Through my free choice," if not because freedom without the grace of God is not freedom but proud rebelliousness?

17. After the Apostle, therefore, said, *The law entered in so that sin might abound, but where sin abounded, grace was even more abundant,* he went on and added, *in order that, as sin reigned in death, so grace also might reign through righteousness in eternal life through Jesus Christ our Lord* (Rom 5: 20-21). But when he said, *in order that, as sin reigned in death,* he did not say, "Through one man," or, "Through the first man," or, "Through Adam," because he had already said, *The law entered in so that sin might abound,* and this abundance of sin does not pertain to the descendants propagated from the first man but to the transgressions committed in human life. To that one sin by which alone infants are held bound these transgressions were added later at an adult age because of the abundance of iniquity. But because the grace of the Savior is, nonetheless, able to remove this totality, even what does not pertain to the origin of that one sin, after he had said, *So grace also might reign through righteousness in eternal life,* he added, *through Jesus Christ our Lord.*

18. And so, let no one's arguments that are brought forth against these words of the Apostle keep infants from the salvation found in Christ Jesus our Lord. We must, after all, speak for them the more insofar as they cannot speak for themselves. *Through one man sin entered the world, and through sin death, and in that way it was passed on to all human beings, in whom all have sinned* (Rom 5:12). Just as they could not come into being apart from that one man, so they cannot be free from the same sin unless they are released from its guilt through the baptism of Christ. *For sin was in the world up to the law* (Rom 5:13). This was not said because from then on sin was found in no one but because what could be removed only by the spirit of grace could not be removed by the letter of the law. Lest anyone, therefore, who puts his trust in the strength, I do not say of his will but rather of his vanity, should think that the law could be enough for free choice and should mock the grace of Christ, the Apostle says, *For up to the law, sin was in the world, but sin was not imputed when the law did not exist* (Rom 5:13). He did not say, "Sin did not exist," but *was not imputed,* because there did not exist a law that by its accusations made sin known, whether the law of reason in an infant or the written law in the people.

19. *But death reigned,* he says, *from Adam to Moses* (Rom 5:14), because the law given through Moses could not take away the reign of death, which only the grace of Christ took away. But see over whom it reigned; he says, *even over those who did not sin in the likeness of the transgression of Adam.* It reigned, therefore, even over those who did not sin. But he showed why it reigned when he says, *in the likeness of the transgression of Adam.* For this is the better interpretation of these words, namely, that, after he had said, *Death reigned over those who did not sin,* as if to teach us why it reigned over those who did not sin, he added,

in the likeness of the transgression of Adam, that is, because the likeness of the transgression of Adam was present in their members. It can also be understood in this way: *Death reigned from Adam to Moses even over those who did not sin in the likeness of the transgression of Adam*, because in themselves, when they were already born but did not yet have the use of reason, which he used when he sinned, they had not received the commandment that he transgressed but were held bound only by original sin, by which the reign of death was dragging them to condemnation. This reign of death exists in all except those who have been reborn by the grace of Christ and belong to his kingdom. For, though temporal death was also propagated by original sin, it kills the body in them but does not drag the soul to punishment, by which he wanted us to understand the reign of death. In that way the soul renewed by grace no longer dies in hell, that is, is not estranged, is not separated from the life of God, but the temporal death of the body remains for the time being, even in these people who are redeemed by the death of Christ for the exercise of their faith and the contest of this present struggle, in which the martyrs have also done battle. But this death too is taken away in the renewal of the body that the resurrection promises. For there death, whose reign the grace of Christ is now destroying, will be completely swallowed up by victory[618] so that it does not drag their souls to the pains of hell. Some manuscripts, to be sure, do not have *over those who have not sinned* but *over those who have sinned in the likeness of the transgression of Adam*, by which words this meaning is in no way destroyed. In accord with it, of course, they are understood to have sinned *in the likeness of the transgression of Adam*, in accord with the previous words, *in whom all have sinned* (Rom 5:12). But more Greek manuscripts, from which the Scripture has been translated into Latin, have what we said.

20. But what he added concerning Adam, *who is the pattern of the one to come* (Rom 5:14), is also not understood in one way. For either he is the pattern of Christ by way of contrast so that, as all die in him, so all will also be brought to life in Christ and, *as through* his *disobedience many were made sinners, so through the obedience of Christ many were made righteous* (Rom 5:19), or he called him the pattern of the one to come because he himself inflicted the pattern of his death upon his descendants. The former is, nonetheless, the better interpretation, according to which he is believed to be the pattern by way of contrast, as the Apostle emphasizes. Then, so that the opposites would not be considered entirely equal in this pattern, he added and said, *But the gift is not like the sin; for, if on account of the sin of the one many have died, the grace and gift of God in the grace of the one man Jesus Christ has abounded much more for many* (Rom 5:15). We should not understand "for many more," since the sinful who will be condemned are many more, but "abounded more," because the pattern of death coming from Adam has power for a time over those who are redeemed by Christ, but the pattern of life through Christ will have power over them for eternity.

---

618. See 1 Cor 15:54.

Although, then, he says that Adam is the pattern of the one to come by way of contrast, Christ, nonetheless, benefited those who are reborn more than Adam harmed those who are born. *And the gift is not like the result of the one who sinned, for judgment comes from the one for condemnation, but grace comes from many sins for justification* (Rom 5:16). The pattern, he says, is not equal not only insofar as Adam did temporal harm to those whom Christ redeemed for eternity but also insofar as, unless they are redeemed by Christ, his descendants are handed over to condemnation because of that one sin of his, whereas Christ's redemption also removed the many sins that the abundance of sinful transgression added to that one, about which we spoke above.

21. Yield to no one regarding these words of the Apostle and their sound interpretation if you wish to live for Christ and in Christ. For, if, as they say, the Apostle mentioned these things in order that we might understand that sinners pertain to the first man not because we contracted sin from him by being born but because we sin by imitating him, he would have instead put the devil there, who sinned first and from whom the human race did not derive the propagation of its substance but only followed after him by imitating him. Thus the devil would be said to be the father of the wicked, just as Abraham is said to be our father because of our imitation of his faith, not because of the origin of our flesh.[619] For Scripture said of the devil himself, *But those who are on his side imitate him* (Wis 2:25). Then, if the Apostle mentioned the first man in this passage on account of imitation, because he was the first sinner among human beings, so that for this reason he said that all human sinners belong to him, why did he not put the saintly Abel there, who was the first righteous person among human beings, to whom all would belong by imitating his righteousness? But he put Adam there and put no one but Christ in opposition to him because, just as that man by his sin damaged his posterity, so this God-man by his righteousness saved his heritage, the former by passing on the impurity of the flesh, something the wicked devil could not do, the latter by giving the grace of the Spirit, something the righteous Abel could not do.

22. We have said much about these questions in our other works and sermons in church, because there were also among us certain persons who sowed these new seeds of their error wherever they could, some of whom the mercy of the Lord healed from that disease through our ministry and that of our brothers. And I suspect that there are still some here, especially in Carthage, but they now whisper in hiding, fearing the most well-founded faith of the Church. For in the church of the same city one of them by the name of Caelestius had already deviously begun to seek the honor of the priesthood, but he was brought by the solid faith and freedom of the brothers straight to an episcopal court on account of these discourses opposed to the grace of Christ.[620] He was, however, forced

---

619. See Jn 8:38-39.44.
620. See *The Deeds of Pelagius* 11, 23 for the propositions of Caelestius that were condemned at

to confess that infants must be baptized because they too need redemption. Although at the time he refused to say there anything more explicit about original sin, he did, nonetheless, do considerable harm to his position by the mention of redemption. After all, from what did they need to be redeemed except from the power of the devil in which they could not have been except by the bonds of sin? Or at what price are they redeemed except by the blood of Christ, of which scripture stated most clearly that it was shed for the forgiveness of sins?[621] But because he went off, having been found guilty and detested by the Church rather than corrected and subdued, I was afraid that it was perhaps he himself there who was trying to disturb your faith, and for this reason I thought I should mention his name. But it makes no difference whether it is he or others who partake of his error. For there are more than we would expect. And where they are not refuted, they win over others to their sect, and they are becoming so numerous that I do not know where they will turn up. Yet we prefer that they be healed within the framework of the Church rather than cut off from its body like incurable members, at least if the very gravity of the situation permits this. For we have to fear that more may begin to go bad if the rottenness is spared. But the mercy of our Lord, which would rather set them free from this plague, is able to do so. And it will undoubtedly do this if they faithfully pay attention to and hold what scripture says: *He who calls upon the Lord will be saved* (Jl 2:32).

4, 23. Listen now to a few points about the rich, which is the next question in your letter. For you said that those people claim, "A rich man who remains in his riches cannot enter the kingdom of God unless he has sold all his possessions, and it does not profit him if he has perhaps observed all the commandments by the use of his riches."[622] Our forefathers, Abraham, Isaac, and Jacob, who departed from this life so long ago, avoided the criticisms of these people. All these men, of course, had significant riches, as Scripture, which is most reliable, testifies. He himself, *who for our sake became poor, though he was truly rich* (2 Cor 8:9), foretold in a perfectly true promise that many will come from the east and from the west and will recline in the kingdom of heaven, not above them or apart from them, but with them.[623] And although the proud *rich man who was clothed in purple and linen and feasted splendidly every day* (Lk 16:19) died and was tormented in hell, nonetheless, if he had shown pity for the poor man covered with sores who lay despised before his gate, he too would have merited mercy.[624] And if that poor man's merit was his indigence, not his righteousness, he would certainly not have been carried by the angels into the bosom of Abraham, who was rich in this life. But in order to show us that God did not reward poverty itself in the poor man and did not condemn riches in that other, but that piety in this one and impiety in the other each

---

Carthage in 411 or 412 after Caelestius was accused of heresy by Paulinus of Milan.
621. See Mt 26:28.
622. Letter 156.
623. See Mt 8:11.
624. See Lk 16:20-22.

met with their own recompense, the torment of fire received that impious rich man while the bosom of a rich man received the pious poor man. Abraham, of course, who lived here as a rich man possessed his riches and valued them so slightly in comparison with the commandments of God that he was unwilling to offend God who commanded it, even in the sacrifice of his son whom he both hoped and desired to be the heir of his riches.[625]

24. What they say here, to be sure is that the patriarchs of old did not sell all they possessed and did not give it to the poor because the Lord had not commanded them to do this. For, when the New Testament was not yet revealed, something that had to come about only in the fullness of time, their virtue also did not have to be revealed. For God knew that by their virtue he could most easily bring this about in their hearts, since he offered to them so remarkable a testimony that, though he is the God of all the holy and righteous, he deigned to say as if of his special friends, *I am the God of Abraham and the God of Isaac and the God of Jacob; this is my name for eternity* (Ex 3:15). But afterwards *the great sacrament of piety was revealed in the flesh* (1 Tm 3:16), and the coming of Christ shone forth to call all the nations. Those patriarchs had also believed in him, but they preserved the domesticated olive tree of this faith, which was to be made manifest in its own time, in the root, as it were, of that tree, of which the apostle spoke.[626] Then Christ said to the rich man, *Go, sell all that you have, and give it to the poor, and you will have a treasure in heaven, and come follow me* (Mt 19:21).

25. If they say this, they seem to say something reasonable, but let them listen to the whole context; let them pay attention to the whole context; let them not open their ears in part and close them in part. For whom did the Lord command concerning this? That rich man, of course, who was asking advice for attaining eternal life. For he said this to the Lord, *What should I do to attain eternal life?* (Mt 19:16) But the Lord did not answer him, "If you wish to attain life, go, sell all you have," but, *If you wish to attain life, keep the commandments* (Mt 19:17). When the young man said that he had kept the commandments from the law that the Lord mentioned to him and asked what was still lacking for him, he received the answer, *If you wish to be perfect, go, sell all that you have, and give it to the poor*. And in order that he would not think that he was in this way losing the things that he loved greatly, he said, *And you will have treasure in heaven*. Then he added, *And come, follow me* (Mt 19:21), in order that he would not suppose that it profits anyone, when he does this, if he does not follow Christ. But that man, of course, went off sad who saw how he had observed the commandments of the law. For I think that he replied with more arrogance than truth that he had observed them. The good teacher, nonetheless, distinguished the commandments of the law from that more excellent perfection. For he said there, *If you wish to attain life, observe the commandments*, but here he says, *If you wish to*

---

625. See Gn 22:1-10.
626. See Rom 11:17.

be perfect, go, sell all that you have, and so on. Why, then, should we deny that rich people, though they lack that perfection, still attain life if they have kept the commandments and have given in order that it may be given them and have forgiven in order that it may be forgiven them?[627]

26. We believe that the apostle Paul was a minister of the New Testament when in writing to Timothy he said, *Command the rich of this world not to think proud thoughts and not to place hope in the uncertainty of riches, but in the living God who offers us all things in abundance for enjoyment. Let them do good; let them be rich in good works; let them give readily, share, and store up for themselves a good foundation for the future in order that they may obtain true life.* (1 Tm 6:17-19) With regard to this life it was said to that young man, *If you wish to attain life.* I think that in commanding these things the apostle was instructing and not deceiving the rich; he did not say, "Command the rich of this world to sell all that they have, give it to the poor, and follow the Lord," but, *not to think proud thoughts and not to place their hope in the uncertainty of riches.* It was this pride and this hope in the uncertainty of the riches by which he thought that he was happy because of his purple and linen and splendid feasts, and not the riches themselves, that brought to the torments of hell the rich man who held in contempt that poor man lying at his door.

27. Or do they perhaps, because the Lord went on to say, *Truly I say to you, a rich man will enter the kingdom of heaven with difficulty, and again I say to you, a camel will enter through the eye of a needle more easily than a rich man into the kingdom of heaven* (Mt 19:23-24), think that, even if a rich man does those things that the Apostle writes the rich should be ordered to do, he cannot enter into the kingdom of heaven? What, then, does this mean? Does the Apostle contradict the Lord, or do these people not know what he is saying? Let a Christian choose which of these to believe. I think that it is better that we believe that they do not know what to say than that Paul is contradicting the Lord. Next, why do they not listen to the Lord himself as he speaks in the following verses to his disciples who were saddened over the misfortune of the rich? *What is impossible for human beings is easy for God* (Mt 19:26).

28. But this was said, the Pelagians say, because it will transpire that, once they have heard the Gospel, the rich will follow the Lord after selling their inheritance and giving it to the poor and will enter the kingdom of heaven. And in that way there will come about what seemed difficult. It was not that, while remaining in possession of their riches, they would obtain true life by observing the commandments of the apostle, that is, by not thinking proud thoughts and not placing their hope in the uncertainty of riches but in the living God, doing good, giving readily, and sharing with the needy. Rather, they would fulfill these commandments of the apostle after having sold all their possessions.

---

627. See Lk 6:38.37.

29. If they say this—I know, of course, that they do say this—they do not, first of all, pay attention to how the Lord preached his grace in opposition to their teaching. For he did not say, "What seems impossible for human beings is easy for human beings if they will it," but *What is impossible for human beings is easy for God*, showing that, when these things are done correctly, they are not done by the power of a human being but by the grace of God. Let these people, then, pay attention to this, and if they find fault with those who boast of their riches, let themselves avoid placing their trust in their own strength. For both are blamed together in the psalm, *those who place their trust in their own strength and those who boast of their riches* (Ps 49:7). Let the rich, therefore, hear, *What is impossible for human beings is easy for God*, and whether remaining in possession of their riches and doing good works with them or having sold them and distributed them in accord with the needs of the poor, let them enter the kingdom of heaven; let them attribute their goodness to the grace of God, not to their own strength. For *what is impossible for human beings is easy* not for human beings but *for God*. Let these people also hear this, and if they have already either sold all their possessions and given them to the poor or are still doing this and arranging it and in this way preparing to enter the kingdom of heaven, let them not attribute this to their own strength but to the same grace of God. For *what is impossible for human beings is easy* not for them, since they are human beings, but *for God*. The Apostle also, of course, says this to them, *Work out your own salvation with fear and trembling, for it is God who produces in you both the willing and the action in accord with good will* (Phil 2:12-13). They say, to be sure, that they received from the Lord the counsel of perfection about selling their possessions in order to follow the Lord because this was added: *And come, follow me*. Why, then, do they presume upon their own will alone in these good actions that they do and not hear the Lord, whom they say they follow, upbraiding them and testifying, *Without me you can do nothing* (Jn 15:5).

30. But if the Apostle said, *Command the rich of this world not to think proud thoughts and not to put their hope in the uncertainty of riches*, in order that they would sell all that they possess and, by distributing the income from it to the needy, would do what follows: *Give readily, share, and store up for themselves a good foundation for the future* (1 Tm 6:17-19), and if he believes that they could not otherwise enter the kingdom of heaven, he deceives those whose homes he so carefully puts in order by the soundness of his teaching, when he admonishes and commands wives how they should behave toward their husbands and husbands toward their wives, children toward their parents and parents toward their children, servants toward their masters and masters toward their servants. For how could they do this without a home and without some family property?

31. Or do the words of the Lord disturb them, *Whoever leaves all his possessions on my account will receive a hundredfold in this world and will possess eternal life in the world to come* (Mt 19:29)? It is one thing to leave and another

thing to sell. For a wife is also mentioned among the things that he commands us to leave, but no human laws permit a man to sell his wife. But the laws of Christ do not permit him to leave her *except in the case of fornication* (Mt 5:32). What, then, do those commandments mean—for they cannot be mutually contradictory—if not that at times there arises a moment of crisis in which one must leave either his wife or Christ—to pass over other occasions—if a wife is unhappy with her Christian husband and proposes to him a divorce either from her or from Christ? At this point what should he do but choose Christ and leave his wife in a praiseworthy fashion on account of Christ? In a case where both are Christians the Lord, of course, commanded that one should not leave his wife *except in the case of fornication*. But where either of them is a non-believer, the counsel of the apostle should be followed, namely, that, if the non-believer consents to live with the believing husband, the husband should not divorce his wife. Likewise, as well a believing wife should not dismiss her husband if he consents to live with her. *But if the one who is a non-believer*, he says, *leaves, let him leave; for the brother or sister is not subject to slavery in such matters* (1 Cor 7:12-13), that is, if the non-believer refuses to live with the believing spouse, let the believer in this case recognize his freedom so that he does not regard himself as subject to slavery, leaving the faith to avoid losing an unbelieving spouse.

32. This rule is also understood with regard to children and parents and also with regard to brothers and sisters. We should leave them all on account of Christ, when the condition is set that we should leave Christ if we want to have them with us. This, then, should also be understood with regard to house and fields; it should also be understood with regard to those things that are owned by right of purchase. After all, he does not say of these things, "Whoever sells on my account whatever it is, of course, permissible to sell," but, *Whoever leaves*. For it is possible that some authority might say to a Christian, "Either cease to be a Christian, or, if you choose to remain one, you will not have your house and possessions." But then those rich persons, who had decided to retain their riches in order that they might merit God as their reward on the basis of good works with them, should leave them on account of Christ rather than Christ on account of them, in order that they may receive a hundredfold in this world. For the perfection of this number signifies all things. *A believer, of course, has a whole world of riches* (Prv 17:6 LXX); in this way they become *as if having nothing and possessing all things* (2 Cor 6:10). And in the future world they will possess eternal life; otherwise, if they leave Christ on account of these things, they will be cast down into eternal death.

33. Under this law and condition there stand not only those who by the excellence of their intention have embraced the counsel of perfection so that, having sold their possessions, they distribute the proceeds to the poor and bear the lighter burden of Christ with their shoulders freer from every burden of this world, but also anyone weaker and less suited to this glorious perfection who, nonetheless, remembers that he is truly a Christian when he hears the condition

set before him that, unless he abandons all these things, he will abandon Christ. He will rather seize the tower *of strength from before the enemy* (Ps 61:4) because, when he was building it by his own faith, he calculated the expenses by which it could be completed,[628] that is, he approached the faith with such a spirit that he did not renounce this world only in words, for, even if he bought something, he was like someone who did not own it, and if he used the world, he was like someone who did not use it,[629] not *putting his hope in the uncertainty of riches, but in the living God* (1 Tm 6:17).

34. For everyone who renounces this world undoubtedly renounces everything that belongs to it in order to be a disciple of Christ. For, he himself, after he had first set forth the parables about the expenses necessary for the building of the tower and about preparing for war against another king,[630] added this: *One who does not renounce everything that belongs to him cannot be my disciple* (Lk 14:33). Such a person, then, should certainly also renounce his riches if he has any, either so that, not loving them at all, he may distribute all of them to the poor and be relieved of needless burdens, or so that, loving Christ more, he may transfer his hope from them to him and use them so that, freely giving and sharing them, he may store up a treasure in heaven and also be ready to leave them, like parents and children and brothers and wife, if he were faced with such a condition that, unless he left Christ, he could not have them. For, if he renounces this world in another way when he approaches the sacrament of the faith, he does what blessed Cyprian bemoaned, when he said of apostates, "They renounce the world in words alone and not in actions."[631] With regard to this sort of person it is said, when at the arrival of temptations he feared more to lose these possessions than to deny Christ, *There you see a man who began to build a building and could not complete it* (Lk 14:30). He is also the man who, when his enemy was still far off, sent envoys seeking peace; that is, when temptation is not yet attacking but still threatening and menacing him, he agrees to abandon and deny Christ in order not to lose the things that he loves more. And there are many of this sort who even suppose that the Christian religion ought to help them to increase their riches and to multiply earthly pleasures.

35. But rich Christians are not this sort of people; though they possess riches, they are not, nonetheless, possessed by them so that they prefer them to Christ. For they have renounced the world with a sincere heart so that they place no hope in such things. These men educate with sound discipline their wives and children and their whole families to hold the Christian religion; their homes, warm with hospitality, receive a righteous person in the name of a righteous

---

628. See Lk 14:28.
629. See 1 Cor 7:30-31.
630. See Lk 14:28-32.
631. Cyprian, Letter 7, 1.

person in order that they may receive the reward of the righteous.[632] They break their bread with the needy; they cloth the naked, redeem the captive,[633] and store up for themselves *a good foundation for the future in order that they might attain true life* (1 Tm 6:19). And if monetary losses have to be suffered for the faith of Christ, they place no value on their own riches; if this world threatens them with the losses of or separations from members of their family for the sake of Christ, they hate their parents, brothers, children, and wives. Finally, if they have to negotiate with an enemy over the very life of this body in order that Christ may not abandon them after they have abandoned him, they also hate their own life. With regard to all of these things they have received the commandment that they cannot otherwise be disciples of Christ.[634]

36. And yet, because they received the commandment to hate even their own lives for the sake of Christ, they do not consider that they should sell them or destroy them by laying their own hands upon themselves, but they are ready to lose them by dying for the name of Christ, lest they live as though they were dead for having denied Christ. So too, they ought to be ready, for the sake of Christ, to lose the riches that they were not ready to sell, as Christ counseled, in order that they may not be lost along with them after they have lost Christ. For this reason we have rich and most glorious persons of both sexes who have been exalted by the glory of martyrdom. Many who hesitated before to become perfect by the selling of their possessions have suddenly been made perfect by imitating the suffering of Christ, and those who by some weakness of flesh and blood spared their riches suddenly did battle against sin for the faith to the point of shedding their blood. But those who did not attain the crown of martyrdom and did not accept the great and glorious counsel about selling their possessions and yet, free from grave sins worthy of condemnation, fed the hungry Christ, gave him drink in his thirst, clothed him when he was naked, and welcomed him when he was traveling, will not, of course, sit with Christ to judge from on high, but will stand at his right hand to be judged with mercy.[635] For blessed are the merciful because God will show them mercy,[636] and *judgment will be without mercy for one who has not shown mercy, but mercy triumphs over judgment* (Jas 2:13).

37. Hence, let these people stop speaking contrary to the Scriptures, and in their exhortations let them rouse people to greater goods without condemning lesser ones. Is it true, after all, that with their exhortations they can only lead people to holy virginity by condemning the bonds of marriage, since, as the Apostle teaches, *Each has his own gift from God, one this gift, another that* (1 Cor 7:7)? Let them, therefore, walk in the path of perfection after having sold all

---

632. See Mt 10:41.
633. See Is 58:7; Mt 25:35.
634. See Lk 14:26-27.
635. See Mt 25:34-40.
636. See Mt 5:7.

their possessions and given them away in acts of mercy. But if they are truly the poor of Christ and gather riches not for themselves but for Christ, why should they punish his weaker members before they have received their seats as judges? For, if they are the sort of persons to whom the Lord says, *You shall sit upon twelve thrones, judging the twelve tribes of Israel* (Mt 19:28 and Lk 22:30), and of whom the Apostle says, *Do you not know that we shall judge the angels?* (1 Cor 6:3) let them prepare themselves rather to welcome into eternal dwelling places not rich criminals but the devout rich, who made friends *by means of the mammon of iniquity* (Lk 16:9). For I suspect that some of those who spread about these ideas impudently and imprudently are supported by rich and pious Christians in their needs. For the Church has, in a sense, its own soldiers and its own officials. Hence, the Apostle says, *Who ever serves as a soldier at his own expense?* (1 Cor 9:7) It has its vineyard and its cultivators; it has its flock and its pastors. Hence, he says by way of conclusion, *Who plants a vineyard and does not eat of its fruit? Who shepherds a flock and does not receive milk from it?* (1 Cor 9:7) And yet, to argue for such ideas as they argue for is not to serve as soldiers but to engage in rebellion; it is not to plant a vineyard but to uproot it; it is not to gather sheep to feed them but to separate them for the flock to lose them.

38. These people, however, who are fed and clothed by the pious services of the rich—for they do not receive things for their needs only from those who sell their possessions—are not, nonetheless, judged and condemned by the more excellent members of Christ who, thanks to their greater virtue, which the Apostle commends,[637] support themselves by their own hands. In the same way these people ought not to condemn Christians of lesser merit by whose wealth they are supported but ought rather to say to them, by living well and by teaching correctly, *If we have sown spiritual goods among you, is it too much if we gather in a natural harvest from you?* (1 Cor 9:11) The servants of God, of course, who live by selling the honest work of their own hands, condemn with far less impudence the people from whom they receive nothing than those people do who are unable to work with their hands on account of some bodily weakness and condemn those from whose resources they themselves live.

39. I myself who write these words have deeply loved the perfection about which the Lord spoke when he said to the rich young man, *Go, sell all that you have, and give it to the poor, and you will have treasure in heaven, and come, follow me* (Mt 19:21), and I have done this not by my own strength but by the help of his grace. It is not true that I will receive less credit because I was not rich. For the apostles themselves who first did this were not rich either. But he abandons the whole world who abandons both what he has and what he hopes to have. I, of course, know better than any other human being how far I have made progress in this path of perfection, but God knows this better than I. And with as much energy as I can, I exhort others to this goal, and in the name of the Lord

---

637. See 1 Thes 4:11; Acts 20:34.

I have companions who have been persuaded to this by my ministry in such a way that, above all, we still maintain sound doctrine, and we do not judge with vain pride those who live like us, saying that it profits them nothing that they live chastely, though as married, that they govern their homes and families, and that by works of mercy they store up for themselves treasure for the next life. Otherwise, by arguing for these ideas we might be found not to be interpreters of the Holy Scriptures but attackers of them. I have mentioned this because, when the Pelagians are prevented from saying such things by those who have not accepted this counsel of the Lord, they reply that those people do not want to discuss these points because they are attached to their own vices and refuse to fulfill the commandments of the Lord. Now, not to mention those who, though weaker, still use riches in a religious manner, even the covetous and greedy people who use these riches badly and set their hearts of clay upon an earthly treasure are more tolerable in the Church than these people. For it is necessary that the Church carry even these up to the end, like those nets carried bad fish to the shore.[638] For by preaching and spreading these ideas these Pelagians want to appear great because they have sold their riches and any inheritance in accord with the commandment of the Lord, and they work to disturb and undermine by this unsound doctrine his heritage, which is spread far and wide up to the ends of the earth.

40. Hence, because I have on this occasion already said, though only briefly, what I hold about the Church of Christ in this world, that is, that it must carry within her good and bad people until the end of this world, for you asked this too among your other questions, I shall finally conclude this lengthy letter. But avoid swearing an oath as much as possible. One does better, of course, not to swear to the truth than by the habit of swearing to fall into perjury often and always come close to perjury. But those people—to the extent that I have heard some of them—have no idea at all what it is to swear. For they think that they do not swear when they have on their lips, *God knows* (2 Cor 11:31; 12:2), *God is my witness* (Rom 1:9; Phil 1:8) and, *I call God as witness to my soul* (2 Cor 1:23), because one does not say, "by God," and because such expressions are found in the apostle Paul. But against them that expression, which they admit is an oath, is also found there in the Apostle where he says, *I die every day, brothers; I swear by the boast about you that I have in Christ Jesus our Lord* (1 Cor 15:31). For in the Greek manuscripts this is certainly found to be an oath so that no one should understand in the Latin language that *by the boast about you* was said in the same way as *by my coming to you again* (Phil 1:26) and many other expressions in which there is said, "by something," and there is no oath. But it is not the case that an oath ought to be a joke for us because the Apostle, a man most solid in the truth, swore in his letter. For we act much more safely, as I said, if, to the extent it is up to us, we never swear so that *yes, yes; no, no* (Mt 5:37, Jas 5:12) is on our lips, as the Lord admonishes, not because it is a sin to swear to the truth but

---

638. See Mt 13:47-48.

because it is a very grave sin to swear falsely, and one falls more quickly into this who becomes used to swearing.

41. You see now what I think. Better people—not those whose view I already know must be rejected, but others who can do so with truth—may explain these points better. For I am more ready to learn than to teach, and you will bestow a great benefit upon me if you do not allow me to be ignorant of what the holy brethren there say against the empty chatter of these people. May you live correctly and happily in the Lord, my most beloved son.

LETTER 178
Augustine to Hilary, the bishop of Narbonne in Gaul (416)

In 416 Augustine wrote to Hilary, most probably the bishop of Narbonne in Gaul. He informs him of the emergence of a new heresy and sums up the principal points of the Pelagian teaching (paragraph 1). He claims that such a doctrine undermines "the foundations of the whole Christian faith" and warns Hilary to be on guard against the followers of Pelagius, mentioning that two African councils have spoken against the new heresy and have sent letters to Rome (paragraph 2). Finally, Augustine asks that all Catholics condemn these errors (paragraph 3).

To Hilary, his blessed lord and venerable brother in the truth of Christ and fellow priest, Augustine sends greetings in the Lord.

1. Since our honorable son, Palladius, was setting sail from our shore when he asked for a favor, he bestowed on me an even greater one. For he asked that I not only commend him to Your Grace but also that I commend myself to your prayers, my blessed lord and venerable brother in the love of Christ. When I do this, Your Holiness will, of course, do what we both hope for from you. Your Holiness will hear from the courier whom I mentioned about our situation, since I know that in your love for us you are concerned about us, just as we are concerned about you in our love for you. Now I shall mention briefly what is most necessary. A certain new heresy inimical to the grace of Christ is trying to rise up in opposition to the Church of Christ but has not yet been clearly separated from the Church. This heresy arises from human beings who dare to attribute so much power to human weakness as to claim that the only things that pertain to the grace of God are our having been created with free choice and the ability not to sin and our having received from God commandments that we can fulfill. But they claim that we do not need any help from God to keep and fulfill the commandments. They admit that we need the forgiveness of sins because we are not able to undo the wrong actions that we did in the past. But they say that the human will is by its natural ability, without the help of the grace of God, sufficient from then on, thanks to virtue, for avoiding and conquering future sins and overcoming all temptations. They claim that even infants do not need the grace of the savior in order to be set free from perdition through baptism, since they contracted no infection of sin from Adam.

2. Your Reverence sees perfectly well, along with us, how inimical this idea is to the grace of God that has been granted to the human race through Jesus Christ our Lord and how they are trying to overthrow the foundations of the whole Christian faith. Nor ought we to be silent with you about how, with pastoral concern, you should watch out for such people whom we want and desire to be healed in the Church rather than cut off from it. For, when I was writing

this, I learned that in the church of Carthage a decree of the council of bishops was drawn up against them to be sent by letter to the holy and venerable Pope Innocent, and we ourselves have also likewise written to the same Apostolic See concerning the council of Numidia.[639]

3. For all of us who have hope in Christ ought to resist this pestilential impiety and with one heart condemn and anathematize it. It contradicts even our prayers when it allows us to say, *Forgive us our debts as we also forgive our debtors* (Mt 6:12), but allows it in such a way as to claim that a human being in this corruptible body, which weighs down the soul,[640] can by his own strength attain such great righteousness that it is not necessary to say, *Forgive us our debts*. But they do not accept the words that follow, *Bring us not into temptation* (Mt 6:13), in the sense that we should pray to God in order that he may help us to overcome temptations to sins but in order that no human misfortune may attack our body and afflict us, since it already lies in our power to conquer temptations to sins by the ability of our nature, so that we should think that it is useless to ask for this by prayers. We cannot in one short letter gather together all or even most of the arguments of so great an impiety, especially since, when I was writing these ideas, the couriers who were about to set sail did not allow me to delay longer. I think, however, that I have not been a burden to your eyes because I could not be silent about avoiding so great an evil with all vigilance and with the help of the Lord.

---

639. Augustine refers to the Councils of Carthage (see Letter 175) and of Milevis (see Letter 176), both held in 416.
640. See Wis 9:15.

LETTER 179
Augustine to John, the bishop of Jerusalem (416)

In 416 Augustine wrote to John, the bishop of Jerusalem, concerning the heresy of Pelagius. At the Council of Jerusalem, held in the summer of 415, John had sympathized with Pelagius, probably due at least in part to his feud with Jerome, who opposed Pelagius. Augustine explains that he is taking advantage of the opportunity provided by the courier, who plans to return immediately, and hopes that John will reply to him (paragraph 1). Augustine explains how he obtained a copy of Pelagius' book, *Nature*, and how in reply to it he wrote *Nature and Grace* (paragraph 2). He points out how in his book Pelagius calls grace merely the nature with which we are created and how he claims that free choice suffices itself for acting righteously (paragraph 3). Pelagius' teachings run counter to the prayers of Christians and are opposed to the blessings that priests ask God to bestow on their flocks (paragraph 4). Augustine explains to John why he is sending him a copy of Pelagius' book and a copy of his reply to it (paragraph 5). He tells John to question Pelagius about whether we need to pray to the Lord in order to avoid sin and about whether infants contract original sin from Adam (paragraph 6). In return Augustine asks for a copy of the proceedings of the Council of Diospolis at which Pelagius was allegedly acquitted, since Augustine has thus far only received a document that Pelagius had written in his own defense (paragraph 7). Augustine points out that Pelagius says in his book the opposite of what he said in the document written in his own defense (paragraph 8). Augustine tells John that, from what Pelagius said in his book, he will be able to see whether he ought to believe his other denials (paragraph 9). Augustine also insists that he has proof that the book was written by Pelagius (paragraph 10).

To John, his most blessed lord and rightly venerable brother and fellow bishop, Augustine sends greetings in the Lord.

1. I do not dare to be angry because I have not deserved to receive a letter from Your Holiness. For it is better to believe that a courier was unavailable than to suspect that Your Reverence has regarded me as unworthy of a reply, my most blessed lord and rightly venerable brother. But now, because I have learned that the servant of God, Luke, by whose hands I have sent this, will soon be returning, I shall offer abundant thanks to God and to Your Kindness if you are so gracious as to pay me a visit by letter. I hear that you are very fond of Pelagius, our brother and your son. I suggest that you show him such love that the people who know him and have carefully listened to him do not think that Your Holiness has been deceived by him.

2. For certain young men, sons of the finest families and well educated in the liberal arts, disciples of Pelagius, abandoned the hopes they had in this world

because of his exhortation and devoted themselves to the service of God.[641] But I found in them certain ideas opposed to the sound teaching that is contained in the Gospel of the Savior and explained in the letters of the apostles, that is, they were seen to argue against the grace of God because of which we are Christians and in which *through the Spirit we await in faith the righteousness for which we hope* (Gal 5:5). And when they began to correct their views through our instructions, they gave me a book that they said was by this same Pelagius, asking that I reply to it. After I saw that I ought to do this so that this wicked error might be more completely removed from their hearts, I read the book and replied.

3. In this book Pelagius calls grace only the nature in which we are created with free choice. But the grace which holy scripture commends by so many testimonies, teaching that we are justified by it, that is, made righteous, and are helped by God's mercy in doing or fulfilling every good work, something which the prayers of the saints most clearly reveal when they ask of the Lord what they are commanded by the Lord—this grace he not only does not mention, but he even says much against it. For he states and strongly maintains that by free choice alone human nature can suffice of itself for acting righteously and observing all the commandments of God. Hence, who would not see, when he reads the same book, how Pelagius attacks the grace of God of which the Apostle says, *Wretched man that I am! Who will set me free from the body of this death? The grace of God through our Lord Jesus Christ* (Rom 7:24-25)? Who would not see that he leaves no place for the help of God on account of which we ought to say in prayer, *Bring us not into temptation* (Mt 6:13)? Who would not see that the Lord also seems to have said to Peter without any reason, *I have prayed for you that your faith might not fail* (Lk 22:32), if all this is accomplished in us without any help of God but by the power of our will?

4. These perverse and impious arguments not only contradict our prayers, by which we ask of the Lord whatever we read and hold that the saints asked, but are also opposed to our blessings, which we say over the people, desiring for them and asking from the Lord that *he may make them abound in love for one another and for all human beings* (1 Thes 3:12), that he may grant that they *may be strengthened in virtue according to the riches of his glory by his Spirit* (Eph 3:16), that *he may fill them with every joy and peace in believing*, and that they may abound *in hope and in the power of the Holy Spirit* (Rom 15:13). Why do we ask for them these things, which we know that the Apostle asked from the Lord for the people, if our nature, created with free choice, can now offer all these things to itself of its own will? Why does the same apostle also say, *For whoever are driven by the Spirit of God are the children of God* (Rom 8:14), if we are driven by the spirit of our own nature to become children of God? Why does he likewise say, *The Spirit helps our weakness* (Rom 8:26), if our nature

---

641. Augustine refers to Timasius and James, who had given him Pelagius' *Nature* and for whom he wrote *Nature and Grace*.

was created so that it does not need to be helped by the Spirit toward works of righteousness? Why did scripture say, *But God is faithful who will not permit you to be tempted beyond what you can bear, but will produce a way out along with the temptation in order that you can endure it* (1 Cor 10:13), if we were already created so that we could overcome all temptations by resisting them with the powers of free choice?

5. Why should I cite more texts for Your Holiness? For I feel that I am being a burden, especially since you are listening to my letter through an interpreter. If you love Pelagius, let him also love you, or rather let him not deceive himself and you. For, when you hear him confess the grace of God and the help of God, you think that he is saying what you hold in accord with the Catholic norm, since you do not know what he wrote in his book. For this reason I sent you his book and mine, in which I replied to it, so that Your Reverence may see from them what he calls the grace and help of God when people object to him that he speaks against the grace and help of God. Thereupon, show him by teaching him and exhorting him and by praying for his salvation, which must be found in Christ, so he may confess the grace of God that the saints of God are known to have confessed when they petitioned God for the things that God commanded them to do. For those things were not commanded except to display our will, and there would be no petitioning except so that a weak will would be helped by him who commanded.

6. Let him be asked openly whether he accepts that we must pray to God in order that we may not sin. But if he does not accept this, read in his hearing the words of the Apostle, *But we pray to God that you may do no evil* (2 Cor 13:7). If, however, he accepts it, let him openly preach the grace by which we are helped in order that he himself may not do much evil. For those who are set free are all set free by this grace of God through Jesus Christ our Lord, because no one can be set free in any other way apart from it. On this account it was written, *Just as in Adam all die, so too all will be brought to life in Christ* (1 Cor 15:22), not because no one will be condemned but because no one will be set free in any other way. For, just as none are children of men except through Adam, so none are children of God except through Christ. None, therefore, can become children of men except through Adam, and none of them can become children of God except through Christ. Let him, therefore, openly state what he holds on this. Does he accept that even infants, who cannot yet desire or reject righteousness, are still set free by the grace of Christ? After all, on account of the one man *sin entered the world, and through sin death, and in that way it passed on to all human beings, in whom all have sinned* (Rom 5:12). Does he believe that the blood of Christ, which was certainly shed for the forgiveness of sins,[642] was also shed for them on account of original sin? It is especially on these points that we wish to know what he believes, what he holds, and especially what he confesses

---

642. See Mt 16:28.

and preaches. But on the other points on which objections are raised against him, even if he is proven to have been in error, one can more easily put up with him until he is corrected.

7. I also ask that you send us the proceedings of the ecclesiastical court by which he was allegedly acquitted. I ask this because of the desire of many bishops who are disturbed along with me by the uncertain rumor on this matter. But I alone wrote this letter because I did not want to lose the opportunity of a courier in a hurry to depart from us, who I heard could quickly return to us. Pelagius has already sent us in place of those proceedings not, in fact, any part of them but a sort of defense of himself that he himself wrote, in which he said that he was responding to the objections of the Gauls.[643] In that defense—to omit other things—when he was replying to the objection that he said a human being can be without sin and observe the commandments if he wills, he replied, "We said this, for God gave a human being this ability. We did not say that anyone is found who has never sinned from infancy to old age but that, having turned away from sin by his own effort and having been helped by the grace of God, a person can be without sin, but despite this he will be capable of sinning afterwards."

8. Your Reverence sees in this response of Pelagius that he confessed that the earlier life of a human being, which begins from infancy, is not without sin, but that he can be converted to a life without sin by his own effort and the help of the grace of God. Why, then, does he say in the book to which I replied that Abel lived this life so that he never sinned at all? For these are his words on this subject: "This can be correctly said with regard to those whom scripture recalls neither as good nor as bad. But with regard to those whose righteousness it recalls, it would also undoubtedly have recalled their sins if they were thought to have sinned in any way. Granted that in other times," he says, "because of the large numbers of people, Scripture refrained from mentioning the sins of all. But right at the very beginning or the world, when there were only four human beings, what are we going to say?" he asks. "Why has Scripture refused to mention the sins of everyone? Was it on account of the huge population, which did not yet exist? Or was it because it recalled only those who had committed sins but could not recall the one who had committed none? Certainly," he says, "in the first age Scripture tells us of only four human beings: Adam and Eve and their sons, Cain and Abel. Eve sinned. Scripture tells us that. Adam also fell. The same Scripture does not omit that fact. Moreover, Scripture likewise testified that Cain sinned. It indicates not only their sins but also the nature of their sins. If Abel had also sinned," he says, "Scripture would certainly have said so. If it did not, then he did not sin."[644] I have quoted these words from his book, which Your Holiness will also be able to find in that volume, so that you may understand how you ought

---

643. I.e., to Hero and Lazarus, the Gallic bishops who brought accusations against Pelagius at the Council of Jerusalem in the summer of 415.
644. Pelagius, *Nature*; Augustine quotes the same passage in *Nature and Grace* 37, 43-44.

to believe him when he denies the other charges. Perhaps he will say that Abel himself committed no sin but that he was not for that reason without sin and, hence, cannot be compared to the Lord, who was the only one in mortal flesh without sin. For there was in Abel the original sin that he contracted from Adam but had not committed in his own person. I wish that Pelagius would say at least this so that for the present we could have his certain opinion on the baptism of infants! Or perhaps, because he said, "from infancy to old age," he might mean that Abel did not sin from infancy to old age, because he is shown not to have reached old age. His words do not indicate this; he said that a person's earlier life from the beginning was sinful, but that his later life could be without sin. For he declares that he did not say that "there is anyone who has never sinned from infancy to old age, but that, having turned away from sin by one's own effort and having been helped by the grace of God, a person can be without sin." For, when he says, "having turned away from sin," he shows that a person's earlier life was spent in sins. Let him, therefore, admit that Abel sinned, since he admits that the first part of his life was in the world and did not lack sins, and let him look at his book where it is clear that he said what in his defense he denied that he said.

9. But if he denies that this book or this passage in that book is his, I in fact have suitable witnesses, honest and faithful men, who are without a doubt admirers of his, by whose testimony I can defend myself. For they themselves gave the same book to me, and this passage can be read in it, and they said that it was Pelagius' book. This is at least enough to keep him from saying that it was written or falsified by me. Let each now choose among them whom to believe; it is not my intention to discuss this point any longer. We ask that you at least pass it on to him if he denies that he holds these ideas, which are objected to him as inimical to the grace of Christ. His own defense is so obscure that, if he has not misled by any ambiguous language Your Holy Wisdom, who has not known his other writings, we will congratulate you with great joy, for we do not care much whether he never held these perverse and impious teachings or has at some point turned away from them.

LETTER 186
Alypius and Augustine to Paulinus, the bishop of Nola (416)

Toward the middle of 416, Alypius, the bishop of Thagaste, and Augustine wrote to Paulinus, the bishop of Nola in Italy. Augustine and Alypius explain to Paulinus that, after having read a work of Pelagius, namely, *Nature*, they have come to realize that the Briton is an enemy of the grace of God (paragraph 1). They tell Paulinus that Pelagius' errors were reported to the Apostolic See by those who attended the Councils of Carthage and Milevis and that Pope Innocent had confirmed the condemnation of Pelagius (paragraph 2). The true grace of God not only wipes away sins but also helps us to avoid sin and to live rightly (paragraph 3). It is not our faith, good will, and good works that have saved us from the mass of perdition but the grace of God from which good works come (paragraph 4). Even our good thoughts do not come from ourselves but from God (paragraph 5). Before receiving grace no one has any good but only evil merits, even if his life has lasted only a single day on earth (paragraph 6).

The love that faith obtains is itself a gift of God (paragraph 7). The righteousness that makes us righteous comes from faith as a gift of God (paragraph 8). But the righteousness that comes from the law does not come from God (paragraph 9). Though faith merits righteousness, faith itself is a gift, so that no human merit precedes grace (paragraph 10).

The grace conferred on infants by baptism is obviously given gratuitously (paragraph 11). Yet some Pelagians have dared to deny the gratuitous character of this grace by supposing that infants are guilty of personal sins (paragraph 12). These people appealed to the struggle between Esau and Jacob in the womb as a sign of personal sin in Esau (paragraph 13). Augustine argues that the struggle between these twins was a miraculous sign but not evidence of free choice in them (paragraph 14). The Apostle appealed to these twins as evidence of God's gratuitous choice of Jacob through grace (paragraph 15).

Some Pelagians object that God is unjust if he does not choose one person over another on the basis of merits, but Augustine and Alypius appeal to the teaching of the Apostle that there is no injustice in God (paragraph 16). For the choice of Jacob over Esau did not depend on their works but on God, who showed mercy to Jacob and justice to Esau (paragraph 17). The Apostle foresaw the Pelagian line of argument and answered them with the example of the potter who makes one vessel for an honorable purpose and another for a dishonorable purpose from the same lump of clay (paragraph 18). For through the sin of Adam the whole lump became subject to death, and from it no one is set free by his own merits (paragraph 19). Why one is set free and another is not falls under the inscrutable but just judgments of God (paragraph 20). Thus Esau is not unjustly condemned because he was subject to the sin he inherited from Adam (paragraph 21).

The Pelagians might object that it would have been better if both of the twins were set free, but that line of argument can go on endlessly (paragraph 22). The same question arises about why God creates those who he knows will be damned (paragraph 23). Augustine and Alypius appeal to the Letter to the Romans for an explanation of why God made vessels of anger for destruction (paragraph 24). In God's foreknowledge the number of the predestined is fixed (paragraph 25). Yet God created the others to reveal what free choice could do without grace and to emphasize the gratuity of grace toward the vessels of mercy (paragraph 26).

Augustine warns those who have other ideas and points to the propositions that Pelagius himself condemned when he was tried in Palestine (paragraph 27). In claiming that infants can have eternal life even if they die without baptism, Pelagius speaks against the words of the Lord, against the authority of the Apostolic See, and against what he himself condemned (paragraph 28). Augustine and Alypius warn Paulinus about those who persist in this condemned error of the Pelagians (paragraph 29). They insist that, if there is no original sin derived from Adam in newborn infants, the infants would be unjustly condemned if they died without baptism (paragraph 30). All those whom God calls and saves are called and saved by God's choice through grace (paragraph 31).

Augustine and Alypius cite the twelve propositions that Pelagius condemned at the Council of Diospolis and argues that the opposite of each of them must be held by a believer (paragraphs 32 and 33). In his recent books Pelagius continues to be unclear about what he understands by the help of God's grace (paragraph 34). Augustine and Alypius cite Pelagius' claim that grace allows us to carry out more easily what God commands (paragraph 35). They cite the passages of Scripture that John, the bishop of Jerusalem, had used against Pelagius at his trial (paragraph 36). By his praise for human nature Pelagius empties of meaning the cross of Christ (paragraph 37). Though the Pelagians' refusal to believe is due to their will, we still ought to pray for them (paragraph 38).

Augustine and Alypius explain that they have written this letter not to support Paulinus' faith but to support his defense of the faith against these objectors (paragraph 39). They quote a passage from a letter of Paulinus that reveals the desperate need on the part of human beings for God's grace as we await the redemption of our body (paragraph 40). As long as we are in this life, we need to pray that we may not be brought into temptation (paragraph 41).

To Paulinus, their most blessed lord, brother, and fellow bishop, who deserves to be sincerely embraced in the heart of Christ, a brother who is more loveable than can be said, Alypius and Augustine send greetings.

1, 1. At long last God has provided us with a most reliable bearer for our letter, Brother Januarius, who is rightly very dear to us all. Even if we did not write, Your Sincerity could know everything about us by means of him as if he were a living and intelligent letter. We know that you loved as a servant of God Pelagius, who we believe had the surname "the Briton," in order that he might be distinguished from Pelagius, the son of Terence, but we do not know how you are at present disposed toward him. For we too not only have loved him but still love him. But our love for him now is different from what our love for him used to be. For we loved him then because we thought he held the correct faith, but we love him now in order that God's mercy might set him free from the views which he is said to hold that are hostile and contrary to the grace of God. For, though rumor spread this about concerning him for a long time, one ought not, of course, to have readily believed it, for rumor often carries lies. But in order that we might believe the rumor there was in addition the more recent event of our reading a certain book of his that certainly tries to convince us of views that wipe out from the hearts of the faithful a belief in the grace of God that has been given to the human race through the one mediator between God and human beings, the man Jesus Christ.[645] This book was handed over to us by servants of Christ who had heard him teaching such doctrines with great zeal and who had been his followers.[646] At their request we replied to the book with one treatise of ours because we saw that it was necessary to do so, though we did not mention the name of its author for fear that he would be offended and become more difficult to heal. That book of his contains and asserts many times and amply the same thing that he also states in a certain letter sent to Your Reverence in which he says that he should not be thought to defend free choice without the grace of God, since he says that the ability to will and to act, without which we can neither will nor do anything good, was implanted in us by the creator. In that way Pelagius' teaching would have us understand that the grace of God is something common to pagans and Christians, to the good and the bad, and to believers and unbelievers.

2. We were refuting, to the extent we could, these errors which empty of meaning the Lord's coming and of which we can say what the Apostle says of the law, *If righteousness comes through nature, then Christ has died in vain* (Gal 2:21). We were refuting these errors in the hearts of those who held them in order that Pelagius too, once he came to know this, would, if possible, correct these views without being attacked. And in that way the harmfulness of his error would be destroyed, and the man would be spared embarrassment. But after we received a letter from the East that aired the same views in full openness, we ought by no means to have failed to help the Church with whatever episcopal authority we had.[647] Reports from two councils in Carthage and in Milevis

---

645. See 1 Tm 2:5.
646. The two disciples of Pelagius were Timasius and James, who gave Augustine Pelagius' work, *Nature*, against which Augustine wrote *Nature and Grace*. See Letter 168 to Timasius and James.
647. See *The Grace of Christ and Original Sin* II, 35, 38, where Augustine cites Pelagius, who had included the letter to Paulinus in the dossier presented to Pope Innocent so as to establish his innocence.

were sent to the Apostolic See, therefore, before the ecclesiastical proceedings at which Pelagius was said to have been acquitted in the presence of some bishops of the Province of Palestine arrived either in our hands or in Africa.[648] We also wrote to Pope Innocent of blessed memory a personal letter in addition to the reports of the councils,[649] in which we dealt with this issue somewhat more at length. He replied to us on all these points in the way in which it was right and necessary for a bishop of the Apostolic See.[650]

3. You will now be able to read all these documents if perhaps some or all of them have not reached you. In them you will see that due moderation was preserved toward human beings so that they would not be condemned if they condemned these wicked teachings but that this new and deadly error was suppressed by the authority of the Church, with the result that we are very surprised that there are still certain people who try to oppose the grace of God through any error—at least if they have come to know that these actions have been taken. This grace of God through Jesus Christ our Lord, as the true and Catholic Church always holds, causes children along with adults to pass from the death of the first man[651] to the life of the second man[652] not only by wiping away sins but also by helping those who can already use the choice of the will not to sin and to live correctly. Hence without the help of this grace we can have no piety and righteousness either in our actions or even in our own will itself. *For it is God who produces in us both the willing and the action in accord with good will* (Phil 2:13).

2, 4. For who separates us from that solid mass of perdition except him who *came to seek and to save what was lost* (Lk 19:10)? For this reason the Apostle asks, *For who sets you apart?* And if a man says, "My faith, my good will, my good work," he receives the answer, *For what do you have that you have not received? But if you have received, why do you boast as if you have not received?* (1 Cor 4:7) Of course he said all of this not so that a human being would not boast but so that *he who boasts would boast in the Lord* (1 Cor 1:31; 2 Cor 10:17), *not on the basis of works, lest anyone perhaps be filled with pride* (Eph 2:9). It is not that good works are rendered useless by that pious thought, for *God repays each one according to his works* and *everyone who does good has glory, honor, peace* (Rom 2:6.10). Rather it is that works come from grace, not grace from works. For *the faith that works through love* (Gal 5:6) would do nothing unless *the love of God* were poured out *in our hearts by the Holy Spirit who has*

---

648. Pelagius was acquitted by a council of bishops at Diospolis in Palestine in December of 415. Augustine was unable to obtain a copy of the acts of that council until 417. The letter he mentions was written by Bishops Hero and Lazarus, who had been present at Diospolis; see Letter 175, 1. The Councils of Milevis and of Carthage in 416 sent Letters 175 and 176 to Pope Innocent to notify him of their condemnation of Pelagius.
649. I.e., Letter 177.
650. I.e., in Letters 181-183.
651. See Rv 11:18.
652. See 1 Cor 15:47.

been given to us (Rom 5:5). Nor would faith itself be present in us *unless God imparted to each the measure of faith* (Rom 12:3).

5. It is, therefore, good for a human being to say truthfully with all the strength of free choice, *I shall preserve my strength with you* (Ps 59:10). For the man who thought that he could preserve what God gave him without God's help left for a distant region and used up everything, living wastefully. And worn down by the misery of hard servitude, he came to his senses and said, *I shall rise up and go to my father* (Lk 15:18). When would he have had this good thought if the most merciful Father had not secretly inspired him with it? Understanding this, that minister of the New Testament said, *It is not that we are able to think something by ourselves, as if from ourselves; rather, our ability comes from God* (Eph 3:6-7). Hence, when the Psalmist said, *I shall preserve my strength with you*, so that he would not arrogate to his own strength the fact that he preserves it, as if it had come to his mind that, *unless the Lord preserves the city, those who guard it keep watch in vain* (Ps 127:1) and that *he who guards Israel does not slumber nor sleep* (Ps 121:4), he adds the reason why he became able to guard it or rather is the guard who preserves it. He says, *For God is my helper* (Ps 59:10).

6. Let this fellow,[653] then, recall, if he can, his own merits because of which God deigned to become his helper as if it were God who was helped. Let him recall whether he sought or was sought, that is, by him who *came to seek and to save what was lost* (Lk 19:10). For, if he wants to seek what he merited before grace in order that he might receive grace, he will be able to find his own evil merits, not good ones, even if the grace of the Savior finds him having life for one day on earth.[654] For, if a human being does some good action in order to merit grace, *his reward is assigned to him not as grace but as something owed. But if he believes in him who makes the sinner righteous* so that *his faith is counted as righteousness* (Rom 4:4-6)—for *the righteous live by faith* (Hb 2:4; Rom 1:17; Gal 3:5; Heb 10:38)—before he is justified by grace, that is, before he is made righteous, what is a sinner but a sinner? If he received what he deserved, what would he receive by his merit but punishment? *If*, then, *it is by grace, it does not come from works; otherwise, grace is no longer grace* (Rom 11:6). What is owed is payment for works, but grace is given gratuitously; that is where it gets its name.

3, 7. But if anyone says that faith merits the grace of doing good actions, we cannot deny it; in fact, we most gratefully admit it. For we want these brothers of ours, who boast much of their good works, to have this faith by which they might obtain the love that alone truly produces good works. But love is so much a gift of God that it is called God.[655] Those, then, who have the faith by which they obtain justification have come through the grace of God to the law of righteousness;

---

653. Augustine refers to Pelagius without naming him.
654. See Jb 14:5 LXX.
655. See 1 Jn 4:8.

for this reason Scripture says, *I heard you at an acceptable time, and I helped you on the day of salvation* (Is 49:8; 2 Cor 6:2). Hence, in those who are being saved through the choice of his grace,[656] God as a helper *produces the willing and the action in accord with good will* (Phil 2:13), *because for those who love God all things work out for the good* (Rom 8:28)—and if all things, then certainly the love itself that we obtain by faith in order that we may love through his grace him who first loved us[657] so that we might believe in him and so that by loving him we might do good works, which we did not do in order that we might be loved.

8. But the people who look for rewards as if they were owed to their merits, and who do not attribute their merits to the grace of God but to the strength of their own will, do not attain the law of righteousness, as it was said of Israel according to the flesh, though they pursue the law of righteousness. Why? Because they pursue it not on the basis of faith but on the basis of works. For this is the righteousness coming from faith that the Gentiles attained, of whom Scripture says: *What, then, shall we say? For the Gentiles, who did not know righteousness, have attained righteousness, but the righteousness that comes from faith. But Israel, while pursuing the law of righteousness, did not attain to the law of righteousness. Why? Because they pursued it not on the basis of faith but as if on the basis of works. For they stumbled on the stumbling block, as it is written, See, I set a stumbling block in Zion, a stone of scandal, and one who believes in him will not be put to shame.* (Rom 9:30-33; Is 28:16; 8:14) This is the righteousness from faith by which we believe that we are justified, that is, made righteous by the grace of God through Jesus Christ our Lord so that we may be found in him, not having our own *righteousness that comes from the law, but that which comes through faith in Christ. This righteousness from God is found in faith* (Phil 3:9), in the faith, of course, by which we believe that righteousness is given to us by God and is not produced in us by us by our own strength.

9. For why did the Apostle say that the righteousness that comes from the law was his own and not from God, as if the law does not come from God? Who but an unbeliever would have such an idea? But because the law commands by the letter and does not help by the Spirit, whoever hears the letter of the law so that he thinks that it is sufficient for him to have known what it commands or forbids and is confident that he will fulfil it by the power of his choice and does not in faith take refuge in the life-giving Spirit for help in order that the letter may not kill him in his guilt—that man certainly has a zeal for God, but not with knowledge. For, not knowing the righteousness of God, that is, the righteousness that is given by God, and wanting to establish his own righteousness so that it comes only from the law, he is not subject to the righteousness of God.[658] *For the end of the law is Christ for the righteousness of everyone who believes* (Rom

---

656. See Rom 11:5; Phil 2:13.
657. See 1 Jn 4:19.
658. See Rom 10:2-4.

10:2-4), as the same Apostle says, *in order that we may be the righteousness of God in him* (2 Cor 5:21). *Made righteous, then, by faith, let us have peace with God through our Lord Jesus Christ* (Rom 5:1), but *made righteous gratuitously by his grace* (Rom 3:21), so that faith is not proud.

10. And let him not say to himself, "If it comes from faith, how is it gratuitous? For why is what faith merits not a repayment rather than a gift?" Let a believer not say this because, when he says, "I have faith in order to merit justification," he receives the answer, *For what do you have that you have not received?* (1 Cor 4:7) Though faith, then, obtains justification, as God has also granted to each the measure of faith itself,[659] no human merit precedes the grace of God, but grace itself merits an increase in order that, once increased, it may also merit to be made perfect with the will accompanying, not leading, following along, not preceding. Hence, he who said, *I shall preserve my strength with you* (Ps 59:10), and went on to give the reason, *Because God is my helper*, as if he were looking for the merits by which he got this and found nothing in himself prior to the grace of God, says, *My God, his mercy will precede me* (Ps 59:11). As much as I shall ponder antecedent merits, he says, *his mercy will precede me.* Hence, in preserving with God the strength that God gave him, he does not lose it because God preserves what that man received as God's gift. And he does not merit more grace except by knowing in piety and in faith him from whom all good gifts come to him and by knowing that this realization does not come from himself so that he does not have even this without its also coming from God. For this reason the Apostle says very well, *We have not received the spirit of this world, but the Spirit who is from God, in order that we may know what God has given us* (1 Cor 2:12). And for this reason even the merit of a human being is a gratuitous gift, and no one merits to receive anything good from the Father of lights, from whom every best gift comes down,[660] except by receiving what he does not merit.

4, 11. But it is much more merciful and undoubtedly more gratuitous that the grace of God through Jesus Christ our Lord is offered to infants so that their birth from Adam may not harm them and their rebirth in Christ may profit them, for in them the mercy of God comes long before even the awareness of their receiving it. And if at this early age they leave the body, they certainly receive eternal life and the kingdom of heaven knowingly by the merit of that gift that they did not know here, when of course it was of benefit to them. In these infants the merits of the later gifts are nothing else than the earlier gifts, and in giving the earlier gifts the grace of God works in such a way that the will of the recipients does not precede it, accompany it, or follow it. For such a great benefit is given not only to those infants who do not desire it but even to those who struggle against it—

---

659. See Rom 12:3.
660. See Jas 1:17.

something that would be counted as a great sacrilege on their part if the choice of the will were already capable of anything in them.

12. We said this for the sake of those who, being unable to search out the inscrutable judgments of God in the area of grace,[661] ask why from the mass coming from Adam, which because of only one person fell as a whole into condemnation, God makes one vessel for honor and another for dishonor.[662] And yet they dare to make infants guilty of personal sins, and thus those who cannot have either a good or a bad thought are supposed to be able to merit punishment or grace through free choice, though the truth from the lips of the Apostle who says, *Because of the one* all entered *into condemnation* (Rom 5:16), in fact shows quite well that they are born subject to punishment so that they may be reborn in grace not by merit but by mercy. *Otherwise, grace is no longer grace* (Rom 11:6) if it is not given as grace from God's riches but is a recompense for human merits. It alone sets one apart from punishment in such a way that, though punishment is owed to all because of Adam, grace through the one Jesus Christ is owed to no one but is gratuitous. In that way grace can truly be grace. Thus the judgments of God, like God himself, can be inscrutable, when he separates infants whom no merits distinguish. But his judgments can never be unjust because *all the ways of the Lord are mercy and truth* (Ps 25:10). Therefore when one person is offered the gift of mercy, he has no reason to boast of human merit, because this does not come *from works, lest anyone be filled with pride* (Eph 2:9). But when another person receives punishment in accord with the truth, he has no reason for just complaint, for he receives in recompense what is rightly owed to sin. For the one *in whom all sinned* (Rom 5:12) is certainly not unjustly punished in each individual as well. In their punishment we are more clearly shown what is given to the vessels of mercy through a grace that is not owed but is true grace, that is, gratuitous.

5, 13. The Apostle says most clearly, *Through one man sin entered the world, and through sin death, and in that way it was passed on to all human beings in whom all sinned* (Rom 5:12). It is annoying to notice and displeasing to state, but we are in fact compelled to say how they argue against him, saying that even infants have personal sins through free choice. For it would be either a sign of our helplessness to omit through silence or a sign of our arrogance to pass over in contempt what those great and clever minds were able to think up. They say, "Look, Esau and Jacob fought in the womb of their mother and, when they are born, one takes the place of the other, and the hand of the second found holding onto the foot of the first proves that the struggle was in some sense still going on. How, then, is there no choice of their own will either for good or for

---

661. See Rom 11:33.
662. See Rom 9:21.

evil in infants performing these acts, as a result of which rewards or punishments follow upon preceding merits?"[663]

14. To this we say that those movements and the supposed fight of the infants were signs of important things not because they involved choice but because they were a miracle. After all, we are not going to assign free choice of the will to donkeys because an animal of this kind, as Scripture says, *a beast of burden without a voice, replying with the voice of a human being, restrained the madness of the prophet* (2 Pt 2:16). But what are these people, who claim that such movements were not prodigies but voluntary acts and were produced not with regard to the infants but by them, going to reply to the Apostle? For, since he saw that he should mention these twins as a proof of the gratuitousness of grace, he said, *When they were not yet born and did nothing either good or bad, in order that God's plan might remain in accord with his choice, it was said not because of works but because of his call that the older would serve the younger* (Rom 9:11-13). And then adding the testimony of a prophet who said these things afterward, but who was explaining God's ancient plan regarding this matter, he says, *As Scripture said, I loved Jacob, but I hated Esau* (Rom 9:13; Mal 1:2-3).

15. The teacher of the nations in faith and truth testifies that those as yet unborn twins did nothing good or bad in order that he might emphasize grace. And so when he said, *The older will serve the younger*, we understand that this *was said not because of works but because of his call in order that God's plan might remain in accord with his choice*, not in order that human merit might come first. He does not mean the choice of the human will or of nature since the condition of death and condemnation was equally present in both of them, but he undoubtedly means the choice of grace, which does not discover those to be chosen but makes them such. Speaking of this grace in the following parts of the letter, he says, *So, then, in this time as well a remnant has been saved by the choice of grace. But if it is grace, it is not because of works; otherwise, grace is no longer grace.* (Rom 11:5-6) This passage agrees well with the one where it is mentioned that it said, *The older will serve the younger, not because of works but because of* God's *call*. Why, then, do they so impudently oppose the most illustrious teacher of grace with regard to the free choice of infants and the actions of those not yet born? Why do they say that grace is preceded by merits? It would not be grace if it were assigned in accord with merits. Why do they argue against the salvation that was sent to those who were lost and that came to those who were unworthy with a line of argument that, however clever, however lengthy and eloquent, is hardly Christian?

6, 16. "But how," they ask, "is there not injustice in God if by his love he separates those whom no merits from their works separate?" They say this to us as if the Apostle himself did not see this, did not pose this question, and did not an-

---

663. See Gn 25:22.25; Hos 12:3.

swer it. He certainly saw what human weakness or ignorance could think up when it heard these ideas and, posing the same question for himself, he asked, *What, then, shall we say? Is there injustice in God?* and he immediately replied: *Heaven forbid!* And giving the reason why he said, *Heaven forbid!* that is, why there is no injustice in God, he did not say, "For he judges the merits or works even of the infants, even if they are still located in the womb of their mother." For how could he say this who had said of those who were not yet born and of those who had done nothing good or bad that *it was not said because of works but because of his call: The older will serve the younger* (Rom 9:11-12)? But when he wanted to show why there is no injustice in God in these matters, he said, *After all, God said to Moses: I will take pity on whom I will take pity and I will show mercy to whom I will show mercy* (Rom 9:15; Ex 33:19). What did he teach us here but that it pertains not to the merits of human beings but to the mercy of God that anyone is set free from that mass coming from the first man,[664] which rightly deserved death, and that thus there is no injustice in God? For he is not unjust either in canceling or in exacting what is owed. After all, forgiveness is gratuitous only in a case where punishment could be just. And from this it is seen more clearly how great a benefit is conferred upon one who is set free from the punishment he deserved and is made righteous gratuitously,[665] because the other who is equally guilty is punished without injustice on the part of God who punishes him.

17. Finally, he goes on to add, *And so, it does not depend on the one who wills or on the one who runs, but on God who shows mercy* (Rom 9:16-18; Ex 9:16). This was said on account of those who were set free by grace and made righteous. But on account of those on whom the anger of God remains,[666] because God also makes good use of them to teach the others whom he deigns to set free, he went on to add, *For Scripture says of Pharaoh: I have raised you up in order to reveal my power in you and in order that my name might be proclaimed in the whole world* (Rom 9:17). Then, concluding with regard to both, he said, *Hence, he shows mercy to whom he wills, and he hardens whom he wills* (Rom 9:18); of course he does neither out of any injustice but both out of mercy and truth. And yet the brazen weakness of human beings is disturbed, that is, of those who try to fathom the inscrutable depth of the judgments of God[667] in accordance with the conjectures of the human heart.

18. Posing this question for himself as an objection, the Apostle says, *And so, you say to me: What complaint still remains? For who can resist his will?* (Rom 9:19) Let us suppose that this objection is made to us. What else, then, ought we to answer but what the Apostle answered? Or if such questions trouble us too, because we too are human beings, we ought all together to listen to him

---

664. See Rom 9:21.
665. See Rom 3:24.
666. See Jn 3:36.
667. See Rom 11:33.

as he says, *Who are you, O human being, to answer back to God? Does the pot say to him who fashioned it, Why did you make me that way? Or does the potter not have the power to make from the same lump of clay one vessel for honor and another for dishonor?* (Rom 9:20-21; Is 45:9; 29:16) If this lump were so positioned in the middle that, as it merited nothing good, so it merited nothing bad, it would seem with good reason to be an injustice that vessels were made from it for dishonor. But since the whole lump fell into condemnation because of the one sin through the free choice of the first human being, the fact that vessels are made from it for honor is not due to his righteousness, because no righteousness preceded grace, but to the mercy of God. The fact, however, that a vessel is made for dishonor is not to be attributed to the injustice of God—heaven forbid that there should be any injustice in God!—but to his judgment. Whoever holds this along with the Catholic Church does not argue against grace in favor of merits but sings to the Lord of his mercy and judgment,[668] so that he does not ungratefully reject his mercy or unjustly accuse his judgment.

19. For it is another mass of dough of which the same Apostle says, *But if the dough offered is holy, then the whole lump is holy, and if the root is holy, then the branches are too* (Rom 11:16). That lump comes from Abraham, not from Adam, that is, from the sharing in the sacrament and the similarity in faith, not from our mortal lineage. But this latter lump or, as we read in many manuscripts, this mass, is wholly subject to death because *through one man sin entered the world, and through sin death, and thus it was passed on to all human beings in whom all sinned* (Rom 5:12). Because of mercy there is made out of it *one vessel for honor*, but by judgment there is made *another for dishonor* (Rom 9:21). In the first case no merits precede the grace of God who sets free, nor in the latter do sins escape the justice of God who punishes. In more adult ages, of course, this is not seen so clearly to be opposed to the quarrelsome when they fight on behalf of human merits, as if protected by some sort of obscurity. But against their argument the Apostle discovered those of whom, *though they were not yet born and had not done anything good or bad, it was said, not because of works but because of his call: The older will serve the younger* (Rom 9:11-12).

20. Because in this area *the judgments of God are* too deep and *inscrutable and his ways unsearchable*, let a human being for the present hold that there is no injustice in God. But let him admit that, as a human being, he does not know the justice by which God shows mercy to whom he wills and hardens whom he wills.[669] And thus let him know by reason of the unshakeable truth that he holds, namely, that there is no injustice in God, that, though no one is made righteous by him because of any preceding merits, neither is anyone hardened except by merit. For it is piously and truthfully believed that, by making sinners and unbelievers righteous, God sets them free from the punishment they deserve, but

---

668. See Ps 101:1.
669. See Rom 9:18.

if it is believed that God condemns anyone who does not deserve it and who is subject to no sin, it is not believed that God is free from injustice. In a case, then, in which someone unworthy is set free, God deserves more gratitude to the extent that the punishment the person deserved was more just. But in a case where someone who does not deserve it is condemned, neither mercy nor truth prevails.

21. "How," they ask, "was Esau not undeservedly condemned if *it was said, not because of works but because of God's call: The older will serve the younger* (Rom 9:11-12)? For, just as no good works of Jacob came first in order that he would receive grace, so no evil works of Esau came first in order that he should meet with punishment." There were no works either good or bad in either of the two, that is, no personal works, but both were subject to him *in whom all sinned* (Rom 5:12) so that all died in him. For those who from that one man were going to be many in themselves were then one in him. Hence, that sin would have been his alone if no one had come from him. But now no one is exempt from the sin of him in whom our common nature existed. If, then, the two, who had not done any good or bad actions of their own, were nonetheless born guilty because of their origin, let the one who is set free praise God's mercy and let the one who is punished not blame his judgment.

7, 22. If we say here, "How much better it would be if both were set free!" nothing more appropriate will be said to us than, *Who are you, O human being, to answer back to God?* (Rom 9:20). For he knows what he is doing and what number there ought to be, first, of all human beings and, secondly, of the saints, just as he knows what the number should be of the stars, of the angels, and—to speak of earthly things—of cattle, of fish, of birds, of trees, of plants, and of the hairs on our heads. Now we can still say in our human way of thinking, "Because all the things he made are good, how much better it would be if he doubled their number or multiplied them so that there were many more than there are." For if the world could not contain them, could he not make it larger to the extent he wanted? And yet, to whatever extent he made them more or made the world more capacious and larger, the same things could still be said about making them more, and there would be no limit to limitless things.

23. For, whether it is the grace by which persons without righteousness are made righteous, about which we are not permitted to doubt, or free choice, as certain people want, that always comes first, and either punishment or reward follows upon its merit, it can still be objected: "Why were they created at all, since God undoubtedly foreknew that they would sin so that they would be condemned to eternal fire?" For, though he did not cause their sins, who but God, nonetheless, created their natures? The natures by themselves were no doubt good, but in them the defects of sins were going to come into existence from the choice of their will—and in many cases the sort of sins that would receive eternal punishment. Why did he do this except because he willed to? But why did he will to? *Who are you, O human being, to answer back to God? Does the pot say to him who fashioned it: Why did you make me so? Does the potter not have the*

power to make from the same lump of clay one vessel for honor and another for dishonor? (Rom 9:20-21)

24. And now let us cite what follows: *But if God, wanting to reveal his anger and to demonstrate his power, endured with great patience the vessels of anger that were made for destruction in order to make known the riches of his glory toward the vessels of mercy* (Rom 9:22-23). See, there the reason is given to a human being to the extent it ought to be given to him, at least if one who defends the freedom of his choice in the slavery of such weakness grasps this. See, the reasons have been stated. Who are you, then, to answer back to God if, wanting to reveal his anger and to demonstrate his power, God endured in great patience the vessels of anger destined for destruction? After all, the all-good God can make good use even of evil persons, for the evil are not such because of their creation by God but because their nature, which was created good by God the creator, was damaged by the wickedness of their will. *He endured with great patience the vessels of anger that were made for destruction* (Rom 9:22) not because he needed the sins of either angels or human beings, for he does not need even the righteousness of any creature, but *in order to make known the riches of his glory toward the vessels of mercy* (Rom 9:23), so that in their good works they would not be filled with pride as if over their own abilities but would humbly understand that, unless God's grace, which is not owed to them but is gratuitous, came to their help, their merits would receive the recompense that they saw was given to the others in the same lump.

25. The predetermined number and multitude of the saints is, therefore, certain in God's foreknowledge. *For those who love God*, a gift which he gave them through the Holy Spirit poured out in their hearts,[670] *all things work together for the good for those who have been called according to his plan. For those whom he foreknew he also predestined to be conformed to the image of his Son, in order that he might be the firstborn among many brothers. But those whom he predestined he also called.* (Rom 8:28-30) Here we ought to understand: *according to his plan.* For there are also others who are called but not chosen.[671] And for this reason they are not called according to his plan. *But those whom he called*—that is, *according to his plan*—*he also made righteous. But those whom he made righteous he also glorified* (Rom 8:30). These are *the children of the promise* (Rom 9:8); these are the chosen who are being saved by his choice through grace, when it says, *But if it is because of grace, it is not because of works; otherwise, grace is no longer grace* (Rom 11:5-6). These are the vessels of mercy,[672] in whom God makes known even through the vessels of anger the riches of his glory. The Holy Spirit makes these to have *one heart and one soul* (Acts 4:32), which blesses God and does not forget all the gifts of him who par-

---

670. See Rom 5:5.
671. See Mt 20:16; 22:14.
672. See Rom 9:22-23.

dons all their sins, who heals all their illnesses, who redeems their life from their corruption, who crowns them in his mercy,[673] because *it does not depend on the one who wills or on the one who runs, but on God who shows mercy* (Rom 9:16).

26. But the other human beings, who do not belong to this company, though their soul and body were made by the goodness of God, and whatever their nature has apart from the defect, which the audacity of a proud will inflicted upon it, was created by God in his foreknowledge. He created them so that in these human beings he might show what the free choice of one who abandons him is capable of without grace and so that the vessels of mercy, which have been separated from that lump not by the merits of their works but by the gratuitous grace of God, might realize the gift that has been given to them *in order that every mouth might be shut* (Rom 3:19) and in order that *he who boasts might boast in the Lord* (1 Cor 1:31; 2 Cor 10:17).

8, 27. *Whoever teaches another doctrine and does not agree with the sound words of our Lord, Jesus Christ* (1 Tm 6:3), who said, *The Son of Man came to seek and to save what had been lost* (Lk 19:10 Mt 18:11)—for he did not say, "what was going to be lost," but, *what had been lost*, in order to show that the nature of the whole human race had perished by the sin of the first human being—*Whoever*, therefore, *teaches another doctrine and does not agree with the teaching that is in accord with piety* (1 Tm 6:3), defending human nature as if it were safe and free, in opposition to the grace of the Savior and in opposition to the blood of the Redeemer, and pretending to bear the name "Christian"—what is such a person going to say about the separation of infants? Why is one taken up into the life of the second man, while another is left in the death of the first man? If he says that the merits of free choice came first, the Apostle has answered what we said above about those who were not yet born and did nothing good or bad.[674] But if he says what is still defended in the books that Pelagius is reported to have published quite recently, although he is now seen to have condemned in the episcopal court in Palestine those who say that the sin of Adam harmed Adam alone and not the human race, that is, if he says that both infants were born without sin and did not contract anything from the condemnation of the first human being, since he certainly does not dare to deny that one who has been reborn in Christ is adopted into the kingdom of heaven, let him reply what will happen with one who has been carried off by this temporal death before being baptized and without any sin of its own. We do not think that he will say that God will condemn to eternal death an innocent human being who does not have original sin prior to the years in which he could have had personal sin. And so he is forced to reply what Pelagius was forced to condemn in the ecclesiastical court in order that he might somehow be declared Catholic, namely, that infants

---

673. See Ps 103:2-4.
674. See Rom 9:11.

have eternal life even if they are not baptized. For, if he does not say this, what else will remain but eternal death?

28. And in this way he will argue against the statement of the Lord, who says, *Your fathers ate manna in the desert and died. This is the bread coming down from heaven so that, if anyone eats it, he may not die.* (Jn 6:49-50) For he was not talking about the death that even those who eat this bread must suffer. And a little later he says, *Truly, truly, I say to you: Unless you eat the flesh of the Son of Man and drink his blood, you will not have life in you* (Jn 6:54)—that life, of course, which will exist after this death. And he will argue against the authority of the Apostolic See where, when it dealt with this issue, it used this testimony from the Gospel lest unbaptized infants be thought capable of having life.[675] And he will argue against the words of Pelagius himself before the bishops who heard his case, the words he expressed when he condemned those who said that unbaptized infants have eternal life.[676]

29. We have mentioned this because some people with you or rather in your city, at least if what we have heard is true, fight with such stubbornness in defense of this error that they say that it is easier for them to abandon and despise even Pelagius, who condemned the people who hold these views, than to give up the truth, as they see it, of this opinion. But if they yield to the Apostolic See or rather to the very teacher and Lord of the apostles, who says that they will not have life in them unless they eat the flesh of the Son of Man and drink his blood—something that only the baptized, of course, can do—they will finally admit that unbaptized infants cannot have life and, for this reason, are still punished by eternal death, though less harshly than all those who have also committed personal sins.

30. Since this is the case, let them be so bold as to argue and let them strive to persuade those whom they can that the just God, in whom there is no injustice,[677] will condemn to endless death infants who are innocent of personal sins if they are not bound by and subject to that sin from Adam. If this is absolutely absurd and completely alien to the justice of God, and if no one who bears in mind that he is a Christian of the Catholic faith denies or doubts that infants do not have life in themselves if they have not received the grace of rebirth in Christ and are without the food of his flesh and the drink of his blood[678] and that they are, for this reason, subject to everlasting punishment, there then remains the fact that, because they have not done anything good or bad,[679] the punishment of their death is just because they died in him *in whom all sinned* (Rom

---

675. See Letter 182, 5.
676. *The Deeds of Pelagius* 11, 23.
677. See Rom 9:14.
678. See Jn 6:54.
679. See Rom 9:11.

5:12). Hence, they are brought to life only in him who could neither contract original sin nor commit personal sin.

31. He himself *called us, not only from the Jews, but also from the Gentiles* (Rom 9:24). For he gathered the children whom he willed even, despite her unwillingness, from the Jerusalem that killed the prophets and stoned those sent to her both before his incarnation as prophets and, after *the Word was made flesh* (Jn 1:14), as apostles and as the thousands who laid at the feet of the apostles the money from the sale of their possessions.[680] All these were, of course, children of the Jerusalem that was unwilling to be gathered, but they were still gathered against her will. Of them he says, *If I cast out demons by Beelzebub, by whom do your children cast them out? Hence, they will be your judges.* (Mt 12:27) Of these it was foretold, *If the children of Israel will be like the sand of the sea, a remnant will be saved* (Rom 9:27; Is 10:22; Hos 1:10). The word of God cannot fail to be true, nor *has he rejected his people whom he foreknew* (Rom 11:2), and *this remnant was saved by his choice through grace* (Rom 11:5). *But if it is by grace*—which must be said with frequency—*it is not because of works; otherwise, grace is no longer grace* (Rom 11:6). These are, of course, not our words but the words of the Apostle. What, therefore, he cried out to the Jerusalem that was unwilling that her children be gathered, we shout out against those who do not want the children of the Church, who are willing, to be gathered and against those who have not been corrected, even after the judgment that was pronounced concerning Pelagius in Palestine. He would have emerged from there as a condemned man if he himself had not condemned the statements against the grace of God that were raised as objections to him, statements that he could not disguise.

9, 32. Besides those statements that he dared to defend by some sort of argument, however he could, certain statements were raised as objections, and if he had not anathematized them without any ambiguity he himself would have left anathematized. For it was objected that he said: "Adam was created mortal so that he was going to die whether he sinned or did not sin," and, "His sin harmed him alone and not the human race," and, "Newborn infants are in the same state in which Adam was before his transgression," and, "The whole human race does not die through the death or transgression of Adam, nor does the whole human race rise through the resurrection of Christ," and, "Infants attain eternal life, even if they are not baptized," and, "If wealthy persons who have been baptized do not renounce all their possessions, they have no merit, even if they seem to do something good, and they cannot possess the kingdom of God,"[681] and, "God's grace and help is not given for individual actions, but consists in free choice or in the law and teaching," and, "The grace of God is given in accord with our merits,"[682] and, "Only those who have become completely without sin can be called children of God," and, "Free

---

680. See Acts 4:23-35; 2:41; 4:4.
681. See *The Deeds of Pelagius* 11, 23-24; 33, 57; 35, 65.
682. See ibid. 14, 30-31; 17, 40; 35, 65.

choice does not exist, if one needs the help of God, because each person has in his own will the power to do or not to do something," and, "Our victory comes not from the help of God but from free choice," and, "Pardon is not given to penitents in accord with God's grace and mercy but in accord with their merit and labor, since they were worthy of mercy because of their penance."[683]

33. Pelagius condemned all these statements, and the proceedings themselves sufficiently testify that he in no way produced any argument in their defense. For this reason it follows that whoever accepts the authority of that episcopal court and the confession of Pelagius himself ought to hold what the Catholic Church has always held: Adam would not have died if he had not sinned. His sin harmed not him alone but also the human race. Newborn infants are not in the same state in which Adam was before the transgression, and so the Apostle's brief statement applies to them: *Death came through one man, and the resurrection of the dead came through one man. For, just as all die in Adam, so all will also be brought to life in Christ.* (1 Cor 15:21-22) For this reason it turns out that, if they are not baptized, infants are unable to attain not only the kingdom of heaven but also eternal life. It must be admitted as well that wealthy persons who have been baptized, even if they do not give up their riches, cannot be excluded from the kingdom of God. The Apostle described people of this sort in writing to Timothy, *Command the rich people of this world not to have proud thoughts and not to place their hope in the uncertainty of riches, but in the living God who gives us all things in abundance for our enjoyment. Let them be rich in good works; let them give readily, share with others, and store up for themselves a good foundation for the future in order that they may attain true life.* (1 Tm 6:17-19) It must be confessed that the grace and help of God is given for individual actions and that it is not given in accord with our merits so that it may be true grace, that is, given gratuitously through the mercy of him who said, *I will take pity on whom I will take pity, and I will show mercy to whom I will show mercy* (Ex 33:19 LXX). It must be confessed that they can be called children of God who say daily, *Forgive us our debts* (Mt 6:12; Lk 11:4). Of course they would not truthfully say this if they were absolutely without sin. It must be confessed that free choice exists even if it needs God's help. It must be confessed that, when we fight against temptations and sinful desires, though we do in that case have a will of our own, our victory does not come from it but from the help of God. Otherwise, the words of the Apostle would not be true, *It does not depend on the one who wills or on the one who runs, but on God who shows mercy* (Rom 9:16). It must be confessed that to those who repent pardon is granted in accord with the mercy of God, not in accord with their merits, since the Apostle said that repentance itself is a gift of God, when he says of certain people, *In case God should perhaps give them repentance* (2 Tm 2:25). Whoever assents to the Catholic authority and to the words expressed in the ecclesiastical proceedings against

---

683. See ibid. 18, 42; 35, 65.

Pelagius must confess all these things unconditionally and unambiguously. For we should not believe that the statements opposed to these are truly condemned if these statements to which they are opposed are not held in a believing heart and uttered in an open confession.

10, 34. Nor is what Pelagius holds on this issue seen clearly enough in the more recent books that the same Pelagius is said to have published after that trial, though he seems to acknowledge the help of divine grace. For at times he considers the power of the will like a balanced scale, so that he holds that it is as capable of not sinning as it is of sinning. But if that is so, no room remains for the help of the grace without which we say that the choice of the will is incapable of not sinning. At times, however, he admits that we are protected by the daily help of grace, though we have a strong and healthy free choice for not sinning, which he ought to admit is weak and sick until all the illnesses of our soul are healed.[684] For he did not pray for the weakness of his body who said, *Have mercy on me, Lord, because I am weak; heal me, Lord, because my bones are troubled* (Ps 7:3), since, in order to show that he was praying for his soul, he went on to say, *And my soul is greatly troubled* (Ps 7:4).

35. Pelagius, then, seems to believe that the help of grace is granted as something extra, that is, so that, even if it were not granted, we would still have a strong and healthy free choice for avoiding sin. But so that we may not be thought to be rash in suspecting him of this and so that no one might say that Pelagius holds that free choice is strong and healthy for avoiding sin, though it cannot accomplish and carry this out without the grace of God, just as we say that sound eyes are healthy for seeing, though they can in no way do this if they lack the help of light, in another passage he shows more clearly what he meant or thought where he says, "The grace of God is given to human beings in order that they may more easily accomplish by grace what they are commanded to do by free will."[685] Where he says, "more easily," what does he want us to understand but that, even if grace is lacking, one can through free choice carry out either easily or even with difficulty what is commanded by God?

36. Where, then, are the words, *What is a human being that you are mindful of him* (Ps 9:5)? Where, finally, are those testimonies that the bishop of the church of Jerusalem mentions that he cited for Pelagius himself, as you can read in the proceedings, when it was reported to him that Pelagius said that a human being could be free from sin without the grace of God?[686] For he set forth three very important testimonies against such an impious presumption, in the words of the Apostle, *I have labored more than all those; not I, however, but the grace of God with me* (1 Cor 15:10), and, *It does not depend on the one who wills or*

---

684. See Mt 4:23.
685. See *The Grace of Christ and Original Sin* 1, 8, 9 and 27, 28.
686. See *The Deeds of Pelagius* 14, 37.

on the one who runs, but on God who shows mercy (Rom 9:16), and, *Unless the Lord builds the house, in vain have its builders labored* (Ps 127:1). How, then, is what God commands carried out, even with difficulty, without his help, since, if the Lord does not build, the builder is said to have labored in vain? And Scripture does not say, "It does in fact depend on the one who wills and on the one who runs, but it is easier when God shows mercy." Rather Scripture says, *It does not depend on the one who wills or on the one who runs, but on God who shows mercy*, not because a human being has no will and does not run, but because one can do nothing unless God shows mercy. Nor did the Apostle say, "I too." Rather he said, *Not I, however, but the grace of God with me*, not because he himself did nothing good, but because he would do nothing if grace did not help. And yet, that perfect equilibrium of the capability of free choice for both good and evil did not leave room for even the ease that he at least seems to have confessed when he said, "They can more easily fulfil God's commands through grace." For, if the good is done more easily through grace, while evil is done most easily without grace, this capability is not in perfect equilibrium.

11, 37. But what else? We ought not only to be careful to avoid these people, but we ought also not to be hesitant to teach and admonish them, if they allow us. Yet we undoubtedly offer them more if we pray that they may be corrected so that they may neither perish with their fine minds nor cause others to perish because of their damnable presumption. For *they have zeal for God, but not in accord with knowledge* (Rom 10:2); but *not knowing the righteousness of God*, that is, the righteousness that comes from God, *and wanting to establish their own, they are not subject to the righteousness of God* (Rom 10:3). Since they are called Christians, they ought certainly to be on guard against this more than the Jews, about whom the apostle said this. Otherwise they will trip over *the stumbling block* (Rom 9:32), when they craftily defend nature and free choice, just like the philosophers of this world who worked hard in order to be thought or in order to think that they achieved for themselves the happy life by the power of their own will. Let these people beware that they do not empty of meaning the cross of Christ by their wordy wisdom.[687] For them this is to trip over the stumbling block. For, even if human nature remained in that state of wholeness in which it was created it would not in any way preserve itself without the help of its creator. Since, then, without the grace of God it could not guard the well-being it received, how could it without the grace of God repair the well-being it lost?

38. But we ought not to cease to pray for them on the grounds that, if they are not corrected, it must be attributed to the will of those who refuse to believe that they need the grace of the Savior, even for what they think lies in the power of their will alone. On this issue the Pelagians resemble very closely the Jews, of whom the Apostle said that, *not knowing the righteousness of God and wanting to establish their own, they are not subject to the righteousness of God* (Rom

---

687. See 1 Cor 1:17.

10:3), and the Jews certainly failed to believe because of a sin of their own will. For they were not forced against their will to be unbelievers, but by refusing to believe they were guilty of the sin of unbelief. And yet the will is not sufficient by itself to come to believe the truth unless God helps it by grace, since the Lord himself said when he was speaking of those who did not believe, *No one comes to me unless it has been given him by my Father* (Jn 6:66). For the same reason, though the Apostle zealously preached the Gospel to them, he saw that it was still not enough unless he also prayed for them. For he said, *Brothers, the good desire of my heart and my prayer to God aims at their salvation*, and then he added the words that we mentioned, *For I bear witness to them that they have zeal for God, but not in accord with knowledge* (Rom 10:1-2), and so on. Therefore, holy brother, let us pray for them.

12, 39. You surely see along with us the wicked error that holds them captive. For your letters are fragrant with the most pure odor of Christ; in them you are seen to love and confess his grace most sincerely. But we thought that we should speak with you on this at length. We did so, first of all, because it is most pleasant. For what ought to be more pleasing to the sick than the grace by which they are healed or more pleasing to the sluggish than the grace by which they are roused or more pleasing to the willing than the grace by which they are helped? Secondly, we did this in order that, if we could do anything by our argumentation with God's help, we might lend support not to your faith but to your defense of the faith against persons such as these just as we have also been helped by the letter of Your Fraternity for this purpose.

40. For what could be richer or more filled with a most true profession than that passage in a letter of yours where you humbly deplored that our nature did not remain as it was created, but was damaged by the father of the human race. You said, "*I am poor and sorrowing* (Ps 69:30), since I am still fashioned from the squalor of the earthly image and still carry more of the first than of the second Adam in the senses of my flesh and in my earthly actions.[688] How shall I dare to make a portrait of myself for you when I am shown to reject the image of the heavenly man by my earthly corruption?[689] Shame encloses me from both sides. I am ashamed to portray what I am; I do not dare to portray what I am not. I hate what I am; I am not what I love. But what good will it do wretched me to hate iniquity and to love virtue,[690] since I do rather what I hate and I do not in my laziness strive to do what I love? In my discord I am torn apart by inner warfare, while *the spirit has desires opposed to the flesh and the flesh has desires opposed to the spirit* (Gal 5:17) and the law of the body attacks the law of the mind with

---

688. See 1 Cor 15:47-49.
689. Paulinus wrote this letter to Bishop Severus, who had asked him to have a painting of him and his wife sent to him.
690. See Ps 45:8; Heb 1:9.

the law of sin.[691] Unhappy man that I am, who have not eliminated the poisoned taste of the hostile tree even by the wood of the cross![692] For there remains in me that paternal poison by which through his transgression our father infected the whole of his race,"[693] and the many other things that you put together concerning this misery, while groaning in expectation of the redemption of your body, in the knowledge that you are not yet saved in fact but in hope.[694]

41. But perhaps, when you said these things, you portrayed someone else rather than yourself, and you do not endure any untimely and odious difficulties from the flesh with its desires opposed to the spirit, though you do not consent to it. Yet you and anyone else who experiences this and awaits the grace of God by which we might be set free *from the body of this death* (Rom 7:4) were clearly not present at the time openly and in your own person but were present in that man in a hidden way when he touched the forbidden food and contracted the perdition that was going to spread far and wide through all human beings, unless he who was not lost came, thanks to a virgin, by another path *to seek and to save what was lost* (Lk 19:10; Mt 18:11). But what letter of yours is not filled with fervor about praying for and demanding with groans the help to make progress and to live correctly? What writing is there of yours, of whatever length, in which there is not scattered amid the groans of piety what we say in prayer, *Do not bring us into temptation* (Mt 6:13; Lk 11:4)? Let us, therefore, console, exhort, and help one another in all these ways to the extent that the Lord grants. But those things we have heard about some people, things over which we grieve and which we do not want readily to believe, Your Holiness will hear from our common friend by means of whom, when he returns in good health by God's mercy, we hope to be assured about everything.

---

691. See Rom 7:23.
692. See Gn 3:6.
693. Paulinus of Nola, Letter 30, 2.
694. See Rom 8:23-24.

LETTER 188

Alypius and Augustine to Juliana, the widow of Olybrius and daughter-in-law of Proba (417-418)

At the end of 417 or the beginning of 418 Alypius and Augustine wrote to Juliana, the widow of Olybrius and daughter-in-law of Proba, concerning Demetrias, the daughter of Juliana and Olybrius, who had recently taken vows as a consecrated virgin. Augustine dedicated his work *The Excellence of Widowhood* to Juliana and wrote Letters 130 and 131 to Proba. Like many Roman aristocrats, the family had fled Rome and come to Africa after 410, and like many Christian aristocrats of Rome, the family was influenced by the ascetic teachings of Pelagius, who in 414 wrote a letter to Demetrias at the request of Juliana to exhort her to the life of virginity.

Augustine and Alypius thank Juliana for her letter, which is no longer extant, in which she informed them of Demetrias' having taken vows as a virgin (paragraph 1). Because of their close relationship Augustine and Alypius venture to warn Juliana and Demetrias about those who destroy the faith (paragraph 2). Though Juliana claimed that no one in her family has ever been tainted with heresy, the bishops warn her of the heresy of Pelagius, which claims that we can have from ourselves whatever virtue we might have (paragraph 3).

The bishops warn that Demetrias must not believe that she has the good of virginity from herself alone, as Pelagius said in his letter to her (paragraph 4). Pelagius' claim that spiritual goods can only come from Demetrias is poison and is opposed to the words of the Apostle (paragraph 5). Virginity is a gift of God and a treasure that we carry in vessels of clay (paragraph 6). The human will needs to be helped by God, who not merely teaches us what to do but inspires us with love so that we do it (paragraph 7). Scripture clearly teaches that continence is a gift of God for which one ought to pray to God (paragraph 8).

Hence Demetrias should boast only in the Lord, since all her reasons for boasting are found only in the Lord (paragraph 9). Juliana and her family may have always had the correct faith about the Trinity, but there are other ways in which one can fall into most dangerous errors, as Pelagius has done (paragraph 10). Careful examination will show that Pelagius admits grace only in the sense of the nature with which we were created, in the sense of free choice, in the sense of teaching, or in the sense of the forgiveness of sins (paragraph 11). The bishops challenge Juliana to find in Pelagius' book the grace by which the will is helped to do the good (paragraph 12). His book lacks the grace that the Apostle commends, by which we are helped by the gift of love to live pious and righteous lives (paragraph 13). The bishops especially want Demetrias to boast only in the Lord. They ask Juliana whether the book is really the work of Pelagius, as they are convinced it is (paragraph 14).

Alypius and Augustine send greetings in the Lord to Juliana, their lady who deserves to be honored in Christ with due regards and their rightly illustrious daughter.

1, 1. It was a cause of joy and pleasure for us that your letter, revered lady, found us both present together in Hippo. We are together sending this reply to it, rejoicing to know of your good health and with mutual love reporting to you ours in turn, which we are confident is dear to you, our lady, who deserves to be honored in Christ with due regards, and rightly illustrious daughter. We know very well, however, that you are aware of the great religious love we owe you and the great concern we have for you both before God and among human beings. Although our humble selves came to know first by letter and then also by your physical presence that you were pious and Catholic, that is, true members of Christ, *when,* nonetheless, *you received the word of God that we preached* through our ministry, *you received it*, as the Apostle says, *not as the word of human beings, but as the word of God, which it truly is* (1 Thes 2:13). With the help of the Savior's mercy and grace, such great fruit has emerged from our ministry in your house that, though her human marriage was already arranged, the saintly Demetrias preferred the spiritual embrace of that husband, more handsome than the sons of men,[695] whom virgins marry in order to have a greater fecundity of spirit and in order not to lose the integrity of their flesh. But we would not have known how that faithful and noble virgin received at that time that exhortation of ours if we had not learned from your most joyful message and truthful testimony that, shortly after our departure, she had taken vows as a holy virgin and that we workers had been given this great gift of God, which he plants and waters through his servants but gives through himself.[696]

2. Since this is the case, no one will blame us if we are concerned, because of our closeness to you, to warn you to avoid teachings opposed to the grace of God. For, though the Apostle commands us to continue to preach the word not only when it is opportune but also when it is inopportune,[697] we do not in any event consider you to be among those to whom our words or writing would seem inopportune, when we say that you should carefully avoid what does not pertain to sound doctrine. For this reason, then, you were so grateful to receive our admonition that you said in the letter to which we are now replying, "I sincerely give abundant thanks for so pious an admonition, since Your Reverence urges me not to give a hearing to these people who often corrupt the venerable faith with their evil writings."

3. You then go on to say, "But Your Holiness knows that I and my home are far removed from such persons, and all our family follows the Catholic faith

---

695. See Ps 45:3.
696. See 1 Cor 3:5-7.
697. See 2 Tm 4:2.

to the point that it has never strayed into any heresy and has never fallen not only into those sects from which it is difficult to free oneself but even into those which are seen to have some small errors." It is this that compels us more and more not to remain silent with you about those who try to corrupt even those teachings that are sound. For we regard your home as no small church of Christ. Nor, of course, are those people in a small error who think that we possess it from ourselves if we have any righteousness, continence, piety, or chastity, because God created us so that, besides the fact that he discloses knowledge to us, he gives us no further help so that by loving we may do what by learning we know that we should do. That is, they claim that nature and doctrine are by themselves the grace and help of God for living righteously and correctly. But they deny that we are helped by God so as to have the good will in which is found our living righteously and the love of God itself, which among all the gifts of God is so outstanding that it is also said to be God.[698] By it alone we carry out whatever we carry out of the law and counsels of God. They say instead that we ourselves are by our own choice sufficient by ourselves for this. It should not seem to you that it is a slight error to want to claim to be Christians, but to refuse to listen to the Apostle of Christ. For, after he said, *The love of God has been poured out in our hearts*, lest anyone should think that we have this only from our own choice, he immediately added, *through the Holy Spirit who has been given to us* (Rom 5:5). You understand what a great and what a deadly mistake one makes if one still does not confess that this is a great grace of the Savior, who, ascending on high, took captivity captive and gave gifts to human beings.[699]

2, 4. How, then, could we hold back from warning you, to whom we owe so much love, that you should avoid such teachings, since we read the book for the holy Demetrias, and we want rather to learn from your reply who wrote it and whether it reached you. In that book a virgin of Christ might read, if this were not wrong, reasons to believe that she has her virginal holiness and all her spiritual riches from herself alone and in that way, before she has attained perfect happiness, she might learn to be ungrateful to God. God keep her from this! For the following are words written to her in the same book: "And so you have even here," he says, "reasons by which you are rightly placed ahead of others; in fact, even more on this account. For the nobility of your birth and the wealth of your family are understood not to be yours, but no one but you yourself will be able to bestow spiritual riches upon you. For these riches, then, which can only come from you and can only exist in you, you are rightly to be praised; for these riches you are rightly to be placed ahead of others."[700]

5. You certainly see the great harm to be avoided in these words. For the statement, "These goods can exist only in you," is very well and most truly said.

---

698. See 1 Jn 4:8.16.
699. See Eph 4:7-8; Ps 68:19.
700. Pelagius, *A Book for Demetrias* 11.

This is clearly solid food. But the statement, "They can come only from you," is entirely poisonous. God forbid that this virgin of Christ should willingly listen to this if she piously understands the proper poverty of the human heart and, for this reason, knows that she is in her heart adorned only by the gifts of her spouse. Let her rather hear the Apostle when he says, *I have betrothed you to one man, to present a chaste virgin to Christ. But I am fearful that, as the serpent seduced Eve by his cunning, so your minds may also be drawn away from chastity, which is found in Christ.* (2 Cor 11:2-3) And for this reason, concerning these spiritual riches let her also not listen to the man who says, "No one apart from you yourself will be able to bestow these upon you," and, "They can come only from you and can exist only in you." Rather, let her listen to the man who says, *We have this treasure in vessels of clay in order that the excellence of virtue may be God's and not ours* (2 Cor 4:7).

6. Let her also listen to the same true and pious teacher concerning the sacred continence of a virgin, which she does not have from herself but which is a gift of God, though one bestowed upon someone who believes and is willing. When he was dealing with this topic, he said, *I would wish all to be like me, but each has his own gift from God, one this gift, another that* (1 Cor 7:7). Let her listen to him who is not only her spouse but the only spouse of the universal Church when he says of such chastity and integrity, *All do not accept this teaching, but only those to whom it has been given* (Mt 19:11), so that she may understand that she ought to thank God and our Lord that she has such a great and outstanding gift rather than listen to the words of anyone that she has it as from herself. We do not say that they are the words of someone who flatters and humors her for fear that we might seem to judge rashly the secrets of human hearts, but at least they are the words of someone who praises her erroneously. Indeed, *every best gift and every perfect gift,* as the apostle James also says, *is from above, coming down from the Father of lights* (Jas 1:17). From this source, then, holy virginity also comes, in which you are willing and glad to be surpassed by your daughter, after you by birth, before you by action, from you by generation, ahead of you in honor, coming after you in age, going before you in holiness. In her that begins to be yours which could not be in you. She has not married in terms of the flesh so that beyond you she might be made spiritually greater not only for herself but also for you. For by that reckoning you are also less than her because you married so that she might be born. These are God's gifts, and they are certainly yours, but they *do not come from you* (Eph 2:8). For you have *this treasure* in earthly and still fragile bodies, as if *in vessels of clay so that the excellence of virtue may be God's and not yours* (2 Cor 4:7). Do not be surprised when we say that they are yours but do not come from you, for we also speak of our daily bread, and yet say, *Give us,*[701] so that it may not be thought to come from us.

---

701. See Lk 11:3.

7. Hence, as Scripture says, *Pray without ceasing; in all things give thanks* (1 Thes 5:17-18). For you pray in order that you may persevere and make progress; you give thanks because this does not come from yourselves. For who has separated you from that mass of death and destruction stemming from Adam? Was it not he who *came to seek and to save what was lost* (Lk 19:10; Mt 18:11)? Or, when a person hears the Apostle saying, *Who has set you apart?* will he reply, "My good will, my faith, my righteousness," without hearing what immediately follows, *For what do you have that you have not received? And if you have received, why do you boast as if you have not received?* (1 Cor 4:7, 9-11) We do not want, therefore, when a consecrated virgin hears or reads, "No one but you yourself will be able to bestow spiritual riches upon you. For these riches, which can only come from you and can only exist in you, you are rightly to be praised; for these riches you are rightly to be placed ahead of others"—we certainly do not want her to boast as if she had not received. Let her say, *In me, O God, are the vows of praise that I will pay to you* (Ps 56:12), but because they are in her and do not also come from her, let her also remember to say, *O Lord, by your will you have given virtue to my beauty* (Ps 30:8). For, even if they come from her on account of personal choice, without which we do no good work, still they do not come only from her, as this fellow said. Unless one's own choice is helped by the grace of God, a good will cannot exist in a human being. *For it is God*, the Apostle says, *who produces in you both the willing and the action in accord with good will* (Phil 2:13), not, as they think, merely by revealing the knowledge in order that we might know what we ought to do, but also by instilling love in order that by loving we may do what we have come to know through learning.

8. For he knew what a great good continence was who said, *And since I knew that no one can be continent unless God grants this* (Wis 8:21-22). Hence he knew not only how great a gift it was and with what desire we should want it but also that it could not exist unless God grants it. For wisdom had taught him; for he says: *And this too was a mark of wisdom: to know whose gift this was.* And yet knowledge was not enough for him; but he says *I approached the Lord, and I begged him for this* (Wis 8:21-22). God, then, helps us not only so that we may know what we should do but also so that by loving we may do what we know from learning. No one, therefore, can have not only knowledge but also continence unless God grants it. For this reason, though he already had knowledge, he begged that he might also have continence in order that there might be in him what he knew did not come from him. Or if on account of his own free choice it came from him to some small degree, it still did not come only from him, *because no one can be continent unless God grants this.* But concerning the spiritual riches among which is certainly also included this bright and beautiful continence, he does not say, "They can exist in you and come from you." Rather, he says, "They can only exist in you and come from you," so that she might believe that, just as they can exist nowhere but in her, so they can come from no one

but her and so that she might for this reason boast as if she had not received.[702] May *the merciful Lord* (Ps 103:8) keep this from her heart!

3, 9. With regard to the Christian discipline and humility of the holy virgin in which she was raised and educated, we too certainly think that when she read these words, if she did in fact read them, she groaned, humbly beat her breast, perhaps even wept, and with trust prayed to the Lord, to whom she was consecrated and by whom she was made holy, in order that, just as those words were not hers but someone else's, so her faith might not be such that she would believe that she has something about which she might boast, but not in the Lord.[703] For her reasons for boasting are in fact in her and not in the words of others, as the Apostle says, *But let each one test his own work, and then each will find reason to boast in himself and not in another* (Gal 6:4). But God forbid that her reason for boasting is she herself rather than he to whom she says, *O my reason for boasting, you who raise up my head* (Ps 4:4). In that way her reason for boasting is in her in a salutary manner when God, who is in her, is himself her reason for boasting. From him she has all the good gifts because of which she is good, and she will have all those by which she will be better to the extent that she can be better in this life and by which she will be perfect when God's grace, not human praise, will make her perfect. For her *soul will be praised in the Lord* (Ps 34:3), *who satisfied* her *desire with good gifts* (Ps 103:5). For he also inspired her with this desire so that his virgin would not so boast of some good as if she had not received it.[704]

10. Please assure us by replying, then, whether we are mistaken about this attitude of hers. For we know very well that you are and have been, along with all your family, worshipers of the undivided Trinity. But human error does not sneak up on one on this point alone, so that one holds something different concerning the undivided Trinity. For there are other doctrines on which one errs in a most destructive way, such as the one on which we have spoken in this letter, perhaps longer than was sufficient for your faith-filled and chaste wisdom. And yet we do not know to whom one does injury if not to God and, for this reason, to that Trinity, if one denies that some good, which comes from God, does come from God. May God keep that sin from you, as we believe he has. May God absolutely forbid that this book, from which we believed that we should cite some readily intelligible words, produce some such idea—I do not say in your soul or in that of your daughter, a consecrated virgin, but even in the souls of any male or female servant of yours of the lowest rank.

11. But if you pay more careful attention to the things in it that he seems to say in defense of grace and the help of God, you will find them so ambiguous

---

702. See 1 Cor 4:7.
703. See 1 Cor 1:31.
704. See 1 Cor 4:7.

that they can refer either to nature or to doctrine or to the forgiveness of sins. For they are forced to admit that we ought to pray in order that we may not enter into temptation,[705] and they can understand this in terms of their reply that we are helped toward this insofar as, when we pray and knock, the understanding of the truth is opened up for us. In that way we learn what we should do, but our will does not receive the strength to do what we learn. And when they say that, by the grace and help of God, Christ the Lord was set before us as a model for living a good life, they limit this to the same teaching, that is, insofar as we learn from his example how we ought to live, but they do not want us to be helped so that by loving we might also do what we know through learning.

12. Or at least find something in that same book, if you can, where, apart from nature, apart from the choice of the will which belongs to nature, apart from the forgiveness of sin and the revelation of doctrine, he admits the sort of help of God that he admits who said, *Since I knew that no one can be continent unless God grants this, and this too was a mark of wisdom: to know whose gift this was, I approached the Lord and begged him for this* (Wis 8:21). For, when he prayed, this man did not want to receive the nature in which he was created. Nor was he concerned about the natural choice of the will with which he was created. Nor did he desire the forgiveness of sins, for he desired instead the continence by which he might avoid sin. And he did not desire to know what he should do, since he admitted that he already knew whose gift this was. But he wanted to receive such a strength of will, such an ardor of love from the Spirit of wisdom as would suffice for carrying out the great task of continence. If, then, you can find anything of the sort in that book, we will give you most ample thanks if you would be so kind as to let us know by replying.

13. For words fail me to express how much I desire that a clear confession of the grace that the Apostle strongly commends[706] be found in the writings of those people, which many read because of their cleverness and eloquence. The Apostle says that God gives to each person a measure of the faith[707] without which it is impossible to please God,[708] the faith from which the righteous live,[709] the faith *that works through love* (Gal 5:6), the faith before which and without which no one's works are to be judged good, since *everything that does not come from faith is sin* (Rom 14:23). He says that, in order that we may live piously and righteously, God does not help us only by the revelation of knowledge, for knowledge without love puffs one up with pride,[710] but also helps us by inspiring us with the love *that is the fullness of the law* (Rom 13:10), which builds up our

---

705. See Mt 26:4; Mk 14:38; 22:46.
706. See Rom 12:3.
707. See Rom 12:3.
708. See Heb 11:6.
709. See Rom 1:17; Gal 3:11; Heb 10:38; Hab 2:4.
710. See 1 Cor 8:1.

heart without puffing it up with pride as knowledge does. But up to now we have never found anything of the sort in their writings.

14. Yet we would very much wish that these things were in this book from which we have taken the words that we cited. There, in praising Christ's virgin as if no one besides herself could bestow on her spiritual riches and as if she could have these only from herself, he does not want her to boast in the Lord[711] but to boast as if she had not received.[712] Though he did not explicitly name her or you, revered lady, he nonetheless mentions that he was asked by the mother of a virgin to write to her. In a certain letter of his in which the same Pelagius very clearly puts his own name and does not pass over the name of the virgin, he says that he wrote to her and strives to prove by the testimony of the same book that he most openly confesses the grace of God, which he is said either not to mention or to deny. But we ask that you be so good as to inform us whether this is the book in which he set forth those words about spiritual riches or whether it reached Your Holiness.

---

711. See 1 Cor 1:31; 2 Cor 1:17; Jer 9:23-24.
712. See 1 Cor 4:7.

LETTER 193
Augustine to Marius Mercator (418)

In approximately 418 Augustine wrote to Marius Mercator, a Catholic layman, an Italian who later lived in Constantinople. He wrote two works against Pelagianism, which he sent to Augustine and which are no longer extant.[713] In the present letter Augustine apologizes for not having replied to Mercator's first letter and expresses his pleasure at receiving his second one (paragraph 1). He thanks Mercator for sending him his books against the Pelagian teaching (paragraph 2).

Augustine notes that, if the heretics hold that baptized infants believe through those who present them for baptism, they have taken a big step in the right direction, since they thereby admit that without baptism infants are non-believers who will, according to the Lord's words, be condemned (paragraph 3). In fact, if they admit that baptized infants believe, the whole controversy is practically speaking settled (paragraph 4).

As Mercator reported, the Pelagians pointed to Enoch and Elijah as having escaped death, but Augustine does not see how this helps their case (paragraph 5). God could bring about eternal life without the intervention of death for those he wanted to (paragraph 6). The question as to why the penalty for sin remains once the sin itself has been wiped out in baptism presents more of a problem, and on this issue Augustine refers Mercator to his books on the baptism of infants (paragraph 7). Or perhaps the Pelagians are troubled that no one now lives without sin as Enoch supposedly did so that he merited to escape death. Augustine points out that it is not certain that Enoch has escaped death (paragraph 8).

Paul's words about those found living at the coming of Christ present another problem (paragraph 9). Augustine would like to hear what more learned persons have said on the passage (paragraph 10). Whether those living at Christ's coming are taken to be the righteous or those still in their bodies, it remains true that Christ will judge the living and the dead (paragraph 11). Whichever interpretation one takes, it does not seem relevant to the Pelagian cause (paragraph 12). Augustine asks Mercator to let him know if he has found a definite resolution to the question about those found living at Christ's coming and says that he prefers to learn rather than to teach (paragraph 13).

To Mercator, his most beloved lord and son worthy of praise and of most sincere love among the members of Christ, Augustine sends greetings in the Lord.

---

713. Marius Mercator later wrote a *Memorandum on the Name of Coelestius* and a *Memorandum against the Heresy of Pelagius and Coelestius on the Writings of Julian*. These works are no longer extant.

1, 1. The letter of Your Charity, which you sent earlier and which I received in Carthage, filled me with such great joy that I was most grateful to receive even your later letter, in which you were angry with me because I had not replied to you. For your anger was not the beginning of a state of animosity but a proof of love. The fact that I did not reply from Carthage was not due to a lack of couriers, but other more urgent matters kept us very occupied with and intent upon them until we left there. But after we left there, we went on to Caesarean Mauretania where the needs of the Church carried us. While the different things thrust upon our senses through all those lands pulled our attention this way and that, no one was insistently reminding me to reply to you and there was no opportunity to find a courier. Then, upon returning from there, I found the other letter of Your Sincerity already filled with sharp complaints and another book against the new heretics filled with testimonies from the Holy Scriptures. After I had read it somewhat in haste, I felt obliged to reply also to the first one you sent since a very good opportunity presented itself in your dearest brother, Albinus, an acolyte of the church of Rome.

2. Heaven forbid, therefore, my dearest son, that I should be negligent in welcoming you when you write to me or send me your writings to examine or that I should hold you in scorn because of proud vanity, especially since my joy over you is greater to the extent that it comes to me unexpected and unforeseen. For I admit that I did not know that you had made so much progress. And what should be more desirable for us than that they become more and more numerous who refute the errors that attack the Catholic faith and lay ambushes for weak and ignorant brethren and who fiercely and faithfully defend the Church of Christ against *profane innovations in language* (1 Tm 6:20)? For, as Scripture says, *The multitude of the wise is the good health of the world* (Wis 6:26). I looked into your heart in your writings as much as I could, and I found a heart that I should embrace and exhort to stretch out with most persevering diligence toward the things that are ahead,[714] as the Lord helps your strength, for he has given you that strength in order that he may make it grow.

2, 3. But the people who wandered off, whom we are trying to call back to the way, have drawn close to the truth to no small degree concerning the baptism of infants, when they admit that an infant, no matter how recently born from its mother, nonetheless believes through those who present the child to be baptized. For they say, as you write, that infants do not believe in the forgiveness of sins in the sense that infants, who they think have no sin, receive the forgiveness of sins. But since infants also receive the same bath that produces the forgiveness of sins in whoever receives it, they believe that this forgiveness, which is not produced in them, is produced in others. When, therefore, they say, "They do not believe in that sense, but they believe in this sense," they certainly are clear that infants believe. Let them, therefore, hear the Lord: *Whoever believes in the*

---

714. See Phil 3:13.

Son has eternal life, but whoever does not believe in the Son will not have life, but the anger of God remains over him (Jn 3:36). Hence, because infants become believers through others who present them to be baptized, they are certainly unbelievers through those people (if they are among such) who do not believe that they should be presented for baptism, since they do not believe that it does them any good. And for this reason, if infants in that way believe through believers and have eternal life, they are certainly unbelievers through unbelievers and will not see life, but the anger of God remains over them. For Scripture did not say "comes over them" but *remains over them*, because it was already in them from their origin, and it is by no means taken away from them except by *the grace of God through Jesus Christ our Lord* (Rom 7:25). Concerning this anger we read in the Book of Job, *A man born of a woman has a short life and one full of anger* (Job 14:1 LXX). Why, then, does the anger of God remain over the innocence of an infant if not because of the condition and defilement of original sin? Concerning this defilement it is likewise written in the same book that no one is immune from it, not even an infant *who has lived one day on the earth* (Job 14:5 LXX).

4. The fact that we argue against them most persistently has, therefore, not failed to accomplish something in these people, and Catholic voices echo in their ears from one side and another, since, though they wanted to argue against the sacraments of the Church, they admitted, nonetheless, that infants believe. They do not, therefore, promise them life even if they have not been baptized. Of what other life is it said, *Whoever does not believe the Son will not see life* (Jn 3:36)? And let them not say that they are excluded from the kingdom of heaven in such a way that they still defend them from condemnation. For what but condemnation is signified by the anger that the Lord testifies remains over one who does not believe? They have in fact come quite close to us, and apart from a dispute over minor points the case is ended. For, if they grant that infants believe, just as the statement, *One who is not reborn of water and the Spirit will not enter the kingdom of heaven* (Jn 3:5), is binding for them, so undoubtedly is this one, which is also from the same Lord, *One who believes and is baptized will be saved, but one who does not believe will be condemned* (Mk 16:16). Because, then, these people admit that infants are believers when they are baptized, they should not doubt that, if they do not believe, they are condemned, and they should be so bold as to say, if they can, that they are condemned by a just God, though they contract no sin from their origin and have no infection of sin.

5. But regarding the point that you mentioned in your letter, namely, that they raise as an objection to us that Enoch and Elijah did not die but were taken from this life from the midst of human beings along with their bodies, I do not understand how it helps them with respect to the issue that we are dealing with. For I omit the fact that it is said that they too are going to die afterward, as most people interpret the Revelation of John concerning those two prophets. He says about them without mentioning their names that these two holy men will at some time appear with the bodies in which they are now living in order that they too

might die for the truth of Christ, like the other martyrs.[715] Having, then, omitted this interpretation, however it stands with the question that they have raised, how, I ask you, does it help them? For, if God, who pardons sins for so many of his faithful, also willed to spare some of them this punishment of sin, who are we to answer back to God[716] and ask why one person receives this gift and another that one?[717]

6. We state, therefore, what the Apostle states with full openness: *The body is indeed dead on account of sin, but the spirit is life on account of righteousness. But if the Spirit of him who has raised up Christ from the dead dwells in you, he who has raised up Christ from the dead will also bring to life your mortal bodies through his Spirit dwelling in you.* (Rom 8:10-11) But we do not say this in the sense that we deny that God can now, in those whom he wants, produce without death what we believe he will doubtlessly produce in so many after their death, nor is that statement for this reason false, that *through one man sin entered this world and through sin death, and in that way it was passed on to all human beings* (Rom 5:12). For this was said because, if death had not entered through sin, there would be no death. For, when we also say, "All are sent to hell on account of sins," do we say something false because all human beings are not sent to hell? That statement is certainly true not because every human being is sent there but because no one is sent there except as punishment for sins. The statement, *Through the righteousness of one all human beings come to righteousness of life* (Rom 5:18), is also a statement of this sort to the opposite effect. For all human beings do not share in the righteousness of Christ, but this was said because no one is made righteous except by Christ.

7. That question, then, is not without reason more disturbing, namely, why the punishment of sin remains when the sin does not remain. That is, if the death of the body is punishment for sin, it is a greater problem that an infant dies after it has been baptized than that Elijah did not die after he had been justified. For, after the sin of the infant is canceled, it is a problem that the punishment of sin takes place; it ought not to be a problem if, after Elijah's sin is canceled, the punishment of sin does not take place. If, then, in the books on the baptism of infants,[718] with which I know that you are quite familiar, we resolved as best we could with the Lord's help the question about the death of the baptized, namely, why, once sin has been abolished, the punishment of sin still follows, how much less should we be disturbed by the question that we are asked: "Why did the righteous Elijah not die if death is the punishment for sin?" It is as if the question were: "Why did the sinful Elijah not die if death is the punishment of sin?"

8. But these people might raise another objection from another angle and ask: "If Enoch and Elijah were so sinless that they did not suffer even death,

---

715. See Rev 11:3-7.
716. See Rom 9:20.
717. See 1 Cor 7:7.
718. See *The Merits and Forgiveness of Sins and Baptism of Infants* 2, 3, 49-34, 56.

which is the punishment for sin, how is it that no one lives in this life without sin?" They might ask this as if we would not give them the more probable answer: "Those whom the Lord wanted to live after their sins had been removed were not allowed to live here because here no one can live without sin." But these and similar responses could be given to them if they proved from elsewhere that those men were never going to die. But since they cannot prove this, it is better to believe that Enoch and Elijah will die at the end of the world, and, since it is better to believe that they will meet death, there is no reason that they should want to raise those two men as an objection to us since they will in no way help their case.

4, 9. But those of whom the Apostle said, when he was speaking of the resurrection of the dead, *And we, the living who remain, will be snatched up with them in the clouds to meet Christ in the air, and in that way we will be with the Lord forever.* (1 Thes 4:16) certainly raise a question, but on account of those people themselves, not on account of our opponents. For, even if they are themselves not going to die, I do not at all see how it helps our opponents, since the same sort of things can be said of these people as were said of those two prophets. But, with regard to the words of the blessed Apostle, he really seems to state that at the end of the world, at the Lord's coming, when the resurrection of the dead will take place, certain persons will not die but will be found alive and will be changed suddenly into that immortality that is also given to the other saints and will be snatched up along with them, as he says, in the clouds. Nothing else has come to my mind whenever I have chosen to think about these words.

10. But I would prefer to hear from more learned persons on this. Otherwise we may find that the Apostle also said to those who think that some living people will be transferred to perpetual life without death having preceded, *You fool, what you sow is not brought to life unless it first dies* (1 Cor 15:36). For how is what we read in most manuscripts, *All of us will rise* (1 Cor 15:51), possible unless all of us die? There is certainly no resurrection unless death has come first. And what some manuscripts have, namely, *All of us will fall asleep*, makes us understand this same point much more easily and clearly, and anything else of the sort that is found in the holy writings seems to force us to the conclusion that no human being should be thought to attain immortality unless death has come first. Hence, when the Apostle said, *And we, the living who remain at the coming of the Lord, will not arrive ahead of those who have already fallen asleep. For the Lord himself at the sound of a command, at the word of an archangel, at the blast of a trumpet, will come down from heaven, and those who have died in Christ will rise first; then we, the living who remain, will be snatched up with them in the clouds to meet Christ in the air, and in that way we will be with the Lord forever.* (1 Thes 4:14-16) I would like, as I said, to hear from more learned persons on these words and, if they can explain them so that we can understand from them that all human beings who are living or who will live after us are going to die, I would like to correct what I once held on this. For we ought not

to be teachers who cannot be taught, and it is certainly better that a little fellow be corrected than that a rigid one be broken, for what we have written exercises and trains our weakness or that of others, even though our writings are not established with anything like the authority of the canon of Scripture.

11. For, if no other meaning can be found in these words of the Apostle and if it is clear that he wanted us to understand what the words themselves seem to cry out, that is, that at the end of the world and at the coming of the Lord there will be some persons who will not be stripped of the body but will be clothed over with immortality, *in order that what is mortal may be swallowed up by life* (2 Cor 5:4), what we confess in the rule of faith will undoubtedly be in accord with this view, namely, that the Lord will come to judge the living and the dead.[719] Thus we would not understand here the living as the righteous and the dead as those lacking righteousness, though the righteous and those lacking righteousness are going to be judged. Rather we would understand the living as those whom his coming will find not yet to have left their bodies and the dead as those who have already left them. If it is established that this is the case, we must examine how we should then interpret the words, *What you sow is not brought to life unless it first dies* (1 Cor 15:36), and, *All of us will rise*, or, *All of us will fall asleep* (1 Cor 15:51), in order that they may not be opposed to this view by which it is believed that they will live with their bodies for eternity without having tasted death.

12. But whichever of these interpretations is found to be truer and clearer, how is it relevant to their case whether all are punished by the death they deserve or some are spared suffering death? For it is clear that death not only of the soul but also of the body would not take place if sin had not come first and that the power of grace is more wonderful in the coming to life of the righteous into eternal blessedness than in their not meeting with the experience of death. Enough has been said on account of the people about whom you wrote to me, though I do not think that they now say that, even if Adam had not sinned, he would have died at least in the body.

13. But, with regard to the question of the resurrection, we must bring to bear a more careful examination on account of those who, it is thought, are not going to die but to pass from this mortality to immortality without death intervening, and if you have either heard or read something or have been able to think of something on this question that has been resolved and settled by arguments that are reasonable and complete, I ask that you not hesitate to send it to me. For I prefer—something I must admit to Your Charity—to learn rather than to teach. We are also admonished about this by the apostle James, who says, *Let each be quick to listen and slow to speak* (Jas 1:19). The sweetness of the truth, therefore, ought to invite us to learn, but the necessity of charity ought to force us to teach.

---

719. See 2 Tm 4:1.

Here we should rather hope that this necessity passes away, because of which one human being teaches another, so that we may *all be taught by God* (Jn 6:45; Is 54:13). And yet we are taught by God when we learn those matters that pertain to true piety, even when a human being seems to teach them, because *neither the one who plants nor the one who waters is important, but only God who gives the increase* (1 Cor 3:7). Since, therefore, if God did not give the increase, the apostles who planted and watered would not be important, how much more are you or I or any human beings of this time unimportant, when we think that we are teachers!

LETTER 194
Augustine to Sixtus, the future pope (418)

In 418 Augustine wrote to the Roman priest Sixtus, to whom he had written Letter 191 and who was elected the bishop of Rome in 432. The letter subsequently played an interesting role in the controversy on grace when some monks from a monastery in Hadrumetum found a copy of it in the library of Evodius, the bishop of Uzalis. Shocked by Augustine's teaching on grace, the monks concluded that their superior ought not to rebuke them for misconduct but should simply pray that God would give them grace since, if they misbehaved, it was due to a lack of grace. As a result, Augustine had to write two works for the abbot of the monastery, Valentine, namely, *Rebuke and Grace* and *Grace and Free Choice*. See Letters 214 and 215 for further background on the controversy.

Augustine begins by expressing his joy at hearing that Sixtus, whose letter to Augustine is no longer extant, has now condemned the Pelagians, though it has been rumored that he earlier favored their views (paragraph 1). He distinguishes various kinds of supporters of the Pelagian position and the different manners in which they should be dealt with (paragraph 2). The Pelagians are simply wrong in claiming that free choice is done away with if one holds that it is impossible to have a good will without God's help (paragraph 2). They wrongly charge God with favoritism on the grounds that grace is not given in accord with previous merits (paragraph 3). They claim that it is unjust if, when two people are in the same situation, God shows mercy to one and not to another (paragraph 4) and that it is unjust that one is set free and the other is condemned (paragraph 5).

Augustine insists that God justifies sinners without any preceding merits but that why he justifies one person and not another is hidden in the unsearchable ways of God (paragraph 6). Although at the Council of Diospolis Pelagius condemned those who say that grace is given in accord with merits, he continues to teach what he condemned (paragraph 7). Pelagius teaches that the grace given without any preceding merits is the human nature with which we are created (paragraph 8). Pelagians also say that this grace given previous to any merits is the forgiveness of sins, but they hold that faith obtains this forgiveness (paragraph 9). Augustine shows from Paul that even faith is a gift of God (paragraph 10). After all, Christian faith must include love, which is a gift of the Holy Spirit (paragraph 11). God's foreknowledge of believers differs from his foreknowledge of those who do not believe (paragraph 12). The Pelagian defenders of free choice ask what complaint God can have with them since no one can resist his will (paragraph 13). Some people do merit to have their hearts hardened, but there is no merit by which others obtain mercy (paragraph 14). We do not merit to receive faith (paragraph 15). Even prayer is a gift of God (paragraph 16). When the Holy Spirit is said to intercede for us with inexpressible groans, we must understand that he makes us groan (paragraph 17). Without the Spirit no one prays correctly (paragraph 18).

Prior to grace we have no merit by which we can earn grace, since grace produces in us all our good merits, and in crowning our merits God crowns his own gifts (paragraph 19). Augustine points out how Paul taught that even eternal life, which Scripture often calls a recompense, is grace (paragraphs 20 and 21).

Augustine answers those who try to excuse themselves for living sinful lives on the grounds that they did not receive grace to live good lives, for, if they live sinful lives, they do so because of sin, either original sin alone or original sin along with personal sins (paragraph 22). Augustine turns against them the words of the apostle who asks who they are to answer back to God (paragraph 23). Of adults one can say that they refuse to understand or refuse to obey so that they are without excuse (paragraph 24). Those who know the law and do not carry it out are especially without excuse (paragraph 25). The Jews who rejected Christ would not have had that sin if Christ had not come, but they would still have had other sins (paragraph 26). Every sinner is without excuse either because of the guilt of original sin or because of the guilt of personal sin as well (paragraph 27). Knowledge of the law without grace is useless (paragraph 28). For those who are set free from the bondage of sin are set free only by grace (paragraph 29). No one is set free from sin, whether original sin or personal sin, except by the grace of Jesus Christ (paragraph 30).

Those who think that God shows favoritism have to face the fact that many infants die without baptism, though God is not unjust (paragraph 31). The lot of infants, some of whom die without baptism while others die after having been baptized, proves the gratuity of grace (paragraph 32). One can, when confronted with their different ends, only exclaim over the inscrutable judgment of God (paragraph 33).

Augustine appeals to the twin sons of Isaac, who did nothing either good or bad before they were born, in order to show that God's choice of Jacob was a gift of grace, while his rejection of Esau was just in view of original sin (paragraph 34). He rejects the idea that God foresaw their future works in choosing Jacob over Esau (paragraph 35). Paul used the example of these twins to teach the gratuity of grace (paragraph 36). He emphasized their conception from a single act of intercourse in order to exclude any difference in merits on their part or on the part of their parents (paragraph 37). Paul wanted to teach that Jacob had no reason to boast except in the Lord (paragraph 38). His choice had no preceding merits and involved no injustice on the part of God (paragraph 39). Again, Augustine asks those who excuse themselves Paul's question about who they think they are to answer back to God (paragraph 40).

Even if God did foresee the future works of Isaac's twin sons who grew up, he could not foresee the future works of infants who were going to die in infancy, because there were not going to be any (paragraph 41). If the Pelagians appeal to God's foreknowledge of what such infants would have done if they had lived, they are faced with even worse problems (paragraph 42).

The Pelagians are confronted with the authority of scripture and with the practice of infant baptism, which includes the rites of exorcism and exsufflation (paragraph 43). Augustine appeals to the example of the wild and domesticated olive trees to show that the child of baptized parents still needs to be baptized for the removal of original sin (paragraph 44). Baptism truly brings about the forgiveness of sin even in infants (paragraph 45), just as it truly drives out the devil who has dominion over them only because of sin (paragraph 46). Finally, Augustine urges Sixtus to exercise pastoral vigilance in the face of the restlessness of the Pelagian heretics (paragraph 47).

To his lord who is most beloved in the Lord of lords, his holy brother and fellow priest Sixtus, Augustine sends greetings in the Lord.

1, 1. In the letter that I sent by means of our dearest brother, the acolyte Albinus, I promised that I would send a lengthier one by means of our holy brother and fellow priest Firmus, who brought us the letter of Your Holiness full of the purity of your faith, which provided us with such great joy that we can more easily possess it than we can express it. For I must admit to Your Charity that we were very sad when rumor spread it about that you sided with the enemies of the grace of Christ. But in order that this sadness might be wiped from our hearts, first of all, that same rumor was not silent about the fact that you first declared them anathema in a large crowd of people; secondly, along with the letter of the Apostolic See sent to Africa concerning their condemnation,[720] your letter also was delivered to the primate, Aurelius.[721] Although it was short, it sufficiently indicated the strength of your opposition to their error. But now in your letter the very faith of the Roman church states more openly and more at length what you hold about and in opposition to that teaching along with us. For it was especially to that church that the blessed apostle Paul said many things in many ways about *the grace of God through Jesus Christ our Lord* (Rom 7:25). Hence, not only has all that cloud of sadness fled from our hearts, but such a great light of joy has also flowed into them that that sadness and fear seem to have had no effect on us apart from increasing the flame of the joys that were to follow.

2. And so, my dearest brother, though we do not see you with the eyes of the flesh, yet with our spirit we hold you, embrace you, and kiss you with the heart in the faith of Christ, in the grace of Christ, and in the members of Christ. And I now reply to your letter as the most holy and reliable courier, whom you wanted to serve for us not merely as a carrier of your letter but also as someone

---

720. That is, the *Tractoria* of Pope Zosimus, issued in the summer of 418. The work is no longer extant.
721. Aurelius was the bishop of Carthage, and thus primate of Africa, during the years 391/2-c.430.

to recount and to bear witness to your actions, goes back from us to you. And we converse with you at somewhat greater length, advising you to press on to teach those people whom you have, as we learned, begun to cause to have some fear. For there are certain people who think that they should still quite freely defend those impious teachings that have been justly condemned, and there are some who secretly enter homes[722] and do not cease to spread in secret what they are afraid to proclaim in the open. But there are some who are completely silent, overwhelmed by great fear, but who still hold in their heart what they do not dare now to utter with their lips. Yet they may be very well known to the brethren because of their previous defense of this teaching. Hence, some should be subjected to stronger means of coercion, others should be more carefully watched, and still others should be dealt with more gently, but they should be not taught in a halfhearted manner. For, if we do not fear that they may cause others to perish, we still should not neglect them lest they themselves perish.

2, 3. For, when they suppose that free choice is taken away if they agree that a human being cannot have a good will without the help of God, they do not understand that they do not strengthen human choice but inflate it with pride so that it is carried off amid vanities rather than set down upon the Lord as if upon solid rock. For *the will is prepared by the Lord* (Prv 8:35 LXX).

4. But when they think that they believe that God shows favoritism if they believe that without any preceding merits *he shows mercy to whom he wills* (Rom 9:18; 2 Thes 1:11), calls whom he wills, and makes devout whom he wills, they do not pay enough attention to the fact that the one condemned is given the punishment that was deserved, while the one set free is given grace that was not deserved. Hence, the former cannot complain that he did not deserve it, nor can the latter boast that he did deserve it. And there is no favoritism present where one and the same mass of condemnation and sin includes that the one set free learns from the one not set free what punishment would be appropriate for him if grace had not come to the rescue. But if it is grace, it is certainly not repayment for any merits but given out of gratuitous goodness.

5. "But it is unjust," they say, "that in one and the same situation the one is set free and the other is punished." It is just, therefore, that both be punished. Who would deny this? Let us, then, give thanks to the Savior since we see in the condemnation of those like us that we have not received what we recognize that we also deserved. For, if both were set free, what was owed to sin through justice would certainly remain hidden; if no one were set free, what grace bestows would remain hidden. Instead, in this most difficult question we use the words of the Apostle, *Wanting to display his anger and to demonstrate his power, God endured with much patience the vessels of anger that were made for destruction and in order to make known the riches of his glory toward the vessels of*

---

722. See 2 Tm 3:6.

mercy (Rom 9:22-23). The clay pot cannot say to him, *Why have you made me so?* since he has *the power to make from the same lump of clay one vessel for honor and another for dishonor* (Rom 9:20-21). And because this whole lump has deservedly been condemned, justice gives the dishonor that was deserved and grace gives the honor that was not deserved, not because of a title to merits, not because of the necessity of fate, not because of the fickleness of fortune, but because of *the depth of the riches of the wisdom and knowledge of God* (Rom 11:33). The Apostle does not explain this but stands in awe at its hiddenness when he cries out, *O the depth of the riches of the wisdom and knowledge of God! How inscrutable are his judgments and unsearchable his ways! For who has known the mind of the Lord? Or who has been his counselor? Or who first gave to him and will be repaid? For from him and through him and in him are all things; to him be glory for age upon age! Amen.* (Rom 11:33-36)

3, 6. But they do not want him to receive glory for justifying sinners by gratuitous grace since, not knowing his righteousness, they want to establish their own.[723] Or, when they are pressured by the outcries of religious and pious people who protest, they admit that they are helped by God to have or to produce righteousness in such a way that some merit of theirs comes first, as if they wanted first to give in order to be paid back by him of whom Scripture says, *Who first gave to him and will be repaid by him?* (Rom 11:35) And they believe that their own merits anticipate him of whom they hear, or rather refuse to hear, *For from him and through him and in him are all things* (Rom 11:36). From the depth of the riches of his wisdom and knowledge[724] there pour forth the riches of his glory toward the vessels of mercy, which he calls to be his adopted children.[725] He wants to make known these riches even through the vessels of anger, which were made for destruction. And what are his unsearchable ways but those of which the Psalm sings, *All the ways of the Lord are mercy and truth* (Ps 25:10)? And so, his mercy and truth are unsearchable, because *he shows mercy to whom he wills*, not out of justice but out of the grace of mercy, and *he hardens whom he wills* (Rom 9:18), not out of injustice, but out of the truth of punishment. Yet, because it says in Scripture, *Mercy and truth have met each other* (Ps 85:11), this mercy and truth meet in such a way that mercy does not impede the truth by which one who deserves it is punished, nor does the truth impede the mercy by which one who does not deserve it is set free. Of what merits of his own is the one set free going to boast? For, if his merits received their due recompense, he would only be condemned. Are there, then, no merits of the righteous? Clearly there are because they are righteous. But they had no merits in order to become righteous. For they were made righteous when they were justified. But, as the Apostle says, *They were justified gratuitously by his grace* (Rom 3:24).

---

723. See Rom 10:3.
724. See Rom 11:33.
725. See Rom 9:22-23.

7. Though these people, then, are bitter enemies of this grace, yet Pelagius anathematized in the Palestinian court those who say that the grace of God is given in accord with merits, for otherwise he would not have left that court without punishment.[726] But nothing else is found even in their later arguments than that this grace is given in accord with merits, the grace that the Apostle's Letter to the Romans especially commends in order that its proclamation might spread out to the whole world from there as if from the capital of the world. For this is the grace by which the sinner is justified, that is, by which someone who was first a sinner is made righteous. And no merits precede the reception of this grace because to the merits of a sinner there is due not grace but punishment. Nor would this grace be grace if it were not given gratuitously but as a recompense that was owed.

8. But when these people are asked what grace Pelagius thought was given without any preceding merits when he condemned those who say that the grace of God is given in accord with our merits, they reply that the grace without any preceding merits is the human nature in which we are created. For, before we existed, we could not merit to be anything. This fallacy should be banished from the hearts of Christians. The Apostle certainly does not refer to the grace by which we were created so that we might be human beings. For this is *the grace through Jesus Christ our Lord*. For Christ did not die for people in order that they might be created but for sinful people in order that they might be justified. The man, of course, already existed who said. *Wretched man that I am! Who will set me free from the body of this death? The grace of God through Jesus Christ our Lord.* (Rom 7:24-25)

9. They can surely say that the forgiveness of sins is a grace that is not given because of any preceding merits. For what good merit can sinners have? But not even the forgiveness of sins is without any merit if faith wins it. Nor does faith lack all merit, for with faith that man said, *O God, be merciful to me, a sinner*, and *he returned justified* (Lk 18:13-14) by the merit of his faithful humility, *because one who humbles himself will be exalted* (Lk 14:11; Mt 23:12). It remains, then, that the very faith from which all righteousness takes its beginning, because of which it is said to the Church in the Song of Songs, *You will come and pass from the beginning of faith* (Sg 4:8 LXX)—it remains, I repeat, that we not attribute faith itself to human choice, which they extol, or to any preceding merits, because any good merits there are begin from faith, but rather that we admit that it is a gratuitous gift of God, if we have in mind true grace, that is, without any merits. For, as we read in the same letter, *God imparts to each a measure of faith* (Rom 12:3). Good works are, to be sure, produced by a human being, but faith is produced in a human being, and without it no good works are produced by any human being. For *whatever does not come from faith is sin* (Rom 14:23).

---

726. I.e., at the Council of Diospolis held in December of 415. See *The Deeds of Pelagius* for Augustine's account and interpretation of that council, which found Pelagius innocent.

10. Hence, in order that a man at prayer might not extol himself or the merit of his prayer, even if help is given to him as he prays in order to conquer the desires for temporal goods and in order to love eternal goods and God, the source of all good things, the faith prays that was given to him when he did not pray, and unless it had been given, he could not pray. For *how will they call upon him in whom they have not believed? Or how will they believe in him of whom they have not heard? How will they hear without someone to preach? And so, faith comes from hearing, and hearing come through the word of Christ.* (Rom 10:14,17) Hence the minister of Christ, the preacher of this faith, plants and waters in accord with the grace that was given him.[727] And yet *neither the one who plants nor the one who waters is anything, but only God who gives the increase* (1 Cor 3:7,6), God *who imparts to each a measure of faith* (Rom 12:3). For this reason it is said elsewhere, *Peace to the brothers and love along with faith* and, in order that they would not attribute this to themselves, he immediately added, *from God the Father and our Lord Jesus Christ* (Eph 6:23). For not all who hear the word have the faith, but only those to whom God imparts a measure of faith, just as not every seed that is planted and watered sprouts but only that seed to which God gives the increase. But why one person believes and another does not, when they both hear the same word and when, if a miracle occurs before their eyes, they both see it, pertains to *the depth of the riches of the wisdom and knowledge of God* (Rom 11:33), whose *judgments are inscrutable* (Rom 9:14), and in whom there is no injustice when *he shows mercy to whom he wills and hardens whom he wills* (Rom 9:18). Nor are these judgments unjust because they are hidden.

11. Then, after the forgiveness of sins, unless the Holy Spirit has a house that has been cleansed, will not the unclean spirit return with seven others *and the last condition of that man be worse than the first* (Mt 12:45)? But in order that the Holy Spirit might dwell there, does he not breathe where he wills?[728] And is not the love of God, without which no one lives a good life, *poured out in our hearts* not by us but *through the Holy Spirit who has been given to us* (Rom 5:5)? The Apostle described this faith when he said, *Neither circumcision nor the lack of circumcision counts for anything, but the faith that works through love* (Gal 5:6). This indeed is the faith of Christians, not of demons, for even *the demons believe and tremble* (Jas 2:19). But do they also have love? After all, if they did not believe, they would not say, *You are God's Holy One* (Lk 4:41), or, *You are the Son of God* (Mk 3:11). But if they had love, they would not say, *What do we have to do with you?* (Mt 8:29)

12. Faith, then, draws us to Christ, and unless it were given to us from above as a gratuitous gift, he would not say, *No one can come to me unless the Father, who sent me, draws him* (Jn 6:44). For this reason he also says a little later, *The words that I have spoken to you are spirit and life. But there are some among you*

---

727. See Rom 12:3; 15:16.15; 1 Cor 3:5-6.
728. See Jn 3:8.

who do not believe. Then the evangelist adds, *For Jesus knew from the beginning who was going to believe and who was going to betray him* (Jn 6:64-65). And so that no one would suppose that those who believe come under his foreknowledge in the same way as those who do not believe, that is, not insofar as faith is given them from above, but only insofar as their future will is foreknown, he immediately goes on to say, *And he said, For this reason I told you that no one can come to me unless it has been given to him by my Father* (Jn 6:66). This is why some of those who heard him speaking of his flesh and blood went away scandalized, but some remained because they believed, because no one can come to him unless it has been given to him by the Father and, hence, by the Son and by the Holy Spirit. For the gifts and works of the inseparable Trinity are not separate. But, in honoring the Father in that way, the Son does not introduce a proof of any distance between them but offers a great example of humility.

13. Here again, what else are these defenders of free choice—or rather these deceivers of it because they inflate it with pride, and they inflate it with pride because they put their trust in it—going to say, not against us but against the Gospel? What else are they going to say but what the Apostle said as an objection to himself, as if such people said it? *And so you say to me: Why does he still blame us? For who resists his will?* (Rom 9:19) He raised this objection for himself as if coming from someone else, as if coming from the mouth of those who refused to accept what he had said previously, *And so, he shows mercy to whom he wills and he hardens whom he wills* (Rom 9:18). To such people, then, let us say with the Apostle, for we cannot find anything to say better than *Who are you, a human being, to answer back to God?* (Rom 9:20)

14. We look for what merits this hardening, and we find it. For the whole mass was condemned as punishment for sin, and God does not harden by imparting malice but by not imparting mercy. For those to whom he does not impart it do not deserve it, nor do they merit it. Rather, they deserve and merit that he not impart mercy. This is what they deserve; this is what they merit. But we look for what merits mercy, and we do not find it, because there is nothing. Otherwise, grace is done away with if it is not given gratuitously but as recompense for merits.[729]

15. For if we say that faith, by which one would merit grace, came first, what merit did a person have before faith in order to receive faith? For what did he have that he did not receive? But if he received, why does he boast as if he had not received?[730] For, just as a person would not have wisdom, understanding, counsel, fortitude, knowledge, piety, and fear of the Lord if he had not, in accord with the words of the prophet, received the Spirit *of wisdom and understanding, of counsel and fortitude, of knowledge, piety, and fear of the Lord* (Is 11:2-3), neither would he have courage, love, and continence if he had not received the

---

729. See Rom 11:6.
730. See 1 Cor 4:7.

Holy Spirit, of whom the Apostle says, *You have not received a spirit of fear, but of courage, love, and continence* (2 Tm 1:7). So too, he would not have faith if he had not received the Spirit of faith, of which the same Apostle says, *But having the same Spirit of faith in accord with what scripture says: I believed, and for this reason I spoke, we also believe and for this reason we speak* (2 Cor 4:13; Ps 116:10). But he shows most clearly that he did not receive faith by merit but by the mercy of him who *shows mercy to whom he wills* (Rom 9:18), when he says of himself, *I obtained mercy in order that I might be a believer* (1 Cor 7:25).

4, 16. If we say that the merit of prayer comes first in order to obtain the gift of grace, prayer shows by its very petitions that whatever it obtains by petition is a gift of God, lest a peson think that it comes from himself. For, if it were within his own power, he would certainly not ask for it. But so that it would not be thought that at least the merits of prayer come first and that grace is given to those merits not as gratuitous (and then it would not be grace since it would be paid as something owed) even prayer is found among the gifts of grace. The teacher of the nations[731] says, *We do not know what we should pray for in the proper manner, but the Spirit himself pleads for us with indescribable groans* (Rom 8:26). But what does *pleads* mean but "makes us plead"? For to plead with groans is a most certain sign of someone in need. But it is not right to believe that the Holy Spirit is in need of anything. Rather, it was said that he pleads because he makes us plead and inspires us with the desire to plead and to groan. In the same sense it was said in the Gospel, *For it is not you who speak, but the Spirit of your Father who speaks in you* (Mt 10:20). For this does not come about in our regard while we, so to speak, do nothing. The help of the Holy Spirit is described in such a way, therefore, that he is said to do what he makes us do.

17. For the Apostle himself shows clearly enough that we should not understand our spirit to be the one of which it was said that he *pleads for us with indescribable groans* but the Holy Spirit who helps our weakness. For he began in this way: *The Spirit,* he said, *helps our weakness,* and then he added as follows: *For we do not know what we should pray for in the proper manner* (Rom 8:26), and so on. Elsewhere he says more clearly about this Spirit, *For you have not received the spirit of slavery once again in fear, but you have received the Spirit of adoption as children in whom we cry out, Abba, Father* (Rom 8:15). See, he does not say here that the Spirit himself cries out in praying but, *in whom we cry out, Abba, Father.* In another passage, nonetheless, he says, *Because you are children of God, God has sent the Spirit of his Son into your hearts crying out, Abba, Father* (Gal 4:6). Here he did not say, *in whom we cry out,* but preferred to say that the Spirit himself cries out who makes us cry out. In the same way we should understand the words, *The Spirit pleads for us with indescribable groans* (Rom 8:26), and, *It is the Spirit of your Father who speaks in you* (Mt 10:20).

---

731. See 1 Tm 2:7.

18. Just as no one, then, is truly wise, truly understanding, truly endowed with counsel and fortitude, just as no one is knowledgeably pious or piously knowledgeable, just as one fears God with a chaste fear, unless he has received the Spirit *of wisdom and understanding, of counsel and fortitude, of knowledge, piety, and fear of the Lord* (Is 11:2-3), so no one has any true courage, sincere love, or religious continence except through *the Spirit of courage, love, and continence* (2 Tm 1:7). And in the same way no one is truly going to believe anything without the Spirit of faith or to pray in a salutary manner without the Spirit of prayer. It is not that there are so many spirits, *but one and the same Spirit produces all these things, distributing the appropriate gifts to each one, as he wills* (1 Cor 12:11), because *the Spirit breathes where he wills* (Jn 3:8). But we must confess that he helps in one way before he dwells in a person and in another way when he dwells in a person. For, when he does not yet dwell in a person, he helps him to become a believer, and when he dwells in a person, he helps a person who is already a believer.

5, 19. What merit, then, does a person have before grace so that by that merit he may receive grace, since only grace produces in us every good merit of ours and since, when God crowns our merits, he only crowns his own gifts? For, just as we have obtained mercy from the very beginning of faith, not because we were believers but in order that we might be believers, so in the end, when there will be eternal life, he will crown us, as Scripture says, *in compassion and mercy* (Ps 103:4). It is not in vain, therefore, that we sing to God, *And his mercy will come before me* (Ps 59:11), and, *His mercy will follow after me* (Ps 23:6). For this reason even eternal life itself, which we shall certainly have in the end without end, is given as recompense for preceding merits, but because the same merits to which it is given as recompense were not produced by us through our own abilities but were produced in us through grace, it too is called grace for no other reason than that it is given gratuitously, not because it is not given to our merits but because even the very merits to which it is given were given to us. But in the place where we find that eternal life is also called grace, we have in the same magnificent defender of grace, the apostle Paul, the words, *The wages of sin is death, but the grace of God is eternal life in Christ Jesus our Lord* (Rom 6:23).

20. See, I beg you, the great brevity with which he vigilantly sets down his words, and, if they are examined carefully, the obscurity of this question is somewhat cleared up. For, when he said, *The wages of sin is death*, who would not judge that he would go on most properly and logically if he said, "But the wages of righteousness is eternal life, and it is true that, just as death is paid as wages to the merit of sin, so eternal life is paid as wages to the merit of righteousness." Or, if he did not want to say "of righteousness," he would say "of faith," because *the righteous person lives from faith* (Rom 1:17; Gal 3:11; Heb 10:38; Hb 2:4). For this reason it is also called a recompense in many passages of the sacred scriptures, but righteousness or faith is never called a recompense,

because a recompense is given to righteousness or faith. But what a recompense is for a worker, wages are for a soldier.

21. But pride tries so much to come upon great persons unawares that the blessed Apostle said that an angel of Satan was given to him to strike him lest he raise up his head in presumption.[732] Against this plague of pride, then, he fought most vigilantly, saying, *The wages of sin is death* (Rom 6:23). It is correctly called *wages* because it is owed, because it is deservedly given, because it is recompense for merit. Then, lest righteosness extol itself over human good merit, just as human bad merit is undoubtedly sin, he did not say by way of contrast, "The wages of righteousness is eternal life," but, *The grace of God is eternal life*. And so that we would seek no other way apart from the mediator, he added, *in Christ Jesus our Lord* (Rom 6:23), as if to say, "Having heard that the wages of sin is death, why do you try to extol yourself, O human pride—not righteousness, but clearly pride under the name of righteousness? Why do you try to extol yourself and demand eternal life, the very opposite of death, as if it were the wages you deserved? It is true righteousness to which eternal life is owed. But if it is true righteousness, it does not come from you, but *it is from above, coming down from the Father of lights* (Jas 1:17). In order to have it, if in fact you have it, you have certainly received; *for what* good *do you have that you have not received?* (1 Cor 4:7) Hence, if you, a human being, are going to receive eternal life, it is the wages of righteousness, but it is grace for you, since righteousness itself is grace for you. For it would be given to you as a recompense owed to you, if you had from yourself the righteousness to which it is owed. But now *we have received from his fullness* not only the grace by which we are now living righteously in the midst of our labors up to the end but also *grace in return for this grace* (Jn 1:16), so that we might afterward live in rest without end." Faith believes nothing more salutary than this, because the intellect finds nothing truer, and we should listen to the prophet as he says, *Unless you believe, you will not understand* (Is 7:9 LXX).

6, 22. "But," he says, "people excused themselves who did not want to live a good and faithful life, saying, 'What did we do who are living a bad life, since we did not receive the grace by which we might live a good life?'" They cannot truthfully say that they do no evil because they live a bad life. For, if they do no evil, they are living a good life. But if they are living a bad life, they live a bad life because of their own sin—either that which they contracted from their origin or that which they added to it. But if they are *vessels of anger that were made for destruction* (Rom 9:22), which is given them as their recompense, they should ascribe this to themselves, because they were made from that lump of clay[733] which God rightly and justly condemned on account of the one sin in which all

---

732. See 2 Cor 12:7.
733. See Rom 9:21.

sinned.[734] But if they are *vessels of mercy* (Rom 9:23) made from that same lump, to whom he chose not to give the punishment due to them, they should not puff themselves up but glorify him who showed them the mercy they did not deserve, and if they think otherwise, he will perhaps reveal this to them as well.[735]

23. Finally, how will these people excuse themselves? They will undoubtedly do so by that brief question which the Apostle raised for himself as an objection, as if coming from their lips, so that they say, *Why does he still blame us? For who can resist his will?* (Rom 9:19) For this is to say, "Why is there a complaint about us because we offend God by living bad lives, since no one can resist the will of him who hardened our hearts by not showing us mercy?" If, then, they are not ashamed to contradict not us but the Apostle with this excuse, why should we be ashamed to say the very same thing that the Apostle said, *Who are you, a human being, to answer back to God? Does the clay pot say to the potter: Why did you make me so? Does not the potter of the clay have power to make from the same lump*, which was, of course, justly and deservedly condemned, *one vessel for honor*, which it did not deserve, on account of gratuitous mercy, *and another vessel for dishonor*, which it deserved, on account of righteous anger, *and in order to make known the riches of his glory toward the vessels of mercy* (Rom 9:20-21,23)? In that way he shows what he gives to these latter when the vessels of anger receive the punishment that all equally deserved. For the time being it is enough for a Christian, who is still living by faith and does not yet see what is perfect but knows only in part, to know or to believe that God sets no one free except out of gratuitous mercy through our Lord Jesus Christ and condemns no one except in accordance with the most just truth through the same Lord of ours, Jesus Christ.[736] But as to why he sets free or does not set free one person rather than another, let him who is able search out the great depth of his judgments, but let him beware of falling off the cliff.[737] For *is there injustice in God? Heaven forbid!* (Rom 9:12) But *his judgments are inscrutable, and his ways unsearchable* (Rom 11:33).

24. On the other hand, it can with reason be said of those of an adult age: These people refused to understand in order that they might do good.[738] And, what is worse, these others understood and did not obey because, as Scripture says, *A stubborn servant will not be corrected by words. For, even if he understands, he will not obey.* (Prv 29:19 LXX) Why will he not obey except because of his most evil will? And he deserves a more severe condemnation from God's justice. For more will be demanded of one to whom more is given.[739] Scripture,

---

734. See Rom 5:12.
735. See Phil 3:15.
736. See Rom 1:17; Gal 3:11; Heb 10:38; Hab 2:4.
737. See 1 Cor 13:9.10.12; Rom 9:14.
738. See Ps 36:4.
739. See Lk 12:47-48.

of course, says that they are without excuse who are not ignorant of the truth, and in them wickedness persists. *For the anger of God is being revealed from heaven*, the apostle says, *against all the impiety and injustice of those human beings who hold the truth in their iniquity, since what is known about God is obvious to them. For God has shown it to them. For from the creation of the world the invisible reality of God is seen, having been understood through those things that have been made, even his everlasting power and divinity, so that they are without excuse.* (Rom 1:18-20)

25. The Apostle says that they are without excuse who were able to see his invisible reality, which had been understood through the things that have been made, and who still did not obey the truth but remained unjust and sinful. For they did not lack knowledge, but *knowing God*, he says, *they did not glorify him as God or give him thanks* (Rom 1:21). How much more, then, are they without excuse who, instructed by his law, presume to be leaders of the blind and, though teaching others, do not teach themselves, who preach that one should not steal, and they steal, and all the other things of which the Apostle speaks! To them he says, indeed, *For this reason you are inexcusable, every one of you who judge. After all, in judging another you condemn yourself. For you do the same acts that you condemn.* (Rom 2:1)

26. The Lord himself also says in the Gospel, *If I had not come and spoken to them, they would have no sin. But now they do not have an excuse for their sin.* (Jn 15:22) He certainly did not mean that those people would have no sin who were filled with many other and great sins. Rather, he meant that, if he had not come, they would not have had the sin of not believing in him when they heard him. He says that they do not have an excuse to say, "We did not hear him, and for that reason we did not believe in him." Human pride, of course, as if presuming upon the strength of free choice, thinks that it has an excuse when the fact that it sins seems to be due to ignorance and not to the will.

27. In terms of this excuse the Divine Scripture says that they are all without excuse whom it proves guilty of sinning knowingly. And yet the just judgment of God does not spare those either who did not hear him, *For whoever have sinned without the law will perish without the law* (Rom 2:12). And although they think that they have an excuse, he does not accept this excuse who knows that he made man righteous[740] and gave him the command to obey and that the sin which was also passed on to his descendants stemmed only from the choice of his will, which he used wrongly. For those who have not sinned are not condemned, since that sin was passed on to all from the one in whom all sinned in common prior to any personal sins in their individual lives.[741] And for this reason every sinner is without excuse either because of the guilt of origin or because

---

740. See Eccl 7:30.
741. See Rom 5:12.

of what is added by one's own will, whether or not one has knowledge, whether or not one judges.[742] For ignorance itself in those who refuse to understand is undoubtedly a sin, but in those who could not understand it is the punishment of sin. In neither, then, is there a just excuse but only just condemnation.

28. For this reason the words of God declare that they are without excuse who sin not in ignorance but with knowledge; thus they may see that they are without excuse in terms of the condemnation of the pride by which they presume too much upon the strength of their own will. For they do not have an excuse because of their ignorance, and they do not as yet have the righteousness for which they were presuming that their own will was sufficient. But that man to whom the Lord gave the grace of both knowing and obeying said, *Knowledge of sin came through the law* (Rom 3:20), and, *I knew sin only through the law, for I would not have known concupiscence if the law had not said: You shall not desire* (Rom 7:7; Ex 20:17; Dt 5:21; 7:25). Nor does he want us to understand someone ignorant of the law with its commands but lacking the deliverance of grace when he says, *I take delight in the law of God in accord with my inner self* (Rom 7:22). And not only with this knowledge of the law but also with delight in it he afterward says, *Wretched man that I am! Who will set me free from the body of this death? The grace of God through Jesus Christ our Lord!* (Rom 7:24-25) No one, therefore, sets anyone free from the wounds of that butcher except the grace of the one Savior. No one sets free those sold into subjection to sin from the chains of the jailer except the grace of the redeemer.

29. And for this reason all who want themselves to be excused for wickedness and sinfulness are punished with full justice because those who are set free are set free only by grace. For, if their excuse were just, it would not be grace but justice that set them free from punishment. But since only grace sets one free, it finds nothing righteous in the one it sets free: no will, no action, not even an excuse. For, if this excuse were just, whoever uses it would be set free by merit, not by grace. For we know that certain people are set free by the grace of Christ, even from among those who say, *Why does he still complain? For who can resist his will?* (Rom 9:19) If this excuse is just, then grace is no longer gratuitous, but they are set free on account of the justice of this excuse. But if it is grace by which they are set free, this excuse is by no means just. For it is true grace by which one is set free when one does not receive this as a debt of justice. Nothing else, then, happens in those who say, *Why does he still complain? For who can resist his will?* but what we read in the Book of Solomon, *The stupidity of a man corrupts his ways, but in his heart he makes God his excuse* (Prv 18:22).

30. God, therefore, makes *the vessels of anger for destruction* in order to show his anger and to demonstrate his power, by which he makes good use even of evil, and *in order to make known the riches of his glory toward the vessels of mercy*

---

742. See Rom 2:1.

(Rom 9:21-23), which he makes for an honor not owed to the mass that deserves damnation but given by the generosity of his grace. And yet in those same vessels of anger made for dishonor, which they deserved on account of what the mass merited, that is, in human beings created on account of the good- ness of their nature but destined for punishment on account of their sins, God himself could condemn but not produce the sinfulness that the truth blames with full justice.[743] For, just as human nature, which is undoubtedly worthy of praise, is attributed to his will, so sin, which deserves condemnation without anyone's objecting to this, is attributed to the will of the man. This will of the man either passed on hereditary sin to his descendants, whom he contained in himself when he sinned, or in addition it acquired other sins when each human being lived wickedly in his own life. But neither from the sin contracted from our origin nor from the sins that each person accumulates in his own life, whether by not understanding or by refusing to understand, or that, after having also learned of the law, one increases by adding transgression, is anyone set free and justified except by *the grace of God through Jesus Christ our Lord* (Rom 7:25). One is set free not merely by the forgiveness of sins but also, first, by the infusion of faith and fear of God and by the salutary gift of love for prayer and its practice, until God heals all our illness, redeems our life from corruption, and crowns us in compassion and mercy.[744]

7, 31. But the people who think that God shows partiality,[745] if in one and the same situation his mercy descends upon some while his anger remains over others, lose all the force of their human arguments when it comes to infants. For I want to pass over for the moment the punishment that includes even the infants, however recently born from their mothers' wombs, of which the Apostle says, *Through the sin of the one all human beings entered into condemnation*, a condemnation from which only he sets us free of whom the same Apostle says, *Through the righteousness of one all human beings come to the righteousness of life* (Rom 5:18). I will pass over this for the moment, then, and will say only that, frightened by the authority of the Gospel or rather crushed by the completely unanimous agreement of the Christian peoples in the faith, the Pelagians also concede without the least opposition that no infant enters the kingdom of the heaven without having been reborn of water and the Spirit.[746] What reason, I ask, will they give as to why one is cared for so that it leaves this life after being baptized, while another expires after being entrusted to the hands of non-believers or even of believers before being presented by them for baptism? Are they going to ascribe this to fate or to fortune? I do not think that they will plunge into such great madness if they want to hold onto the name of Christians to some slight degree.

---

743. See Ps 45:8; Heb 1:9.
744. See Ps 103:3-4.
745. See Acts 10:34.
746. See Jn 3:5.

32. Why, then, will no infant enter the kingdom of the heavens without having received the bath of rebirth?[747] Has an infant chosen for himself non-believing or negligent parents to be born from? What shall I say of the countless unexpected and sudden deaths by which the infants of even pious Christians are overtaken and snatched away from baptism, while, on the other hand, the children of sacrilegious folks and enemies of Christ somehow come into the hands of Christians and leave this world with the sacrament of rebirth? What will those people say at this point who maintain that some human merits come first in order that grace may be given lest God show favoritism?[748] What merits, finally, came first in this case? If you have in mind the merits of the same infants, they have none of their own, and both in common belong to that mass of condemnation. If you look to the merits of the parents, those whose children perished by sudden deaths without Christ's baptism had good merits, while those whose children came to the sacraments of the Church though the intervention of Christians had evil merits. And yet the providence of God, for whom the hairs of our head are numbered and without whose will not even a sparrow falls to the earth,[749] is not subject to fate, nor is it impeded by chance events or defiled by any injustice. Yet his providence does not take care of all the infants of his own children so that they may be reborn for the heavenly kingdom but does take care of the infants of some unbelievers. This infant, born of believing parents and welcomed with the joy of parents, suffocated by the sleepiness of its mother or nurse, becomes a stranger to and is excluded from the faith of his parents; that infant is born of wicked adultery, exposed by the cruel fear of its mother, taken up by the merciful goodness of strangers, baptized out of their Christian concern, and becomes a member and partaker of the eternal kingdom. Let them think of these examples; let them ponder them; let them dare at this point to say that God either shows favoritism with his grace or rewards preceding merits.

33. For, though they try to find some merits, either good or bad, at a later age, what will they say about these infants, since one of them could not merit the violence of suffocation for any evil merits of its own and the other could not merit the care of the one who baptized it? They are filled with excessive folly and blindness if, after considering these examples, they still do not agree to cry out with us, *O the depth of the riches of the wisdom and knowledge of God! How inscrutable are his judgments and unsearchable his ways!* (Rom 11:33) Let them not, then, oppose the gratuitous mercy of God with a most stubborn insanity. Let them allow the Son of Man *to seek and save* at any age *what was lost* (Lk 19:10; Mt 18:11). And let them not dare to judge about his inscrutable judgments why in one and the same situation his mercy descends upon one and his anger remains over another.

---

747. See Tit 3:5.
748. See Acts 10:34.
749. See Mt 10:30.29.

8, 34. For who are these people that they should answer back to God?[750] For Rebecca was carrying twins from a single union with Isaac, our father. Though, when they were not yet born, they had not done anything good or bad, in order that the plan of God might remain in accord with his choice, a choice based on grace, not on a debt, a choice by which he made, not found, those worthy of being chosen not because of their works but because of God's call, he said that the older would serve the younger.[751] The blessed Apostle also used in support of this statement the testimony of a much later prophet, *I loved Jacob, but I hated Esau* (Rom 9:13; Mal 1:2-3), in order that what was present in the predestination of God through grace before they were born might be understood clearly afterward through the prophet. For what did he love in Jacob before he was born and had done anything good or bad but the gratuitous gift of his own mercy? And what did he hate in Esau before he was born and had done anything bad but original sin? For in the former he would not love righteousness that he had not made, nor would he hate in the latter the nature that he made good.

35. But it is surprising to see the steep cliffs they hurl themselves over when they are trapped by these difficulties and fear the nets of the truth. They say, "He hated one and loved the other of those not yet born because he foresaw their future works." Who would not be surprised that the Apostle lacked this very clever idea? He certainly did not see this when, as if the question were raised as an objection for him by an opponent, he did not instead give this reply that is so short, so clear, and—as they suppose—so absolutely true. For, when he proposed an awesome question, namely, how it could be correctly said of those who were not yet born and had not done anything either good or bad that God loved the one and hated the other, after having posed the question for himself and expressed the concern of his hearer with the words, *What then shall we say?* He replied, *Is there injustice in God? Heaven forbid!* (Rom 9:14) This, then, was the place for him to say what these people think, "For God foresaw their future works when he said that the older would serve the younger." Yet the Apostle did not say this but rather, so that no one would be able to boast of the merits of his own works, he wanted what he said to be able to emphasize the grace and glory of God. For, when he said, "*Heaven forbid* that there should be *injustice in God,*" it was as if we said to him, "How do you explain this since you say that it is not because of works but because of God's call that it was said, *The older will serve the younger?*" (Rom 9:11-12; Gn 25:23) The Apostle said that God *said to Moses, I will show pity to whom I will show pity, and I will be merciful to whom I will be merciful. Therefore, it does not depend on the one who wills or the one who runs, but upon God who shows mercy.* (Rom 9:15-16; Ex 33:19) Where now are the merits, where are the works either past or future, carried out or to be carried out, by the strength of free choice? Did not the Apostle make a clear statement of his

---

750. See Rom 9:20.
751. See Rom 9:10-12; Gn 25:21-23.

endorsement of gratuitous grace, that is, of true grace? *Has not God made foolish the wisdom* (1 Cor 1:20) of the heretics?

36. But what was at issue that the Apostle should say this when he mentioned the example of the twins? What was he trying to persuade them of? What did he want to teach? It was what their madness opposed, what the proud do not grasp, what they refuse to believe who, *not knowing the righteousness of God and wanting to establish their own righteousness, are not subject to the righteousness of God* (Rom 10:4). The Apostle was, of course, concerned with grace, and for this reason he mentioned the children of the promise. For only God does what God promises, for it is reasonable and true that a human being makes a promise and God carries it out, but it is a sign of proud impiety and a wicked idea that a human being should say that he does what God promises.

37. Emphasizing the children of the promise, then, he showed that this was first symbolized by Isaac, the son of Abraham. For the work of God is seen more clearly in him who was born contrary to the usual order of nature from a sterile womb worn out with old age so that, in the children of God who were foretold to be coming, this would be a sign of the work of God, not of human beings. *From Isaac*, he says, *your descendants will take their name. That is, it is not children of the flesh who are children of God; but the children of the promise will be counted as offspring. For this is the word of the promise: At that time I shall come, and Sarah will have a son. And not only that, but Rebecca also conceived twins from one union with Isaac, our father.* (Rom 9:7-10) What did it mean that he added *from one union* except to prevent Jacob from boasting not only of his own merits or of the merits of other ancestors but even of the will of that one father, which was perhaps changed for the better? It meant to prevent him from saying that the creator loved him because, when his father begot him, he was more praiseworthy for his better conduct. He said *from one union* because their father had at that point the same merit in fathering them and their mother had the same merit in conceiving them. For, even if their mother carried them enclosed in her womb until she gave birth to them and perhaps changed in her desire and loves, she of course changed not regarding one but regarding both, whom she bore equally in her womb.

38. We must, then, look to the intention of the Apostle to see how, in order to emphasize grace, he did not want the one of whom it was said, *I loved Jacob* (Mal 1:2), to boast except in the Lord. For, before they did anything good or bad, God loves the one and hates the other, though they were from the same father, from the same mother, and from the same union. In that way Jacob could understand that only by grace could he have been set apart from that mass of original sinfulness when he sees that his brother, with whom he shared a common situation, merited to be condemned. He says, *When they were not yet born and had not done anything good or bad, in order that the plan of God might remain in accord with his choice, not because of works but because of God's call it was said to him, The older will serve the younger* (Rom 9:11-12).

39. In another passage the Apostle shows most clearly that God's choice is made by grace without any preceding merits from works. He says, *In that way a remnant was saved also at that time according to a choice that was grace. But if it is by grace, it is no longer by works; otherwise, grace is no longer grace.* (Rom 11:5-6) In accord with this grace he also logically makes use of the testimony of the prophet; he says, *As Scripture says, I loved Jacob, but I hated Esau,* and he immediately adds, *What then shall we say? Is there injustice in God? Heaven forbid!* But why should heaven forbid this? Is it on account of the future works of both of them that God foresaw? On the contrary; heaven forbid this as well! *For he said to Moses, I will show pity to whom I will show pity, and I will be merciful to whom I will be merciful. Therefore, it does not depend on the one who wills or the one who runs, but upon God who shows mercy.* And in order that in the vessels that were made for the destruction that was owed to the condemned mass the vessels that were made from the same mass for honor might recognize what the divine mercy has given them, he says, *For Scripture says to Pharaoh, I have raised you up in order that I may reveal my power in you and in order that my name may be glorified in the whole world.* Finally, he concludes with regard to both, *Therefore, he shows mercy to whom he wills and he hardens whom he wills.* (Rom 9:13-18) He in whom there is no injustice does this. He shows mercy, therefore, by a gratuitous gift, but he hardens by most just punishment.

40. But the unbelieving presumption of the proud and the damnable excuse of someone punished may still say, *Why does he still blame us? For who resists his will?* Let him say this, and let them hear what answer is appropriate for such a human being, *Who are you, a human being, to answer back to God?* (Rom 9:19-20), and the rest that I have already discussed often enough to the extent that I could. Let him hear this and not scorn it. But if he does scorn it, let him realize that his heart has been hardened in order to scorn it. If, however, he does not scorn it, let him believe that he too has been helped in order not to scorn it—but hardened as he deserved and helped by grace.

9, 41. For, even if God foresaw the future works of the twin sons of the patriarch Isaac, for they both lived and reached old age, and for this reason loved Jacob but hated Esau—an idea whose great blindness we have already made clear—one cannot say that God foresees the works of infants who are going to die so that he may take care that one receives baptism and not take care of the other. For how can we call those works future works since there will not be any?

42. "But," they object, "God foresees in those whom he takes from this life how each one would live if he were going to live and for this reason he also causes to die without baptism one who he knows was going to live sinfully. And in that way he punishes in him evil works, not those he did but those he was going to do." If, then, God also punishes evil actions that were not done, let them first notice how false is their promise that infants who die without baptism will not enter into condemnation. For, if they were not baptized because they were going to live bad lives if they lived, they will undoubtedly be condemned on account

of this bad life, if even those sins that were not going to be committed are condemned. Secondly, if God takes care that they receive the sacrament of baptism who he knows were going to live good lives if they lived, why does he not keep in this life all those who he knows will adorn it with good works? Why do some of those who are baptized also live long and very bad lives and at times even go as far as apostasy? If even sins that are not yet committed are justly punished, why did God not throw out of paradise beforehand that first pair of sinners, who he certainly knew were going to sin, in order that they might not commit in paradise a sin that was so inappropriate to so holy a place? Then, what does God give to one who is carried off *so that malice does not change his mind and so that deception does not mislead his soul* (Wis 4:11), if those sins are also punished that, though he did not commit them, he was nonetheless, going to commit if he continued to live? Finally, why does God not provide better for a person about to die, so that he might receive the bath of rebirth[752] if he was going to live a bad life if he lived? For in that way the sins he was going to commit would be forgiven in baptism. For who is so stupid as to deny that those sins can be forgiven in baptism that he says can be punished without baptism?

10, 43. But in arguing against those people who, though they have been completely refuted, try to persuade others that God punishes even sins that have not been committed, we have to fear that we may be thought to have made up these charges against them. They may in no way be believed so foolish as either to hold these views or to try to convince anyone of them. And yet, if I had not heard them say these things, I would not think that they had to be refuted. For they are bound by the authority of the Divine Scriptures and by the rite of the Church handed down from of old and held firmly in the baptism of infants. There it is most clearly shown that infants are set free from the dominion of the devil when they undergo exorcism and when they reply through those who present them that they renounce the devil. And since these heretics find nowhere to go, they continue on headlong into stupidity as long as they refuse to change their mind.

44. They certainly think that it is with great insight that they say, "How is sin passed on to the children of believers, since we have no doubt that it was forgiven in the parents through baptism?" They imply that carnal generation cannot have what only spiritual regeneration takes away or that in true baptism the weakness stemming from concupiscence of the flesh is immediately healed, just as its guilt is immediately abolished, but by the grace of being reborn, not by the condition of being born. Hence, if anyone is born through this concupiscence, even from someone reborn, it will undoubtedly harm him when he is born, unless he himself is likewise reborn. But whatever difficulty there is regarding this question, the workers in Christ's field are not kept from baptizing infants for the forgiveness of sins, whether they are born from believers or non-believers, just as farmers are not kept from turning wild olive trees into domesticated olive trees

---

752. See Tit 3:5

through the practice of grafting, whether they arise from wild olive trees or domesticated ones. For, if a farmer is asked why, though a domesticated olive tree is different from a wild olive tree, only a wild olive tree comes from the seed of both of them,[753] the farmer does not stop the work of grafting, even if he cannot answer the question. Otherwise, while thinking that the saplings sprung from the seed of the domesticated olive tree are domesticated olive trees, his stupid laziness causes that whole field to fill up with harsh barrenness.

45. Now when they were pressed by the weight of the truth, they thought up another idea. But *the Lord is faithful in his words* (Ps 145:13), and for this reason his Church in no way falsely baptizes infants for the forgiveness of sins, but, if the rite is performed with faith, there certainly takes place what the words say. What Christian, then, would not laugh at the idea they thought up when the most obvious weight of the truth was crushing them, no matter how clever he might find it? For they say, "Infants in fact respond truthfully by the lips of those who present them that they believe in the forgiveness of sins, yet not because their sins are forgiven but because they believe that sins are forgiven in the Church or in baptism in those people in whom they are found, not in those who have none." And for this reason they deny that "infants are baptized for the forgiveness of sins in the sense that this forgiveness is produced in them, since they maintain that infants have no sin but that, though they are without sin, they are still baptized in that baptism by which the forgiveness of sins is produced in certain sinners."

46. It is certainly possible for this slippery sophism to be refuted with greater subtlety and cleverness at leisure. Given all their cunning they still do not find anything to say to the fact that infants undergo exorcism and exsufflation. For these rites are undoubtedly not carried out truthfully if the devil does not have dominion over them. If, however, he does have dominion over them and they truly undergo exorcism and exsufflation, how does he, who is of course the prince of sinners, have dominion over them except through sin? Hence, if they now blush with shame and do not dare to say that these rites are carried out in the Church as lies, they should admit that even in infants Christ seeks what had been lost. For only through sin had there been lost what can only be sought and can only be found through grace. But thanks be to God that, though they argue against the forgiveness of sins so that people will not believe that it takes place in infants, they at least still admit that infants already believe, though they do so through the hearts and the lips of adults. Just as, then, they hear the Lord who says, *Whoever is not reborn of water and of the Spirit will not enter the kingdom of heaven* (Jn 3:5), for which reason they grant that the infants must be baptized, so let them hear the same Lord when he says, *One who does not believe will be condemned* (Mk 16:16). For, just as they admit that they are reborn by the ministry of those who baptize them, so they admit that they also believe through the hearts and lips of those who make the responses. If, then, infants are not bound

---

753. See Rom 11:24.

by any chain of original sin, let them dare to say that the just God will condemn them in their innocence.

47. If this letter is long and adds a burden to your work, pardon me, because I forcibly interrupted my work in order to write to you and discuss these topics with you, after your letter invited me to do so by the signs of your good will toward us. If you know of any other argument that they think up against the Catholic faith, and whatever you teach in opposition to them out of a faithful and clearly pastoral love so that they do not ravage the weak among the Lord's flock, inform us of this. The restlessness of the heretics certainly rouses us as if out of a lazy sleep to search the Scriptures with great watchfulness in order to confront the heretics so that they do not harm the flock of Christ. In that way, by the manifold grace of the savior, God transforms what the enemy devises for our destruction into a help for us, *because for those who love God all things work together for the good* (Rom 5:28). My dearest brother, may you always live for God and be mindful of us.

LETTER 214

Augustine to Valentine, the abbot of the monastery of Hadrumetum (426-427)

Just before Easter in 426 or more probably in 427, Augustine wrote to Valentine, the abbot of the monastery of Hadrumetum. Florus, a monk of that monastery, had discovered Augustine's Letter 194 on the subject of grace, which had been addressed to Sixtus in Evodius' monastery in Uzalis. He had the letter copied and brought it back to his own monastery, where it created a disturbance among the monks. Some argued that, in light of Augustine's doctrine on grace, superiors should not rebuke monks for wrongdoing but should simply pray for them. Augustine wrote two works for Valentine, *Rebuke and Grace* and *Grace and Free Choice*.

Augustine tells Valentine of the arrival in Hippo of two monks, Cresconius and Felix, who reported to him the disturbance in the monastery of Hadrumetum over free choice and grace (paragraph 1). He exhorts the monks to come to an understanding in which they will maintain the existence of free choice as well as the need for grace (paragraph 2). He explains that his letter to Sixtus, which had caused the disturbance at Hadrumetum, was written against the Pelagians, who claimed that grace was given in accord with human merits so that human beings might boast in their own strength and not in the Lord (paragraph 3). On account of that heresy, Augustine explains, he wrote the letter to Sixtus in which he insisted that we have our good works, our pious prayers, and our faith only from the grace of God (paragraph 4).

Augustine tells Valentine that he wanted to send him a variety of documents on the Pelagian heresy but was not able to do so, since the monks were in a hurry to return to Hadrumetum for Easter, though they did not in fact return until after Easter, as we learn from another letter (paragraph 5). He admits that the question of grace and free choice is very difficult to understand and encourages Valentine to send him the monk who has difficulties with his work (paragraph 6). He urges Valentine to believe in the meanwhile the words of God and to pray that he may come to understand what he believes (paragraph 7).

To our brother, Valentine, our most beloved lord worthy of honor among the members of Christ, and to the brothers with you, Augustine sends greetings in the Lord.

1. Two young men, Cresconius and Felix, came to us, saying that they were from your community. They reported to us that your monastery was troubled by some disagreement because certain men among you preach grace in such a way as to deny that human beings have free choice. And what is worse, they say that on the day of judgment God will not recompense *each one in accord*

with his works (Mt 16:27; Rom 2:6; Rev 22:12). Yet they also indicated that the majority of you do not hold these views but admit that free choice is helped by the grace of God in order that we may think and do what is right so that, when the Lord comes to recompense *each one in accord with his works*, he may find our good works, which *God has prepared in order that we may walk in them* (Eph 2:10). Those who hold these latter views are correct.

2. *I beg you, therefore, my brothers*, as the Apostle begged the Corinthians, *in the name of our Lord Jesus Christ that you all say the same thing, and let there be no divisions among you* (1 Cor 1:10). For the Lord Jesus, as is written in the Gospel of John the apostle, *did not* first *come in order to judge the world, but in order that the world might be saved by him* (Jn 3:17). But afterwards, as the apostle Paul writes, *God will judge the world* (Rom 3:6) when, as the whole Church professes in the creed, "he will come to judge the living and the dead."[754] If, then, there is no grace of God, how will he save the world? And if there is no free choice, how will he judge the world? Hence, understand in accord with this faith my book or letter,[755] which those I mentioned above brought with them to you so that you may neither deny the grace of God nor defend free choice in such a way that you make it independent of the grace of God, as if without grace we could think or do anything at all as God wants. For we absolutely cannot! On this account, after all, when the Lord was speaking of the fruit of righteousness, he said to his disciples, *Without me you can do nothing* (Jn 15:5).

3. Hence you should know that the previously-mentioned letter to Sixtus of the Roman church was written in answer to the new Pelagian heretics. They say that the grace of God is given in accord with our merits so that one who boasts may boast not in the Lord but in himself, that is, in a human being, not in the Lord. The Apostle forbids this when he says, *Let no one boast in a human being* (1 Cor 3:21), and in another place he says, *Let one who boasts boast in the Lord* (1 Cor 1:31; 2 Cor 10:17). But when these heretics suppose that they themselves can make themselves righteous, as if God did not give this to them but they themselves gave it to themselves, they certainly boast not in the Lord but in themselves. The Apostle says to such people, *Who has set you apart?* (1 Cor 4:7) The reason he says this is that, from the mass of that perdition which Adam produced, only God sets a human being apart in order to make him into a vessel of honor, not into a vessel of dishonor.[756] But because, when a carnal and vainly proud human being hears, *Who has set you apart?* he could reply and say, whether by word or in thought, "My faith has set me apart; my prayer has set me apart; my righteousness has set me apart," the Apostle immediately counters

---

754. These words found in 2 Tm 4:1 and 1 Pt 4:5 appear in most Christian creeds from the beginning of the third century. In his *Faith and the Creed*, Augustine explained the creed to the bishops of Africa. For the creed used at Hippo see J. N. D. Kelly, *Early Christian Creeds*, 3rd ed. (New York 1972) 176.

755. Augustine refers to Letter 194 to Sixtus.

756. See Rom 9:21.

his thoughts and says, *What do you have that you have not received? But if you have received, why do you boast as if you have not received?* (1 Cor 4:7) For they boast in this way, as if they have not received, when they suppose that they make themselves righteous and therefore boast in themselves, not in the Lord.

4. For this reason, in this letter that reached you, I proved by the testimonies of the Holy Scriptures, which you can examine in them, that we could never have our good works and pious prayers and correct faith if we did not receive them from him of whom the apostle James says, *Every good gift and every perfect gift comes from above, descending from the Father of lights* (Jas 1:17). Let no one, therefore, say that he has received the grace of God because of the merits of his works or because of the merits of his prayers or because of the merits of his faith. That is utterly false. It is not that there is no merit, whether the good merit of pious people or the bad merit of sinners. Otherwise, how will he judge the world? Rather, the mercy and grace of God produces a person's conversion. Of this the Psalm says, *My God, his mercy will go ahead of me* (Ps 59:11), in order that the sinner may be justified, that is, be made a righteous person from a sinner, and may begin to have the good merit which the Lord will crown when he judges the world.

5. There were many documents that I wanted to send you; by reading them you could acquaint yourself more precisely and fully with this whole issue, which has been dealt with in episcopal councils in opposition to the same Pelagian heretics. But the brothers who came to us from your number were in a hurry, and through them we have not written a reply to you but have simply written to you. For they did not bring to us any letter of Your Charity. We nonetheless welcomed them, for their simplicity made it quite clear to us that they could not have made up any such story for us. They were, however, in a hurry so that they could celebrate the feast of Easter with you.[757] By the help of the Lord, may so holy a day find you at peace rather than at odds with one another.

6. You will, however, do better—something for which I pray very much—if you do not hesitate to send me that monk by whom they say that they were disturbed.[758] For he either does not understand my book, or he himself may be misunderstood when he tries to resolve and untangle a most difficult question, which only a few can understand. For it is the question about the grace of God which caused those who did not understand to suppose that the apostle Paul said, *Let us do evil that good may come of it* (Rom 3:8). For this reason the apostle Peter says in his Second Letter, *Hence, my dear brothers, while we await these things, strive that God may find you in peace without blemish and without fault, and consider the patience of our Lord as salvation, as our beloved brother, Paul, wrote to you in accord with the wisdom that was given him. For in all his letters*

---

757. From the following letter we learn that the monks did in fact remain with Augustine past Easter for further instruction on the Pelagian heresy.
758. In light of the final sentence of Letter 215 it would seem that Augustine means Florus.

he spoke of these topics. In them there are some things difficult to understand, and the unlearned and unstable distort them to their own destruction, just as they also do with the other scriptures. (2 Pt 3:14-16)

7. Be attentive, then, to the frightening words of such a great Apostle, and where you think that you do not understand, believe for the time being the words of God that there exist both the free choice of a human being and the grace of God, without the help of which free choice can neither turn back to God nor make progress toward God. And pray that you may also wisely understand what you piously believe. You have free choice, after all, for this very purpose, that is, that you may wisely understand. For, if we did not have understanding and wisdom through free choice, we would not have been commanded in the words of Scripture, *Have understanding, then, you among the people who are lacking in wisdom, and become wise at last, you fools* (Ps 94:8). By the very fact that we have been commanded and ordered to have understanding and wisdom, our obedience is required,[759] and that obedience cannot exist without free choice. But if we could bring it about by free choice without the help of grace that we have understanding and wisdom, we would not say to God, *Give me understanding that I may learn your commandments* (Ps 119:125). Nor would it be written in the Gospel, *Then he opened their minds that they might understand the Scriptures* (Lk 24:45). Nor would the apostle James say, *But if anyone among you lacks wisdom, let him ask for it from God who gives to all generously and without reproach, and it will be given to him* (Jas 1:5). The Lord, however, is powerful, and I pray that he may grant to you and to us that by the fastest means possible we may rejoice over your peace and agreement. I send you greetings not only in my own name but also in the name of the brothers with me, and I beg you to pray for us in harmony and with persistence. May the Lord be with you. Amen.

---

759. R. Teske has followed the reading of *requiritur* found in PL in place of *requirit* in the CSEL edition.

LETTER 215

Augustine to Valentine,
the abbot of the monastery of Hadrumetum (427)

Shortly after Easter, most probably in 427, Augustine again wrote to Valentine, the abbot of Hadrumetum. He tells Valentine that the monks who had come to him from Hadrumetum have spent Easter with him and will be returning to Valentine better instructed concerning the errors of the Pelagians (paragraph 1). He says that he has written *Grace and Free Choice* for him and is sending with it a number of papal letters and conciliar documents (paragraph 2). He mentions that he also read Cyprian's work, *The Lord's Prayer*, with the visiting monks as well as his own letter to Sixtus (paragraph 3). He explains that he has done all he could so that the monks would neither deny free choice nor suppose that free choice could do anything good without the grace of God (paragraph 4).

Augustine then turns to a passage from the Book of Proverbs, which he uses to illustrate both the existence of free choice and the need for God's grace for any good actions (paragraphs 5 to 8).

To our brother, Valentine, our most beloved lord worthy of honor among the members of Christ, and to the brothers with you, Augustine sends greetings in the Lord.

1. May I inform Your Charity that Cresconius, Felix, and the other Felix, servants of God, who came to us from your congregation, have celebrated the feast of Easter with us. We have kept them a little longer so that they might return to you better instructed against the new Pelagian heretics. A person falls into the Pelagian error if he thinks that the grace of God, which alone sets a human being free through our Lord Jesus Christ, is given in accord with some human merits. But on the other hand a person is also and no less in error who thinks that, when the Lord comes for judgment, he will not judge human beings in accord with their works—I mean those human beings who could already by reason of their age use the free choice of the will. For only small children who do not yet have their own actions, whether good ones or bad ones, will be condemned by reason of original sin alone if the grace of the savior does not come to their aid by the bath of rebirth.[760] But all the rest who, in using free choice, have added their own personal sins to original sin, will, if they are not rescued from the power of darkness by the grace of God and transferred to the kingdom of Christ,[761] receive judgment not only in accordance with the merits of their origin but also in accordance with the merits of their own will. But good persons will also receive

---

760. See Tit 3:5.
761. See Col 1:13.

their reward in accordance with the merits of their good will; they have attained this good will itself, however, through the grace of God. And in that way there are fulfilled the words of Scripture, *There will be anger and indignation, tribulation and anguish, for every human soul that does evil, the Jews first and then the Greeks, but there will be glory, honor, and peace for one whose works are good, the Jews first and then the Greeks* (Rom 2:8-10).

2. I had no need to discuss at greater length in this letter as well this most difficult question, namely, concerning the will and grace, because I had already given the monks another letter on the supposition that they were going to return earlier. And I also wrote a book for you;[762] if you read it carefully with the help of the Lord and understand it with a lively mind, I think that there will no longer be any disputes among you on this topic. The monks, however, also carry with them other writings that we believed we ought to send to you by which you may know how, by the mercy of God, the Catholic Church repelled the venom of the Pelagian heresy. These are the letters to Pope Innocent, the bishop of the city of Rome—one from the Council of the Province of Carthage, another from the Council of Numidia,[763] a more detailed letter sent to him by five bishops,[764] and his responses to these three letters.[765] There is also a letter to Pope Zosimus from an African Council[766] and his reply sent to all the bishops of the world.[767] There are also the decrees drawn up in brief statements by a later plenary council of the whole of Africa against this error,[768] and there is the previously–mentioned book of mine that I have just written for you. We have also read all these documents on the present question together with the monks, and we sent them to you along with them.

3. We also read to them the book of the blessed martyr Cyprian entitled *The Lord's Prayer*, and we showed how he taught that we must ask from our Father who is in heaven for everything that pertains to our moral conduct and the way we live correctly, so that we do not put our trust in free choice and fall away from God's grace. There we also demonstrated how the same most glorious martyr warned us that we ought to pray even for our enemies who have not yet believed in Christ, so that they may come to believe. This would, of course, be a pointless act if the Church did not believe that even the evil and unbelieving wills of human beings can be converted to the good by the grace of God. But since they said that this book of Saint Cyprian was already available in the monastery, we did not

---

762. The book is *Grace and Free Choice*.
763. These are Letters 175 and 176.
764. This is Letter 177 from the bishops Aurelius, Alypius, Augustine, Evodius, and Possidius.
765. These are Letters 181, 182, and 183.
766. This African council met in the winter of 417-418; it probably included only the bishops of Proconsular Africa.
767. Augustine refers to the *Tractoria* of Zosimus written in the summer of 418; it is extant only in fragments.
768. This was the plenary Council of Carthage held on May 18, which drew up nine canons on original sin and grace. For a translation of the canons, see St. Augustine. Answer to the Pelagians I, trans. by Roland J. Teske (Hyde Park, N.Y. 1997) 389-391.

send it to you. We also read with them the letter that I sent to Sixtus,[769] a priest of the church of Rome, which they brought with them to me, and we showed that it was written in opposition to those who say that the grace of God is given in accordance with our merits, that is, in opposition to the same Pelagians.

4. To the extent, then, that we were able, we worked with these brothers, both yours and ours, in order that they might persevere in the sound Catholic faith, which does not deny that there is free choice, whether for a good life or a bad one, but does not attribute to it such power that, apart from the grace of God, it is able to do something, whether it turns from bad to good, or makes progress toward the good with perseverance, or attains the everlasting good where it no longer fears that it may fall. In this letter I exhort you too, my dear brothers, as the Apostle exhorts all of us, *not to be more wise that one ought to be, but to be wise in moderation, as the Lord has given to each one a measure of faith* (Rom 12:3).

5. Pay attention to the warning which the Holy Spirit gives through Solomon. He says, *Make straight paths for your feet, and direct your ways so that you do not turn aside to the right or to the left. But turn your foot away from the evil way. For the Lord knows the ways on the right, but those on the left are perverse. But he will make your paths straight and will guide your journeys in peace.* (Prv 4:26-27)[770] In these works of Scripture, my brothers, consider that, if free choice did not exist, it would not say, *Make straight paths for your feet, and direct your ways so that you do not turn aside to the right or to the left.* And yet, if one could do this apart from the grace of God, it would not say later, *He will make your paths straight and will guide your journeys in peace.*

6. Do not, therefore, turn aside to the right or to the left, although the ways on the right are praised and those on the left are blamed. This, after all, is the reason he added, *But turn your foot away from the evil way*, that is, from the left. He makes this clear in the following words when he says, *For the Lord knows the ways which are on the right, but those on the left are perverse.* We ought, then, to walk in those ways which the Lord knows; of them we read in the Psalm, *The Lord knows the way of the righteous, and he will destroy the way of the wicked* (Ps 1:6). For the Lord does not know this latter way, which is on the left, just as he is going to say to those placed on the left, *I do not know you* (Mt 15:12; 7:23; Lk 13:27). But why is it that he does not know them, since he certainly knows everything good or bad about human beings? What does *I do not know you* mean but "I did not make you such"? So too, what does the statement about the Lord Jesus that he *did not know sin* (2 Cor 5:21; 1 Pt 2:22) mean but that he did not commit sin? And for this reason how should we interpret the words, *The Lord knows the ways on the right*, if not in the sense that he made the ways on the right, that is, the ways of the righteous? These are, of course, the good works that

---

769. This is the work which the monk Florus found in the monastery of Evodius at Uzalis and had transcribed and sent to Hadrumetum.
770. Augustine's Latin text is closer to the wording of the Septuagint than to that of the Vulgate.

God has prepared, as the Apostle says, *in order that we might walk in them* (Eph 2:10). But he certainly does not know the perverse ways on the left, that is, the ways of the wicked, because he did not make them for human beings, but human beings made them for themselves. For this reason he says, *But I hate the perverse ways of the evil* (Ps 119:4); these are on the left.

7. But they reply to us, "Why, then, did he say, *Do not turn aside to the right or to the left* (Prv 4:27), since it seems that he ought to have said, 'Hold to the right, and do not turn aside to the left,' if the ways on the right are good?" Why do we suppose he said this if not because the ways on the right are good such that it is nonetheless not good to turn to the right? He must be understood to turn to the right, indeed, who wants to attribute to himself and not to God the good works that pertain to the ways on the right. And so, when he said, *For the Lord knows the ways on the right, but the ways on the left are perverse,* as if someone said to him, "Why then do you not want us to turn to the right?" he continued, *But he will make your paths straight and will guide your journeys in peace* (Prv 4:27). Understand in that sense, then, the commandment given you, *Make straight paths for your feet, and direct your ways* (Prv 4:26), in order that, when you do this, you may know that the Lord God grants it to you that you do it. And you shall not turn aside to the left, though you walk in the ways on the right, not trusting in your own virtue, and he will be your virtue *who will make your paths straight and will guide your journeys in peace* (Prv 4:27).

8. Hence, dearest brothers, whoever says, "My will is sufficient for me to do good works," turns aside to the right. But, on the other hand, those turn aside to the left who think that they should give up their efforts to live well when they hear that the grace of God is preached in such a way that it is believed and understood to make human wills good from bad and also to preserve the good wills it makes. Hence they say, *Let us do evil that good may come of it* (Rom 3:8). This is the reason why I said to you, "Do not turn aside to the right or to the left," that is, neither defend free choice so that you attribute to it good works without the grace of God nor defend grace so that, as if you were safe because of it, you love evil works. God keep you from this! Posing such an objection to himself, the Apostle says, *What then shall we say? Shall we remain in sin in order that grace may abound?* (Rom 6:1) And he replies, as he ought, to these words of human beings in error who do not understand the grace of God; he says, *Heaven forbid! For, if we have died to sin, how shall we continue to live in it?* (Rom 6:2) He could have said nothing briefer or better. After all, what greater benefit does the grace of God bestow in this present evil world than that we die to sin? And for this reason the person who wants to live in sin because of that by which we die to sin is found ungrateful to grace itself. But may *God who is rich in mercy* (Eph 2:4) grant that you have sound wisdom and persevere up to the end, making progress in the good you have undertaken. Pray for this grace for yourselves; pray for it for us; pray for it for all those who love you and for those who hate you; pray for it persistently and vigilantly in brotherly peace. May you live for God. If I have merited anything from you, let brother Florus come to me.

LETTER 215A

Augustine to Valentine, the abbot of the monastery of Hadrumetum (soon after Letter 215)

Sometime after having written the previous letter Augustine again wrote to Valentine, thanking him for sending Florus to him for instruction and asking that he be sent back to Hippo again in order that Augustine might instruct the monk still further.

To Valentine, his most beloved lord and brother worthy to be embraced in the heart of Christ, Augustine sends greetings in the Lord.

I am indeed most grateful to Your Charity because you sent Brother Florus to me as I desired, and I am even more grateful to our God because I found him to be the sort of man I had hoped. But though he may seem to have returned to you somewhat late, he was with me less time than I wanted. In fact, when he was present, such weakness of the body held me in its grip for so many days that I could not be with him, my beloved lord and brother worthy to be embraced in the heart of Christ. Hence, I ask you again that you be so good as to fulfill not merely my own desire but that of both of us, and that you send him again that he may be with us for some time. For I think that this will be beneficial both for him and for us and that his fuller instruction, which he will be able to obtain through us with the help of the Lord, will be profitable for the brothers as well. May you always be pleasing to God.

LETTER 217

Augustine to Vitalis, a Catholic layman in Carthage (426-427)

Between 426 and 428, approximately, Augustine wrote to Vitalis, a Catholic layman in Carthage. From some source unknown to us Augustine had heard that Vitalis held that believing in God and assenting to the gospel were not a gift of God but something that we did by our own will. Augustine points out that Vitalis is consequently opposed to the prayers of the Church for non-believers (paragraph 1). He challenges Vitalis to state openly that Catholics should not pray for the conversion of non-believers but should only preach to them, contrary to the teaching of Cyprian and even contrary to the teaching of Paul (paragraphs 2 and 3).

Augustine warns that Vitalis is holding the error of the Pelagians, who say that grace consists only in free choice and in the law and doctrine (paragraph 4). The genuine grace of God precedes any human good will and does not find such good will but produces it (paragraph 5). Augustine appeals to Cyprian's interpretation of the Lord's Prayer to show that we should pray for the conversion of non-believers (paragraph 6). If we pray sincerely, it makes no sense to ask God to do what we ourselves could do by our own wills (paragraph 7).

Augustine argues that, if we want to defend free choice, we should not attack grace, by which our choice is made free to avoid evil and to do good (paragraph 8). As a result of the sin of Adam even newborn infants need to be rescued from the power of the devil by the grace of baptism (paragraph 9). The angels who fell now try to keep human beings from the faith without which it is not possible to please God (paragraph 10). Hence we need the help of the grace brought by the second Adam, not the help of the nature damaged by the first Adam (paragraph 11).

Grace does not consist in the nature of free choice or in the law and teaching, but is given for individual actions by the will of God (paragraph 12). In his providence God has arranged it so that he brings some persons to the faith through answering the prayers of others (paragraph 13). We should also pray for believers that they may persevere in the faith up to the end (paragraph 14). Why some are given the gift of final perseverance and others are not remains hidden from us (paragraph 15).

Augustine lists twelve propositions that embody the Catholic faith in opposition to the Pelagian errors concerning the relation between God's grace and the human will (paragraphs 16 and 17). Then he goes on to explain how grace precedes any good will on our part, as is evident especially in the case of infants (paragraph 18). The fact that all human beings are not saved points to the gratuity of grace (paragraph 19). The human will does not merit grace, which is given to those to whom it is given by God's gratuitous mercy (paragraph 20). Final perseverance too is a gratuitous gift of God (paragraph 21). Furthermore, God's grace and judgment do not depend upon what one would have done, had one lived longer (paragraph 22). And yet anyone who believes in God does so by his free will (paragraph 23). The fact that we thank God for the conversion of non-believers is a sign that their beginning to believe is his gift (paragraph 24).

Augustine points out that all twelve propositions together (mentioned in paragraphs 16-17) as well as each of them individually teach that God's grace anticipates the human will, and he asks Vitalis to write back to him if he disagrees with any of the statements (paragraph 25). Once again he shows how the prayer of the Church presupposes that faith is a gift of God (paragraph 26). The prayers of Saint Paul for non-believers and those making progress in the faith show that it is God who produces and preserves faith in the hearts of human beings (paragraph 27). As prayers for the conversion of non-believers show that faith is God's gift, so our thanking God once they have been converted shows that it is God who produces their faith (paragraphs 28 and 29). Finally, Augustine expresses his hope that Vitalis will agree that the prayers of Christians prove that faith is a gift of God's grace (paragraph 30).

Bishop Augustine, a servant of Christ and through him a servant of his servants, sends greetings in Christ to his brother Vitalis.

1, 1. Since the news reported to me about you was not good, I begged the Lord, and I still beg him until good news is reported to me, that you may not receive my letter with scorn but read it in a way conducive to salvation. If he hears this prayer of mine for you, he also gives me reason to offer thanksgiving for you. If I obtain this favor, you will undoubtedly not speak against this beginning of my letter. After all, my prayer for you is that you may be a man of correct faith. If, then, you are not displeased that we pray for this for our friends, if you recognize that this is a Christian prayer, if you either recall that you also make such prayers for your friends or recognize that you ought to, how do you say what I hear that you say—that the fact that we have the correct faith in God and assent to the Gospel is not a gift of God, but that we have this from ourselves, that is, from our own will, which God has not produced in our heart? And when you hear, "Why is it, then, that the Apostle said, *God produces in you even the will*" (Phil 2:13), you reply to this, "God causes us to will through his law, through his scriptures, which we either read or hear, but to assent or not to assent to them is up to us so that, if we will to, we do, but if we do not will to, we cause God's activity to be without effect in us. Of course," you say, "he causes us to will to the extent he can when his words become known to us. But if we refuse to go along with them, we bring it about that his activity accomplishes nothing in us. If you say this, you certainly speak in opposition to our prayers."

2. State most openly, then, that we should not pray that those to whom we preach the Gospel may believe, but that we should only preach to them. Employ your arguments against the prayers of the Church, and, when you hear a priest

of God at the altar exhorting the people of God to pray for non-believers that God may convert them to the faith and for catechumens that he may inspire them with the desire for rebirth and for the faithful that by his gift they may continue in what they have begun to be, sneer at such pious words, and say that you do not do what he urges, that is, that you do not ask God on behalf of non-believers that he may make them believers, on the ground that these things are not benefits of God's mercy but tasks of the human will. And as a learned man in the church of Carthage, condemn as well the book of the most blessed Cyprian on *The Lord's Prayer*. When that teacher explained this prayer, he showed that we petition from God the Father what you say is given to a human being by a human being, that is, by oneself.

3. But if you believe that what I said about the prayers of the Church and the martyr Cyprian is not enough, be bolder; rebuke the apostle who said, *We pray to God that you may do no evil* (2 Cor 13:7). After all, you are not going to say that one who does not believe in Christ or who gives up faith in Christ does no evil. And for this reason he who says *that you may do no evil* does not want us to do these actions. And it is not enough for him to give the command, but he confesses that he asks God that we may not do these actions, knowing that God corrects and directs the will of human beings so that they do not do them. For *the steps of a man are directed by the Lord, and he will choose the Lord's way* (Ps 37:23). He did not say, "And he will learn the Lord's way," or, "He will hold onto it," or, "He will walk in it," or some such thing that you could say is indeed given by God, but to a person who already wills it, that is, so that the gift of God by which he directs the steps of a man so that he may learn, hold onto, and walk in the Lord's way are preceded by the man's will, and the man merits this gift of God by his antecedent will. Rather, he said, *The steps of a man are directed by the Lord, and he will choose the Lord's way*, in order that we might understand that the good will itself, by which we begin to will to believe (for what is God's way but the correct faith?), is a gift of him who first directs our steps in order that we may will. After all, Scripture does not say, *The steps of a man are directed by the Lord* because the man chose his way, but it says that they *are directed* and that *he will choose*. They are not, then, directed because the man chose, but he will choose because they are directed.

2, 4. Here you are again perhaps going to say that the Lord does this when we read or hear his teaching, if a person assents with his will to the truth that he reads or hears. You say, "For, if God's teaching were concealed from him, God would not direct his steps in order that, once they had been directed, a man would choose God's way." And for this reason you think that the Lord directs the steps of a man to choose God's way only in the sense that without God's teaching he could not come to know the truth to which he assents by his will. You say, "If a man assents to it (something that lies within his free choice), the Lord is correctly said to direct his steps in order that he may choose the way of him whose teaching he follows because he was first persuaded and then assented, which he does by his natural freedom if he wills to, but does not do if he does not will to. And he will receive a reward or punishment in accord with what he has done." This is the teaching of the Pelagians that is wrongly spread about and rightly condemned, and Pelagius himself, fearing that he would be condemned in the courtroom of the Eastern bishops, condemned the view by which they say that the grace of God is not given for individual actions but lies in free choice or in the law and teaching.[771] Will we be hardhearted to such a point, my brother, that we hold that Pelagian view on the grace of God, or rather against the grace of God, that Pelagius himself condemned with a false heart, but still in fear of Catholic judges?

5. And how, you will ask, shall we reply? How do you suppose we shall do so more easily or more clearly than by embracing what we said above about praying to God so that no invasion of forgetfulness, no clever argument may tear it from our mind? For Scripture says, *The steps of a man are directed by the Lord, and he will choose the Lord's way* (Ps 37:23), and, *The will is prepared by the Lord* (Prv 8:35 LXX), and, *For it is the Lord who produces in you even to will* (Phil 2:13). And there are many such passages by which the true grace of God is taught, that is, the grace that is not given according to our merits, but that gives our merits themselves when it is given, because it precedes a person's good will and does not find it in anyone's heart, but produces it. If, then, God so prepares and so produces a person's will that he only proposes his law and teaching to the person's will and does not move his mind by that deep and hidden calling, so that he gives his assent to the same law and teaching, it would undoubtedly be enough to read it or to understand it through reading or even to explain and preach it, and it would not be necessary to pray that God might convert the hearts of non-believers to his faith and that, by the bounteousness of the same grace of his, he might give to those already converted growth and perseverance. If, then, you do not deny that we must ask for this from the Lord, what remains, Brother Vitalis, but that you admit that he—from whom you agree that we must ask for them—gives these things? But if you deny that we ought to ask him for them, you contradict the same teaching of his, because we also learn in it that we should ask for these things from him.

6. You know the Lord's Prayer, and I do not doubt that you say to God, *Our Father, who are in heaven* (Mt 6:9), and so on. Read the most blessed Cyprian, who has explained it,[772] and pay careful attention to how he explained the words, *May your will also be done on earth as it is in heaven* (Mt 6:10), and humbly understand what he said. He will certainly teach you to pray for non-believers who are enemies of the Church, in accord with the command of the Lord who says, *Pray for your enemies* (Mt 5:44; Lk 6:28), and to pray that God's will also be done in those who, because of their unbelief, bear only the image of the earthly man and for this reason are rightly called *earth*, just as it is done in those

---

771. See *The Deeds of Pelagius* 14, 30.
772. See Cyprian, *The Lord's Prayer* 14-17.

who are already believers and who bear the image of the heavenly man and are for this reason called *heaven*.[773] The former, of course, are the enemies for whom the Lord commanded us to pray, and the most glorious martyr explained in that sense what we say in the prayer, *May your will also be done on earth as it is in heaven* (Mt 6:10), in order that we might also ask for them the faith that believers have. Of course those enemies of the Christian faith either do not at all want to hear the law and teaching of God by which the faith of Christ is preached, or they listen to it and also read it in order to mock, despise, and blaspheme it with as much opposition as they can. Vainly and perfunctorily rather than truthfully do we pour forth prayers to God for them, so that by believing they may assent to the teaching they oppose, if it does not pertain to his grace to convert to his faith the wills of persons who are opposed to that faith. Uselessly and insincerely rather than truthfully do we thank God in exultation, when some of them come to believe, if he does not cause this in them.

7. Let us not deceive human beings, for we cannot deceive God. We surely do not pray to God, but we pretend to pray to him, if we believe that it is we ourselves, not God, who do what we pray for. We surely do not thank God, but pretend that we do, if we think that he does not do that for which we thank him. If we have deceitful lips[774] in any conversations with human beings, let us at least not have them in our prayers. Far be it from us to deny in our hearts that God does what we ask him to do with our lips and voices. And—what is worse—far be it from us to remain silent about this in our discussions in order to deceive others; and, when we want to defend free choice before human beings, to lose before God the help of prayer; and not to give true thanks, since we do not acknowledge true grace.

3, 8. If we truly want to defend free choice, we should not attack that by which it becomes free. For one who attacks the grace by which our choice is set free in order to turn away from evil and to do good wants his will to be still captive. Answer me, I beg you: How does the Apostle say, *Giving thanks to the Father who makes us fit to partake of the lot of the saints in light, who has rescued us from the power of darkness and transferred us into the kingdom of his beloved Son* (Col 1:12-13), if he himself does not set our choice free but our choice sets itself free? We lie, therefore, when we give thanks to the Father as if he himself does what he does not do, and the Apostle was mistaken when he said that *he makes us fit to partake of the lot of the saints in light because he has rescued us from the power of darkness and transferred us into the kingdom of his beloved Son.* Answer me: How did we have free choice in order to turn away from evil and to do good when it was under the power of darkness? If, as the Apostle says, God has rescued us, he certainly set our choice free from it. If he causes so great a good as this only through the proclamation of his teaching, what shall we say of those whom he has

---

773. See 1 Cor 15:47-49.
774. See Pss 12:3-4; 17:1; 31:19.

not rescued from the power of darkness? Are we only to preach God's teaching to them, or should we also pray for them that they may be rescued from the power of darkness by God's power? If you say that we should only preach to them, you contradict the command of the Lord and the prayers of the Church. But if you admit that we should pray for them, you admit that we should pray that they assent to the same teaching by their choice, which has been set free from the power of darkness. In that way it happens that they do not become believers except by free choice, and yet they become believers by the grace of him who has set free their choice from the power of darkness. Thus the grace of God is not denied but shown to be true grace without any preceding human merits, and free choice is defended in such a way that it is strengthened by humility, not hurled down by pride, so that *he who boasts may boast not in a human being,* whether someone else or himself, but *in the Lord* (1 Cor 1:31; 2 Cor 10:17).[775]

9. After all, what is the power of darkness but the power of the devil and his angels,[776] who, though they were angels of light,[777] because they did not remain standing in the truth by free choice[778] but fell from there, became darkness? I am not teaching you these things, but I am admonishing you to recall what you know. The human race, then, was made subject to this power of darkness through the fall of that first human being, who was persuaded to transgress the commandment by that power and in whom we all fell.[779] On this account even infants are rescued from this power of darkness when they are reborn in Christ. And this is not seen in their choice, which has been set free, except when they come to an age when they have the use of reason, have a will that assents to the saving doctrine in which they have been raised, and end this life with that will, if they were chosen in Christ before the creation of the world in order that they might be holy and spotless in his sight in love, predestined for adoption as his children.[780]

10. But this power of darkness, that is, the devil, who is also called the prince of the power of the air, is at work in the children of unbelief.[781] This prince, the devil, the ruler of darkness, that is, of those children of unbelief, rules them by his choice. Nor does he possess his choice as free to do good but as hardened into the greatest malice as punishment for his sin.[782] From this no one of sound faith believes or says that those rebel angels are converted to their former goodness once their will has at some point been corrected. What, then, does this power produce in the children of unbelief but its own evil works and, first of all and especially, the very unbelief and infidelity by which they are enemies of the faith? For by that

---

775. See Jer 9:23-24.
776. See Mt 25:41.
777. See 2 Cor 11:14.
778. See Jn 8:44.
779. See Gn 3:1-6; 1 Tm 2:14; Rom 5:12.
780. See Eph 1:4-5.
781. See Eph 2:2.
782. See 2 Tm 2:26.

faith this power knows that the children of unbelief can be purified, can be healed, and can reign as perfectly free in eternity, which he intensely hates. And so he allows some of them, through whom he tries to deceive more extensively, to have some seemingly good works for which they are praised. There are found among any number of peoples, but especially in the people of Rome, those who have lived illustrious and most glorious lives. But, as Scripture says, which is perfectly true, *Everything that does not come from faith is sin* (Rom 14:23), and, *Without faith it is* indeed *impossible to please God* (Heb 11:6)—not human beings. Hence this prince aims at nothing but that people not believe in God or, by believing, come to his mediator, by whom his works are destroyed.

11. But the mediator himself enters *into the house of a strong man* (Mt 12:29), that is, into the world of mortals situated under the power of the devil insofar as it belongs to him; of him Scripture says, to be sure, that he has the power of death.[783] The mediator enters *into the house of a strong man*, that is, of him who has the human race under his dominion, and he first ties him up, that is, checks and restrains his power by the mightier chains of his own power. And in that way he carries off whichever of his vessels he predestined to carry off, setting free from his power their choice so that, without the devil's interference, they might believe in him by their free will. Hence this is a work of grace, not of nature. It is, I say, a work of the grace that the second Adam brought us, not of the nature that the first Adam destroyed as a whole in himself. It is a work of grace that takes away sin and gives life to the dead sinner, not a work of the law that reveals the sin but does not give life to the sinner. For that great preacher of grace says, *I knew sin only through the law* (Rom 7:7), and, *If a law were given that could give life, righteousness would certainly come from the law* (Gal 3:21). This is a work of grace by which those who receive it are made friends of that salutary teaching of Holy Scripture, though they were its enemies, not the work of that teaching by which those who hear it and read it without the grace of God become that much fiercer enemies of it.

4, 12. The grace of God, then, is not found in the nature of free choice and in the law and teaching, as the Pelagian error foolishly supposes. Rather, it is given for individual actions by the will of him of whom Scripture says, *You will set apart a voluntary rain, O God, for your heritage* (Ps 68:10), because we lost free choice for loving God by the enormity of the first sin, and the law and teaching of God, though holy and righteous and good,[784] nonetheless kills if the Spirit does not give life.[785] The Spirit brings it about that we hold on to the law not by hearing it but by obeying it, not because we read it but because we love it. Hence, that we believe in God and live a pious life *does not depend upon the one who wills or the one who runs, but upon God who shows mercy* (Rom 9:16), not because

---

783. See Heb 2:14.
784. See Rom 7:11-12.
785. See 2 Cor 3:6; Jn 6:63.

we ought not to will and to run but because God produces the willing and the running in us.[786] For this reason, when the Lord Jesus himself distinguished those who believe from those who do not believe, that is, the vessels of mercy from the vessels of anger,[787] he said, *No one comes to me unless it has been given him by the Father* (Jn 6:65-66), and his disciples who afterwards did not follow him[788] were of course scandalized that he said this. Let us, therefore, not call teaching grace, but let us acknowledge the grace that makes teaching beneficial. If that grace is lacking, we see that even teaching is harmful.

13. For this reason, though God foreknew all his future actions in his predestination, he arranged them so that he would convert certain non-believers to faith in him by answering the prayers of believers for them. And in this way those who think that grace is the nature of free choice with which we are born or that grace is teaching, however useful, which is proclaimed aloud and in writing, are refuted, and, if he is merciful to them, they are corrected. After all, we do not pray for non-believers that God may cause their nature, that is, that they may be human beings, or that they may be given the teaching that they hear to their misfortune if they do not believe it—and we very often pray for those who, when they read or hear it, refuse to believe. Rather, we pray that their will may be corrected, that they may assent to the teaching, and that their nature may be healed.

14. But now believers pray even for themselves, that they may persevere in what they have begun to be. It is, of course, beneficial for all or for almost all, for the sake of a most salutary humility, that they cannot know the sort of persons they are going to be. For this reason Scripture says, *Let him who seems to be standing firmly see to it that he does not fall* (1 Cor 10:12). Because of the usefulness of this fear that, after we have been reborn and begin to live a holy life, we might have proud thoughts,[789] as if we were safe, certain persons who are not going to persevere are by God's permission, provision, or disposition mingled with those who are going to persevere in order that, terrified by their fall, we may follow the righteous road *with fear and trembling* (2 Cor 7:15; Eph 6:5; Phil 2:12) until we pass from this life, which *is a temptation upon the earth* (Job 7:1), to the other life, where pride no longer has to be suppressed and we do not have to struggle against its suggestions and temptations.

15. But concerning this issue, that is, why certain people who are not going to remain in Christian faith and holiness still receive this grace for a time and are allowed to live here until they fall away, though they could be snatched from this life *so that malice would not change their mind* (Wis 4:11), as was written in the Book of Wisdom about one who died at a tender age, let each person investigate as he can. And, if he finds another credible account apart from the one that I have

---

786. See Phil 2:13.
787. See Rom 9:22-23.
788. See Jn 6:61-62.67.
789. See Rom 11:20; 12:8.

given, without deviating from the rule of the correct faith, let him hold it, and I will hold it along with him if I come to know it. Let us nonetheless, if we have some other idea, continue to walk on the path to which we have come until God makes it clear to us, as we are taught in the letter of the Apostle.[790] But we have come to those truths, which we most firmly know belong to the true and Catholic faith and in which, with the help and mercy of him to whom we say, *Lead me, O Lord, on your path, and I will walk in your truth* (Ps 86:11), we should walk in such a way that we never turn aside from them.

Twelve Propositions against the Pelagians[791]

5, 16. Because by the mercy of Christ we are Catholic Christians:

1. We know that those not yet born have done nothing good or bad in their own life and did not come into the miseries of this life in accord with the merits of some previous life of their own, which as individuals they could not have, but that those born in the flesh after Adam contract by their first birth the contagion of the ancient death and are not set free from the punishment of eternal death that a just condemnation carries with it, passing from the one to all,[792] unless they are reborn in Christ through grace.

2. We know that the grace of God is given neither to infants nor to adults in accord with our merits.

3. We know that it is given to adults for individual actions.

4. We know that it is not given to all human beings and that it is not only not given to those to whom it is given according to the merits of their actions but that it is also not given to those to whom it is given according to the merits of their wills, something that is seen especially in infants.

5. We know that the mercy of God is given as gratuitous to those to whom it is given.

6. We know that by the just judgment of God it is not given to those to whom it is not given.

7. We know that *we shall all stand before the judgment seat of Christ in order that each may receive recompense in accord with what he did in the body* (Rom 14:10; 2 Cor 5:10), not in accord with what one would have done if one had lived longer.

---

790. See Phil 3:16.15; 2 Jn 6.
791. The CSEL edition omits this subtitle and the numbering of the propositions.
792. See Rom 5:12.

8. We know that infants too will receive either reward or punishment in accord with what they did in the body. They did nothing by themselves, however, but by those who make the responses for them and by whom they are said to renounce the devil and to believe in God. Hence they are counted in the number of believers, included in the Lord's statement when he says, *One who believes and is baptized will be saved* (Mk 16:16). For this reason there also applies to those who do not receive this sacrament what follows: *But one who does not believe will be condemned* (Mk 16:16). Hence, if they die at that early age, they too, as I said, are certainly judged in accord with what they did in the body, that is, at the time when they were in the body, when by the hearts and lips of those presenting them they believed or did not believe, when they were or were not baptized, when they ate or did not eat the flesh of Christ, when they drank or did not drink the blood of Christ.[793] They are not judged in accord with what they were going to do if they had lived here longer.

9. We know that the dead *who die in the Lord* (Rv 14:13) are happy and that whatever they would have done if they had lived for a longer time does not pertain to them.

10. We know that those who believe in the Lord in their own heart do this by will and by free choice.

11. We know that we who already believe act in accord with the correct faith when we pray to God for those who refuse to believe so that they may will to believe.

12. We know that we correctly and truly both should and are accustomed to offer thanks to God for those who have come to believe, as for so many benefits.

17. You recognize, I think, that I did not want to mention all the truths that pertain to the Catholic faith in those that I said that we know but only those that pertain to what we are discussing regarding the grace of God, namely, whether this grace precedes or follows upon the will of a human being, that is (to speak more plainly), whether grace is given to us because we will it or, by grace, God also makes us will it. If, then, you, my brother, also hold along with us these twelve propositions that I have said we know pertain to the correct and Catholic faith, I give thanks to God, and I would not truthfully give thanks unless the grace of God brought it about that you held them. If you hold them, there will remain no dispute at all with us on this question.

---

793. See Jn 6:54-55.

6, 18. Let me run through these twelve propositions with a brief explanation. How does grace follow upon the merit of the human will when it is given even to infants who are not yet able either to will or not to will? How are merits of the will said to come before grace even in adults if, in order to be true grace, grace is not given according to our merits? Pelagius himself was so afraid of this Catholic statement that, without any hesitation, he condemned those who say that the grace of God is given in accord with our merits, for fear that he would be condemned by Catholic judges.[794] How is grace said to be found in the nature of free choice or in the law and teaching since Pelagius also condemned this statement, confessing without any doubt that the grace of God is given for individual actions to those who of course already have use of free choice?

19. How can one say that all human beings would receive grace if those to whom it is not given would not reject it by their own will, because *God wills that all human beings be saved* (1 Tm 2:4), since it is not given to many infants? For very many die without it who do not have a will opposed to it, and at times their parents desire it and hasten to it, and the ministers are also willing and ready. But, because God does not will it, it is not given, when the infant suddenly dies before the sacrament is given to which his parents had hastened so that he might receive it. Hence it is obvious that those who resist this truth, which is so clear, do not at all understand the sense in which it was said that *God wills that all human beings be saved*, though so many are not saved not because they do not will it but because God does not will it, which is perfectly clear in the case of infants. But just as the statement, *All will be brought to life in Christ* (1 Cor 15:22), though so many are punished with eternal death, was said in the sense that all who receive eternal life receive it only in Christ, so the statement, *God wills that all human beings be saved*, though he does not will that so many be saved, was said in the sense that all who are saved are saved only by his will. And if these words of the Apostle can be understood in any other way, they still cannot contradict this absolutely obvious truth by which we see that so many are not saved because God does not will this, though human beings do.

20. And how does the human will merit that God's grace be given, if it is given out of gratuitous mercy to those to whom it is given in order that it may be true grace? How are the merits of the human will weighed in this case, since by the just judgment of God—for there is no injustice in God[795]—this grace is not given to those to whom it is not given, though they do not differ by any merit or any will from those to whom it is given, but are with them in one and the same condition? As a result, those to whom it is given should understand how gratu-

---

794. At the Council of Diospolis Pelagius condemned those who said that grace was given according to human merits and confessed that it is given for individual actions. See *The Deeds of Pelagius* 14, 30.
795. See Rom 9:14.

itously it is given when of course it might justly not be given, since it is justly not given to those who are in a similar condition.

21. How is not only the will to believe from the beginning but also the will to persevere up to the end[796] not due to the grace of God, since the end of this life is not in the power of a human being but in God's power, and God could certainly also bestow this benefit on someone who was not going to persevere, so that he would be taken from the body *in order that malice might not change his mind* (Wis 4:11)? For a human being will not receive either reward or punishment[797] except in accord with what he has done in this life, not in accord with what he would have done if he had lived longer.

22. How is it said that the grace of God is not given to certain infants and is given to certain others who are going to die, because he foresees their future wills, which they would have had if they had lived? For, as the Apostle says, each person will receive either reward or punishment in accord with what he did in the body, not in accord with what he would have done if he had lived longer in the body.[798] How are human beings judged in accord with their future wills, which it is said that they would have had if they lived longer in the flesh, since scripture says, *Happy are the dead who die in the Lord* (Rv 14:13)? Their happiness is undoubtedly not certain and secure if God will also judge those actions that they did not do but were going to do if their life were longer, and he receives no benefit who is carried off *in order that malice might not change his mind* (Wis 4:11), because he also suffers the punishment for that malice from which he was removed when it was perhaps imminent. Nor should we rejoice over those who we know have died in the correct faith after a good life, lest they be judged in accord with some crimes that they perhaps would have committed if they had lived. Nor are they to be mourned and despised who have ended this life in unbelief and corrupt morals, because, if they had lived, they would perhaps have done penance, would have lived piously, and would have been judged in terms of this. We would have to disagree with and reject in its entirety the book *Mortality* of the most glorious martyr Cyprian,[799] in which his whole aim is that we should know that we ought to rejoice over the good faithful when they die, since they are removed from the temptations of this life and will thereafter remain in most blessed security. But since this is not false and because *the dead who die in the Lord are* undoubtedly *happy* (Rv 14:13), we should mock and curse the error by which it is supposed that human beings are going to be judged according to the future dispositions of their wills, which are not going to exist in the case of those who die.

---

796. See Mt 24:13.
797. See 2 Cor 5:10.
798. See 2 Cor 5:10.
799. See Cyprian, *Mortality* 7, 20-21.

23. How are those said to deny the free choice of the will who confess that every human being who believes in God from his heart believes only with his free will? For they, rather, attack free choice who attack the grace of God by which choice becomes truly free for choosing and doing good. How does someone say that the law and teaching of God and not rather the hidden inspiration of the grace of God bring about what the same Scripture says: *The will is prepared by the Lord* (Prv 8:35, LXX)? For, on behalf of those who contradict the same teaching and refuse to believe it, we beg God with the correct faith that they might desire to believe.

24. How does God wait for the wills of human beings so that those to whom he gives grace may anticipate him, though we correctly thank him for those to whom he granted mercy when they did not believe in him and were attacking his teaching with their wicked will and whom he converted to himself with his omnipotent ease, making them willing instead of unwilling? Why do we thank him for this if he himself did not do it? Why do we glorify him more to the extent that those who we rejoice have come to believe used to refuse to believe with greater obstinacy, if the human will is not changed for the better by God's grace? The apostle Paul says, *I was unknown by appearance to the churches of Judea that are in Christ. They only heard that he who once was persecuting us is now spreading the good news of the faith that he once ravaged, and they glorified God in me.* (Gal 1:22-24) Why did they glorify God if God had not converted the heart of that man to himself by the goodness of his grace, since, as he himself admits, he obtained mercy in order that he might become a believer[800] in the faith that he once ravaged? Who but God produced this great good, according to the expression that he used? After all, what does *they glorified God in me* mean but "they declared God glorious because of me"? But how did they declare God glorious if God himself had not produced that great deed of Paul's conversion? And how did he himself do it if he did not, from being unwilling, make him willing to believe?

25. It is, of course, evident from those twelve propositions, which you are not permitted to deny pertain to the Catholic faith, that not only all of them together but also each of them individually makes us confess that the grace of God precedes human wills and that they are prepared by grace rather than that grace is given on account of their merit. Or if you deny that one of those twelve is true, whose number I also mention so that they may more easily be committed to memory and held there more distinctly, do not hesitate to write back in order that I may know and reply with the ability that the Lord has given me. For I do not in fact believe that you are a Pelagian heretic, but I want you to be such a man that none of that error passes into you or remains in you.

7, 26. But you will perhaps find some point among those twelve which you think that you should deny or hold as doubtful and over which you would force us

---

800. See 1 Cor 7:25.

to argue in more detail. You surely do not, do you, forbid the Church to pray for non-believers in order that they may become believers, for those who refuse to believe in order that they may will to believe, for those who disagree with its law and teaching in order that they may agree with its law and teaching, in order that God may give them what he promised through the prophet: *a heart for knowing him and ears for hearing* (Bar 2:31)? Those of whom the Lord said, *Let those hear who have ears for hearing* (Mt 13:9; Mk 4:9; Lk 8:8), had of course received these ears. When you hear the priest of God at his altar exhorting the people to pray to God, or when you hear him praying aloud that God would compel unbelieving peoples to come to faith in him, will you not respond "Amen?" Or will you argue in opposition to the soundness of this faith? Will you cry out or whisper that the most blessed Cyprian was in error on this point, when he teaches us to pray for the enemies of the Christian faith that they too might be converted to it?

27. Finally, will you blame the apostle Paul, who made prayers of this sort for the non-believing Jews? He says of them, *The good will of my heart and my prayer to God is of course for their salvation* (Rom 10:1). He also says to the Thessalonians, *Finally, brothers, pray for us, that the word of God may spread rapidly and may be glorified, as it is also among you, and that we may be rescued from wicked and evil persons. For not all have the faith.* (2 Thes 3:1-2) How would the word of God spread rapidly and be glorified if not by the conversion to the faith of those to whom it was preached, since he says to those who already believe, *as it is also among you*? He surely knows that God, whom he wants them to ask to do this, is the one who acts in order that he may also be rescued from wicked and evil persons who were certainly not going to believe despite their prayers. For this reason he added, *For not all have the faith*, as if to say, "For the word of God will not be glorified among all despite your prayers," because they were certainly going to believe *who were destined for eternal life* (Acts 13:48), predestined *for adoption as his children through Jesus Christ and chosen in him before the creation of the world* (Eph 1:5.4). But by means of the prayers of believers God makes those who are still non-believers believe in order to show that he himself does this. For there is no one so ignorant, so carnal, so slow in mind as not to see that God does what he commands us to ask him to do.

28. These and other divine testimonies, which it would take too long to mention, show that by his grace God removes from non-believers their heart of stone[801] and that he anticipates in human beings the merits of their good wills so that he might prepare their wills by his antecedent grace, not so that grace might be given because of the antecedent merit of their wills. Thanksgiving indicates the same thing as prayer: prayer for non-believers, thanksgiving for believers. For to him to whom we must pray that he might do this we must offer thanksgiving when he has done it. For this reason the same Apostle says to the Ephesians,

---

801. See Ez 11:19; 36:26.

On this account, having heard of your faith in the Lord Jesus and of your love for all the saints, I too do not cease to offer thanks for you (Eph 1:15-16).

29. But we are now speaking about the very beginnings, when people who were turned away from and set against God are turned back to him and begin to will what they did not will and to have the faith that they did not have. In order that this may come about, prayer is offered *for* them, even though it is not offered *by* them. After all, *how will they call upon him in whom they have not believed?* (Rom 10:14) But when what is prayed for has come about, thanksgiving is offered both for them and by them to him who did this. I do not, however, think that it is necessary to dispute with you about the prayers of those who are already believers, which they offer both for themselves and for others of the faithful in order that they may make progress in what they have begun, and about their thanksgiving because they are making progress. This dispute with the Pelagians is something that you and I have in common. They of course attribute to the free choice of the will all the things that have to do with the faithful and holy life of human beings in such a way that they think that they are to be had from ourselves, not asked for from God. But if what I hear about you is true, you do not want the beginning of faith, in which there is also found the beginning of a good, that is, of a pious will, to be a gift of God; rather, you claim that we have it from ourselves that we begin to believe. Yet you agree that through his grace God grants the other goods pertaining to a religious life to those who ask, seek, and knock with faith.[802] You do not notice that we pray to God on behalf of non-believers in order that they may believe because God also gives faith, and that we give thanks to God on behalf of those who have come to believe because he also has given faith.

30. Hence, in order to bring this letter to you to an end, if you deny that we should pray that those who refuse to believe may will to believe, if you deny that we should give thanks to God because those who refused to believe have willed to believe, we must deal with you in another way so that you may not be in such an error or so that, if you persist in error, you may not bring others into error. But if, as I prefer to believe of you, you hold and agree that we ought to pray to God and often do pray to God for those who are unwilling to believe in order that they may will to believe and for those who are opposed to and contradict his law and teaching in order that they may believe and follow it, if you hold and agree that we also ought to give thanks to God and often do give thanks to God for such people when they have been converted to his faith and teaching and become willing from having been unwilling, you ought undoubtedly to admit that the wills of human beings are anticipated by the grace of God and that God, whom we ask to do this and whom we know it is right and just to thank when he has done this, brings it about that human beings will the good that they did not will. May the Lord grant you understanding on all these points, my lord and brother.

---

802. See Mt 7:7-8; Lk 11:9-10.

LETTER 4*
Augustine to Cyril, the bishop of Alexandria (417)

In the fall of 417 Augustine wrote to Cyril, the bishop of Alexandria, who was to lead the opposition to Nestorius at the Council of Ephesus in 431. Augustine commends himself to Cyril's prayers and expresses his pleasure at the opportunity that the servant of God Justus has provided for him to write to Cyril (paragraph 1). He recalls the circumstances that led to his composing *The Deeds of Pelagius*, in which he showed that Pelagius was acquitted at the Council of Diospolis in Palestine only because he condemned parts of his own teaching (paragraph 2). Augustine explains that Justus is returning to Cyril after having come to Hippo in order to check his copy of *The Deeds of Pelagius* against better exemplars, for he had been accused of falsifying his copy of Augustine's work where it said that not all sinners were destined for eternal fire (paragraph 3). Augustine warns Cyril that those who found this idea objectionable might very well be proponents of the Pelagian heresy (paragraph 4). Finally, he asks Cyril to investigate the matter and to defend Justus against those who slander him (paragraph 5).

To his most blessed lord and brother and fellow priest, Cyril, who deserves honor and reverence with the due signs of love, Augustine sends greetings in the Lord.

1. I commend myself greatly to your holy prayers as I pay Your Reverence the duty of greeting you by the intermediary of the servant of God, Justus by name, whom I have very recently come to know as a good brother. Since he had come to us from you and was returning to you from us, he offered us a very attractive opportunity to carry out these duties to Your Beatitude. Nor do I think that I should pass over in silence the reason that forced him to make the journey to us. I know of it, of course, because he told me.

2. Your Sincerity, I think, recalls that you sent us the ecclesiastical proceedings held in the province of Palestine where Pelagius was acquitted because he was thought to be Catholic. For he had concealed his true self in the shrewd hiding places provided by words and deceived our brothers who then sat in judgment, since no opponent from the other side argued against him.[803] After I had considered and examined those proceedings as carefully as I could, I wrote a book on them for our venerable brother and fellow priest, Aurelius, the bishop of Carthage.[804] In it I showed, to the extent that the Lord granted me, what guided

---

803. Augustine refers to the Council of Diospolis held in December of 415.
804. After Augustine received the proceedings from the Council of Diospolis he wrote *The Deeds of Pelagius*. Aurelius was the bishop of Carthage and hence the primate of Africa as well as Augustine's friend for many years.

the Catholic judges in the replies of Pelagius, so that they acquitted him as being Catholic. Of course many people caught up in his error were boasting that, since he was acquitted, his heretical teachings were confirmed as Catholic by the judgment of the Catholic bishops, and, since they were spreading these ideas everywhere, very many people who were ignorant of what had occurred believed that such was the case, to the great scandal of the churches.

3. In order to destroy this opinion, then, I produced the book I mentioned in which I showed, as well as I could, that, even though Pelagius was acquitted—not before God, whom no one deceives, but before human beings, whom Pelagius was able to deceive—those deadly teachings were nonetheless absolutely condemned, since he himself declared them anathema. The servant of God, Justus, who is the bearer of this letter to Your Reverence, had this book of mine. It shocked certain people because it argued that not all sinners are punished by eternal fire, and they said, as he reported to me, that I had not written that passage in that way but that he himself had falsified it. Hence he was upset and sailed to us with the same book in case he perhaps had a defective copy, though he was fully conscious that he had falsified nothing in it. And so, by comparing that copy with our volumes, and with my own full awareness of the matter, he found that he had a copy free from defects.

4. Then the suspicion struck us—may God keep all malice from it and make it rather full of love, though it should not in any case be disregarded—that the statement we made, that not all sinners but only certain ones are condemned to endless punishment, displeases those who say that even in this mortal life there are holy persons without sin. As a result they say that they do not need the Lord's Prayer, in which the whole Church cries out, *Forgive us our debts* (Mt 6:12), for the forgiveness of their own sins, because they have no sins. Your Holiness undoubtedly sees that these people must be corrected from the wickedness of their error. For it is certain that these ideas stem from that unhealthy Pelagian teaching that claimed that all sinners are punished by eternal fire such that no hope of pardon would be left for those who truthfully admit that they are not without sin. In that way they either swell up with pride, supposing that this life of theirs has no sin, or they waste away in despair, as if they were already destined for everlasting punishment. To be sure, the blessed Apostle says, *Fire will test the quality of each person's work. If the work of anyone that he built on the foundation survives, he will receive a reward. If the work of anyone is consumed by fire, he will suffer a loss, but he himself with be saved, but as by fire.* (1 Cor 3:13-15) But these words of the Apostle should be interpreted so that we may understand what was said in terms not of the fire of the last judgment but of a fire before that judgment, either in this life or after death. In any case, that error is certainly to be avoided by which all sinners are thought to be destined for the punishment of everlasting fire if they do not live a life here that is utterly without sin. We must also be on guard that those who hold this view are not also found to hold other Pelagian teachings, no less unsound or even worse, and that their dreadful infection does not spread

among unwary people, when we do not suppress or heal the evil that the care of brotherly love has discovered in some of them.

5. I commend our brother Justus to Your Most Faithful Holiness, so that you may not only defend him from slanderers but also be so good as to correct those whom he rightly holds suspect, lest they lose their souls and inject the Pelagian poison into them. Correct them with your pastoral care and with your fatherly gentleness or even with remedial severity, if there is need. Or, if you find them sound in the faith,[805] be so good as to remove this worry from the mind of this man. For both he and they are Latins, and they have come to those places from the Western Church, where we are too. Hence we ought especially to bring them to Your Reverence's attention, so that they may not seem to have chosen for themselves those lands, in order to hide unpunished among the Greeks, where, when they discuss these topics, they are less well understood and their error is thus not easily refuted. We are doing this, however, so that we may not be saddened by the loss of anyone but instead may rejoice, as far as possible, over the salvation of all.

---

805. See Tit 1:13.

AUGUSTINE AS EXEGETE

LETTER 28
Augustine to Jerome (394-395)

Between 394 and 395 Augustine wrote from Hippo to Jerome in Bethlehem this letter, which reached Jerome only nine years later after it had circulated among others in Rome and elsewhere. As result, Jerome came to hear that Augustine had written a book to attack him long before he saw the actual letter. The series of letters between them reveals a spirited and at times angry debate, though by the time of the Pelagian controversy Jerome and Augustine are close friends and collaborators. In the present letter, after praising Jerome whom he has come to know better through the report of Alypius, he commends Brother Profuturus to Jerome (paragraph 1). Augustine urges Jerome to translate the Scriptures from the Greek Septuagint rather than from the Hebrew (paragraph 2). He warns Jerome against the view that Paul used a useful or advantageous lie in rebuking Peter in Galatians (paragraph 3) and argues that to admit any sort of lie in the Scriptures completely undermines their authority (paragraph 4). Hence, Augustine begs Jerome to avoid appealing to useful lies in interpreting the Scriptures (paragraph 5) and sends to Jerome some of his own writings for criticism (paragraph 6).

To my most beloved lord, Jerome, a brother and fellow priest, who should be served and embraced with the most sincere devotion of love, Augustine sends greetings.

1, 1. Never has physical presence made anyone as well known to someone else as your peaceful joy and truly liberal pursuit of your studies in the Lord has made you known to me. Hence, although I desire very much to know you in every respect, there is, nonetheless, a certain aspect of you of which I have less, namely, your physical presence. After brother Alypius,[806] now a most blessed bishop, but then already worthy of the episcopacy, saw you and, returning here, was seen by me, I cannot deny that your physical appearance was to a large extent impressed upon me by his report. And before his return, when he saw you there, I saw you, but with his eyes. For one who knows us would say that we are two, not in mind, but in body, at least in terms of our harmony and most trustworthy friendship, not in merits by which he surpasses me. Since, then, you already love me, first, because of the communion of the Spirit by which we strive for unity, second, because of his words, I am by no means acting impudently, as if I were someone unknown, in commending to you, my brother, Brother Profu-

---

806. Alypius had traveled to Palestine where he met Jerome; upon his return to Africa he was consecrated bishop of Thagaste.

turus,[807] who we hope will truly profit[808] from our efforts and your help, and yet he is perhaps such a good man that he will rather commend me to you than I will commend him to you. I ought perhaps to have written only this far if I wanted to be content with the type of letter one usually writes, but my mind bubbles over to share ideas with you concerning our studies, which we undertake in Christ Jesus, our Lord, who also graciously provides to us in no small amount through your love many benefits and provisions for the journey that he himself has shown us.

2, 2. We, therefore, beg you, and the whole zealous society of the African churches begs you along with us, not to hesitate to devote your careful effort to translating the books of those who have so excellently commented on our Scriptures in Greek. For you can bring it about that we too have those fine men, and that one especially, whom you preferably cite in your writings.[809] But I do not want you to labor over translating the canonical Holy Books into the Latin language, except in the way in which you translated Job so that it may be seen by the use of signs what is the difference between your translation and the Septuagint[810] which has the very weightiest authority. I, however, cannot say how astonished I would be if there were still something found in the Hebrew texts that has escaped so many expert translators of that language. For I leave aside the seventy; concerning the harmony of either their mind or spirit, which is greater than if there were only one man, I do not pass a certain judgment for some side except that I think that they should be given a preeminent authority in this task without any controversy. Those men bother me more who, though they have translated later and have clung tooth and nail, as they say, to the method and rules of Hebrew words and expressions, not only do not agree with one another, but have left many points that need to be dug out and disclosed so much later. For, if they are obscure, we believed that you too can also be mistaken on them. But if they are evident, we do not believe that they could have been mistaken in them. By explaining, therefore, the reasons for this in accord with your love, I beg you to assure me about this.

3, 3. I also read certain writings on the letters of Paul the apostle, which were said to be yours. When you wanted to explain the Letter to the Galatians from among them, you took up that passage where the apostle Peter is called back from his deadly pretense. There, I admit, the fact that a man as fine as you are or someone else undertook the defense of a lie leaves me in more than a little in

---

807. Profuturus did not carry this letter but was consecrated bishop of Cirta in Numida. For this reason Letter 28 was not delivered to Jerome, but circulated in Rome and elsewhere before Jerome saw it.
808. Augustine puns on Profuturus' name and the verb for profiting.
809. Augustine means Origen, of whom Jerome was quite fond before the crisis a few years later over his thought.
810. The Greek translation of the Hebrew Scriptures that was made in the third and second centuries before Christ, according to the legend, by seventy-two translators who, though working separately, each produced the same translation.

pain, until those points that trouble me are refuted, if they can perhaps be refuted. For I regard it as absolutely disastrous to believe that there is a lie in the Holy Books, that is, that those men who gave us and put into writing that Scripture lied in their books. It is, of course, one question whether good men ought to lie at some time, and it is another question whether a writer of the Holy Scriptures ought to lie. In fact, it is not another question; it is no question at all! For, if a useful lie has once been admitted into so lofty a peak of authority, no section of those Books will remain that will not, as soon as anyone finds it either difficult in terms of conduct or incredible in terms of faith, be attributed by the same most deadly rule to the plan and purpose of a lying author.

4. After all, suppose that the apostle Paul lied when he said, in reproaching Peter, *If, though you are a Jew, you live like a Gentile and not like a Jew, why do you force the Gentiles to live like Jews?* (Gal 2:14); suppose that he thought that Peter acted correctly and both said and wrote that he had not acted correctly in order to mollify, as it were, the minds of those in an uproar. What, then, shall we reply when wicked men arise, forbidding marriage, the very men whom he foretold?[811] They might say that everything that the same apostle said in upholding the law of marriage[812] was a lie he told on account of persons who could have been upset because of the love of their spouses. That is, he did not hold this, but spoke to calm their opposition. There is no need to mention many examples. For lies can be seen as useful even in the praises of God in order that the sluggish might be set afire with love for him, and in that way the authority of holy and pure truth will nowhere be certain in the Holy Books. Do we not see that the same Apostle says with great concern for teaching the truth, *But if Christ has not risen, our preaching is empty, your faith is also empty. We, however, are found to be false witnesses of God, since we have given testimony against God that he raised up Christ whom he has not raised up* (1 Cor 15:14-15)? If anyone says to him, "Why are you horrified at this lie since you have said something that, even if it is false, pertains very much to the praise of God?" Would the Apostle not detest the insanity of this man, and would he not, by whatever words and ideas he could, open the inner chambers of his heart to the light, crying out that false praise for God is no less a crime or perhaps even a greater crime than finding fault with the truth about him. Our aim must, therefore, be that a man occupies himself with the knowledge of the Scriptures who regards them as so holy and so true that he refuses to find satisfaction in any part of them through useful lies and rather passes over what he does not understand than prefers his own ideas to that truth. For, when he appeals to such lies, he wants us to believe him, and he tries to make us not believe the authorities of the Divine Scriptures.

5. With all the strength that the Lord has supplied me, I myself would, of course, prove that all those testimonies that have been used to defend the useful-

---

811. See 1 Tm 4:1-3.
812. See 1 Cor 7:10-16.

ness of a lie must be interpreted in some other way in order that we may teach that the truth of those books is solid in every respect. For, just as testimonies ought not to be lies, so they ought not to favor a lie. But I leave this point to your intelligence. Once you have given more careful consideration to the passage, you will perhaps see this more readily than I. But your piety will force you to this consideration, for because of it you recognize that the authority of the Divine Scriptures is crumbling so that each person believes in them what he wants and does not believe what he does not want, once one is convinced that those men from whom we have received them could have told useful lies in their writings. Or are you perhaps going to give us some rules by which we might know where it is necessary to lie and where it is not. If this is possible, please, do not in any way explain it with lying and dubious reasons, and I beg you by the most true humanity of our Lord, do not judge me burdensome and impudent. For, to be brief, it is surely not a great fault by which my error favors the truth, if in your case the truth can correctly favor a lie.

4, 6. I would like to say many other things and discuss Christian studies with your most sincere heart, but no letter suffices for this desire of mine. I do this more fully through the brother whom I am happy to have sent to be exposed to and nourished with your sweet and profitable conversations. And, nonetheless, even he perhaps does not absorb as much as I would like—something I say without offense to him—though I in no sense hold myself superior to him. For I admit that I have more capacity for taking you in, but I see that he is becoming fuller— and in that respect he undoubtedly surpasses me. And after he returns, as I hope he will do successfully with the Lord's help, and after I have become a sharer in his heart that you have filled, he will not fill up my still remaining emptiness and eagerness for your thoughts. Thus it will turn out I will even then have a greater need and he a greater abundance. The same brother, of course, carries with him some of our writings; if you do me the kindness of reading them, please, also apply to them the sincere, but severe judgment of a brother. For I understand the words of Scripture, *The righteous man will correct me with mercy and reproach me, but the oil of the sinner will not anoint my head* (Ps 141:5), to mean that one who heals with his reproaches shows more love than a flatterer who anoints the head. I, however, find it very difficult to read as a good judge what I myself have written, for I am either more cautious or more enthusiastic than is correct. I also at times see my defects, but I prefer to hear of these from my betters for fear that, after I have correctly found fault with myself, I do not again go easy on myself and think that I have judged myself meticulously rather than justly.

LETTER 71
Augustine to Jerome (403)

Perhaps in 403, Augustine wrote to Jerome. He pleads with Jerome to take advantage of the courier, the deacon Cyprian, to reply to his letters (paragraph 1). Augustine mentions the three previous letters to Jerome to which Jerome has not replied (paragraph 2). He tells Jerome that he has learned of his translation of Job from the Hebrew and expresses regret that Jerome has omitted from the Greek text the indications of the variant readings (paragraph 3). Augustine also expresses his preference for the Greek Septuagint text over the Hebrew (paragraph 4) and recounts a problem that arose in one congregation when the bishop introduced Jerome's translation of Jonah from the Hebrew (paragraph 5). Augustine compliments Jerome on his translation of the Gospel and asks for Jerome's opinion on passages where the Septuagint differs from the Hebrew (paragraph 6).

To his venerable lord and lovable holy brother and fellow priest, Jerome, Augustine sends greetings in the Lord.

1, 1. From the time I began to write to you and to long for your replies, I have never had a better opportunity than to have my letter brought to you by a servant and most faithful minister of God and someone very dear to me, such as our son, Cyprian, the deacon. Through his hands I so certainly hope for a letter from you that we could not hope for anything more certain in this sort of matter. For our son whom I mentioned will not lack zeal in seeking a reply; he will not lack charm in gaining one, nor carefulness in guarding it, speed in carrying it, and reliability in delivering it. If I somehow merit so much, may the Lord grant his help and be present in your heart and in my desire so that no more important desire may hinder your brotherly good will.

2. And so, since I already sent two letters, but afterward received none from you, I chose to send the same letters again in the belief that they have not arrived. Even if they did arrive and your letters rather were perhaps unable to reach me, send once again those letters that you already sent if you perhaps kept copies. If not, dictate again something for me to read, provided that you do not, nonetheless, delay to answer this letter because it has already been a long time that I am waiting for it. When I was still a priest I had prepared my first letter to be sent to you by the hands of a certain brother of ours, Profuturus,[813] who later became a colleague of ours and has already left this life. He was not able at that time to deliver it because, right when he was arranging to leave, he was prevented by the burden of the episcopacy and then soon died. I have decided to send this

---

813. See Letter 28.

letter now as well in order that you may know how ardently I then desired to converse with you and how much I suffer because the senses of your body are so far distant from me by which my mind might have access to your mind, my most charming brother worthy of honor among the members of the Lord.

2, 3. In this letter, however, I add what I learned later, namely, that you translated Job from the Hebrew, though we already have your translation of the same prophet made from the Greek language into Latin in which you marked with asterisks what is found in the Hebrew and is missing in the Greek and marked with obelisks what is found in the Greek and is not in the Hebrew. You did this with such a wonderful care that in certain passages we see stars for every word, signifying that those words are in the Hebrew, but not in the Greek. Now, however, in this later version that was made from the Hebrew, I do not find the same fidelity to the words, and it disturbs me no small amount as I ponder why in the first translation asterisks are inserted with such great care that they indicate that even the smallest particles of speech that are present in the Hebrew are lacking in the Greek or why in this second translation made from the Hebrew less care was used in order that these same particles might be found in those passages. I wanted to cite something from it as an example, but the book that was translated from the Hebrew was not available to me at the time. Because, nonetheless, you soar ahead of me in natural talents, you understand well enough, I think, not merely what I said, but also what I wanted to say, so that you may reply to what bothers me once the reason has been presented.

4. I would, of course, prefer that you translate for us the canonical Greek Scriptures, which are said to have had seventy translators.[814] It will, after all, be extremely annoying if your translation begins to be read more frequently in many churches because the Latin churches will be out of harmony with the Greek churches, especially since, when the Greek book is produced, that is, in a widely known language, your translation will easily be proven to be in opposition to it. But if anyone is upset by something unfamiliar in the translation from the Hebrew and raises the charge of falsification, he will rarely or never have access to the Hebrew texts by which your translation might be defended against the objection. But even if one had access to the Hebrew, who would tolerate the condemnation of so many Latin and Greek authorities? In addition, even the Hebrews, when consulted, can offer a different response so that you alone seem indispensable since you can prove even them wrong. But who will be the judge? I would be surprised if you can find one.

3, 5. For, when a certain brother bishop of ours began to have your translation read in the church over which he presides, a particular passage in the prophet Jonah caused a disturbance because it was presented in far different language

---

814. The Septuagint version is so named because, according to legend, it was translated by seventy men.

than had become familiar to the senses and memory and had been chanted for so many ages. There was produced so great an uproar among the people, especially when the Greeks brought accusations and stirred up the charge of falsification, that the bishop—this took place in the city of Oea[815]—was forced to demand the testimony of Jews. But, whether out of ignorance or out of malice, they replied that what both the Greek and Latin texts had and said was in the Hebrew books. What then? The man was forced to correct the text as if it were incorrect, since he did not want to be left without any people after the grave crisis. Hence, it seems to us as well that you could have been mistaken at times on some points. And see what a problem this presents in those writings that cannot be corrected by a comparison with the texts in familiar languages.

4, 6. So then, we offer to God no small thanks for your work by which you translated the Gospel from Greek because there is no problem in almost all the passages when we compare it with the Greek Scripture. Hence, if anyone for the sake of argument favors the old incorrect version, he will be either easily instructed or refuted when the books are brought out and compared. Even if certain very rare passages rightly trouble someone, who is so hardhearted that he will not readily pardon a work so useful that he is not able to praise it as it deserves? I wish, however, you would be so good as to explain to me what you think as to why in many passages the authority of the Hebrew book is quite different from the Greek books that are called the Septuagint. For that version has no small authority; it has deservedly, after all, been widely used and was used by the apostles. Not only does the text itself indicate this, but I also remember that you testified to it. And for this reason you will do very much good if you render that Greek Scripture, which the seventy produced, into correct Latin, for the Latin we have is so different in different manuscripts that it is barely tolerable. And it rouses such suspicions that something else may be found in the Greek that one hesitates to quote or to prove something from it. I thought this letter would be short, but somehow or other it became very pleasant for me to go on with it as if I were conversing with you. But I beg you by the Lord not to delay in answering all these questions and in offering me your presence as far as possible.

---

815. The modern city of Tripoli in Lybia.

LETTER 149

Augustine to Paulinus, the bishop of Nola (416)

Toward the end of 416 Augustine wrote to Paulinus, the bishop of Nola, in reply to his letter (Letter 121), in order to answer for him a series of questions on the interpretation of various difficult passages of Scripture. Augustine first thanks God for the good news he has received from Paulinus' letter and expresses regret that Paulinus did not receive certain other letters, of which Augustine now sends him copies (paragraphs 1 and 2). Then Augustine turns to a series of questions on the meaning of various verses from different psalms (paragraphs 3 to 10).

Augustine next deals with the meaning of various verses from the apostle, such as Ephesians 4:11 (paragraph 11) and 1 Timothy 2:1 (paragraph 12). In the latter verse Paulinus wanted to know the difference between the different sorts of prayer mentioned: entreaties, prayers, intercessions, and thanksgiving, and Augustine spends several paragraphs distinguishing the terms as they are found in the Greek text and as the terms are used in the liturgy (paragraphs 13 to 16). He also indicates the reason why such prayers are to be made (paragraph 17).

Augustine then turns to Paulinus' question about Romans 11:28 and explains what Paul meant by the blindness of the Jews that was produced until the fullness of the Gentiles had entered (paragraphs 18 and 19). He points out that it need not be thought that the same Jews were enemies in terms of the Gospel and beloved in terms of their election (paragraph 20) and asserts that only the elect who have been called according to God's plan belong to the predestined (paragraph 21). Though God's judgments may be hidden, they can never be unjust (paragraph 22).

Augustine next considers the Apostle's words in Colossians 2, specifically his words, *Do not handle; do not taste; do not touch* (Col 2:21), which he argues were said with irony (paragraph 23), and then proceeds to set them within the context of the whole chapter, doing an exegesis of the chapter verse by verse both before and after verse 21 (paragraphs 24 to 30).

Finally, Augustine takes up a series of questions on the Gospel, first, regarding why some did not recognize Christ after the resurrection (paragraph 31), then, about the words the risen Christ spoke to Mary Magdalene at the tomb (paragraph 32), and about the words of Simeon to the Virgin Mary in the temple (paragraph 33). He brings the letter to a close with greetings and commends a monk also called Paulinus to Paulinus of Nola.

To his most blessed and venerably dear and dearly venerable brother and fellow bishop, Paulinus, who is holy and most beloved to us in a holy way, Augustine sends greetings in the Lord.

1, 1. We give thanks to God, who comforts the afflicted and consoles the humble,[816] because the Lord has quickly brought us joy by the reports of the letter of Your Holiness about the successful arrival of our brother and fellow priest, Quintus, and of those who sailed with him. Now by the opportunity furnished by our son and fellow deacon, Rufinus, which was the next opportunity we had, I am writing in reply. For he left from the port of Hippo. And I approve the counsel of mercy with which the Lord has inspired you and of which you have been so good as to tell me. May God also help this along; may he make it go well who has eased our concern to a large extent, because a man most dear to me has set out, commended not only by good works but also by your holy prayers.

2. The letter of Your Reverence, in which you asked many questions and advised me to investigate them and by asking them taught me, has arrived.[817] But the letter that I immediately wrote back by the intermediary of those same holy men, who are our consolation, was not, as I found out from this more recent letter of yours, delivered to Your Reverence. I was not able to recall the extent to which I replied in it to your questions, nor did I find a copy in which I might be able to find this out when I looked for one. I am, nonetheless, absolutely certain that I replied to some of them and not to all of them, because the courier's haste was pressing me to finish. Along with it I had sent, as you directed, a copy of that letter that I had written to Your Charity at Carthage on the resurrection of the body, in which the question arose about the use of our members.[818] Now, therefore, I sent this copy and another of another letter since I suspected that it too did not come into your hands, because you have again asked me certain questions that I find and recognize in it that I have already answered. But I do not know by whom I sent it. As the letter also indicates, the writings of Your Charity, to which I replied by my letter, were sent to me by our brothers from Hippo, since I was staying with our holy brother and fellow bishop, Boniface[819] (for I did not see its bearer), and I did not put off an immediate reply.

3. Because at that time, as I wrote, I had not been able to look at the Greek manuscripts on account of certain verses of Psalm Sixteen, I later looked at those I found. And one of them had what our Latin books have: *Lord, removing them from the land, scatter them* (Ps 17:14). Another has, as you quoted: *From the few from the land.* And the meaning of the former is, of course, clear: *Removing them from the land* that you gave them, *scatter them* among the nations, and this took place when they were defeated and wiped out in a terrible war.[820] But I have no idea how the other version should be interpreted, unless in comparison with the great number of them who were lost a remnant was saved, namely, among the

---

816. See 2 Cor 7:6.
817. Letter 121.
818. Letter 95.
819. Boniface was the bishop of Cataqua.
820. Jerusalem was destroyed by the Romans in 70 A.D.

few from whom Scripture foretold they were going to be scattered, that is, divided and separated. It said: *O Lord, from the few*, that is, from the remnant that you made from that people, *scatter them from the land*, where we understand the land to be the Church and the heritage of believers and saints, which is called the land of the living.[821] We can also correctly understand this from that passage: *Blessed are the meek because they shall possess the land as their heritage* (Mt 5:4). But after it said, *From the few divide them from the land*, it added, *in their life*, in order that it would be clearly understood that this will be while they live this life. For many are separated from the Church, but only when they die, for when they are living they seem to be united to the Church by sharing in the sacraments and in the Catholic unity. These, then, have been divided from the few who came to believe from among them from the land that the Father, like a farmer, cultivates like his own field.[822] They have, however, been divided in this life, that is, here in a clear manner, as we now see. There follows, however: *And their belly has been filled from your secrets*. That is, besides the fact that they have been clearly divided, *their belly has been filled* even *from your secrets*, which you secretly repay to the conscience of the wicked. The Psalmist used "belly" for the secret places of what is internal and hidden.

4. But I have already said what I thought about the next words, *They have been sated with pork*. But the reading of the other manuscripts, which are regarded as more accurate because the more careful copies remove the ambiguity by the accent mark on this same Greek word in the Greek way of writing,[823] is, of course, more obscure, but it seems to fit better with a preferable meaning. For, since it said, *And their belly has been filled from your secrets*, which words signified the hidden judgments of God, those people are wretched in a hidden way, even if they are happy in their sins, since God has abandoned them to the desires of their heart.[824] And as if the Psalmist were asked how they could be known who are filled with the wrath of God in secret, and as if he gave the answer found in the Gospel, *From their fruits you will know them* (Mt 7:16), there was immediately added, *They were sated with their children*, that is, with their fruits, and it is expressed more clearly as "with their works." For this reason we read elsewhere, *See, he brought to birth injustice; he conceived pain and bore iniquity* (Ps 8:15), and elsewhere, *Then, after it has conceived, concupiscence begets sin* (Jas 1:15). Bad children, then, are the bad actions by which they are known who have been filled as if in the belly of their own thoughts by the hidden judgments of God. Good children are good works. Hence, he says to the Church, his spouse, *Your teeth are like a flock of shorn sheep climbing out of the bath; all of them produce twins, and none of them is sterile* (Sg 4:2). In the twin offspring the twofold

---

821. See Pss 27:13; 142:6; Is 38:11; 53:8; Jer 11:19.
822. See Jn 15:1.
823. That is, in some manuscripts there is found υἱῶν (children); in others ὑῶν (pigs) or ὑειῶν (pork). The difference is not due to accent marks but to the vowels.
824. See Rom 1:24.

work of love is seen, namely, of the Lord God and of the neighbor, on which two commandments the whole law and the prophets depend.[825]

5. This interpretation, however, by which the words, *They were sated with their children,* are explained had not occurred to me when I wrote to you before, but I reexamined a very brief explanation of the same Psalm that I had long ago dictated, and I found that I had quite briefly said this. I also examined the Greek manuscripts to see whether *children* was in the dative case or the genitive, which that language uses in place of the ablative, and I found the genitive. If this were translated word for word, it would read: *They were sated of their children.* But the translator correctly followed the sense and said in the Latin way, *They were sated with their children.* But with regard to what follows, *And they left the remnants for their little ones,* I think that we should understand the little ones as the obvious children of the flesh. Hence, even according to this explanation, not about pork but about children, the sense remains the same as that by which they said: *His blood be upon us and upon our children* (Mt 27:25). For in that way they left the remainder of their work to their little ones.

6. But in Psalm Fifteen it says, *He has made marvelous,* or *Let him make marvelous all his desires among them* (Ps 16:3). Nothing prevents us from understanding not *among them* but *in them*; in fact, it seems better to do so. For the Greek manuscripts have it that way. But our people often translate *in them,* which that language has as *among them.* Let us take it, then, as follows: *For the holy ones who are in his land, he has made marvelous all his desires in them,* which most manuscripts have. And let us understand *all his desires* as the gifts of grace that are given freely, that is, because he wanted to, not because they were owed. Hence it says, *With the shield of your goodwill you have crowned us* (Ps 6:13), and *Willingly he begot us by the word of truth* (Jas 1:18), and *You set aside a free rain, O God, for your heritage* (Ps 68:10), and *apportioning to each one his gifts as he wants* (1 Cor 12:11), and countless others. Hence, *He made marvelous all his desires in them.* In whom but in *the holy ones in his land*? If *land* can, as we showed above, be taken in a good sense, even where *his* is not added,[826] how much more can it be where it says *his land*! *He made,* therefore, *all his desires marvelous in them*; he made his desires absolutely marvelous, because he set them free in a marvelous way from despair.

7. As a result of that admiration the Apostle cried out, *O the depth of the riches of the wisdom and knowledge of God!* (Rom 11:33). He had, of course, said above, *For God enclosed all in unbelief in order that he might show mercy to all* (Rom 11:32). For this also follows here: *Their infirmities were made many; afterward they hurried* (Ps 16:4). He used *infirmities* instead of "sins," just as the Apostle says to the Romans, *For if, when we were infirm, Christ died for sin-*

---

825. See Mt 22:40.
826. See above 1, 3, where it stands for the Church.

ners at the appointed time (Rom 5:6). He calls the same people infirm whom he calls sinners. Then shortly after this sentence, he says in repetition, *God proves his love for us, because, when we were still sinners, Christ died for us* (Rom 5:8). Those whom he called infirm above, he here called sinners. So too, in the following verses he says the same things in other words: *For if, when we were enemies, we were reconciled to God through the death of his Son* (Rom 5:10). And for this reason in the verse that says, *Their infirmities were made many*, we understand that their sins were made many. For the law entered in order that sin might abound. But since where sin abounded grace was even more abundant,[827] for this reason *afterwards they hurried*. For he did not come to call the righteous, but sinners,[828] since *it is not those in good health, but the sick who need a doctor* (Mt 9:12), that is, those whose infirmities were made many in order that the medicine of so great a grace might be needed for healing them and in order that one who is forgiven many sins may love much.[829]

8. The ashes of a cow and the sprinkling of blood and the multiplication of victims signified this but did not bring it about. For this reason it goes on to say, *I will not gather their assemblies for the sake of blood* (Ps 16:4), that is, for the sake of the sacrifices that were immolated as a symbol of the blood of Christ. *Nor will I be mindful of their names with my lips*. Their names signified a multitude of infirmities: fornicators, idolaters, adulterers, the effeminate, sodomites, thieves, the greedy, robbers, drunks, revilers, and all those who will not possess the kingdom of God.[830] But where, because sin abounded, grace was even more abundant,[831] *afterwards they hurried*. They were indeed these things, but they were washed; they were made holy; they were made righteous in the name of the Lord Jesus Christ and in the Spirit of our God.[832] For this reason he will not be mindful of their names with his lips.[833] The more correct manuscripts and those of greater authority do not have *his own desires* but *my desires*. This is just as good since it is said in the person of the Son. It is he, of course, who speaks as those words clearly show that the apostle also used: *You will not leave my soul in the underworld, nor will you allow your holy one to see corruption* (Ps 15:10).[834] The gifts of grace of the Father and of the Son and of the Holy Spirit are, of course, the same, and for this reason the Son also can say: *His own desires*.

9. But in Psalm Fifty-Eight it says, *Do not kill them lest they forget your law* (Ps 59:12); this is understood of the Jews. It seems to me that this can be suitably understood to have been a prediction that the same people even when

---

827. See Rom 5:20.
828. See Mt 9:13.
829. See Lk 7:47.
830. See 1 Cor 6:9-10.
831. See Rom 5:22.
832. See 1 Cor 6:11.
833. See Ps 16:4.
834. See Acts 2:31; 13:35.

conquered and defeated, would not give in to the superstitions of the conquering people but would abide by the old law in order that in that law there might be found the testimony of the Scriptures in the whole world, from which the Church was going to be called. For the Gentiles are shown by no more evident proof than this a fact that they notice for their salvation, namely, that it was not something unexpected and unforeseen initiated by the spirit of human presumption that the name of Christ enjoys such great authority in terms of the hope of salvation, but this was foretold and written down long ago. For what else would they think but that our people made up the prophecy if it were not proven from the manuscripts of our enemies? And so, *do not kill them*, lest the name of this people be wiped out, *in order that they may not forget your law*, something that would happen if, when they were compelled to observe fully the rites and sacrifices of the pagans, they did not retain any mention of their own religion. As a symbol of them Scripture says of Cain that the Lord put on him a mark so that no one would kill him.[835] Next, after the Psalmist had said, *Do not kill them so that they do not forget your law*, as if he were asked what should be done with them in order that they might not be killed, that is, in order that they might not become extinct and might not forget the law, but might be of service in testimony to the truth, he immediately added, *Scatter them by means of your power* (Ps 59:12). For, if they were in one place on the earth, they would not by their testimony help the preaching of the Gospel, which bears fruit in the whole world. For this reason, *Scatter them by means of your power*, in order that by the law, which they do not forget, they may be witnesses everywhere to him whom they denied, persecuted, and killed. For that law foretold the one whom they do not follow. Nor, after all, does it do them any good that they do not forget it; it is one thing to have the law of God in one's memory and another to have it in one's intellect and actions.

10. In Psalm Sixty-Seven, however, you ask about what this means: *God, nonetheless, will crush the heads of his enemies, the top of the hair of those who walk in their sins* (Ps 68:22). I do not think that it means anything but that God will crush the heads of his enemies, of those who are excessively proud, of those who are too exalted in their sins. By hyperbole he of course signified pride that is so exalted and walks in such elation, as if one were treading upon the top of a hair in walking. So too, the words in the same Psalm, *The tongue of your dogs* [comes] *from enemies by him* (Ps 68:24).[836] Dogs are not always to be taken in the bad sense. Otherwise, the prophet would not criticize the silent dogs that do not know how to bark and love to sleep.[837] For the dogs would certainly be praiseworthy if they knew how to bark and liked to keep watch. And certainly those three hundred—those who lapped up water like dogs[838]—who were des-

---

835. See Gn 4:15.
836. Augustine's Latin is a word-for-word translation of the Septuagint: ἡ γλῶσσα τῶν κυνῶν σου ἐχθρῶν παρ' αὐτου.
837. See Is 56:10.
838. See Jgs 7:7.

ignated by that most sacred number signifying the cross,[839] would not be chosen to bring about victory if they did not signify something important. For good dogs keep watch and bark in defense of the house, the master, the flock, and the shepherd. Finally, this is also expressed in praises of the Church as prophecy; the tongues, not the teeth, of the dogs are mentioned. But *your dogs*, it said, come *from your enemies*; that is, in order that those who were your enemies may become your dogs and that those who raged against you may bark in your defense. But he added: *By him*, that is, in order that they might understand that this was not done by themselves, but by him, that is, by his mercy and grace.

2, 11. I understand the Apostle's words regarding the prophets, *God made certain persons in the Church apostles, but certain others prophets* (Eph 4:11), in the same way as you yourself wrote, namely, that those were called prophets in this passage whose number included Agabus,[840] not those who foretold that the Lord would come in the flesh. But we find evangelists who were not apostles, for example Mark and Luke. I, however, think that shepherds and teachers, whom you especially wanted me to distinguish, are the same, just as you thought, so that we do not understand that some are shepherds and others teachers. But, after he had first said shepherds, he added teachers in order that shepherds would understand that teaching pertains to their office. For this reason he does not say, "But certain persons shepherds and certain others teachers," though he had distinguished the previous kinds of persons by this sort of language when he said, *Certain persons apostles, but certain others prophets, and certain others evangelists*. Rather he included this like a single office under two names: *But certain others pastors and teachers*.

12. It is clearly difficult to distinguish those terms where in writing to Timothy he says: *I beg you, therefore, first of all that entreaties, prayers, intercessions, and thanksgiving be made* (1 Tm 2:1). They must be distinguished in terms of the Greek language, for it is hard to find our translators who have taken care to translate them with diligence and knowledge. For, look, the Apostle who of course wrote that letter in Greek did not express both of these by the same word as you quoted it: *I beg* (*obsecro*) *that entreaties* (*obsecrationes*) *be made*. But instead of the Latin, *obsecro*, he said in Greek: παρακαλῶ (I urge). But for *obsecrationes*, which our Latin has, he used δεήσεις (petitions). Hence, other manuscripts, including ours, do not have *entreaties* but *petitions*. Most Latin manuscripts have the following three terms in this way: *prayers, intercessions, thanksgiving*.

13. Hence, if we want to distinguish these terms according to the proper meanings in the manner of speaking the Latin language, we will perhaps hold our view or some other, but it would be surprising if we got the sense for the Greek language or usage. Many of ours think that "prayer" (*precatio*) and "deprecation" (*deprecatio*) are the same, and this has absolutely prevailed in our daily

---

839. The Greek letter tau has the shape of a cross and is the sign for the number 300. Gideon had only 300 warriors, those who lapped up water like dogs, to deliver Israel from the Medianites.
840. See Acts 11:27-28.

usage. But those who have spoken Latin with more precision use "prayers" for desiring good things, but "deprecations" for avoiding evils. For they said "to pray" (*precari*) is to desire good things by praying, but "to imprecate" (*imprecari*), which is commonly said, is to curse, while "to deprecate" (*deprecari*) is to ward off evils by praying. Let us rather follow the usual manner of speaking and, whether we find "prayers" or "petitions," which the Greeks call δεήσεις, let us not suppose that it should be corrected. But it is very difficult to distinguish "orations," which in Greek is προσευχάς, from "prayers" and "petitions." But certain manuscripts do not have "orations" but "adorations," because in Greek it did not say εὐχάς but προσευχάς. I do not think that this was translated wisely. For it is very well known that for "orations" the Greeks use προσευχάι. And to pray is something other than to adore. Finally, we do not find this verb but another in Greek, where it says, *You shall adore the Lord your God* (Mt 4:10), and *I will adore at your holy temple* (Ps 5:8).

14. But instead of "intercessions," which our manuscripts have, you put "petitions" in accord with your manuscripts, I believe. Regarding these two words, that is, which some translated as "petitions" and others as "intercessions," they wanted to translate the one word that the Greek has: ἐντεύξεις. And you certainly notice and know that to intercede is different than to petition. For we do not usually say, "They intercede in order to petition," but "They petition in order to intercede." Nonetheless, a word used because of the closeness of its meaning, which gets its meaning from this nearness, should not be blamed as an error. For Scripture even said of our Lord Jesus Christ that *he intercedes on our behalf* (Rom 8:34 and Heb 7:25). Does he intercede and not also petition? On the contrary, precisely because he petitions, "intercedes" was used in its place. It is clearly said of him in another passage: *And if anyone sins, we have an advocate before the Father, Jesus Christ the righteous one, and he is the intercession on behalf of our sins* (1 Jn 2:1-2). Although the manuscripts that you have perhaps do not say in that place, *He intercedes on our behalf*, but *He petitions on our behalf*, in the Greek, because of which "intercessions" was used here, where you quoted "petitions," it is the same verb as where Scripture says: *He intercedes on our behalf*.

15. Since, then, one who beseeches prays and one who prays beseeches and one who intercedes with God intercedes in order to pray and to beseech, what does it mean that the apostle used these words in such a way that we ought not to neglect this distinction? If you leave aside the general meaning and keep the customary way of speaking, whether you say "beseech," "pray," "intercede," or "petition," one and the same action is understood. But we should look for some particular meaning for each of these individual acts. It is, however, difficult to come to that meaning clearly. Many things can, of course, be said here that should not be criticized.

16. But I choose to understand in these words what the whole or almost the whole Church usually understands, and thus we take *precationes* as those prayers which we make in the celebration of the sacraments before we begin to

bless the offerings on the Lord's table. We take *orationes* to be those prayers said when the offerings are blessed and sanctified and broken for distribution, and almost every church concludes this whole prayer with the Lord's Prayer. The origin of the Greek word also helps us for understanding this. For scripture rarely uses what they call ευχή in order to express "prayer." But usually and much more frequently it calls a vow ευχή but it always called prayer προσευχή, which is the word used in the passage we are dealing with. For this reason some less learned people looked to the origin of this word and wanted to say that it was not prayer (*oratio*), but adoration (*adoratio*), which is rather said to be προσκύνησις. But since prayer (*oratio*) is at times called ευχή, adoration was thought to be προσευχή. But if, as I said, a vow is called ευχή in Scripture, apart from the general term for prayer, that is called prayer in the proper sense which we make by a vow, that is, πρὸς ευχήν. For everything we offer to God, especially the sacrifice of the altar, is offered as a vow. That sacrament declares that greatest vow of ours by which we vow that we will remain in Christ, that is, in the unity of the body of Christ. It is a sacred sign of the reality that we are one bread, one body.[841] And so I think that the Apostle commanded that in preparation for this sanctification we make προσευχάι, that is, "prayers" or, as some have translated less learnedly, "adorations." For this means "as a vow," which is more usually called ευχή in Scripture. "Intercessions," however, or "petitions," as your manuscripts have, are made when the people are blessed. For then the bishops, like defense lawyers, offer to God's most merciful power those under their protection by the imposition of hands. After they have done this and have partaken of the sacrament, everything is ended with the thanksgiving, which the Apostle also emphasized with these last words.

17. But the main reason for saying these things was that, after he briefly marked off and indicated these forms of prayer, we would not think that we should neglect what follows: *for all people, for kings and those in a lofty position, in order that we might lead a quiet and peaceful life in all piety and love* (1 Tm 2:1). Otherwise someone might think, given the weakness of the human mind, that we should not make these prayers for those from whom the Church suffers persecution, since the members of Christ are to be gathered from every kind of human being. For this reason he says in addition, *for this is good and pleasing in the sight of God, our Savior, who wants all people to be saved and come to the knowledge of the truth* (1 Tm 2:3-4). And lest anyone say that the way of salvation can consist in living a good life and the worship of God without partaking of the body and blood of Christ, he says, *for there is one God and one mediator between God and human beings, the man Jesus Christ* (1 Tm 2:5), in order that his words, *he wants all people to be saved*, might be understood in no other sense than that this salvation is offered only through the mediator, not

---

841. See 1 Cor 10:17.

God, who as the Word always existed, but the man Jesus Christ, since the Word became flesh and dwelled among us.[842]

18. Hence, do not let the words of the same Apostle about the Jews disturb you. He says, *In terms of the gospel they are enemies on your account, but in terms of the election they are beloved on account of the patriarchs* (Rom 11:28). That depth, of course, of the riches of wisdom and knowledge and those inscrutable judgments of his and his unsearchable ways[843] produce this great awe in believing hearts that do not doubt his wisdom, which stretches from one end to another mightily and arranges all things gently,[844] but do not know why it pleases him that these people are born, grow, and multiply who, though he did not make them evil, he nonetheless foreknew would be evil. For his plan is too deeply hidden by which he makes good use even of the evil for the betterment of the good, revealing the marvels of the omnipotence of his goodness even in this. For just as it is a mark of their wickedness to make bad use of his good works, so it is a mark of his wisdom to make good use of their bad works.

19. The Apostle, then, sets forth the depth of this mystery as follows: *In order that you may not be wise in yourselves, I do not want you, brothers and sisters, to be ignorant of this mystery. For blindness has been produced in a part of Israel until the fullness of the Gentiles has entered, and in that way all of Israel will be saved.* (Rom 11:25) He said *in a part* because not all were blinded; after all, there were some from them who came to know Christ. The fullness of the Gentiles enters in these who have been called according to his plan, and in that way all of Israel will be saved, because those who have been called according to his plan both from the Jews and from the Gentiles are the true Israel. Of these the same Apostle says, *and over the Israel of God* (Gal 6:16), but he calls the others Israel according to the flesh. He says, *See Israel according to the flesh* (1 Cor 10:18). Then he inserts the testimony of the prophet, *He will come from Zion to remove and turn aside impiety from Jacob, and this is my testament with them when I shall take away their sins* (Rom 11:26-27; Is 59:20), not the sins of all the Jews, but of the chosen ones.

20. Here he adds those words that you set forth to be investigated: *They are enemies in terms of the gospel on your account.* The price of our redemption is, of course, the blood of Christ who certainly could be killed only by enemies. This exemplifies that use of the evil for the betterment of the good. Yet by the addition, *but beloved in terms of the election on account of the patriarchs*, he shows that it is not those enemies but the chosen who are beloved. But it is the custom of scripture to speak in this way of a part as if it were the whole. Thus he praised the Corinthians in the first parts of his letter as if all were like that because some of them deserved praise, and later in some passages of the same letter

---

842. See Jn 1:14.
843. See Rom 11:33.
844. See Wis 8:1.

he criticizes them as if all deserved blame on account of certain ones who did. Whoever takes careful note of this custom of the Divine Scriptures, which is evident in many places through the whole body of these writings, resolves numerous apparent contradictions. The Apostle, therefore, calls some people enemies and others beloved, but, because they were in one people, he seems to say that they were the same ones. And yet many even from the enemies who crucified the Lord were converted and were seen to be chosen. They were chosen at the time when they were converted in terms of the beginning of salvation, but in terms of the foreknowledge of God they were not chosen then but before the creation of the world, as the same Apostle says, *Because he chose us before the creation of the world* (Eph 1:4). In two ways, then, the same people were enemies who were beloved, either because they were both in one people or because, from enemies raging to the point of shedding Christ's blood, certain of them became beloved according to the election that was hidden in the foreknowledge of God. For to this he added: *On account of the patriarchs*, because it was necessary that the promise made to the patriarchs be fulfilled, as he says near the end of the Letter to the Romans, *For I say that Christ was a minister to the circumcision on account of the truthfulness of God in order to confirm the promises made to the patriarchs. But the Gentiles glorify God because of his mercy.* (Rom 15:8-9) In accord with this mercy Paul said *enemies on your account*, in the same sense as he said above, *from their sin came the salvation of the Gentiles*.

21. But after he said, *Beloved in terms of the election because of the patriarchs*, he added, *For the gifts and calling of God are without any repentance.* You surely see that he meant those who belong to the number of the predestined. Of them he says in another passage, *We know that for those who love God all things work together to the good, for those who are called according to his plan* (Rom 8:28). For many are called, but few are chosen.[845] But the chosen are those who are called according to his plan. Regarding these the foreknowledge of God undoubtedly cannot be deceived. *He foreknew and predestined these to be conformed to the image of his Son in order that he might be the firstborn among many brothers. But those he predestined he also called.* (Rom 8:28-29) This is the calling according to his plan; this is the calling without repentance. *But those he called he also made righteous, and those he made righteous he also glorified. If God is for us, who is against us?* (Rom 8:30-31)

22. They are not included in this calling who, even though they live for some time in the faith that works through love,[846] do not persevere up to the end. And of course they could have been carried off so that malice would not change their mind[847] if they belonged to that predestination and calling that is according to his plan and without repentance. But no one should be so presumptuous and

---

845. See Mt 22:14.
846. See Gal 5:6.
847. See Wis 4:11.

judgmental concerning the hidden sins of others as to say, "They were not taken from this life before they abandoned the faith because they were not living this life faithfully, and the Lord knew this in their hearts, even though they looked other- wise to human beings." What is such a presumptuous person going to say about tiny infants? After receiving the sacrament of Christian grace at that age, they undoubtedly would belong to eternal life and the kingdom of heaven if they immediately departed from this life, but many are allowed to grow up, and some of them become apostates. Why, except that they do not belong to that predestination and the calling according to his plan and without repentance? But the reason why some belong to it and others do not may be hidden but cannot be unjust. After all, is there injustice in God? Heaven forbid![848] For this too belongs to that profundity of God's judgments that left the Apostle as if astonished and amazed. And of course he calls them judgments in order that no one would think that such things happen through either injustice or the thoughtlessness of the agent or because any parts of the ages that God has arranged according to his great wisdom pass by chance and without design.

23. You said that the words in the Letter to the Colossians, *Let no one mislead you by wanting to feign humility* (Col 2:18), and the rest that follow are extremely obscure to you, nor do I myself as yet understand them clearly. I wish that you had asked me this face to face, for, in order to bring out to some degree the meaning that I think I find in these words, I have to use a certain expression of the face and tone of voice that cannot be expressed in writing, and the words become more obscure because they are not, I think, correctly pronounced. For the words of Scripture, *Do not handle; do not taste; do not touch* (Col 2:21), are thought to be like a command of the apostle forbidding us to handle, to taste, and to touch something or other. But, unless I am mistaken amid such great obscurity, it is just the opposite. With irony, in fact, he quoted the words of those by whom he did not want the Colossians to be deceived and misled; those people distinguish foods in accord with the worship of the angels, and in that way they judge concerning this world. They say, *Do not handle; do not taste; do not touch*, though all things are clean for the clean,[849] and every creature of God is good,[850] something that he clearly teaches in another passage.[851]

24. Let us look, then, at the whole context of this phrase, for in that way, once we have seen the Apostle's intention, we will perhaps grasp his meaning to the extent we can. For he feared that those to whom he writes this are being misled by the shadows of things, under the sweet name of knowledge, and being turned away from the light of the truth which is found in Christ Jesus, our Lord. He saw, however, that this concern for empty or superfluous observances under

---

848. See Rom 9:14.
849. See Tit 1:15.
850. See 1 Tm 4:4.
851. See Rom 14:20.

the guise of wisdom and knowledge, stemming both from the superstition of the Gentiles, especially from those who are called philosophers, and from Judaism, must be avoided. There the shadows of future things had to be removed since Christ, their light, had come. He therefore mentioned and emphasized the great struggle he had for them and for those who were from Laodicea and for all who did not personally know him in order that they might be consoled in their hearts, united in love and in all the riches of the fullness of understanding, in order to know the mystery of God, which is Christ, in whom are hidden all the treasures of wisdom and knowledge.[852] Then he says, *I say this so that no one may deceive you in words with the appearance of truth* (Col 2:4); because they were attracted by the love of the truth, the apostle feared that they would be deceived by the appearance of truth. And for this reason he emphasized that they have in Christ a most sweet treasure, namely, a treasure of wisdom and knowledge, for they could be led into error by the mention and promise of it.

25. The Apostle says, *For, even if I am absent in terms of the body, I am present with you in spirit, rejoicing and seeing your discipline and what is lacking in your faith in Christ* (Col 2:5). He was afraid for them because he saw what they still lacked. He says, *Just as you accepted Jesus Christ our Lord, so live in him, rooted in and built upon him and made strong in faith, just as you were taught, abounding in acts of thanksgiving* (Col 2:6). He wants them to be nourished in faith in order that they may be capable of partaking of the treasures of wisdom and knowledge, which are hidden in Christ. Otherwise, before they are suited for these, they might be taken in by words that seem true and wander away from the path of truth. Then, more openly showing what he fears for them, he says, *See that no one deceives you through philosophy and empty enticement according to human tradition, according to the elements of the world, and not according to Christ. For in him dwells all the fullness of divinity in a bodily manner.* (Col 2:8-9) He says *in a bodily manner* because they were being misled by shadows, using a metaphor, just as the term "shadow" in these matters is not used in its proper sense but metaphorically by reason of a certain likeness. He says, *And you have been filled with him who is the head of every principality and power* (Col 2:10). For the superstition of the pagans or the philosophers was misleading them by principalities and powers, proclaiming what they call theology through the elements of this world. But he wanted us to understand that the head of all things is Christ, the principle of all things, just as, when he was asked, *Who are you?* he replied: *The principle, I who am also speaking to you* (Jn 8:25). For all things were made through him, and without him nothing was made.[853] In a wonderful way the Apostle, however, wants the Colossians to hold in contempt these so-called wonders when he shows that they had become the body of that head, saying: *And you have been filled with him who is the head of every principality and power.*

---

852. See Col 2:1-3.
853. See Jn 1:3.

26. So that they would not be misled by the shadows of Judaism, he adds: *In whom you have also been circumcised, not by a circumcision made by hand in the removal of part of the body of flesh*—or as some manuscripts have, *in the removal of a part of the body of sins of the flesh*—*but in the circumcision of Christ. You have been buried with him in baptism, and you have also risen with him through faith in the act of God who raised him from the dead* (Col 2:12). See how here too he shows them the body of Christ in order that they may hold these things in contempt, clinging to their great head, Jesus Christ, the mediator between God and human beings, and not looking for a false and powerless intermediary by which they might cling to God. He says, *And when you were dead in your sins and in the foreskin of the flesh.* He called the foreskin what is signified by the foreskin, that is, sins of the flesh that we must remove. He says, *He brought you to life along with him, forgiving you all your sins, wiping out the decree of condemnation that was against us and was opposed to us* (Col 2:14). For the law, which entered in, in order that sin might abound, made them guilty. He said, *Taking it from our midst and nailing it to the cross, he stripped himself of the flesh and made an example of the principalities and powers, triumphing over them in himself confidently* (Col 2:15). He made an example not, to be sure, of good but of evil principalities and evil powers, that is, diabolical and demonic ones. He produced an example by them to show that, just as he stripped himself of the flesh, so the Colossians must be stripped of their carnal vices by which they were subject to those principalities and powers.

27. Now pay careful attention to how he introduced that on account of which we have mentioned all this. He says, *Let no one judge you regarding food* (Col 2:16), as if he said all this because they were being led astray by such observances from the truth that had freed them. In the Gospel it says of that truth, *And the truth will set you free* (Jn 8:32), that is, will make you free. He says, *Let no one judge you regarding food or drink or with respect to a feast day or the new moon or the sabbath days, for this is a foreshadowing of what was to come* (Col 2:16-17). This was said on account of Judaism. Next there follows what was said on account of the superstitions of the pagans. He says, *But the body is Christ's. Let no one condemn you*; he says that it is shameful and highly incongruous and foreign to the nobility of your freedom that, though you are the body of Christ, you are led astray by shadows and seem to be proven guilty like sinners if you fail to observe these things. *But the body is Christ's. Let no one condemn you by wanting to feign humility of heart.* (Col 2:17-18) Although this was said in Greek, it would sound quite familiar in the Latin usage of the people. For in that way one who pretends to be rich is commonly called a would-be rich man, and one who pretends to be wise is called a would-be wise man,[854] and other expressions of the sort. Hence, this would-be humble man, which is expressed in greater detail as "wanting to be humble," that is, wanting to appear humble,

---

854. Augustine uses *thelodives* and *thelosapiens* and *thelohumilis*, words that are half Greek, but

pretending to be humble. This means wanting to be seen as humble, feigning humility. And he added, *and the cult of the angels*, or as our manuscripts have, *the religion of the angels*, which in Greek is θρησκηία. He wants us to understand by the angels the principalities that they think should be worshiped by these observances as the rulers of the elements of this world.

28. Let no one, he says, who wants to appear humble of heart in the cult of the angels condemn you since you are the body of Christ. He says, *teaching what he did not see*, or as certain manuscripts have, *teaching what he saw*. He either said, *teaching what he did not see*, because people carry out these practices because of suspicions and suppositions, not because they see that they should do them, or he said, *teaching what he saw*, that is, thinking them important, because he saw that those practices are observed in certain places by men in whose authority he put his trust, even if an argument was not given. And he thinks that he is someone important because he happens to see the secrets of certain sacred rites. But the fuller meaning is the following: *teaching what he does not see, vainly puffed up in his carnal mind*. He said that he was puffed up in a surprising way in his carnal mind where he said previously "a would-be humble man." For it happens in strange ways in the human soul that one is more puffed up from false humility than if one is just plain proud. *And not holding onto the head*, where he wants us to understand Christ, *from whom the whole body, joined together and connected, having received nourishment and cohesion, grows into the development God wills. If, then, you have died with Christ to the elements of this world, why do you judge as if you were still living in the world?* (Col 2:19-20)

29. Having said this, he inserts the words of those who judge concerning the world on the basis of these supposedly reasonable observances and are puffed up with their vain pretense of humility: *Do not handle; do not taste; do not touch*. Let us recall what we said previously in order to understand this. For he does not want them to be judged regarding these observances when he says, *Do not handle; do not taste; do not touch; all these things*, he says, *are destined for corruption by their use* (Col 2:22). All these things, he says, serve more for corruption when one abstains from them through superstition so that a person misuses them, that is, does not use them, *in accord with the precepts and teachings of human beings*. This is clear, but on what follows you have many questions. *These things have the appearance of wisdom in their observance, in humility of the heart and in the affliction of the body*, or as others have translated it, *for not sparing the body, nor in some honor for the satisfaction of the flesh* (Col 2:23). Why, you ask, does he say that these things, which he blames in this way, have the appearance of wisdom?

30. I will say what you yourself can see in the Scriptures, namely, that wisdom is often attributed to the positions of this world, and Scripture quite explic-

---

apparently at least the first two were in popular usage.

itly calls it the wisdom of this world. Do not let it bother you that he did not here add "of the world." For in another passage where he said, *Where is there a wise man? Where is there a scribe?* (1 Cor 1:20), he did not also add "of this world," so as to say, "Where is there a wise man of this world?" And yet, it is understood. And so it is with this *appearance of wisdom*. For they say nothing in the observances of such superstition where they do not seem to give a certain appearance of wisdom regarding the elements of this world and the natures of things. For even when he says, *Beware that no one deceives you through philosophy*, he does not say "of this world," and what is philosophy in Latin but the pursuit of wisdom? *These things have*, he says, *the appearance of wisdom*, that is, those things about which they give some explanation in accord with the elements of this world and the principalities and powers. *In their observance, in humility of the heart*, for they do these things so that the heart is humbled by the vice of superstition. *For not sparing the body*, when it is deprived of these foods from which they are forced to abstain. *Nor in some honor for the satisfaction of the flesh*, not because the flesh is more honorably satisfied by this food rather than by that, since only refreshment and sustenance by any food suitable for one's health pertains to what is necessary.

3, 31. Your question about the Gospel often causes problems for many people, namely, how after the resurrection, though he rose in the same body, certain persons of both sexes who knew him recognized him and certain others did not. Here it is usually asked first whether something was brought about in his body or rather in their eyes in order that they could not recognize him. For when we read, *Their eyes were prevented from recognizing him* (Lk 24:16), it seems that a certain impediment for recognizing him was produced in the eyes of those who saw him. But when it clearly says elsewhere, *He appeared to them in another guise* (Mk 16:12), it seems that something was produced in the body itself whose appearance was different, and they were prevented by that impediment; that is, their eyes suffered a delay in recognizing him. But since there are two things in a body by which the appearance of anyone is recognized, the features and color, I wonder about this. Why does it cause problems of recognition for no one that, before the resurrection when he was so transfigured on the mountain that his face became as bright as the sun,[855] he was able to change the color of his body to so great an excellence of brightness and light? But after the resurrection it causes problems that his features were slightly changed so that he could not be recognized and that by the ease of his power he then regained his same color, just as after the resurrection he also got back his same features. For those three disciples before whose eyes he was transfigured on the mountain would not recognize him if he had come to them from elsewhere, but, because they were with him, they held it for certain that it was he. But it was the same body in which he rose. How is this pertinent? After all, the body in which he was transfigured on the mountain

---

855. See Mt 17:2.

was certainly the same as the body he had as a young man and as the body in which he was born, and yet, if someone who knew only the little baby suddenly saw him as a young man, he would certainly not recognize him. Or is the power of God unable to change the features quickly, something that the age of a man can only do over many years?

32. But you know that I understood Christ's words to Mary, *Do not touch me, for I have not yet ascended to the Father* (Jn 20:17), just as you did. For he wanted to convey in that way that he asks for a spiritual touch, that is, that an approach with a faith that believes that he is on high with the Father. And as for the fact that he was recognized by those two in the breaking of the bread,[856] no one should doubt that it signifies the sacrament that gathers us together in order to recognize him.

33. Concerning the words of Simeon, where he says to the Virgin, the mother of the Lord, *And a sword shall pierce your soul* (Lk 2:35), I said what I thought in another letter, a copy of which I just sent you. And that is what you also thought among other things. I think that the next words, *in order that the thoughts of many hearts might be laid bare*, ought to be understood in the sense that the Lord's passion revealed the plotting of the Jews and the weakness of the disciples. It is, then, credible that the term *sword* signified the tribulation by which her maternal soul was wounded by the feeling of sorrow. The sword was in the mouth of his persecutors, of whom the Psalm says, *And the sword was in their mouth* (Ps 59:8). They were the sons of men whose teeth were weapons and arrows, and their tongue a sharp sword.[857] For I think that the sword that pierced the soul of Joseph[858] stood for severe tribulation; for Scripture clearly says, *A sword pierced his soul until his word came about* (Ps 105:18), that is, he was in severe tribulation until what he predicted happened. Because of this he was highly esteemed and was set free from that tribulation. But in order that it would not be attributed to human wisdom that his word came about, that is, that what he predicted happened, Holy Scripture gives glory to God for it in its usual manner and immediately adds, *The word of the Lord set him ablaze* (Ps 105:19).

34. I answered your questions as well as I could with the help of your prayers and your arguments that you sent. For, when you argue as you ask questions, you both ask with acuteness and teach with humility. It is useful, however, to discover many opinions on the obscure passages of the Divine Scriptures, which God wanted to be there in order to provide exercise for our minds, when different people have different views, though they are all nonetheless in accord with the teaching of sound faith. You will surely pardon my style since I am in a great hurry in order to catch the courier who has already boarded the ship. I greet in

---

856. See Lk 24:30-31.
857. See Ps 57:5.
858. See Gn 39:20.

return in this letter our son Paulinus,[859] who is most dear in the love of Christ, and I exhort him in a few words in my rush that he may give as many thanks as he can to the mercy of the Lord. For he knows how to give relief from tribulation, and he has sent Paulinus by a very violent storm into the harbor where you made your way by a calmer sea, though not trusting the sea's calmness, and God gave you to him to take up and nourish his beginnings in the spiritual life. And let all his bones cry out: *O Lord, who is like you?* (Ps 35:10). For he does not read or listen to me with greater benefit as I teach him, converse with him, or set him afire with any exhortation than he looks upon you as you live your life. My brothers and the fellow servants of God with me greet Your Graciousness in return. From the time, however, when our fellow deacon Peregrinus left me along with our holy brother Urbinus, when he went to take up the burden of the episcopacy, he has not returned to Hippo. From their letters and by word of mouth we nonetheless know that they are safe and sound in the name of Christ. We greet with brotherly love our fellow priest Paulinus and all who enjoy your presence in the Lord.

---

859. This Paulinus was probably a monk.

LETTER 5*

Augustine to Valentinian, the primate of Numidia (?)

In this letter, whose date cannot be determined, Augustine wrote to Valentinian, the Catholic bishop of Baiana and primate of Numidia. Augustine tells Valentinian that he would have preferred a visit rather than a letter from him with questions (paragraph 1). He explains why the Lord's Prayer is recited immediately after baptism, even in the case of infants (paragraph 2). Then he answers Valentianian's question about Genesis 6:3, where he points out two errors in the text that Valentinian was using and explains the meaning of *spirit* in that verse (paragraph 3).

To his most blessed lord and venerable and loveable brother and fellow bishop, Valentinian, Augustine sends greetings in the Lord.

1. You promise a visit, and in place of it you send us questions to answer that, as you write, trouble your heart. Though I would prefer to have you here, I still respond somehow to you in your absence by writing, despite how busy I am, but I could have replied more easily in conversation if you were present.

2. Your first question is why the baptized immediately confess their debts in [the Lord's][860] Prayer and ask that they be forgiven, since they were all forgiven in baptism. And though you resolved this same question for yourself on the basis of the harmful desires and illicit impulses of the heart, which easily sneak up on human weakness, you say that another question came to mind about infants who can neither think nor speak, as if anyone would command or force infants to be reborn, [like adults],[861] if they did not have to be washed in baptism on account of original sin. Or do you say this as if adults do not respond with words from the Lord's Prayer on their behalf, as they do with words from the symbol of faith? Without that they cannot be baptized at all, and for this reason those who bring them to baptism reply on their behalf to the words when they are questioned. There is nothing, then, that ought to upset you in the case of infants with regard to the debts that the baptized ask to be forgiven immediately after the bath in which all past sins are forgiven. They do this because of those debts that overtake us due to the readiness of the human mind [to sin].[862]

3. You likewise ask how we should interpret what God said: *My spirit will not remain in these men in this age* (Gn 6:3). Our own manuscripts, however, have it like this: *My spirit will not remain in these men for eternity*. Let the mis-

---

860. The Bibliothèque Augustinienne (BA) edition has added the words in brackets.
861. The BA edition has added the words in brackets.
862. The BA edition has added the words in brackets.

take of your book or books be corrected, and there will be no question over which to labor in asking why God said *in this age*, as if to signify that the punishment of the present death suffices for wicked sinners. For he threatened eternal death, rather, when he said, *My spirit will not remain in these men for eternity*. But the ambiguity of the Greek word misled the translator, who translated it so as to say *in this age*, though it should at least have said *for this age* and not *in this age*. For the Greek expression, εἰς αἰῶνα, can be expressed in Latin as *for this age* or *for eternity*. The translator should consider the meaning of Scripture in that passage so that he is not misled by an ambiguity. For, when you ask about which spirit he said this, whether about the spirit that gives life to the body or about the spirit that sanctifies the soul, there is no problem, since you hear God say *my spirit*. After all, he would say "their spirit" if he wanted us to understand the spirit by which the body is alive, since it belongs to human nature, and he could have correctly said *My spirit will not remain in these men* of the spirit that does not pertain to human nature and that could remain in them if they were not overcome by the pleasure of the flesh and did not abandon God and thus deserve to lose the Holy Spirit, who is the gift of God.[863] For, if you understand their spirit, by which they are human beings, in relation to their bodies, how could it remain in them since they were going to die at some point? But, if you understand it in relation to that part of them by which their body is living, how could it not remain in them since these are spirits that leave the body at death and necessarily exist wherever they are, whether they are happy or not? I think that I have sufficiently answered your questions. But I would not demand your physical presence if you had not promised it, and, since you did promise it, I demand it as a debt that you owe me.

---

863. See Rom 5:5.

AUGUSTINE AS BISHOP

LETTER 96

Augustine to Olympius, a Catholic layman and a high official at the imperial court in Ravenna (408)

In the beginning of September of 408, Augustine wrote to Olympius, a Catholic layman, newly appointed to the highest ministerial post of the imperial court (*magister officiorum*). Augustine congratulates Olympius on the attainment of his high office (paragraph 1). He then commends to Olympius the petition of Boniface, bishop of Cataqua, who has come into possession of ecclesiastical property that was acquired by his predecessor, Paul, through fraud and tax evasion and who is seeking a remission of the back taxes so that the church can own the property with a clear conscience (paragraph 2). Hence, Augustine asks Olympius to support Boniface's petition and even suggests that he might obtain the lands from the emperor in his own name and give them to the church (paragraph 3).

To his most beloved lord and son, Olympius, who is to be embraced with honor among the members of Christ, Augustine sends greetings.

1. Whatever you may have become in your career in this world, we, nonetheless, write with confidence to our dearest and most sincere fellow servant and Christian, Olympius. For we know that this is for you more glorious than all glory and more lofty than every loftiness. Rumor has, of course, brought us the news that you have attained a higher honor; whether or not this is true had not yet been confirmed for us when we obtained this opportunity for writing you. But since we know that you learned from the Lord not to think proud thoughts, but to associate with the humble,[864] we are confident that you will welcome our letter no differently than usual, no matter to what height you have attained, my dearest lord and son who are to be embraced with honor among the members of Christ. We have no doubt that you will wisely use temporal happiness for eternal gains in order that, the more power you have in this earthly state, the more you will use it for that heavenly city, which has brought you to birth in Christ, and you will be more richly repaid in the land of the living[865] and in the true peace of joys that are secure and that last without end.

2. I commend to Your Charity the petition of my holy brother and fellow bishop, Boniface,[866] in the hope that what was impossible before might perhaps now be possible. For, though he could perhaps without any question logically have himself retained what his predecessor had obtained, though under another name, and had already begun to possess in the name of the Church, we do not

---

864. See Rom 12:16; 11:20.
865. See Pss 115:9; 27:13.
866. Boniface was the recently ordained bishop of Cataqua in Numidia.

want him to have this worry on his conscience that he was in debt to the treasury. After all, this fraud did not cease to be fraud because it was committed against the government. And after that Paul, to whom we referred, became a bishop, he was going to renounce all his possessions on account of the immense amount of taxes he owed. Having received a pledge by which a certain amount of silver was owed to him, he bought, as if for the Church, these small fields from which he might support himself, under the name of a family that was very powerful at the time, in order that, when according to his custom he did not pay his taxes from them, he would suffer no problems from the tax collectors. But when Boniface was ordained for the same church at Paul's death, he was afraid to take possession of these fields, and though he could have asked the emperor for the pardon of the back taxes alone, which his predecessor had contracted from these small possessions we mentioned, he preferred to confess to the whole situation, since Paul bought those fields from his own money at an auction, when he was in debt to the government for taxes. Boniface did this in order that the Church might own them, if possible, not by the hidden injustice of a bishop, but by the evident generosity of a Christian emperor. But if it cannot be done, it is better that the servants of God endure the hard work of poverty than that they obtain the means to live with fraud on their conscience.

3. We beg that you be so kind as to give this petition your support, for he did not want to claim the benefit that was first obtained for fear that he would preclude for himself the possibility of a second petition. For the reply was not in accord with his desires. But now, since you have the same kindness as usual, but are greater in power, we do not give up hope that, with the Lord's help, this petition can easily be granted in accord with your merits. For, even if you asked for those places in your own name and yourself gave them to the previously mentioned church, who would find fault? Or who would not very highly praise your petition made, not in the service of earthly desire, but in that of Christian piety? May the mercy of the Lord our God protect you, my lord and son, and make you happier in Christ.

LETTER 97
Augustine to Olympius (408)

At the end of 408, Augustine again wrote to Olympius at the imperial court in Ravenna. Augustine thanks Olympius for replying to his letter (paragraph 1). He asks Olympius to make it known that the laws concerned with the destruction of idols and the correction of heretics were promulgated by the emperor, not by Stilicho (paragraph 2). He assures Olympius that he is acting in union with his fellow bishops in urging Olympius to implement the imperial laws and in asking Olympius to deliberate along with the bishops about the best means of implementing them (paragraph 3). Finally, Augustine expresses his concern for the weakness of some of those who were converted at the occasion of the imperial laws, but are now suffering persecution (paragraph 4).

To his illustrious lord and son, Olympius, who is rightly outstanding and worthy of much honor in the love of Christ, Augustine sends greetings in the Lord.

1. As soon as we heard that you were deservedly raised to your lofty position, though we did not yet have a fully certain report, we believed nothing else concerning your attitude toward the Church of God, whose son we rejoice to know you truly are, than what you soon disclosed to us by your letter. But now we also read the letter by which you of your own accord were so good as to send, despite our slowness and hesitance, your exhortation filled with good will in order that the Lord, by whose gift you are the man you are, might at last come to the aid of his Church through our humble instruction and your religious obedience. And we write to you with greater confidence, my excellent and rightly outstanding lord and son, who are worthy of much honor in the love of Christ.

2. And many brothers, holy colleagues of mine, went off, when the Church was severely disturbed, almost in flight to the most glorious imperial court. Either you have already seen them, or you have received their letters from the city of Rome when they found some opportunity. Though I was unable to share in some planning with them, I could not, nonetheless, pass up the chance to greet Your Charity, a charity which you have in Christ Jesus the Lord, by means of this brother and my fellow priest, who was forced to go to those parts somehow or other, even in the middle of winter, because of the urgent need for the safety of his fellow citizens. I also want to advise you to speed up your good work with much diligence and concern in order that the enemies of the Church may know that those laws which were sent to Africa concerning the destruction of idols and the correction of heretics, when Stilicho[867] was still alive, had been established

---

867. Stilicho was Olympius' predecessor in the post of *magister officiorum*.

by the will of the most pious and faithful emperor.[868] They deceitfully boast or rather choose to think that these laws were established without his knowledge or against his will, and for this reason they cause the minds of the ignorant to be very upset and dangerous and deeply hostile toward us.

3. I have no doubt that this advice, which I give to Your Excellency in asking this or rather suggesting it, is in accord with the will of all my colleagues throughout Africa. I think that, wherever the occasion first arises, you can most easily and ought quickly, as I said, to inform those foolish people whose salvation we are seeking, though they oppose this, that it was the son of Theodosius[869] rather than Stilicho who had taken care to send the laws that were sent for the defense of the Church of Christ. For this reason, of course, the priest I mentioned who carried them, since he was from the region of Milevis, was ordered by his venerable bishop, my brother, Severus,[870] to pass through Hippo Regius, where I am. Along with me Severus heartily greets Your Most Sincere Charity. For, since we happened to be at the same time suffering great tribulations and disturbances of the Church, we were looking for an opportunity to write to Your Excellency, and we did not find any. I, in fact, sent you one letter concerning the business of my holy brother and colleague, Boniface, the bishop of Cataqua,[871] but at that time there had not yet come upon us the more serious problems that would trouble us more deeply. To suppress or to correct these problems in a way that would bring help by a better plan in accord with the way of Christ, the bishops who have set sail on this account[872] will more suitably deal with the great kindness of your heart; for they were able to come to a decision that was more carefully thought out in a common plan to the extent that the limitations of time permitted. You must in no way, nonetheless, delay that action by which the province might know the mind of that most gentle and most religious emperor toward the church, but even before you see the bishops who have left here, I suggest, beg, plead, and demand that in your most excellent vigilance you hasten to do as soon as possible what you can for the members of Christ who are suffering very great tribulation. For the Lord offered us no small consolation amid these evils in that he willed that you have more power than you had when we already were rejoicing over your many and great good works.

4. We are very pleased at the firm and stable faith of certain persons, and these not few in number, who have converted to the Christian religion or to the Catholic peace at the occasion of these very laws. For their everlasting salvation we are delighted even to face dangers in this temporal life. For this reason, after

---

868. The emperor was Honorius.
869. Theodosius was Honorius' father and predecessor as emperor.
870. Severus was bishop of Milevis in Numidia from 396 to 426.
871. I.e., Letter 96.
872. These bishops were Restitutus and Florentius, who by the decree of the Council of Carthage on October 13, 408 were sent to the emperor to protest the actions of the pagans and heretics.

all, we now endure the more serious attacks of hatred, especially from men who are excessively and cruelly perverse, and some of the converts endure them most patiently along with us. But we fear very much for their weakness until they learn and have the ability, with the help of the most merciful grace of the Lord, to scorn the present age and the day of man with a greater strength of heart. Let the memorandum that I sent to my brother bishops be presented to them by Your Excellency when they arrive, unless, as I suspect, they are already there. We have such great confidence in your most sincere heart that, with the help of the Lord our God, we want you not only to be a source of help, but also to share in our deliberations.

LETTER 113

Augustine to Cresconius, a Catholic layman and tribune of the harbor at Hippo (409-423)

Sometime between 409 and 423 Augustine wrote this letter and the following on behalf of Faventius, who had sought asylum in the church of Hippo because of legal problems but became careless and was arrested and carried off. Augustine writes to Cresconius, a Catholic layman and tribune of the harbor at Hippo, asking him to intercede with the magistrate to allow Faventius the thirty-day period prescribed by imperial law to prepare his case and raise money while under moderate surveillance.

To his most beloved lord and rightly honorable and praiseworthy brother, Cresconius, Augustine sends greetings in the Lord.

If I turn a blind eye to this case concerning which, you see, I am again writing Your Eminence, not only Your Excellency, but also that man, whoever he is, because of whom Faventius[873] was seized in that manner, will deservedly blame me and rightly reprehend me. He will, of course, think that, if he himself had fled to the Church for help,[874] if something of the sort had happened to him, I would have turned a blind eye to his need and trouble. Moreover, if we should scorn the opinion of men, what shall I say to the Lord our God and what account shall I give him if I do not do as much as I can for the safety of one who entrusted himself for protection and help to the Church I serve, my most beloved lord and venerable son? I, therefore, beg Your Grace, since it is all but impossible and hard to believe that you either do not already know or cannot come to know the reason why he is being held, be so good in the meanwhile as to further my petition before the magistrate who is holding him in order that he may do what is prescribed by the emperor's law,[875] namely, that he should have him questioned in the municipal court whether he wants to be granted thirty days during which he might act under moderate surveillance in that city in which he is detained in order to prepare his case and to provide for his expenses. If, with the consent of Your Benevolence, we can in that period of time bring his case to an end through an amicable discussion, we shall have reason to rejoice. But if we cannot, he will face the decision of the courts that is pleasing to God in accord with the merits of the case itself or in accord with the will of the omnipotent Lord.

---

873. Faventius was arrested by Florentinus, an officer of the count of Africa, despite his having sought asylum in the church of Hippo.
874. The Christian churches enjoyed the right of asylum, as the pagan temples previously had.
875. Augustine refers to the law issued by Honorius on January 22, 409, which allowed someone arrested to request thirty days in which to prepare his case and to put his affairs in order. See Letter 114 where Augustine spells out the details of the law

LETTER 114

Augustine to Florentinus, an imperial official (soon after Letter 113)

Shortly after the previous letter Augustine wrote to Florentinus, an imperial official. He asks Florentinus for help with the case of Faventius and appeals to the imperial law, a copy of which he enclosed with this letter.

To his most beloved lord and son, Florentinus[876] *Augustine sends greetings in the Lord.*

It is up to you to see what authority gave the orders by which you seized Faventius. I, however, know this, namely, that all authority that is located under the imperial authority is subject to the laws of the emperor. Now, I sent to you by my brother and fellow priest, Coelestius, the text of the law of which you ought, of course, not to have been ignorant, even before I sent it. By that law it is permitted to those who are ordered by some authority to present themselves to the courts that they be brought before the municipal court and asked whether they want to spend thirty days under moderate surveillance in that city in which they are detained in order to prepare resources for themselves and set their case in order, as is needed. As the priest I mentioned reported to me, this law was read out for your revered self. I have, nonetheless, also now sent the same text along with this letter, not in order to threaten but in order to plead and to intercede for a human being in a human way and with the mercy of a bishop, to the extent that humaneness itself and piety permit. Be so good, my lord and son, as to add this to your reputation and grant my request, and do not hesitate to do on the occasion of my intervention and petition what the law of the emperor, whose country you serve, commands.

---

876. Florentinus was an officer of the governor of Africa and a Catholic layman; he had Faventius arrested. See Letter 113.

LETTER 153
Augustine to Macedonius (413-414)

In 413 or 414, Augustine replied to Macedonius's questions about intercession by bishops on behalf of the guilty (Letter 152). Macedonius, the vicar of Africa, had asked why Augustine supposes that it is the duty of a bishop to intercede on behalf of the guilty given the fact that the Church allows penance only once. Moreover, such intercession seems to make one an accomplice in the crime (paragraph 1). Augustine, first of all, agrees with Macedonius that all sins seem deserving of pardon when the guilty party promises amendment (paragraph 2). Next, he explains that he makes intercession for the guilty not because he approves of their sin but in order that they may be corrected in this life, where they still have a chance of amendment (paragraph 3). Augustine shows that the duty of intercession on behalf of the guilty stems from the teaching of Christ (paragraph 4). In commanding us to love our enemies and to do good to sinners, God certainly does not implicate us in their sins (paragraph 5). Excommunication of sinners aims only at bringing them to do penance for their sins (paragraph 6). Although the Church grants public penance only once to those who have committed serious sin, God continues to be merciful to those who repent (paragraph 7). There are different roles for the prosecutor, for the defense attorney, for the judge, and for the intercessor, but all should remember that they are sinners and need God's mercy (paragraph 8).

Augustine appeals to the examples of Christ who did not punish the adulteress and of Joseph who did not accuse Mary of adultery (paragraph 9). Augustine also points to Macedonius's act of interceding with the bishop of Carthage on behalf of a cleric and argues that, if he could do so to spare the man a rebuke, Augustine ought for far better reason to intercede to spare a man's life (paragraph 10). We should follow Christ's example of mercy in dealing with the adulteress (paragraph 11). In this life we cannot say that we are without all sin (paragraph 12). Rather, we are good insofar as we are children of God and bad insofar as we are sinners (paragraph 13). Jesus called the same people both good and bad, and even Seneca reminds us that we are all bad (paragraph 14). In dealing with the woman taken in adultery, Jesus condemned the sin but pardoned the woman (paragraph 15). The power of the state was instituted for good reason, and Christian clemency does not interfere with it (paragraph 16). A person can be merciful in punishing someone and cruel in sparing someone (paragraph 17). At times intercession leads to bad results, but Christian mercy should be judged in terms of its aims (paragraph 18). Both the severity of the officials of the state and the intercession of a bishop are beneficial (paragraph 19).

Augustine insists that a thief should not be pardoned if he has not made restitution, provided that he has the means to do so (paragraph 20). Someone who intercedes on behalf of a thief and does not insist upon his making restitution, when he can, shares in the guilt of the theft (paragraph 21). It is, however, possible that we are deceived about whether a thief can make restitution (paragraph 22). A judge ought not to sell his judgment, even if it is true, nor ought a witness to sell his testimony, even if it is true (paragraph 23). It is a tolerable custom for some lower officials to accept gifts from both parties to a transaction, and after their conversion to give such acquisitions to the poor rather than restore them to their givers (paragraph 24). But justice demands that a lawyer return what he wrongfully took in a court of law (paragraph 25). Finally, Augustine points out that justice, unlike money, can never be wrongfully possessed, and he wishes Macedonius happiness in Christ (paragraph 26).

Augustine, bishop and servant of Christ and his family, sends greetings in the Lord to his beloved son, Macedonius.

1, 1. We ought neither to leave you without a reply nor take up your time with an introduction, you who are the busiest man in the state and most attentive not to your own advantage but to that of others, for we are happy not only for you but for human affairs, that you are such a man. Receive, then, what you wanted either to learn from me or to test whether I myself knew it. If you judged it something slight or superfluous, you would by no means think that in the midst of such important and necessary concerns you should be concerned about this. You ask me why we say that it is part of our priestly responsibility to intercede on behalf of the guilty and to be offended if we do not get what we asked for, as if we do not get what pertains to our office. On this point you say that you are deeply in doubt about whether this comes from our religion. Then you add the reason why you are so upset. "For," you say, "if the Lord forbids sins so that after the first penance, he does not give a chance for a second penance, how can we claim in the name of religion that we should forgive a crime, no matter of what sort it is?" And you add a more serious point and say that we approve what we want to go unpunished, and "if it is clear that in all sins not merely the one who commits a sin but also the one who approves of it is guilty, it is certain that we are bound together as accomplices in guilt as often as we want a person who is guilty of sin to go unpunished."[877]

2. Whom would you not frighten with these words, if he were unaware of your gentleness and kindness? Hence, we who know you do not doubt that you wrote this for the sake of raising a question, not for the sake of pronouncing judgment, and we reply to this with other words of yours. For, as if you did not want us to linger over this question, you either foresaw what we were going to say or taught us what we ought to say. You said, "Then, in addition, there is something more serious. For all sins seem to be more deserving of pardon when the one who is guilty promises correction." Before, then, I discuss what that

---

877. Letter 152,2.

more serious point is that follows in your letter, I shall in the meanwhile take what you gave and use it to remove this weight that might seem to be able to suppress our acts of intercession. As far as we have the chance, we of course intercede on behalf of all sins because all sins seem more deserving of pardon when the one who is guilty promises correction. This is your view, and this is ours too.

3. In no way, then, do we approve of the sins that we want to be corrected, nor do we want the wrongdoing to go unpunished because we find it pleasing. Rather, having compassion for the person and detesting the sin or crime, the more we are displeased by the sin the less we want the sinful person to perish without having been corrected. For it is easy and natural to hate evil persons because they are evil, but it is rare and holy to love those same persons because they are human beings. Thus in one person you at the same time both blame the sin and approve of the nature, and for this reason you more justly hate the sin because it defiles the nature that you love. He, therefore, who punishes the crime in order to set free the human being is bound to another person as a companion not in injustice but in humanity. There is no other place for correcting our conduct save in this life. For after this life each person will have what he earned for himself in this life. And so, out of love for the human race we are compelled to intercede on behalf of the guilty lest they end this life through punishment so that, when it is ended, they cannot have an end to their punishment.

2, 4. Do not, therefore, have any doubt that this duty of ours comes from our religion, since God, with whom there is no injustice, whose power is supreme, who not only sees what sort of person each one is but also foresees what sort of person one will be, who alone cannot make a mistake in judging because he cannot be deceived in knowing, *makes*, nonetheless, as the Gospel says, *his sun to rise over the good and the evil and sends rain upon the just and the unjust* (Mt 5:45). Christ the Lord exhorts us to imitate this marvelous goodness; he says, *Love your enemies; do good to those who hate you, and pray for those who persecute you in order that you may be children of your Father, who is in heaven, who makes his sun to rise over the good and the evil and sends rain upon the just and the unjust* (Mt 5:4-45). Who can fail to know that many have misused this leniency and gentleness to their own destruction? The Apostle blames them and severely rebukes them; he says, *But do you think, every one of you who judges those who do such things, though you yourself do them, that you will escape the judgment of God? Do you hold in contempt the riches of his goodness and patience and tolerance? Do you not know that the goodness of God is leading you to repentance? But according to the hardness of your unrepentant heart you store up for yourself wrath on the day of wrath and of the revelation of the just judgment of God, who will pay back each according to his works.* (Rom 2:3-6) Does God not persevere in his patience because these people persevere in their wickedness? He punishes very few sins in this world, lest people suppose that there is no divine providence, and he reserves many for the last judgment in order to emphasize that judgment.

5. For that heavenly teacher does not, I think, command us to love wickedness when he commands us to love our enemies, to do good to those who hate us, and to pray for those who persecute us. For, if we worship God piously, we undoubtedly can have only wicked persons as enemies and as people roused against us with most bitter hatred and as persecutors. Should we, then, love the wicked? Are we to do good to the wicked? Are we also to pray for the wicked? Yes, of course! After all, it is God who commands this. Yet he does not in this way put us in league with the wicked, nor is he himself, of course, in league with them when he pardons them and gives them eternal life. The Apostle explains his plan to the extent that a pious person is permitted to know it; he says, *Do you not know that the patience of God is leading you to repentance?* (Rom 2:4). We want to lead to this repentance those for whom we make intercession; we do not spare or favor their sins.

3, 6. For we remove from the fellowship of the altar certain persons whose grave sins are public, although they were released from your severity, in order that by doing penance and by punishing themselves they may appease him whom they held in contempt by sinning. For someone who truly repents does nothing else but makes sure that the evil he did does not go unpunished. For in that way God, whose deep and just judgment no one escapes if he holds it in contempt, spares those who do not spare themselves. But if in sparing the unjust and wicked and granting them life and salvation, even to many of them whom he knows will not do penance, he nonetheless shows patience, how much more ought we to be merciful toward those who promise correction, even if we are uncertain whether they will do what they promise! For we act in order to mitigate your rigor by interceding for those for whom we also pray to the Lord, from whom none of their actions are hidden, even their future actions. And yet we do not do this impudently because the Lord himself commanded it.

7. At times, however, the wickedness of human beings advances to such a point that they commit either similar sins or more serious ones, even after having done penance and after the reconciliation of the altar. And still God makes his sun to rise even over such people, nor does he give them his most bounteous gifts of life and salvation less than before. And though they are not given in the Church that place of penance, yet God does not forget his patience in their regard. If anyone from their number says to us, "Either give me again the same place of doing penance, or leave me, a hopeless case, to do whatever I want, to the extent that I can help myself with my money and am not prevented by human laws, with prostitutes and in every form of dissoluteness, something that God condemns but that is even praiseworthy in the eyes of most men. Or if you call me back from this sinfulness, tell me whether it does me some good for the life to come, if in this life I scorn the enticements of pleasure with its powerful attractions, if I rein in the impulses of sexual desires, if I deprive myself even of many licit and permissible things to chastise my body, if I torment myself by doing penance more vigorously than before, if I groan more pitifully, if I weep

more abundantly, if I live a better life, if I care for the poor more generously, if I burn more ardently with the love that covers a multitude of sins."[878] Who of us would be so foolish as to say to this man, "These acts will do you no good for the next life. Go, enjoy at least the sweetness of this life"? May God prevent such monstrous and sacrilegious insanity! And yet it was a cautious and salutary provision that a place for that most humble penance be granted only once in the Church for fear that cheap medicine might become less beneficial for the sick. After all, it will be more salutary to the extent that it is held less in contempt. Who, nonetheless, would dare to say to God, "Why do you still once more spare this man who, after his first penance, again entangles himself in the snares of iniquity?" Who would dare to say that God does not do regarding these people what the Apostle says: *Do you not know that the patience of God is leading you to repentance?* (Rom 2:4). Or that, with the exception of these people, the words of scripture hold true: *Blessed are all who put their trust in him* (Ps 2:13)? Or that these words do not pertain to them: *Act courageously, and let your heart be strong, all you who hope in the Lord* (Ps 31:25)?

8. Since, then, God has such great patience and such great mercy for sinners that, if they have corrected their conduct in this life, they are not condemned for eternity, though God does not look for mercy to be shown him from anyone, since no one is more happy, no one more powerful, and no one more just than he, how should we human beings behave toward other human beings? For, no matter how much praise we have accumulated for this life of ours, we do not say that it is free from sin. After all, as Scripture says, *if we say* that, *we deceive ourselves, and the truth is not found in us* (1 Jn 1:8). Hence there are distinct roles for the prosecutor, for the defense attorney, for the intercessor, and for the judge, and it would take too long and is not necessary to discuss their particular duties in this letter. So even those who punish crimes should not be moved by personal anger in their office but should be servants of the laws, avenging not their own injuries but those of others, just as judges ought to do. The judgment of God has filled them with fear so that they keep in mind that they need God's mercy on account of their own sins and do not suppose that it counts as a failure in their office if they act mercifully in any way toward those over whom they have the legitimate power of life and death.

4, 9. For, when the Jews brought to Christ the Lord the woman caught in adultery and said, to test him, that the law commanded that she be stoned, they then asked him what he himself commanded in her regard. He answered them, *Let whoever of you is without sin be the first to throw a stone at her* (Jn 8:7). Nor did he in this way show his disapproval of the law that commanded that those guilty of such a sin be put to death. But by frightening them, he called back to mercy those by whose judgment she could have been put to death. I suspect that, if her husband was also present and was asking that the fidelity of his bed be

---

878. See 1 Pt 4:8.

vindicated, once he heard these words of the Lord, he was filled with fear and turned his mind away from the desire for vengeance to the will to pardon. For how was her accuser not warned not to pursue the injuries he suffered when the judges themselves were forbidden to exact punishment, though in punishing the adulteress they were not driven to satisfy their personal pain but the law? For this reason, when Joseph, to whom the Virgin Mary, the mother of the Lord, was engaged, discovered that she was pregnant, though he knew that he had not had intercourse with her and for this reason believed that she was an adulteress, he still did not want her to be punished. Nor did he approve of the sin. For this desire of his is attributed to justice; Scripture, of course, speaks of him as follows: *And since he was a just man and was unwilling to make public knowledge of her, he decided to send her off privately. While he was thinking of this, an angel appeared to him* (Mt 1:18-20) in order to explain to him that what he had thought was a sin was the work of God.

10. If therefore a consideration of our common weakness breaks down the indignation of the prosecutor and the rigor of the judge, what then do you think should be the duty of either the defense attorney or the intercessor? Since even you good men who are now judges once worked in court and took up the cases of human beings, you know how you used to defend a case more gladly than prosecute one. And yet a defense attorney is very different from an intercessor. For the defense attorney puts most effort into undermining or obscuring the charges, but the intercessor shows concern to remove or to lessen the punishment, even when the guilt is clear. The righteous do this before God on behalf of sinners; the sinners themselves are admonished to do this for one another. For Scripture says, *Confess your sins to one another, and pray for one another* (Jas 5:16). Every human being claims for himself before another, when he can, this duty of human kindness. For each person wants that crime to go unpunished in the house of another that he would punish if it were committed in his own. For, if the appeal is before a friend or if in our presence the man with the power to punish becomes angry at someone or if we by chance come upon someone who is angry, we are judged not most just but most inhuman if we do not intercede. I know that you yourself have interceded along with other friends of yours in the church of Carthage on behalf of a cleric with whom the bishop was rightly angry, and there was certainly no fear of condemnation to death under that discipline, which involves no bloodshed. And though you wanted that wrong, which was displeasing even to you, to go unpunished, we did not judge that you approved of the sin but heard that you interceded in a most kind manner. If you are permitted to mitigate the severity of an ecclesiastical rebuke by interceding, how is it that a bishop should not intercede with you who have the power of the sword? For the former punishment was employed in order that the person might live a good life, while the latter is employed in order that this man not continue to live!

11. Finally, the Lord himself interceded before human beings so that the adulteress was not stoned, and he commended to us in that way the duty of in-

tercession, except that he did by causing fear what we do by begging. For he is the Lord, while we are his servants. But he caused fear in such a way that we all ought to have fear. For who of us is without sin? After he had said to those who presented the adulteress to him for punishment that the one who knew that he was without sin should be the first to throw a stone at her, their anger collapsed as their conscience trembled. For at that point they slipped away from that gathering and left the poor woman to the merciful Lord. Let the piety of Christians yield to the words to which the impiety of the Jews yielded. Let the humility of his followers yield to him to whom the pride of his persecutors yielded. Let faithful confession yield to him to whom the hypocrisy of a tempter yielded. Spare the evil, O good man. Be gentler the better you are. Become humbler in piety to the extent you are higher in power.

5, 12. I who see your good conduct have called you a good man, but you who see the words of Christ, say to yourself, *No one is good except God* (Mk 10:18). Though this is true, because the Truth said it, you should not think that what I said was a false statement and that I was more or less contradicting the words of the Lord by calling you a good man, although he says, *No one is good except God.* After all, the Lord did not contradict himself when he said, *A good man brings forth good things from the storehouse of his heart* (Lk 6:45). God, then, is good in a singular way, and he cannot lose this. After all, he is not good by participation in some good, because he is for himself the good by which he is good. But when a human being is good, his goodness comes from God, and it cannot come from himself. For whoever of us becomes good does so by his Spirit, because our nature was created capable of partaking of him by our will. If we are to be good, therefore, it is up to us to receive and to hold on to what he gives, whose goodness comes from himself. Anyone who neglects this is evil because of himself. Hence, one is good to the extent that he acts correctly, that is, knowingly, lovingly, and piously produces good, and one is evil to the extent that he sins, that is, turns away from the truth, from love, and from piety. But who is there in this life without some sin? Yet we call a person good if goodness predominates, and we call a person best who sins the least.

13. For this reason the Lord himself also calls the same people evil on account of the sins of human weakness whom he calls good on account of their participation in divine grace, until our whole being is healed of all sinfulness and passes into that life where there will be no sin at all. After all, he taught good people, not evil ones, to pray when he commanded them to say, *Our Father, who art in heaven* (Mt 6:9). For they are good because they are children of God, not born such by nature but made such by grace, inasmuch as they are those to whom he gave the power to become children of God because they received him.[879] This spiritual generation is also called adoption in accord with the custom of the scriptures in order to distinguish it from that generation of God from God,

---

879. See Jn 1:12.

of the coeternal from the eternal, of which Scripture says, *Who will recount his generation?* (Is 53:8) Though he showed that they were good whom he wanted to say to God, *Our Father, who are in heaven*, he still commanded that they say in the same prayer, among other things, *Forgive us our debts as we forgive our debtors* (Mt 6:12). Although it is evident that these debts are sins, he afterward explained this more clearly when he said: *For, if you forgive human beings their sins, your Father will also forgive you your sins* (Mt 6:14). The baptized say this prayer, nor are there any past sins at all that are not forgiven in those baptized in the Church. But unless, as they live in this mortal frailty, they contracted some sin afterward that needed to be forgiven, they would not truthfully say, *Forgive us our debts*. They are good people, then, inasmuch as they are children of God, but insofar as they sin—something they admit by their honest confession—they are, of course, evil.

14. Someone might perhaps say that the sins of good people are different from the sins of evil people, and this is not said without good reason. But clearly the Lord Jesus called those same people evil, though he said that God was their father. For in the same sermon in which he taught that prayer, when exhorting them to pray to God, he said in another passage, *Ask and you will receive; seek and you will find; knock and the door will be opened for you. For everyone who asks receives, and everyone who seeks finds, and for everyone who knocks the door will be opened* (Mt 7:7-8). And a little later he says, *If, then, though you are evil, you know how to give good gifts to your children, how much more will your Father who is in heaven give good things to those who ask him?* (Mt 7:11) Is God, therefore, the father of evil people? Heaven forbid! How, then, does he say, *Your heavenly Father*, to those to whom he says, *Though you are evil*, unless the Truth is indicating two things: what we are by the goodness of God and what we are by human sinfulness, praising the one and correcting the other? Seneca, a man who lived at the time of the apostles and whose letters to Paul we also read, was right to say, "One who hates bad people hates everyone."[880] And yet we should love those who are bad in order that they might cease to be bad, just as we love the ill not in order that they may remain ill but in order that they may be healed.

15. But after that destruction of sins that takes place in baptism, whatever sin we commit while abiding in this life, even if it is not the sort of sin that forces a person to be separated from the altar of God, is wiped away not by fruitless sorrow but by sacrifices of mercy. Know, then, that we offer to God on your behalf what we get you to do by our intercession. After all, you need the mercy that you show, and see who said, *Forgive, and you will be forgiven; give, and it will be given to you* (Lk 6:37-38). And yet, even if we lived so that there was

---

880. Seneca was the Roman philosopher who taught the emperor Nero. Augustine alludes to an apocryphal correspondence between the philosopher and the Apostle. In *Illustrious Men* 12 Jerome says, "I would not put [Seneca] in a catalogue of the saints if I were not called to do so by those letters of Paul to Seneca and of Seneca to Paul that are read by many."

no reason why we should say, *Forgive us our debts*, to the extent that our mind is freer from sinfulness it ought to be more full of clemency. Thus, even if we were not smitten by the words of the Lord when he said, *Let the one of you who is without sin throw the first stone at her* (Jn 8:7), we should follow the example of him who, though he was certainly without sin, said to the woman whom her frightened accusers left alone, *Nor will I condemn you; go, sin no more* (Jn 8:11). After all, the sinful woman could have feared that, when those men left who reflected upon their own sins so that they spared the sin of another, he who was without sin might himself condemn her with full justice. But he, not fearful in his conscience but full of clemency, said when she answered that no one had condemned her, *Nor will I condemn you*, as if to say, "If the guilty could spare you, why do you fear the innocent?" And so that he would not be thought to condone sins but to pardon them, he said, *Go, sin no more*, in order to show that he spared a human being and not that he approved of her sin. You now see that the fact that we, though not criminals, often intercede even for criminals, and that we, though sinners, intercede for sinners, stems from our religion and that we do not become implicated in their crimes, and I think that you understand that we said truthfully rather than insultingly that we intercede before sinners.

16. Nor does it follow, of course, that the power of the sovereign, the judge's right over life and death, the executioner's instruments of torture, the weapons of the soldier, the discipline of the ruler, and the severity of a good father were instituted to no avail. All these have their limits, causes, reasons, and utility. When these are feared, the evil are held in check and the good live more peaceful lives among the evil. It is not that those who do not sin because they fear such things should be declared to be good. For no one is good out of a fear of punishment but out of a love of righteousness. But it is not without benefit that human audacity is held in check even by fear of the laws in order that the innocent might be safe amid the wicked and in order that, by calling upon God, the will might be healed in the wicked themselves, while the possibility of their committing sin is held in check by the fear of punishment. The intercession of bishops is not opposed to this arrangement of human affairs; in fact, there would be neither a reason nor a place for any intercession if they did not exist. After all, the benefits of those who intercede and of those who pardon are more gratifying to the extent that the punishments of the sinners are more just. Nor, in my opinion, did a more severe punishment of the law prevail in the Old Testament in the time of the ancient prophets for any other reason than to show that punishments were rightly instituted for the wicked. Thus the fact that we are taught to pardon them with the forgiveness of the New Testament is either the remedy of salvation by which sins, including our own, are pardoned or an instruction in gentleness in order that, because of those who grant pardon, the truth they preach may not only be feared but also loved.

17. The attitude with which one grants pardon is, however, very important. For just as at times mercy punishes, so cruelty also pardons. After all, to set forth something obvious as an example, who would not more correctly call him cruel

who gave in to a boy who was most insistent about wanting to play with snakes? But who would not call a person merciful who forbade such actions and chastised even with a beating the boy who scorned his words? And for this reason discipline should not be carried to the point of death in order that the person may still live who can benefit from it. And yet, when one human being kills another, there is a big difference whether one kills out of a desire to do harm or to take something unjustly, as an enemy or a thief does, or whether one kills in a situation of punishing or obeying, as a judge or an executioner does, or whether one kills out of the need to escape attack, as a traveler kills a robber, or out of the need to help someone, as a soldier kills an enemy. And, at times, the one who was the reason for the death is guilty rather than the killer, such as when one deceives his bail bondsman and the latter pays the legitimate penalty instead of him. Nor is everyone guilty who is the reason for another's death. After all, what if someone tries to commit an immoral act and kills himself if he does not get what he wants? What if a son fears his father's well-meant beatings and throws himself over a cliff? What if one man causes his own death because another has been released or for fear that he might be released? Must we on account of these reasons for the deaths of others either consent to a sinful act or abolish the punishment of a sin, if the punishment is carried out with the desire not to do harm but to correct, even by a father? Or must we curtail works of mercy? When these deaths occur, we ought to feel a sorrow that is human, but we do not on their account hold back our desire for correct actions in order that these deaths may not occur.

18. So, even when we intercede for a sinner who is about to be condemned, at times there follow results that we do not want. These occur in the person who is set free because of our intercession and in his unpunished audacity prowls about even more savagely, since he is subject to passion and ungrateful for leniency, and one man rescued from death slays many. Or another man perishes by living a bad life and commits the same sins or worse ones, because he set before his eyes the impunity of this man, after he was by our help changed for the better and corrected in his conduct. These evils should not, in my opinion, be imputed to us when we intercede with you, but rather those good things that we look to and want. I mean the emphasis upon gentleness to win love for the word of truth and the hope that those who are set free from temporal death may live so that they do not incur eternal death, from which they will never be set free.

19. Your severity, therefore, is beneficial, by means of which our tranquility is also secured; and our intercession is beneficial, by means of which your severity is also tempered. Let it not displease you that good people petition you, because it also does not displease good people that you are feared by the evil. For even the apostle Paul frightened wicked men not only with the judgment to come but also with your present powers as judge, and he said that they belong to the plan of divine providence. He said, *Let every soul be subject to the higher authorities. For there is no authority except from God. But those that exist have been established by God. Hence, one who resists authority resists the order es-*

tablished by God. But those who resist bring condemnation upon themselves. For rulers are not feared on account of good deeds but on account of evil ones. Do you want to have no fear of someone in authority? Do good, and you will have praise from him. For he is the minister of God for your good. But if you do evil, fear. For he does not carry the sword for no purpose. He is, after all, the minister of God to punish in anger one who does evil. And so, you must be subject not only on account of his anger but also on account of your conscience. For this reason, after all, you also pay taxes. The authorities are the ministers of God, continuing in this role. Pay your debts to all: tribute to whom you owe tribute, taxes to whom you owe taxes, fear to whom you owe fear, honor to whom you owe honor. Owe no one anything except that you love one another.* (Rom 13:1-8) These words of the Apostle show the usefulness of your severity. Hence, just as those who fear are commanded to owe love to those who cause fear, so those who cause fear are commanded to owe love to those who fear them. Nothing should be done out of the desire to do harm, but everything should be done out of a love to show concern. And let nothing be done cruelly, nothing inhumanely. In that way the punishment of the judge will be feared so that the religion of the intercessor is not held in contempt, because both punishing and pardoning are done well only in order to correct the life of human beings. But if the wickedness and impiety is so great that neither discipline nor pardon can do any good for correcting it, good men fulfill the duty of love with the intention and conscience that God sees, whether by severity or by leniency.

20. As for what follows next in your letter, where you say, "But now, given our bad habits, human beings want the punishment of the crime to be relaxed in their case and to keep that for the sake of which they committed the crime,"[881] you mention the very worst kind of human beings for whom the remedy of repentance is absolutely useless. For, if the property of another on account of which the sin was committed is not returned, though it can be returned, one does not do penance but only pretends to. But if one truly does penance, the sin is not forgiven unless the stolen property is returned, but only, as I said, when it can be returned. For quite often the one who takes it loses it, either because he meets with other bad persons or because he lives a bad life himself, and he does not have anything else by which he might make restitution. We certainly cannot say to this person, "Return what you took," except when we believe that he has it and denies that he does. In this case, if he endures some torture from the one demanding the return of his property, when he is thought to have it to return, there is no injustice, because, even if he does not have the means to return the stolen money, he nonetheless rightly pays the penalty of the sin by which it was taken when he is being forced to restore it by physical punishment. But it is not inhuman to intercede even for such persons, as if for those guilty of crimes. The purpose is not that the property of another might not be restored but that one human being

---

881. Letter 152, 2.

not uselessly rage against another, especially a man who has already forgiven the sin but is asking for the money and who, even if he feared being cheated, does not seek vindication. Finally, if we can in such cases convince the judge that those people for whom we intercede do not have what is being demanded, we immediately have less trouble from them. At times, however, merciful persons, precisely in such a doubtful case, do not want to impose certain punishments for uncertain money. It is fitting that we also challenge and exhort you to this mercy. For it is better that you lose it, even if he has it, than that you either torture or kill him if he does not. But for these persons it is appropriate for us to intercede with those who are seeking a return of their money rather than with the judges. Otherwise, the judge might seem to take it away if, though he has the power, he does not force him to restore what was stolen. And yet, in using force, he ought to maintain his integrity so that he does not lose his humanity either.

21. But this I would say with full confidence: Someone who intercedes for another in order that he might not restore what he wrongly took and who does not force a man who has recourse to him to make restitution, to the extent that he honestly can, shares in his fraud and crime. For we are more merciful in withdrawing our help than in giving it in such cases. After all, someone who helps him to sin does not offer him aid but rather destroys and kills him. But for this reason can we or should we either exact the penalty or hand him over for the exaction of it? We act within the limits of our episcopal power when we threaten a person at times with the judgment of men but most of all and always with the judgment of God. But we blame, rebuke, and despise those who refuse to make restitution and who we know stole something and have the means to make restitution. We do this in some cases privately and in some cases publicly as different persons are seen to be able to accept different medicine and are not roused to greater madness to the destruction of others. At times we also deprive them of communion at the holy altar if a more urgent concern does not prevent us.

22. But it often happens that they deceive us either by denying that they stole or by claiming that they do not have the means to make restitution. And you yourself are often deceived when you think that we are not trying to get them to make restitution or that they have the means to make restitution. And all or almost all of us human beings like to call or consider as knowledge our suspicions when we are moved by credible indications of what is the case, though some credible indications are false just as some incredible ones are true. And so, in recalling certain persons who "both want the punishment of the crime to be relaxed for them and to keep that on account of which they committed the crime," you went on to say, "Your priesthood thinks that it should also intervene on behalf of these persons." After all, it is possible that you know what I do not know and that for this reason I think that I should intercede for someone because he was able to deceive me, though he was not able to deceive you, and in that way I would not believe that he possesses what you know that he possesses. So it turns out that, though our judgment about the guilty person is not the same, still neither of

us is happy with the fact that the property of another person is not restored. As human beings, we have different views of human beings, but we are together on the question of justice. In the same way, it can also happen that you are not absolutely certain, but have reasons to suspect, that a person has what I know that he does not have, and for this reason you think that I intercede for a person who wants to have the punishment of the crime to be relaxed in his case and to keep that on account of which he committed the crime. In conclusion, then, neither before you nor before others—if they are found to be such men as we are happy that you are—nor before those who with a great desire seek to possess the goods of others that do not benefit them and that are very dangerous and harmful,[882] nor before my own heart, of which God is a witness, would I dare to say, think, or decide that I should intercede for someone in order that he might possess with his crime unpunished what he stole by his crime, but only that he might return what he wrongfully took, once his wrongdoing has been forgiven, provided he has what he stole or other means to make restitution.

23. Not everything, of course, that is taken from someone against his will is wrongfully taken from him. For many people do not want to pay the doctor his fee nor the worker his wage, and still those who receive these against the will of the people from whom they receive them do not receive them wrongfully, since it is rather through wrongfulness that they are not given them. But a judge ought not to sell his just judgment nor a witness his true testimony because an advocate sells his just advocacy and a lawyer his true counsel. For the former are used by both parties to a hearing, but the latter are on just one side. But when judgments and testimonies, which should not be sold when they are just and true, are sold when they are unjust and false, it is much worse to take the money. For it is taken wrongfully, even though it is being taken from people who are willing. The person, nonetheless, who buys a just judgment often seeks to recover the money, as if it were wrongly taken from him, because it ought not to have been for sale. But someone who paid for an unjust judgment would, of course, want to ask for his money back if he were not afraid or were not ashamed to have bought it.

24. There are other persons of a lower type who shamelessly take money from both sides, such as an official who takes money both from someone from whom a service is provided and from someone for whom it is provided. People usually demand back what has been extorted by these types through gross dishonesty; they usually do not demand back what has been given through a custom that is tolerable. And we blame those people more who asked for such things back contrary to custom than those who took them according to custom, because many persons who are needed for managing human affairs are either enticed or held onto by such advantages. If these people change their way of life or rise to a level of more excellent holiness, they are more ready to give to the poor what they acquired in this way as if it were their own than to restore it to those from

---

882. See Sallust, *The War against Jugurtha* 1, 5.

whom they received it as if it were not theirs. But we judge that those who took things contrary to the law of human society by thefts, robberies, slanders, assaults, and attacks ought to make restitution rather than to give them to the poor. This is in accord with the gospel example of Zacchaeus. When he received the Lord as his guest, he was suddenly converted to a holy life. He said, *I give half of my possessions to the poor, and if I have taken something from someone, I repay it fourfold* (Lk 19:8).

25. If, nonetheless, one considers justice more carefully, one says with more justice to the advocate, "Return what you took when you stood opposed to the truth, sided with injustice, deceived the judge, defeated a just case, or won a case by lies." And you see many very distinguished and eloquent lawyers think that they do this not only with impunity but even with glory. One says this with more justice to an advocate than one says it to anyone else serving in some office, "Return what you received when by order of a judge you arrested a man needed for some case, put him in chains so that he would not resist, locked him up so that he would not flee, and finally either presented him to the court if the dispute lasted or dismissed him if it was ended." But it is obvious why one does not say this to the advocate, namely, because a man does not want to ask back what he gave to his defense counsel in order to win the case unjustly, just as he does not want to repay what he received from his adversary when he won the case unjustly. Finally, where can one easily find a lawyer or a man of honor who was once a lawyer who says to his client, "Take what you gave me when I wrongly took your case, and repay to your adversary what you wrongfully took through my action"? And yet, someone who most correctly repents of his former unjust life ought also to do this so that, if the lawyer who argued the unjust case does not want to correct the injustice after having been admonished, his client, nonetheless, does not want to keep the reward of that injustice. Or are we supposed to restore the property of another that was taken secretly by theft, while we are not supposed to restore the property of another that was obtained through deceiving the judge and circumventing the laws in the court where wrongdoing is punished? What shall I say about the interest that the laws and the judges themselves command to be repaid? Or is he more cruel who steals or snatches something from a wealthy man than he who ruins a poor person through usury? These gains and others of the sort are, of course, wrongly possessed, and I would demand their restitution, but there is no judge under whom they can be claimed.

26. Now, if we wisely consider the words of Scripture, *A faithful man has a whole world of riches, but an unfaithful man does not have even a penny* (Prv 17:6 LXX), do we not prove guilty of possessing the goods of others all those who seem to themselves to be happy over their gains but certainly do not know how to use them? For what is lawfully possessed is certainly not someone else's property. But what is lawfully possessed is justly possessed, and what is justly possessed is correctly possessed. Everything, then, that is wrongly possessed is someone else's property, but one who uses it wrongly possesses it wrongly. You

see, then, how many people ought to return the property of others, if at least a few people are found to whom they might return it. These people, wherever they are, hold these things more in contempt to the extent that they could possess them with more justice. No one, of course, wrongly possesses justice, and one who does not love it does not have it. But money is both wrongly possessed by bad people and possessed by good people in a better way to the extent that it is loved less. But in these circumstances the injustice of people who possess goods wrongly is tolerated, and certain laws are established among them that are called civil laws. These laws do not make people good users of such goods but make those who use them wrongly less troublesome until faithful and pious people, to whom all things rightly belong, who either emerge from them or who, living among them in the meanwhile, are not implicated in their sins but are tested by them, come to that city where their eternal inheritance is. There, only a just person has a place, only a wise person a position of power; all who will be there will truly possess their own property. But still, even here we do not intercede in order that the property of others may not be restored in accord with earthly laws and customs, although we want you to be merciful to sinners not in order that they may be loved or remain sinners but because all who become good persons become such from them and because God is pleased with a sacrifice of mercy. For, if he were not merciful to sinners, there would be no good people. I have been burdensome to you for a long time, I think, given all the things you have to do, though the questions you asked could have been quickly resolved by a clever and learned man like you. But I ought long ago to have concluded, if I knew that you alone were going to read this. May you live happily in Christ, my dearest son.

LETTER 209

Augustine to Celestine, the pope (423)

Probably in the beginning of 423 Augustine wrote to Celestine, who became pope after the death of Boniface on 4 September 422 and died on 27 July 432. Augustine congratulates Celestine on his peaceful election to the papacy (paragraph 1). He explains to the pope how it came about that Antoninus[883] was ordained bishop of Fussala when the man whom Augustine wanted to be ordained refused to be ordained at the last minute (paragraphs 2 and 3). Augustine explains to Celestine that Antoninus was accused of serious crimes by the people of Fussala (paragraph 4). When brought to trial, Antoninus was required to make restitution to the people from whom he had stolen property and was allowed to retain the dignity of the episcopacy, though not over the people whom he had mistreated (paragraph 5). Augustine pleads for Celestine's help and calls his attention to how Antoninus had induced the primate of Numidia to intercede on his behalf with Pope Boniface (paragraph 6). Antoninus is now insisting that he should be bishop over the people of Fussala or should not be a bishop at all (paragraph 7). Augustine points to examples of penalties imposed on other bishops similar to that imposed on Antoninus (paragraph 8). Augustine begs the pope for his help in order that Antoninus may not do further harm to the people of Fussala or to himself (paragraph 9). Augustine tells Celestine of his sorrow and fear over the whole affair, which has brought him to consider resigning from the episcopacy (paragraph 10). In Letter 20* to Fabiola, a Roman laywoman, Augustine presents further details about the problems that Antoninus had caused.

To Celestine, his most blessed lord and holy father to be venerated with due love, Augustine sends greetings in the Lord.

1. First, I congratulate you for your merits because the Lord our God has placed you in that great see without, as we have heard, any division among his people.[884] Secondly, I report to Your Holiness our situation in order that you may help us not only by praying for us but also by counseling us and bringing us relief. Finding myself in great trouble, I have sent this letter to Your Beatitude, because, though I wanted to do good to certain members of Christ in our neighborhood, I inadvertently and carelessly caused them a great loss.

---

883. Some editions have "Antonius" rather than "Antoninus," but the latter seems to be correct. See Letter 20*.
884. The election of Celestine's predecessor, Boniface, had been disputed, with one part of the people favoring Boniface and another favoring Eulalius. Zosimus died in December 418, but Boniface was not recognized as the sole bishop of Rome until Easter of 419.

2. A town bordering on the territory of Hippo bears the name Fussala; previously there was never a bishop there, but it belonged to the diocese of the church of Hippo along with the adjoining region. The country had few Catholics; the error of the Donatists held in wretched captivity the remaining people there, who were very great in number, so that in the same town there was no Catholic at all. It came about through the mercy of God that all these places were brought to the unity of the Church. It would take a long time to explain the many labors and perils of ours by which this was accomplished. The priests who were first sent there by us to bring back the people were robbed, beaten, injured, blinded, and killed. Yet their sufferings were not useless and without fruit since unity was securely attained. But the town I mentioned is at a distance of forty miles from Hippo. Since for governing the faithful and bringing back those few persons of both sexes who were still in schism, no longer in a threatening way but in flight, I saw that I was extended further than I ought to be and that I was unable to give them the attention that I realized with most certain evidence needed to be given them, I arranged to ordain and establish a bishop there.

3. In order to achieve that goal, I looked for someone apt and suitable for that place, who was also trained in the Punic language. And I had a priest in mind who was prepared, and to ordain him I got the holy old man who was then the primate of Numidia[885] to come from a distance, pleading with him by letter. And when he was already present and the hearts of all were eagerly awaiting so important an event, the man who I thought was suited backed down at the last minute, absolutely refusing. Of course I ought to have postponed things rather than to have rushed into such a dangerous action, as the outcome has proved. But since I did not want the most reverend and holy primate, who was so exhausted in coming to us, to return home without accomplishing the purpose for which he had come so far, I presented a certain youth, Antoninus, who was with me at that time, though the people had not asked for him. He had been raised by us in the monastery from an early age, but apart from the office of lector[886] he had not attained any level or functions of the clergy. But those poor people most obediently obeyed me when I offered him to them, for they did not know what was going to happen. Why should I say more? He was ordained; he began to be their bishop.

4. What am I to do? I do not want to worsen in the eyes of Your Reverence a man whom I undertook to raise to the episcopacy, and I do not want to abandon those people whom I have brought to birth in Christ, gathering them to the Church amid fear and sorrow. And I cannot find a way to do both. The situation has developed into so great a scandal that the people who obeyed us by accepting him as bishop, thinking that they were looking out for their interests, presented their accusations against him here before us. But since in those accusations they

---

885. This was probably Silvanus of Zumma, the predecessor of Valentine of Baia, who was primate by 419.

886. The office of lector was one of the minor orders.

could not prove capital charges of sexual misconduct, which were raised not by people of whom he was bishop but by certain others, and since he seemed to have been acquitted of those charges that were so hatefully spread about, he became so pitiful in our eyes and those of others that, whatever accusations were made by the people of the town and of that region concerning his unbearable domination of them, concerning robberies, various acts of oppression, and harassment, they did not seem to us such that we thought that he should, for this reason or for all of them put together, be removed from the episcopacy. But we determined that he should restore the things that it was proven that he stole.

5. Finally, we tempered our verdicts so that, while he retained the episcopacy, those actions nonetheless were not left entirely unpunished that ought not to have been proposed either for him to repeat in the future or for others to imitate. And so we preserved the full episcopal dignity of the young man who was to be corrected, but in correcting him we diminished his power, that is, so that he did not preside over those people with whom he had behaved in such a way that with just resentment they absolutely could not bear his being over them and showed that their impatience would perhaps burst forth into some crime with danger to themselves and to him. Their frame of mind was also clearly seen to be such when the bishops dealt with them concerning him, though Celer,[887] a respected man about whose use of excessive power against him Antoninus had complained, no longer holds any position of power either in Africa or anywhere.

6. But why should I delay over the many details? Work together with us, I beg you, my most blessed lord, who are venerable for piety and worthy of reverence with due love, O holy father, and command that everything that has been sent to you be read out. See how he has exercised the episcopacy, how he was in such agreement with our verdict that he would be excommunicated unless he first restored everything to the people of Fussala and how afterward, once the proceedings were over, he set aside a sum of gold for the estimated value of the property in order that he might be restored to communion. Consider how with a cunning argument he induced the holy old man, our primate, a highly respected man, to commend him to the venerable Pope Boniface as completely exculpated. What need is there for me to recall all the other things since the venerable old man I mentioned has reported all of them to Your Holiness?

7. But in those many records which contain our judgment about him, I would have to fear more that we may be thought to have pronounced judgment less severely than we ought to have, if I did not know that you were so inclined toward mercy that you would think that you should spare not only us because we spared him but also the man himself. But that man is trying to turn what we did out of kindness or negligence into a precedent in his favor and to use it as such.

---

887. This is perhaps the same Celer, a wealthy landowner of Hippo Regius, to whom Augustine addressed Letters 56 and 57.

He cries out, "I either ought to sit upon my episcopal throne or I ought not to be a bishop," as if he now sits on any throne but his own. For on this account those places over which he was previously a bishop were left and entrusted to the same man lest he be said to have been illicitly transferred to another see contrary to the statutes of our predecessors.[888] Ought anyone to be a judge of such severity or of such leniency that either those who he decides should not be deprived of the dignity of the episcopacy should not be punished in any way or those who he decides deserve any punishment should be deprived of the dignity of the episcopacy?

8. There exist cases in which the Apostolic See judged or upheld the judgment of others that for certain sins certain men were neither to be stripped of their episcopal dignity nor to be left entirely unpunished. In order not to seek out examples far removed from our times, I shall mention recent ones. Let Priscus, a bishop of the province of Caesarea, cry out, "Either access to the primacy ought also to be open to me as it is to the others or the episcopacy ought not to remain mine." Let Victor, another bishop of the same province, who was left in the same punishment Priscus was and who was in communion with no bishop anywhere but in his own diocese, cry out. Let him cry out, I say, "Either I ought to be in communion with bishops everywhere, or I ought not to be in communion with them in my own area." Let Lawrence, a third bishop of the same province, cry out even in the words of Antoninus, "Either I ought to sit on the episcopal throne for which I was ordained or I ought not to be a bishop." But who would find fault with these punishments except someone who does not pay enough attention to the fact that not all wrongdoing should be left unpunished nor all wrongdoing be punished in the same way?

9. Since, therefore, with the vigilant caution of a shepherd Pope Boniface stated in his letter when speaking of the bishop Antoninus, "If he has honestly revealed to us the sequence of events," be informed now of the sequence of events that Antoninus did not mention in his report and then of what was done after the letter of that man of holy memory was read in Africa. Then come to the aid of the people who are asking for your help through the mercy of Christ much more eagerly than Antoninus, from whose disruptiveness they long to be set free. He himself or very frequent rumors threaten those people with legal proceedings, public officials, and attacks by the military as if they were charged with carrying out the judgment of the Apostolic See. As a result poor Catholic Christian people fear worse things from a Catholic bishop than they feared from the laws of the Catholic emperors for having been heretics. Do not allow this to go on, I beg you by the blood of Christ, by the memory of Peter the apostle, who warned the leaders of Christian peoples not to lord it over brethren with violence.[889] I commend to the kindness and love of Your Holiness both the people of Fussala,

---

888. That is, the participants of the councils of Nicaea, Sardica, and Antioch, who had forbidden that a bishop move from one see to another.

889. See 1 Pt 5:3.

my Catholic children in Christ, and Bishop Antoninus, my son in Christ, because I love them both. I am not angry at the people of Fussala for having brought a just complaint about me to your hearing because I afflicted them with a man by whom they were so mistreated, who was not yet tested by me and not yet grown strong with age. Nor do I want Antoninus to be harmed, for the more I resist his evil desire the more sincerely I love him. Both of them deserve your mercy—the people in order that they may not suffer wrongs, Antoninus in order that he may not cause them; they in order that they may not hate the Catholic Church if they do not receive help from Catholic bishops, especially from the Apostolic See itself, against a Catholic bishop, but he in order that he may not involve himself in such a great crime that he alienates from Christ those whom he wants to make his own against their will.

10. Amid this danger to both of them so great a fear and sorrow torments me, as I must confess to Your Goodness, that I would consider withdrawing from the office of administering the episcopacy and devoting myself to lamentations suited to my mistake if I saw that the Church was being ravaged by that man whose episcopacy I supported through imprudence and that it was even perishing—may God prevent this!—along with the destruction of the one who was ravaging it. For, recalling the words of the Apostle, *If we would judge ourselves, we would not be judged by the Lord* (1 Cor 11:31), I will judge myself so that he may spare me, *who will judge the living and the dead* (2 Tm 4:1). But if you also want to revive the members of Christ in that area from their deadly fear and sadness and console my old age with this merciful justice, may God who comes to our aid through you in this tribulation and who has established you in that great see, reward you in the present life and also in the life to come.

LETTER 7*

Augustine to Faustinus, a deacon in Hippo (426-427)

Probably in 426 or 427, during the absence of Count Boniface from Africa, Augustine wrote to his deacon, Faustinus—undoubtedly the same man who is mentioned in Sermon 356,4 as having given up military life and entered the monastery of Hippo, where he was later baptized and ordained a deacon. In the present letter Augustine asks Faustinus to urge Novatus, the bishop of Sitifis in Mauretania Sitifensis, to help settle a financial issue concerning money that a widow may or may not owe to the Church. Augustine describes the situation (paragraph 1) and asks Novatus to investigate the matter in order that the Church might do what is right (paragraph 2).

A memorandum to the deacon Faustinus.

1. Although in the matter of the priest Heraclius you were sent to the Gauls in order to ask for a ship, if you have the opportunity, urge my brother and fellow bishop Novatus to be so good as to assist in the business of the Church. It is a question of the money that the widow of Bassus had sequestered until the first of July, after having requested a delay. For afterwards the tribune Felician wrote to the man who held the sequestered money that he should not give the Church the same money that Count Sebastian[890] had written should be given. It is the sort of case regarding which you ought to inform the bishop. Several years ago, when the domesticus,[891] Florentinus, was still alive, Count Boniface gave the Church a certain sum of money. The consignment was made to two men with whom the tribune Bassus had deposited it from his own funds, and he received from them the receipts issued in his name. One of these men, then, who was ready to hand over to the Church the part of the same money that he had in his possession demanded back the receipt that he had issued to Bassus. But the same Bassus had already died, and the receipts had remained with his wife. This man, nonetheless, made a payment to the Church of eighty gold coins, more or less, if I am not mistaken. The Church used them for her needs as if they came from her own resources. Then the banker[892] died, leaving heirs. Afterward, however, the widow of Bassus came to Hippo, and she received in coins the remaining money, which was the larger part of it, from the heirs of the same banker, and she returned to them the receipts for the deposit. But she said that she was prepared to give the Church the same gold coins and the receipt that remained in her possession from the man who had the other part of the money. For we said that the

---

890. Sebastian, the son-in-law of Boniface, was acting count of Africa during Boniface's absence.
891. A domesticus was a member of a household, or an escort or bodyguard of some person.
892. "Banker" (*collectarius*), i.e., a money-changer or cashier.

consignment was made to two different men. She said, therefore, that she wanted to give the Church the same coins that she received from the heirs of the one man and the receipt of the other. With regard to her husband's record, which he had sent to the count concerning this affair, she wanted it either to be restored to her or, if it could not be restored, to be voided. After this had been done, she began to refuse to turn over to the Church what she earlier said she was willing to turn over. Rather, she left it with the trustee[893] and asked for a delay until the first of July. Then she left Hippo for Sitifis, either in order to do something there, as she said, or to go on to Tipasa. But after a few days the tribune Felician wrote to the trustee that, according to the wishes of the woman, he should not turn over to the Church the coins that Count Sebastian demanded be returned to her after her husband's bill had been voided.

2. Hence, ask my brother Novatus to be so good as to investigate this case carefully, especially so that we do not seem to oppress the widow. If he ascertains that the same money belongs to her, he should make this known to Count Sebastian, especially because of the coins that the Church used from there, as if they were hers. For it is no problem if he has them restored to the woman so that the Church lays no claim to them. But if the bishop ascertains that the woman's case is unjust, he should act so that the trustee is ordered or permitted to hand over to the Church what was deposited with him, once the prohibition of the tribune Felician is removed. If, however, the woman is not at Sitifis, my brother Novatus should see to it that the tribune Felician replies concerning this matter and that the case is brought to the attention of Count Sebastian, who can determine regarding it what he sees is just.

---

893. "Trustee" (*sequester*), i.e., an official who held property whose ownership was disputed.

LETTER 8*

Augustine to Victor, an African bishop
(sometime during Augustine's episcopacy)

At an undetermined date Augustine wrote to Victor, an African bishop who is otherwise unknown. Augustine tells Victor of his sorrow over what the Jew Licinius has reported to him regarding the property that Victor bought from Licinius' mother, though she in fact had sold it to Licinius. Victor had allegedly evicted Licinius and told him to take his mother to court if he had any complaints. Augustine warns Victor that it seems that he has acted unjustly and tells him to bear in mind the words of Saint Paul, who urged that we give no offense to anyone (paragraph 1). Augustine explains how he had inquired further about whether Licinius had offended his mother, who in turn was seeking vindication. Licinius denied having done anything to his mother, though he admitted that his mother did complain about his wife and one of his wife's servants. Augustine goes on to suggest disciplinary measures against either Licinius or his wife, should such measures need to be taken (paragraph 2).

A memorandum of Augustine to his holy brother Victor.

1. Please consider how precious to me is Your Holiness's life and reputation. If they are true, the actions that the Jew Licentius deplored in my presence sadden me very much. He in fact proved to me by the tablets he brought that he had purchased some small fields from the people to whom his mother had sold them and that he gave a part of them to his wife as a dowry when he married her. But what he went on to say in his complaint is quite incredible, namely, that Your Holiness bought all his property from the same old woman, his mother, and drove him out, though he owned it with full right. And when he complained to you about what you yourself had done, you said to him, "I bought it. If your mother was wrong in selling it to me, take her to court. Do not ask anything of me since I owe you nothing." If he lied to me about this, please write back to me. But if through ignorance of the law you thought that you should answer him in that way, Your Charity should know that a person who has possession of property cannot legally be driven off of it and that she was not right in selling what her son possessed as his own, even if part of it belonged to her. For she ought first to have won her case against him and then to have sold what she had been able to obtain when he lost the case. The son, after all, had a real case. He certainly does not intend to take his own mother to court but the man who invaded his property, a situation in which I wish that Your Fraternity did not find himself. It is very odious and foreign to your way of life. If, then, he told me the truth, please restore his property to him and recover the price from his mother, if you paid her. But if she perhaps refuses to return to you the price you paid, this man must not,

even in that case, be deprived of his property. For he must get it back because justice is on his side and the laws cry out in his favor. I beg you to bear in mind the words of the Apostle, *Give no offense to the Jews or the Greeks, nor to the Church of God* (1 Cor 10:32). But it is better that, after having been admonished by your most dear brother, you do what is just than that this case come before an episcopal court.

2. Of course, when I asked him if he had perhaps done an injustice to his mother and you wanted in this way to vindicate her without any desire to possess the man's property but were doing this instead to frighten him, he answered that his mother had complained of an injustice from his wife and her serving girl but that he himself had done her no injustice. Hence I beg Your Holiness that, if these are the facts, you either discipline him with a beating in the presence of his mother if you discover that he has been unjust to his mother, for he said that he would be willing to endure that, or discipline his wife with a beating if she is at fault. For she can also be disciplined with a beating from her husband in the presence of her mother-in-law in accord with the judgment of Your Reverence. Now with regard to the serving girl the case is simple, since his mother can more easily punish her. He says that he has not done this because he was unaware of the injustice she did to his mother. For he says that his mother complained about this only after the property was already sold.

LETTER 9*

Augustine to Alypius, Augustine's closest friend
and the bishop of Thagaste (422-429)

On 27 August of a year between 422 and 429, Augustine wrote to his friend Alypius, the bishop of Thagaste, who was at the time in Italy and was charged with hearing the case of a man who had carried off a professed nun and used her for his pleasure. After the man was discovered by clerics and allegedly beaten, he appealed to Pope Celestine against the clerics in order to obtain reparation. Augustine tells Alypius that he finds it hard to believe that the clerics involved would have refrained from inflicting bodily injury on the unnamed man whom they caught (paragraph 1). He discusses the difficulties involved either in letting sins, such as this man is accused of, go unpunished or in finding the proper punishment for them. He points out the ineffectiveness of excommunication in some cases and the inability to punish those who hold positions of honor, as does the man in question. Hence he wonders how the clerics in this case could have refrained from beating the man (paragraph 2). Augustine suggests to Alypius that they need first to establish a regular penalty for persons who commit crimes of this type and that clerics who do bodily harm to someone guilty of such a crime should not be penalized unless they go beyond the sort of penalties provided by civil law (paragraph 3). Augustine suggests that in the present case the pope would not have thought that the man deserved reparation if he had truthfully stated in his complaint what he had done. He tells Alypius that he simply does not know what to say if the man who has suppressed facts in his petition to the Holy See not merely goes unpunished but even receives reparation (paragraph 4).

A memorandum of Augustine to his holy brother Alypius.

1. I received the memorandum of Your Holiness on 26 August, and I have replied on the next day. I had already seen the priest Commodian, and I had not sent anything about the matter by means of him because I had not wanted to see him in order to do that. Rather, because I was worried that something might be done about the man, which reason could not justify, I wanted to know how those events about which he complained had really occurred. After this priest had given me his account, I saw that nothing should be done if the matter had come before your tribunal, except to make known to you what happened inasmuch as it pertains to the case of the same priest. For, regarding the violence inflicted, which was all Pope Celestine[894] wanted to be punished, he could tell me nothing because, he answered, he knew nothing. Hence I had a single remaining worry about this matter: I found it hard to believe that those who found the man with that

---

894. Celestine was the pope from 422 to 432.

woman, a professed nun whom he had taken from her native town to make her the plaything of his debauchery, would have refrained from doing him bodily injury.

2. You know, after all, how this question tends to wear us down, that is, how these sins are left unpunished without harm to ecclesiastical discipline, or how they ought to be punished by the Church when they cannot be punished by civil laws. What, then, is a bishop or what are other clerics going to do in the case of such crimes and not of just any sins of human beings? We must, first, ask this of those who think that no corporeal punishment at all should be imposed on anyone, especially on account of the sort of persons who do not have the least care about ecclesiastical excommunication at all, either because they are not Christians or Catholics or because they live such lives that they might as well not be. But if honors that anyone holds or has held in the world mean anything, we are not permitted to lessen them or to take them away in the case of such sins in order that we might hold in check the license for wrongdoing in those persons whom you cannot jail or beat. Yet if men who have a position of honor in the government or in the legal profession, which this fellow with whom we are dealing seems to have, wanted to dance in church, I do not see how those who hold in their hands the means for imposing the discipline of a beating could spare them. And it is much more serious to subject to one's lust someone vowed to holiness than to dare to dance within the walls of a church.

3. Those who want to deliver the correct judgment when these matters are brought to trial, then, ought first to investigate and determine what should be done with such people who in such cases as these are caught in the commission of their sinful actions. Otherwise, if we are moved by their complaints when they receive bodily punishment but are not moved by their actions when they do a most wicked injury to God and disturb by their restless wickedness the Church's reputation for goodness and holiness as well as her peace, or if we are moved by the wrongful actions of most wicked men, which they perpetrate in the church out of their unspeakable audacity, so that we punish the light penalties they suffer for the sake of discipline but judge that we should leave unpunished those serious crimes that they commit against discipline, or we are unable to find how to punish them, I certainly do not see what sort of account of our judgments we are going to give to our Lord.[895] We must therefore first seek, find, and establish a regular penalty for these restless and wicked persons. Thereafter we would only need to impose a penalty if it could be proved that any irregular or excessive punishment had been imposed upon them. Until that happens, I do not at all see what sentence should be pronounced against servants of God who, in defense of the house of their Lord, do to criminals something incomparably less than the civil laws provide for, in order that there might be something to fear on the part of those who have no fear that the bishop or clerics can bring the civil laws to bear against them.

---

895. See Mt 12:36; Heb 13:17.

4. But I certainly do not doubt that, if our deplorable son had set down in his statement what he himself had done, the venerable pope would by any means think that the plaintiff ought to receive reparation because he was beaten by clerics, unless the man who did this to him exceeded the limits set by Christian moderation. I think, however, that in the tribunal of Your Holiness he cannot deny so obvious a matter, that is, the action of his about which he did not remain silent in his statement. Now, I do not know what to say if in ecclesiastical tribunals we do not preserve the justice that the civil laws have most wisely established so as to avoid having anyone brought to trial unjustly by means of an imperial rescript—I mean so that a man loses the favor he asked for and so that a person does not go unpunished if, in the petitions submitted to the emperor, he suppresses something that clearly pertains to his case. And I do not know what to say if the man who did this in the request he submitted to so holy a see is seen not only to escape punishment by the bishops but even to obtain reparation.

LETTER 14*

Augustine to Dorotheus, a Catholic layman and landowner in the neighborhood of Thagaste (419)

In October 419 Augustine wrote to Dorotheus, a Catholic layman and landowner in the neighborhood of Thagaste in Numidia. Augustine tells Dorotheus that his reputation as a Christian and as the head of a Christian family is well known (paragraph 1). Augustine informs him that he has a complaint about one of Dorotheus' men but that he will not disclose the man's name or his crime until he has Dorotheus' promise not to punish him more severely than is proper and fitting to punish someone because of a bishop's complaint (paragraph 2). Letter 15* reveals the name of the man who has been complained about and provides details about the nature of the complaint.

To his excellent lord and rightly distinguished and honorable son, Dorotheus, Augustine sends greetings in the Lord.

1. I know how much you love Christ, and all of us who know you know that your whole house is his family and, as the Apostle says, *a household church* (Rom 16:5), and how you want the possessions of Christ to bear fruit and to grow in your possessions, my excellent lord and rightly distinguished and honorable son.

2. I had reason to complain about one of your men, though I have not dared to make known to you by this letter either his name or his sacrilegious crime lest perhaps you become more seriously angry and punish him more severely than is proper or necessary because of a bishop's complaint. And so I have revealed by a memorandum: to these brothers from whom Your Excellency is receiving this letter what the issue was. And I asked that they first obtain the most trustworthy promise of Your Reverence that you will not punish him more than I indicated in the same memorandum and that, when they have your promise, they should give it to you to read. If you are unwilling to make the promise, however, they should reveal nothing. But I beg you by Christ rather to make the promise so that we can confidently bring to you whatever our pastoral care demands so that you may correct it if we cannot.

LETTER 15*

Augustine to unnamed clerics in Thagaste (419)

In October 419 Augustine wrote to certain unnamed clerics in Thagaste. He explains that a memorandum from Alypius, the bishop of Thagaste, who we know from other sources was at the time on a mission in Italy, had arrived with the ship used for the mail (paragraph 1). Augustine quotes from the memorandum, in which Alypius indicates the progress he has made in obtaining pardon for some Carthaginians and explains that he is still awaiting the arrival of an important personage in order to bring his business to completion (paragraph 2). The rest of the letter concerns the misconduct of Cresconius, about whom, without mentioning his name, Augustine had written to Dorotheus in Letter 14*. From the present letter we find out that Cresconius, a married man and a supervisor of Dorotheus's estate, had raped a nun who came to the estate to work with the wool (paragraph 3). Augustine here explains how he believes that Cresconius, who has been excommunicated, should be further punished by being removed from his position as supervisor, although he hopes that Dorotheus will not punish him with excessive severity (paragraph 4).

A memorandum: Augustine to the holy brothers whose names my letter contains.

1. After our letter to be sent to Your Benevolence was already finished, a memorandum came from Brother Alypius that he addressed to Thagaste, since the same ship used for the mail was driven into our harbor. I have taken care that Your Holiness knows what we learned from that memorandum, inserting the words of the same memorandum into this letter of mine.

2. A memorandum of Alypius to his priests.

Our son Severian has left us. We were still waiting for the reply of the highly placed man and his arrival, because it was announced by those who stated that he had most certainly left Gaul that he would be here by the Ides of October.[896] And so, may the prayers of Your Charity assist us in order that with the help of the Lord we may accomplish something before winter, so that, by the Lord's aid and in accord with both your desire and mine, we may return to you before winter. Much has already been granted as a result of our letter, to be sure. For on the day we dictated this a silentiary departed with the pardon sent to the people of Carthage. It remained, therefore, for us to deal with the people who took refuge in the church of Carthage for the same reason.

3. These are the extracts from the memorandum sent to Thagaste that I thought were necessary to copy and send to you. In addition, I ask that you gra-

---

896. In the Roman Calendar the Ides of October fell on the 15th day of this month.

ciously give the other letters that I sent to those to whom they were addressed and to give those letters your backing in interceding before them, each as he can. For, if you all want to do everything at the same time, it will be difficult for you to accomplish what you want, because it is extremely rare that you are all free at a single time. I wrote to the honorable and pious man, our son Dorotheus,[897] that he should not be angry at his man, who brutally violated a nun who came from another village to do woolworking, so that he punishes him more severely than is proper on account of our complaint. For it is sufficient that he should remove him from the supervision of the place where he put him so that he may not tempt others to imitate himself if he goes completely unpunished. He in fact is already doing penance, but this is precisely because, after he was proven guilty and was obliged because of his conviction to make a confession of what he had done, he was immediately forbidden communion. For, if he had willingly confessed and had revealed out of fear of God's judgment what was not known and what no one had accused him of, who would have been so misguidedly severe as to seek a further correction?

4. But now, just as he would lose the honor of his rank if he were a cleric, so this man also ought to lose the honor of his position as procurator, in which his impunity is inflated with pride, and for this reason we must take care that he not have any imitators. This man, however, is Cresconius, the procurator of Saltus Hispaniensis,[898] who has a wife, a factor that adds to the seriousness. But do not reveal either the action or its author unless you have first obtained the promise of Dorotheus, with God as his witness, that he will not punish him further, and do not specify the manner of punishment before he has promised that he will not do anything with greater severity than what he shall have found in this memorandum. For he, given the faith and piety that he has in Christ, although he could be very upset. . . .[899] Surely, if he is willing to punish more leniently than I had asked, without any consideration of corporeal punishment, I do not forbid it, but he should not be more severe. Let him promise this first, then, and after he has promised, without going out of your way to explain it, make him read the part of this memorandum that pertains to the issue.

---

897. Dorotheus was the addressee of Letter 14*.
898. Saltus Hispaniensis was in the diocese of Hippo, undoubtedly the same place mentioned in Letter 35, 2.
899. The sentence is incomplete in the Latin text.

LETTER 20*

Augustine to Fabiola, a Roman laywoman (422-423)

In the fall of 422 or the winter of 422-423, Augustine wrote to Fabiola, a Roman laywoman, to whom he had written Letter 267. The present letter throws further light on Augustine's problems with Antoninus of Fussala, the young bishop about whom Augustine had written Letter 209 to Pope Celestine. Augustine thanks Fabiola for her response and asks her forgiveness for bothering her with his troubles by this letter (paragraph 1). He also thanks Fabiola for welcoming Antoninus and narrates the early life of the young man, his entrance into the monastery, and his ordination to the priesthood (paragraph 2). He explains how Antoninus came to be made bishop of Fussala when the man whom Augustine had originally wanted backed out at the last moment (paragraph 3). He tells how Antoninus, who was in his early twenties and quite inexperienced, began to use his episcopal power so that he was feared rather than loved (paragraph 4). Antoninus ordained to the priesthood a renegade monk and made another monk his deacon, both men like himself (paragraph 5). With these men and a few others Antoninus robbed and plundered the people of Fussala, even helpless widows (paragraph 6). The lists of their crimes are so long that there is not a sufficient number of judges to hear the cases (paragraph 7). Augustine explains the penalties imposed upon Antoninus, namely, that he was removed from Fussala and assigned to another parish in his diocese and that he was excommunicated until he made restitution for the properties he had stolen (paragraph 8).

Antoninus tried to appeal these decisions but did so too late. He then asked to have, along with the other communities assigned to him, the estate of Thogonoetus, which was very close to Fussala (paragraph 9). The mistress of the estate and her workers all protested having Antoninus present in their community (paragraph 10). When Antoninus saw that he was not going to get what he wanted, he set sail to lodge a complaint with Pope Boniface, though he did not disclose that he had been excommunicated at least briefly (paragraph 11). Boniface appointed judges to hear the case, and the bishops gathered in Tegulata, where Antoninus demanded that the church of Fussala be returned to him (paragraph 12). The priests and people of Fussala, however, made it clear by letter that they would never accept him back. Antoninus challenged the authenticity of the letter but agreed to accept Thogonoetus instead, if the people of Fussala did not want him back (paragraph 13). The people of Thogonoetus, however, were equally opposed to having him there (paragraph 14).

A delegation was sent to Fussala to ascertain the true attitude of the people, though Augustine himself did not go there because of the hostility of the people toward him (paragraph 15). The people of Fussala showed that they were even more strongly opposed to having Antoninus back than their letter had expressed (paragraph 16). Meanwhile Augustine received a letter from the mistress of Thogonoetus in which she denied that she had said that she was willing to accept Antoninus (paragraph 17). When the bishops returned to Tegulata to continue hearing the case, Augustine produced that letter from the mistress of Thogonoetus, and Antoninus gave another interpretation of the events (paragraph 18). Augustine, however, produced still another letter from the mistress of the estate that contradicted Antoninus's version of events (paragraph 19).

Because of further complaints from Antoninus it was decided to question the people of Fussala once again. Augustine meanwhile interceded with the primate of Numidia to restore the people of Thogonoetus to communion (paragraph 21). When questioned, the people of Thogonoetus complained of everything that they had suffered from Antoninus, though they did not want what they said to be recorded for fear of reprisals (paragraph 22). Meanwhile a message from the people of Fussala arrived in which they expressed similar concerns about being questioned again. The people of Fussala were questioned again, however, and records were kept, which the bishops brought back to Tegulata (paragraph 23). Antoninus was summoned to hear the decision of the bishops, including the primate. When told that he should be content with the communities assigned to him, he expressed his desire to go off alone and live as a servant of God, though he would not commit his plans to writing (paragraph 24). Once again, Antoninus insisted on being bishop in Fussala, at which point Augustine urged the primate to draw up proceedings that could be sent to the Apostolic See (paragraph 25).

Hence Augustine tells Fabiola that the bishops sent a letter and a copy of the proceedings to the Apostolic See, and he prays that all this disturbance may not result in the loss of the souls of those in Fussala who have recently been converted from Donatism (paragraph 26). Augustine counsels Fabiola on how she should provide for the needs of Antoninus's soul as well as those of his body and prays that Antoninus will be content to be a good bishop over the communities assigned to him (paragraph 27). He urges her to counsel Antoninus to seek the things of God rather than worldly power in the Church (paragraph 28).

Augustine adds that Antoninus, who became a bishop with only the clothes on his back, has managed to acquire property in his own name by various dishonest means (paragraphs 29 and 30). He used one property to make restitution to a man whose house he had plundered in order to build his own house in Fussala, and Augustine laments the fact that he still demands that house for himself (paragraph 31). He tells Fabiola of his concern for Antoninus, who is seeking not merely property for himself but also the people whom Christ has redeemed (paragraph 32). Hence Augustine begs Fabiola for her help with the whole problem so that Antoninus does not do further harm to himself (paragraph 33).

To his most devout lady and most revered and excellent daughter, Fabiola, Augustine sends greetings in the Lord.

1. I was overjoyed at the reply of Your Holiness, which came by means of my lord and brother. . . .[900] Would that I were repaying the word of greeting without annoying you. But now, first of all, tormented as I have been by my affliction, I have made myself unwelcome and troublesome to your holy repose, but tolerate me patiently. By progressing in that way, may you persevere in the grace of Christ up to the end.[901] I know that a letter from me is never a burden but rather a joy for you. Pardon this letter, for it has many things over which you will grieve; share my pains with me by mutual love in Christ; and add your prayers to the Lord our God that he may console us.

2. I have heard of the pious goodness with which you welcomed my beloved son and fellow bishop, Antoninus, and of the Christian kindness with which you eased his destitute travels. Learn, then, what I mean to Antoninus, what I owe to him, and what I ask of you. As a child he came to Hippo with his mother and stepfather; they were so poor that they lacked what they needed for daily sustenance. At length, when they had taken refuge in the church and I had discovered that the father of Antoninus was still alive and that his mother was united to another man after having been separated from her husband, I convinced both of them to lead lives of continence. And so all of them, he with the boy in a monastery and she in a home for the poor whom the Church supports, began in this way to live under our care by the mercy of God. Finally, as time went on—not to dwell on many events—he died, she grew old, and the boy grew up. Among his comrades he performed the office of lector and soon began to be viewed as a man of such qualities that Brother Urbanus (who at that time was a priest among us and superior of the monastery but is now bishop of the church of Sicca) wanted him, in my absence, to become a priest in a certain large estate situated in our diocese. For I had, when departing, given orders that he should find someone whom the neighboring bishop might ordain for that place without waiting for my return. This of course could not have been done if he had refused. Nonetheless, when I learned of this afterwards, I began to consider him as fit for such an office—not because I had come to know him as I ought to have but on account of the testimony of his superior.

3. Meanwhile, because I was not capable of governing, as the need demanded, a diocese that was so spread out, since many people not only in the city but also in the countryside had come over from the sect of Donatus, I decided, after having consulted with the brothers, that in a certain town called Fussala, which is subject to the see of Hippo, someone should be ordained as bishop, to whom the care of the region would fall. I sent a request to the bishop of the primatial see. He agreed to come. At the last moment the priest whom I thought I had ready disappeared. What ought I to have done at that point, if I were to do the right thing, but postpone such an important action? But I was afraid that, if the

---

900. The name of the courier is missing.
901. See Mt 10:22; 24:13.

holy primate,[902] who had with great difficulty come to us from a distance, went back from us without accomplishing anything, the spirits of all those who needed the ordination to take place would be crushed and that there would be some people whom the enemies of the Church would begin to lead astray by mocking the failure of our action. Hence I believed it useful to present for ordination the man who was there, because I had heard that he also knew the Punic language. And when I presented him, they trusted me. After all, they did not ask for him on their own, but, as one of my men who was acceptable to me, they did not dare to reject him.

3. I introduced to such a great burden, then, a youth not much more than twenty years old, who had not been proven in any tasks of the clerical ranks and who was unknown to me in those respects that ought to have been known about him beforehand. You see, of course, my great mistake; look at what ensued. Not having merited anything by previous service, the soul of the young man was seized with awe and suddenly swept away by the honor of the episcopacy. Then, seeing that the clergy and people were subject to him, as the affair itself reveals, he was puffed up with the arrogance of power, and, teaching nothing verbally but compelling people to everything by his power, he was happy to be feared when he saw that he was not loved.

4. To carry out this role, he sought men of his own kind. There was in our monastery a certain former secretary who, much to my distress, did not turn out well. Subjected to a beating by the superior of the monastery because he was found conversing alone with certain nuns at an inappropriate hour, he was considered a scoundrel. He abandoned the monastery, and, as soon as this fellow presented himself to the bishop under discussion, he was ordained a priest by him, without consulting me and without my knowledge. For I heard that the deed was done before I could have believed it possible, even if I had been informed by someone whom I ought to have believed. But I wish that you would believe the great sorrow that filled my heart, because I feared the destruction of that church which he would one day bring about, for I cannot describe it. When I found the opportunity, because the same bishop himself presented to me serious complaints about the sort of person that his priest was, I tried to have him excommunicated and returned to his native land, from which he had been given to me. And it happened—but I do not know how, and again without my having been consulted—that Antoninus restored him to his communion and friendship. He also created another deacon, following the correct procedure, who was given to him from our monastery, but he was not seen as troublesome until he was a deacon.

5. Anyone whom it would not disgust to read the records can easily learn what evils that town and the surrounding region suffered because of these two

---

902. I.e., Silvanus of Summa.

clerics, the priest and the deacon, and because of the defender of the church[903] and a certain other man, a former soldier or deserter, to whom he gave orders as friends, and because of those men from the same town whom he made into guards for night watches and whom he used when there was need of a slightly larger number. These records were compiled before the bishops in the church of Hippo, where I myself presided, after many people with lists of grievances had complained. Anyone will find in them the pitiful complaints of men and women and—what is worse—of widows, whom neither their name, which holy scripture especially recommends to our defense,[904] nor even their elderly age could protect to some extent from the robberies, plunderings, and unspeakable injustices that those people committed. Whoever fell into their hands lost money, furniture, clothing, cattle, harvests, timber, and even building stones. The homes of some were occupied; those of others were torn down in order that what the construction of new buildings demanded might be carried off from there. At times they made purchases but did not pay the price. The fields of some were invaded and were returned after the harvests had been seized over the course of several years, but some of them were retained and occupied up to the time of the episcopal judgment.

7. Besides the facts that are recorded in the judicial proceedings we have come to know many things from a different source, and on the lands of those who suffered them they are spread about not by the groans of grumbling people but by the outcries of screaming mobs, and they are piled up waiting to be proved, if judges would hold court where the small number of them would not be exhausted or where even those who do hold court might be sufficient to hear all the cases. For hardly anyone would endure the review of these cases that we have heard about from the ecclesiastical proceedings. Of these a very small number were settled somehow or other, but many were set aside or postponed in part because of the absence of those who committed the acts. It would, however, take a long time to say how the appearance of those clerics, that is, of the priest and the deacon, was kept from and is still kept from the episcopal tribunal. Yet we do have the words of the bishop[905] in which he himself admitted that they were warned by him to come because they were with him and that they had wanted to come.

8. We, however, commanded the restitution of what they plundered, but we left to the bishop the full and complete possession of his episcopacy. But, so that those evils might not remain unpunished and be left either for him to continue or for others to imitate, we imposed punishment to this extent: that the bishop

---

903. The defenders of the church (*defensores ecclesiae*) were advocates who, by a decree of the Emperor Honorius in 407, were given the task of being legal representatives of the Church and of defending its interests. See Serge Lancel, "L'affaire de Antoninus de Fusala," in *Les lettres de saint Augustin découvertes par Johannes Divjak* (Paris 1983) 277.
904. See 1 Tm 5:3.
905. I.e., Antoninus

would indeed sit on one of his seats—in order that he might not be said to have been transferred contrary to the canons into another see—but that he would no longer preside over the people of Fussala against their will. I think that this kind of punishment should even have been considered a benefit for him insofar as he would not be living with those whose most bitter hatred his very presence would most dangerously exacerbate. We of course judged that he should be deprived of communion until he had first restored what he had taken. He himself embraced this sentence of ours to the point that he did not appeal and within a few days paid with borrowed gold coins for the goods he had stolen in order that he might no longer be denied communion. And many of our brothers and sons had, along with us, taken pity on him because he was acquitted, and quite probably justly, of four grave and capital charges of adultery. It was not the people of Fussala but other people whom he harmed, who on some grounds had raised these charges against him and had caused them to be raised against him. And so these brothers and sons of ours were delighted with fraternal joy that such a judgment had been rendered concerning him.

9. He also asked by a petition that the holy primate of the primatial see in Numidia[906] graciously postpone until the council the desire of the people of Fussala by which they most ardently demanded that a bishop be ordained for them, and he postponed it. When it had been convened and all who were present decided to implement our decisions, he did not appeal against them. And if he had done so, he would certainly have done so too late, since he had not appealed against our decisions several months before. Then our superior, the primate, sent bishops to Fussala in whose presence the faithful would choose by votes who would be ordained bishop for them and would be sent to them for ordination, and that was done. But when the day of ordination dawned, then the idea of appealing entered his mind. Yet he remained quiet after the holy primate had given him an explanation, and, because he was appealing such a long time after judgment had been passed concerning him, he understood that he was appealing in vain, and he agreed that eight communities, which for some reasons had not come to the church of Fussala to vote for the ordination of a bishop, should be assigned to him. But, in order to sow discord once again,[907] he obtained by his insistence that it be added to the letter of the holy primate that one community should also be given to him from those which had come to Fussala to ask for a bishop, namely, the estate of Thogonoetus, where he might have a seat to which his others would be subject.

10. This estate, however, was so close to the town that it seemed that he was seeking nothing in it but occasions for quarrels by which to disturb the peace of the church. Then, since the same tenant farmers had already had experience of him from nearby and had borne those evils with the others, they wrote to the

---

906. I.e., Aurelius of Macomades.
907. See Prv 6:19.

mistress of the property that, if she permitted this to take place, they would immediately move away, and they likewise wrote to me that I should intervene on their behalf in order that this would not take place. On their account she and I wrote to the primate.

11. When Antoninus saw that he was not going to be granted this, then, he thought that he should set sail, carrying a letter of recommendation from the same superior, the primate, not one that he had received at that time, but one that he had received before, when that grave man had naively believed that he had absolutely no guilt and had wanted to set sail in order to obtain the release of persons whom the vicar of Africa held prisoner. At that time he had not clearly come to know from the church records the woes of the people of Fussala and their righteous sorrow. Antoninus, therefore, gave a formal complaint to the venerable Pope Boniface in which he stated falsely that he had remained in communion from the time that judgment had been pronounced concerning him—for, as I mentioned above, he had been excommunicated until he returned the goods that he had taken from the people of Fussala. On this account he had paid the gold coins after only a few days, of course, but still after some days, so that he might be restored to communion. He also passed over in silence the whole sequence of events that was necessary in order to understand the case, and he obtained from the pope a letter that was clearly very tentative.

12. For Pope Boniface of venerable memory assigned judges to learn whether the explanation he gave was supported by the facts, whether he had faithfully reported the sequence of events, and whether the facts were such as he had set them forth in the text of his complaint. Only then would the church of Fussala be returned to him as to someone having no sins for which it would justly have been taken from him. Those who were able to come assembled in a certain place in Numidia, that is, in the church of Tegulata. Other bishops were also present there whom Antoninus had not asked for and who had other reasons for coming, and though the number of bishops that he had demanded had not appeared, he nonetheless said that they were enough for him. We were also present, that is, Brother Alypius and I, alerted by the letter of the primate, not in order that we might pronounce judgment on him again—after all, what could be worse than that?— but in order that we might give an account of our judgment, if the situation demanded. All this was to be referred to the Apostolic See. After the complaint that Antoninus brought was read out, the primate of Numidia, the elderly Aurelius,[908] explained the reason why he had ordained a bishop for the people of Fussala.[909] In his explanation it became clear what Antoninus had omitted in order to obtain from Rome such a letter and that he had not faithfully reported the sequence of events.

---

908. I.e., Aurelius of Macomades.
909. I.e., Antoninus' successor.

13. Then Bishop Antoninus asked that the priest whom the people of Fussala had sent be brought in. When he entered, the letter of the priests and of the people of Fussala was read out. When he saw that it was full of pitiful complaints against him, on account of which they were refusing by every means to accept as bishop a man from whom they had been justly and rightly freed, he refused to believe that the letter was sent by them and asked the holy primate that, with some bishops from the number of those who had been granted him, he himself would deign to visit those places and explore the attitudes of the priest and the people under the following condition. If the people of Fussala raised a protest about taking him back, he would accept the community of Thogonoetus added to those eight communities that he had already had before, and the holy primate would also ask me to give him a confirmation by entering into the records the promise concerning those five communities that I had already made him apart from the proceedings so that he would not act with hostility toward the people of Fussala.

14. After I had done this without any difficulty, we parted as if in peace, except for the fact that I saw that the locality of Thogonoetus was resisting him no less than the people of Fussala and that the mistress of the property would not agree to this, something that the venerable primate Aurelius also saw. Finally, the primate promised in the proceedings, as he had been asked, that he would come to Fussala, but no one promised Thogonoetus to Antoninus in those proceedings. The declaration of the same bishop, Antoninus, was to the effect that the bishops should recognize from the response of the people of Fussala what ought to be done.

15. After some days, as had been decided, they came to Fussala; there were present with the primate two bishops whom Antoninus asked for from those who had been in the city,[910] and those were also granted him whom he was able to find closer to the same town. Another three also accompanied the primate out of respect, as is usually done. I myself was absent, because I do not dare to face the people of Fussala. They were already at peace after having received a bishop in accord with our judgment, and, now that they were again in turmoil on account of the restlessness of this man, I myself have also become odious to them. They no longer complain in hushed murmurs but shout out in clear cries and wailing that I have brought a great disaster upon them, and Antoninus himself in his utter ingratitude suspects nothing of me but that I am his enemy. Brother Alypius, who had returned to his own town, was also absent.

16. And so, under the eyes of six bishops, that community, having assembled quickly and in large numbers, was questioned and was found to have the same disposition as when it had sent a letter to the church of Tegulata by a priest, and in fact it was more vehement and bitter. It is not necessary to write what

---

910. I.e., Tegulata; see the following paragraph.

Antoninus did in advance out of a desire to terrify them. He himself will perhaps admit it if he is constrained, though these people who hand you our letter can also reliably make it known to Your Reverence. After the crowd had been questioned and had expressed well enough in a single day what they thought of him, they most insistently demanded the presence of their own bishop, because he was not present either when the first interrogation was held. And so, after an interval of one day, with their bishop now present, they gave many answers in their own defense and against Antoninus and did much shouting, and everything was written down.

17. Then the primate wrote to me so that I would meet him at some place where all of us together might see what should be done. When I was traveling to that place, I received en route a letter of the illustrious lady who owns the estate of Thogonoetus. She informed me that her steward had written her that the holy primate said to him that he had heard from Bishop Antoninus that she had agreed to his being at Thogonoetus. "I know nothing about that," she said. "Rather, when he came to me, he himself asked that I not agree." I carried with me this letter from the pious woman since I saw that it was very necessary, although I had already learned that he acted in this way, but I did not see by what certain proof he could be shown to be guilty if he denied it in the absence of that honorable woman.

18. After we had assembled, then, at a certain place ten miles away from Fussala, to which I did not want to go, we all began to deal with him as each was able, in order that a Catholic bishop would not devise further trouble and ruin for Catholic Christians. And when it was a matter of the estate of Thogonoetus, I brought out the letter of the mistress of the property. After it was read, when all the brothers and our fellow bishops who were present began to be horrified and to reproach him gravely, he replied that he had not spoken in that way but that, when she first said that she would not grant him that place, he had said, not in the tone of a petitioner but in that of someone indignant, "If you do not want to, do not grant it, nor do I want it." From this we turned to other terms by which we were trying to bring it about, if possible, that he would accept two other places instead of that estate and that he would in the future be troublesome to no one from those communities that had already begun to belong to the bishop of Fussala. But this could not be done since they all rejected him most emphatically.

19. We were also in a certain place from among the eight that had been assigned to him and where he presided without any dispute. For the manager of that estate had asked that we meet, and we dealt with Antoninus on many issues, but in vain. There, in any case, I received another letter from the mistress of the estate of Thogonoetus, because I had written in reply to her what Antoninus had answered, and I had asked that she indicate by letter the order in which events had taken place. She wrote, however, that Antoninus had informed her by means of her son-in-law that he would ask her to do him the favor of not agreeing to his

being at Thogonoetus nor to his being in its parish[911] if he was going to have his see as bishop anywhere else but in Fussala. And afterwards she confirmed from her own lips that he had asked this of her. She wrote with perfect clarity that not merely her son-in-law but also the bishop of the place where they were at that time were witnesses to this.

20. When this letter was read out in the presence of the brothers, Antoninus was so disturbed that he replied with nothing but abuse for me. And since the primate had said to me that he had complained that their bishop was present on the day when the people of Fussala were questioned for the second time, it was decided that the people be consulted a third time with that bishop absent, separating the tenant farmers of each area with the supervisors or procurators, but without the managers. But to get to Fussala it was necessary to pass through Thogonoetus, and I asked repeatedly that the primate restore its people to communion, because he had excommunicated them when they produced a serious disturbance in his presence against Bishop Antoninus. And I deeply feared that they might utterly perish because of their peasant despair. For between the two bishops they had been abandoned in such a way that I knew that they had begun to apostatize in some instances. For this reason I feared that this wound to my heart would increase, and I hastened to heal it as fast as I could.

21. Since we arrived there in the evening, we saw them gathered in the church on the next day. But when the venerable primate began to speak to them about Antoninus in the Punic tongue, they made known their will with great shouts, and when he asked them how the man had injured them to whom they were opposed with such great stubbornness, they began to say individually what they had suffered. When they were ordered to do this by name for the records, they replied that they were afraid that he would come to know them and would pursue and destroy them individually. But when they were ordered even more insistently to do what was said, all of them suddenly abandoned us and departed with very angry protests so that not even a single nun remained. Who could say how much we were all upset with the fear that, in the judgment of Christ, their loss would be tied around our neck as an object heavier than that millstone turned by an ass, of which the Gospel speaks?[912] They were scarcely called back when the primate promised that he would do nothing that they would not want with regard to giving them a bishop.

22. And so, when we had left the church after celebrating the divine rites, we found that two inhabitants of Fussala had been sent with a dispatch in which they said that the rumor had reached them that we wanted to question them separately, although their will had already been made indisputably clear so often regarding whom they considered their bishop and that they were not individually

---

911. The Latin word is *diocesi*, which in the context seems to have the meaning not of "diocese" but of "parish."
912. See Mt 18:6; Mk 9:42.

going to say anything other than what they were all able to say together. But if this were being done in order that their enemy might know whom he ought to pursue once their names were taken down, we should understand that they would be handing themselves over to death by this provision, and that it certainly ought to have been enough that we killed their souls by giving them to Antoninus without handing over their bodies so that they might die again at the hands of Antoninus. In the same dispatch they also set down that, if it seemed good to us, we should order their case to be heard again after the documents containing the charges against Antoninus that they had submitted at Hippo Regius were returned to them, as well as other things that it would take too long to mention. But because someone could say that the dispatch did not reflect the will of the people but was sent by one or by two or surely by only a very few, we decided that we should not change our plan of going to them.

23. Then the primate arrived at noon in Fussala with those who were required; their bishop and I remained in the same place.[913] But on the following day, when the primate questioned the people for the third time, we met him at a certain place through which he was going to pass on his way from there, and we spent the whole day there while he was situated in Fussala. After this, the bishops came from there to us along with the holy primate, carrying the written record of the groans and cries of the poor people, in which they did not think that even I was to be spared. For they also shouted about me things that I deserved to hear because I was the author of such a great disaster for them, since I had given them a man for whom they had not asked and who afflicted them with such great evils.

24. Then a letter was sent to the same Bishop Antoninus, and he met us in a certain town called Gilva, where the needs of the church required the primate to go. For Antoninus had left us with the proviso that he would meet us wherever he had been told to go by letter. When he had heard even from the very bishops, whom among others he had asked for as judges, what they had seen and heard in person, and after all of them tried to persuade him, as each was able to do, that he ought to do nothing else if he considered himself a bishop but to govern in peace the communities that had accepted him without any scandal to the Church and without any disturbance, he replied that they did not want to have him either and that he had the firm resolve to sit as bishop in some very remote place, at a distance from the crowds, away from hatred, and as a servant of God. He desired, if we were willing, to prove this even by witnesses to whom he said that he had told this before he saw us. Since I was unwilling to believe readily so favorable a disposition of mind in his regard, I said to him that, if he were sincerely thinking and saying such things, he should not hesitate to offer that sacrifice of mercy to our God whereby he would make his church secure by removing the fear that it had of him and by expressing this will of his in the episcopal records. And after he had said that he would state nothing for the records, we said that he should at

---

913. I.e., in Thogonoetus.

least express it in his own writing. And after he answered that he would not do this either, he heard what he deserved, namely, that he was not sincerely thinking of being a servant of God, when he took pleasure in leaving in such an upheaval of fear the church of him whose servant he was going to be.

25. But then, when he saw that he was pressed by the words of the bishops to which he had not been able to reply, he blurted out at long last what he was hiding in his heart, and he said with a frightening countenance and voice that he could in no way be persuaded not to try somehow or other to return to the church of Fussala. After hearing that, I began to insist with the holy primate that, in accord with the records of the church of Tegulata, he should set something down in the ecclesiastical records that could be referred to the Apostolic See. He said, "I am not saying anything for the record," and in much agitation he got up and left, and, immediately returning in a distraught mood of body and soul, he announced that he would go to the Apostolic See, as if we were going to send to some other see whatever we accomplished with him in the records.

26. It remained, then, for the Apostolic See to be informed by sending a letter and the proceedings to it. We took care to do this with as much speed as possible. See what a long tale we have become for the Jews and the Gentiles,-[914] for heretics and also for any who are our enemies within. May this be without the loss of those who have been set free from heresy and are already aspiring for some light of unity, for whom we are making the name Catholic something odious, if their weakness is not at least consoled to the point that they do not have as bishop the man whom they shout with righteous sorrow that they cannot have.

27. I thought, however, that I should write this to Your Excellency so that you might know how you ought to advise him if he comes to see you. You will, of course, do much better to give the poor fellow counsel for eternal life than sustenance for the present life. For he lacks much more dangerously the former alms, for want of which the heart dies[915] even if the flesh is unharmed. May he stop desiring to lord it over the members of Christ gathered together by the blood that others have shed. For, from the time he began to be bishop there, he suffered no losses or wounds from the Donatists—neither he himself nor any of his priests and clerics nor anyone placed under his authority. But in order that he might find such peace there, it is horrifying to state what sufferings our people have endured there. Let the communities that God wanted him to receive without scandal satisfy him, for governing even one of them with piety and care earns a great reward in God's eyes. But this man does not bear this in mind, for he desires to rejoice, with blasphemy to the name of Christ and with the dying groans of wretched human beings, over the number of his communities, not seeking to gain many persons for

---

914. See Acts 19:17.
915. See Prv 10:21.

God but to boast of having many. Otherwise he would not desire with such a great effort to make his own those people he sees are already Christ's.

28. Let him hear this from you, I beg, and do not keep from him whatever the Lord gives you to say to the man over whose soundness of heart I desire to rejoice. After all, you have in relation to him such an age that you can properly show him the affection of a mother. For, unless he is living under God's very great anger, he does not disdain in you the advice of his own mother. I know that you have risen with Christ so that *you seek the things that are above, not those on earth* (Col 3:1); do not, then, be afraid to give the advice of a believer to a bishop who is seeking the things of earth. You are in fact seeking God in this world; he is seeking this world in the Church.

29. For (this is something that you perhaps would not believe if someone else told it to you) he has not hesitated to buy farms in his own name, not in the Church's—he, a man who became a bishop right from the monastery, who had nothing but the clothing he wore that day. You perhaps ask with what he bought them. I do not want to say from those robberies that the people of Fussala complain that they suffered. The things that were stolen in that way were immediately consumed. But for his own sustenance and that of those who were with him I gave him an estate belonging to the church of Hippo, which was located in the same territory of Fussala. He rented it out, and, after having received the rent for five full years, he found the sum by which he could buy it. But, as for the complaint that the seller lodged about him before the emperor in a petition and the risks of a trial that he faced or how the defender of the church of Fussala, with whom the seller complained that he was held in a private jail so that he would sell his property to the bishop at the lowest price, just barely escaped the penalty of public condemnation through our efforts because he had already admitted that he did this under orders of the bishop, though this bishop said that he had commanded him to be held in custody, not in order to force him to sell him this farm but on account of another wrong—if I wanted to recount all this, when will there be an end to this letter?

30. He also bought another small property, it too in his own name, but with what I do not know. But in this affair also it was said in a complaint from the partner in our court that he dealt with him, with whom he owned a half of the undivided property, in such a fashion that he took all the harvest and stripped the tiles from the house they owned in common. We heard the case; proof was given us; we ordered restitution. This partner also produced a letter of his brother, and it was read out in our court. He wrote that he was forced by the bishop to sell his part of the property and had not received the price that he ought to have had. But because it was not proven to us that it was really his brother's letter, we somehow ended the debate among those present and reserved action for the man who was absent.

31. But Antoninus gave that property to another man whose house he had torn down, and he carried off to his own building all the materials out of which

the man's house had been built. I myself made intercession with this man so that he would not charge the bishop in our court by a formal petition and complaint. And the case was settled between them by private arbitration in such a way that, for his share, he would receive from Antoninus that farm, by which he might make up for his losses. And this miserable monk who had become a bishop still said to the people of Fussala,"Give me back my house, which I have built in your town"—the house that he was thought to have built not for himself, of course, but for the church. And would that he had built it by good means and from just offerings, not from robberies! For it is said that there is almost nothing in the fabric of that house that one cannot show was stolen from someone else and point with one's finger at the place from which it was stolen.

32. But there is another aspect to this affair. I wanted to pour out my groans before Your Sincerity because a young man raised by us in the monastery—who, when we accepted him, abandoned nothing that was his own either to distribute it to the poor or to contribute it to our community—now prides himself over farms and a house as if they were his own, and he wants not only to make them his own but also the flock of Christ, insofar as he wants to belong to the number of those who *seek their own interests, not those of Jesus Christ* (Phil 2:21), and he who would heal this wound of my heart sees how great a wound it is.

33. I beseech you by Christ and by his mercy and judgment to help me in this affair both for his sake and for the sake of the Church. After all, I wanted you to be informed, perhaps with more words than moderation, not in order that you might hate him but rather that you would look after him in a true and spiritual fashion, to the extent that the Lord chooses to give you the ability, by not allowing him to do harm to himself. For whom will he harm more grievously than himself if he tries to disturb and destroy a church that he ought to want to gain for Christ, not for himself? I believe that he will obey Your Holy Benevolence and will not raise up his pride against you if the fountain of mercy hears my weeping for him, which is so frequent and so abundant.

AUGUSTINE AS MONK AND MONASTIC FOUNDER

LETTER 48

Augustine to Eudoxius, the abbot of the monks on the island of Capraria (398)

In 398 Augustine wrote to Eudoxius, the abbot of the monks on the island of Capraria.[916] Augustine first recalls the oneness he shares with Eudoxius and his monks in the body of Christ (paragraph 1). He then urges them to steer a middle path between the contemplative and the active life (paragraph 2) and exhorts them to do whatever they do for the glory of God (paragraph 3). Finally, he expresses the hope that his exhortation will lead them to keep him in their prayers, and he tells Eudoxius of the death of one of his brothers (paragraph 4).

To his beloved lord, most desired brother, and fellow priest, Eudoxius, and to those brothers who are with you, Augustine sends greetings in the Lord.

1. When we think of the peace that you enjoy in Christ, we too find rest in your love, even though we are caught up in the midst of various difficult labors. For we are one body under one head in such a way that you are also busy in us and we are at leisure in you,[917] because *if one member suffers, all the members suffer with it, and if one member receives glory, all the members rejoice with it* (1 Cor 12:26). Let us admonish, then, and ask and implore through Christ's deepest lowliness and most merciful height that you be mindful of us in your holy prayers for we believe that your prayers are more vigilant and attentive. The dark tumult of worldly courtroom procedures, after all, often wounds and weakens our prayers. Even if we do not have such cases of our own, those who force us to go one mile, and with whom we are commanded to go another two,[918] impose upon us such great burdens that we can scarcely catch our breath. We believe, nonetheless, that, with the help of your prayers, he into whose sight the groaning of prisoners enters[919] will set us free from every difficulty, as we persevere in that ministry in which he has deigned to place us with the promise of a reward.

---

916. It is disputed whether this island is the one located to the north of Corsica or the one of the same name in the Balearics.
917. In the Latin original: *ut et vos in nobis negotiosi, et nos in vobis otiosi sumus*. The traditional Roman contrast between *otium* ("rest") and *negotium* ("activity," usually social and/or political) is not reflected in this case. Augustine adapts the term *otium* for his monastic language and understands it in an entirely positive way. According to him, monks should begin their ascetic life as people free from the temporal concerns that could hinder their progress, *ex otio* (see Letter 83,3). This freedom had for Augustine a positive character also with regard to monks already living in the monastery.
918. See Mt 5:41.
919. See Ps 79:11.

2. But we exhort you in the Lord, brothers, that you keep to the way of life you have undertaken and that you persevere in it up to the end,[920] and if your mother, the Church, desires any services from you, do not undertake them with an eager burst of pride or reject them because of the attraction of indolence. Rather, obey God with a meek heart, submitting yourselves with gentleness to him who rules you, who guides the meek in justice, who teaches the meek his ways.[921] Do not prefer your leisure to the needs of the Church. If no good men were willing to minister to her as she brings to birth new children, you would not have found a way to be born in Christ. But just as we must hold to the path between fire and water so that we are neither burned nor drowned, so we ought to steer our journey between the peak of pride and the whirlpool of indolence, as Scripture says, *Do not turn aside either to the right or to the left* (Dt 17:11; Prv 4:27). For there are some who, while too afraid of being filled with pride and carried off, as it were, to the right, are drowning because they have fallen to the left. And again there are some who, while restraining themselves too much from the left for fear of being swallowed up by the torpid softness of idleness, disappear in ashes and smoke, corrupted and consumed by the pride of boastfulness. So, my brothers, love leisure in such a way that you hold yourselves back from all earthly delight and that you remember that there is no place where he who fears our flying back to God cannot set his snares. Let us condemn the enemy of all good persons, for we were once his captives. Let us consider that we have no complete rest *until iniquity passes away* and *justice is turned into judgment* (Ps 57:2; 94:15).

3. Likewise, when you eagerly do something strenuous and work unstintingly, whether in prayers or in fasting or in almsgiving, when you give something to the needy or forgive injuries, *as God has also forgiven us in Christ* (Eph 4:32; Col 3:13), when you subdue harmful habits and chastise the body, subjecting it even to servitude,[922] when you bear with tribulation and, above all, bear with one another in love—for what does one bear with who does not bear with his brother?—or when you are guarding against the cleverness and ambushes of the tempter and are repelling and extinguishing his fiery darts with the shield of faith,[923] then, *singing and chanting in your hearts to the Lord* (Eph 5:19), or with words in harmony with your hearts, *do all for the glory of God who does all things in all* (1 Cor 10:31, 12:6). And be so fervent in spirit[924] that your soul may receive praise in the Lord.[925] For this is the action of someone on the straight road who always has his eyes on the Lord, because the Lord rescues his feet from the

---

920. See Mt 24:13; 10:22.
921. See Ps 25:9.
922. See 1 Cor 9:27.
923. See Eph 6:16.
924. See Rom 12:11.
925. See Ps 34:3.

snare.[926] Such action is not broken because of work, and it is not cold because of leisure. It is neither turbulent nor flagging, neither too bold nor cowardly, neither too hasty nor idle. Do all this, and the God of peace will be with you.[927]

Let not Your Charity regard me as forward because I wanted to speak to you, at least by means of a letter. For I do not admonish you about this matter because I think that you are not now acting in this way, but I believed that you would commend me to God to no small degree, if you do those actions that you do by his grace with a recollection of our words. For your reputation came to our attention even before, and now the brothers who have come from you, Eustasius and Andrew, have brought to us from your holy way of life the good odor of Christ.[928] Of these Eustasius has gone on to that peace that is not battered, like an island, by the waves, nor does he long for Capraria because he now no longer desires to don his shirt of a penitent.[929]

---

926. See Ps 25:15.
927. See Phil 4:9; 2 Cor 13:11.
928. See 2 Cor 2:15.
929. It is likely that the monks of Capraria were engaged in the manufacture of penitential vestments.

LETTER 60

Augustine to Aurelius, the bishop of Carthage and primate of Africa (401-402)

In late 401 or 402 Augustine wrote to Aurelius, the bishop of Carthage and primate of Africa, about a certain Donatus and his brother who had left the monastery. Augustine counsels Aurelius against allowing monks who have abandoned the monastery to be readily chosen as clerics, since even a good monk does not necessarily make a good priest (paragraph 1). Augustine points out that Donatus and his brother did not leave the monastery with his authorization and that the case of Donatus, who was ordained before any decision of a council, is different from that of his brother, who has not yet been ordained (paragraph 2).

To his most blessed lord and truly most dear brother worthy of reverence with due obedience, his fellow priest, Bishop Aurelius, Augustine sends greetings in the Lord.

1. I received no letter from Your Reverence since we physically parted from each other. But I have now read the letter of Your Grace concerning Donatus and his brother, and I have wavered back and forth for a long time about what reply I should make. But as I pondered again and again what would be conducive to the salvation of those whom we serve in Christ by providing them with spiritual nourishment, nothing else occurred to me but that we should not open this path to the servants of God so that they suppose that they are more likely to be chosen for a better position if they have become worse men. And it is, after all, easy for them to fall, and a most shameful injury is done to the clerical order if those who abandon their monastery are chosen for the army of the clergy since from those who remain in their monastery we usually choose only the more tested and better to be members of the clergy, unless as the common folk say, "A bad flute player makes a good singer." In the same way the common folk joke about us and say, "A bad monk makes a good cleric." It is something highly deplorable if we raise monks up to such ruinous pride and think that clerics, among whom we are counted, are worthy of grave abuse. After all, at times even a good monk does not make a good cleric if he has sufficient continence and, nonetheless, lacks the necessary instruction and the personal integrity required. But I am sure that Your Beatitude has thought concerning these men that they withdrew from the monastery by our decision in order that they might be more useful to the people of their region, but that is not true. They left of their own accord; they went off of their own accord while we resisted as much as we could for the sake of their salvation. And with regard to Donatus, since his ordination had already taken place before we

determined anything about this in a council,[930] if he has perhaps been corrected from the perversity of his pride, let Your Wisdom do as you see fit. But with regard to his brother, who was the main reason why Donatus himself left the monastery, I do not know what answer I should give, since you understand what I think. I do not dare to speak in opposition to Your Wisdom, Your Honor, and Your Charity, and I, of course, hope that you will do what you see will be salutary for the members of the Church.

---

930. I.e., in the Council of Carthage on September 13, 401 (canon 80).

LETTER 83

Augustine to Alypius (404-405)

In 404 or 405 Augustine wrote to his lifelong friend, Alypius, who was now the bishop of Thagaste, Augustine's hometown, concerning the possessions of Honoratus, a priest from Thiave, who died in the monastery of Thagaste. The faithful of Thiave claimed his money as their own. Augustine tells Alypius that the disturbance of the faithful of Thiave must be settled immediately and offers him his own resolution of the problem (paragraph 1). He warns that bishops must avoid giving scandal and should avoid even the appearance of greed (paragraph 2). Augustine points out that the problem with Honoratus could have been avoided if he disposed of his goods before entering the monastery (paragraph 3). Augustine suggests the rule that the possessions of a cleric should belong to the church where he was ordained if he dies without selling or giving them away. He reports that he sought the advice of another bishop who was horrified at the first decision of Augustine and Alypius (paragraph 4). Augustine begs Alypius to sign and send on the letter he has drafted in the name of both of them so that they can avoid further harm to the faithful of Thiave (paragraph 5). He agrees to pay half of what the people are claiming if Alypius really thinks that it is just, when his monastery has such a sum (paragraph 6).

To his most blessed and venerably most dear and most beloved brother and fellow bishop, Alypius, and to those brothers who are with you, Augustine and the brothers who are with me send greetings in the Lord.

1. The sadness of the church of Thiave does not permit my heart to rest until I hear that they have been restored to their original relation with you, something that must be done quickly. For, if the Apostle had tried to do so much because of one man, when he said, *Lest such a person be swallowed up by greater sadness* (2 Cor 2:7), where he also said, *For fear that we should be taken over by Satan, for we are not unaware of his wiles* (2 Cor 2:11), how much more ought we to act with vigilance for fear that we should have to grieve over this in a whole flock and especially in those who have now entered the Catholic peace[931] and whom I can in no way abandon. But since the shortness of time has not permitted us to carefully work out together a well-considered statement on this, I ask Your Holiness to accept what I have decided in thinking about it for a long time since our parting. And if you also like it, let the letter that I wrote to them in the name of both of us be sent on without delay.

---

931. Augustine is probably referring here to those Donatists who, following the edict of unity issued against them by emperor Honorius in 405, were forced to reunite with the Catholic Church.

2. You said that the faithful of Thiave should have half of their inheritance[932] and that I should somehow or other provide them with the other half. I, however, think that, if we provide[933] them with whole of it, it would be the case that people said that we labored so greatly, not for money, but for justice. But when we grant them half and in that way compromise with them at some point, people will see quite clearly that our concern has been only financial, and you see what damage results. For to them we will give the impression that we have taken the half belonging to them, and to us they will give the impression that they have suffered a wrong and an injustice in receiving a half, while the whole of it belonged to the poor. For your words, "We must be careful that, when we want to correct a doubtful matter, we do not inflict more serious wounds," will have the same validity if they are granted a half. For on account of a half, of course, those whose entrance into monastic life we want to foster are going to delay the selling of their property through those periods in which they excuse themselves in order that they might be dealt with in accord with this example. Finally, if there is so great a scandal of a whole people over a doubtful matter, would it be a surprise that they think that their bishops, whom they hold in high esteem, are tainted with filthy greed, if the appearance of wrongdoing is not avoided?

3. For, when anyone enters a monastery, if he enters with a sincere heart, he does not think about that problem, especially after having been warned how wrong it is. If, however, he is pretending and is seeking his own interests, not those of Jesus Christ,[934] he surely does not have love. And what good does it do him if he distributes all he has to the poor and hands his body over to be burned?[935] Besides this, as we have already said, that problem can be avoided hereafter and handled with the one entering the monastery if he cannot be admitted to the society of the brothers before he strips himself of all those impediments and enters free from business concerns since those possessions have ceased to be his. But we can only avoid this death for the weak and so great an impediment to the salvation of those for whom we have labored so greatly in order to gain them for the Catholic peace, if they understand with absolute clarity that we are by no means after their money in such cases. And they will never understand this unless we leave for their use that property that they thought always belonged to the priest, because, even if it was not his, they ought to have known this from the beginning.

4. It seems to me, then, that this rule should be observed in matters of this sort: whatever belongs to the man who is ordained a cleric anywhere, by whatever law he owns such things, should belong to the church in which he is ordained. Now that property we are dealing with belongs to the priest, Honora-

---

932. The dispute concerned the property of the priest, Honoratus, who died without a will.
933. R. Teske has followed here the reading in one manuscript of *provideretur* in place of *auferetur*, which is found in the CSEL.
934. See Phil 2:21.
935. See 1 Cor 13:3.

tus, by the same law so that, having been ordained elsewhere, but still living in the monastery of Thagaste, if he died with some property not sold nor transferred to someone by a public gift, only his heir would enter into possession of it, just as Brother Aemilian came into possession of those thirty silver pieces of Brother Privatus. These precautions, then, should be taken in advance; if, however, they were not taken, it is necessary for them to observe those laws that have been established in civil society for acquiring or not acquiring possession of such things, in order that we may avoid, as far as possible, not only all wrongdoing, but even the appearance of wrongdoing,[936] and that we may preserve our good reputation, which is quite necessary for our ministry. Let Your Wisdom consider how damaging the appearance of wrongdoing can be. Leaving aside the sorrow of those people that we experienced, for fear that I myself might be deceived in some way, as often happens when I err by being more inclined to my own view, I recounted the whole case to our brother and colleague, Samsucius,[937] without as yet telling him what I now think, but rather including what the two of us thought when we were opposing those people. He was deeply horrified and was amazed that we had that idea, disturbed by nothing else but the appearance of wrongdoing, which is most inappropriate not only for our life and conduct, but for the life and conduct of anyone.

3. Hence, I beg you not to delay in sending on with your signature the letter that I wrote to them under both of our names. And if you see with great clarity that my proposal in it is just, let the weak not now be forced to learn what I do not as yet understand, but in this case let us observe in their regard to the words of the Lord, *I have many things to say to you, but you cannot now bear them* (Jn 16:12). While sparing, of course, such weakness, he also said this about paying the tribute, *Therefore, the children are exempt, but for fear that we cause them scandal* (Mt 17:26), and so on, when he sent Peter in order that they might pay the two drachmas, which were then demanded. For he knew another law in accord with which he owed nothing of the sort, but he paid the tribute in accord with that law by which we said that the heir of the priest, Honoratus, would have come into possession of his goods if he died before he gave away or sold his possessions. And yet, with regard the very law of the Church the apostle Paul spares the weak and does not exact the wages they owe him, certain in his conscience that he would demand them with full justice. But he avoided nothing other than the suspicion that disturbs the good odor of Christ and held himself back from that appearance of wrongdoing, in those regions where he knew this was necessary,[938] and perhaps before he had experienced the sorrow of the people. But let us, though slower, at least after we have experienced this sorrow, correct what we ought to have foreseen.

---

936. See 1 Thes 5:22.
937. Samsucius was the bishop of Turris in Numidia.
938. See 1 Cor 9:1-23.

Finally, because I fear every eventuality and recall what you proposed at our departure, namely, that the brothers of Thagaste should consider me as owing half of that sum, if you clearly see that this is just, on that condition at least I will not refuse to pay it when I have it, that is, when so great an amount is obtained by the monastery of Hippo that this can be done without difficulty, that is, that, when so great a sum has been removed, our brothers receive a part no less than equal in proportion to the number of members of the community.

LETTER 210

Augustine to Felicity, the superior of the women's monastery at Hippo (423)

In approximately 423 Augustine wrote to Felicity, the superior of the women's monastery at Hippo, who had taken the place of Augustine's sister at the latter's death, and to Rusticus, who probably was the chaplain to this monastery. Augustine points out that among God's great acts of mercy is the tribulation that he occasionally sends to sinners as a warning that they should bring their lives into harmony with the word of God and thus avoid the wrath to come (paragraph 1). He insists that a rebuke is usually felt to be painful when it is received but often brings much good to the person who receives it. He tells them that one who gives a rebuke ought never to do so in order to repay evil with evil and urges the two to put more effort into achieving harmony than into giving rebukes (paragraph 2).

To his most beloved and most holy mother, Felicity, to his brother, Rusticus, and to the sisters who are with you, Augustine and those with me send greetings in the Lord.

1. *The Lord is good* (Lm 3:25), and his mercy is poured out everywhere, consoling us in his heart by your love. For he shows how much he loves those who believe and hope in him and love him and one another and what he reserves for them hereafter. He does this especially insofar as, though he threatens with eternal fire and with the devil[939] the wicked who are without faith and without hope if they persevere in their bad will up to the end, yet he bestows great blessings upon them in this world. For he *makes his sun rise over the good and the bad and sends rain upon the just and the unjust* (Mt 5:45). For he said this in a few words in order that we might think of more gifts. For who is able to count how many blessings and gratuitous gifts the wicked have in this life from him whom they hold in contempt? Among these there is this great gift: Through examples of occasional tribulations, which like a good doctor he blends in with the sweetness of this world, he warns them, if they are willing to pay attention, to flee from the wrath to come,[940] and, while they are on the road, that is, in this life, to bring themselves into harmony with the word of God, which they make into their enemy by living bad lives.[941] What, then, does the Lord God not give to human beings out of mercy when even tribulation is a benefit from him? For prosperity is a gift from the God who consoles us, but adversity is a gift from the God who warns us. And if he gives this, as I said, even to the evil, what does he

---

939. See Mt 25:41.
940. See Mt 3:7; Lk 3:7.
941. See 1 Pt 4:11.

prepare for those who are awaiting him in patience? Rejoice that you have been gathered by his grace into their number, *supporting one another in love, striving to preserve the unity of the Spirit in the bond of peace* (Eph 4:2-3). For you will not lack something to tolerate in one another except when the Lord has purified you, after death has been swallowed by victory, so that God may be all in all.[942]

2. We should, however, never love disagreements, but at times they arise, nonetheless, from love and are a test of love. For can we easily find anyone who is willing to be rebuked? And where is that wise person of whom Scripture says, *Rebuke a wise man, and he will love you* (Prv 9:8)? Should we not, then, rebuke and correct a brother in order that he may head toward death without a worry? For it is likely to happen, and it often does happen, that, at the time when he is rebuked, a person becomes sad, resists, and objects. And yet afterwards he considers the rebuke alone in silence, where there is only God and he himself and where he does not fear the displeasure of human beings because he is rebuked but fears the displeasure of God because he is not corrected. And afterwards he will avoid committing the sin for which he was rightly rebuked. And to the extent he hates his sin, he loves his brother who he saw was opposed to his sin. But if he belongs to that number of people of whom Scripture said, *Rebuke a fool, and it will cause him to hate you* (Prv 9:8 LXX), then the disagreement of that person does not arise from love, but it still actualizes and tests the love of the one who gives a rebuke. For he does not display hatred toward him, but the love that leads him to give the rebuke continues undisturbed, even when the one rebuked hates it. If, however, the one giving the rebuke wants to return evil for evil to someone who is angered at the person giving the rebuke, he was not worthy to give the rebuke but clearly deserves to be rebuked himself. Do this so that cases of anger either do not exist among you or so that they are done away with by a most speedy reconciliation as soon as they arise. Put more effort into establishing harmony among yourselves than into rebuking one another. For, just as vinegar spoils a container if it is kept there too long, so anger ruins a heart if it lasts until the next day. *Do this, then, and the God of peace will be with you* (Phil 4:9), and at the same time pray for us also that we may quickly carry out the good admonitions we give.

---

942. See 1 Cor 15:57.54.28.

LETTER 211
Augustine to the nuns of the women's monastery at Hippo (424)

In approximately 424 Augustine wrote this letter in which, first, he calls back to harmony some nuns in the monastery at Hippo who, in trying to change their superior, had created a state of disorder in the monastery. Then he goes on to prescribe a set of rules for their life. The first part of the letter, namely, paragraphs 1 to 4, is often treated as a separate work, *The Reprimand for Quarreling Nuns* (*Objurgatio*), while the second part is commonly called *The Rule for Nuns* (*Regularis informatio*).[943]

Augustine admonishes the nuns for having caused a disturbance (paragraph 1). He tells them that, as Saint Paul said to the Corinthians, he has not come to them so that he might spare them his anger. Rather, he has been praying for them to the Lord (paragraph 2). He tells them of his desire that they may not be corrupted but may be changed for the better (paragraph 3). He expresses his astonishment at the nuns' desire for a new superior in view of all the good the present superior has done for them (paragraph 4).

Then he begins to spell out the rules for the monastery. He first prescribes that the nuns possess all things in common as the members of the early Church did (paragraph 5). He warns them against pride, whether because of the families from which they have come or because of the community into which they have entered (paragraph 6). He adds prescriptions about set times for prayer, about fasting and abstinence, and reading at meals (paragraphs 7 and 8). He provides rules touching upon the nuns' care of the sick (paragraph 9) and the cleanliness of their clothing and the modesty of their behavior (paragraph 10). He lays down guidelines for rebuking a sister, for reporting her to the superior, and for expelling her from the monastery if she refuses to reform (paragraph 11). He establishes various norms for the common care and custody of clothing and for the reception of gifts (paragraph 12). He spells out further norms for the washing of clothes, for bathing, for caring for the sick, and for the dispensation of food, clothing, and books (paragraph 13). He warns about the evils of quarreling and the need for quickly forgiving a sister who has injured another (paragraph 14). He prescribes obedience to the superior and to the priest and describes what the superior's behavior toward her subjects should be (paragraph 15). Finally, he tells the sisters that they should use this letter, which he refers to as a book, as a mirror in which they can see how much progress they have made or have failed to make, and he asks that it be read to them weekly (paragraph 16).

---

943. See George Lawless, *Augustine of Hippo and His Monastic Rule* (Oxford 1987) for an analysis of the various Augustinian legislative texts as well as their translations.

1. Just as severity is ready to punish the sins that it finds, so love does not want to find any to punish. This is the reason that caused me not to come to you, though you were asking for my presence, not in order that I might enjoy you peace but in order that I might increase your dissension. After all, how would I overlook it and leave it unpunished if your uproar was as great in my presence as it was in my absence when it pummeled my ears with your words, though it was hidden from my eyes? For your rebelliousness might perhaps be even greater in my presence. After all, it would be necessary to refuse you those things that you asked for contrary to sound discipline, because they would set a most destructive precedent and would not be beneficial for you. And thus I might find you to be the sort of persons I do not want you to be, and you might find me to be the sort of person you did not want me to be.

2. As, therefore, the Apostle writes to the Corinthians, *I call God as witness to my soul that, in order to spare you, I have not yet come to Corinth. We do not want to dominate your faith. Rather, we are working with you for your joy.* (2 Cor 1:23-24) I also say to you that I have not come to you in order to spare you. I have also spared myself, *so that I would not have sadness upon sadness* (Phil 2:27; 2 Cor 2:3), and I chose not to show my face to you but to pour out my heart to God for you,[944] and I pleaded the case that involves great peril for you, not with words in your presence but with tears in God's presence. I prayed that he would not turn into grief the joy with which I often rejoice and am at times consoled over you amid the great scandals with which this world everywhere abounds. For I am consoled when I consider your large community, your chaste love, your holy way of life, and the more abundant grace that God has given you so that you would not only renounce carnal marriage but also choose a community where you might dwell together in a house with oneness of heart in order to be one soul and one heart for God.[945]

3. Considering these goods you have, these gifts of God, my heart usually quiets down somewhat amid the many storms by which it is shaken because of other evils. *You were running well. Who has bewitched you? That idea does not come from God who has called you.* (Gal 5:7-9) *A small amount of yeast* (1 Cor 5:6)—I do not want to say what follows. After all, I desire more, and I pray and urge that the yeast may be changed for the better so that the whole lump of dough does not change for the worse, as it had almost done. If, then, you have come to your senses, *pray that you may not enter into temptation* (Mt 26:41; Mk 14:38; Lk 22:46), in order that you may not fall back *into quarrels, rivalries, anger, dissensions, backbiting, rebelliousness, and murmuring* (2 Cor 12:20).[946]

---

944. See Lam 2:19.

945. See Acts 4:32. Augustine usually quotes this Lucan verse (*anima una et cor unum*) in a specific way, adding the phrase *in Deum* ("for God") at the end of the sentence, which is missing from the known versions of this biblical text. See, e.g., Letter 238, 13; *Expositions of the Psalms* 83,4; 101, 14-15; 132, 2.

946. See Gal 5:20; Rom 13:13.

For we did not plant and water the Lord's garden in your midst [947]so that we should reap these thorns from you.[948] But if your weakness is still in an uproar, pray that you may be rescued from temptation.[949] If, however, those who were disturbing you still disturb you, they will receive judgment, whoever they are, if they are not corrected.[950]

4. Think what an evil it is that, though we rejoice over the Donatists[951] in the unity of the Church, we mourn over internal divisions in the monastery. Persevere in your good resolve, and you will not want to change your superior by whom you have grown both in number and in age in that monastery, which has lasted through so many years and which received you like a mother, not in her womb but in her heart. For all of you who entered there found her either serving and obeying the holy superior, my sister,[952] or found her as the superior herself who received you.[953] Under her you were trained; under her you received the veil; under her you have grown many. And you are in such an uproar in order to have her replaced, though you ought to be in a state of grief if we wanted to replace her for you. She is the one you have known; she is the one to whom you came; she is the one under whom you grew many through having her. You have only received a new priest.[954] Or if on his account you are seeking change and have rebelled against your mother out of hatred for him, why did you not rather ask that he be replaced for you? If you are horrified at this, because I know how much you reverently love him in Christ, why do you not rather love her? For the basic principles of the priest for directing you are so thrown into confusion that he himself would prefer to abandon you rather than that she suffer hateful gossip from you, namely, that it is being said that you would not have sought another superior if he had not begun to be your priest. May God make your hearts calm and composed; let not the work of the devil prevail among you, but *let the peace of Christ win out in your hearts* (1 Jn 3:8). And may you not shamefully run to your destruction with sorrow in your heart because you do not get what you want or because you are ashamed to have wanted what you ought not to have wanted. Rather, by doing penance, may you return to virtue,[955] and may you not have the repentance of Judas the betrayer but rather the tears of Peter the shepherd.[956]

---

947. See Sir 24:42; 1 Cor 3:6-8.
948. See Jer 12:13.
949. See Ps 18:30; 2 Pt 2:9.
950. See Gal 5:10.
951. The CSEL edition has *de Deo natis* ("over those born for God") in place of *de Donatistis*.
952. The name of Augustine's sister is not known. At the time he wrote this letter she had already died.
953. The letter is dealing with two superiors, one of which was Augustine's own sister.
954. The priest was assigned by the bishop as chaplain and spiritual director to the nuns. From Letter 210 we know that his name was Rusticus.
955. See Mt 27:3-5.
956. See Mt 26:75; Mk 14:72; Lk 22:62.

5. These are the rules that you should observe when you are living in the monastery. The first reason on account of which you are gathered together is that you may dwell in the house in unity of mind and that you may have *one heart and one soul for God* (Acts 4:32). And you should not call anything your own, but everything ought to be yours in common, and food and clothing[957] should be distributed to each of you by your superior, not equally to all, because you are not all equally well, but to each one according to her need. After all, you read this in the Acts of the Apostles, *They held everything in common, and it was distributed to individuals according to need* (Act 4:32.35). Those who owned something in the world should gladly want it to be owned in common when they have entered the monastery. But those who did not own anything should not seek in the monastery what they could not have owned outside. Still, what is necessary should be provided for their infirmity, even if their poverty when they were in the world could not obtain for them what they needed. And let them not now consider themselves fortunate because they have found food and clothing of the sort that they could not find in the world.

6. Nor should they act in a haughty manner because they are in community with those whom they would not dare to approach in the world, but let them lift up their heart and not seek earthly goods,[958] for fear that monasteries may begin to be useful for the rich, not for the poor, if the rich are humbled in them and the poor are puffed up with pride. But, on the other hand, let those who considered themselves to be important in the world not show disdain for their sisters who came to that holy community from poverty. They should, however, strive to boast not over the social status of their rich relatives but over their community with their poor sisters. And let them not be filled with pride if they have contributed something to common life from their own wealth, for fear that they should be more proud over their own riches because they gave them to the monastery than if they enjoyed them in the world. Any other form of sinfulness is, of course, found in the commission of bad actions, but pride lies in ambush for good actions in order to destroy them. And what good does it do to distribute one's goods by giving them to the poor and to become poor, if a wretched soul becomes more proud when it scorns them than it was when it possessed them? All of you, then, live in unity of mind and in oneness of heart, and reverence in one another God, whose temples you have become.[959]

7. Be diligent about the prayers appointed for the various hours and seasons.[960] In the oratory let no one do anything but that for which it was built, from which it also derives its name, so that, if any wish to pray, if they are free, even apart from the appointed hours, those who wanted to do something else there

---

957. See 1Tm 6:8.
958. See Col 3:1-2.
959. See 1 Cor 3:16; 2 Cor 6:16.
960. See Col 4:2.

may not prevent them. When you pray to God in psalms and hymns, let what you utter with your voice be weighed in your heart, and sing only what you read is to be sung. But anything that is not prescribed for singing should not be sung.

8. As much as your health permits, subdue your flesh by fasts and abstinence from food and drink. When, however, some sister cannot fast, let her not, nonetheless, take any nourishment apart from the hour of dinner, except when she is ill. From when you approach the table until you get up from it, listen without disturbance and arguments to what is read to you according to custom, and let not only your mouths receive food but let your ears receive the word of God as well.

9. If those who are infirm as a result of their previous manner of life are treated differently in terms of food, it ought not to be troubling or seem unjust to the others, whom another manner of life has made stronger. And let them not suppose that those others are more fortunate because they eat what they themselves cannot eat. And if something in the line of food, clothing, bed, and blankets is given to those who have come to the monastery from a more delicate lifestyle, though it is not given to others who are stronger and for this reason more fortunate, those who do not receive such treatment should consider how far the others have come down from their life in the world to this present life, though they could not attain the frugality of the others who are stronger in body. Nor should they be disturbed because they see them receive more, for they are not being honored but are being tolerated. Otherwise, there might result the detestable perversity that in the monastery where, as far as possible, wealthy ladies become working women, poor women become dainty and delicate ladies. Certainly, those nuns who are ill must receive less food so that they are not made worse. And after their illness they should be treated in such a manner that they recover more quickly, even if they came from the very lowest poverty in the world, as if their rather recent illness provided for them what rich women's previous manner of living bestowed on them. But when they recover their original strength, let them return to their happier way of life, which is more fitting for the servants of God to the extent that they need less. Nor should their desire keep them, once restored to health, at a level to which necessity raised them when they were infirm. Those who are stronger in enduring scarcity ought to judge themselves richer. For it is better to need less than to have more.[961]

10. Let your habit not stand out, and do not aim to please people by your clothing but by your way of life. Let the veils on your heads not be so fine that your hairnets are seen beneath them. Nowhere should your hair be uncovered; let neither carelessness spread it outside the veil nor meticulousness arrange it. When you go out, walk together; when you arrive where you are going, stay together. In your walk, your posture, your habit, and all your movements let

---

961. See Seneca, *Moral Letters to Lucilius* 2,6.

there be nothing that might arouse the desire of anyone but only what might fit with your holiness. Even should your eyes fall upon someone, they should not be fixed upon anyone. For, when you go out, you are forbidden not to see men but to desire them or to want to be desired by them. A woman is desired and has desires not only because of touches but also because of affection and glances. Do not say that you have modest minds if you do not have modest eyes, for an immodest eye is the messenger of an immodest heart. And when, even if the tongue is silent, immodest hearts send messages to each other by glances at each other and find delight in terms of concupiscence of the flesh from each other's passion, chastity itself flees from their manner of life, even if their bodies are untouched by any impure violation. Nor should the sister who fixes her eye upon a man and likes to have his eye fixed upon her think that she is not seen by others when she does this; she certainly is seen—and by those who she does not think see her. But suppose that she is concealed and is not seen by any human being. What will she do about that observer on high from whom nothing can be hidden?[962] Should we think that he does not see because he sees with more patience to the extent he sees with more wisdom? Let a holy woman, then, fear to be displeasing to him so that she does not want to be pleasing to a man in the wrong way. Let her bear in mind that God sees all things so that she does not want a man to see her in the wrong way. For fear of God was taught to us even in this matter where Scripture says, *She who fixes her eye on someone is an abomination to the Lord* (Prv 27:20, LXX). When, therefore, you are together in church and wherever there are also men, mutually guard your chastity. For in this way God, who dwells in you, will guard you by means of one another.[963]

11. And if you notice this flirting with the eye, of which I am speaking, in one of yours, admonish her immediately so that she does not continue what she has begun but is corrected right away. But if you see her do this same thing again after the admonition or on any other day, let any sister who was able to discover this report her, for she is now like someone who has been wounded and is in need of being healed. But she should first be made known to a second or third sister in order that she can be accused by the lips of two or three[964] and corrected with adequate severity. And do not consider yourselves as having bad will when you report this. You are in fact more lacking in innocence if you allow your sisters, whom you can correct by reporting them, to perish by keeping silence. After all, if your sister had an ulcer in her body that she wanted to hide because she feared surgery, would you not be cruel in keeping silent about it and merciful in reporting it? Ought you not that much more to report her for fear that she may be more dangerously infected in her heart? But if, after having been admonished, she does not take care to correct herself, she ought to be reported to the supe-

---

962. See Prv 24:12.
963. See 1 Cor 3:16; 2 Cor 6:16.
964. See Dt 19:15; Mt 18:16; 2 Cor 13:1.

rior before she is made known to others who would have to bring accusations against her if she denies it. Thus she can perhaps be privately rebuked and not made known to others. But if she denies it, then others are to be summoned for the sister who is lying so that, in the presence of all, she may not be accused by one witness but proven guilty by two or three. But once proven guilty, she must submit to the corrective penalty according to the judgment of the superior or the priest, and if she refuses to submit to it and if she does not go away on her own, she should be thrown out of your community. After all, this is not done out of cruelty but out of mercy, so that she may not destroy a great number with a deadly infection. And what I said about making eyes at someone should also be observed with love for the persons and a hatred for their vices in discovering, prohibiting, reporting, proving, and punishing other sins. But any sister who has gone so far in wrongdoing that she secretly receives a letter or any little gifts from a man should be forgiven if she confesses this on her own, and you should pray for her. But if she is caught and proven guilty, she should be more severely corrected according to the judgment of the superior or of the priest or even of the bishop.

12. Keep your clothing in one place under one or two custodians or however many are enough to air them out in order that they may not be damaged by moths. And just as you are fed from one storeroom, so clothe yourselves from one wardrobe. And, if possible, it should not be up to you what you will be given to wear in accord with the needs of the season, whether each sister receives the garment she had left there or another that another sister had worn, provided, nonetheless, that each is not denied what she needs. If, however, quarrels and murmuring arise among you over this, and if some sister complains that she has received something worse than she previously had, and if the one who is dressed in that way considers herself not to deserve to be dressed as the other sister was dressed, you who are quarreling about the habit of the body can learn from this how much you are lacking in that interior *holy habit* (Tit 2:3) of the heart. If, nonetheless, your weakness is tolerated so that you receive back what you left in the wardrobe, at least keep what you put away in one place under common custodians. In that way no one may make something for herself, whether to wear or to lie on or to use as a cincture or a cloak or a veil for the head. Rather, you should make everything that you make for the common good with greater zeal and greater speed than if you were making something for yourself. For the love of which scripture says that *it does not seek what is its own* (1 Cor 13:5) is understood to mean that it sets the common good before one's own good, not one's own good before the common good. And so you can know that you have made more progress the more concern you show for the common good than for your own. As a result, in all the things that passing necessity makes use of, the love that lasts should stand out.[965] Hence it follows that, if a man or woman gives

---

965. See Eph 3:19; 1 Cor 13:8.

clothing or any other necessity either to his or her own daughters or to any others in the monastery in some way related to him or her, it should not be accepted secretly. Rather, it should be in the control of the superior in order that, as something given to the community, it may be offered to one who needs it. But if a sister conceals some gift given to her, she should be judged guilty of theft.

13. Your clothing should be washed according to the judgment of the superior, either by you or by laundresses, lest an excessive desire for clean clothes soil the soul interiorly. The washing of the body and the use of the baths should not be too frequent, but it should be permitted at the usual interval of time, that is, once a month. But if the demands of some illness necessitate bathing the body, it should not be postponed too long. Let it be done without complaint at the advice of a physician so that, even if a sister is unwilling, she may do what needs to be done for her health when the superior commands. But if she wants to and it is perhaps not good for her, she should not follow her desire, for at times what causes pleasure is thought to be beneficial, even if it is harmful. Finally, if the source of a pain in the body of a servant of God is not apparent, the sister who says that she is in pain should be believed without hesitation. But if it is not certain whether something that causes pleasure is useful for healing that pain, a physician should be consulted. Nor should fewer than three go to the baths or wherever it is necessary to go. Neither should the sister who needs to go somewhere go with those with whom she wants but with those whom the superior commands. The care of the ill or of those recovering after illness or suffering under some infirmity, even without fevers, ought to be assigned to some sister in order that she may ask from the storeroom for whatever she sees is necessary for anyone. But those placed in charge of the storeroom or clothing or books should serve their sisters without complaint. Books should be asked for at a certain hour each day; those who ask for them outside that hour should not receive them. But when clothes or sandals are necessary for one who asks, the sisters under whose keeping they are should not delay giving them.

14. Either have no disputes or end them as fast as possible for fear that anger may grow into hatred and make a beam out of a piece of straw and make the soul murderous.[966] For the words of Scripture are not true of men alone: *He who hates his brother is a murderer* (1 Jn 3:15). For in the male sex, which God created first, the female sex also received the commandment. Let, then, whoever offends another by insolence, cursing, or even by the accusation of a crime, remember to make reparation for her action as soon as possible, and let her who was offended forgive without discussion. But if they offend each other, they ought to forgive each other their debts on account of your prayers, which ought to be more holy the more frequently you offer them. But the sister who, though she is often tempted by anger, quickly asks the one whom she recognizes that she has wronged to forgive her is better than the sister who grows angry more slowly and

---

966. See Mt 7:3-5; Lk 6:41-42.

finds it more difficult to ask for forgiveness. If she is unwilling to forgive a sister, she should not expect to have her prayer heard, but one who is never willing to ask for forgiveness or does not ask from the heart is living in a monastery for no reason, even if she is not thrown out. Hence, keep yourselves from harsh words, and, if they have passed from your lips, do not be slow to bring forth the remedies from the same lips by which you produced the wounds. But when the need for discipline forces you to speak harsh words to your subjects in order to keep them in line, it is not required of you that you ask pardon of them even if you feel that you have exceeded the limit in their regard. Otherwise, while you show too much humility, you may diminish your authority for governing in the eyes of those who should be subordinate. But you should, nonetheless, ask pardon from the Lord of all, who knows the great good will with which you love even those whom you perhaps rebuke more than is just. The love between you ought to be spiritual, however, not carnal. For the actions of persons not mindful of modesty, even of women with one another, in shameful jokes and games, ought to be avoided not only by widows and virgin servants of Christ living in their holy profession but even by married women or young girls destined for marriage.

15. Obey the superior as a mother, giving her due honor in order that you may not offend God in her person; obey much more the priest who has care for all of you. It pertains especially to the superior, therefore, that all these points be observed and that, if something is not observed, it not be passed over in negligence but care be taken to rectify and correct it. What exceeds her limits and powers[967] he should refer to the priest who directs you. But she should not consider herself fortunate because of the power by which she rules but because of the love with which she serves. She is raised above you in honor before human beings; she is prostrate at your feet in fear before God. Let her show herself to be a model of good actions for all.[968] Let her rebuke the restless, console the faint-hearted, help the weak, be patient toward all,[969] gladly have discipline, but fearfully impose it. And though both are necessary, still let her seek to be loved by you rather than to be feared, always having in mind that she will give an account to God concerning you. For this reason, by obeying, show mercy not only to yourselves but also to her, because among you a sister is in greater danger to the extent that she is in a higher position.

16. May the Lord grant that you observe all these norms with love, like lovers of spiritual beauty and persons fragrant with the good odor of Christ[970] because of your good way of life, not like serving girls under the law but like free women living under grace.[971] But in order that you may see yourselves in

---

967. See Dn 11:4; Gal 5:13.
968. See Tit 2:7.
969. See 1 Thes 5:14.
970. See 2 Cor 2:15.
971. See Rom 6:14-15.

this little book as in a mirror, have it read to you once a week lest you overlook anything through forgetfulness, and, where you find yourselves doing what has been written, give thanks to the Lord, the giver of all good gifts. But where anyone of you sees that she is lacking something, let her be sorry for the past and watch out for the future, praying that her debt may be forgiven and that she may not be led into temptation.[972]

---

972. See Mt 6:12-13; Lk 11:4.

LETTER 243

Augustine to Laetus, a young man who left the monastery in Hippo (during Augustine's episcopacy)

Sometime during his episcopacy Augustine wrote to Laetus, a Catholic layman from Africa who had entered a monastery but left after his father's death because of his attachment to his mother and his family. Augustine tells Laetus of his sorrow over the temptations Laetus has encountered in his first steps in following Christ (paragraph 1). He refers to the words of Christ about the need to hate one's father, mother, brothers and sisters, and wife and children if one is to be Christ's disciple, and also to the two parables about the man who sets out to build a house and the king who is outnumbered by an enemy army (paragraph 2). He explains that each follower of Christ must renounce everything that is temporal and that belongs to him alone in order to possess what is eternal and common to all (paragraph 3). He points out that it is Laetus' carnal love for his mother that holds him back from being a disciple of Christ (paragraph 4). Augustine explains the meaning of Christ's words about hating one's parents and one's own soul (paragraph 5). He tells Laetus that the heavenly trumpet calls him, a soldier of Christ, to battle, but that his mother holds him back (paragraph 6). He looks at the claims that Laetus' mother has on him and urges him to get rid of such carnal love (paragraph 7). Mother Church is also making claims upon him, and these are more important than those of his bodily mother (paragraph 8). Augustine points to Christ's treatment of his own mother as a model of how Laetus should treat his mother, though Christ by no means denied Mary's motherhood (paragraph 9). The carnal love of Laetus' mother comes from original sin (paragraph 10). Augustine tells Laetus that the cross that a disciple of Christ must carry is his own flesh, which torments us in this life until death is swallowed up in victory (paragraph 11). Finally, he counsels Laetus on the disposition of his inheritance and urges him to greater alacrity in following the Lord (paragraph 12).

To Laetus, his most beloved lord and most longed-for brother, Augustine sends greetings in the Lord.

1. I read the letter that you sent to the brothers, and I want to console you because your first steps in religious life[973] are troubled by many temptations. In that letter you also indicated that you desired a letter from me. I felt sorrow with you, my brother, and I could not refrain from writing for fear that I would deny not only to your desire but also to mine what I saw that I owed to the duty of charity. If, then, you profess to be Christ's recruit, do not abandon the camp; in it you must

---

973. Augustine uses here the term *tirocinium*, which actually means the beginning of military service. He also consistently calls Laetus, the beginner in the monastic way, a *tiro*, i.e., a recruit.

build that tower of which the Lord speaks in the Gospel.⁹⁷⁴ When you are standing on it and soldiering under the arms of the word of God, no temptations can wound you from any direction. From it weapons hurled at the enemy come down with great force, and those you see coming are deflected by its solid bulwark. Consider too that our Lord Jesus Christ, though he is our king, has nonetheless, in that society in which he has also deigned to be our brother, called kings as his soldiers and has warned that each person ought to be ready to go to war with a king who has twenty thousand soldiers when he has only ten thousand.⁹⁷⁵

2. Pay attention to what he said shortly before he proposed the exhortatory parables about the tower and the king: *If anyone comes to me and does not hate his father, mother, wife, children, brothers, and sisters, and even his own soul, he cannot be my disciple. And if he does not carry his cross and come after me, he cannot be my disciple.* Then he added, *Who of you, if he wants to build a tower, does not first sit down and calculate whether he has the funds to complete it for fear that, having laid the foundation, he might be unable to build the tower? And then all who pass by and see it may start to say, This man began to build, and he could not complete it. Or what king going to wage war with another king does not first sit down and consider whether with ten thousand men he can confront the one who is coming at him with twenty thousand? If not, when he is far off, he sends a delegation in order to ask for peace.* (Lk 14:26-32) He shows the point of these parables quite clearly, however, at the very conclusion. For he says, *In the same way, then, any one of you who does not renounce everything that belongs to him cannot be my disciple* (Lk 14:33).

3. And so the funds for building the tower and the capabilities of ten thousand against a king who has twenty thousand signify nothing else than that each person should renounce everything that belongs to him. The beginning of the discourse above, however, fits with the final conclusion. For, in the precept that each person should *renounce everything that belongs to him*, there is also included the precept that he should *hate his father, mother, wife, children, brothers, and sisters, even his own soul.* For all these are his personal goods, which generally tie one down and prevent one from obtaining not the personal goods that pass away in time but the common goods that last for eternity. After all, by the very fact that a certain woman is your mother, she is of course not mine. Hence this is something temporal and passing, just as you see that it already belongs to the past that she conceived you, that she bore you in her womb, that she gave birth to you, and that she nursed you with milk. But insofar as she is a sister in Christ, she belongs to you and to me and to everyone who is promised the one heritage in heaven and God as Father and Christ as brother.⁹⁷⁶ These are eternal; these do not wear out with the passing of time; these we more firmly hope to possess

---

974. See Lk 14:28.
975. See Lk 14:31.
976. See Rom 8:16-17.

to the extent that we are taught that they are to be obtained not by a private but rather by a common claim.

4. You can easily recognize this in your own mother. For why does she hold you like someone trapped in a net and, after you have been impeded, why does she turn and divert you from the course you have undertaken except because she is your own mother? For, because she is the sister of everyone whose father is God and whose mother is the Church, she holds back neither you nor me nor any of our brothers who love her not with a private love as you do in your house but with a public love in the house of God. The fact, then, that you are connected to her by a blood relationship ought to give you the chance to converse with her more familiarly and to see to it more readily that the love by which she loves you as an individual may be put to death in her, so that she does not consider it more important that she gave birth to you from her womb than that she was born along with you from the womb of the Church. But what I said about one's mother should be understood of any other relationship of the sort. This is what everyone should think concerning his own soul, so that he may hate in it a private love, which is undoubtedly temporal. But he should love the community and society of which Scripture said, *They had one soul and one heart for God* (Acts 4:32). For in that way your soul belongs not just to you but to all the brothers, whose souls are also yours, or rather whose souls are not souls along with yours but are one soul, that single soul of Christ, of which we sing in the Psalm that it may be rescued *from the grasp of the dog* (Ps 22:21). At that point it is very easy to attain to a contempt of death.

5. Nor should parents be angry that the Lord commanded that we hate them, since the same thing is commanded us regarding our own soul.[977] For, just as we have a command concerning the soul, that we should hate it along with our parents for the sake of Christ, so what the same Lord says in another passage concerning the soul can most appropriately be applied to our parents as well. He says, *One who loves his own soul will lose it* (Jn 12:25; Mt 10:39, 16:25; Mk 8:35; Lk 17:33). I shall also say with confidence, "One who loves his parents will lose them." For in the former passage he said *hates* in regard to the soul, but here he says *loses*. This commandment, however, by which we are commanded to lose our soul, does not mean that anyone should kill himself, which is an unforgivable crime, but what it does mean is that one should kill in oneself the soul's carnal love because of which the present life causes delight and presents an obstacle to the life to come. After all, this is what the words *hates his own soul* and *will lose it* mean. This is accomplished, however, by loving, since he most clearly mentions in the same commandment the benefit of gaining one's own soul when he says, *But one who loses it in this world will find it for eternal life*. In the same way it is perfectly correct to say about one's parents that one who loves them loses them. He does not kill them like a parricide, but by the

---

977. See Lk 14:26.

spiritual sword of the word of God he piously and confidently strikes and slays the carnal love of theirs by which they try to bind themselves and their children in the entanglements of this world, and he causes that love to live in them by which they are brothers and sisters, by which along with their children in time they acknowledge God and the Church as their parents in eternity.

6. See, the desire for the truth and for knowing and finding the will of God in the Holy Scriptures attracts you; the duty of preaching the Gospel attracts you. The Lord gives the signal that we should keep watch in the camp, that we should build the tower from which we may be able to look down on and drive off the enemy of eternal life. The heavenly trumpet calls you, a soldier of Christ, to battle, and your mother holds you back. She is clearly not a mother of the sort that the Maccabees had, nor one like the mothers of Sparta, of whom it was recorded that they roused their sons for the conflicts of war much more persistently and much more passionately than the sounding of trumpets in order that they might shed their blood for their earthly fatherland.[978] For your mother, who does not allow you to withdraw from worldly concerns in order to learn of the true life, shows well enough how she would not allow you to repudiate this world in order to face death, if that were necessary.

7. But what does she say or what reasons does she give? Perhaps those ten months during which you weighed heavily in her womb, the pains of childbirth, and the work of raising you. Slay this; slay this with the word of salvation. Lose this love of your mother that you may find her for eternal life. Remember to hate this in her if you love her, if you are Christ's recruit, if you have laid the foundation of the tower. Otherwise the passers-by will say, *This man began to build and could not finish it* (Lk 14:30). For this is carnal affection and still smacks of the old human being.[979] Christ's militia exhorts us to put to death this carnal affection both in ourselves and in our dear ones, yet not so that anyone is ungrateful to his parents and mocks those very same benefits we mentioned, by which he was born into this life, raised, and nourished. Let him rather observe filial piety everywhere, and let these duties hold where more important ones do not call us.

8. Mother Church is also the mother of your mother. She has conceived both of you from Christ; she has been in travail for you with the blood of martyrs; she has given birth to you into everlasting light; she has fed and feeds you with the milk of faith, and, though she prepares more solid foods, she sees with horror that you want to wail like small children without teeth. This mother, spread throughout the whole world, is troubled by such varied and multiple attacks from errors that her aborted offspring now do not hesitate to war against her with unrestrained arms. Because of the neglect and laziness of certain ones whom she holds on her lap, she grieves that her members become cold in many

---

978. See Plutarch, *Moralia* III, 241-242.
979. See Eph 4:22; Col 3:9; Rom 6:6.

places and become less able to embrace the small children. From where but from other children, from other members, in whose number you are included, does she demand the help that is due her in justice? Are you going to neglect her needs and turn to the words that the flesh speaks? Does she not strike the ears with more serious complaints? Does she not have a womb that is more precious and breasts filled with heavenly food? Add to this the assumption of the flesh of that man,[980] in order that you might not cling to the things of the flesh, and everything assumed by the eternal Word, of which this mother reminds you, so that you may not become entangled in them. Add to them the insults, the scourging, *and death, even death upon the cross* (Phil 2:8).

9. Though you were conceived from such seed and were brought into new life by such a union, you languish and waste away into the old human being. Did your king not have an earthly mother? And yet, when her presence was reported to him as he was doing God's work, he replied, *Who is my mother and who are my brothers?* And *stretching out his hand toward his disciples*, he said that only those who did the will of his Father belonged to his family.[981] In that number he certainly, like a loving son, included Mary herself; after all, she also did the will of the Father. In that way the best and divine teacher rejected the term "mother," which they had reported to him as something private and personal to him, because it was earthly, in comparison with the close relationship of heaven. And, in mentioning the same close relationship of heaven among his disciples, he showed the kind of society in which that virgin was again united with him along with the other saints. And, in order that this most salutary teaching, by which he taught us to place little value on carnal affection for our parents, might not lend support to the error by which some deny that he had a mother, he warned his disciples in another place not to say that they have an earthly father.[982] In that way, just as it was evident that they had fathers, so he showed that he had a mother, and yet, by taking no account of his earthly relation to her, he offered his disciples an example of how to treat such relationships as of little account.

10. Are these teachings, then, interrupted by the outcries of your mother, and does the memory of her being pregnant with you and nursing you, so that you were born as a child of Adam and Eve and fed as another Adam, find a place among them? Turn your eyes, rather; turn them to the second Adam from heaven, and bear now the image of the heavenly one as you did bear that of the earthly one.[983] In fact, even here those gifts of your mother that are listed for you to weaken your resolve should find a place; they should certainly have a place. Do not be ungrateful; thank your mother; return spiritual gifts in exchange for carnal ones, eternal gifts in exchange for temporal ones. Does she not want to be converted

---

980. I.e., the humanity assumed by the Word of God.
981. See Mt 12:47-50; Mk 3:32-35; Lk 8:20-21.
982. See Mt 23:9.
983. See 1 Cor 15:47-49.

for the better? Watch out that she does not twist and overturn you for the worse. What difference does it make whether it is in a wife or in a mother, provided that we nonetheless avoid Eve in any woman?[984] For this shadow of a son's love for his mother comes from the leaves of that tree with which our parents first clothed themselves in that damnable nakedness. And whatever she offers you in those words and in that suggestion supposedly as a duty of love, in order to turn you aside from the most genuine and pure love of the Gospel, comes from the cunning of the serpent[985] and from the duplicity of that king who has twenty thousand men, for we are taught to overcome that duplicity by the simplicity of ten thousand, that is, the simplicity of the heart by which we seek God.

11. Keep your mind on these ideas, instead, my dearest friend, and take up your cross and follow the Lord.[986] For, when you were here, I noticed that you were held back from the love of God by family concerns, and I perceived that you were carried and dragged by your cross instead of carrying and dragging it. After all, what else does our cross, which the Lord commands us to carry in order that we may follow him with the least impediment, signify but the mortality of this flesh? For it is what torments us until death is swallowed up in victory.[987] This cross itself, then, must be crucified and pierced by the nails of the fear of God.[988] Otherwise, with our members loose and free, we might not be able to carry it if it resists us. For you absolutely cannot follow the Lord except by carrying it. After all, how can you follow him if you do not belong to him? But *those who belong to Jesus Christ*, the Apostle says, *have crucified their flesh along with its passions and desires* (Gal 5:24).

12. Of course, if your share of the family property, in whose management it is neither necessary nor proper that you be involved, includes some cash, it really should be given to your mother and to the others in your family. Their needs should certainly hold first place in your eyes if, in order to be perfect, you have decided to distribute such money to the poor. *For, if anyone*, the Apostle says, *does not provide for his own and especially for the members of his family, he has denied the faith and is worse than a non-believer* (1 Tm 5:8). If you have left us in order to deal with these matters and in order to remove your neck from these chains and to put on wisdom, how will your mother's tears flowing for her flesh and blood harm you? How will they tear you away? Or what about the flight of a slave, the death of female servants, or the ill health of brothers? If you have a well-ordered love, you should know how to prefer more important to less important things and to be touched by mercy in order that the Gospel may

---

984. See Gn 3:7.
985. See Gn 3:1.
986. See Mt 16:24; Mk 8:34; Lk 9:23.
987. See 1 Cor 15:54.
988. See Ps 119:120.

be preached to the poor.[989] Otherwise the bountiful harvest of the Lord may fall prey to birds through a lack of workers. And you should know how to have a heart ready to follow the will of the Lord,[990] insofar as he has decided to deal with his servants either by scourging them or by pardoning them. *Meditate on these ideas; take your stand upon them in order that your progress may be evident to all* (1 Tm 4:15). I beg you to avoid causing your brothers greater sadness by your sluggishness than you caused them joy by your alacrity. But I considered it needless to recommend you by letter to those you wanted as if someone had wanted to recommend you to me in the same way.

---

989. See Mt 11:5; Lk 7:22.
990. See Mt 13:4; Mk 4:4; Lk 8:5.

SELECT BIBLIOGRAPHY

Adamiak, Stanisław. "Asking for Human Mercy. Augustine's Intercession with the Men in Power," in *Scrinium Augustini. The World of Augustine's Letters. Proceedings of the International Workshop on Augustine's Correspondence, Toruń, 25-26 June 2015*, ed. by Przemysław Nehring, Mateusz Stróżyński and Rafał Toczko. Turnhout 2017. Pp. 19-40.

Brown, Peter R. L. *Augustine of Hippo: A Biography. A New Edition with an Epilogue*. Berkeley and Los Angeles 2000.

De Bruyne, Donatien. "Les anciennes collections et la chronologie des lettres de Saint Augustin," in *Revue Bénédictine* 43 (1931) 284-295.

Cain, Andrew. *The Letters of Jerome. Asceticism, Biblical Exegesis, and the Construction of Christian Authority in Late Antiquity*. Oxford 2009.

Cameron, Michael. "Augustine and Scripture," in *A Companion to Augustine*, ed. by M. Vessey. Malden-Oxford 2012. Pp. 200-214.

Ciccarese, Maria Pia. "La tipologia delle lettere di S. Agostino," in *Augustinianum* 11 (1971) 471-507.

Clark, Gillian. "Influential Friends? Augustine's Episcopal Networks," in *Episcopal Networks in Late Antiquity*, ed. by Carmen A. Cvetkovic and Peter Gemeinardt. Berlin-Boston 2019. Pp. 63-81.

Clarke, Graeme W., introd. and trans. *The Letters of St. Cyprian of Carthage* I. New York 1984.

Conybeare, Catherine. "Spaces between Letters: Augustine's Correspondence with Women," in *Voices in Dialogue: Reading Women in the Middle Ages*, ed. by L. Olson and K. Kerby-Ulton. Notre Dame, Ind. 2005. Pp. 55-72.

Conybeare, Catherine. *Paulinus Noster: Self and Symbols in the Letters of Paulinus of Nola*. Oxford 2000.

Dalmon, Laurence. *Un dossier de l'Épistolaire augustinien: la correspondance entre l'Afrique et Rome à propos de l'affaire pélagienne (416-418)*. Leuven 2015.

Divjak, Johannes. "Zur Struktur Augustinischer Briefkorpora," in *Les lettres de Saint Augustin découvertes par Johannes Divjak: communications présentées au colloque des 20 et 21 septembre 1982*. Paris 1983. Pp. 13-27.

Divjak, Johannes. "Epistulae," in *Augustinus-Lexicon* II 5/6 (2001) 893-1057.

Doyle, Daniel E. *The Bishop as Disciplinarian in the Letters of St. Augustine*. New York 2002.

Ebbeler, Jennifer V. "The Letter Collection of Augustine of Hippo, in" in *Late Antique Letter Collections. A Critical Introduction and Reference Guide*, ed. by Cristiana Sogno, Bradley K. Storin and Edward J. Watts. Oakland 2017. Pp. 239-253.

Ebbeler, Jennifer V. *Disciplining Christians. Correction and Community in Augustine's Letters.* Oxford 2012.

Eno, Robert B. "Epistulae," in *Augustine through the Ages,* ed. by Allan D. Fitzgerald. Grand Rapids 1999. Pp. 298-310

Frend, William H.C. "The Divjak Letters: New Light on St Augustine's Problems, 416-28," in *Journal of Ecclesiastical History* 34(1983) 497-513.

Frend, William H.C. "Fussala, Augustine's Crisis of Credibility (*Epist. 20*),*" in *Les lettres des saint Augustin découvertes par Johannes Divjak: communications présentées au colloque des 20 et 21 septembre 1982.* Paris 1983. Pp. 251-265.

Frend, William H.C. *The Donatist Church: A Movement of Protest in Roman North Africa.* Oxford 1952; repr. 1970.

Fürst, Alfons. *Augustinus Briefwechsel mit Hieronymus.* Münster 1999.

Gibson, Roy K. and Ruth Morello, eds. *Reading the Letters of Pliny the Younger: An Introduction.* Cambridge 2012.

Gibson, Roy. "On the Nature of Ancient Letter Collections," in *Journal of Roman Studies* 102 (2012) 56-78.

Hollingworth, Miles. *Saint Augustine of Hippo. An Intellectual Biography.* London 2013.

Humfress, Caroline. "Bishops and Law Courts in Late Antiquity: How (Not) to Make Sense of the Legal Evidence," in *Journal of Early Christian Studies* 19/3 (2011) 375-400.

Hunter, David G. "Between Discipline and Doctrine: Augustine's Response to Clerical Misconduct. St. Augustine Lecture-2019," in *Augustinian Studies* 51 (2020), pp. 3-22.

Kuhn, Eva M. "Justice Applied by the Episcopal Arbitrator: Augustine and the Implementation of Divine Justice," in *Etica & Politica / Ethics & Politics* 9/2 (2007) 71-104.

Lamoraux, John C. "Episcopal Courts in Late Antiquity," in *Journal of Early Christian Studies* 3/2 (1995) 143-167.

Lawless, George P. *Augustine of Hippo and His Monastic Rule.* Oxford 1987.

Lenski, Noel. "Evidence for the Audientia episcopalis in the New Letters of Augustine," in *Law, Society, and Authority in Late Antiquity*, ed. by Ralph W. Mathisen. Oxford 2001. Pp. 83-97.

Liebeschuetz, John H. W. G. "Letters of Ambrose of Milan (374-397). Books I-IX," in *Collecting Early Christian Letters from the Apostle Paul to Late Antiquity*, ed. by Bronwen Neil and Pauline Allen. Cambridge 2015. Pp. 97-112.

Liebeschuetz, John H. W. G. "General Introduction," in *Ambrose of Milan: Political Letters and Speeches*, trans. with an introduction and notes by J.H.W.G. Liebeschuetz with the assistance of Carole Hill. Liverpool 2005. Pp. 27-46.

Lietzmann, Hans, "Zur Entstehungsgeschichte der Briefsammlung Augustins," in *Sitzungsberichte der Preussischen Akademie der Wissenschaften* (Berlin 1930) 356-388.

Malherbe, Abraham J. *Ancient Epistolary Theorists.* Atlanta 1988.

McLynn, Neil. "Augustine's Black Sheep: The Case of Antoninus of Fussala," in *Istituzioni, carismi ed esercizio del potere, IV-VI secolo*, ed. by G. Bonamente and R. L. Testa. Bari 2010. Pp. 305-321.

Merdinger, Jane E. *Rome and the African Church in the Time of Augustine.* New Haven and London 1997.

Monceaux, Paul. "La formule 'Qui mecum sunt fratres' dans la correspondance de saint Augustin," in *Mélanges Paul Thomas*. Bruges 1930. Pp. 529-537.

Morello, Ruth and Andrew D. Morrison. *Ancient Letters. Classical and Late Antique Epistolography.* Oxford 2007.

Morgenstern, Frank. *Die Briefpartner des Augustinus von Hippo. Prosopographische, sozial- und ideologiegeschichtliche Untersuchungen.* Bochum 1993.

Mratschek, Sigrid. "The Unwritten Letters of Augustine of Hippo," in *Scrinium Augustini. The World of Augustine's Letters. Proceedings of the International Workshop on Augustine's Correspondence, Toruń, 25-26 June 2015*, ed. by Przemysław Nehring, Mateusz Stróżyński and Rafał Toczko. Turnhout 2017. Pp. 57-77.

Mratschek, Sigrid. *Der Briefwechsel des Paulinus von Nola. Kommunikation und soziale Kontakte zwischen christlichen Intellektuellen.* Göttingen 2002.

Nauroy, Gérard. "The Letter Collection of Ambrose of Milan," in *Late Antique Letter Collections. A Critical Introduction and Reference Guide*, ed. by Cristiana Sogno, Bradley K. Storin and Edward J. Watts. Oakland 2017. Pp. 146-156

Nehring, Przemysław. "Literary sources for everyday life of the early monastic communities in North Africa," in *La vie quotidienne des moines en Orient et en Occident (IVe-Xe siècles)* I. *Etat des sources*, ed. by Olivier Delouis and Maria Mossakowska-Gaubert. Cairo 2015. Pp. 325-336.

Nehring, Przemysław. "Disposal of Private Property: Theory and Practice in the Earliest Augustinian Monastic Communities," in *La vie quotidienne des moines en Orient et en Occident (IVe-Xe siècles)* II. *Questions transversales*, ed. by Olivier Delouis and Maria Mossakowska-Gaubert. Cairo 2019. Pp. 393-411.

Nehring, Przemysław. "Misbehaviour of Clergy in the Light of Augustine's Letters," in *Scrinium Augustini. The World of Augustine's Letters. Proceedings of the International Workshop on Augustine's Correspondence, Toruń, 25-26 June 2015*, ed by Przemysław Nehring, Mateusz Stróżyński and Rafał Toczko. Turnhout 2017. Pp. 79-112.

Neil, Bronwen. "Continuities and Changes in the Practice of Letter-Collecting from Cicero to Late Antiquity," in *Collecting Early Christian Letters from the Apostle Paul to Late Antiquity*, ed. by Brownen Neil and Pauline Allen. New York 2015. Pp. 3-17.

Rapp, Claudia. *Holy Bishops in Late Antiquity: The Nature of Christian Leadership in an Age of Transition*. Berkeley 2005.

Rist, John. *Augustine. Ancient Thought Baptized*. Cambridge 1994.

Shaw, Brent. "Augustine and Men of Imperial Power," in *Journal of Late Antiquity* 8 (2015) 32-61.

Shaw, Brent, *Sacred Violence. African Christians and Sectarian Hatred in the Age of Augustine*. Cambridge 2011.

Sirks, A. J. B. "The *episcopalis audientia* in Late Antiquity," in *Droit et cultures* 65/1 (2013).

Sotinel, Claire. "Augustine's Information Circuits," in *A Companion to Augustine*, ed. by Mark Vessey. Chichester 2012. Pp. 125-137.

Squires, Stuart. *The Pelagian Controversy: An Introduction to the Enemies of Grace and the Conspiracy of Lost Souls*. Eugene, Or. 2019.

Stróżyński, Mateusz. "Neoplatonism in Augustine's Letters," in *Scrinium Augustini. The World of Augustine's Letters. Proceedings of the International Workshop on Augustine's Correspondence, Toruń, 25-26 June 2015*, ed. by Przemysław Nehring, Mateusz Stróżyński and Rafał Toczko. Turnhout 2017. Pp. 113-148.

Sumruld, William A. *Augustine and the Arians: The Bishop of Hippo's Encounters with Ulfilan Arianism*. Selinsgrove, Penn. 1994.

Teske, Roland J. *Augustine of Hippo. Philosopher, Exegete, Theologian. A Second Collection of Essays*. Milwaukee 2009.

Tilley, Maureen A. "General introduction," in *The Donatist Controversy* I, trans. by Maureen Tilley and Boniface Ramsey. New York 2019. Pp. 13-28.

Tilley, Maureen A. "No Friendly Letters: Augustine's Correspondence with Women," in *The Cultural Turn in Late Ancient Studies*, ed. by Dale B. Martin and Patricia Cox Miller, Duke University Press 2005, pp. 40-62.

Tilley, Maureen A. *The Bible in Christian North Africa: The Donatist World.* Minneapolis 1997.

Toczko, Rafał. "Debating through the Letters vs. Live Discussions. The Patterns of *ars disputandi* in Augustine's Correspondence," in *Scrinium Augustini. The World of Augustine's Letters. Proceedings of the International Workshop on Augustine's Correspondence, Toruń, 25-26 June 2015*, ed. by Przemysław Nehring, Mateusz Stróżynski and Rafał Toczko. Turnhout 2017. Pp. 149-178.

Toczko, Rafał. *Crimen obicere. Forensic Rhetoric and Augustine's anti-Donatist Correspondence.* Göttingen, 2020.

Trapp, Michael. "Introduction," in *Greek and Latin letters: An Anthology, with Translation*, ed. by Michael Trapp. Cambridge 2003. P. 12.

Trout, Dennis. "The Letter Collection of Paulinus of Nola," in *Late Antique Letter Collections. A Critical Introduction and Reference Guide*, ed. by Cristiana Sogno, Bradley K. Storin and Edward J. Watts. Oakland 2017. Pp. 254-268.

Wankenne, Ludovic-Jules. "La langue de la correspondance de Saint Augustin," in *Revue Bénédictine* 94 (1984), 102-153.

Williams, Michael S. "Augustine as a Reader of His Christian Contemporaries," in *A Companion to Augustine,* ed. by M. Vessey. Chichester 2012. Pp. 227-239.

Zumkeller, Adolar. *Augustine's Ideal of the Religious Life.* New York 1986.

INDEX OF SCRIPTURE

(Prepared by Michael Dolan)

The numbers after the scriptural reference
refer to the Letters and their parts.

Old Testament

Genesis
3:8   148, 4, 14
22:17   93, 9, 30
22:18   185, 1, 5
25:23   194, 8, 35; 194, 8, 38;
26:4   93, 5, 19; 93, 6, 20; 185, 1, 5

Exodus
3:15   157, 4, 24
9:16   186, 6, 17; 194, 8, 39
20:17   157, 2, 6; 157, 2, 9; 194, 6, 28
28:3   157, 1, 2
33:19   186, 6, 16; 186, 9, 33

Leviticus
22:4.6   108, 3, 7

Deuteronomy
5:21   157, 2, 6; 194, 6, 28;
6:4   238, 3, 18
6:13   170, 2
7:25   157, 2, 6; 194, 6, 28;
17:11   48, 2

Job
7:1   217, 4, 14
14:1   193, 2, 3
14:5 LXX   193, 2, 3

Nehemiah
9:26   87, 3

Psalms
2:1-2   93, 3, 9; 185, 5, 19
2:7   185, 1, 3
2:7-8   43, 9, 25
2:8   185, 1, 3
2:10-11   93, 3, 9; 185, 5, 19
4:4   188, 3, 9
5:8   149, 2, 13
6:13   149, 1, 6
7:3   186, 10, 34
7:4   186, 10, 34
8:15   149, 1, 4
9:5   186, 10, 36
11:3   93, 9, 30
11:6   155, 4, 15
12:2   93, 9, 33
12:8   93, 9, 33
14:3   108, 5, 14; 108, 5, 15
15:10   149, 1, 8
16:3   149, 1, 6
16:4   149, 1, 7; 149, 1, 8
17:14   149, 1, 3
18:2   155, 2, 6
18:37   185, 2, 11
19:5   93, 6, 21
22:17-19   185, 1, 3
22:21   243, 4
22:28   51, 5
22:28-29   185, 1, 3
23:6   194, 5, 19
25:10   186, 4, 12; 194, 3, 6
27:9   157, 2, 10
30:8   188, 2, 7
32:9   185, 2, 7

33:16	157, 2, 7	103:8	188, 2, 8
34:3	188, 3, 9	104:4	238, 2, 15
35:10	149, 3, 34	105:18	149, 3, 33
36:12	157, 3, 16	105:19	149, 3, 33
36:23	157, 3, 16	108:6	93, 1, 1
37:23	217, 1, 3; 217, 2, 5	116:10	157, 3, 14; 194, 3, 15
41:5	157, 3, 16	118:8	185, 1, 4
42:3	185, 6, 21	119:29	157, 3, 16
43:1	185, 2, 9	119:40	157, 3, 16
45:12	93, 9, 29	119:53	93, 9, 28
45:17	93, 9, 29	119:86	185, 2, 9
48:3	93, 8, 25	119:119	157, 3, 15
49:7	157, 4, 29	119:125	214, 7
49:21	23, 1	119:133	157, 2, 8; 157, 3, 16
50:18	108, 3, 8	119:158	93, 9, 28
51:3	157, 3, 16	121:4	186, 2, 5
55:14-16	93, 9, 28	122:6-7	185, 10, 46
55:19	93, 11, 46	127:1	186, 2, 5; 186, 10, 36
56:12	188, 2, 7	133:1	185, 9, 36
57:2	48, 2	139:3	108, 5, 15
59:8	149, 3, 33	141:5	28, 4, 6; 33, 3; 108, 2, 6
59:10	186, 2, 5; 186, 3, 10	144:11-15	155, 2, 7
59:11	186, 3, 10; 194, 5, 19; 214, 4	145:13	194, 10, 45
59:12	149, 1, 9		
61:3	93, 9, 28	Proverbs	
61:4	157, 4, 33	4:27	48, 2
67:2-3	93, 10, 35	8:35 LXX	194, 2, 3; 217, 2, 5; 217, 6, 23
68:10	149, 1, 6; 217, 4, 12	9:8 LXX	210, 2
68:22	149, 1, 10	9:9	93, 5, 17
68:24	149, 1, 10	9:18 LXX	108, 1, 1; 108, 2, 6
69:30	186, 12, 40	13:22	93, 12, 50; 185, 9, 37; 185, 9, 40
72:8	93, 5, 19; 185, 1, 5		
72:11	87, 8	13:24	185, 6, 21
72:17-19	93, 6, 20	17:6 LXX	157, 4, 32
73:28	155, 3, 12	18:22	194, 6, 29
78:39	238, 2, 15	23:14	185, 6, 21
86:11	217, 4, 15	27:6	93, 2, 4
90:12	93, 9, 28	27:20 LXX	211, 10
94:8	214, 7	29:19	93, 5, 17
94:9	148, 4, 14	29:19 LXX	185, 6, 21; 194, 6, 24
94:15	48, 2	30:12 LXX	93, 10, 37; 93, 10, 41; 108, 3, 12; 108, 7, 20
101:5	93, 2, 8		
103:4	194, 5, 19		
103:5	188, 3, 9		

Ecclesiastes
3:21   238, 2, 15

Song of Songs
1:6   93, 8, 4; 93, 8, 25; 93, 9, 28
1:7   93, 9, 29
2:2   93, 9, 28
4:2   149, 1, 4
4:8 LXX   194, 3, 9

Wisdom
1:5   185, 11, 50
2:25   157, 3, 21
4:11   194, 9, 42; 217, 4, 15; 217,
            6, 21; 217, 6, 22
5:1   185, 9, 41
6:26   193, 1, 2
7:24-25.27 238, 4, 23
7:26   238, 4, 24
8:21   157, 2, 9; 188, 3, 12
8:21-22   188, 2, 8
9:15   185, 9, 39
10:19   185, 9, 37; 185, 9, 40

Sirach
4:25   93, 13, 51
11:7   43, 3, 11
34:30   108, 2, 6

Isaiah
2:2   93, 9, 29
3:12   33, 3
7:9 LXX   194, 5, 21
8:14   186, 3, 8
10:22   186, 8, 31
11:2-3   194, 3, 15; 194, 4, 18
28:16   186, 3, 8
29:16   186, 6, 18
45:9   186, 6, 18
49:8   186, 3, 7
52:11   108, 3, 7
53:8   238, 4, 24; 242, 4
54:1   93, 8, 26
54:2-5   93, 9, 29

54:13   193, 4, 13
59:20   149, 2, 19
65:5   108, 7, 20
66:5 LXX   108, 1, 3

Jeremiah
2:30   93, 1, 3
15:18   108, 2, 6
17:5   89, 5; 155, 2, 8

Lamentations
3:25   210, 1

Baruch
2:31   217, 7, 26

Ezekiel
18:4.20   44, 5, 20

Daniel
3:36   93, 9, 30

Hosea
1:10   186, 8, 31

Joel
2:32   157, 2, 7; 157, 3, 22

Habakkuk
2:4   186, 2, 6; 194, 5, 20

Malachi
1:1   93, 6, 20
1:2   194, 8, 38
1:2-3   186, 5, 14; 194, 8, 34; 194,
            8, 39; 196, 3, 13
1:11   185, 1, 5

New Testament

Matthew
3:11   194, 3, 11
4:10   149, 2, 13
5:4   149, 1, 3

5:8	148, 2, 9; 148, 3, 11; 148, 3, 12; 242, 4	19:26	157, 4, 27
		19:28	157, 4, 37
5:9	43, 1, 2	19:29	157, 4, 31
5:10	44, 2, 4; 87, 7; 93, 2, 8; 108, 5, 14	21:25	93, 11, 47
		22:30	148, 2, 7
5:10	185, 2, 9	23:12	194, 3, 9
5:14	93, 9, 29	24:12	93, 9, 33
5:32	157, 4, 31	24:14	93, 7, 22
5:37	23, 1; 157, 4, 40	24:31	93, 9, 33
5:40	93, 3, 11	26:41	211, 3
5:44	217, 2, 6	27:25	149, 1, 5
5:45	93, 2, 4; 210, 1		
6:9	187, 5, 16; 217, 2, 6	Mark	
6:10	217, 2, 6	4:9	217, 7, 26
6:12	157, 1, 2; 185, 9, 39; 186, 9, 33; 4*, 4	8:35	243, 5
		12:35	148, 2, 7
6:13	157, 2, 5; 178, 3; 179, 3; 186, 12, 41	14:38	211, 3
		14:62	193, 2, 4; 194, 10, 46
7:14	93, 9, 30	16:12	149, 3, 31
7:15.16	44, 2, 4		
7:16	149, 1, 4	Luke	
8:11	93, 9, 30	2:35	149, 3, 33
8:29	194, 3, 11	4:41	194, 3, 11
9:12	149, 1, 7; 157, 2, 7	6:28	217, 2, 6
9:13	157, 2, 7	7:47	157, 3, 16
10:20	194, 4, 16; 194, 4, 17	8:8	217, 7, 26
10:39	243, 5	11:4	186, 9, 33; 186, 12, 41
12:27	186, 8, 31	12:10	238, 4, 21
12:29	217, 3, 11	14:11	194, 3, 9
12:32	185, 11, 48; 185, 11, 49; 238, 4, 21	14:16. 21. 23	185, 6, 24
		14:23	93, 2, 5
12:45	194, 3, 11	14:26-32	243, 2
13:9	217, 7, 26	14:30	157, 4, 34; 243, 7
13:24-3	43, 8, 21	14:33	157, 4, 34; 243, 2
16:25	243, 5	15:18	186, 2, 5
17:26	83, 5	15:32	185, 10, 43
18:11	186, 8, 27; 186, 12, 41; 188, 2, 7; 194, 7, 33	16:9	157, 4, 37
		16:19	157, 4, 23
18:18	185, 10, 45	16:22	187, 2, 6
19:16	157, 4, 25	16:23	187, 2, 6
19:17	157, 4, 25	16:26	187, 2, 6
19:21	157, 4, 24; 157, 4, 25; 157, 4, 39	17:33	243, 5
		18:8	93, 9, 33; 93, 11, 49
19:23-24	157, 4, 27	18:9-10	93, 11, 49

18:13-14	194, 3, 9	14:6	238, 4, 22
19:10	186, 2, 4; 186, 2, 6; 186, 8, 27; 186, 12, 41; 194, 7, 33	14:16	33, 3
		14:16-17	148, 2, 6
20:4	93, 11, 47	14:21	148, 3, 11
20:36	148, 2, 7	14:27	33, 2; 108, 1, 3
22:30	157, 4, 37	14:28	170, 9; 238, 2, 10
23:43	187, 2, 3	15:2	93, 10, 40
24:16	149, 3, 31	15:5	157, 4, 29; 214, 2
24:44-47	93, 6, 21	15:22	185, 11, 49; 194, 6, 26
24:46	93, 7, 23; 185, 1, 3; 211, 3	16:12	83, 5; 185, 11, 49
24:47	93, 7, 23; 185, 1, 3	17:3	238, 4, 22
24:45	214, 7	17:11	238, 4, 28
		17:20-23	238, 4, 28
John		20:17	120, 3, 15; 149, 3, 32
1:1	157, 3, 14; 170, 4; 185, 1, 3	20:28-29	238, 3, 18
1:3	242, 2	21:17	93, 9, 29; 108, 6, 17
1:14	185, 1, 3; 186, 8, 31;		
1:16	194, 5, 21	Acts of the Apostles	
1:33	51, 5; 108, 1, 3	1:8	93, 6, 21
3:5	193, 2, 4; 194, 10, 46	2:21	157, 2, 7
3:8	194, 4, 18	4:32	185, 9, 36; 186, 7, 25; 211, 5; 238, 2, 13; 243, 4
3:17	214, 2		
3:36	193, 2, 3; 193, 2, 4	4:32.35	211, 5
4:22	23, 4	13:48	217, 7, 2
4:24	238, 2, 15		
5:19	93, 9, 32	Romans	
6:44	93, 2, 5	1:9	157, 4, 40
6:45	193, 4, 13	1:17	186, 2, 6; 194, 5, 20
6:49-50	186, 8, 28	1:18-20	194, 6, 24
6:54	186, 8, 28	1:21	194, 6, 25
6:64-65	194, 3, 12	2:1	43, 3, 10; 194, 6, 25
6:65-66	217, 4, 12	2:4	185, 11, 49
6:66	186, 11, 38; 194, 3, 12	2:5	185, 11, 49
8:25	149, 2, 25	2:6	214, 1
8:32	149, 2, 27	2:6.10	186, 2, 4
10:16	93, 5, 19; 108, 6, 17	2:12	194, 6, 27
10:30	170, 9; 238, 2, 10; 238, 2, 12; 238, 4, 28; 241, 2	3:4	238, 1, 8
		3:6	214, 2
11:43	157, 3, 15	3:8	214, 6
12:25	243, 5	3:19	186, 7, 26
13:10	44, 5, 10; 108, 3, 8	3:20	194, 6, 28
13:30	108, 6, 17	3:24	185, 9, 40; 194, 3, 6
13:35	108, 6, 17	4:4-6	186, 2, 6
13:36	93, 1, 3	4:5	185, 9, 37

4:15	157, 3, 15	9:11-12	186, 6, 16; 186, 6, 19; 186, 6, 21; 194, 8, 35; 194, 8, 38
5:5	157, 2, 4; 157, 3, 16; 185, 11, 50; 186, 2, 4; 194, 3, 11	9:11-13	186, 5, 14
5:6	149, 1, 7	9:12	194, 6, 23
5:8	149, 1, 7	9:13	186, 5, 14; 194, 8, 34
5:10	149, 1, 7	9:13-18	194, 8, 39
5:12	157, 3, 11; 157, 3, 18; 157, 3, 19; 186, 4, 12; 186, 5, 13; 186, 6, 19; 186, 6, 21; 186, 8, 30; 193, 2, 6	9:14	194, 3, 10; 194, 8, 35
		9:15	186, 6, 16
		9:15-16	194, 8, 35
5:13	157, 3, 18	9:16	186, 7, 25; 186, 9, 33; 186, 10, 36; 217, 4, 12
5:14	157, 3, 19; 157, 3, 20;		
5:15	157, 3, 20	9:16-18	186, 6, 17
5:16	157, 3, 11; 157, 3, 12; 157, 3, 20; 186, 4, 12;	9:17	186, 6, 17
		9:18	186, 6, 17; 194, 2, 4; 194, 3, 6; 194, 3, 10; 194, 3, 13; 194, 3, 15
5:17	157, 3, 15		
5:17-19	157, 3, 11		
5:18	193, 2, 6; 194, 7, 31	9:19	186, 6, 18; 194, 3, 13; 194, 6, 23; 194, 6, 29
5:19	157, 3, 20		
5:20	157, 2, 6; 157, 3, 15; 157, 3, 16	9:19-20	194, 8, 40
5:20-21	157, 3, 17	9:20	186, 7, 22; 194, 3, 13
5:28	194, 10, 47	9:20-21	186, 6, 18; 186, 7, 23; 194, 2, 5
6:23	194, 5, 19; 194, 5, 21		
7:4	186, 12, 41	9:20-21. 23	194, 6, 23
7:7	157, 2, 6; 194, 6, 28;	9:21	186, 6, 19
7:22	194, 6, 28	9:21-23	194, 6, 30
7:22-25	157, 3, 16	9:22	186, 7, 24; 194, 6, 22
7:23	157, 3, 15; 194, 3, 8; 194, 6, 28; 193, 2, 3; 194, 1, 1; 194, 6, 30	9:22-23	186, 7, 24; 194, 2, 5
		9:23	186, 7, 24; 194, 6, 22
		9:24	186, 8, 31
8:2	157, 3, 15	9:27	186, 8, 31
8:10-11	193, 2, 6	9:30-33	186, 3, 8
8:14	179, 4	9:32	186, 11, 37
8:15	194, 4, 17	10:1	217, 7, 27
8:17	238, 2, 13	10:1-2	186, 11, 38
8:26	179, 4; 194, 4, 16; 194, 4, 17	10:2	186, 11, 37
8:28	149, 2, 21; 186, 3, 7	10:2-3	93, 3, 10
8:28-29	149, 2, 21	10:2-4	186, 3, 9
8:28-30	186, 7, 25	10:3	157, 2, 4; 185, 9, 37; 186, 11, 37; 186, 11, 38; 196, 2, 7
8:30	186, 7, 25		
8:30-31	149, 2, 21	10:3-4	157, 2, 6
8:32	93, 2, 7	10:4	194, 8, 36
8:34	149, 2, 14	10:8	93, 6, 21
9:7-10	194, 8, 37	10:13	157, 2, 7
9:8	186, 7, 25	10:14	157, 2, 8; 217, 7, 29

10:14. 17	194, 3, 10	3:3	93, 9, 32
11:2	186, 8, 31	3:6	93, 11, 47
11:5	186, 8, 31	3:7	120, 3, 14; 185, 10, 44; 193, 4, 13
11:5-6	186, 5, 15; 186, 7, 25; 194, 8, 39;	3:7. 6	194, 3, 10
11:6	177, 8; 186, 2, 6; 186, 4, 12; 186, 8, 31	3:13-15	4*, 4
		3:21	214, 3
11:16	186, 6, 19	3:22-23	185, 9, 36
11:25	149, 2, 19	4:7	157, 2, 10; 185, 9, 38; 186, 2, 4; 186, 3, 10; 194, 5, 21; 214, 3
11:26-27	149, 2, 19		
11:28	149, 2, 18	5:5	93, 2, 7
11:32	149, 1, 7	5:6	108, 3, 7; 211, 3
11:33	149, 1, 7; 194, 2, 5; 194, 3, 10; 194, 6, 23; 194, 7, 33	6:3	157, 4, 37
		6:16	238, 2, 11
11:33-36	194, 2, 5	6:16-17	241, 2
11:34-36	238, 3, 19	6:17	238, 2, 11
11:35	194, 3, 6	6:19-20	170, 2; 238, 4, 21
11:36	170, 3; 194, 3, 6	7:7	157, 4, 37
12:2	120, 4, 20	7:12-13	157, 4, 31
12:3	186, 2, 4; 194, 3, 9; 194, 3, 10	7:25	194, 3, 15
		8:2	238, 2, 16
12:3-5	185, 9, 42	8:5-6	238, 2, 18
12:12	155, 1, 4	8:6	238, 3, 20; 238, 4, 22
13:1-3	93, 6, 20	9:7	157, 4, 37
13:2-4	87, 7	9:11	157, 4, 38
13:9	157, 2, 6	10:12	217, 4, 14
13:10	157, 2, 4; 157, 2, 9; 157, 3, 16; 167, 3, 11; 188, 3, 13	10:13	157, 2, 5
		10:17	185, 11, 50
14:4	87, 5; 95, 3	10:18	149, 2, 19
14:10	217, 5, 16	10:32	8*, 1
14:23	188, 3, 13; 194, 3, 9	12:6	48, 3
15:8-9	149, 2, 20	12:11	149, 1, 6; 194, 4, 18
16:5	14*, 1	12:26	48, 1
		13:5	211, 12
1 Corinthians		13:12	120, 1, 4; 148, 1, 1; 148, 2, 7; 242, 5
1:4-7	93, 9, 32		
1:10	214, 2	13:13	238, 2, 13
1:12	108, 1, 3	14:14-15	238, 2, 15
1:20	149, 2, 30; 194, 8, 35	15:10	186, 10, 36
1:22	185, 6, 24	15:12	93, 9, 32
1:31	157, 2, 10; 214, 3; 217, 3, 8	15:14-15	28, 3, 4
2:11	238, 2, 15	15:21-22	157, 3, 14; 186, 9, 33; 187, 9, 30
2:12	186, 3, 10		
2:12-14	242, 1	15:22	179, 6; 217, 6, 19

15:28	148, 5, 17; 238, 2, 13	2:14	28, 3, 4; 93, 9, 31
15:31	157, 4, 40	2:18	93, 13, 52
15:33-34	93, 9, 32	2:20	93, 2, 7
15:36	193, 4, 10; 193, 4, 11	3:1.3	93, 9, 31
15:51	193, 4, 10; 193, 4, 11	3:21	217, 3, 11
15:55-56	185, 9, 38	3:5	186, 2, 6
		3:11	194, 5, 20
2 Corinthians		3:19	157, 3, 15
1:23	157, 4, 40	3:21-22	157, 3, 15
1:23-24	211, 2	4:4	238, 2, 10
2:3	211, 2	4:6	194, 4, 17
2:7	83, 1; 95, 3	4:27	93, 9, 30
2:11	83, 1; 95, 3	4:29	93, 2, 6
3:5	186, 2, 6	4:47	93, 8, 26
3:11	194, 5, 20	5:5	179, 2
3:15	148, 2, 8	5:6	186, 2, 4; 188, 3, 13; 194, 3, 11
3:18	148, 2, 7; 148, 2, 8		
3:19	157, 3, 15	5:7-9	211, 3
3:21-22	157, 3, 15	5:13	23, 1
4:6	194, 4, 17	5:17	186, 12, 40
4:7	188, 2, 5; 188, 2, 6	5:19-21	93, 11, 48
4:13	157, 3, 14; 194, 3, 15	5:24	243, 11
5:4	193, 4, 11	6:5	87, 5
5:5	179, 2	6:9-10	185, 2, 8
5:6	186, 2, 4; 188, 3, 13; 194, 3, 11	6:16	149, 2, 19
5:10	217, 5, 16	Ephesians	
5:17	186, 12, 40	1:4	149, 2, 20
6:9-10	185, 2, 8	1:5.4	217, 7, 27
6:10	157, 4, 32	1:15-16	217, 7, 28
7:15	217, 4, 14	2:8	188, 2, 6
8:9	157, 2, 10; 186, 2, 4; 186, 7, 26; 155, 3, 9; 157, 4, 23	2:9	186, 2, 4; 186, 4, 12
		3:6-7	186, 2, 5
10:6	185, 6, 24	3:15-16	108, 3, 9; 120, 1, 4
10:17	214, 3; 217, 3, 8	3:16	179, 4
11:31	157, 4, 40	3:20	120, 2, 12; 238, 2, 15
12:2	157, 4, 40	4:2-3	44, 5, 11; 210, 1
12:14	185, 9, 36	4:3	43, 8, 23; 185, 6, 24; 185, 10, 43
12:20	211, 3		
13:7	179, 6; 217, 1, 3	4:5-6	238, 3, 20
		4:11	149, 2, 11
Galatians		4:32	48, 3
1:22-24	217, 6, 24	5:1	148, 1, 5
1:9	93, 7, 23	5:19	48, 3

5:25-26	108, 1, 3	2:22	149, 2, 29
5:26	185, 9, 39	2:23	149, 2, 29
5:27	93, 9, 34; 185, 9, 38; 185, 9, 39	3:1	20*, 28
		3:13	48, 3
6:5	217, 4, 14	3:13	108, 5, 15; 148, 1, 5
6:23	194, 3, 10		

1 Thessalonians

3:12	43, 1, 1; 179, 4
4:14-16	193, 4, 10
4:16	193, 4, 9
5:17-18	188, 2, 7
5:23	238, 2, 15

Philippians

1:8	157, 4, 40
1:23	185, 6, 21
1:26	157, 4, 40
2:6	242, 4
2:7	33, 5; 170, 9
2:8	243, 8
2:12	217, 4, 14
2:12-13	157, 4, 29
2:13	186, 1, 3; 186, 3, 7; 188, 2, 7; 217, 1; 217, 2, 5
2:21	43, 8, 23; 87, 2; 20*, 32
2:27	211, 2; 211, 2
3:13	238, 2, 16
3:15-16	93, 10, 35
4:7	238, 2, 16
4:9	210, 2

2 Thessalonians

2:11	194, 2, 4
3:1-2	217, 7, 27

1 Timothy

1:17	148, 3, 11; 238, 2, 11; 238, 4, 23
1:20	93, 2, 7
2:1	149, 2, 12; 149, 2, 17
2:3-4	149, 2, 17
2:4	217, 6, 19
2:5	149, 2, 17
4:15	243, 23
5:8	243, 12
5:22	108, 3, 7
6:16	148, 2, 10; 238, 2, 11

Colossians

1:6	185, 1, 5
1:12-13	217, 3, 8
1:24	185, 9, 40
2:4	149, 2, 24
2:5	149, 2, 25
2:6	149, 2, 25
2:8-9	149, 2, 25
2:10	149, 2, 25
2:12	149, 2, 26
2:14	149, 2, 26
2:15	149, 2, 26
2:16	149, 2, 27
2:16-17	149, 2, 27
2:17-18	149, 2, 27
2:18	149, 2, 23
2:19-20	149, 2, 28
2:21	149, 2, 23; 149, 2, 29

2 Timothy

1:7	194, 3, 15; 194, 4, 18
2:20	108, 3, 11
2:25	186, 9, 33
2:25-26	185, 7, 31
2:26	43, 1, 1
4:3	35, 3

Titus

1:11	34, 4; 35, 3
2:3	211, 12
2:14	93, 9, 30
3:10	43, 1, 1

Index of Scripture

Hebrews
2:9   170, 9
7:25   149, 2, 14
10:38   186, 2, 6; 194, 5, 20
11:6   217, 3, 10
12:14   185, 10, 43

James
1:5   214, 7
1:15   149, 1, 4
1:17   188, 2, 6; 194, 5, 21; 214, 4
1:18   149, 1, 6
1:19   193, 4, 13
2:13   157, 4, 36
2:19   194, 3, 11
4:6   93, 11, 49; 157, 2, 10
5:12   23, 1; 157, 4, 40

1 Peter
4:8   93, 10, 40; 108, 2, 5; 185, 10, 43; 185, 10, 44

2 Peter
2:16   186, 5, 14
3:14-16 214, 6

1 John
1:8   185, 9, 40
1:8-9   185, 9, 39
1:18   157, 1, 2
2:1-2   149, 2, 14
2:2   93, 9, 32
2:19   93, 9, 29
3:2   148, 3, 11; 148, 5, 17
3:8   211, 4
3:9   185, 9, 40
3:15   211, 14
4:8   148, 5, 18
4:12   148, 2, 6; 148, 2, 10
4:18   185, 6, 21; 185, 6, 22

Jude
19   185, 11, 50

Revelation
2:1-3   43, 8, 22
2:7   43, 8, 22
4:5   43, 8, 22
7:9   93, 9, 30
14:13   217, 6, 22
22:12   214, 1

General Index

(prepared by Kathleen Strattan and adapted by Przemek Nehring)

The first number in the Index is the Letter number.
The number after the colon is a paragraph number.

Aaron: idol worship, as tolerating, 43:23
abandoned woman, the, 93:26, 30
Abednego (Shadrach, Meshach, and), 3:9(3)
Abel, 179:8–9
Abiram, 87:4; 93:28(9), 52
Abraham, 186:19 :
   God's promises to, 89:4
   offspring of, 93:15, 19, 51(13)
Absalom, 185:32(8);
Academics, the,118:16;
Acts of the Apostles:
   Holy Spirit filling one hundred and twenty, 93:21
Adam, 179:8; 217:9, 11
   Christ as second, 157:14; 217:11
adoption, 153:13
adultery, 153:9(4),
adulterers, rules regarding, 93:41–42
Aeneid, the, 7:4;
Africa, 185:29; 186:2;
   Donatists as only in, 52:2; 87:1; 93:24(8)–25
   schisms in, 93:24(8)–25 *See also* schisms
Agabus, 149:11(2)
Ahab, King, 185:41
Alexandria, 4* :
   Athanasius as bishop of, 44:6
allegories:
   interpretation of, 93:24(8)
Alypius, 238:4; 20*:12

   as bishop of Thagaste, 28:1(1);
   Jerome, as link to, 28:1(1);
   memorandum to Thagaste clerics, 15*:1–2
Alypius and Augustine:
   on Demetrias, consecrated virgin, 188:1(1)–14
   letter to Maximus from on Arianism, 170:1–10
Ambrose,
   asking Fortunius about, 44:7(4)
   Commentary on the Gospel of Luke, 148:6(2)–7, 10
Ananias, in Acts, 185:22
Anaxagoras, 118:12, 23(4)–27
Anaximenes, 118:12, 23(4)
anathema, 93:23
angel(s), 148:7:
   bad, 217:9–108
   and circumcision of Moses, 23:4
   "devil and his angels," 43:22
   "even an angel from heaven ... should be anathema," 93:23
   in Revelation, Book of, 43:22–23
   wicked, 194:20
anger, 9:3–4; 93:48; 193:3(2); 210:2; 211:14
   of God, 186:24–25; 194:5
   wild, 93:11
anthropomorphites, 148:13(4)–14
Antioch:
   quarrel between Paul and Peter, 28:3(3)–5

See also under Paul; Peter
Antoninus, 209:1–10; 20*:1–33
Anulinus, proconsul of Africa, 89:3; 93:13
Apocalypse, the,
 many thousands seen in, 93:30
apostle(s) 149:11(2); 185:22
 See also individual names
 the Church in time of, 93:9(3)
 true and false, 43:22–23
Arcesilas of Pitane, 118:16
Arianism, Arians, 44:6; 93:31; 148:10; 170:1–2, 8; 185:1(1), 47–48(9); 238–239, 241–242
Arles:
 Caecilian, acquittal of, 89:3
arts, liberal:
 salvation as not from, 87:1
Arzuges, the, 46:1–5; 93:24(8)
ashes, 48:2
Asia:
 Hilary of Poitiers on, 93:31–32
Athanasius, Catholic bishop of Alexandria, 44:6; 148:10
atomism:
 of Epicurus, rejecting, 3:2
 physical (Democritus), 118:12,27–28, 30–31
Audians, 148:14
Aurelius, bishop of Carthage; primate of Africa, 44:12; 60; 194:1(1); 4*:2; 20*:12, 14.
Aurelius of Macomades, 20*:9, 12
authority:
 resisting, 87:7
Auxentius, 38:4

Bagai:
 Catholic bishop of, 185:26–27
 council of, 88:11; 108:1(1), 5–6, 13(4)–15
baptism, 89:5, 108:3, 149:26; 153:15; 185:39–40; 193:7; 194:45–46
 See also John the Baptist
 bad behavior after, 194:42
 of Christ, 89:5; 185:30(9
 Christ, as belonging to, 51:5 of by disciples, 44:10(5)
 Donatists accepting Maximianist, not Catholic, 51:4–5
 infant, 149:22
 of John's, 44:10(5)
 of John's vs. Christ's, 93:47
 the Lord's Prayer at, 5*:2
 Paul as rebaptizing (after John), 93:47–48 by Peter, 93:47
 Peter wanting to be washed, 44:10(5)
 rebaptism, Donatist practice of, *See* rebaptism. righteousness and, 93:10
 schismatics, of former, 93:46(11)
 Second Coming as eliminating need for, 23:4
 true, 89:5
 validity of, 89:5
beauty120:20:
 of body and soul, 3:4
being, the hierarchy of, 18:2
"belly," 49:3–4
bishop(s):
 Donatist, council in Carthage, 93:43
 letters on Pelagian heresy, 215:2
 removal of abusive, 20*:1–33
 role of Catholic, 153:1(1)–26
 rules among (letter from Cyprian regarding), 93:41
blindness, 7:6(3)
 bodily, 155:3
 Didymus of Alexandria: spiritual, 93:1(1)
 of Jews, 149:18–20
 "those that strike even blind eyes," 51:5
blood of Christ, 179:6; 186:28
boasting, 48:2
body (-ies):
 beauty of, 3:4

and good, supreme, 118:13–16
redemption of, 186:40
senses as deceptive, 7:2, 3
soul making use of senses, 7:2, 3–7
soul vs., 120:18(4); 238:12
spiritual,,120:17; 148:16–18
body of Christ, 185:50;
Boniface, bishop of Cataqua, 96:2–3; 97:3, 149:2
Boniface, pope, 209:6,9; 20*:11–12
Boniface, tribune and count of Africa, 7*:1; 185:1(1)–51
books, 211:13
books, sacred,
  burning of, 51:1, 2
  surrendered in time of persecution, 35:4; 43:10; 44:4; 53:4(2); 89:4
boyhood:
  manhood and, 4:1–2
branches:
  broken, reattachment of, 87:9
bread, 185:50; 186:28:
brethren, false, 87:2–3
bribery, 153:23
bull of Phalaris, 155:2
Byzacium: Maximianist schism, 93:24(8)

Caecilian (bishop of Carthage), 185:4–7, 10, 16, 47
  case of (Donatist condemnation of), 43:1–20, 25(9)–26; 93:13–16(5); 108:2
  Donatist reaction to verdict, 89:3
  false charges against, 93:19
  judgment regarding, validity of, 93:14
Caelestius, Caelestian heresy, 157:22;
caelicolae, 44:13(6)
Caesar, Emperor, 185:28
Caesarea, 209:8:
  Emeritus as Donatist bishop of, 87:1–10
Cain, 149:9, 179:8

Canaan, 185:41
canonical books (Scriptures), 148:15
See also Scripture
  authority of, 93:35(10)
  on reprimands, benefit of, 93:32
  translations and preservation of, 93:38
capi, 3:5
Capraria, 48:4
carnal, 93:32
carnal persons,
  Ishmael as symbolizing, 93:6
carousing, 93:48
Cartenna:
  Rogatists in, 93:21–22(7)
  Rogatus as bishop, 87:10
  Vincent as Rogatist bishop, 93:1(1)–53
Carthage, 43:7; 15*:2.
  council of Donatist bishops in, 93:43
  Donatist promise in, 51:1
  Genethlius as bishop before Aurelius, 44:12
  Majorinus as first Donatist bishop of, 93:13 *See also* Majorinus
Casae Nigrae, Numidia:
  Donatus as bishop in, 43:4 *See also* Donatus
Catholic Church, Catholics, 93:23
  as body of Christ, 185:50
  Donatist converts to (rejoining), 3:16(5)–17
  and Donatist schism, *See* Donatists.
  false, 93:17
  fish, bad among the good (as like), 93:33–34, 50(12)
  persecution of, 93:6
  spread of, 52:1; 87:1
  as true Church, 93:51(13); 118:32(5);
cattle:
  shepherds and, 93:5
  theft of, 93:5
  wandering, 93:5

Celer, 209:5
Celestine, possibly deacon and pope, letters from Augustine to:
  on the hierarchy of being, 18:1–2
Celestine, pope, letters from Augustine to:
  on Antoninus of Fussala, 209:1–10
celibacy, 157:39
  See also virginity, chastity
chaff, *See also* harvest; weeds; wheat.
  removal at last winnowing, 93:33, 42, 50(12)
  wheat, amid, 93:33–34; 108:12
charity, 48:3; 243:12
chastity, 157:39; 188:6, 8
  nuns and, 211:10–11
child (-ren):
  of abandoned woman, 93:26, 30
  bad, 89:2
  chosen, the, 149:19–22
  sated with their children, 49:4–5
  "where even the children praise the Lord," 93:50(12)
Chremes, 7:4
Christian unity, 44:13(6)
  bringing about, ways discussed, 93:17
  Donatists exhorted to return to, 76:1–4; 87:9; 108:17–20
  Donatists (former) as desiring, 93:16(5)
  force used to bring about, 93:16(5)–18
  importance of, 93:28(9)
  love, bearing with one another in, 48:3
  parables supporting, 108:10–12
  scattered members gathered together, 93:31
  tolerance and, 44:11
Christianity
  hierarchy of being, task in relation to, 18:2
  humility in, 118:22–23(4)
  Jerusalem, as beginning in, 93:21, 23
  spread of, 93:22(7)
Christians, 194:23:
  false brethren, 87:2–3
  God's foreknowledge of, 194:12
  living for Christ, 157:31–36
  numerical superiority over Jews, 93:26
  prayer for, 217:14, 28
  and self-righteousness, 157:37–39
  weak, help for, 118:32(5)
  wealthy, 157:23(4)–38
Church, the, 93:30–31
  asylum in, 113
  of Christ, 87:9,
  Christ as king of, 89:4
  coercion, use by, 185:21(6)–25(7)
  "defenders of," 20*:6
  Donatist claim to be, 93:24(8)
  Mary as symbolizing, 120:15
  as mother, 48:2; 89:6
  "no one wipes out from the earth the Church of God," 43:27
  Rogatist claim to be, 93:23–26
  serving, steering middle path while, 48:2–3
  sin of some as not destroying, 93:30–34
  spread of, 93:21, 26–30 *See also* Catholicism true, 44:3(2); 93:11
  unity in, 173:5–6; 185:42–44
  without spot or wrinkle, 185:38–40
Cicero, 17:3; 155:3–4; 242:5
  Dioscorus, questions of, 118:1(1)–34
Circumcellions, 23:6–7; 35:2; 93:2; 108:19; 185:25(7), 41
Catholicism, converts to, 93:2
  Donatists as tolerating, 43:24
  savagery of, 93:11; 108:13(4); 149:20, 26
circumcision, circumcised, 23:4; , 194:11

Cirta, Numidia:
  Fortunius, meeting with, 44:1(1)
  Sylvanus as bishop of, 43:17(6)
city (-ies) 155:9(4)
City of God, 91:3; 155:2
clean of heart, 148:9, 11
cleanliness: of clothing, 211:10
cleric(s):
  monks and, 60:1–2
clothes:
coercion, use of, 185:1(1)–51
commandments of Christ, 155:14–15
concupiscence, 194:44
  nuns and, 211:10–11
Conference of Carthage, 173:7; 185:6(2), 30
Consentius, Catholic layman, letter from Augustine to:
  answering theological questions, 120:1–20
Constantina, 34:5
Constantine, 43:4; 185:6(2)
Caecilian, case of, 89:3; 93:13–16(5)
Corinthians, 43:25(9)
  baptism of, 93:47
Corinthians, Letter(s) to:
  on resurrection, beliefs regarding, 93:32
correction (being corrected), 93:1(1)
  See also punishment shame regarding, 93:52
Correction of the Donatists, The, 185:1(1)–51
Council of Bagai, 108:1(1), 5–6, 13(4)–15
Council of Carthage, 215:2
Council of Diospolis, 4*:2
Council of Jerusalem, 179:7
Council of Nicaea, 238:4
Council of Numidia, 215:2
courage 155:12–13(4), 16
crazy person:
  "Someone who ties down a crazy person," 93:4(2)

Cresconius, letter from Augustine to:
  on behalf of Faventius, 113
Cresconius, estate supervisor, 14*:2; 15*:3–4
Cresconius, monk, 214:1; 215:1
crime: guilt vs. innocence, 93:15
Crispinus, letters from Augustine to:
  on the schism, 51:1–5
criticism, constructive, 28:6(4)
crosses, the three, 93:7
cruelty:
  comparative, 93:7
  in persecution, 97:4
cupi, 3:5
cupiri, 3:5
Cyprian, bishop of Carthage, 93:36
  Christian unity, regarding, 93:36–42, 45
  Donatists, as seeming to favor, 93:37–42
  on *The Lord's Prayer,* 217:2–3, 6
  as martyr, 93:36; 108:9–12; *Mortality,* 217:22
  Paul and Peter, regarding, 93:31
  as Saint, 93:36
Cyril, letter from Augustine to: on *The Deeds of Pelagius,* 4*

Daniel, 93:19; , 157:2; 185:7
  Shadrach, Meshach, and Abednego, 93:9(3)
Dathan, 87:4; 93:28(9), 52
daughter as thorns, 93:28(9)
David, King:
  Saul, as tolerating, 43:23
  Saul's anointing, respect for, 87:9
debate: with Pascentius, 238:1–9
deafness, 155:3
death:
  escaping (Enoch and Elijah), 193:5, 7–8
  and eternal life, 193:6
  of the soul (as impossible), 3:4
"defenders of the church," 20*:6

General Index 529

Demetrias: as consecrated virgin, 188:1(1)–14
Democritus, 118:12, 27–30
demons, 194:11
desire: "desired," Latin conjugations, 3:5
devil, the, 185:47; 217:8(3)–11
driving out, 194:46.
Dioscorus, letter from Augustine to: on Cicero, 118:1(1)–34
disagreements, 210:2
dishonor: vessels made for, 93:50(12)
Donatist leaders, Augustine's letters to
on Caecilian and peacemaking, 43:1–27
on Fortunius, meeting with, and the true Church, 44:1–14
Donatist(s), 118:12; 208:3
Africa, as only in, ; 52:2; 87:1; 93:24(8)–25, 27
beliefs of (Christ's glory), 93:1(1)
bishops, council in Carthage, 93:43
Christian guilt, beliefs regarding, 89:4
Circumcellions as, 23:6–7; 93:1
The Correction of the Donatists, 185:1(1)–51
doctrine as false, 89:1
Eusebius, Augustine's correspondence with regarding, 34:2–6
as false, 89:1
Fortunius, Augustine meeting with, 44:1–14
Hippo, around, 89:8
Holy Spirit, as lacking, 93:46(11)
laws, imperial, complaints regarding, 89:3
laws issued against, 93:16(5)–17
love shown to, 89:6
Macarius, the time of, 23:6; 44:4–5(3)
martyrdom, as claiming, 89:2
mass conversion (to Catholicism), 93:16(5)–17

matricidal young man, rebaptism of, 34:2–6
Maximianists, accepting back, 51:2, 4–5;
Maximianists, persecution of, 51:3, 5
Optatus, as not expelling, 87:4–5
See also Optatus persecution of, 44:4, 7(4)–8, 11; 87:8; 89:2; 108:14
reason for, primary, 87:6, 10
rebaptizing, practice of, 23:1–8; 34:2–6; 43:21(8); 44:7(4)–8, 12
Rogatus, the Rogatist split from, 87:10 *See also* Rogatists
Roman authorities appealed to regarding, 87:8
sacraments of, 87:9
schism with Catholic Church, 33:1–6; 43:1–27
secular power to control, 93:1(1)
Severinus, letters from Augustine to (re: schism), 52:1–4
suppressing, Paul's words to justify, 87:7
unity with, appealing for, 43:1–27
See also Christian unity
wickedness of, 93:10
Donatus, bishop of Casae Nigrae, 43:4, 15, 26; 44:6
See also Donatists
Donatus, former monk, 60:1–2
Dorotheus, 15*:3–4:
letter from Augustine to on employee accused of crime, 14*
dove:
Holy Spirit as, 89:5

earth
See also world
glory of Christ over, 93:1(1)
kingdom of Christ, 93:19
east, 93:30
Easter:
baptism at, 51:4

vigil, 34:2
Egypt:
  "souls" going with Jacob to, 97:
Eleusius, 93:31
Eli: Samuel tolerating wicked sons, 43:23
Elijah, 193:5, 7–8
  false prophets, killing, 44:9; 93:6
Elpidius:
  letter from Augustine to on the Trinity, 242
Emeritus, Donatist bishop of Caesarea:
  letter from Augustine to on sin, Optatus, schism, 87:1–10
emperor(s) 185:6(2), 19(5)–20, 27–29
  See also individual names
  petitioning, 93:13
end of the world
  See also Apocalypse;
  harvest God's elect at, 93:33
  seashore as, 93:34
enemy (-ies):
  God...will crush the heads of his enemies, 149:10
  of all good persons, 48:2
  of Christian faith, 217:6, 10
  Donatists as, 93:2
  loving, 153:4(2)–5
  praying for, 215:3
  "Not everyone who scourges is an enemy," 93:4(2)
  In terms of the gospel they are enemies on your account, 149:18–20
Enoch, 193:5, 8
Epicureans, sect of, 88:10; 118:12, 14, 20–21, 26; 155:2–3
  body as highest good, 118:16–19, 19
  on mind, 118:29
  on nature, 118:28
Epicurus, 155:2
  rejecting atomism of, 3:2
eternal fire, 4*:3
eternal life, 217:19:
  attaining, 155:16–17

bodily death and, 193:6
grace and, 194:20–21
eternity: permanence of, 7:2
Eudoxius, abbot on Capraria, letters from Augustine to:
  on steering a middle path, 48:1–4
Eunomians, 185:48(9)
Eunomius, 238:4
Eusebius, Catholic, Roman official, letters from Augustine to:
  on Donatist rebaptism, 34:1–6
  messages for Proculeian, 35:1–5
Eustasius, monk, 48:4
evangelists, 149:11(2); 185:8, 47; 194:43(10), 4
Eve, 179:8;
evil:
  See also sin
  Church treatment of, 93:6
  correction of, 93:7
  free choice and, 217:8(3)–10
  good vs., 93:6; 215:4–8
  good use made from, 149:18; 215:8
  hidden, 93:10
  motives as showing, 93:6
  persecution of, 93:8
  punishment for, 91:6
  repaying, 93:14 tolerated, for good, 93:15
Evodius:
  apology to Proculeian for language of, 33:2–3
exorcism, 194:43(10), 46
exsufflation, 34:3; 43:21(8), 25(9); 51:5; 52:2–3; 108:3
  sacraments subjected to, 43:25(9)
external things:
  as present to us as we are to ourselves, 4:2
eyes:
  of body and mind, 4:2
Ezekiel, 87:2; 185:31:
  on the sins of children and parents, 44:12

Fabiola, letters from Augustine to:
  on Antoninus of Fussala, 20*
faith, 186:7(3)–10; 217:10:
  differing between spouses, 23:4 as gift, 194:10–11, 15
  grace and, 187:32; 194:15; 214:4; 217:24–30
  and reason, 120:2–3, 5–6, 8
  as shield, 48:3
  strong, 97:4
  weak, 97:4 *See also under* weak
false prophets:
  Elijah killing, 44:9
family (ies):
  abandoning, 157:32
  charity beginning with, 243:12
  relations, 170:6
  religious differences in, 33:5
  renouncing for Christ, 243:2–10
"fantasies," 7:1, 4
farmer:
fasting, 48:3; 11:8
Faventius, 113; 114
fear:
  of government, 93:20(6)
  salvation, as catalyst for, 93:3,
  of secular authority, 93:20(6)
feet:
  "the Lord rescues his feet from the snare," 48:3
Felician, tribune, 7*:1–2
Felician of Musti, 51:2, 4–5; 108:1(1), 4(2)–6, 13(4)–15;
Felicity and Rusticus, letter from Augustine to:
  on tribulations and giving rebukes, 210:1–2
Felix, monk, 214:1; 215:1
Felix of Aptungi, 43:3(2)–4, 12–13(4)
fervent in spirit, 48:3
Festus, letters from Augustine to:
  on dealing with Donatists, 89:1–8
fiery furnace, the, 3:9(3); 185:8
fire, 48:2

Dathan and Abiram consumed, 87:4
eternal, 4*:3
schism, punishment for, 51:1
Firmus, 87:10
fish: bad among the good, 93:33–34, 50(12); 108:12
five caves of the nation of darkness, 7:4
flattery, 28:6(4)
Flavian, vicar for Africa, 87:8
flesh, the
  See also body; sensual pleasures
  desires of, 149:6, 8
  Ishmael as symbolizing, 93:6
  pleasures of, 118:14, 17
  spirit vs., 93:31
flirtation, 211:10–11
Florentinus, imperial official, letter from Augustine to:
  on behalf of Faventius, 114
Florentius, 97:3
Florentinus, domesticus, 7*:1
Florus, monk, 214:6; 215A; 215:3, 8
flute:
  "a bad flute player makes a good singer," 60:1–2
food:
  Do not handle; do not taste; do not touch, 149:23, 29–30
  Let no one judge you regarding food, 149:26
  sweet foods, 93:28(9)
fool(s), folly:
  happiness and, 3:1
forgiveness, 148:5; 153:15; 185:38–39; 186:16(6); 211:14
  of injuries, 48:3
  of sins, in Christ's name, 93:21,
Fortunatian (bishop of Sicca),
  letter from Augustine to:
    on seeing God, 148:1(1)–18
fortune: neither fearing nor desiring, 3:5
Fortunius, Donatist bishop of Thaive:
  Augustine meeting with, 44:1–14

fraud: property acquired through, 96:2
free choice, 157:5
  faith and, 217:23
  God as causing, 217:1
  grace and, 214:1–3, 6–7; 215:4–8; 217:4–24
  sin and, 157:2–4(2); 217:12(4)
friends, friendships, 82:1; 155:1(1)
  as good fortune, 3:4
  "Not everyone who is merciful is a friend," 93:4(2)
furnace, the fiery, 93:9(3)
Fussala, bishop of, 209:1–10; 20*:1–33

Galatians, Letter to:
  Paul, rebuke of Peter by, 28:3(3)–5
Gaul, 157:41; 175:1; 179:7
Gelizi, Church of, 43:5
generation:
  Who will recount his generation?, 153:13
Genesis, 5*:3
Genethlius, bishop of Carthage before Aurelius, 44:12
Gentiles, 149:18–20:
gentleness:
  obeying God with, 48:2
gifts:
  of God, 157:29; 186:10; 194:10–11, 14–16(4)
  nuns and material, 211:12
Gildo, Count, 87:5
glory:
  of Christ, 93:1(1)
  of humans, as empty, 93:15
goats:
  sheep, separating from, 93:49–50(12); 108:12
God:
  in heaven, 120:14
  as just, 217:20
  as love, 186:7(3)
  nature of, 118:23(4); 120:7
  seeing, 148:1(1)–18
  as severe and gentle, 93:4(2)
  truth in teaching about, as crucial, 28:3(3)–5
  wrath of, 93:5
good, goodness, 153:12(5)–13
  doing, civil authorities and, 93:20(6)
  evil, returning for, 153:4(2)–5
  evil tolerated for, 93:15
  evil vs., 93:6
  fear and, 93:20(6)
  the highest, 118:13–16;
  motives as showing, 93:6
  persecution of, 93:8
  seeking common, 211:12
good will:
  grace and, 215:1, 4–8; 217:5, 16(5)–17
good works, 217:10
  among non-believers, 217:10
Gospel:
  spread of, 93:21–23
Goths, 185:1(1)
government
  See also secular power
  Christianity and, 153:16–19
  doing good and, 93:20(6)
  fear of, 93:20(6)
  officials of, 153:8, 19, 23–25,
  See also specific titles
  as God's servant, 87:7
  resisting authority of, 87:7
grace, 93:32; 186:3–6, 31; 4:19(5); 214–217; 225–226
  in (sinners) and, 82:20; 149:7–8
  vs. free choice, 157:5–8, 10, 16–18; 179:1–10; 186:1(1)–41; 188:1(1)–14; 194:1(1)–47
  as gratuitous, 217:19–21
  and law, 217:11–12(4), 23
  teaching and, 217:12(4)
  the Twelve Propositions, 217:16(5)–18(6), 25–26(7)
Grace and Free Choice, 215:1, 2

grain:
    weeds, separating from, 108:11–12
    wheat, amid, 93:33–34;
    wheat and chaff, 108:12; 142:3
    at winnowing, the last, 93:50(12)
Greek (language), 149:12–16; 238:4; 5*:3
    Scripture translations, 71:3(2)–6(4);
Greek mythology:
    Medea, 7:4
Greeks, 4*:5:
    Paul and, 93:7
Gregory (Phoebatius of Agen), 148:10
guilt:
    innocence vs., 93:15
    habits, bad, 89:6, 7
    fear as breaking, 93:3
    subduing, 48:3

Hagar 185:9, 11; 196:12–13
    Sarah and, 93:6
happiness, 3:1–5; 55:26,
    attaining, 118:13–15;
    as not from sensual pleasure, 3:4
    the happy life, 155:1(1)–10
    wisdom and, 3:1, 5
harmony 93:28(9)
harvest, 93:15
    end-time, 87:8; 93:31, 33
hatred, 210:2:
    and persecution, 97:4
    preaching from, 93:15
heart:
    Blessed are the clean of heart, 148:9,
    hardness of, 194:14
    heaven, 55:17–19
    Christ in, 120:15
    God in, 120:14,
    glory of Christ over, 93:1(1)
Hebrew (language)
    scripture translations from, 28:2(2); 71:3(2)–6(4)
hierarchy of being, 18:

heresies, heretics, heresies,118:12; 120:13(3); 185:2, 47; 194:47;
    bishops sent to emperor regarding, 97:3
    caelicolae, 44:13(6)
    conversion of, forcible, 93:17
    correction of, 89:1; 97:2–3; 98:5
    See Donatists.
    false Catholics, 93:17
    laws concerning, 97:2
    schism as, 87:4; 89:7
    secular authority against, 93:12
Hero and Lazarus, bishops,179:7
Hilary, Catholic layman:
    on Pelagian teaching in Sicily, 157:1(1)–41
Hilary, bishop of Narbonne, letter from Augustine to:
    on Pelagian heresy, 178:1–3
Hilary Bishop of Poitiers, 75:20(6); 93:31–32
    on Asia, 93:31–32
    Synods as by, 93:21
Hippo, 209:1–10
holiness, 148:18
    "All we want is holiness," 93:14, 43
    of Scriptures, 28:3(3)–5
Holy Spirit, the:
    Donatist(s) as lacking, 93:46(11)
    as dove, 89:5
    prayer and, 194:16(4)–18
    sin against, 185:48(9)–50
Holy Week:
    criminal suits ceased during, 34:
honorable: use of word, 23:1
Honorius, 97:2
hope:
    account of, giving, 120:4
    faith and, 120:8
    placing, in humans vs. Christ, 89:5
humility, 22:7(2)
    of Christ, 118:17, 22–23(4)
    feigned, 149:23, 27–29

idol(s), idolatry, 87:2; 185:8, 12(3)
   Julian and, 93:12(4)
   laws concerning, 93:26; 97:2
   Nebuchadnezzar forcing worship, 93:9(3)
   schism punished more severely than, 51:1
images, three kinds:
   arrived at by reason, 7:4–7
   ones we make up, 7:4–7
   from previous sensations, 7:1, 4–7
imagination:
   memory and, 7:1–7
   memory impossible without, 6:1
   sensation vs., 6:1–2
   the soul and, 7:1–7
immortality: of Christ, 120:9;
immutability of God, 148:11
incense, 87:2
infant baptism, 149:22
   Catholic view, 86:11(4); 194:44–46
   infant death and, 194:31(7)–32
   Pelagian view, 157:11(3); 186:12, 30; 193:3(2)–4; 194:42–43(10)
Innocent:
   letters regarding Pelagians, 186:2;
insanity: advantage of, 7:2, 3
intellect, intelligence
   See also mind; soul
   maturity and, 4:2
   as seat of truth, 3:4
intelligible nature:
   sensible nature compared to, 4:1–2; 3:2–3
invisible realities, 120:9
irony, 149:23
Isaiah, 43:23
Ishmael:
   and Isaac, 93:6
Israel, 149:19; 185:41

jaci, 3:5
Jacob:
   and Esau, 186:13(5)–21; 194:34(8)–39;
Januarius, 186:1(1)
jealous (-y), 93:32, 48
Jeremiah, 43:23
Jerome, 148:6(2)–9, 13(4)–14:
Jerome, letters from Augustine to:
   on Jerome's Scripture translations, 71:1(1)–6(4)
   the letter delivered after nine years, 28:1(1)–6(4)
Jerusalem:
   Council of, 179:7
Jesus Christ
   as circumcised, 23:4
   death of, 120:9
   glory of, 93:1(1)
   immortality of, 120:9;
   in heaven, 120:15
   kingdom of, 93:19
   as mediator, 149:17, 26
   prophecy, as fulfillment of, 93:21
   as servant, 33:5; 170:9
   sins, as propitiation for, 93:32
   sins forgiven in name of, 93:21, 23
   suffering as necessary, 93:21, 23
   as the truth, 155:14
   truth in teaching about, as crucial, 28:3(3)–5
   the way of, 93:35(10)
   as wisdom of God, 120:19
Jew(s) 149:24, 26–27
   as non-believers, 149:18–20
   "flogged Christ, and Christ flogged the Jews," 93:8
   numerical superiority of Christians, 93:26
   Paul rebuking Peter for living like Gentile, 28:4
   scattering of, 149:3, 9
   unity, regarding, 93:26
Jezebel, 93:6
Job, Book of: Jerome, translation by, 28:2(2); 71:3
John the Baptist:

baptism of, 44:10(5)
Christ, baptism of, 89:5
Paul as rebaptising people from, 93:48
John, bishop of Jerusalem, 186:36
letter from Augustine to
on Pelagianism, 179:1–10
Jonah, Book of:
Jerome, translation by, 71:5(3)
Jordan River, 93:26
and circumcision of Moses, 23:4
Joseph, husband of Mary, 153:9(4)
Joseph, son of Jacob, 149:33
Josiah, 185:19(5)
joy, 10:2:
effects of (Nebridius), 3:1–5
Jubaianus,
letter from Cyprian to, 93:36
Judaism, 149:24, 26–27
Judas, 108:7(3), 8
Christ in regard to, 43:23; 44:10(5); 93:15
Last Supper, as sharing, 93:15
Satan as entering, 93:7
Judea, 93:21
judge (state official), 153:8, 16, 19–20, 23
judges, human, 89:4
judgment:
by God, 149:22; 153:4(2) ; 167:20; 186:12, 20; 194:6(3), 33
the last, 23:3
judging others, 157:37–39;
Julian the Apostate, emperor, 93:12(4):
Donatists appealing to, 93:12(4)
Juliana:
letter from Alypius and Augustine to:
on Demetrias as consecrated virgin, 188:1(1)–14
Julius, bishop of Roman church, 44:6
justice, 153:26; 155:12–13(4),16; 194:4–5
persecution on account of, 87:7; 93:7
justification, 186:10; 194:6(3)–8;

killing:
in name of Christianity, wrongness of, 44:8–9
king(s)
Christ as, 89:4
to serve Christ, 93:19
know yourself, 93:29
Korah, 93:52

land ownership, 149:3
languages:
Scripture translations, 71:3(2)–6(4);
Last Supper, the:
Judas as sharing, 93:15
Latin grammar:
points of, 3:5
Latin language, 149:12–13
law, the:
Do not kill them lest they forget your law, 149:9
grace and, 149:26; 186:10; 194:6(3)–8
and the prophets, 155:14–15
and Psalms, 93:21
Lawrence of Caesarea, 209:8
lawyers, 153:8, 25
laziness, 89:6
avoiding, 48:2
"Someone who . . . rouses a lazy person," 93:4(2)
leisure:
putting Church before, 48:2
letters, Augustine's
characteristics of (described by Nebridius), 6:1
liberal arts:
salvation as not from, 87:1
licentiousness, 93:48
lies, lying, 157:40
Paul's rebuke of Peter, 28:3(3)–4;
as undermining authority of Scriptures, 28:3(3)–5
nature of, 120:18(4)
lily: in the midst of thorns, 93:28(9)

lion(s), 93:19
logic, 118:19
"lord": as salutation, 23:1
Lord's Prayer, the, 153:13–14
Lot, 93:27
love, 43:1; 148:6(2); 155:13(4)–15; 186:7(3); 194:11
   Christian unity, 48:3
   commandments to,; 153:15
   disagreements and, 210:2
   faith and, 186:7(3); 194:11
   fruit of, 52:2
   for God, 155:13(4)–15
   God as, 148:18
   as healer, 89:6
   maternal, 89:6
   for others, 153:14
   with severity, 93:4(2)
Lucifer, bishop of Cagliari, 185:47
Lucilla, 43:17(6), 25(9)–26
Luke, 149:11(2)

Macarius, 23:6; 44:4–5(3); 87:10; 93:43
Macedonians, 85:48(9)
Macrina: Deuterius as bishop, 93:43
Majorinus, 43:4; 43:26; 44:8;
   schism sect of, 93:13
manhood: boyhood and, 4:1–2
Manicheans
   five caves of the nation of darkness, 7:4
Mark, 149:11(2)
marriage:
   chastity in, 157:39
   religious differences in, 33:5
martyrs, martyrdom
   the Church in time of, 93:9(3)
   Circumcellions demanding honor of, 88:9
   Donatist(s) claiming, 89:2
   suffering alone as not making, 89:2
Mary, mother of Jesus, 149:32–33; 153:9(4)
   Church, as symbolizing, 120:15
Mary Magdalene, 149:32 materialism, See Democritus
maturity: of mind and intellect, 4:2
Mauritania Caesariensis, 87:1,10; 93:24(8)
   Cartenna as in, See Cartenna.
Maximian, Donatist bishop of Bagai, 108:5, 13(4)
Maximianists, 51:3; 87:6; 93:24(8); 108:1(1); 118:12;
   Donatist persecution of, 51:3, 5; 108:14
   Donatists, breaking away from, 43:26
   Donatists, split from, 43:26; 87:6
   Donatists accepting back, 51:2; 76:3
   Donatists accepting baptism of, 51:4–5; 108:5–6;
   Donatists appealing against, 93:12(4)
Maximinus, Donatist bishop on Siniti in Numidia,
   letters from Augustine to, on rebaptism, 23:1–8
Maximus, physician,
   letter from Alypius and Augustine to on Arianism, 170:1–10
Medea, 7:4
meek, the, 149:3
meekness:
   obeying God with, 48:2
Melchiades, 43:16
memory:
   imagination and, 7:1–7
   impossible without imagination, 6:1
Mercator, Marius, letter to Augustine from:
   on Pelagians and second coming, 193:1(1)–13
mercy, 194:14:
   Christian, 153:3–19
   in criticism, 28:6(4)
   of God, 149:7; 153:26; 194:4, 6(3), 14

"Not everyone who is merciful is a friend," 93:4(2)
Meshach (Shadrach, and Abednego), 93:9(3)
middle path:
  steering, serving the Church, 48:2–3
mile, going the extra, 48:1
Milevis, 34:5:
  region of, 97:3
Mincius, 118:6
mind, 118:24–27, 29, 32
  See also intelligence; intelligible nature;
  sensual pleasures vs., 3:4; 4:1–2
  truth, as seat of, 3:4
mirror(s), 3:3
miracles:
  early Christian, 118:20
  non-believers doubting, 120:5
monad, the, 3:2
monasteries:
  entering, 83:3
money, 93:5; 153:26
  silver, 96:2
monks:
  Donatus and his brother, 60:1–2
  morals, 118:17:
  bad conversations as ruining, 93:32
Moses:
  murmuring against God, tolerating, 43:23
  punishing sinful actions, 93:6
mother:
  the Church as, 48:2; 89:6; 93:6;
  still needing . . . the milk of his mother, 93:21
Mount Zion, 93:25
murder
  See also killing
  matricidal young man, 34:2–6
Mutugenna, 23:2
mysteries, divine, 120:5
myths, 7:4

nature, 118:17–18, 28
  as mutable (hierarchy of being), 18:2
Nature and Grace (book by Augustine), 179:2
Nature (book by Pelagius), 179:2–10; 186:1(1)
Nebridius, letters from Augustine to:
  on happiness, 3:1–5
  on memory and imagination (images), 7:1–7
  on sensible vs. intelligible natures, 4:1–2
Nebuchadnezzar, 93:9(3); 185:8, 19(5)
neighbor(s):
  he who prepares a pit for his neighbor, 93:19
  love of, 153:14
Nineveh, 164:2; 185:19(5)
Noah, 108:20(7).
non-believers:
  God's foreknowledge of, 186:26; 194:12
  infants as, 193:3(2)–4
  praying for, 186:38
North Pole, 7:4
numbers, 3:2
  and images arrived at by reason, 7:4
  the monad, 3:2
  pebbles used as means of calculation 7:4
  power of soul illustrated by, 7:(3), 6
  raven set, 7:(3), 6
Numidia:
  Casae Nigrae, Donatus as bishop in, 43:4
  Mutugenna, 23:2
Nundinarius, 43:17(6);
nun(s):
  farmer's daughter as, 35:4
  Primus' improper conduct with, 35:2

oaths (swearing), 157:40
Oea, 71:5(3
Old Testament,

See law; law and the prophets; Scriptures:
  patriarchs, faith of, 157:14;
  prophecy, Christ as fulfillment of, 89:4
olive trees, 194:44
Olympius, letters from Augustine to:
  on church and property matters, 96:1–3
  on laws regarding idolatry and heretics, 97:1–4
one hundred and twenty:
  Holy Spirit filling, 93:21
Optatus, bishop of Milevis, 185:6(2)
Optatus (the Gildonian), Donatist bishop of Thamugadi, 43:25(9); 51:3; 53:6(3); 76:3; 87:2–5; 108:5
orgies, 35:2
Origen, 28:2(2)
original sin, 157:12–13, 19–21; 186:33

pagan(s), 149:25:
  bishops sent to emperor regarding, 97:3
  Christians, relationship with, 93:26
  laws passed against, 93:10
Palestine, 186:2, 27(8)
parable(s), 108:11–12 :
  bad fish in with good, 93:33–34
  banquet, 185:24
  chaff amid the wheat, 93:33–34; , 108:12
  of Pharisee and publican, 93:49
  weeds amid the grain, 93:33–34
parents:
  of bad children, 89:2
Parmenian, Donatist bishop of Carthage, 93:43–44
Parmenon, 7:4
Passion of the Lord, 55:2; 149:33; 155:4
past, the: memories, 7:1–7
Paul, apostle, 108:8; 118:20; 185:22–24, 22–28

  armed escort for, 87:8
  baptizing after John, 93:17–48
  on destruction of flesh to save spirit, 93:7
  Donatist schism, words used to justify, 87:7
  on fear of government, 93:20(6)
  on government, fear of, 93:20(6)
  Greeks defending, 93:7
  imprisonment of, 93:7
  on Ishmael and Isaac, 93:6
  persecution of, 93:7
  and Peter, 28:3(3)–5; 93:31
  tolerance, as living life of, 43:23
  violence of Christ used, 93:5
Paul, bishop of Cataqua:
  property acquired by, 96:2
Paulinus, bishop of Nola:
  letter from Augustine to:
  on Pelagianism as heresy, 186:1(1)–41
  response to biblical questions, 149:1(1)–33
peace, 148:18
  "Do all this, and the God of peace will be with you," 48:3
Pelagians, 178:1
  See also free choice; grace; infant baptism
  dealing with, 178:2–3
  in Sicily, 157:1(1)–41
Pelagius, 86:1(1), 27(8):
  letter from Augustine to:
  brief, of greeting, 146
Peregrinus, 139:2, 4; 149:34
perjury, 157:40
persecution, 93:8; 108:14(5); 185:9–11
  of Catholic Church, 93:6
  of Catholics by Circumcellions, *See* Circumcellions.
  Catholics called persecutors, 35:4
  cruelty in, 97:4
  of Diocletian, 43:3(2)
  of Donatists, 44:4, 7(4)–8, 11

Donatist(s) claiming, 89:2
hatred in, 97:4
just, 93:8
justice, on account of, 44:4; 87:7; 93:7
of Maximinianists by Donatists, 51:3, 3, 5
motives for, bad and good, 93:50(12) nonresistance to, 93:11
praiseworthiness of, factors in, 93:7
pray for those who persecute you, 153:4(2)–5
resisting, 93:11
Persius, 118:3
person(s)
spiritual and carnal, 93:6
Peter, apostle, Saint, 185:22, 46
baptism by, 93:47
correction of failure, 93:38
merits of, 93:38
Paul and, 28:3(3)–5; 93:31
sword of, Christ stopping, 93:7
Phalaris, bull of, 155:2
Pharaoh, the, 93:6
Pharisee(s):
and publican, parable of, 93:49
Zechariah tolerating, 43:23
philosophy, 149:24–25, 30; 155:2, 4–6, 9(3):
Phlegethon, 7:4
Phoebatius, of Agen, 148:10
Photinians, 185:48(9)
Photinus, 120:15
piety, 155:2, 4–5(2), 17
Plato, Platonic doctrine:
intellectual learning and memory, 7:2
sensible world as mere copy/image of ideas, 3:1
Platonists, 118:16, 20
and Christians, early, 118:33
as concealing views, 118:20–21, 33
highest good as divine, 118:16, 20
on logic, 118:19

on morality, 118:17
on nature, 118:18
truth and error of, 118:16–19
Plotinus, 118:33
Plotonian thought:
the monad, 3:2
Plutarch, 243:6
Po, 118:6
Polemon, of Athens, 118:16
pork, 149:4
possessions, 31:5–6; 93:5
See also wealth love of, 93:15
poverty:
virtue and, 157:157:23(4)–38
Praetextatus, of Assuri, 51:2, 4–5; 108:5–6, 13(4)–15
praise, 118:6–7;:
for doing good, 93:20(6)
false praise as criminal, 28:3(3)–5
praising God:
"be fervent in spirit, that your soul may receive praise in the Lord," 48:3
prayer, 48:3:
daily, for forgiveness, 185:38
different sorts of, 149:13–17
as gift, 194:15
the Lord's Prayer, 153:13–14
against temptation, 186:41
predestination, 186:25;
pride, 93:20(6); 165:1(1); 194:21
avoiding, 48:2
of carnal persons, 93:6
vanity, 155:4, 6–9(3).
Primian, 43:26; 108:1(1)–5,13(4)–14(5);
Primus: rebaptism of, 35:2
Priscus, of Caesarea, 209:8
prisoners: the groaning of prisoners, 48:1
Proculeian, discussed with Eusebius (re: matricidal young man), 34:4–6
letters from Augustine to: hoping to mend their differences, 33: 1–6

Profuturus, 28:1(1)
  and correspondence between Augustine and Jerome, 71:2;
promise(s):
  of God, 43:25(9)
property:
  See also possessions; wealth defending, 93:11
prophecy:
  Christ as fulfillment of Old Testament, 89:4
prophet(s) 149:11(2)
  See also individual names
  Jezebel killing, 93:6
  and persecution, 93:8
  tolerance by, 93:15
prophets, false:
  Elijah killing, 44:9; 93:6
prudence, 155:12–13(4), 16
Psalms:
  law and the prophets and, 93:21
publican(s):
  and Pharisee, parable of, 93:
punishment, 186:12, 16(6):
  bishops interceding, 53:1(1)–26
  coercion, use by Church, 185:21(6)–25(7)
  as correction, 93:8 *See also* correction
  fear, use of, 93:3
  rebukes, giving, 210:2
purity, 93:48
Purpurius, bishop of Limate, 43:6(3)
Pythagoras, 118:23(4

rain: on the just and unjust, 93:4(2)
raven set, 7:6(3)
reason:
  faith and, 120:2–3, 5–6, 8
  images resulting from, 7:4–7
rebaptism, 23:1–8; 34:2–6; 43:21(8); 44:7(4)–8, 12; 89:4; 108:1(1)–20; 185:22, 43(10)
  Christian standards regarding, 93:46(11)–48
  Cyprian regarding, 93:36
  Donatist practice of, 23:1–8; 34:2–6; 43:21(8); 44:7(4)–8, 12
  Jubaianus, letter from Cyprian to, on 93:36
  of matricidal young man, 34:2–6
  Paul baptizing after John, 93:47–48
  of Primus, 35:2
rebukes, giving, 210:2
religion
  See also Catholicism; Christianity
  faith differences of, in same family, 33:5
remnant, the, 149:3
repentance, 93:52
reputation:
  of bishops, 83:2
rest:
  complete, 48:2
Restitutus, 97:3; 108:13(4)–14(5)
resurrection of Christ, 120:9
  belief in, 120:9
  spiritual body at, 120:17
  the third day, 93:21, 23
Revelation, Book of, 43:22
  See also Apocalypse
righteousness, 120:18(4)–20; 149:21; 153:12(5); 185:37–38, 41
  baptism and, 93:10
  establishing, 93:10
  of God, 93:10
  parable regarding pride over, 93:49
  persecution not proof of, 44:7(4)
  Rogatists as far from, 93:27
  source of, 157:5, 13–14; 185:42; 186:8–10;
Rogatist(s), 87:10; 93:11, 23, 26, 49
  in Cartenna, 93:21–22(7) Catholicism, claim of, 93:23
  Donatists, compared to, 93:11
  Rogatus as founder, 93:11
  Vincent, Rogatist bishop of Cartenna, letter from Augustine to, 93:1(1)–53
Rogatus, 87:10; 93:1(1), 11

See also Rogatists
root: life from, 87:9
rope(s):
 Stretch out further your ropes, 93:29
Rusicca, 87:10
Rustician, 108:19
Rusticus, Felicity and, letter from Augustine to:
 on tribulations and giving rebukes, 210:1–2

sacrament(s), 149:16; 186:28
 See also specific sacraments
 baptism, 23:4 *See also* baptism
 circumcision, 23:4
 of Donatists, 87:9
 of Donatists vs. Christians, 89:7
 sin of others sharing, 93:37
sacred books:
 burning of, 51:1, 2
 surrendered in time of persecution, 35:4; 43:10; 44:4; 89:4
saints, 186:25
Salvation, 118:32; 149:17; 186:31:
 fear as catalyst for, 93:2–3
 force used to bring about, 93:1(1)–7
Samsucius, bishop of Turris, 34:6
Samuel, 43:23
sanctification, 89:5
sand, 93:30
Sarah 185:9, 11; 194:37:
 and Hagar, 93:6
Sardica:
 Donatist appeal to Council of, 44:6
Satan:
 apostles handing men over to, 93:7–8
 cleverness of, 48:3
 "devil and his angels," 43:22 Judas, as entering, 93:7
 as tempter, 48:3
Saul, King, 87:9; 185:9
 David tolerating, 43:23
Saul (later Paul), 93:5

saved, *See* salvation.
scandal(s):
 abundance of, 93:33
 Church clouded over by, 93:30
schism, schismatics, 51:1–5; 93:25; 185:2, 44–45, 47; 204:2; 208:3
 See also heretics; names of individual groups
 as crime, 76:1–4; 87:4
 See Donatists.
 force, use against, 93:1(1)–7
 as heresy, 87:4; 89:7
 punished in Scripture, 51:1
 secular authority against, 93:12
 as sin, 87:4
 as unjustifiable, 108:11–12
scourge
 See also punishment
 "Not everyone who scourges is an enemy," 93:4(2)
scribes:
 Zechariah tolerating, 43:23
Scripture(s)
 See also canonical books holy and true, 28:3(3)–5
 promise(s) in, 43:25(9)
 understanding, 120:13(3)
 "useful lies" as undermining authority of, 28:3(3)–5
Sebastian, count, 7*:1-2
Second Coming:
 baptism, as eliminating need for, 23:4
 the living at time of, 193:9(4)–13
secrets, 149:3–4
secular power:
 Church, on behalf of, 93:1(1)–20, 50
 fear of, 93:20(6)
Secundus, of Tigisi, 43:5–12, 14(5), 17(6), 26
seeing Christ:
 after resurrection, 149:31(3)
seeing God, 148:1(1)–18

seed:
  good, Church found in, 93:31–32
self-righteousness, 157:37–39
Seneca, 153:14
senses, the:
  deceptiveness of, 7:2, 3
  sight, 7:6(3)
  taste, 7:6(3)
  truth of, 7:5
sensible nature and world:
  as image of intelligible one, 3:3
  intelligible nature compared to, 3:2–3;
sensual pleasures, 95:6
  doing without, 3:4
  mind and intelligence vs., 3:4
Septuagint, the:
  translations of, 28:2(2); 71:4, 6(4);
servant(s):
  Jesus Christ as, 33:5; 170:9
Severinus, Donatist relative:
  letters from Augustine to:
    on Donatist schism, 52:1–4
shadow(s), 149:24–27
Shadrach, Meshach, and Abednego, 93:9(3)
shame, 186:40
sheep:
  goats, separating from, 93:49–50(12)
  rebaptizers as like wolves preying on, 35:4
shepherd(s), 149:11(2)
  the good shepherd, 93:49
  "If you are good shepherds, be silent," 35:4
Sicily, 156; 157:1(1)–41
sight:
  See also under eyes
  sense of, 7:(3), 6
  three kinds of things we see, 120:11
  visible events and realities, 120:8–11
signs, 185:24
silver, 83:4; 96:2
Simeon, 149:33

sin, sinners, 87:3; 149:3–4; 153:11:
  of children and parents, 44:12
  Christ, as forgiven in name of, 93:21, 23
  correction of, 108:20(7)
  and death, 193:6–7, 12
  early Church as tolerating, 43:22–23
  excuses for, 194:22(6)–29
  of good vs. evil people, 153:14
  grace and, 149:7–8; 194:29–30
  against the Holy Spirit, 185:48(9)–50
  the law and, 157:9, 15; 194:25
  of one as not defiling others, 93:15, 33–34, 37, 42, 45, 49
  of others, 93:37; 153:2, 14, 21
  participation in, 100:1–2; 108:7(3)–8,16(6)–17
  personal, 194:27
  repentance of, 93:52
  sinful person, what constitutes, 87:3
  sinners, known, effect of, 87:2
  sinners, unknown, the presence of, 87:1
  unknown, guilt regarding, 89:4
  wicked, destruction of, 87:2
singing:
  "a bad flute player makes a good singer," 60:1–2
Sitifis, 185:6(2)
Sixtus, letters from Augustine to:
  on grace, baptism, and God's judgment, 194:1(1)–47
sleep:
  advantage over waking, 7:2, 3
smoke, 48:2
Socrates:
  about learning and memory, 7:2
Soliloquies, 3:1, 4
Sosthenes, 93:7
soul, 120:18(4);
  activities of, many, 7:7
  beauty of, 120:20
  body vs., 3:4
  death of (as impossible), 3:4

decreasing or increasing, power of, 7:6(3)
highest good as in, 118:13–16,
image of God, 120:20
imagination and, 7:1–7
making use of body's senses, 7:2, 3–7
righteousness as from, 120:20
as seat of truth, 3:4
sower:
Christ as, 93:15, 31
Spanianum, 35:2, 4
spirit:
flesh vs., 93:31
spiritual persons:
Isaac as symbolizing, 93:10
stars:
believers as, 93:15
Stilicho, 97:2–3
Stoics, 118:12, 15, 19–21, 26
soul as highest good, 118:16
straw: wheat, separated from, 87:8
strife, 93:32, 48
stubbornness, 93:20(6)
suffering, 210:1:
See also sorrow
of Jesus Christ, 93:21, 23
happiness in, 155:2–4
suicide, 153:17; 155:2–3; 185:12(3), 14, 32(8)–34(10)
superstitions, 7:4
surgeon, 93:8
swearing, 157:40
sweet foods, 93:28(9)
sword, 149:33:
of Peter, 93:7
Sylvanus, bishop of Cirta, 43:17(6)
Synods, 93:21, 31
Syracuse in Sicily, 156; 157:1(1)–41

taste, sense of, 7:6(3)
tax evasion: property acquired through, 96:2
taxes, 96:2

teachers, 149:11(2)
temperance, 155:12–13(4), 16
temples of God, 170:2
temptation, 178:3:
guarding against, 48:3
prayer regarding, 186:41
struggles with, 186:33
Terence, 155:14; 85:21(6):
comedy of, 7:4
Thagaste:
Donatists, mass conversion of, 93:17
Thiave:
Honoratus of, 83:1–6
letter to Donatist leaders in, 43
Thamugadi:
Optatus as Donatist bishop of, 43:25(9); 51:3
theft, 153:20–26
Themistocles, 118:13
Theodosius, 97:3; 185:25(7)
thief, thieves:
crucified with Christ, 93:7
third day: Christ rising on, 93:21, 23
thorns: lily in the midst of, 93:28(9)
Timasius and James, 179:2; 186:2
tolerance:
and Christian unity, 44:11
of evil on account of good, 93:15
unity, for the sake of, 43:22–23
tomb of Jesus, 149:32
torture, 153:20; 155:2
the torturer, 93:8
traditor(s), 35:4; 44:10(5); 108:2
See also sacred books, 89:4
Transfiguration, the, 149:31(3)
trial: of Caecilian, bishop of Carthage, 43:1–20
Trinity, the, 120:6–7(2), 12–13(3), 16–17; 170:2–9
Tripoli: Maximinianist schism, 93:24(8)
truth:
Christ as Truth made man, 118:32; 155:14

imagination and, 7:4
knowing, yet fighting against, 93:10
mind thought to be, 118:24–27
Paul's concern for teaching, 28:4
progression toward (with age), 4:1
of Scripture, 28:3(3)–5
of senses (as greater than that of thoughts), 7:5
soul as seat of, 3:4
vs. flattery, 33:3
Tusculan Disputations, Cicero, 155:3–4
Tychonius, 93:14, 43–44, 43–45

underworld, 7:4
unhappiness: and happiness, discussion of, 3:1

veiled woman, 93:28(9)
Victor of Caesarea, 209:8
Victor, priest of Proculeian, 34:5; 35:1
Vincent, Rogatist bishop of Cartenna, 93:1(1)–53, 21
See also Rogatists
vine:
    Jesus as, 52:2
violence:
    of Christ, 93:5
    value of, 89:7 *See also under* force
Virgil, 17:3
    The Aeneid, 7:4
virgin, virginity, 188:6
    See also chastity virgins, consecrated:
    Demetrias as, 188:1(1)–14
virtue, 155:6
    and self-righteousness, 157:38
visible events and realities, 120:8–11
vows:
    to God, 149:16

water, 48:2
    salvation of the, 93:31
    support of the, 93:3

weak, weakness, 120:6; 118:32(2)
wealth:
    Christians and, 157:23(4)–38; 186:33
    of the wicked, 185:35(9)–37, 40–42
    wrongful possession of, 153:24–26
weeds, 93:15:
    seed among, 93:31–32
west, 93:30
wheat:
    chaff amid, 93:33–34; 108:12
    chaff (weeds) as not choking, 93:33
    grain, amid, 93:33–34
    not uprooting weeds *for fear that they might . . . uproot the wheat*, 43:21(8)
    in sacrament(s), 55:13
    straw, separated from, 87:8
white:
    clothes at Easter Vigil, 34:2–3
White Sunday, 34:3
wicked (-ness), 93:10
    See also evil; sin
    of carnal persons, 93:6
    destruction of, 87:2
    of Donatists, 93:10
widow (-hood), 93:29
    the matricidal young man, 34:2–6; 93:11
winnowing
    See also harvest
    the last, 93:33, 42, 50(12)
wisdom, 149:30; 155:5(2), 12
    incorporeal, 118:18; 120:11
    mind thought to be, 118:24–27
    true and false, 120:6
wisdom of God:
    Christ as, 120:19; 170:4
wolf, wolves:
    rebaptizers as like, 35:4
woman, women:
    "roving bands of women who have shamelessly refused to have husbands," 35:2

woman, abandoned, 93:26, 30
woman, veiled, 93:28(9)
works, good
   grace vs. free choice free choice and, 157:5
world, the:
   Christ as propitiation for sins of whole, 93:32
   spread of Christianity, 93:22(7)
   wheat spread throughout, 93:32
   "three worlds," 7:4

worship, 155:5(2), 17
   See also praise
wrath of God: salvation, as bringing about, 93:5

Xenocrates, 118:16

Zechariah, 43:23
Zenophilus, 43:17(6
Zion, Mount, 93:25
Zosimus, the pope, 194:1(1)

THE COMPLETE WORKS OF ST. AUGUSTINE
A Translation for the 21st Century

Part I — Books

Autobiographical Works

The Confessions (I/1)
  cloth, 978-1-56548-468-9
  paper, 978-1-56548-445-0
  pocket, 978-1-56548-154-1
  Mobile App for iOS & Android available

Revisions (I/2)
  cloth, 978-1-56548-360-6

Dialogues I (I/3) forthcoming

Dialogues II (I/4) forthcoming.

Philosophical-Dogmatic Works

The Trinity (I/5)
  cloth, 978-1-56548-610-2
  paper, 978-1-56548-446-7

The City of God 1-10 (I/6)
  cloth, 978-1-56548-454-2
  paper, 978-1-56548-455-9

The City of God 11-22 (I/7)
  cloth, 978-1-56548-479-5
  paper, 978-1-56548-481-8

On Christian Belief
  cloth, 978-1-56548-233-3
  paper, 978-1-56548-234-0

Pastoral Works

Marriage and Virginity (I/9)
  cloth, 978-1-56548-104-6
  paper, 978-1-56548-222-7

Morality and Christian Asceticism (I/10)
  forthcoming

Exegetical Works

Teaching Christianity (I/11)
  (On Christian Doctrine)
  cloth, 978-1-56548-048-3
  paper, 978-1-56548-049-0

Responses to Miscellaneous Questions (I/12)
  cloth, 978-1-56548-277-7

On Genesis (I/13)
  cloth, 978-1-56548-175-6
  paper, 978-1-56548-201-2

Writings on the Old Testament (I/14)
  cloth, 978-1-56548-557-0

New Testament I and II (I/15 and I/16)
  cloth, 978-1-56548-529-7
  paper, 978-1-56548-531-0

The New Testament III (I/17) forthcoming

Polemical Works

Arianism and Other Heresies (I/18)
  cloth, 978-1-56548-038-4

Manichean Debate (I/19)
  cloth, 978-1-56548-247-0

Answer to Faustus, a Manichean (I/20)
  cloth, 978-1-56548-264-7

Donatist Controversy I (I/21) forthcoming

Donatist Controversy II (I/22) forthcoming

Answer to the Pelagians (I/23)
  cloth, 978-1-56548-092-6

Answer to the Pelagians (I/24)
  cloth, 978-1-56548-107-7

Answer To The Pelagians (I/25)
  cloth, 978-1-56548-129-9

Answer to the Pelagians (I/26)
  cloth, 978-1-56548-136-7

Part II — Letters

Letters 1-99 (II/1)
  cloth, 978-1-56548-163-3

Letters 100-155 (II/2)
  cloth, 978-1-56548-186-2

Letters 156-210 (II/3)
  cloth, 978-1-56548-200-5

Letters 211-270 (II/4)
  cloth, 978-1-56548-209-8

Part III — Homilies

Sermons 1-19 (III/1)
  cloth, 978-0-911782-75-2

Sermons 20-50 (III/2)
  cloth, 978-0-911782-78-3

Sermons 51-94 (III/3)
  cloth, 978-0-911782-85-1

Sermons 94A-150 (III/4)
  cloth, 978-1-56548-000-1

Sermons 151-183 (III/5)
  cloth, 978-1-56548-007-0

Sermons 184-229 (III/6)
  cloth, 978-1-56548-050-6
Sermons 230-272 (III/7)
  cloth, 978-1-56548-059-9
Sermons 273-305A (III/8)
  cloth, 978-1-56548-060-5
Sermons 306-340A (III/9)
  cloth, 978-1-56548-068-1
Sermons 341-400 (III/10)
  cloth, 978-1-56548-028-5
Sermons Newly Discovered Since 1990
  (III/11)
  cloth, 978-1-56548-103-9
Homilies on the Gospel of John 1-40
  (III/12)
  cloth, 978-1-56548-319-4
  paper, 978-1-56548-318-7
Homilies on the Gospel of John (41-124)
  (III/13) forthcoming
Homilies on the First Letter of John (III/14)
  cloth, 978-1-56548-288-3
  paper, 978-1-56548-289-0
Expositions of the Psalms 1-32 (III/15)
  cloth, 978-1-56548-126-8
  paper, 978-1-56548-140-4
Expositions of the Psalms 33-50 (III/16)
  cloth, 978-1-56548-147-3
  paper, 978-1-56548-146-6
Expositions of the Psalms 51-72 (III/17)
  cloth, 978-1-56548-156-5
  paper, 978-1-56548-155-8

Expositions of the Psalms 73-98 (III/18)
  cloth, 978-1-56548-167-1
  paper, 978-1-56548-166-4
Expositions of the Psalms 99-120 (III/19)
  cloth, 978-1-56548-197-8
  paper, 978-1-56548-196-1
Expositions of the Psalms 121-150 (III/20)
  cloth, 978-1-56548-211-1
  paper, 978-1-56548-210-4

**Essential Texts
Created for Classroom Use**

*Augustine Catechism: Enchiridion on
Faith Hope and Love*
  paper, 978-1-56548-298-2
Essential Expositions of the Psalms
  paper, 978-1-56548-510-5
Essential Sermons
  paper, 978-1-56548-276-0
Instructing Beginners in Faith
  paper, 978-1-56548-239-5
Monastic Rules
  paper, 978-1-56548-130-5
Prayers from The Confessions
  paper, 978-1-56548-188-6
Selected Writings on Grace and Pelagianism
  paper, 978-1-56548-372-9
Soliloquies: Augustine's Inner Dialogue
  paper, 978-1-56548-142-8
Trilogy on Faith and Happiness
  paper, 978-1-56548-359-0

E-books Available
*Essential Sermons, Homilies on the First Letter of John, Revisions,
The Confessions, Trilogy on Faith and Happiness, The Trinity,
The Augustine Catechism: The Enchiridion on Faith, Hope and Love.*

Custom Syllabus
Universities that wish to create a resource that matches their specific needs using selections from any of the above titles should contact New City Press.

Free Index
A free PDF containing all of the **Indexes** from *The Works of Saint Augustine, A Translation for the 21st Century* published by NCP is available for download at www.newcitypress.com.

New City Press — The Works of Saint Augustine Catalog
For a complete interactive catalog of *The Works of Saint Augustine, A Translation for the 21st Century* go to New City Press website at: www.newcitypress.com

www.ingramcontent.com/pod-product-compliance
Lightning Source LLC
Chambersburg PA
CBHW022005300426
44117CB00005B/41